Lecture Notes in Computer Science 11192

Commenced Publication in 1973
Founding and Former Series Editors:
Gerhard Goos, Juris Hartmanis, and Jan van Leeuwen

More information about this series at http://www.springer.com/series/7410

Joonsang Baek · Willy Susilo
Jongkil Kim (Eds.)

Provable Security

12th International Conference, ProvSec 2018
Jeju, South Korea, October 25–28, 2018
Proceedings

 Springer

Editors
Joonsang Baek
University of Wollongong
Wollongong, NSW
Australia

Jongkil Kim
University of Wollongong
Wollongong, NSW
Australia

Willy Susilo
University of Wollongong
Wollongong, NSW
Australia

ISSN 0302-9743 ISSN 1611-3349 (electronic)
Lecture Notes in Computer Science
ISBN 978-3-030-01445-2 ISBN 978-3-030-01446-9 (eBook)
https://doi.org/10.1007/978-3-030-01446-9

Library of Congress Control Number: 2018955834

LNCS Sublibrary: SL4 – Security and Cryptology

This Springer imprint is published by the registered company Springer Nature Switzerland AG
The registered company address is: Gewerbestrasse 11, 6330 Cham, Switzerland

Preface

This volume contains the papers presented at ProvSec 2018 – the 12th International Conference on Provable Security held during October 25–28, 2018, in Jeju, Republic of Korea. The conference was organized by the Institute of Cybersecurity and Cryptology at the University of Wollongong and the Laboratory of Mobile Internet Security at Soonchunhyang University.

The first ProvSec conference was held in Wollongong, Australia, in 2007. The series of ProvSec conferences continued successfully in Shanghai, China (2008), Guangzhou, China (2009), Malacca, Malaysia (2010), Xi'an, China (2011), Chengdu, China (2012), Malacca, Malaysia (2013), Hong Kong, SAR China (2014), Kanazawa Japan (2015), Nanjing, China (2016) and Xi'an, China (2017). This was the first ProvSec held in Korea.

This year we received 48 submissions of high quality from 23 countries. Each submission was allocated to at least three Program Committee members. The submission and review process was conducted through the EasyChair conference management system. In the first phase of the review process, the submitted papers were evaluated by the Program Committee members. In the second phase, the papers were scrutinized through extensive discussions. This phase includes the "shepherding" process, which gives a few authors the chance to address issues raised by some reviewers. Finally, the committee decided to accept 21 regular papers and four short papers. The review process was conducted anonymously to make sure that the submissions receive fair marks and comments.

Among the accepted regular papers, the paper that received the highest weighted review mark was given the Best Paper Award:

- "Security Notions for Cloud Storage and Deduplication" by Colin Boyd, Gareth T. Davies, Kristian Gjøsteen, Håvard Raddum, and Mohsen Toorani

The program also included an invited talk presented by Prof. Jung Hee Cheon from Seoul National University, Korea, titled "Recent Development of Homomorphic Encryptions and Their Applications."

We thank all the authors of the submitted papers. We also greatly appreciate the time and effort that the Program Committee members and external reviewers put in to evaluate and select the papers for the program. Our gratitude extends to our sponsors – Jeju National University, Korea, and Innovation Information Science and Technology Research Group, Korea. We are also grateful to the team at Springer for their continuous support of the conference and for their assistance in the production of the conference proceedings.

October 2018

Joonsang Baek
Willy Susilo

Organization

The 12th International Conference on Provable Security

Jeju, Republic of Korea
October 25–28, 2018

Program Chairs

Joonsang Baek	University of Wollongong, Australia
Willy Susilo	University of Wollongong, Australia

General Chairs

Ilsun You	Soonchunhyang University, Republic of Korea
Kyung Hyune Rhee	Pukyung National University, Republic of Korea

Publication Chair

Jongkil Kim	University of Wollongong, Australia

Organization Chair

Namje Park	Jeju National University, Republic of Korea

Program Committee

Elena Andreeva	K.U. Leuven, Belgium
Man Ho Au	The Hong Kong Polytechnic University, SAR China
Donghoon Chang	IIIT-Delhi, India
Jie Chen	East China Normal University, China
Liqun Chen	University of Surrey, UK
Xiaofeng Chen	Xidian University, China
Cheng-Kang Chu	Huawei, Singapore
Bernardo David	The Tokyo Institute of Technology, Japan
Jean Paul Degabriele	TU Darmstadt, Germany
Robert Deng	Singapore Management University, Singapore
Keita Emura	NICT, Japan
Zekeriya Erkin	TU Delft, The Netherlands
Jinguang Han	University of Surrey, UK
Ryo Kikuchi	NTT, Japan
Jongkil Kim	University of Wollongong, Australia

Hyung Tae Lee	Chonbuk National University, Republic of Korea
Jooyoung Lee	KAIST, Republic of Korea
Joseph Liu	Monash University, Australia
Bernardo Magri	Friedrich Alexander University, Germany
Barbara Masucci	University of Salerno, Italy
Bart Mennink	Radboud University, The Netherlands
Chris Mitchell	Royal Holloway, University of London, UK
Kirill Morozov	University of North Texas, USA
Khoa Nguyen	Nanyang Technological University, Singapore
Abderrahmane Nitaj	Université de Caen Normandie, France
Josef Pieprzyk	CSIRO/Data61, Australia
Kouichi Sakurai	Kyushu University, Japan
Rainer Steinwandt	Florida Atlantic University, USA
Chunhua Su	Osaka University, Japan
Katsuyuki Takashima	Mitsubishi Electric, Japan
Atsushi Takayasu	The University of Tokyo, Japan
Qiang Tang	New Jersey Institute of Technology, USA
Joseph Tonien	University of Wollongong, Australia
Damien Vergnaud	ENS, France
Shota Yamada	AIST, Japan
Chung-Huang Yang	National Kaohsiung Normal University, Taiwan
Guomin Yang	University of Wollongong, Australia
Xun Yi	RMIT University, Australia
Yong Yu	Shaanxi Normal University, China
Tsz Hon Yuen	The University of Hong Kong, SAR China
Aaram Yun	UNIST, Republic of Korea

Additional Reviewers

Arcangelo Castiglione	Byeonghak Lee
Yu Long Chen	Jinhui Liu
Stelvio Cimato	Sweta Mishra
Hui Cui	Binanda Sengupta
Sabyasachi Dutta	Jie Shi
Chengfang Fang	Boaz Tsaban
Katharina Fech	Valentin Vasseur
Yaokai Feng	Luping Wang
Manuela Flores	Yohei Watanabe
Junqing Gong	Yanhong Xu
Atsunori Ichikawa	Takashi Yamakawa
Arkadius Kalka	Rupeng Yang
Shuichi Katsumata	Zuoxia Yu
Seongkwang Kim	Kai Zhang
Tarun Kumar Bansal	Mingwu Zhang
Amit Kumar Chauhan	Yinghui Zhang
Mario Larangeira	Qian Zhao

Contents

Foundation

On the Leakage of Corrupted Garbled Circuits

Aurélien Dupin[1,2(✉)], David Pointcheval[3,4], and Christophe Bidan[2]

[1] Thales Communications & Security, Gennevilliers, France
dupin.aurelien@gmail.com
[2] CentraleSupélec, Rennes, France
[3] DIENS, École normale supérieure, CNRS, PSL University, Paris, France
[4] INRIA, Paris, France

Abstract. Secure two-party computation provides a way for two parties to compute a function, that depends on the two parties' inputs, while keeping them private. Known since the 1980s, Yao's garbled circuits appear to be a general solution to this problem, in the semi-honest model. Decades of optimizations have made this tool a very practical solution. However, it is well known that a malicious adversary could modify a garbled circuit before submitting it. Many protocols, mostly based on cut-&-choose, have been proposed to secure Yao's garbled circuits in the presence of malicious adversaries. Nevertheless, how much an adversary can modify a circuit and make it still executable has not been studied yet. The main contribution of this paper is to prove that any modification made by an adversary is equivalent to adding/removing NOT gates arbitrarily in the original circuit, otherwise the adversary can get caught. Thereafter, we study some evaluation functions for which, even without using cut-&-choose, no adversary can gain more information about the inputs by modifying the circuit. We also give an improvement over most recent cut-&-choose solutions by requiring that different circuits of the same function are used instead of just one.

Keywords: Garbled circuits · Malicious adversaries
Corruption of garbled circuits · Cut-and-choose

1 Introduction

The pioneering work of Yao [19], known as garbled circuits, is a general solution to the secure two-party computation problem, with a generator that builds the garbled circuit to be evaluated, and the evaluator that executes it on its inputs. It was originally designed in the semi-honest model and it was clear that a malicious generator could modify the logic gates of the garbled circuit before sending it

D. Pointcheval—This work was supported in part by the European Research Council under the European Community's Seventh Framework Programme (FP7/2007-2013 Grant Agreement no. 339563 – CryptoCloud).

© Springer Nature Switzerland AG 2018
J. Baek et al. (Eds.): ProvSec 2018, LNCS 11192, pp. 3–21, 2018.
https://doi.org/10.1007/978-3-030-01446-9_1

to the evaluator for execution. Applying *cut-&-choose* to garbled circuits soon appeared to fix this issue, but requires to generate and evaluate a large number of garbled circuits.

Since then, a lot of work has been made to optimize the garbled circuits on the one hand [2,8,13,20], and the cut-&-choose on the other hand [1,9–12,16–18]. The best of these approaches requires s garbled circuits for statistical security 2^{-s}. Other interesting solutions based on a gate-level cut-&-choose have emerged [4,14,15]. While these protocols have good asymptotic performances, their implementations still have a higher running time in practice than the best circuit-level cut-&-choose protocols. However, all these techniques aim at avoiding any kind of modification on the circuit. Nevertheless, it has never been studied which modifications a malicious generator can make to a single garbled circuit, still leading to an accepted execution, and then why the cut-&-choose is necessary.

Before the most recent general optimization of semi-honest garbling schemes of Zahur, Rosulek and Evans [20], such a study would have been meaningless. Indeed, it was obvious that an adversary could apply any modification of his choice as long as the topology of the circuit remains the same. In other terms, any binary gate could be turned into any other binary gate and the resulting corrupted garbled circuit would be still executable for any input. However, the recent improvement [20] manages to reduce the size of a garbled gate to only two ciphers (instead of three since the work of Naor et al. [13], or even four before that). Whereas this improvement can be seen as just a nice improvement for an honest party, it is clearly an extra constraint for a malicious party, given that he can now change only two variables instead of three or four. Since then, it is not clear which modifications can actually be made, and we prove in this paper that it is much more limited than suggested in the previous state-of-the-art.

More specifically, our first contribution is to show that an adversary is only able to add NOT gates to a circuit or to allow abortion of the protocol. The latter case is already known in the state-of-the-art as *selective failure attacks*. This result leads to our second contribution: we show some evaluation functions for which no such addition of NOT gates can help an adversary to learn more information about the inputs than the honest circuit. For such functions, this shows that a single circuit, without any cut-&-choose, is the best solution even against malicious adversaries (under the assumption that learning more information is not worth being caught). These results hold for the generic garbling scheme presented in [20].

When one of the parties does not have any inputs, privacy-free garbling schemes should be used instead. Privacy-free garbling schemes were used by Jawurek et al. [6] to build very efficient zero-knowledge proof of knowledge protocols. In this context, a prover has a secret, that satisfies some given statement, and wants to convince a verifier about his knowledge without revealing it. The works of [5] and later [20] showed that in this setting, the size of garbled circuits can be drastically reduced. Our results also hold for the optimal privacy-free scheme of [20], and thus limit a malicious verifier to add NOT gate or to make selective failure attacks.

Table 1. Garbled truth table   **Table 2.** Commitments of outputs

$H(k_A^0)$	$H(k_B^0)$	$E_{k_A^0}(E_{k_B^0}(k_C^{g(0,0)}))$
$H(k_A^0)$	$H(k_B^1)$	$E_{k_A^0}(E_{k_B^1}(k_C^{g(0,1)}))$
$H(k_A^1)$	$H(k_B^0)$	$E_{k_A^1}(E_{k_B^0}(k_C^{g(1,0)}))$
$H(k_A^1)$	$H(k_B^1)$	$E_{k_A^1}(E_{k_B^1}(k_C^{g(1,1)}))$

The next section is a reminder of how to garble a circuit with the most recent optimizations. Then, we show in Sect. 3 how an adversary can add NOT gates to a circuit or make selective failure attacks. The main contribution of our paper comes in Sect. 4: we prove that no other modification can be made for a large class of circuits that we define. Section 5 gives a construction of garbled circuits that reduces the possible deviations. Finally, we study in Sect. 6 the impact of our contribution on some real-case circuits and show that some of them do not require cut-&-choose based solutions to ensure privacy, and that for the others, cut-&-choose can be improved for free by recommending that different circuits of the same function are used instead of just one.

2   A Reminder of the Garbled Circuit Optimizations

Let us remind how garbled circuits are designed. The point-and-permute technique [2], the 25-%-row reduction [13] and the free-XOR [8] are briefly explained in the beginning of this section. We refer the reader to these papers for details.

2.1   The Basic Construction

We assume both parties agree on the function to evaluate and the circuit representation of it. One party, called the generator (noted $\mathcal{G}$), randomly chooses two garbled keys k_i^0 and k_i^1 for each wire w_i of the circuit, representing respectively 0 and 1. Then, for the Boolean gate g taking as input the wires w_A and w_B and returning the output in w_C, $\mathcal{G}$ computes the garbled truth table as shown in Table 1, using a hash function H and a symmetric encryption function E.

The rows of this table are randomly shuffled before they are sent to the other party, the evaluator (noted $\mathcal{E}$). Then, with the keys k_A^a and k_B^b, $\mathcal{E}$ is able to compute $k_C^{g(a,b)}$. $\mathcal{G}$ sends the keys corresponding to his inputs, whereas the keys of $\mathcal{E}$ are exchange through oblivious transfers. That way, $\mathcal{E}$ evaluates the circuit and obtains output garbled keys. $\mathcal{G}$ also provides commitments of the garbled keys of the output of the circuit (shown in Table 2) that allow $\mathcal{E}$ to get an exploitable result, and check the correct evaluation. If $\mathcal{E}$ is not supposed to learn the result, these commitments can be randomly shuffled and sent to $\mathcal{E}$. If the result does not match any commitment, then a misbehavior in the generation of the garbled circuit may have occurred.

2.2 The Point-and-Permute Trick

The point-and-permute trick of Beaver, Micali and Rogaway [2] allows to get rid of the two input columns of Table 1. For every wire w_i, $\mathcal{G}$ picks a random bit p_i, called *permute bit*. The least significant bit of a garbled key (later called *select bit*) is now the clear value masked with the permute bit. For example, the select bit of k_A^a is $a \oplus p_A$. Remark that the select bit of every garbled key is arranged so that the two garbled keys of a wire have opposite select bits. Then, the garbled truth table can be arranged by these select bits, as shown in Table 3. Then, $\mathcal{E}$ uses the select bit of the garbled keys to determine which row he should decrypt.

In the rest of the paper, we call $s()$ the function that takes a garbled key as input and outputs the select bit of that key. It tells $\mathcal{E}$ which line of Table 3 he should use while executing: $s(k_A^a) = a \oplus p_A$, $s(k_A^{p_A}) = 0$, and $s(k_A^0) = p_A$.

2.3 The 25%-Row Reduction

The 25%-row reduction of Naor, Pinkas and Sumner [13] allows to reduce the number of ciphertexts per garbled gate. The main idea is to choose one of the output keys so that the first ciphertext is nullified. Then, one less ciphertext has to be transmitted. For example, in Table 4, $k_C^{g(p_A, p_B)}$ is the decryption of zero.

2.4 The Free-XOR Trick

The free-XOR trick of Kolesnikov and Schneider [8] allows to garble XOR gates for free. The idea is to choose a *global offset* Δ that will be used to differentiate the two garbled keys of a same wire. In other words, for any wire, the bitwise XOR of the two garbled keys is Δ. That way, when the evaluator has to evaluate a XOR gate, he just bitwise XOR the two input garbled keys to obtain the output garbled key. Note that, in order to make it compatible with the point-and-permute technique, Δ has to be odd.

Table 3. Garbled truth table with permute bit

$E_{k_A^{p_A}}(E_{k_B^{p_B}}(k_C^{g(p_A,p_B)}))$
$E_{k_A^{p_A}}(E_{k_B^{\overline{p_B}}}(k_C^{g(p_A,\overline{p_B})}))$
$E_{k_A^{\overline{p_A}}}(E_{k_B^{p_B}}(k_C^{g(\overline{p_A},p_B)}))$
$E_{k_A^{\overline{p_A}}}(E_{k_B^{\overline{p_B}}}(k_C^{g(\overline{p_A},\overline{p_B})}))$

Table 4. 25% reduced garbled truth table

$E_{k_A^{p_A}}(E_{k_B^{p_B}}(k_C^{g(p_A,p_B)})) = 0$
$E_{k_A^{p_A}}(E_{k_B^{\overline{p_B}}}(k_C^{g(p_A,\overline{p_B})}))$
$E_{k_A^{\overline{p_A}}}(E_{k_B^{p_B}}(k_C^{g(\overline{p_A},p_B)}))$
$E_{k_A^{\overline{p_A}}}(E_{k_B^{\overline{p_B}}}(k_C^{g(\overline{p_A},\overline{p_B})}))$

2.5 The Two Half-Gates Technique

We now describe how to garble an AND gate using only two ciphertexts. As noticed in the original paper of Zahur, Rosulek and Evans [20]:

$$\forall \gamma \in \mathbb{F}_2, a \wedge b = \underbrace{(a \wedge \gamma)}_{\text{First half-gate}} \oplus \underbrace{(a \wedge (b \oplus \gamma))}_{\text{Second half-gate}}$$

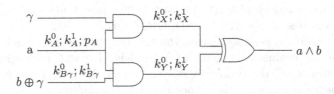

Fig. 1. The two half-gates of an AND gate

Then, an AND gate is replaced by the sub-circuit shown in Fig. 1 with the bit γ randomly chosen by $\mathcal{G}$. A *half-gate* is defined as a gate for which one of the inputs is known by one of the parties. In the first half-gate, γ is known by $\mathcal{G}$, whereas in the second, $b \oplus \gamma$ can be revealed to $\mathcal{E}$ without leaking b (by revealing the permute bit of the corresponding wire). Using this knowledge, each half-gate can be reduced to one ciphertext (called G and E). $\mathcal{G}$ computes these ciphertexts as described in Table 5 and send them to $\mathcal{E}$. We note i and j two distinct and public indexes used as salts for hash function, as detailed in [20].

Table 5. Garbling the half-gates

First half-gate			Second half-gate	
Garbled table if $\gamma = 0$	Garbled table if $\gamma = 1$	$b \oplus \gamma$	Garbled table	
$k_X^0 \oplus H(k_A^{p_A}\|i) = 0$	$k_X^{p_A} \oplus H(k_A^{p_A}\|i) = 0$	0	$k_Y^0 \oplus H(k_{B\gamma}^0\|j) = 0$	
$k_X^0 \oplus H(k_A^{\overline{p_A}}\|i) = G$	$k_X^{\overline{p_A}} \oplus H(k_A^{\overline{p_A}}\|i) = G$	1	$k_Y^0 \oplus k_A^0 \oplus H(k_{B\gamma}^1\|j) = E$	

To simplify notations, we will omit the salts i and j unless they are necessary to our proofs. Then, $\mathcal{E}$ executes the garbled gate using the garbled inputs. Table 6 shows the four different algorithms of evaluation, depending on the garbled inputs the evaluator has. Of course, three of them output the same garbled key (for an output 0 to the AND gate). Knowing the clear value of $b \oplus \gamma$ and the select bit of k_A^a, the evaluator is able to choose the correct algorithm.

Table 6. Evaluating the half-gates

Inputs		First half-gate	Second half-gate	Garbled output key
k_A^{PA}	$k_{B\gamma}^0$	$H(k_A^{PA})$	$H(k_{B\gamma}^0)$	$K_1 = H(k_A^{PA}) \oplus H(k_{B\gamma}^0)$
k_A^{PA}	$k_{B\gamma}^1$	$H(k_A^{PA})$	$E \oplus H(k_{B\gamma}^1) \oplus k_A^{PA}$	$K_2 = E \oplus H(k_A^{PA}) \oplus H(k_{B\gamma}^1) \oplus k_A^{PA}$
k_A^{PA}	$k_{B\gamma}^0$	$G \oplus H(k_A^{\overline{PA}})$	$H(k_{B\gamma}^0)$	$K_3 = G \oplus H(k_A^{\overline{PA}}) \oplus H(k_{B\gamma}^0)$
k_A^{PA}	$k_{B\gamma}^1$	$G \oplus H(k_A^{\overline{PA}})$	$E \oplus H(k_{B\gamma}^1) \oplus k_A^{PA}$	$K_4 = E \oplus G \oplus H(k_A^{\overline{PA}}) \oplus H(k_{B\gamma}^1) \oplus k_A^{PA}$

2.6   Linear and Non-linear Gates

The two half-gates technique works for "any gate whose truth table contains an odd number of ones (e.g. AND, NAND, OR, NOR, etc.)" [20]. Let's call them *non-linear gates* in $\mathbb{F}_2$. For these gates, the garbling scheme of Table 5 is slightly different, but the evaluation scheme of Table 6 is identical. By opposition, we call *linear gates* in $\mathbb{F}_2$ the eight others (e.g., XOR, XNOR, True, False, etc.). Only non-linear gates are garbled, since linear gates are free.

2.7   The Case of Privacy-Free Garbled Circuits

Jawurek et al. [6] demonstrated that garbled circuits can be used as a practical solution to zero-knowledge proof protocols. The evaluator (i.e. the prover) can prove any statement "$\exists x : f(x) = 1$" without revealing x, using a single garbled circuit for f.

Frederiksen et al. [5] showed that in this context, the size of the garbled circuits can be significantly reduced. Since the evaluator knows the entire input, he also knows the value of each intermediate wire. The work of [20] provides an optimal garbling scheme in this context. Since the evaluator knows every value, the non-linear gates can be viewed as half-gates, and thus require a single ciphertext.

Although only the general case is presented in this paper, our results also hold for the privacy-free garbling scheme of [20].

3   Corruption of a Garbled Circuit

Now that we have seen how to garble a circuit, let us see how the generator $\mathcal{G}$ can cheat. We consider two kinds of corruptions: those that can not be detected, since the evaluation always succeeds, and those that may lead the adversary to get caught, because of an invalid output (inconsistent with the commitments).

3.1   Selective Failure Attacks

We first consider the latter category, that leads to the so-called *selective failure attacks*. These are corruptions of the garbled circuit that make it executable only if a condition on internal values is met. If not, the protocol aborts: $\mathcal{E}$ does not obtain a correct output and thus can not send back a result to $\mathcal{G}$. Then $\mathcal{G}$ learns whether the condition is met, but, if not, $\mathcal{E}$ detects the corruption and

$\mathcal{G}$ gets caught. More specifically, the malicious $\mathcal{G}$ could use inconsistent keys to construct a garbled gate or to exchange inputs during the OT phasis.

Let us see two examples, first, with the modification of an internal gate, and then with a corrupted OT during the initialization phasis.

Alteration of an Internal Garbled Gate. We consider an internal gate garbled as in Table 5. Suppose a key $k_{B_\gamma}^{1*}$ has been used for the garbling instead of $k_{B_\gamma}^1$. During the evaluation, if $\mathcal{E}$ gets $k_{B_\gamma}^1$, then after this corrupted gate, he will get an inconsistent key, that will be used to evaluate the rest of the circuit. It will not be detected until the last gate of the circuit, the output of which will not match any commitment. An example of this corrupted garbled gate is shown in the full version [3].

Because he can not return a valid output, $\mathcal{E}$ is forced to abort the protocol. If the protocol aborts, $\mathcal{G}$ learns that $k_{B_\gamma}^1$ should have been used and $\mathcal{E}$ detects the attack. But if the protocol runs correctly, $\mathcal{G}$ learns the normal output, plus an internal bit $k_{B_\gamma}^0$, and the $\mathcal{E}$ does not detect it. In the previous works, as any other corruption of the circuit, this attack is prevented by cut-&-choose solutions.

Corruption During the OT. We now consider $\mathcal{E}$ has some input bit b and $\mathcal{G}$ generates honestly the circuit using k_B^0 and k_B^1. However, during the OT phasis, $\mathcal{G}$ uses k_B^0 and k_B^{1*}. Then, if $b = 1$, $\mathcal{E}$ gets an inconsistent key and the leakage of information is just as before. Note that the circuit itself is not modified, meaning that cut-&-choose does not solve this issue. More specific and efficient solutions have been designed, such as *s-probe-resistant matrices* [10,17].

Information vs. Detection. In both above cases, the malicious generator can get detected since the failure is part of the way to learn information. Hence, the adversary must make the protocol fail with non-negligible probability to learn something. In the rest of the paper, we restrict the study to context where the potential gain of information is not worth the risk of getting caught by the honest party. Moreover, if the garbled circuit and the inputs were signed by the generator, the evaluator could easily prove to some authority that the garbled circuit is indeed non-executable. This seems reasonable in many real-life cases. We thus limit alterations to the protocol that do never lead to a failure.

3.2 Undetectable Corruptions

In order to be undetectable, the corrupted circuit must keep the same topology and the outputs must match the commitments. We later prove that this limits modifications to turning any non-linear gate into any other non-linear gate.

But before showing this is the only possible alteration, let us show how such an alteration can work: if $\mathcal{G}$ garbles the half-gates by switching some garbled keys, as shown in Table 7, it is easy to prove that the resulting gate computes $\bar{a} \wedge b$, and that the execution algorithm of $\mathcal{E}$ remains unchanged. Moreover, this modified garbled truth table is actually the correct way of garbling $\bar{a} \wedge b$.

Table 7. Turning $a \wedge b$ into $\bar{a} \wedge b$

First half-gate		Second half-gate	
Garbled table if $\gamma = 0$	Garbled table if $\gamma = 1$	$b \oplus \gamma$	Garbled table
$k_X^0 \oplus H(k_A^{p_A}) = 0$	$k_X^{\overline{p_A}} \oplus H(k_A^{p_A}) = 0$	0	$k_Y^0 \oplus H(k_{B_\gamma}^0) = 0$
$k_X^0 \oplus H(k_A^{\overline{p_A}}) = G$	$k_X^{p_A} \oplus H(k_A^{\overline{p_A}}) = G$	1	$k_Y^0 \oplus k_A^1 \oplus H(k_{B_\gamma}^1) = E$

With similar modifications, we obtain (in the full version [3]) a correct garbling of $a \wedge \bar{b}$ and $\overline{a \wedge b}$ from a corrupted AND gate. Combining these three modifications, one can turn a AND gate into any of the eight non-linear gates. Note that other ways exist to obtain the same results, but we chose these ones because they represent the honest ways of garbling $\bar{a} \wedge b$, $a \wedge \bar{b}$ and $\overline{a \wedge b}$.

These modifications can be made arbitrarily by the generator and it will not be detected by the evaluator, unless some cut-&-choose solution is used. In the rest of the paper, we are proving that no other modification can be made by a probabilistic polynomial-time adversary, or the protocol may abort, but the adversary does not want to take the risk of getting caught.

4   Delimitation of the Corruption

Let us now prove that the above modifications and their combinations are the only ones that can be made by an adversarial generator $\mathcal{G}$, if it does not want to get detected. We call f the function to evaluate and C_f a Boolean circuit representation of it.

We assume in this section that the (possibly corrupted) garbled circuit is executable for all inputs, since the adversary does not want to get detected.

Let us start with the obvious limitations. First, as already noticed, the topology of the Boolean circuit to evaluate is public, which ensures that $\mathcal{G}$ can not cheat on the number of gates or the way they are connected. Second, because of the free-XOR trick [8], XOR gates have no garbled truth tables to transmit, then they can not be corrupted either.

But $\mathcal{G}$ can still garble "correctly" another circuit $\mathsf{C}_{f'}$ (computing some other function f' instead of f). By correct garbling, we mean that $\mathcal{G}$ garbles $\mathsf{C}_{f'}$ in accordance with the garbling algorithm (and its optimizations), and keeps the number of gates and the way they are connected to each other unchanged, as if f' was the correct function to evaluate. XOR gates of C_f must also be present in $\mathsf{C}_{f'}$. More specifically, we have the following restrictions:

1. Only two ciphers are sent for each non-linear gates.
2. XOR gates are not transmitted.
3. There is a global offset that differentiates the two garbled keys of each wire of $\mathsf{C}_{f'}$ (in accordance with the free-XOR trick [8]) and this offset is odd (as required by the point-and-permute technique [2]).
4. $\mathsf{C}_{f'}$ is Boolean: for every wire of the circuit, there are two garbled keys.

It is obvious that the first two requirements are met. Otherwise, $\mathcal{E}$ will refuse to evaluate the circuit. In this section, we show that if the input wires of C_f are correctly garbled (i.e. have a common odd offset), then the rest of the circuit is also correctly garbled, or the protocol may abort. Thereafter, we provide a construction to ensure that input wires are correct. This will help to prove that the adversary is only able to turn a non-linear gate into another non-linear gate.

For the sake of simplicity, we consider that the original circuit is only composed of XOR and AND gates and we show later that the same result applies for the other gates.

4.1 Impossibility of Reducing the Number of Garbled Keys to One

The first thing to prove is that, for any garbled gate, there are at least two output garbled keys. Consider the case where an adversary wants to alter an AND gate (w.l.o.g.) so that it always outputs True (or always False), whatever the inputs are. Then, he must choose E and G in Table 6, so that the four garbled output keys are equal. Then, we have the following system of equations:

$$\begin{cases} K_2 = K_1 \\ K_3 = K_1 \\ K_4 = K_1 \end{cases} \iff \begin{cases} E = H(k_{B\gamma}^0) \oplus H(k_{B\gamma}^1) \oplus k_A^{p_A} \\ G = H(k_A^{p_A}) \oplus H(k_A^{\overline{p_A}}) \\ k_A^{p_A} = k_A^{\overline{p_A}} \end{cases}$$

Lemma 1. *For any garbled gate, if the first operand has two garbled keys with an odd offset, then the output wire has at least two possible garbled keys.*

Proof. If we indeed have $k_A^{p_A} \oplus k_A^{\overline{p_A}} = \Delta$ that is odd, then the four keys can not be equal. $\square$

4.2 Impossibility of Three-Key Wires - Part 1

In the last part, we showed that if the input wires are correct, there are at least two garbled keys per wire. In this section, we aim to prove there is no wire having more than two possible garbled keys, while the circuit remains evaluable. As described in Sect. 2, the garbled circuit is considered to have two commitments on the garbled keys of its output wires. This ensures that output wires have at most two possible keys, or the protocol aborts when a third key is obtained. Then, if some wire of the circuit has three possible keys or more, then there must be a gate that reduces it to only two. We show that such a gate is impossible.

As defined in Sect. 2, $s()$ refers to the function that takes a garbled key as input and outputs the select bit of that key. This function tells the evaluator what line of Table 6 he should use while evaluating: $s(k_A^{p_A}) = 0$ and $s(k_A^0) = p_A$.

Since the previous notations are irrelevant, if there are more than two keys or if the point-and-permute trick is not followed, we now call k_X, k_X' the two distinct garbled key of a wire, and k_X'' a third garbled key when needed.

We remind that $H()$ is a hash function that is assumed to behave like a random function from $\mathbb{F}_{2^N}$ to $\mathbb{F}_{2^N}$ and we expect the following problems to be computationally unfeasible by any polynomially bounded adversary:

Fig. 2. Reducing the number of keys of the first operand: impossible

Fig. 3. Modification of the offset: impossible

1. Finding distinct $k_1, k_1' \in \mathbb{F}_{2^N}$, so that $H(k_1) = H(k_1')$ requires $2^{N/2}$ evaluations of $H()$ on average (Birthday paradox).
2. Finding distinct $k_1, k_1' \in \mathbb{F}_{2^N}$, so that $H(k_1) \oplus k_1 = H(k_1') \oplus k_1'$ requires $2^{N/2}$ evaluations of $H()$ on average (Equivalent to the birthday paradox).
3. For given i and j, finding $k_1, k_1', k_2, k_2' \in \mathbb{F}_{2^N}$, so that $k_1 \neq k_1'$, $k_2 \neq k_2'$ and $H(k_1|i) \oplus H(k_1'|i) \oplus H(k_2|j) \oplus H(k_2'|j) = 0$ requires $2^{N/4}$ evaluation of $H()$ on average.
4. For given i and j, finding $k_1, k_1', k_2, k_2' \in \mathbb{F}_{2^N}$, so that $k_1 \neq k_1'$, $k_2 \neq k_2'$ and $H(k_1|i) \oplus k_1 \oplus H(k_1'|i) \oplus k_1' \oplus H(k_2|j) \oplus H(k_2'|j) = 0$ requires $2^{N/4}$ evaluations of $H()$ on average.

All these properties can be proven if H is modeled as a random oracle, using the birthday paradox bound. Note that in the definition of these problems, the adversary can freely choose the garbled keys k_1, k_1', k_2 and k_2', whereas for garbled gates, they are constrained by the garbling of the previous gates. Intuitively, solving these problems requires a lot more evaluations than listed above. These properties lead to the following lemma, which proof can be found in the full version [3], illustrated in Fig. 2:

Lemma 2. *For any garbled gate, if the first operand has at least three possible garbed keys, and the second has at least two, then the output wire has at least three garbled keys.*

4.3   Impossibility of Three-Key Wires - Part 2

In this part, we study the opposite problem, where the second operand has at least three garbled keys and the first has at least two. The proof being more tricky, we need Lemma 3 as a preliminary step:

Lemma 3. *For any gate, if the operands have two garbled keys and have the same odd offset, then the output wire has the same offset or at least three keys.*

The proof of Lemma 3 is given in the full version [3]. We now aim at concluding the last case with the following lemma:

Lemma 4. *If the input wires of the circuit have garbled keys with an odd global offset, then the garbled circuit cannot have a gate such that the second operand has at least three possible garbed keys, and the first has at least two, while the output wire has only two garbled keys.*

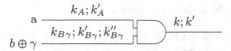

Fig. 4. Reducing the number of keys of the second operand: impossible

Proof. From Lemma 2, we know this is true if the two operands have at least three keys. We thus focus to the case where the first operand has two keys and the second operand has three keys, as illustrated in Fig. 4. For this proof, we consider that the input wires of the circuit are correctly garbled: these wires have two garbled keys and they have an odd global offset Δ. We study the case of the first gate, called $\mathcal{F}$, of the circuit (in topological order) that has two garbled inputs for the first operand and three (or more) for the second.

Since $\mathcal{F}$ is the first of its kind in the circuit and because of Lemma 2, the sub-circuit that links the inputs of the circuit to the first operand wire of $\mathcal{F}$ have only wires with exactly two garbled keys. Moreover, since all input wires of this sub-circuit have the global offset Δ and because of Lemma 3, all wires of the sub-circuit, including the first operand of $\mathcal{F}$, have this same odd offset Δ.

Remark that an input wire of the circuit can not have three keys. Then the three keys (or more) of the second operand of $\mathcal{F}$ come from a corrupted gate $\mathcal{F}'$ that outputs three distinct keys (or more). However, the two operand wires of $\mathcal{F}'$ have two possible garbled keys, and, with a similar approach, we can show that they have the same offset Δ as the first operand of $\mathcal{F}$. Then, the three keys of the second operand engages the choice of Δ. Using this fact and Table 6, we show in the full version that no such gate can exist.   □

4.4   Impossibility of Turning a Non-linear Gate into a Linear Gate

In Sect. 3, we showed how to turn a non-linear gate into any other non-linear gate. We will now prove that, since an adversarial generator is limited to Boolean circuits and can not deviate from the global offset, he can not turn a non-linear gate into a linear gate. We focus on the case of an AND gate.

Lemma 5. *For any non-linear gate, if the two operands have two garbled keys and have the same odd offset, then it can not be turned into a linear gate.*

Proof. We already demonstrated that an AND gate can not be corrupted into a gate that always outputs True (or False). All other cases are proven to be impossible in the full version [3].   □

Two particular cases of this lemma clearly reduce the possibilities of a malicious generator. First, an adversary can not force the output of a non-linear gate, and thus can not trivially force the output of the entire garbled circuit. Moreover, the adversary can not alter a gate so that it always outputs the first input a ($K_1 = K_2$ and $K_3 = K_4$). This last example is interesting: it actually means that the malicious generator cannot modify the circuit so that the evaluator's inputs go directly to the output through the circuit.

4.5   About Other Non-linear Gates

We showed in Sect. 3 how to turn $a \wedge b$ into $\bar{a} \wedge b$, $a \wedge \bar{b}$ and $\overline{a \wedge b}$. It appears that these deviations and their combinations are identical to the honest ways of garbling these respective gates, described in [20].

Then, an honest garbling of $\overline{a \wedge b}$ (or any other non-linear gate) can be obtained from a corruption of $a \wedge b$. Thus, there is no modification that can be made on $\overline{a \wedge b}$ and that cannot be made on $a \wedge b$. Therefore, any non-linear gate can only be turned into another non-linear gate.

4.6   Fitting Everything Together

Assembling the lemmata previously proved, we obtain Theorem 6, which is the main contribution of this paper.

Theorem 6. *If all the operands of the first garbled gates can take the two values according to the evaluator's inputs (while the generator's inputs are fixed), and if there are output commitments, then the adversarial generator is limited to turn any non-linear gates into other non-linear gates.*

This theorem means that if we can guarantee that the first garbled gates (the non-linear gates that are the closest to the input wires) can take the two possible inputs, independently on each wire, according to the evaluator's choice, then all the garbled gates can only be altered into any non-linear gates.

Proof. Using Lemma 1, if the input wires of the first garbled gates all have two possible garbled keys, then there is no wire in the rest of the circuit that has only one possible key. Combining Lemmata 2 and 4, if the input wires of the first garbled gates of the circuit all have the same odd global offset and if the circuit has output commitments, then no wire of the rest of the circuit has more than two possible garbled keys. Moreover, with the same conditions, Lemma 3 shows that all wires share the same odd global offset. Then, Lemma 5 comes last and shows that non-linear gates can only be turned into other non-linear gates, and that this is the only possible corruption.   □

It remains to study the conditions so that the starting point of this theorem is satisfied: all the inputs of the first garbled gates have two possible garbled keys. How to guarantee some wires to have two possible garbled keys, with the same global odd offset? We will show below that it is possible to make sure that all the evaluator's inputs are converted into garbled keys with a common global odd offset. But there is no way to do the same for the generator's inputs. Indeed, he can not be forced to choose his inputs after generating the garbled circuit. On the other hand, XOR gates can not be corrupted, and so a XOR gate with an evaluator's input will necessarily have two distinct outputs. Hence, here are some interesting cases that will meet our above requirements:

– one wants to evaluate $f(y)$, for a public function f, so that the evaluator chooses y, but the generator will get the result;

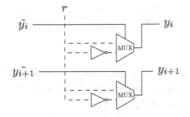

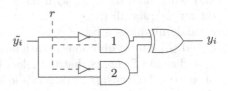

Fig. 5. Overview of the sub-circuit   **Fig. 6.** Implementation of the MUX

- one evaluates $f(x, y)$, and any input wires of the first non-linear gates is either an y_j chosen by the evaluator, or $x_i \oplus y_j$, where x_i is chosen by the generator. Indeed, in both cases, y_j or $x_i \oplus y_j$, when x_i is fixed, the inputs of the first gates can take the two possible values according to y_j.

The latter case applies to a large class of circuits, including the addition, the greater-than, the equality test, combination of those, or even more complex circuits, such as AES. The former case is known as *privacy-free* garbled circuits [5] and was shown to be efficient zero-knowledge proof protocols [6]. As mentioned in Sect. 2, there are more efficient garbling schemes in this context. The work of [20] also provides an optimal garbling scheme for this purpose. Our results also hold with this garbling scheme.

5   Ensuring the Correct Garbling of Input Wires

In this section, we describe a construction to guarantee that input wires of the evaluator $\mathcal{E}$ are correctly garbled by the generator $\mathcal{G}$. Rather than modifying the garbling scheme, we propose to modify the circuit representation of the function to evaluate, by adding a sub-circuit in front of the original circuit. This sub-circuit is illustrated in Fig. 5. Figure 6 gives details of the multiplexer, but is not required for the correctness. We call x the input of $\mathcal{G}$, and y the input of $\mathcal{E}$.

5.1   Construction

The main idea is that rather than transmitting the input garbled keys of $\mathcal{E}$ through an oblivious transfer, the inputs are now connected to the outputs of this sub-circuit. The sub-circuit has the same number of inputs of $\mathcal{E}$ as the original circuit plus one: a bit r that is randomly chosen by $\mathcal{E}$. For each input y_i of the original circuit, the sub-circuit has an input $\tilde{y}_i = y_i \oplus r$ and an output y_i. The new inputs are transmitted as usual through an oblivious transfer.

We also give restrictions on some permute bits: the permute bit of w_R (the wire carrying r) and $w_{\tilde{Y}_i}$ (carrying $\tilde{y}_i$) must be zero. Also the permute bit of w_{Y_i} (the wire carrying y_i) must be public. This is to ensure that $\mathcal{G}$ does not force the inputs of $\mathcal{E}$ during the oblivious transfer phase.

Because of r and of those permute bits, the protocol has to be slightly modified, as suggested by the following sketch:

1. $\mathcal{G}$ garbles the concatenation of the two circuits using the usual garbling scheme and sends it to $\mathcal{E}$, along with his garbled input keys for x and the permute bit for w_{Y_i}, for all i;
2. $\mathcal{E}$ randomly picks a bit r;
3. $\mathcal{E}$ and $\mathcal{G}$ perform oblivious transfers in order $\mathcal{E}$ to obtain the garbled keys of $\tilde{y}_i$ and r, and $\mathcal{E}$ checks that the select bits of these keys match the clear values or aborts. This ensures two possible keys for the evaluator's inputs;
4. $\mathcal{E}$ evaluates the sub-circuit and checks if the select bits of the keys for the input y match the clear value, or aborts;
5. $\mathcal{E}$ evaluates the rest of the circuit and returns the result.

Since the functionality of the circuit is not changed by the sub-circuit (as long as the new input $\tilde{y}$ is chosen according to r), the correctness is preserved.

5.2 Analysis

Our security goal is to ensure that all output wires of the sub-circuit (i.e. inputs of the rest of the circuit) share the same odd global offset, or the protocol aborts for some specific inputs. To prove it, we need two more lemmata.

Lemma 7. *For any garbled gate, if the two operands have distinct but odd offsets, then the offset of the first operand is propagated to the output wire.*

Proof. The proof of this lemma is identical to the proof of Lemma 3. Indeed, in the proof of Lemma 3, the offset of the second operand ($k_{B_\gamma}^0 \oplus k_{B_\gamma}^1$) never appears.   □

Lemma 8. *For any XOR gate, if the offsets of the operands are different or if one of the operands has more than two garbled keys, there are at least four distinct garbled keys at the output.*

Proof. The proof of this lemma is trivial since the output keys of a XOR gate are the input keys XORed together.   □

Let us analyze the propagation of offsets in one of the multiplexer of the sub-circuit. Remark that there can not be only one possible garbled key for w_{Y_i}. Indeed, since the permute bit of this wire is known by the evaluator, then there must be at least two possible keys with opposite select bits. We consider the multiplexer illustrated in Fig. 6. We stress that the order of the operands matters. Let w_1 and w_2 refer to the output wires of the AND gates noted respectively 1 and 2. We also note Δ the offset of wire w_r carrying r and $\Delta_{\tilde{Y}_i}$ the offset of the wire carrying $\tilde{y}_i$. We can enumerate the different corruption cases:

1. The offsets Δ and $\Delta_{\tilde{Y}_i}$ are different but odd.
2. Δ is even and $\Delta_{\tilde{Y}_i}$ is odd.
3. Δ is odd and $\Delta_{\tilde{Y}_i}$ is even.
4. Both offsets are even (distinct or not).

Consider the first case. According to Lemma 7, the different offsets propagate so that w_1 has offset $\Delta_{\tilde{Y}_i}$ and w_2 has offset Δ, or one of them two wires have more than two keys. In either case, using Lemma 8, the output of the XOR gate gives at least three different keys. Given that these three (or more) keys engages the value of Δ, we can show that it can not be reduced back to two in the rest of the circuit, using the same method as for Lemma 4.

Consider the second case, if Δ is even, then the garbled keys of w_R have equal select bits. In other words, the select bit of one of the garbled keys does not match the clear value of r. Since r is known to evaluator and since the permute bit must be set to zero, this situation is detected and leads the evaluator to abort. The exact same reasoning works for the third and fourth cases.

We can now conclude that the output wires of the sub-circuit have exactly two possible garbled keys with the same odd global offset, or the protocol aborts for some inputs of the evaluator or some r.

6   Applications to Real Circuits

In the previous sections, we have defined precisely how a malicious generator can corrupt a garbled circuit. Turning non-linear gates into other non-linear gates is equivalent at adding NOT gates to the circuit. Then, we consider in this section that the adversary is able to add a NOT gate to any wire of the circuit. An important consequence is that a circuit can not be modified so that the inputs of the evaluator's inputs go trivially through the gates to the outputs of the circuit. Thus, the question "does a corrupted circuit leak more information than the original circuit?" turns out to be trickier than suggested in the previous works.

In this section, we don't provide a general answer, but we see the impact of corruptions on some real circuits. We measure this impact with the Shannon entropy of the evaluator's input. We call x and y the respective inputs of the generator and the evaluator. Let $z = f(x, y)$ be the function to evaluate and C_f a boolean circuit computing it. We note $\mathcal{C}_f$ the set of all circuits that can be obtained by corrupting C_f (i.e. by adding NOT gates to C_f). In other words, there exists a corruption of C_f that leads to $C_{f'}$, that computes some other function f', if and only if $C_{f'} \in \mathcal{C}_f$. We formalize the problem as follows:

Problem: *For a circuit C_f does it exist a corrupted circuit $C_{f'} \in \mathcal{C}_f$, such that the obtained function f' leaks more information on the evaluator's input:*
$$H(Y|X = x, Z = f(x,y)) > H(Y|X = x', Z = f'(x',y))?$$

Remark that in the entropy equation, the generator knows x since this is his input. In our computations, we consider that the adversarial generator chooses his input in order to increase the leakage.

To help us answer that question, we implemented a tool to exhaustively compute all corruptions $C_{f'}$ of a circuit C_f and check if one of them leaks more information. More details about this tools are given in the full version [3].

6.1   The Greater-Than Function

Let us now see a practical example: the greater-than function, that returns a single bit (1 if $x > y$, 0 otherwise). Assuming the adversary takes the middle of the set as input (which leaks the most information), the original function leaks one bit of entropy. Since there is a single output wire, whatever the modification made on the circuit, it does not leak more than one bit of entropy on y. But it is interesting to see that the adversary is limited in the choice of that bit. For example, if we consider the greater-than circuit defined in [7], it can not be modified to output the parity bit of y. This can be proven exhaustively for the 3-bit greater-than circuit and then recursively.

In the particular case of greater-than circuit, remark that the best strategy of an adversarial $\mathcal{G}$, willing to retrieve the input y, consists in not modifying the circuit. If y is ℓ-bit long, then it would require ℓ evaluations for $\mathcal{G}$ to find y, and it can not be reduced by corrupting it. Thus, in this context, using cut-&-choose based solutions does not enhance privacy (but ensures the correctness).

6.2   The Addition Function

Let us study now the addition function f, the circuit C_f of which is defined and optimized in [7]. Consider that $\mathcal{E}$ has two inputs $y, y' \in \mathbb{F}_2^\ell$ and the generator none. This circuit computes the addition of y and y' in $\mathbb{F}_2^\ell$ (the carry bit is not returned). The original function f does not leak any information on y (or on y'). Up to $\ell = 10$, we exhaustively demonstrated that no modification leaks any information on y: $H(Y|Z = f'(y,y')) = H(Y|Z = f(y,y')) = \ell$ This result can be extended recursively for larger values of ℓ.

6.3   The Equality-Test Function

Unfortunately, it is not the case for all circuit. Consider now the equality-test function, that returns 1 if and only if $x = y$. The Boolean circuit we study for the 4-bit case is shown in Fig. 7. Inputs are 4-bit long and after the evaluation of the original function, it remains 3.66 bits of entropy. This circuit is vulnerable to the addition of NOT gates. Indeed, we demonstrated exhaustively that the best corruption required to add a single NOT gate, as shown in red in Fig. 7. Now, the remaining entropy is $H(Y|X = x', Z = f'(x',y)) = 3.01$ bits. Consequently, almost 1 bit is leaked by this function f'. Actually, f' returns $x_3 \oplus y_3$ if x_{0-2} and y_{0-2} are different and 0 otherwise. Clearly, this same attack would work for larger equality-test circuits.

But note that this attack is entirely based on the topological representation of the function. If we inverted the direction of the cascade of AND gates (as shown in Fig. 8), the leaked bit would be $x_0 \oplus y_0$. Based on this fact, we propose a generic solution to reduce the leakage of a circuit in the full version. Unfortunately, this fix also requires to increase the size of the circuit.

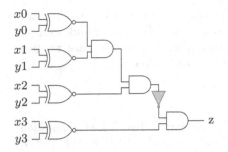

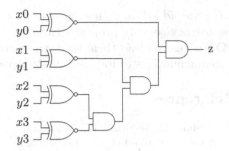

Fig. 7. Circuit for the 4-bit-equality test and its best corrupted circuit in red (Color figure online)

Fig. 8. Another circuit for the 4-bit-equality test

6.4   Trade-Off with Cut-&-Choose

Then, for some classes of circuits, there exist corrupted circuits that leak more information than the original function. In such cases, cut-&-choose remains necessary if we want to avoid this leakage. Based on the fact that this leakage depends on the topology of the circuit, our results still allow to improve for free any cut-&-choose based solutions since [9].

Since several garbled circuits are generated, we recommend to use different circuits of the same function (with different topologies). Then, even if the adversary manages to guess correctly which circuits are opened, he is limited to corruptions that can be obtained from all unopened circuits and their respective topologies. Indeed, if different corrupted circuits do not compute the same (corrupted) function, then they may output different results, which allows the evaluator to learn the adversarial inputs thanks to [1,9].

For example, let us consider the two circuits of Figs. 7 and 8 of the same function. Say that cut-&-choose is used with half of the circuits with the first topology and the other half with the second. Assume that at least one circuit of each is unopened. Then, we demonstrated exhaustively that any corrupted function that can be obtained from both topologies does not leak any information on the evaluator's inputs more than the original function already does.

7   Conclusion

The main contribution of this paper is to show that, for a large class of circuits, a malicious generator can corrupt a garbled circuit by only two ways. He can add NOT gates arbitrarily in the circuit, or make selective failure attacks on inputs/outputs of a non-linear gate. This is drastically lower than the previous state-of-the-art suggests. We believe this work can lead to some more optimized secure solutions in the malicious setting, more efficient than the regular cut-&-choose schemes.

The second contribution is the analysis of the impact of NOT gates in real-life circuits. We show that some circuits do not leak more information when NOT gates are added, and thus cut-&-choose solutions are unnecessary to enhance the privacy security property. However, for some other circuits, the addition of NOT gates can lead them to reveal more information, but in that case we give recommendations to improve cut-&-choose solutions for free.

References

1. Afshar, A., Mohassel, P., Pinkas, B., Riva, B.: Non-interactive secure computation based on cut-and-choose. In: Nguyen, P.Q., Oswald, E. (eds.) EUROCRYPT 2014. LNCS, vol. 8441, pp. 387–404. Springer, Heidelberg (2014). https://doi.org/10.1007/978-3-642-55220-5_22
2. Beaver, D., Micali, S., Rogaway, P.: The round complexity of secure protocols (extended abstract). In: 22nd ACM STOC, pp. 503–513. ACM Press, May 1990
3. Dupin, A., Pointcheval, D., Bidan, C.: On the leakage of corrupted garbled circuits. Cryptology ePrint Archive, Report 2018/743, August 2018. https://eprint.iacr.org/2018/743
4. Frederiksen, T.K., Jakobsen, T.P., Nielsen, J.B., Nordholt, P.S., Orlandi, C.: MiniLEGO: efficient secure two-party computation from general assumptions. In: Johansson, T., Nguyen, P.Q. (eds.) EUROCRYPT 2013. LNCS, vol. 7881, pp. 537–556. Springer, Heidelberg (2013). https://doi.org/10.1007/978-3-642-38348-9_32
5. Frederiksen, T.K., Nielsen, J.B., Orlandi, C.: Privacy-free garbled circuits with applications to efficient zero-knowledge. In: Oswald, E., Fischlin, M. (eds.) EUROCRYPT 2015. LNCS, vol. 9057, pp. 191–219. Springer, Heidelberg (2015). https://doi.org/10.1007/978-3-662-46803-6_7
6. Jawurek, M., Kerschbaum, F., Orlandi, C.: Zero-knowledge using garbled circuits: how to prove non-algebraic statements efficiently. In: Sadeghi, A.R., Gligor, V.D., Yung, M. (eds.) ACM CCS 13, pp. 955–966. ACM Press, November 2013
7. Kolesnikov, V., Sadeghi, A.-R., Schneider, T.: Improved garbled circuit building blocks and applications to auctions and computing minima. In: Garay, J.A., Miyaji, A., Otsuka, A. (eds.) CANS 2009. LNCS, vol. 5888, pp. 1–20. Springer, Heidelberg (2009). https://doi.org/10.1007/978-3-642-10433-6_1
8. Kolesnikov, V., Schneider, T.: Improved garbled circuit: free XOR gates and applications. In: Aceto, L., Damgård, I., Goldberg, L.A., Halldórsson, M.M., Ingólfsdóttir, A., Walukiewicz, I. (eds.) ICALP 2008. LNCS, vol. 5126, pp. 486–498. Springer, Heidelberg (2008). https://doi.org/10.1007/978-3-540-70583-3_40
9. Lindell, Y.: Fast cut-and-choose based protocols for malicious and covert adversaries. In: Canetti, R., Garay, J.A. (eds.) CRYPTO 2013. LNCS, vol. 8043, pp. 1–17. Springer, Heidelberg (2013). https://doi.org/10.1007/978-3-642-40084-1_1
10. Lindell, Y., Pinkas, B.: An efficient protocol for secure two-party computation in the presence of malicious adversaries. In: Naor, M. (ed.) EUROCRYPT 2007. LNCS, vol. 4515, pp. 52–78. Springer, Heidelberg (2007). https://doi.org/10.1007/978-3-540-72540-4_4
11. Mohassel, P., Franklin, M.: Efficiency tradeoffs for malicious two-party computation. In: Yung, M., Dodis, Y., Kiayias, A., Malkin, T. (eds.) PKC 2006. LNCS, vol. 3958, pp. 458–473. Springer, Heidelberg (2006). https://doi.org/10.1007/11745853_30
12. Mohassel, P., Riva, B.: Garbled circuits checking garbled circuits: more efficient and secure two-party computation. In: Canetti, R., Garay, J.A. (eds.) CRYPTO 2013. LNCS, vol. 8043, pp. 36–53. Springer, Heidelberg (2013). https://doi.org/10.1007/978-3-642-40084-1_3

13. Naor, M., Pinkas, B., Sumner, R.: Privacy preserving auctions and mechanism design. In: Proceedings of the 1st ACM Conference on Electronic Commerce, pp. 129–139. ACM, November 1999
14. Nielsen, J.B., Orlandi, C.: LEGO for two-party secure computation. In: Reingold, O. (ed.) TCC 2009. LNCS, vol. 5444, pp. 368–386. Springer, Heidelberg (2009). https://doi.org/10.1007/978-3-642-00457-5_22
15. Nielsen, J.B., Schneider, T., Trifiletti, R.: Constant round maliciously secure 2PC with function-independent preprocessing using LEGO. In: NDSS 2017. The Internet Society (2017)
16. Shelat, A., Shen, C.: Two-output secure computation with malicious adversaries. In: Paterson, K.G. (ed.) EUROCRYPT 2011. LNCS, vol. 6632, pp. 386–405. Springer, Heidelberg (2011). https://doi.org/10.1007/978-3-642-20465-4_22
17. Shelat, A., Shen, C.H.: Fast two-party secure computation with minimal assumptions. In: Sadeghi, A.R., Gligor, V.D., Yung, M. (eds.) ACM CCS 13, pp. 523–534. ACM Press, November 2013
18. Wang, X., Malozemoff, A.J., Katz, J.: Faster secure two-party computation in the single-execution setting. In: Coron, J.-S., Nielsen, J.B. (eds.) EUROCRYPT 2017. LNCS, vol. 10212, pp. 399–424. Springer, Cham (2017). https://doi.org/10.1007/978-3-319-56617-7_14
19. Yao, A.C.C.: How to generate and exchange secrets (extended abstract). In: 27th FOCS, pp. 162–167. IEEE Computer Society Press, October 1986
20. Zahur, S., Rosulek, M., Evans, D.: Two halves make a whole - reducing data transfer in garbled circuits using half gates. In: Oswald, E., Fischlin, M. (eds.) EUROCRYPT 2015. LNCS, vol. 9057, pp. 220–250. Springer, Heidelberg (2015). https://doi.org/10.1007/978-3-662-46803-6_8

Location-Proof System Based on Secure Multi-party Computations

Aurélien Dupin[1,3]($\boxtimes$), Jean-Marc Robert[2], and Christophe Bidan[3]

[1] Thales Communications & Security, Gennevilliers, France
dupin.aurelien@gmail.com
[2] École de Technologie Supérieure, Montréal, Canada
[3] Centrale-Supélec, Rennes, France

Abstract. Location-based services are quite popular. Their variety and their numerous users show it clearly. However, these applications rely on the persons' honesty to use their real location. If they are motivated to lie about their position, they can do so. A *location-proof system* allows a *prover* to obtain proofs from nearby *witnesses*, for being at a given location at a given time. Such a proof can be used to convince a *verifier* later on. Many solutions have been designed in the last decade, but none protects perfectly the privacy of their participants. Indeed, provers and witnesses may want to keep their identity and location private. In this paper, a solution is presented in which a *malicious adversary*, acting as a prover, cannot cheat on his position. It relies on *multi-party computations* and *group-signature schemes* to protect the private information of both the prover and the witnesses against any *semi-honest participant*. Additionally, this paper gives a new *secure multi-party maximum computation* protocol requiring $\mathcal{O}(n \log(n))$ computations and communications, which greatly improves the previously known solutions having $\mathcal{O}(n^2)$ complexities. Although it is designed for our location-proof system, it can be applied to any scenario in which a small information leakage is acceptable.

Keywords: Location proof
Secure multi-party maximum computation
Secure two-party comparison computation · Privacy preserving

1 Introduction

Location-based services are now ubiquitous, mostly through our phones and vehicles. These services generally rely on the persons' honesty to use their real location. Hence, they are limited to situations in which the persons do not have any motivation to lie. However, for some services such as electronic voting, location-based access control, and law enforcement investigation, this is not the case. These services must be based on a *location-proof system* that allows a participant, called *prover*, to obtain proofs from nearby participants, called *witnesses*,

© Springer Nature Switzerland AG 2018
J. Baek et al. (Eds.): ProvSec 2018, LNCS 11192, pp. 22–39, 2018.
https://doi.org/10.1007/978-3-030-01446-9_2

asserting that he has been at a given location at a given time. Such a proof can be used later on to convince a service provider, called *verifier*.

Any location-proof system based on the interaction between a prover and his neighbors has some privacy issues. The prover may not want to broadcast his identity every time he needs location proofs. Similarly, witnesses may want to hide their identity and location. Hence, private information must be kept secret from all the participants but not from an independent trusted third-party, called *judge*. Indeed, the judge must be allowed to retrieve the identities of the participants, in order to detect malicious collusions among them. An ideal location-proof system must then have the following properties [5].

1. **Correctness:** location proofs generated honestly by a prover with the collaboration of honest witnesses must always be accepted by the verifier.
2. **Unforgeability:** a prover cannot obtain/modify valid location proofs for a location where he is not, or at a different time.
3. **Non-transferability:** location proofs are valid only for the prover who generated them. They cannot be exchanged.
4. **Traceability:** given a proof, the judge must be able to retrieve the identity of the witness who signed it. *New property - not in* [5].
5. **Location and identity privacy:** the location and the identity of the witnesses and the prover must be kept secret from other participants.
6. **Unlinkability:** given two distinct location proofs, a participant cannot guess whether they have been generated by the same witness, nor whether they concern the same prover. This obviously does not stand for the judge.
7. **Storage sovereignty:** the prover is responsible for storing his own location proofs. No one is able to access them without the prover's agreement.

Several solutions that partially fulfill these objectives were proposed. Unfortunately, most of them require that the participants broadcast their identity and/or location. Sastry *et al.* [15] introduced the notion of *secure location verification*. Their solution relies on the deployment of impersonal local access points to locate participants in a given region, using *distance-bounding protocols*. Furthermore, the identity and location of the prover have to be transmitted to allow access points to grant access to nearby location-based services. In [14], Saroiu *et al.* introduced the notion of location proofs. The prover can now ask access points to generate proofs that he can store until he has to convince a verifier. However, it still requires an infrastructure to be deployed and does not ensure privacy. Later, other approaches based on impersonal access points (Luo *et al.* [10,11] and Pham *et al.* [13]) start answering the privacy issues using hash functions and pseudonyms. Although the most recent of these schemes achieve a high level of privacy, it is still limited to regions where access points are already deployed.

A complete different approach has been used by Singelee *et al.* [16]. Instead of deploying impersonal devices, they have suggested to involve nearby users. These users, called witnesses, can run distance-bounding protocols with the prover to certify his location. Unfortunately, the scheme still does not provide any privacy property. The solution of Graham *et al.* [6] is somehow similar, but the verifier has to choose himself the witnesses among the nearby volunteers. It reduces the probability of collusion among the participants. Later, Zhu *et al.* proposed a new solution APPLAUS [18] that protects identities through a set of pseudonyms. This allows the witnesses to generate location proofs without leaking their identity. However, all proofs (including pseudonyms and locations) are stored in a centralized authority, raising some privacy and efficiency issues. The protocol Link of Talasila *et al.* [17] is also based on centralized system.

Finally, Gambs *et al.* [5] proposed a solution to get rid of the central authority and to ensure most privacy properties. Identities are protected with a group-signature scheme instead of pseudonyms and the positions of the witnesses are not transmitted. Unfortunately, the location of the prover is still learned by the witnesses. A comparison of all these schemes is provided in Table 1.

Table 1. Comparison of existing protocols

	Echo [15]	[16]	SLVPGP [6]	[14]	[10]	Veriplace [11]	Applaus [18]	Link [17]	[3]	Props [5]	SecureRun [13]	Our work
Prover anonymity P: pseudonyms G: group signatures H: hash function				H				H	G		P	G
Witness anonymity P: pseudonyms G: group signatures NA: not applicable	NA			NA	NA	NA	P	H	G		NA	G
Prover location privacy	✓			✓	✓	✓		~			✓	✓
Witness location privacy	NA			NA	NA	NA			✓	✓	NA	✓
Storage sovereignty						✓				✓	✓	✓
No infrastructure requirement		✓	✓				✓	✓	✓			✓
Traceability	NA		✓	NA	NA	NA	✓	✓	✓		✓	✓

In this paper, we propose a privacy-aware location-proof system that fulfills all these properties. It relies on two protocols: a *location-proof gathering* protocol (allowing a prover to obtain proofs from witnesses) and a *location-proof verifying* protocol (allowing a verifier to validate the correctness of a proof). The first one ensures that both the prover and the witnesses keep their identity and their location secret. Once the location proofs have been obtained from witnesses, a prover must keep them securely and may use them later on to convince verifiers. For efficiency reasons, no centralized server is used during the gathering protocol.

Our scheme relies on *multi-party computations* and *group signature schemes* to protect the identity and the location of all participants. It assumes that the participants have phones/vehicles with directional antenna to locate their neighbors. Such a solution can complement classical distance-bounding protocols [1].

The security of our solution is analyzed against *malicious* and *semi-honest* adversaries. The former is a prover trying to obtain invalid location proofs, whereas the later is any participant (prover, witness or verifier) trying to obtain the private information on other participants. *Static collusions* between a prover and some of the witnesses against other witnesses are also considered.

As already mentioned, our scheme relies on multi-party computations, more specifically a multi-party maximum protocol. Although any existing protocol would be sufficient for our scheme. We design a new multi-party maximum protocol in Sect. 4 requiring $\mathcal{O}(n \log(n))$ computations and communications. All previously known results have their complexity in $\mathcal{O}(n^2)$. However, our construction is based on a trade-off between efficiency and privacy, but can be generalized to any scenario where a small information leakage is acceptable.

2   Problem Statement

Let us suppose the participants have devices (phone or vehicle) equipped with directional antennas, allowing to locate a transmitting device in 90°-quadrants with respect to their position and orientation. Depending on his location and orientation, a witness would be able to locate a prover in one of the four reference orthogonal half-planes (*North, East, South, West*), as shown in Fig. 1.

Our location problem can therefore be stated as follows. Consider n witnesses having located a prover $\mathcal{P}$ in half-planes with respect to their position. Looking for a location proof, $\mathcal{P}$ wants to obtain an authenticated description of the intersection of these half-planes, as shown in Fig. 2, while the witnesses want to protect their identity and private information. This can be reduced to find the maximum (or minimum) of the private x- or y-coordinates of the witnesses.

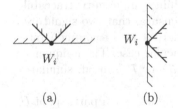

(a)   (b)

Fig. 1. Half-planes from 90°-quadrants

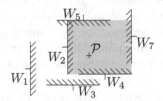

Fig. 2. Intersecting half-planes

2.1   Location-Proof Generation Protocol Outline

Protocol 1 presents the outline of our approach. After sharing among all participants the ephemeral additive homomorphic public keys, and the directions in which the prover is located for all witnesses (**Step 1**), the idea is to find the intersection of the witness-defined orthogonal half-planes approximating the prover's position (**Steps 2–3**), and generate a location proof from it (**Steps 4–5**).

Input: Each participant U knows his position (x_i, y_i) and his group signature
key gsk_U. The encryption function of the verifier $E_V(\cdot)$ is public.

Output: $\mathcal{P}$ obtains an authenticated location proof from his neighbor witnesses.

Step 1 : Initialization

$\mathcal{P}$ broadcasts a request: "*I'd like location proofs at time τ*".

forall the *accepting witness* W_i **do**

> Find the direction d_i of $\mathcal{P}$ (N, S, W or E) and generate an ephemeral
> public key N_{W_i} (Protocol 4).
> Send back (d_i, N_{W_i}) to $\mathcal{P}$.

$\mathcal{P}$ broadcasts to all witnesses $\mu = (\tau, N_\mathcal{P}, (d_i, N_{W_i})_{1 \leq i \leq n})$ and $GS(gsk_\mathcal{P}, \mu)$.
$N_\mathcal{P}$ is his ephemeral public key (Protocol 4).

forall the *accepting witness* W_i **do**

> Find his key N_{W_i} in the properly signed message. If not, abort.
> Return the signature $GS(gsk_{W_i}, \mu)$.

$\mathcal{P}$ broadcasts $\{GS(gsk_{W_i}, \mu) | 1 \leq i \leq n\}$.

forall the *accepting witness* W_i **do**

> Find if all the signatures are valid and different. If not, abort.

Step 2 : forall the *accepting witness* W_i **do**

> Run a min/max computation protocol with all witnesses (Protocol 3).

Step 3 : $\mathcal{P}$ gets $E_V(x_{i_{min}})$, $E_V(x_{i_{max}})$, $E_V(y_{i_{min}})$ and $E_V(y_{i_{max}})$ (Protocol 5).

Step 4 : $\mathcal{P}$ transfers these encrypted results to all witnesses.

Step 5 : All W_i sign the proof, using gsk_{W_i}, and send it to $\mathcal{P}$ (Protocol 2).

Protocol 1: Location proof generation

Our method relies on an *additive homomorphic encryption scheme*, such as
Paillier's cryptosystem [12], and a *unique group-signature* scheme [4], that possesses the following properties: correctness, unforgeability, anonymity, traceability, unlinkability and uniqueness. The last property ensures that two signatures
on the same message by a given group member share a lot of common bits,
breaking the unlinkability property in this very particular case. The uniqueness
property prevents that an accomplice of the prover $\mathcal{P}$, or $\mathcal{P}$ himself, simulates
the presence of multiple witnesses (Sybil attack).

In our scheme, groups can be dynamically managed and each participant U
has a signing key gsk_U. Let $GS(gsk_U, m)$ denote the private signature function
of the message m with gsk_U, and $GV(g_v, m, \sigma)$ the public verification function
that allows anyone to verify the signature σ of m with the public group key g_v.

2.2 Adversary Models

The following definitions of adversary models are extracted from [8]:

Definition 1 (semi-honest adversary model). *A semi-honest adversary follows the protocol specification exactly, but it may try to learn more information
than allowed by looking at the messages that it received and its internal state.
This model is also known as the passive or honest-but-curious adversary model.*

Definition 2 (malicious adversary model). *A malicious adversary may use any efficient attack strategy and thus may arbitrarily deviate from the protocol specification. This model is also known as the active adversary model.*

In this paper, we stress that there are two different motivations for the prover. First, the main motivation of a malicious prover is to obtain a valid proof that he is at a given location at a given time, when in fact he is somewhere else. In this case, the prover has to deviate from the protocol, while remaining undetected. Otherwise, legitimate witnesses would abort and alert the judge.

On the other hand, a curious prover may be interested in getting information about his neighbors (identity or precise location). Since the identity of a witness relies on the security of the group-signature scheme used, the potential risk is low. At best, the prover can expect to get the location of an unknown participant.

The witnesses could be interested in discovering more information on their neighbors. However, since a witness has far less possibilities than a prover, a malicious witness would be better to act as a prover with his neighbors.

Similarly, the verifier does not participate in the gathering location protocol and thus can only follow the semi-honest adversary model to try to get more information about the witnesses and the prover.

Finally, notice that a prover can always obtain a valid but faked location proof from accomplices. The verifier and the judge can always determine the number of witnesses having participated in the protocol. If they determine that this number is too low, they may reject the valid proof anyway.

To sum up, our scheme is secure against the following adversaries:

- A malicious prover willing to obtain fake location proofs.
- A semi-honest prover, witness or verifier trying to violate other participants' privacy.

In the rest of the paper, Sect. 3 presents how to build encrypted location proofs against a malicious adversary, and how to verify them. In Sect. 4, a new solution to the secure multi-party maximum computation problem is described. It relies on a modified version of a classical two-party comparison protocol presented in Sect. 5 and is optimized in the context of our location-proof system.

3 Location-Proof Gathering and Verifying

Let us first assume that the prover $\mathcal{P}$ has obtained somehow the four encrypted optimum values $E_V(x_{i_{min}})$, $E_V(x_{i_{max}})$, $E_V(y_{i_{min}})$ and $E_V(y_{i_{max}})$ describing the rectangle in which he lies. Sect. 4 presents how to obtain them from his neighboring witnesses. Unfortunately, nothing proves that he has not chosen these values himself and encrypted them with the verifier public key. The goal of **Steps 4–5** of **Protocol 1** is specifically to prevent this malicious behavior. In this section, we design a protocol allowing the witnesses to certify these optimum values. In this section, we will focus only on one of these values, say $E_V(x_{i_{max}})$.

Input: $\mathcal{P}$ knows $E_V(x_{i_{max}})$. Each witness W_i has his value x_i and his signature key gsk_{W_i}. Each witness knows the number of participants n, $GS(gsk_{\mathcal{P}}, \mu)$, and the verifier semi-homomorphic encryption function $E_V(\cdot)$.

Output: $\mathcal{P}$ obtains a location proof from each witness.

Step 1 : $\mathcal{P}$ broadcasts the randomized version of $E_V(x_{i_{max}})$.

Step 2 : forall the *witness* W_i **do**

> Choose randomly $k_i \in_R [\![2^{l_x+1}; 2^{l_k} - 1]\!]$ and $r_i \in_R [\![-2^{l_x} + 1; 2^{l_x} - 1]\!]$.
> Compute $E_V(k_i(x_{i_{max}} - x_i) + r_i) = (E_V(x_{i_{max}}) \cdot E_V(-x_i))^{k_i} \cdot E_V(r_i)$.
> Send $E_V(k_i(x_{i_{max}} - x_i) + r_i)$ to $\mathcal{P}$.

Step 3 : $\mathcal{P}$ broadcasts $\{E_V(k_i(x_{i_{max}} - x_i) + r_i) | 1 \leq i \leq n\}$.

Step 4 : forall the *witness* W_i **do**

> Check the presence of $E_V(k_i(x_{i_{max}} - x_i) + r_i)$. If not, abort.
> Define $\nu = ((E_V(k_i(x_{i_{max}} - x_i) + r_i))_{1 \leq i \leq n}, E_V(x_{i_{max}}), n, GS(gsk_{\mathcal{P}}, \mu))$.
> Sign $\sigma_i = GS(gsk_{W_i}, \nu)$ and send it to $\mathcal{P}$.

Step 5 : $\mathcal{P}$ stores ν, $GS(gsk_{\mathcal{P}}, \nu)$ and all witness signatures σ_i.

Protocol 2: Location-proof gathering protocol

3.1 Location-Proof Gathering

Let us assume w.l.o.g. that the public key N_V of the verifier is 2048-bit long and that the witnesses are at most at one kilometre from the prover. If the scale of the grid system is one meter, the difference $x_{i_{max}} - x_i \leq 2^{10}$ uses at most $l_x = 10$ bits. We define $l_k = |N_V| - (l_x + 1)$. Our method for generating the location proofs is presented in **Protocol 2**. If a witness follows the protocol, the verifier would be able to retrieve the value $k_i(x_{i_{max}} - x_i) + r_i$, which is such that:

$$k_i(x_{i_{max}} - x_i) + r_i > 2^{l_x} \text{ iff } x_i < x_{i_{max}} \tag{1}$$

$$-2^{l_x} < k_i(x_{i_{max}} - x_i) + r_i < 2^{l_x} \text{ iff } x_i = x_{i_{max}} \tag{2}$$

$$k_i(x_{i_{max}} - x_i) + r_i < -2^{l_x} \text{ iff } x_i > x_{i_{max}} \tag{3}$$

If all the participants follow the protocols, Case (2) must happen at least once and Case (3) never. This can be confirmed by the verifier V. Thus, V can detect if a malicious prover deviates in **Step 1** and uses an invalid value. On the other hand, if a malicious prover deviates in **Step 3** and drops (or alters) some values, at least one witness can abort the protocol and alert the judge, by sending him any value signed by the prover (such as $GS(gsk_{\mathcal{P}}, \mu)$ of **Protocol 1**), which the judge can trace thanks to the properties of the group-signature scheme. Finally, the prover cannot deviate in **Step 5** due to the unique group-signature scheme.

3.2 Security Properties of the Overall Process

We have now to argue that the overall process to obtain the location proofs respects all the security properties listed in the introduction.

Since the unique group signature scheme [4] is unforgeable, the prover $\mathcal{P}$ cannot forge new proofs, except with his own key. In **Step 5** of **Protocol 1**, such an opportunity is impossible. $\mathcal{P}$ would have to generate two distinct signatures on the same message, contradicting the uniqueness property of the signature scheme. In fact, the judge would identify any transgressing participant in this step, due to the traceability property of the signature scheme. Thus, the unforgeability and traceability properties of our location-proof protocol are ensured.

In **Step 1** of Protocol 1, the prover broadcasts a message μ and its signature $GS(gsk_{\mathcal{P}}, \mu)$. This links the timestamp and the n ephemeral keys of the witnesses. Since this signature is included in the final proofs signed by the witnesses, the location proof is valid only for the participant able to produce the valid signature $GS(gsk_{\mathcal{P}}, \mu)$, confirming the non-transferability property of the protocol.

Due to the unlinkability property of the group signature scheme, the location proof associated to $GS(gsk_{\mathcal{P}}, \mu)$ would not be linkable with another location proof associated to a different signature $GS(gsk_{\mathcal{P}}, \mu')$ done by the same prover. Similarly, the signatures of the witnesses in Protocol 2 would also not be linkable. Thus, the unlinkability property of our location-proof protocol is guaranteed.

The privacy of the identities follows from the property of group signature scheme. Similarly, the privacy of the positions (x_i, y_i) relies on the semantic property of the encryption scheme and the randomization process (see Sect. 5.2). Unfortunately, the last step of Protocol 2 leaks some information through $E_V(k_i(x_{i_{max}} - x_i) + r_i)$. The verifier can guess some bits of x_i. However, we can show that the Shannon entropy $H(X|Y = k_i(x_{i_{max}} - x_i) + r_i)$ is still close to $H(X|X \leq x_{i_{max}})$.

The prover obtains his location proofs during **Step 5**. Then, he stores them until he needs to convince the verifier, ensuring the storage sovereignty property.

3.3   Location-Proof Verifying

Finally, the correctness property has to be shown. The prover $\mathcal{P}$ wants to convince the verifier V that $E_V(x_{i_{max}})$ is indeed the maximum value. So, he sends:

- His position x, the message μ and his signature $GS(gsk_{\mathcal{P}}, \mu)$. The message contains the timestamp τ and the number of witnesses n (Protocol 1).
- The randomized value of maximum $E_V(x_{i_{max}})$ (Protocol 5).
- The n proofs $E_V(k_i(x_{i_{max}} - x_i) + r_i)$ and the witness signatures σ_i of $\nu = ((E_V(k_i(x_{i_{max}} - x_i) + r_i))_{1 \leq i \leq n}, E_V(x_{i_{max}}), n, GS(gsk_{\mathcal{P}}, \mu))$ (Protocol 2).

The verifier proceeds to several verifications. He first decrypts $E_V(x_{i_{max}})$ and checks if $x_{i_{max}} < x$. Then, he checks that the n proofs are generated by n distinct participants, different from $\mathcal{P}$. This verification is based on the uniqueness property of the group signature scheme. All the signatures of the message ν must be different. The verifier also asks the judge to check that $GS(gsk_{\mathcal{P}}, \mu)$ was generated using $gsk_{\mathcal{P}}$, ensuring that $\mathcal{P}$ took place in the proof generation protocol. The final step is to make sure that $E_V(x_{i_{max}})$ is indeed the maximum value of the witnesses. From the values of $E_V(k_i(x_{max} - x_i) + r_i)$ in ν, the verifier can check that there is an index j s.t. $-2^{l_x} < k_j(x_{i_{max}} - x_j) + r_j < 2^{l_x}$, and that there is no index j s.t. $k_j(x_{i_{max}} - x_j) + r_j < -2^{l_x}$.

Input: The witnesses $S_1 = \{W_1, W_2, \cdots, W_n\}$. Each W_i has a private value x_i.
Output: $\mathcal{P}$ determines $i_{max} = \arg\max\{x_i | 1 \leq i \leq n\}$.
for $i = 1$ **to** $\lceil \log(n) \rceil$ **do**

> **for** $j = 2^{i-1}$ **to** $2^i - 1$ **do**
>
> > **Step 1** : $\mathcal{P}$ does the following steps :
> >
> > > $S = \emptyset$
> > > **if** $|S_j|$ *is odd* **then**
> > >
> > > > Select $Single \in_R S_j$ s.t. $Single$ is not marked.
> > > > Mark the witness $Single$ and add it to S.
> > >
> > > Pair the elements of $S_j \setminus S$ − pair the marked witnesses.
> >
> > **Step 2** : Each pair of witnesses uses Protocol 4, and $\mathcal{P}$ obtains the index of the owner of the greater value.
> > **Step 3** : $\mathcal{P}$ selects $k \in_R \{0, 1\}$ and computes the following sets:
> >
> > > $S_{2j+k} = S \cup \{\text{the set of the losing witnesses}\}$
> > > $S_{2j+\overline{k}} = S \cup \{\text{the set of the winning witnesses}\}$

Step 4 : $\mathcal{P}$ determines the index Set i_{max} of this witness.

Protocol 3: Secure maximum computation based on binary tree

If all the verifications succeed, the verifier should be convinced that $\mathcal{P}$ was indeed at the east of $x_{i_{max}}$ at the given time. If any of these steps fails, it reveals a malicious action by either the prover or a witness. But unlike the prover, witnesses do not have any incentive to cheat. If some proofs are missing, the prover might have deleted them on purpose, or a witness may have aborted because of a deviation of the prover.

4   Secure Multi-party Maximum Protocol

In this section, we introduce a new approach for a secure multi-party maximum protocol. The main purpose is to enable a third party (the prover) to determine the owner of the maximum value among a set of n participants (or witnesses). The prover is the only party who gets a result from this protocol.

The basic idea is to use iteratively a dedicated secure two-party comparison protocol, that (i) enables the prover $\mathcal{P}$ to know which one of the two witnesses owns the greater private value without having to know this value, and (ii) guarantees that if one of the witnesses has already lost a comparison against another witness, the prover would not get any further information. This protocol (Protocol 4) is presented in Sect. 5.

4.1   The Protocol Description

Protocol 3 presents our approach for maximum computations. The prover gathers subsets of witnesses in a binary tree. In each node, the witnesses of the associated subset are paired and the dedicated secure two-party comparison protocol (Protocol 4) is used. At the end of each round, the prover gets the results of these comparisons and can eliminate half of the remaining witnesses. If a witness does not participate in any further comparison, he can deduce that he was farther away from the prover than his latest paired witness. Similarly, if one keeps participating in the protocol, he knows he has won every previous comparisons. Thus, the protocol should be adapted to ensure that witnesses keep participating in the protocol even if they have been eliminated. However, the comparisons with eliminated witnesses must be randomized and meaningless for the prover.

First assume that the number of witnesses is a power of 2. In the initial round, the prover pairs the 2^k witnesses all together. Each of these pairs runs the two-party comparison protocol. At the end of the round, the winners and the losers are gathered independently. This process is then applied recursively on each subset. Hence, two witnesses would never be paired twice together. After i iterations, there would be 2^i subsets of 2^{k-i} witnesses. One of these subsets would contain only winners and all the others would contain only losers.

Consider now the general case of n witnesses. The prover pairs the witnesses. If there is an odd number of witnesses in a subset, one of them (called *Single* in Protocol 3) would be *doubled*, and considered as both a winner and a loser.

Finally, notice that the witnesses do not communicate with each other directly. Otherwise, it would be simple to find out which one is closer to the prover due to the directional antennas. Thus, communications must go through $\mathcal{P}$.

4.2   The Protocol Security

The security of our maximum computation protocol relies on these objectives:

1. the prover cannot get any information from the two-party comparison protocol if at least one of the witnesses has been already eliminated previously,
2. the prover cannot get any information on the value of any witness, and
3. the witnesses cannot get any information from the comparison protocol.

The prover does the pairing and acts as the intermediary for the two-party comparison protocol. He can then observe all the messages exchanged between the witnesses. Thus, Objectives (1) and (2) rely on the security of the two-party comparison protocol. This will be addressed in Sect. 5.

Objective (3) relies on the indistinguishability of the subsets $\mathcal{S}_j$ in the round i of Protocol 3, for $2^{i-1} \leq j \leq 2^i - 1$. If the two-party comparison protocol is secure, the only way for a semi-honest witness to get any information on the comparisons is to find if he is in the subset of the winners. Since the indices of the subset are chosen randomly, any of them can be the subset of the winners.

4.3   The Protocol Analysis

The maximum computation problem has already been studied (e.g., [2,7]). However, the computational and communication complexities of these solutions are in $\mathcal{O}(n^2)$. Such complexities are not suitable for portable or embedded devices. In comparison, our method only requires $O(n \log(n))$ two-party comparisons, at the cost of leaking $n - 1$ comparison results involving winning witnesses. This follows directly from the underlying binary tree orchestrating the comparisons. The leaked information is not sufficient to order the witnesses.

In order to determine the complexity of Protocol 3, few facts must be proven. Since some witnesses may be doubled, they may be compared at least twice in any given round. We consider that the comparisons of a marked witness are resolved sequentially. In that case, two consecutive stages of comparisons are required for a round. The first step is to show that in any subset of witnesses at any round, there are at most two marked witnesses. This can be seen as an invariant of the protocol. Let us assume that a subset S_j contains at most two marked witnesses at the beginning of the round. If $|S_j|$ is even, the subsets S_{2j} and S_{2j+1} may contain at most one marked element. Otherwise, if $|S_j|$ is odd, one new witness would be marked, and the subsets S_{2j} and S_{2j+1} may contain at most two marked elements - the new one and an old one. Hence, for any subset of odd cardinality in a non-final round, there are at least one unmarked witness that can be marked and doubled if needed. Marking twice the same witness is unnecessary. As a corollary of this analysis, we have the following fact:

Fact 1. *Sets having two marked witnesses at the end of a round would contain one previously marked witness and a newly doubled witness.*

The second step is to show that any combination of comparisons can always be split into at most two stages in any given round. Consider the hypothetical cycle $\{W_{i_1}, W_{i_2}\}, \{W_{i_2}, W_{i_3}\}, \cdots, \{W_{i_k}, W_{i_1}\}$ of comparisons between marked witnesses in a given round. Each of these pairs belongs to a different subset of witnesses. If k is even, these comparisons can be split into two independent stages. This is optimal since a marked witness may have to be compared with two other witnesses. Now, if k is odd, alternate witnesses would have been just doubled in the round. By Fact 1, this is impossible since the length of the cycle is odd. Hence, no cycle of comparisons of odd length may exist. Two stages per round are enough to orchestrate the comparisons. As a result, the total number of stages is greater than $\lceil \log(n) \rceil$ and lower than $2\lceil \log(n) \rceil$. One can prove that no cycle can actually exist, but it does not improve the complexity further.

5   Secure Two-Party Comparison Protocol

In this section, we propose a specific two-party comparison protocol (Protocol 4) that enables a third party (the prover $\mathcal{P}$) to know which one of the two participants (the witnesses A and B) owns the greater private value without having to know this value explicitly. This can be used iteratively, so that if one of the participants has already lost a comparison against another participant, he should not give any further information to the third party. Such a protocol can be obtained by adapting the protocol of Lin and Tzeng [9], chosen for efficiency.

Given an integer x, let us define the following sets for our comparison protocol: $T_0^x = \{x_1 x_2 ... x_{i-1} 1 | x_i = 0\}$ and $T_1^x = \{x_1 x_2 ... x_i | x_i = 1\}$. Let $T_j^x[i]$ denote the ith element of T_j^x, if it exists. Lin and Tzeng's protocol relies on this lemma:

Lemma 1 [9]. *For $x, y \in \mathbb{N}$, $x > y$ if and only if $T_1^x \cap T_0^y \neq \emptyset$.*

Our comparison protocol has been developed to be used in our multi-party maximum protocol presented in the previous section. It relies heavily on a probabilistic additive encryption scheme such as Paillier's cryptosystem [12]. The participants uses their ephemeral encryption keys broadcast in Protocol 1. These keys are signed by the prover and verified by all the nearby witnesses. This associates the keys to a particular session of the protocol. As mentioned earlier, there should be no direct communication between the participants.

5.1 The Protocol Correctness

Let us first assume that the private values s_A and s_B have been initialized to zero by A and B, respectively. To simplify the notations, let us assume w.l.o.g. that the permutation functions are the identity function. At the end of **Step 2**, there is an index i^* such that $\delta_{i^*} = r_B$, iff $a > b$. This follows from Lemma 1 and the fact that the hash function is collision-free. Consequently, at the end of **Step 3**, if s_A and s_B are both still equal to 0, there would be an element $\mu_{i^*} = r_{A_{i^*}} \cdot r_{A_{i^*}}^{-1} = 1$, iff $a > b$. Thus, $\mathcal{P}$ would know the result of the comparison. On the other hand, if at least one of the participants has randomized his private value $E_{\mathcal{P}}(s_*)$, due to a previous comparison, no element of the vector μ would be equal to 1, except if $\delta_i - r_B + s_A + s_B \equiv 0 \mod \mathbb{Z}_p$. In any case, the result would be meaningless.

5.2 The Protocol Security

To prove the security of Protocol 4 w.r.t. *semi-honest* polynomially-bounded adversaries trying to get more information on other participants, we have to show that these objectives are achieved: (1) A cannot find b, (2) B cannot find a, (3) $\mathcal{P}$ cannot find neither a nor b, (4) the result of the comparison is known only to $\mathcal{P}$, (5) no one knows the first index i^* that differentiates a and b, (6) $\mathcal{P}$ eliminates A or B, (7) there is no information leaking if A or B has been already discarded, and (8) $\mathcal{P}$ cannot simulate A or B and have a coherent result.

First, consider the information sent by A in **Step 1**. T_1^a gives a bit-encoding of a. Due to the semantic security of Paillier's cryptosystem, $\mathcal{P}$ and B cannot get any information on a (Objectives (2) and (3)). Notice that the exact same γ (including random values) must be produced by A at any iteration. Otherwise, a collusion of $\mathcal{P}$ and B can set $E_A(\delta_i) = E_A(\gamma_i) \cdot E_A(\gamma_i')^{-1}$ and have an encoding of a. Either δ_i would be equal to 0, if $a_i = 1$, or be a random value, if $a_i = 0$.

We demonstrate in Annex B that the vector δ in **Step 2** is uniformly random in $\mathbb{Z}_{N_A}^l$ and independent of b, and thus does not leak any information on b to A (Objectives (1)). We also prove in the same Annex B that the elements of the vector μ in **Step 3** are uniformly random in $\mathbb{Z}_{N_{\mathcal{P}}}^l$ and independent of a and b, except one element that may be 1. Then, the vector μ does not leak any information about a or b, except whether $a > b$ (Objective (3)).

Input: The l-bit private values a and b of A and B. The encryption functions $E_A(\cdot)$, $E_B(\cdot)$ and $E_\mathcal{P}(\cdot)$, with keys N_A, N_B and $N_\mathcal{P}$. The private values $E_\mathcal{P}(s_A)$ and $E_\mathcal{P}(s_B)$ of A and B, respectively. The hash function $h(\cdot)$.

Output: $\mathcal{P}$ determines whether $a > b$ or $a \leq b$.

Step 1 : A does the following steps :

Compute T_1^a and the l-element vector γ, so that $\gamma_i = h(T_1^a[i])$ if it exists, otherwise, γ_i is simply a random value.

Pick a random $c \in_R \mathbb{Z}_{N_B}$.

Return $(E_A(\gamma_1), \cdots, E_A(\gamma_l))$ and $E_B(c)$ to B through $\mathcal{P}$.

Step 2 : B does the following steps after decrypting $E_B(c)$:

Compute T_0^b and the l-element vector δ

$$E_A(\delta_i) = E_A(k_i(h(T_1^a[i]) - h(T_0^b[i])) + r_B)$$
$$= (E_A(\gamma_i) \cdot E_A(-h(T_0^b[i])))^{k_i} \cdot E_A(r_B)$$

where $k_i, r_B \in_R \mathbb{Z}_{N_A}$ s.t. $(k_i, N_A) = 1$. Otherwise, δ_i is a random value.

Pick randomly a permutation $\pi_B(\cdot)$ and $\alpha, \beta \in_R \mathbb{Z}_{N_\mathcal{P}}$ s.t. $(\alpha, N_\mathcal{P}) = 1$.

Return $E_\mathcal{P}(s_B - r_B + c)$, $E_A(\alpha)$, $E_A(\beta)$ and

$(E_A(\delta_1^*), \cdots, E_A(\delta_l^*)) = \pi_B(E_A(\delta_1), \cdots, E_A(\delta_l))$ to A through $\mathcal{P}$.

Step 3 : A does the following steps :

Decrypt the elements $E_A(\delta_i^*)$ and compute the vector μ homomorphically

$$E_\mathcal{P}(\mu_i) = E_\mathcal{P}((\delta_i^* - r_B + s_B + s_A + r_{A,i}) \cdot r_{A,i}^{-1})$$
$$= (E_\mathcal{P}(\delta_i^* + r_{A,i}) \cdot E_\mathcal{P}(s_A) \cdot E_\mathcal{P}(s_B - r_B + c) \cdot E_\mathcal{P}(-c))^{r_{A,i}^{-1}}$$

where $r_{A,i} \in_R \mathbb{Z}_{N_\mathcal{P}}$ s.t. $(r_{A,i}, N_\mathcal{P}) = 1$.

Return $(E_\mathcal{P}(\mu_1^*), \cdots, E_\mathcal{P}(\mu_l^*)) = \pi_A(E_\mathcal{P}(\mu_1), \cdots, E_\mathcal{P}(\mu_l))$, where $\pi_A(\cdot)$ is a random permutation, to $\mathcal{P}$.

Step 4 : $\mathcal{P}$ decrypts the cyphertexts $E_\mathcal{P}(\mu_i^*)$.

If one of the elements of μ^* is equal to 1, then $a > b$ and $\mathcal{P}$ sets $s_A' = 0$.

Otherwise, $a \leq b$ and $\mathcal{P}$ sets $s_A' = 1$. $\mathcal{P}$ returns $E_\mathcal{P}(s_A')$ to A.

Step 5 : A does the following steps, once α and β have been retrieved :

Update $E_\mathcal{P}(s_A) \leftarrow E_\mathcal{P}(s_A + k_A \cdot s_A')$ using $E_\mathcal{P}(s_A) \cdot E_\mathcal{P}(s_A')^{k_A}$, where $k_A \in_R \mathbb{Z}_{N_\mathcal{P}}$.

Return $E_\mathcal{P}(\alpha s_B' + \beta) = (E_\mathcal{P}(1) \cdot E_\mathcal{P}(s_A')^{-1})^\alpha \cdot E_\mathcal{P}(\beta)$ to B through $\mathcal{P}$, since $s_B' = 1 - s_A'$.

Step 6 : B does the following steps :

Retrieve $E_\mathcal{P}(s_B') = (E_\mathcal{P}(\alpha s_B' + \beta) \cdot E_\mathcal{P}(-\beta))^{\alpha^{-1}}$.

Update $E_\mathcal{P}(s_B) \leftarrow E_\mathcal{P}(s_B + k_B \cdot s_B')$ using $E_\mathcal{P}(s_B) \cdot E_\mathcal{P}(s_B')^{k_B}$, where $k_B \in_R \mathbb{Z}_{N_\mathcal{P}}$.

Protocol 4: Secure two-party comparison protocol determining which participant has the greater private value.

Due to the permutations, no information on the index differentiating a and b can be inferred (Objective (5)).

The semantic security of Paillier's cryptosystem ensures that A cannot retrieve neither the values of r_B nor μ_i^* in **Step 3** as well as A and B cannot retrieve the value of s_A' in **Step 4** (Objective (4)).

In the last two steps, s_A and s_B are updated. Since $\mathcal{P}$ cannot infer the values of α and β in **Step 2**, it cannot manipulate the value of s_B' in **Step 6** in such a way that $s'_B = 0$. At least one of the participants would then have his value $s_* \neq 0$, achieving Objective (6). Finally, notice that once s_A or s_B is a random number different than 0, μ^* follows an independent uniform distribution of $\mathbb{Z}^l_{N_P}$. Hence, no conclusion follows from the value of μ^* in **Step 4** (Objective (7)).

Finally, note that δ and c are necessary to obtain the result and that they are encrypted respectively with A's and B's public keys. Assuming that these keys have been properly exchanged and have not been tampered with by $\mathcal{P}$, a polynomially-bounded $\mathcal{P}$ cannot simulate A or B successfully. In such a case, the result of the protocol would then be meaningless (Objective (8)).

Let us briefly consider the collusion between A and $\mathcal{P}$ against B. In such a case, A and $\mathcal{P}$ accept to exchange all their private information. Due to $\pi_B(\cdot)$, A and $\mathcal{P}$ cannot obtain the index of the bit that differentiates a and b. Moreover, due to the multiplication of each element of μ by a distinct k_i, A and $\mathcal{P}$ cannot compute $h(T^a_1[i^*]) - h(T^b_0[i^*])$, except if the hashes are equal, which has been discarded anyhow. Thus, $\mathcal{P}$ does not discover more information with the help of A. Similarly, B and $\mathcal{P}$ do not gain more information neither. The index of the bit that differentiates a and b is hidden by the permutation $\pi_A(\cdot)$, and it is impossible to compute δ^* without knowing the values $r_{A,i}$ generated by A.

5.3   The Protocol Complexity

Following the fact that communications are made through $\mathcal{P}$, any message sent between A and B is counted twice. The size of a public key N is denoted by $|N|$. Notice that ciphertexts are $2|N|$-bit long in Paillier's cryptosystem.

For any iteration, there are eight communications and $(10l + 22)|N|$ bits transferred. A maximum of $4l + 6$ cryptographic operations are computed by A, $2l + 8$ by B and only $l + 1$ by $\mathcal{P}$. By cryptographic operations, we mean encryption, decryption and modular exponentiation. If either A or B was eliminated, $\mathcal{P}$ does not have to decrypt the result in **Step 4**: only one encryption is needed.

5.4   The Maximum Transfer

Using Protocols 3 and 4, the prover $\mathcal{P}$ knows the index i_{max} of the witness that has the maximum value. However, $\mathcal{P}$ needs to obtain $E_V(x_{i_{max}})$, which corresponds to the maximum value encrypted with the verifier's public key. $\mathcal{P}$ does not want to inform which witness has been selected, but the discarded witnesses do not want to provide their location uselessly. Protocol 5 manages to reach both objectives. It relies on the fact that $W_{i_{max}}$ ends up with the internal value $E_{\mathcal{P}}(s_{W_{i_{max}}}) = E_{\mathcal{P}}(0)$ at the end of Protocol 4 (which correspond to s_A or s_B in Protocol 4). The other witnesses have a random s_{W_i}.

The security of Protocol 5 is easy to show. The security of all encrypted messages relies on the semantic security of the cryptosystem. In **Step 1**, $\mathcal{P}$ receives only random values from the witnesses. In **Step 2**, he picks one of them and broadcasts it back to all witnesses encrypted with the verifier's public key. A witness would return a meaningful value in **Step 3** if and only if his internal random value α_i is the additive inverse of the value sent by $\mathcal{P}$. In this case,

Input: $\mathcal{P}$ knows i_{max}. Each witness W_i has his values x_i and $E_{\mathcal{P}}(s_{W_i})$. Public keys $N_{\mathcal{P}}$ and N_V with functions $E_{\mathcal{P}}(\cdot)$ $E_V(\cdot)$.

Output: $\mathcal{P}$ obtains $E_V(x_{i_{max}})$.

Step 1 : forall the *witness* W_i **do**
    Generate a random number $\alpha_i \in_R \mathbb{Z}_{N_{\mathcal{P}}}$.
    Compute $E_{\mathcal{P}}(\alpha_i + s_{W_i}) = E_{\mathcal{P}}(\alpha_i) \cdot E_{\mathcal{P}}(s_{W_i})$ and return it to $\mathcal{P}$.

Step 2 : $\mathcal{P}$ does the following steps:
    Compute $\alpha_{i_{max}}$ from $E_{\mathcal{P}}(\alpha_{i_{max}} + s_{W_{i_{max}}})$ received from $W_{i_{max}}$.
    Broadcast to all witnesses $E_V(\alpha_{i_{max}})$.

Step 3 : forall the *witness* W_i *receiving* $E_V(\alpha_{i_{max}})$ **do**
    Compute $E_V(\alpha_{i_{max}} - \alpha_i + x_i) = E_V(\alpha_{i_{max}}) \cdot E_V(-\alpha_i) \cdot E_V(x_i)$.
    and return it to $\mathcal{P}$, only if it is the first request for that proof generation.

Step 4 : $\mathcal{P}$ does the final steps:
    Receive $E_V(x_{i_{max}})$ from $W_{i_{max}}$.
    Randomize it $E_V(x_{i_{max}}) \leftarrow E_V(x_{i_{max}}) \cdot r^{N_V}$, for $r \in_R \mathbb{Z}_{N_V}^*$.

Protocol 5: Maximum transfer protocol

the witness would return his encrypted position. Otherwise, he would return a random encrypted value. Finally, $E_V(x_{i_{max}})$ is randomized to conceal it from the witness $W_{i_{max}}$. In term of complexity, if broadcasting generates only one communication, $2n + 1$ messages of $2|N|$ bits are exchanged during the protocol.

This concludes our secure multi-party maximum protocol and allows to build our location-proof system more efficiently than with previous existing works. The complexity of the full location-proof system and of each sub-protocol is given in Annex A.

6 Conclusion

We have presented a privacy-aware location-proof system, allowing a prover to generate location proofs with the cooperation of nearby witnesses. Our solution is the first of its kind to provide both identity and location privacy. Our scheme relies on secure multi-party computations, allowing the prover to learn which participant is the closest, and thus to approximate more accurately the region in which he is. The proofs are then signed with a group signature scheme, protecting the identity of the participants and allowing the detection of any adversary trying to impersonate multiple witnesses. However, our scheme assumes that participants' devices are equipped with directional antennas. Although this is not a technological challenge, obtaining a similar level of privacy without these antennas is still an open problem.

As a second contribution, we also designed a new multi-party maximum computation based on a trade-off between efficiency and privacy. We showed that by leaking a few intermediate values, we can reduce the asymptotic cost to $\mathcal{O}(n \log(n))$ instead of $\mathcal{O}(n^2)$. Although it was originally designed specifically for our location-proof system, it can be applied to any scenario in which this leakage is acceptable.

A   Complexity of the Overall System

We have detailed the computational and communication complexity in each sub-protocols, but we are now interested in the complexity of the overall location-proof system (Protocol 1), depending on the number of witnesses. For simplicity, let us assume there are $m = 4n$ witnesses, i.e. n in each direction. Let $|N|$ denote the size of the keys (the size of a ciphertext is simply $2|N|$ with the Paillier's cryptosystem) and $|S|$ denote the size of group signatures. We consider that the encryption, decryption functions and homomorphic operations are in $\mathcal{O}(1)$.

Table 2. Complexity of the system

	Cryptographic operations		Communication cost	
	Each witness	Prover	Communications	Bits sent
Protocol 1 (overall system)	negl	negl	$2m + 3$	$(2m + 1)(|N| + |S|)$
	+Protocols 2, 3, 5	+4 × Protocols 2, 3, 5		
Protocol 2	negl	negl	$2n + 2$	$(4n + 2)|N| + m|S|$
Protocol 3	<2⌈log n⌉ × Protocol 4	≈ $\frac{n}{2}$⌈log n⌉ × Protocol 4		
Protocol 4	≤4l + 6	$l + 1$ or 1	≤8	≤ $(10l + 22)|N|$
Protocol 5	negl	negl	$2n + 1$	$(4n + 2)|N|$

Table 2 presents the number of cryptographic operations processed by the prover and by each witness, the number of communications and the bits exchanged during the different protocols. We only deal with the worst case scenario: a marked witness for the computational complexity in Protocol 3, and only a witness A in Protocol 4. This can obviously be optimized by giving role B to marked witnesses as often as possible. The complexity of Protocol 3 is an approximation of the total number of comparisons. An exact formula is given in Sect. 4.3. In Protocol 4, it has been shown that $\mathcal{P}$ runs $l + 1$ operations in $n - 1$ comparisons, and only 1 otherwise. Thus, the number of operations done by the prover in Protocol 3 and 4 is approximately $(n - 1)l + \frac{n}{2}\lceil \log n \rceil$.

To summarize, the global complexity, both in terms of computations and communication, is in $\mathcal{O}(n \log n)$ for the prover and $\mathcal{O}(\log n)$ for a witness. In comparison, most previous location-based systems have a complexity for the prover in $\mathcal{O}(n)$, and $\mathcal{O}(1)$ for a witness. This is due to the fact that witnesses do not need to interact with each other. However, location-privacy requires such interactions, and thus we do not reach the same objectives.

B   Security Proofs of the Two-Party Comparison Protocol

In this annex, we give more details about some security goals of Protocol 4: (1) A cannot find b, (3) $\mathcal{P}$ cannot find neither a nor b and (4) the result of the comparison is known only to $\mathcal{P}$.

Proof (Objective (1)). At the beginning of **Step 3**, A learns $\pi_B(\delta_1, \cdots, \delta_l)$ with

$$\delta_i = k_i(h(T_1^a[i]) - h(T_0^b[i])) + r_B$$

Remember that $h(T_0^b[i])$ can be seen as an encoding of b. Let us prove that the vector δ does not leak any information about b.

W.l.o.g. assume that $\pi_B(\cdot)$ is the permutation identity. Let us take any value $b' \neq b$ and show that the same vector δ can be obtained from b' and thus does not leak any information.

If $a > b'$, let i^* be the index such that $T_1^a[i^*] = T_0^{b'}[i^*]$ and take $r_B = \delta_{i^*}$. On the other hand, if $a \leq b'$, we can choose arbitrarily r_B. Now if we take:

$$k_i = (\delta_i - r_B) \cdot (h(T_1^a[i]) - h(T_0^{b'}[i]))^{-1} \quad \forall i \neq i^*$$

then we obtain the same vector δ.

This can be generalized to permutation $\pi_B(\cdot)$. Hence, δ can be obtained from any value of b' with the same probability, and does not therefore leak any information about b.

It remains to prove that A does not learn the result of the comparison (part of Objective (4)) which would leak partial information about b. The result of the comparison (either in the vector μ, the value s_A or s_B) is always encrypted under the public key of $\mathcal{P}$. We assume the cryptosystem is semantically secure, which ends the proof of Objective (1). □

Proof (Objective (3)). At the beginning of **Step 4**, $\mathcal{P}$ learns $\pi_A(\mu_1, \cdots, \mu_l)$ where

$$\mu_i = (\delta_i^* - r_B + s_B + s_A + r_{A,i}) \cdot r_{A,i}^{-1}$$

and $\delta_i^* = \delta_{\pi_B(i)}$. To simplify notations, assume that $\pi_A(\cdot)$ and $\pi_B(\cdot)$ are the identity permutation. If s_A or s_B is different from 0, this case is simple (Objective (7)): the vector μ follows an independent uniform distribution of $\mathbb{Z}_{N_\mathcal{P}}^l$. Thus, we only study the case:

$$\mu_i = (k_i(h(T_1^a[i]) - h(T_0^b[i])) + r_{A,i}) \cdot r_{A,i}^{-1}$$

Knowing that $a > b$, we will now show that for any couple (a', b') such that $a' > b'$, we can obtain the same vector μ with the same probability. In this case, let i^* be the index such that $T_1^{a'}[i^*] = T_0^{b'}[i^*]$. In this case, k_{i^*} can be chosen arbitrarily. For all other value $i \neq i^*$, $r_{A,i}$ can be chosen arbitrarily, and k_i can be defined as:

$$k_i = (\mu_i \cdot r_{A,i} - r_{A,i}) \cdot (h(T_1^{a'}[i]) - h(T_0^{b'}[i]))^{-1}.$$

Finally, if $a \leq b$, this is simpler. In this case, the index i^* is not defined, and the values of all $r_{A,i}$ and k_i are defined as above.

Thus, the same vector μ can be obtained. This can be done for any values of a' and b', as long as the result remains unchanged, and for any permutation $\pi_A(\cdot)$ and $\pi_B(\cdot)$. Therefore, the vector μ does not leak any information about a or b except whether $a > b$ or not, which ends the proof. □

References

1. Bultel, X., Gambs, S., Gérault, D., Lafourcade, P., Onete, C., Robert, J.M.: A prover-anonymous and terrorist-fraud resistant distance-bounding protocol. In: Proceedings of WISec, pp. 121–133. ACM (2016)
2. Cramer, R., Fehr, S., Ishai, Y., Kushilevitz, E.: Efficient multi-party computation over rings. In: Biham, E. (ed.) EUROCRYPT 2003. LNCS, vol. 2656, pp. 596–613. Springer, Heidelberg (2003). https://doi.org/10.1007/3-540-39200-9_37
3. Davis, B., Chen, H., Franklin, M.: Privacy-preserving alibi systems. In: Proceedings of ASIACCS, pp. 1–10. ACM (2012)
4. Franklin, M., Zhang, H.: Unique group signatures. In: Foresti, S., Yung, M., Martinelli, F. (eds.) ESORICS 2012. LNCS, vol. 7459, pp. 643–660. Springer, Heidelberg (2012). https://doi.org/10.1007/978-3-642-33167-1_37
5. Gambs, S., Killijian, M.O., Roy, M., Traoré, M.: PROPS: a privacy-preserving location proof system. In: Proceedings of SRDS, pp. 1–10. IEEE (2014)
6. Graham, M., Gray, D.: Protecting privacy and securing the gathering of location proofs – the secure location verification proof gathering protocol. In: Schmidt, A.U., Lian, S. (eds.) MobiSec 2009. LNICST, vol. 17, pp. 160–171. Springer, Heidelberg (2009). https://doi.org/10.1007/978-3-642-04434-2_14
7. Hasan, O., Brunie, L., Bertino, E.: Preserving privacy of feedback providers in decentralized reputation systems. Comput. Secur. **31**, 816–826 (2012)
8. Hazay, C., Lindell, Y.: Efficient Secure Two-Party Protocols: Techniques and Constructions. Springer, Heidelberg (2010). https://doi.org/10.1007/978-3-642-14303-8
9. Lin, H.-Y., Tzeng, W.-G.: An efficient solution to the millionaires' problem based on homomorphic encryption. In: Ioannidis, J., Keromytis, A., Yung, M. (eds.) ACNS 2005. LNCS, vol. 3531, pp. 456–466. Springer, Heidelberg (2005). https://doi.org/10.1007/11496137_31
10. Luo, W., Hengartner, U.: Proving your location without giving up your privacy. In: Proceedings of the HotMobile, pp. 7–12. ACM (2010)
11. Luo, W., Hengartner, U.: Veriplace: a privacy-aware location proof architecture. In: Proceedings of SIGSPATIAL, pp. 23–32. ACM (2010)
12. Paillier, P.: Public-key cryptosystems based on composite degree residuosity classes. In: Stern, J. (ed.) EUROCRYPT 1999. LNCS, vol. 1592, pp. 223–238. Springer, Heidelberg (1999). https://doi.org/10.1007/3-540-48910-X_16
13. Pham, A., Huguenin, K., Bilogrevic, I., Dacosta, I., Hubaux, J.P.: SecureRun: cheat-proof and private summaries for location-based activities. In: Proceedings of TMC, pp. 2109–2123. IEEE (2015)
14. Saroiu, S., Wolman, A.: Enabling new mobile applications with location proofs. In: Proceedings of HotMobile, pp. 1–6. ACM (2009)
15. Sastry, N., Shankar, U., Wagner, D.: Secure verification of location claims. In: Proceedings of WISEC, pp. 1–10. ACM (2003)
16. Singelee, D., Preneel, B.: Location verification using secure distance bounding protocols. In: Proceedings of MASS, pp. 7–14. IEEE (2005)
17. Talasila, M., Curtmola, R., Borcea, C.: LINK: location verification through immediate neighbors knowledge. In: Sénac, P., Ott, M., Seneviratne, A. (eds.) MobiQuitous 2010. LNICST, vol. 73, pp. 210–223. Springer, Heidelberg (2012). https://doi.org/10.1007/978-3-642-29154-8_18
18. Zhu, Z., Cao, G.: APPLAUS: a privacy-preserving location proof updating system for location-based services. In: Proceedings of INFOCOM, pp. 1889–1897. IEEE (2011)

Verifiable Homomorphic Secret Sharing

Georgia Tsaloli$^{(\boxtimes)}$, Bei Liang, and Aikaterini Mitrokotsa

Chalmers University of Technology, Gothenburg, Sweden
{tsaloli,lbei,aikmitr}@chalmers.se

Abstract. In this paper, we explore the *multi-server* (*i.e.*, multiple servers are employed to perform computations) and *multi-client* (*i.e.*, multiple clients outsource joint computations on their joint inputs) scenario that avoids single points of failure and provides higher security and privacy guarantees. More precisely, we introduce the notion of *verifiable homomorphic secret sharing* (VHSS) for multi-input, that allows n clients to outsource joint computations on their joint inputs to m servers without requiring any communication between the clients or the servers; while providing the *verifiable capability* to any user to confirm that the final output (rather than each share) is correct. Our contributions are two-fold: *(i)* we provide a detailed example for casting Shamir's secret sharing scheme over a finite field $\mathbb{F}$ as an n-client, m-server, t-secure perfectly secure, additive HSS scheme for the function f that sums n field elements, and *(ii)* we propose an instantiation of an n-client, m-server, t-secure computationally secure, multiplicative VHSS scheme for the function f that multiplies n elements under the hardness assumption of the fixed inversion problem in bilinear maps.

Keywords: Function secret sharing · Homomorphic secret sharing · Verifiable computation

1   Introduction

The emergence of ubiquitous computing has led to multiple heterogeneous devices with increased connectivity and have formed the Internet of Things (IoT). These IoT devices are often constrained regarding resources (*i.e.*, memory, bandwidth and computational resources) and thus, require the assistance of more powerful but often untrusted servers in order to store, process and perform computations on the collected data, leading to what is known as *cloud-assisted computing*. An important challenge in this cloud-assisted computing paradigm is how to protect the *security* and *privacy* of the participants considering the clients' resource-constraints, especially in the *multi-client* setting. Although the classical cloud-computing paradigm traditionally involves one client, we argue that a *multi-client* setting is more realistic since often an aggregator has to perform computations from data collected from multiple users. This is, for instance, the case when it is required to compute statistics for data collected from multiple users in order to monitor electricity consumption via smart metering, clinical

© Springer Nature Switzerland AG 2018
J. Baek et al. (Eds.): ProvSec 2018, LNCS 11192, pp. 40–55, 2018.
https://doi.org/10.1007/978-3-030-01446-9_3

data or even the safety of buildings or environmental conditions from data collected from multiple sensors.

Although a major part of existing work focuses on the *single client, single server* setting (*i.e.*, a single client outsourcing a computation to a single server) [2,10,11,13,17,18,21], we argue that not only the *multi-client* setting [12,15] is more realistic but also the *multi-server* setting (*i.e.*, multiple servers are employed in order to perform the computations) [1] provides better security guarantees and avoids single points of failure. The multi-server setting could also be adopted in multiple online services when users need to perform queries (*e.g.*, statistics on available data) to service providers, while at the same time have guarantees that no information can be inferred from the users' queries by the servers. For instance, a user (client) may split her query into multiple shares and send each share to a different server [22]. Similarly, in a smart electricity consumption application setting, multiple servers could be employed to collect data for the electricity consumption from multiple sensors (clients). As long as at least one of the servers is honest and does not collude with the others, the servers cannot recover any sensitive information. However, given responses from all the servers, the user can compute the answer to her query. This multi-server paradigm provides higher security guarantees since single points of failures are avoided.

In this paper, we consider the problem of outsourcing computations and providing strong security and privacy guarantees when: *(i)* *multiple-clients* outsource joint computations on their joint secret inputs, *(ii)* *multiple-servers* are employed for the computations, and *(iii)* *anyone* can verify that the combination of the shares is correct. More precisely, we investigate how we may outsource computations from multiple clients to multiple untrusted servers without requiring any communication between the clients or the servers *i.e.*, all information required for the computations are shared publicly and thus no communication overhead is required. We consider functional secret sharing schemes that can be employed to compute a function (addition or multiplication) of multiple secrets. This is achieved by enabling the servers to locally convert the shares of the different secrets into a (multiplicative or additive) function of their shares. Furthermore, the servers are able to locally generate shares of a proof that guarantees that the product of all the shares is correct. We focus on specific functions, the addition and the multiplication, and we employ, as building tools, *verifiable homomorphic secret sharing* schemes. The result is the definition and the first concrete construction of a *verifiable multiplicative homomorphic secret sharing* scheme.

Homomorphic Secret Sharing. A threshold secret sharing scheme [20] allows a dealer to randomly split a secret x into m shares, $(x^1, \ldots, x^m)$, such that certain subsets of the shares can be used to reconstruct the secret and others reveal nothing about it. Motivated by the powerful cryptographic functionality of fully homomorphic encryption (FHE) [14,19] which supports arbitrary computations on encrypted inputs, Boyle *et al.* [8] introduced the natural notion of *homomorphic secret sharing* (HSS) that achieves some of the functionality offered by FHE [6]. An HSS scheme supports computations on shared inputs based on local computations on their shares. More concretely, there is a local evaluation algorithm Eval and a decoder algorithm Dec satisfying the following homomorphism requirement. Given a description of a function F, the algorithm $\mathsf{Eval}(F, x^j)$ maps an input share x^j to a corresponding output share y^j, such that $\mathsf{Dec}(y^1, \ldots, y^m) = F(x)$. Analogously to the *output compactness* requirement of FHE, in HSS the output shares are *compact* in the sense that the output length of Eval, and hence the complexity of Dec, depends only on the output length of F and the security parameter, but not on the input length of F. The simplest type of HSS is the *additive HSS*, where the Dec algorithm computes $F(x)$ as the sum $y^1 + \ldots + y^m$ in some finite Abelian group, which is the first instance of HSS considered in the literature by Benaloh [4]. Boyle *et al.* [9] naturally consider a multi-input variant of HSS, where inputs $x_1, \ldots, x_n$ are independently shared, Eval locally maps the j-th shares of the n inputs to the j-th output share, and Dec outputs $F(x_1, \ldots, x_n)$.

Our Contributions. In this paper, we introduce the notion of *verifiable homomorphic secret sharing* (VHSS) for multi-input. We call a multi-input homomorphic secret sharing (HSS) scheme verifiable if the scheme enables the clients (users) to locally generate shares of a proof which confirms that the combination of the shares (rather than each share) is correct. We expect that the verifiability property can be employed for making multi-party computations (MPC) secure in the presence of an active adversary by accepting the output only if the correctness is verified.

Firstly, we provide a detailed example for casting Shamir's secret sharing scheme [20] over a finite field $\mathbb{F}$ as a n-client, m-server, t-secure perfectly secure, additive HSS scheme for the function f that sums n field elements. Such a scheme exists if and only if $m > n \cdot t$. Secondly, we propose an instantiation of an n-client, m-server, t-secure computationally secure, multiplicative VHSS scheme for the function f that multiplies n elements under the hardness assumption of the fixed inversion problem in bilinear maps. More precisely, we present a scheme where there are n clients $c_1, \ldots, c_n$ each of whom shares its secret input x_i to m servers $s_1, \ldots, s_m$. Each server's share of x_i is denoted as x_{ij}. For each $j \in \{1, \ldots, m\}$, the server s_j that possesses n shared inputs $x_{1j}, \ldots, x_{nj}$ generates a share y^j as well as a share σ^j of a proof that the product of m shares is correct. In our multiplicative VHSS instantiation, each client c_i has x_i but also $\widetilde{x}_i$ such that $g^{\widetilde{x}_i} = x_i$ where g denotes a generator of the multiplicative group of $\mathbb{F}$.

1.1   Related Work

Multiplicative Secret Sharing. A multiplicative secret sharing scheme allows two parties to multiply two secret-shared field elements by locally converting their shares of the two secrets into an additive sharing of their product. Barkol *et al.* [3] consider a different natural extension of the basic multiplication property of secret sharing that is called d-multiplication. The d-multiplication property generalizes standard multiplication by considering a multiplication of d (rather than two) secrets. Specifically, a secret sharing with d-multiplication allows multiplying d secret-shared field elements by enabling the players to locally convert shares of d different secrets into an additive sharing of their product. They also proved that d-multiplicative schemes exist if and only if no d unauthorized sets of players cover the whole set of players. In particular, t-private d-multiplicative secret sharing among m players is possible only if $m > d \cdot t$ where t-private means that every set of t players is unauthorized.

In fact, d-multiplicative secret sharing (d-multiplicative SS) among m players is a specific case of Boyel *et al.*'s [9] multi-input variant of HSS, where the Eval algorithm of HSS can be specified as the MULT algorithm of d-multiplicative SS, while the Dec algorithm of HSS can be specified as the summation operation on the outcomes of the m local computations.

Verifiable Multiplicative Secret Sharing. Following Barkol *et al.*'s [3] work on d-multiplicative secret sharing, Yoshida *et al.* [23] introduced the notion of verifiably d-multiplicative SS, which enables the players to locally generate an additive sharing of a proof that the sum of shares (rather than each share) is correct. Actually, our verifiable HSS for multi-input is a more general notion for verifiably d-multiplicative SS, since we generalize the reconstructing operation on local outcomes and local proofs, *e.g.*, using the algorithms FinalEval and FinalProof respectively.

We need to note that in both works of d-multiplicative SS [3] and verifiably d-multiplicative SS [23], no instantiation of a verifiable multiplicative HSS scheme was proposed. On the contrary, the authors assume that the local computation algorithms MULT and PF on d shares exist without though providing any instantiation. In this paper, we instantiate for the first time the MULT and PF algorithms of a verifiable multiplicative secret sharing scheme as a product on the d shares and bilinear map operations respectively.

Verifiable Functional Secret Sharing. Boyle *et al.* [5] after introducing the notion of functional secret sharing (FSS), they have also introduced the notion of verifiable FSS [7], where on the one hand a function f is split into m functions $f_1, \ldots, f_m$, described by the corresponding keys $k_1, \ldots, k_m$, such that for any input x we have that $f(x) = f_1(x) + \ldots + f_m(x)$ and every strict subset of the keys hides f; on the other hand, there is an additional m-parties interactive protocol Ver for verifying that the keys $(k_1^*, \ldots, k_m^*)$, generated by a potentially malicious client, are consistent with some f. Compared to Boyle *et al.*'s notion of verifiable FSS which is applied to the one client (one input) and multi-server setting, our VHSS works on the multi-client (multi-input) and multi-server setting. Furthermore, by employing a verification algorithm, Boyle *et al.*'s VFSS goal is to convince all involved parties that the function effectively shared by the client is consistent with some f. However, in our proposed notion of VHSS, the verification algorithm is employed to enable the servers to locally generate shares of a proof that guarantees that the combination (such as the product) of all shares (rather than each share) is correct.

Organization. The paper is organized as follows. In Sect. 2, we present the general definitions for the homomorphic secret sharing (HSS) and the verifiable homomorphic secret sharing (VHSS) schemes. In Sect. 3, we provide a concrete construction for the additive HSS scheme as well as a proof of its correctness and the corresponding security proof. In Sect. 4, we present our proposed multiplicative VHSS scheme as well as the assumption it relies on, the proposed concrete multiplicative VHSS construction and the corresponding proofs of correctness, verifiability, and security.

2   General Definitions for the HSS and the VHSS

In this section, we will formulate a general definition of homomorphic secret sharing (HSS) inspired by Boyle et al.'s [9] definition, which is the base of our *verifiable homomorphic secret sharing* (VHSS) definition that will follow.

We consider n clients $c_1, c_2, \ldots, c_n$ that split their inputs $x_1, \ldots, x_n$ between m servers using the algorithm **ShareSecret**, in such a way that each x_i is hidden from any t servers that could be corrupted. Each server s_j, having its share of the n inputs, applies the algorithm **PartialEval** in order to get and publish the partial share y^j. Finally, any user may apply the algorithm **FinalEval** in order to obtain $f(x_1, x_2, \ldots, x_n)$ where f is a function such that $f : \mathcal{X} \mapsto \mathcal{Y}$ for $\mathcal{X}$ to be a domain and $\mathcal{Y}$ be a target set respectively.

The verifiable homomorphic secret sharing (VHSS) scheme is based on the HSS, and it provides additionally the notion of *verifiability*. Most precisely, each server s_j applies the algorithm **PartialEval** to obtain the partial share y^j but also it applies the algorithm **PartialProof** to compute σ^j, where the latter is the share of the proof that the final computation is correct. Furthermore, any user that would like to get y by running the algorithm **FinalEval** is also able to run the algorithm **FinalProof** which gives the proof σ that the value y is correct. By employing the algorithm **Verify**, each user is able to check that what she gets is actually the output that corresponds to $f(x_1, x_2, \ldots, x_n)$.

We will now give the definitions of a general *homomorphic secret sharing* (HSS) scheme and a *verifiable homomorphic secret sharing scheme* (VHSS).

Definition 1. *An n-client, m-server, t-secure homomorphic secret sharing (HSS) scheme for a function $f : \mathcal{X} \mapsto \mathcal{Y}$, is a 3-tuple of PPT algorithms (**ShareSecret, PartialEval, FinalEval**) which are defined as follows:*

- *$(x_{i1}, x_{i2}, \ldots, x_{im}) \leftarrow$ **ShareSecret**$(1^\lambda, i, x_i)$: On input 1^λ, where λ is the security parameter, $i \in \{1, \ldots, n\}$ which is the index for the client c_i and $x_i \in \mathcal{X}$ which is her secret input, the algorithm **ShareSecret** outputs m shares for the corresponding secret input x_i.*

- *$y^j \leftarrow$ **PartialEval**$(j, (x_{1j}, x_{2j}, \ldots, x_{nj}))$: On input $j \in \{1, \ldots, m\}$ which denotes the index of the server s_j, and $x_{1j}, x_{2j}, \ldots, x_{nj}$ which are the shares of the n secret inputs that the server s_j has, the algorithm **PartialEval** outputs $y^j \in \mathcal{Y}$.*

– $y \leftarrow \textbf{FinalEval}(y^1, y^2, \ldots, y^m)$: On input $y^1, y^2, \ldots, y^m$, which are the shares of $f(x_1, x_2, \ldots, x_n)$ that the m servers have, the algorithm **FinalEval** outputs y, the final result for $f(x_1, x_2, \ldots, x_n)$.

The algorithms (**ShareSecret, PartialEval, FinalEval**) should satisfy the following correctness and security requirements:

- **Correctness:** For any n secret inputs $x_1, \ldots, x_n$, for all $(x_{i1}, x_{i2}, \ldots, x_{im})$ computed for all $i \in [n]$ from the algorithm **ShareSecret**, for all y^j computed for all $j \in [m]$ from the algorithm **PartialEval**, the scheme should satisfy the following correctness requirement:

$$\Pr\left[\textbf{FinalEval}(y^1, y^2, \ldots, y^m) = f(x_1, x_2, \ldots, x_n)\right] = 1.$$

- **Security**: Let T be the set of the corrupted servers with $|T| < m$. Consider the following semantic security challenge experiment:
  1. The adversary $\mathcal{A}$ gives $(i, x_i, x_i') \leftarrow \mathcal{A}(1^\lambda)$ to the challenger where $i \in [n]$, $x_i \neq x_i'$ and $|x_i| = |x_i'|$.
  2. The challenger picks a bit $b \in \{0, 1\}$ uniformly at random and computes $(\hat{x}_{i1}, \hat{x}_{i2}, \ldots, \hat{x}_{im}) \leftarrow \textbf{ShareSecret}(1^\lambda, i, \hat{x}_i)$ where $\hat{x}_i = \begin{cases} x_i, & \text{if } b = 0 \\ x_i', & \text{otherwise} \end{cases}$.
  3. The adversary outputs a guess $b' \leftarrow \mathcal{A}((x_{ij})_{j|s_j \in T})$, given the shares from the corrupted servers T.

  Let $\mathrm{Adv}(1^\lambda, \mathcal{A}, T) := \Pr[b = b'] - 1/2$ be the advantage of $\mathcal{A}$ in guessing b in the above experiment, where the probability is taken over the randomness of the challenger and of $\mathcal{A}$. The scheme (**ShareSecret, PartialEval, FinalEval**) is t-secure if for all $T \subset \{s_1, \ldots, s_m\}$ with $|T| \leq t$, and all PPT adversaries $\mathcal{A}$, it holds that $\mathrm{Adv}(1^\lambda, \mathcal{A}, T) \leq \varepsilon(\lambda)$ for some negligible $\varepsilon(\lambda)$.

Definition 2. *An n-client, m-server, t-secure verifiable homomorphic secret sharing (VHSS) scheme for a function $f : \mathcal{X} \mapsto \mathcal{Y}$, is a 6-tuple of PPT algorithms (**ShareSecret, PartialEval, PartialProof, FinalEval, FinalProof, Verify**) which are defined as follows:*

– $(x_{i1}, x_{i2}, \ldots, x_{im}, \tau_i) \leftarrow \textbf{ShareSecret}(1^\lambda, i, x_i)$: *On input 1^λ, where λ is the security parameter, $i \in \{1, \ldots, n\}$ which is the index for the client c_i and $x_i \in \mathcal{X}$ which is her secret input, the algorithm **ShareSecret** outputs m shares for the corresponding secret input x_i as well as a publicly available encoded value τ_i related to the secret x_i.*

– $y^j \leftarrow \textbf{PartialEval}(j, (x_{1j}, x_{2j}, \ldots, x_{nj}))$: *On input $j \in \{1, \ldots, m\}$ which denotes the index of the server s_j, and $x_{1j}, x_{2j}, \ldots, x_{nj}$ which are the shares of the n secret inputs that the server s_j has, the algorithm **PartialEval** outputs $y^j \in \mathcal{Y}$.*

– $\sigma^j \leftarrow \textbf{PartialProof}(j, (x_{1j}, x_{2j}, \ldots, x_{nj}))$: *On input j (the server's index) and the n shares $x_{1j}, x_{2j}, \ldots, x_{nj}$, the algorithm **PartialProof** outputs σ^j. This output is the share of the proof that the final output is correct.*

- $y \leftarrow \textbf{\textit{FinalEval}}(y^1, y^2, \ldots, y^m)$: On input $y^1, y^2, \ldots, y^m$ which are the shares of $f(x_1, x_2, \ldots, x_n)$ that the m servers have, the algorithm **FinalEval** outputs y, the final result for $f(x_1, x_2, \ldots, x_n)$.
- $\sigma \leftarrow \textbf{\textit{FinalProof}}(\sigma^1, \sigma^2, \ldots, \sigma^m)$: On input the shares $\sigma^1, \sigma^2, \ldots, \sigma^m$, the algorithm **FinalProof** outputs σ which is the proof that y is the correct value.
- $0/1 \leftarrow \textbf{\textit{Verify}}(\tau_1, \ldots, \tau_n, \sigma, y)$: On input the final result y together with its proof σ, as well as the encoded values $\tau_1, \ldots, \tau_n$ the algorithm **Verify** outputs either 0 or 1.

The algorithms (**ShareSecret, PartialEval, PartialProof, FinalEval, FinalProof, Verify**) should satisfy the following correctness, verifiability and security requirements:

- **Correctness**: For any n secret inputs $x_1, \ldots, x_n$, for all $(x_{i1}, x_{i2}, \ldots, x_{im}, \tau_i)$ computed for all $i \in [n]$ from the algorithm **ShareSecret**, for all y^j and σ^j computed for all $j \in [m]$ from the algorithms **PartialEval** and **PartialProof** respectively, and for y and σ generated by the algorithms **FinalEval** and **FinalProof** respectively, the scheme should satisfy the following correctness requirement:

$$\Pr\left[\, \textbf{Verify}(\tau_1, \ldots, \tau_n, y, \sigma) = 1 \,\right] = 1.$$

- **Verifiability**: Consider n secret inputs $x_1, x_2, \ldots, x_n \in \mathbb{F}$, T the set of corrupted servers with $|T| \leqslant m$ and a PPT adversary $\mathcal{A}$. Any PPT adversary who modifies the shares of the secret inputs for any j such that $s_j \in T$, can cause a wrong value to be accepted as $f(x_1, x_2, \ldots, x_n)$ with negligible probability. We define the following experiment:

$\textbf{Exp}_{\text{VHSS}}^{\text{Verif.}}(x_1, x_2, \ldots, x_n, T, \mathcal{A})$:
1. For all $i \in [n]$, generate $(x_{i1}, x_{i2}, \ldots, x_{im}, \tau_i) \leftarrow \textbf{ShareSecret}(1^\lambda, i, x_i)$ and publish $\tau_i, i \in [n]$.
2. For all j such that $s_j \in T$, give $\begin{pmatrix} x_{1j} \\ x_{2j} \\ \vdots \\ x_{nj} \end{pmatrix}$ to the adversary.
3. The adversary $\mathcal{A}$ outputs modified multiplicative shares $y^{j'}$ and $\sigma^{j'}$ for j such that $s_j \in T$. For j such that $s_j \notin T$, we define the multiplicative shares $y^{j'} = \textbf{PartialEval}(j, (x_{1j}, x_{2j}, \ldots, x_{nj}))$ and $\sigma^{j'} = \textbf{PartialProof}(j, (x_{1j}, x_{2j}, \ldots, x_{nj}))$.
4. Compute the modified final value $y' = \textbf{FinalEval}(y^{1'}, y^{2'}, \ldots, y^{m'})$ and the modified final proof $\sigma' = \textbf{FinalProof}(\sigma^{1'}, \sigma^{2'}, \ldots, \sigma^{m'})$.
5. If $y' \neq f(x_1, x_2, \ldots, x_n)$ and $\textbf{Verify}(\tau_1, \ldots, \tau_n, \sigma', y') = 1$, then output 1 else 0.

We require that for any n secret inputs $x_1, x_2, \ldots, x_n \in \mathbb{F}$, any set T of corrupted servers and any PPT adversary $\mathcal{A}$ it holds:

$$\Pr[\textbf{Exp}_{\text{VHSS}}^{\text{Verif.}}(x_1, x_2, \ldots, x_n, T, \mathcal{A}) = 1] \leq \varepsilon.$$

- **Security:** Let T be the set of the corrupted servers with $|T| < m$. Consider the following semantic security challenge experiment:
  1. The adversary $\mathcal{A}$ gives $(i, x_i, x_i') \leftarrow \mathcal{A}(1^\lambda)$ to the challenger where $i \in [n]$, $x_i \neq x_i'$ and $|x_i| = |x_i'|$.
  2. The challenger picks a bit $b \in \{0, 1\}$ uniformly at random and computes $(\hat{x}_{i1}, \hat{x}_{i2}, \dots, \hat{x}_{im}, \hat{\tau}_i) \leftarrow$ **ShareSecret**$(1^\lambda, i, \hat{x}_i)$ where $\hat{\tau}_i$ is an encoded value related to $\hat{x}_i$ and $\hat{x}_i = \begin{cases} x_i, \text{if } b = 0 \\ x_i', \text{otherwise} \end{cases}$.
  3. The adversary outputs a guess $b' \leftarrow \mathcal{A}((x_{ij})_{j|s_j \in T}, (\tau_i)_{i \in [n]})$, given the shares from the corrupted servers T and the encoded values $\tau_1, \dots, \tau_n$.

Let $\text{Adv}(1^\lambda, \mathcal{A}, T) := \Pr[b = b'] - 1/2$ be the advantage of $\mathcal{A}$ in guessing b in the above experiment, where the probability is taken over the randomness of the challenger and of $\mathcal{A}$. The VHSS scheme is t-secure if for all $T \subset \{s_1, \dots, s_m\}$ with $|T| \leq t$, and all PPT adversaries $\mathcal{A}$, it holds that $\text{Adv}(1^\lambda, \mathcal{A}, T) \leq \varepsilon(\lambda)$ for some negligible $\varepsilon(\lambda)$.

3 Additive Homomorphic Secret Sharing Scheme

In this chapter, we present a detailed example of the additive HSS scheme. Therefore, we consider n clients $c_1, \dots, c_n$, their secret inputs $x_1, x_2, \dots, x_n$ respectively and one or more users that would like to compute the sum of these secret inputs, that is, they want to compute $f(x_1, x_2, \dots, x_n) = x_1 + x_2 + \dots + x_n$ without knowing $x_1, \dots, x_n$.

3.1 Construction of the Additive HSS

We consider m servers $s_1, \dots, s_m$. Let $\mathbb{F}$ be a finite field with $|\mathbb{F}| > m$, λ be the security parameter, let, $\forall i \in [n]$, $\theta_{i1}, \dots, \theta_{im}$ be distinct nonzero field elements, and let, for any $i \in \{1, \dots, n\}$, $\lambda_{i1}, \lambda_{i2}, \dots, \lambda_{im}$ be field elements such that for any univariate polynomial p_i of degree t over $\mathbb{F}$ we have $p_i(0) = \sum_{j=1}^m \lambda_{ij} p_i(\theta_{ij})$. Each client c_i will distribute her secret's share to the servers so that the latter will compute the partial sum y^i and then, any user can easily compute the final sum by adding the partial sums that the servers have computed without having any information about the secret inputs. More precisely, we have the following algorithms:

1. **ShareSecret**$(1^\lambda, i, x_i)$: Pick a polynomial p_i of the form $p_i(X) = x_i + a_1 X + a_2 X^2 + \dots + a_t X^t$ where $\{a_i\}_{i \in \{1, \dots, t\}} \in \mathbb{F}$ are elements selected uniformly at random and t denotes the degree of the polynomial with $t \cdot n < m$. Notice that the free coefficient of p_i is the secret input x_i. Then, output $(x_{i1}, x_{i2}, \dots, x_{im}) = (\lambda_{i1} \cdot p_i(\theta_{i1}), \lambda_{i2} \cdot p_i(\theta_{i2}), \dots, \lambda_{im} \cdot p_i(\theta_{im}))$.
2. **PartialEval**$(j, (x_{1j}, x_{2j}, \dots, x_{nj}))$: For the given j and for all $i \in [n]$, compute the sum of all $x_{ij} = \lambda_{ij} \cdot p_i(\theta_{ij})$. Output $y^j = \lambda_{1j} \cdot p_1(\theta_{1j}) + \lambda_{2j} \cdot p_2(\theta_{2j}) + \dots + \lambda_{nj} \cdot p_n(\theta_{nj}) = \sum_{i=1}^n \lambda_{ij} \cdot p_i(\theta_{ij})$.

3. **FinalEval**$(y^1, y^2, \ldots, y^m)$: Add the partial shares together and output $y = y^1 + \ldots + y^m$.

Now, each client c_i runs **ShareSecret** and gives $\lambda_{ij} \cdot p_i(\theta_{ij})$ to each server s_j. Table 1 shows how each client c_i distributes her secret input x_i to the servers. Then, each server s_j has the shares $\lambda_{1j} \cdot p_1(\theta_{1j}), \lambda_{2j} \cdot p_2(\theta_{2j}), \ldots, \lambda_{mj} \cdot p_m(\theta_{mj})$, thus, she computes the partial sum y^j after running **PartialEval** and she publishes it. Finally, any user is able to get the total sum y by running **FinalEval**.

Table 1. Additive Homomorphic Secret Sharing

Secret inputs	Servers				
	s_1	s_2	$\ldots$	$\ldots$	s_m
x_1	$\lambda_{11} \cdot p_1(\theta_{11})$	$\lambda_{12} \cdot p_1(\theta_{12})$	$\ldots$	$\ldots$	$\lambda_{1m} \cdot p_1(\theta_{1m})$
x_2	$\lambda_{21} \cdot p_2(\theta_{21})$	$\lambda_{22} \cdot p_2(\theta_{22})$	$\ldots$	$\ldots$	$\lambda_{2m} \cdot p_2(\theta_{2m})$
.	.	.			.
.	.	.			.
.	.	.			.
x_n	$\lambda_{n1} \cdot p_n(\theta_{n1})$	$\lambda_{n2} \cdot p_n(\theta_{n2})$	$\ldots$	$\ldots$	$\lambda_{nm} \cdot p_n(\theta_{nm})$
Partial sum	y^1	y^2	$\ldots$	$\ldots$	y^m
Total sum			y		

3.2   Correctness of the Additive HSS

We may now confirm that even though the clients in the additive HSS do not reveal their secret inputs $x_1, \ldots, x_n$, it is still possible for a user to compute the total sum with probability 1. It suffices to show that

$$y = x_1 + \ldots + x_n.$$

We can get to this as follows: By construction, it holds that $y = \sum_{j=1}^{m} y^j$ and $y^j = \sum_{i=1}^{n} \lambda_{ij} \cdot p_i(\theta_{ij})$. This implies that

$$y = \sum_{j=1}^{m} \sum_{i=1}^{n} \lambda_{ij} \cdot p_i(\theta_{ij}) = \sum_{i=1}^{n} \sum_{j=1}^{m} \lambda_{ij} \cdot p_i(\theta_{ij}).$$

However, it is also true that $p_i(0) = \sum_{j=1}^{m} \lambda_{ij} p_i(\theta_{ij})$ which implies that $y = \sum_{i=1}^{n} p_i(0)$. Now, by construction (see **ShareSecret**), $p_i(0) = x_i$ which gives

$$y = \sum_{i=1}^{n} x_i = x_1 + x_2 + \ldots + x_n$$

as we wished.

3.3 Security of the Additive HSS

Theorem 1. *For all $T \subset \{s_1, \ldots, s_m\}$ with $|T| \leq m-1$ and all PPT adversaries $\mathcal{A}$, the additive HSS scheme (**ShareSecret, PartialEval, FinalEval**) is $(m-1)$-secure. It holds that $\mathrm{Adv}(1^\lambda, \mathcal{A}, T) \leq \varepsilon(\lambda)$ for some negligible $\varepsilon(\lambda)$.*

Proof. Let $|T| = m - 1$, that is, there are $m - 1$ corrupted servers.
The adversary $\mathcal{A}$ has $(m-1)n$ shares from the corrupted servers and no information that any $(m-1)$-tuple is related either to x_i or to x_i'. Consider, without loss of generality, that the first $m - 1$ servers are the corrupted ones.

If we denote the shares for any $i \in [n]$ by $\hat{x}_{i1}, \ldots, \hat{x}_{im}$, it is true that $\sum_{j=1}^{m} \hat{x}_{ij} = \hat{x}_i$ for some i. We may also see this equality as $\hat{x}_{im} = \hat{x}_i - \sum_{j=1}^{m-1} \hat{x}_{ij}$. Then, any PPT adversary has no information whether $\hat{x}_{im} \in \mathcal{Y}$ is the m-th share of x_i or x_i' and thus, may guess whether $\hat{x}_m$ corresponds to x_i or x_i' with probability $1/2$. That gives that the adversary can guess whether $\hat{x}_i$ is x_i or x_i' with probability $1/2$ as well. Therefore, it holds that $\mathrm{Adv}(1^\lambda, \mathcal{A}, T) \leq \varepsilon(\lambda)$ for some negligible $\varepsilon(\lambda)$.

4 Multiplicative Verifiable Homomorphic Secret Sharing Scheme

In this chapter, we present a concrete instantiation of the multiplicative verifiable homomorphic secret sharing (VHSS) scheme for which we use the notion of the bilinear maps. A bilinear map is a function that is defined as follows:

Definition 3. *Let $\mathbb{G}_1, \mathbb{G}_2$ and $\mathbb{G}_k$ be cyclic groups of the same order. A bilinear map from $\mathbb{G}_1 \times \mathbb{G}_2$ to $\mathbb{G}_k$ is a function $e : \mathbb{G}_1 \times \mathbb{G}_2 \to \mathbb{G}_k$ such that for all $u \in \mathbb{G}_1, v \in \mathbb{G}_2, a, b \in \mathbb{Z}$,*

$$e(u^a, v^b) = e(u, v)^{ab}.$$

In our instantiation, however, we consider the bilinear map $e : \mathbb{G} \times \mathbb{G} \to \mathbb{G}_k$ where $\mathbb{G}, \mathbb{G}_k$ are cyclic groups of the same order.

For the security of the multiplicative VHSS, we need that the inversion of the bilinear map when one of the inputs is fixed does not exist. We call such an inversion by the fixed inversion problem (FI). More formally, the FI problem is defined as follows:

Definition 4 [16]. *For a fixed $g \in \mathbb{G}$ and any given $h \in \mathbb{G}_k$, the problem which finds an inverse image g' such that $e(g, g') = h$ is called fixed inversion problem (FI).*

In order to meet the multiplicative VHSS's security requirement, we yield the following assumption:

Assumption 1. *Given the bilinear map $e : \mathbb{G}_1 \times \mathbb{G}_2 \to \mathbb{G}_k$ and the values $g \in \mathbb{G}_1, g' \in \mathbb{G}_2$ and $h \in \mathbb{G}_k$, we assume that the fixed inversion problem (FI) is hard.*

What is more, assuming that the FI problem is hard implies that the discrete logarithm problem (DLP) is hard. More precisely, we give what the discrete logarithm problem is as well as the relation between FI and DLP:

Definition 5. *For any given two values g and g^a in a group $\mathbb{G}$ the problem which computes a is called the discrete logarithm problem (DLP).*

Observation 1 [16]. *If the fixed inversion (FI) problem is hard, then the discrete logarithm problem (DLP) in $\mathbb{G}_k$ is hard.*

4.1   Construction of the Multiplicative VHSS

Let us consider n clients $c_1, \ldots, c_n$ who will again split their secret inputs $x_1, x_2, \ldots, x_n$ to m servers $s_1, \ldots, s_m$, $\mathbb{F}$ to be a finite field with $|\mathbb{F}| > m$ and λ be the security parameter. The clients (users) are able to compute their secret inputs' product by multiplying the partial products that have been computed by each server. In other words, a user can compute $f(x_1, x_2, \ldots, x_n) = x_1 \cdot x_2 \cdot \ldots \cdot x_n$ without knowing $x_1, \ldots, x_n$.

In this setting, each client c_i has x_i but also $\widetilde{x}_i$ such that $g^{\widetilde{x}_i} = x_i$ where g denotes a generator of the multiplicative group of $\mathbb{F}$. Furthermore, each server will not only publish the partial product but also a share of a proof. As a result, any user is able to use the shares of the proof in order to obtain the proof and verify that the final product is correct.

Let, for any $i \in \{1, \ldots, n\}$, $\theta_{i1}, \ldots, \theta_{im}$ be distinct nonzero field elements and $\lambda_{i1}, \lambda_{i2}, \ldots, \lambda_{im}$ be field elements ("Lagrange coefficients") such that for any univariate polynomial p_i of degree t over $\mathbb{F}$ we have $p_i(0) = \sum_{j=1}^{m} \lambda_{ij} p_i(\theta_{ij})$. For any $j \in \{1, \ldots, m\}$, the share of the proof that will be published by the server s_j is denoted by σ^j. We consider the following algorithms:

1. **ShareSecret**$(1^{\lambda}, i, \widetilde{x}_i)$: Pick a polynomial p_i of the form $p_i(X) = \widetilde{x}_i + a_1 X + a_2 X^2 + \ldots + a_t X^t$ where $a_i, i \in \{1, \ldots, n\}$ are elements selected uniformly at random, t denotes the degree of the polynomial with $t \cdot n < m$ and $\widetilde{x}_i$ its free coefficient. Then, the algorithm outputs $(x_{i1}, x_{i2}, \ldots, x_{im}, \tau_i) = (g^{\lambda_{i1} \cdot p_i(\theta_{i1})}, g^{\lambda_{i2} \cdot p_i(\theta_{i2})}, \ldots, g^{\lambda_{im} \cdot p_i(\theta_{im})}, e(g, g^{\widetilde{x}_i}))$. Note that $\tau_i = e(g, g^{\widetilde{x}_i})$.
2. **PartialEval**$(j, (x_{1j}, x_{2j}, \ldots, x_{nj}))$: For the given j and for all $i \in [n]$, multiply all x_{ij}, that is, compute $x_{1j} \cdot x_{2j} \cdot \ldots \cdot x_{nj} = g^{\lambda_{1j} \cdot p_1(\theta_{1j})} \cdot g^{\lambda_{2j} \cdot p_2(\theta_{2j})} \cdot \ldots \cdot g^{\lambda_{nj} \cdot p_n(\theta_{nj})} = \prod_{i=1}^{n} g^{\lambda_{ij} \cdot p_i(\theta_{ij})} = y^j$. Output y^j.
3. **PartialProof**$(j, (x_{1j}, x_{2j}, \ldots, x_{nj}))$: For the given j and $x_{1j}, x_{2j}, \ldots, x_{nj}$, compute the partial proof, that is, the share of the proof, $\sigma^j = e(g, x_{1j} \cdot x_{2j} \cdot \ldots \cdot x_{nj}) = e(g, y^j)$ where $e : \mathbb{G} \times \mathbb{G} \to \mathbb{G}_k$. Output σ^j.
4. **FinalEval**$(y^1, y^2, \ldots, y^m)$: Multiply the partial products y^j for $j \in [m]$, that is, compute $y^1 \cdot y^2 \cdot \ldots \cdot y^m = y$. Output y.
5. **FinalProof**$(\sigma^1, \sigma^2, \ldots, \sigma^m)$: Multiply the partial proofs to get $\sigma^1 \cdot \ldots \cdot \sigma^m = \sigma$. Output σ.
6. **Verify**$(\tau_1, \ldots, \tau_n, \sigma, y)$: Check that $\prod_{i=1}^{n} \tau_i = \sigma$ and $\prod_{i=1}^{n} \tau_i = e(g, y)$. Output: 1 if both are satisfied or 0 otherwise.

Each client c_i splits her secret input x_i by running **ShareSecret** for $\tilde{x}_i$ and give to each server s_j the share $x_{ij} = g^{\lambda_{ij} \cdot p_i(\theta_{ij})}$. **ShareSecret** also outputs the encoded value $\tau_i, i \in [n]$ which will be published by the client c_i. Table 2 shows how the secret inputs are distributed. Then, the server s_j runs **PartialEval** to compute and publish the partial product $y^j = \prod_{i=1}^{n} g^{\lambda_{ij} \cdot p_i(\theta_{ij})}$. Each server s_j applies also the algorithm **PartialProof** to compute and publish a partial proof $\sigma^j = e(g, y^j)$. Now, any user, not having any secret input $x_1, \ldots, x_n$, applies **FinalEval** to get the value $y = f(x_1, x_2, \ldots, x_n) = x_1 \cdot x_2 \cdot \ldots \cdot x_n$ and **FinalProof** to get the proof $\sigma = \sigma^1 \cdot \ldots \cdot \sigma^m$ that y is correct. Any user may now run the algorithm **Verify** to confirm that y is actually the product of $x_1, x_2, \ldots, x_n$, which will be the case if **Verify** outputs 1.

Table 2. Multiplicative Homomorphic Secret Sharing

Secret inputs	Public	Servers				
	value	s_1	s_2	$\ldots$	$\ldots$	s_m
x_1	τ_1	$g^{\lambda_{11} \cdot p_1(\theta_{11})}$	$g^{\lambda_{12} \cdot p_1(\theta_{12})}$	$\ldots$	$\ldots$	$g^{\lambda_{1m} \cdot p_1(\theta_{1m})}$
x_2	τ_2	$g^{\lambda_{21} \cdot p_2(\theta_{21})}$	$g^{\lambda_{22} \cdot p_2(\theta_{22})}$	$\ldots$	$\ldots$	$g^{\lambda_{2m} \cdot p_2(\theta_{2m})}$
.	.	.	.			.
.	.	.	.			.
.	.	.	.			.
x_n	τ_n	$g^{\lambda_{n1} \cdot p_n(\theta_{n1})}$	$g^{\lambda_{n2} \cdot p_n(\theta_{n2})}$			$g^{\lambda_{nm} \cdot p_n(\theta_{nm})}$
Partial product		y^1	y^2			y^m
Partial proof		σ^1	σ^2	$\ldots$	$\ldots$	σ^m
(Product, proof)		(y, σ)				

4.2 Correctness of the Multiplicative VHSS

To confirm the correctness of the multiplicative VHSS, it suffices to show that $\prod_{i=1}^{n} \tau_i = \sigma$ and $\prod_{i=1}^{n} \tau_i = e(g, y)$. In fact,

$$\sigma = \sigma^1 \cdot \ldots \cdot \sigma^m = e(g, y^1) \cdot e(g, y^2) \cdot \ldots \cdot e(g, y^m)$$

$$= e(g, \prod_{i=1}^{n} g^{\lambda_{i1} \cdot p_i(\theta_{i1})}) \cdot e(g, \prod_{i=1}^{n} g^{\lambda_{i2} \cdot p_i(\theta_{i2})}) \cdot \ldots \cdot e(g, \prod_{i=1}^{n} g^{\lambda_{im} \cdot p_i(\theta_{im})})$$

$$= e(g, g^{\sum_{i=1}^{n} \lambda_{i1} \cdot p_i(\theta_{i1})}) \cdot e(g, g^{\sum_{i=1}^{n} \lambda_{i2} \cdot p_i(\theta_{i2})}) \cdot \ldots \cdot e(g, g^{\sum_{i=1}^{n} \lambda_{im} \cdot p_i(\theta_{im})})$$

$$= e(g, g)^{\sum_{i=1}^{n} \lambda_{i1} \cdot p_i(\theta_{i1})} \cdot e(g, g)^{\sum_{i=1}^{n} \lambda_{i2} \cdot p_i(\theta_{i2})} \cdot \ldots \cdot e(g, g)^{\sum_{i=1}^{n} \lambda_{im} \cdot p_i(\theta_{im})}$$

$$= e(g, g)^{\sum_{j=1}^{m} \sum_{i=1}^{n} \lambda_{ij} \cdot p_i(\theta_{ij})} = e(g, g^{\sum_{j=1}^{m} \sum_{i=1}^{n} \lambda_{ij} \cdot p_i(\theta_{ij})})$$

$$= e(g, g^{\sum_{i=1}^{n} \lambda_{i1} \cdot p_i(\theta_{i1})} \cdot g^{\sum_{i=1}^{n} \lambda_{i2} \cdot p_i(\theta_{i2})} \cdot \ldots \cdot g^{\sum_{i=1}^{n} \lambda_{im} \cdot p_i(\theta_{im})})$$

$$= e(g, y^1 \cdot y^2 \cdot \ldots \cdot y^m) = e(g, y)$$

and

$$\prod_{i=1}^{n} \tau_i = \tau^1 \cdot \ldots \cdot \tau^n = e(g, g^{\widetilde{x}_1}) \cdot e(g, g^{\widetilde{x}_2}) \cdot \ldots \cdot e(g, g^{\widetilde{x}_n})$$

$$= e(g,g)^{\widetilde{x}_1} \cdot e(g,g)^{\widetilde{x}_2} \cdot \ldots \cdot e(g,g)^{\widetilde{x}_n} = e(g,g)^{\sum_{i=1}^{n} \widetilde{x}_i} \qquad (1)$$

$$= e(g, g^{\sum_{i=1}^{n} \widetilde{x}_i}) = e(g, g^{\widetilde{x}_1} \cdot g^{\widetilde{x}_2} \cdot \ldots \cdot g^{\widetilde{x}_n})$$

$$= e(g, x_1 \cdot x_2 \cdot \ldots \cdot x_n) = e(g, y)$$

Combining the two results we obtain that $\prod_{i=1}^{n} \tau_i = \sigma$ and $\prod_{i=1}^{n} \tau_i = e(g,y)$ which imply that the algorithm **Verify** will output 1.

4.3   Verifiability of the Multiplicative VHSS

Theorem 2. *For any n secret inputs $x_1, x_2, \ldots, x_n \in \mathbb{F}$ and any set T of corrupted servers with $|T| \leqslant m$ in the multiplicative VHSS, it holds that any PPT adversary who modifies the shares of the secret inputs for any j such that $s_j \in T$, can cause a wrong value to be accepted as $x_1 \cdot x_2 \cdot \ldots \cdot x_n$ with negligible probability. It holds that*

$$\Pr[\boldsymbol{Exp}_{VHSS}^{Verif.}(x_1, x_2, \ldots, x_n, T, \mathcal{A}) = 1] \leq \varepsilon.$$

Proof. Consider that $y' \neq f(x_1, x_2, \ldots, x_n)$ where $f(x_1, x_2, \ldots, x_n) = x_1 \cdot x_2 \cdot \ldots \cdot x_n = y$ and **Verify**$(\tau_1, \ldots, \tau_n, \sigma', y') = 1$.
Then:

$$\textbf{Verify}(\tau_1, \ldots, \tau_n, \sigma', y') = 1$$

$$\implies \prod_{i=1}^{n} \tau_i = \sigma' \text{ and } \prod_{i=1}^{n} \tau_i = e(g, y')$$

$$\implies \prod_{i=1}^{n} \tau_i = e(g, y') \quad \text{(see equation (1))}$$

$$\implies e(g, y) = e(g, y')$$

$$\implies e(g, g^{r_1}) = e(g, g^{r_2}) \quad \text{for some } r_1, r_2 \in \mathbb{F}$$

$$\implies e(g, g)^{r_1} = e(g, g)^{r_2} \quad \text{for some } r_1, r_2 \in \mathbb{F}$$

$$\implies r_1 = r_2 \text{ in } \mathbb{F}$$

$$\implies g^{r_1} = g^{r_2} \text{ in } \mathbb{G}$$

$$\implies y = y'$$

$$\implies f(x_1, x_2, \ldots, x_n) = y'$$

which is a contradiction!

4.4   Security of the Multiplicative VHSS

Theorem 3. *For all $T \subset \{s_1, \ldots, s_m\}$ with $|T| \leq m - 1$ and all PPT adversaries $\mathcal{A}$, the multiplicative VHSS scheme (**ShareSecret**, **PartialEval**, **PartialProof**, **FinalEval**, **FinalProof**, **Verify**) is $(m-1)$-secure. It holds that $\text{Adv}(1^\lambda, \mathcal{A}, T) \leq \varepsilon(\lambda)$ for some negligible $\varepsilon(\lambda)$.*

Proof. Let $|T| = m - 1$, that is, there are $m - 1$ corrupted servers.

Consider, without loss of generality, that the first $m-1$ servers are the corrupted ones. The adversary $\mathcal{A}$ has $(m - 1)n$ shares from the corrupted servers and no additional information.

Then, if we denote the shares by $\hat{x}_{i1}, \ldots, \hat{x}_{im}$ with $i \in \{1, \ldots, n\}$, we know that $\prod_{j=1}^{m} \hat{x}_{ij} = \hat{x}_i$ for some i and it holds that:

$$\prod_{j=1}^{m-1} \hat{x}_{ij} \cdot \hat{x}_{im} = \hat{x}_i$$

$$\iff \hat{x}_{im} = (\prod_{j=1}^{m-1} \hat{x}_{ij})^{-1} \cdot \hat{x}_i$$

given the $(\prod_{j=1}^{m-1} \hat{x}_{ij})^{-1}$. Now, $\hat{x}_{im} \in \mathcal{Y}$ is just a value which gives nothing to the adversary regarding whether it is related to x_i or $x_i{}'$. Therefore, any PPT adversary has probability $1/2$ to decide whether $\hat{x}_i$ is x_i or $x_i{}'$.

What is more, the adversary is also able to see the public encoded values $\tau_1 = e(g, g^{\tilde{x}_1}), \ldots, \tau_n = e(g, g^{\tilde{x}_n})$. It holds that the adversary cannot obtain neither $g^{\tilde{x}_i}$ (Assumption 1) nor $\tilde{x}_i$ (Observation 1) from τ_i. Therefore, the adversary gets no additional information from τ_i.

Finally, it holds that $\mathrm{Adv}(1^\lambda, \mathcal{A}, T) \leq \varepsilon(\lambda)$ for some negligible $\varepsilon(\lambda)$.

5   Conclusion

In this paper, we introduced the notion of *verifiable homomorphic secret sharing* (VHSS) for multi-input which is based on the general notion of homomorphic secret sharing (HSS). The VHSS scheme enables the clients (users) to locally generate shares of a proof which confirms that the combination of the shares is correct. We provided a detailed example for casting Shamir's secret sharing scheme [20] over a finite field $\mathbb{F}$ for the function f that sums n field elements. Such a scheme exists if and only if $m > n \cdot t$. Furthermore, we proposed an instantiation of the multiplicative verifiable homomorphic secret sharing (multiplicative VHSS) scheme for the function f that multiplies n elements under the hardness assumption of the fixed inversion problem in bilinear maps.

Acknowledgments. This work was partially supported by the Wallenberg AI, Autonomous Systems and Software Program (WASP) funded by the Knut and Alice Wallenberg Foundation and the VR grant PRECIS.

References

1. Ananth, P., Chandran, N., Goyal, V., Kanukurthi, B., Ostrovsky, R.: Achieving privacy in verifiable computation with multiple servers – without FHE and without pre-processing. In: Krawczyk, H. (ed.) PKC 2014. LNCS, vol. 8383, pp. 149–166. Springer, Heidelberg (2014). https://doi.org/10.1007/978-3-642-54631-0_9

2. Backes, M., Fiore, D., Reischuk, R.M.: Verifiable delegation of computation on outsourced data. In: Proceedings of the 2013 ACM SIGSAC Conference on Computer and Communications Security, pp. 863–874. ACM (2013)

3. Barkol, O., Ishai, Y., Weinreb, E.: On d-multiplicative secret sharing. J. cryptol. **23**(4), 580–593 (2010)

4. Benaloh, J.C.: Secret sharing homomorphisms: keeping shares of a secret secret (extended abstract). In: Odlyzko, A.M. (ed.) CRYPTO 1986. LNCS, vol. 263, pp. 251–260. Springer, Heidelberg (1987). https://doi.org/10.1007/3-540-47721-7_19

5. Boyle, E., Gilboa, N., Ishai, Y.: Function secret sharing. In: Oswald, E., Fischlin, M. (eds.) EUROCRYPT 2015. LNCS, vol. 9057, pp. 337–367. Springer, Heidelberg (2015). https://doi.org/10.1007/978-3-662-46803-6_12

6. Boyle, E., Gilboa, N., Ishai, Y.: Breaking the circuit size barrier for secure computation under DDH. In: Robshaw, M., Katz, J. (eds.) CRYPTO 2016. LNCS, vol. 9814, pp. 509–539. Springer, Heidelberg (2016). https://doi.org/10.1007/978-3-662-53018-4_19

7. Boyle, E., Gilboa, N., Ishai, Y.: Function secret sharing: improvements and extensions. In: Proceedings of the 2016 ACM SIGSAC Conference on Computer and Communications Security, pp. 1292–1303. ACM (2016)

8. Boyle, E., Gilboa, N., Ishai, Y.: Group-based secure computation: optimizing rounds, communication, and computation. In: Coron, J.-S., Nielsen, J.B. (eds.) EUROCRYPT 2017. LNCS, vol. 10211, pp. 163–193. Springer, Cham (2017). https://doi.org/10.1007/978-3-319-56614-6_6

9. Boyle, E., Gilboa, N., Ishai, Y., Lin, H., Tessaro, S.: Foundations of homomorphic secret sharing. In: LIPIcs-Leibniz International Proceedings in Informatics, vol. 94. Schloss Dagstuhl-Leibniz-Zentrum fuer Informatik (2018)

10. Chung, K.-M., Kalai, Y., Vadhan, S.: Improved delegation of computation using fully homomorphic encryption. In: Rabin, T. (ed.) CRYPTO 2010. LNCS, vol. 6223, pp. 483–501. Springer, Heidelberg (2010). https://doi.org/10.1007/978-3-642-14623-7_26

11. Fiore, D., Gennaro, R., Pastro, V.: Efficiently verifiable computation on encrypted data. In: Proceedings of the 2014 ACM SIGSAC Conference on Computer and Communications Security, pp. 844–855. ACM (2014)

12. Fiore, D., Mitrokotsa, A., Nizzardo, L., Pagnin, E.: Multi-key homomorphic authenticators. In: Cheon, J.H., Takagi, T. (eds.) ASIACRYPT 2016. LNCS, vol. 10032, pp. 499–530. Springer, Heidelberg (2016). https://doi.org/10.1007/978-3-662-53890-6_17

13. Gennaro, R., Gentry, C., Parno, B.: Non-interactive verifiable computing: outsourcing computation to untrusted workers. In: Rabin, T. (ed.) CRYPTO 2010. LNCS, vol. 6223, pp. 465–482. Springer, Heidelberg (2010). https://doi.org/10.1007/978-3-642-14623-7_25

14. Gentry, C.: A Fully Homomorphic Encryption Scheme. Stanford University, Stanford (2009)

15. Gordon, S.D., Katz, J., Liu, F.-H., Shi, E., Zhou, H.-S.: Multi-client verifiable computation with stronger security guarantees. In: Dodis, Y., Nielsen, J.B. (eds.) TCC 2015. LNCS, vol. 9015, pp. 144–168. Springer, Heidelberg (2015). https://doi.org/10.1007/978-3-662-46497-7_6

16. Cheon, J.H., Lee, D.H.: A note on self-bilinear maps. Bull. Korean Math. Soc. **46**, 303–309 (2009)

17. Pagnin, E., Mitrokotsa, A., Tanaka, K.: Anonymous single-round server-aided verification of signatures. In: The 5th International Conference on Cryptology and Information Security (Latincrypt) (2017)

18. Parno, B., Raykova, M., Vaikuntanathan, V.: How to delegate and verify in public: verifiable computation from attribute-based encryption. In: Cramer, R. (ed.) TCC 2012. LNCS, vol. 7194, pp. 422–439. Springer, Heidelberg (2012). https://doi.org/10.1007/978-3-642-28914-9_24
19. Rivest, R.L., Adleman, L., Dertouzos, M.L.: On data banks and privacy homomorphisms. Found. Secure Comput. **4**(11), 169–180 (1978)
20. Shamir, A.: How to share a secret. Commun. ACM **22**(11), 612–613 (1979)
21. Tang, C., Chen, Y.: Efficient non-interactive verifiable outsourced computation for arbitrary functions. IACR Cryptology ePrint Archive, 2014:439 (2014)
22. Wang, F., Yun, C., Goldwasser, S., Vaikuntanathan, V., Zaharia, M.: Splinter: practical private queries on public data. In: NSDI, pp. 299–313 (2017)
23. Yoshida, M., Obana, S.: Verifiably multiplicative secret sharing. In: Shikata, J. (ed.) ICITS 2017. LNCS, vol. 10681, pp. 73–82. Springer, Cham (2017). https://doi.org/10.1007/978-3-319-72089-0_5

Single Private-Key Generator Security Implies Multiple Private-Key Generators Security

Atsushi Fujioka[1] and Kazuki Yoneyama[2(✉)]

[1] Kanagawa University, 3-27-1 Rokkakubashi, Kanagawa-ku, Yokohama-shi,
Kanagawa 221-8686, Japan
fujioka@kanagawa-u.ac.jp
[2] Ibaraki University, 4-12-1 Nakanarusawa, Hitachi-shi, Ibaraki 316-8511, Japan
kazuki.yoneyama.sec@vc.ibaraki.ac.jp

Abstract. This paper discusses the security of identity-based cryptography with multiple private-key generators (mPKG-IBC). Most mPKG-IBC schemes and protocols are statically secure where private-key generators (PKGs) cannot control a binding between a party and its PKG. We propose adaptive security notions for identity-based key encapsulation mechanism with multiple private-key generators, identity-based signature with multiple private-key generators, and identity-based authenticated key exchange with multiple private-key generators, respectively. In additions, we provide their generic constructions of those from identity-based key encapsulation mechanism, identity-based signature, and identity-based authenticated key exchange which are secure in a single PKG model, respectively.

Keywords: Identity-based cryptography
Multiple private-key generators · Adaptive security
Identity-based key encapsulation mechanism
Identity-based signature · Identity-based authenticated key exchange

1 Introduction

It is well known that *identity-based cryptography* (IBC) has several advantages than *public-key cryptography* (PKC). One of the advantages is that IBC does not need a mechanism to ensure an identity and its public key such as *public-key infrastructure* (PKI).

However, IBC requires an additional authority, *private-key generator* (PKG). Upon a request, a PKG generates a private key for a entity using on a string which identifies the entity, and the string is called *identity* (ID). It is worth to note that in conventional IBC, a single PKG manages all entities belong to a domain.

Although many researches on IBC have been investigated [1,3,11], most of them assume that there exists a single PKG in the system. It may be unrealistic that a single PKG manages all.

© Springer Nature Switzerland AG 2018
J. Baek et al. (Eds.): ProvSec 2018, LNCS 11192, pp. 56–74, 2018.
https://doi.org/10.1007/978-3-030-01446-9_4

Here, consider a PKI system. An ideal PKI system assumes the existence of a single root CA. However, several root CAs exist in a real PKI system. Thus, it is natural to consider the multi-authority situation in IBC, also. It is common that some E-mail address such as a Gmail address can be used as a login ID for other services like Facebook, LinkedIn, and so on. In such situation, an user who is indicated with a mail address obtains different private keys from Google, Facebook and LinkedIn, respectively. Therefore, this leads us to a multiple PKG scenario.

1.1   Related Works

Several schemes and protocols in IBC with multiple PKG (mPKG-IBC) have been researched in literature: *identity-based encryption with multiple PKG* [10, 12], *identity-based signcryption with multiple PKG* [9,13], and *identity-based authenticated key exchange with multiple PKG* (mPKG-IBAKE) [2,4,5,8].

In those schemes and protocols, a PKG manages a domain and another PKG manages a different domain. Even in such situation, a entity can securely communicate or establish a key with each other.

However, most of the above assume a security model that a party is statically bound to its PKG. Therefore, an adversary cannot control the binding between a party and its PKG, that is, the domain which the party belongs to.

In the previous works of [4,5], Fujioka discusses the following security models in mPKG-IBAKE:

- When we assume that there is a binding between an identifier and its PKG, we call this *static binding model*.
- When an adversary adaptively indicates a binding between an identifier and its PKG, we call this *adaptive binding model*.
- When an adversary can get the private key of an user only once, we call this *separated domain model*.
- When an adversary is allowed to obtain several private keys from different PKGs, we call this *overlapped domain model*.

Roughly speaking, a mPKG-IBAKE protocol is statically secure when its security is proven in the static binding and separated domain model, and a mPKG-IBAKE protocol is adaptively secure when its security is proven in the adaptive binding and overlapped domain model. Fujioka proposes a dedicated mPKG-IBAKE protocol and proves that it is adaptively secure [5].

It is worth to note here that schemes and protocols in mPKG-IBC can be classified into two types: *common parameter type* and *independent parameter type*. In a scheme of common parameter type (e.g., [2]), each PKG can generates master keys based on the same parameter (e.g., groups, generators, a pairing function, and so on) used in the scheme, and in a scheme of independent parameter type (e.g., [8]), each PKG can generates not only master keys but also the parameter used in the scheme.

1.2   Our Contributions

This paper formally defines adaptive security notions in *identity-based key encapsulation mechanism with multiple PKG* (mPKG-IBKEM) and *identity-based signature with multiple PKG* (mPKG-IBS), respectively. In addition, we provide another adaptive security notion in mPKG-IBAKE different from the id(m)-eCK model defined in [5] as the former is based on the id-CK$^+$ model [6] and the latter is on the id-eCK model [7].

Roughly speaking, a scheme/protocol is said to be *multiple private-key generators secure* (mPKG secure) when it is adaptively secure in the above sense. It is worth to note there that a scheme/protocol is said to be *single private-key generators secure* (sPKG secure) when it is secure in the single PKG model, i.e., for conventional IBC.

We propose generic constructions from a conventionally secure IBC scheme, called *single private-key generator secure* IBC scheme, to a multiple private-key generators secure one for *identity-based key encapsulation mechanism* (IBKEM), *identity-based signature* (IBS), and *identity-based authenticated key exchange* (IBAKE), respectively. Precisely,

- When there exists a IBKEM scheme which is secure in the single PKG model, i.e., satisfies *indistinguishablity* against a attack, we have a mPKG-IBKEM scheme which is mPKG secure against the attack.
- When there exists a IBS scheme which is secure in the single PKG model, i.e., satisfies *unforgeability* against a attack, we have a mPKG-IBS scheme which is mPKG secure against the attack.
- When there exists a IBAKE protocol which is secure in the single PKG model, i.e., satisfies *indistinguishablity*, we have a mPKG-IBAKE protocol which is mPKG secure.

Regarding to generation of a system parameter, we describe the schemes and constructions in the independent parameter type. You may feel that it is a drawback of our approach. However, the master key generation algorithm in most of conventional IBC schemes and protocols, i.e., with a single PKG, can be divided into two parts: parameter generation one and exact master key generation one. Thus, we may use the parameter generation part to generate the global parameter, and we can assume that such algorithm exists.

2   mPKG Secure IBKEM from sPKG Secure IBKEM

In this section, we show that mPKG secure IBKEM can be generically constructed from sPKG secure IBKEM.

2.1   Our Model for mPKG-IBKEM

We propose a security model for mPKG-IBKEM. Besides the ordinary security model for sPKG-IBKEM, we can also consider some variants according to the selection timing of the target ID (i.e., selective ID (sID) or full adaptive ID (aID)) and the target PKG's ID (i.e., selective PKG's ID (sPID) or full adaptive PKG's ID (aPID)) and the usage of the decryption oracle (i.e., CPA or CCA). Hence, we define eight variants of security notions for mPKG-IBKEM.

sPKG-IBKEM. First, we recall the syntax and security notions for sPKG-IBKEM. In this paper, we suppose that the global parameter (e.g., groups, generators, and the order) of IBKEM is already determined outside the master public key if necessary.

Definition 2.1 (Syntax of sPKG-IBKEM Schemes). *An sPKG-IBKEM scheme consists of the following four algorithms,* sKEM.KeyGen, sKEM.KeyDer, sKEM.EnCap, *and* sKEM.DeCap*:*

$(mpk, msk) \leftarrow$ sKEM.KeyGen$(1^\lambda; r_g)$: *a key generation algorithm which on inputs* 1^λ *and* $r_g \in \mathcal{RS}_G$, *where* λ *is the security parameter and* $\mathcal{RS}_G$ *is a randomness space, outputs master public key and secret key* (mpk, msk).

$dk_i \leftarrow$ sKEM.KeyDer$(mpk, msk, \mathrm{id}_i; r_k)$: *a key derivation algorithm which on inputs master public and secret keys* (mpk, msk), *identity string* id_i *and* $r_k \in \mathcal{RS}_K$, *where* $\mathcal{RS}_K$ *is a randomness space, outputs decapsulation key* dk_i *corresponding to* id_i.

$(K, ct) \leftarrow$ sKEM.EnCap$(mpk, \mathrm{id}_i, r_e)$: *an encapsulation algorithm which on inputs master public key* mpk, *identity string* id_i, *and* $r_e \in \mathcal{RS}_E$, *outputs session key* $K \in \mathcal{KS}$, *and ciphertext* $ct \in \mathcal{CS}$, *where* $\mathcal{RS}_E$ *is a randomness space,* $\mathcal{KS}$ *is a session key space, and* $\mathcal{CS}$ *is a ciphertext space.*

$K \leftarrow$ sKEM.DeCap$(mpk, dk_i, ct, \mathrm{id}_i)$: *a decapsulation algorithm which on inputs master public key* mpk, *decapsulation key* dk_i, *ciphertext* $ct \in \mathcal{CS}$, *and identity string* id_i, *outputs session key* $K \in \mathcal{KS}$.

Definition 2.2 (IND-{sID/aID}-{CPA/CCA} Security for sPKG-IBKEM). *A sPKG-IBKEM scheme,* Σ, *is* (ρ, ϵ)-*IND-id-atk-secure for sPKG-IBKEM if the following property holds for security parameter* λ; *For any adversary* $\mathcal{A} = (\mathcal{A}_1, \mathcal{A}_2)$ *with a time-complexity at most* ρ, *advantage* $\mathbf{Adv}_\Sigma^{\text{ind-id-atk}}(\mathcal{A}) = |\Pr[r_g \leftarrow \mathcal{RS}_G; (mpk, msk) \leftarrow$ sKEM.KeyGen$(1^\lambda; r_g)$; $(\mathrm{id}_T^*,$ STATE$) \leftarrow \mathcal{A}_1^{\mathcal{O}(\cdot,\cdot),\mathcal{O}'(\cdot)}(1^\lambda,$ INPUT$)$; $b \leftarrow \{0,1\}$; $r_e \leftarrow \mathcal{RS}_E$; $(K_0^*, ct^*) \leftarrow$ sKEM.EnCap$(mpk, \mathrm{id}_T^*; r_e)$; $K_1^* \leftarrow \mathcal{KS}$; $b' \leftarrow \mathcal{A}_2^{\mathcal{DO}(\cdot,\cdot),\mathcal{KO}(\cdot)}(mpk, K_b^*, ct^*,$ STATE$)$; $b' = b] - 1/2| \leq \epsilon$, *where* $\mathcal{KO}(\mathrm{id}_i)$ *is the key derivation oracle, and* STATE *is state information which* $\mathcal{A}$ *wants to preserve from* $\mathcal{A}_1$ *to* $\mathcal{A}_2$,

if $\mathrm{id} = \mathrm{sID}$ *then* INPUT $= \emptyset$, $\mathcal{O} = \emptyset$ *and* $\mathcal{O}' = \emptyset$,
if $\mathrm{id} = \mathrm{aID}$ *then* INPUT $= mpk$, $\mathcal{O} = \mathcal{DO}$ *and* $\mathcal{O}' = \mathcal{KO}$,
if atk $= \mathrm{CPA}$ *then* $\mathcal{DO}(ct, \mathrm{id}_i)$ *outputs* $\bot$, *and*
if atk $= \mathrm{CCA}$ *then* $\mathcal{DO}(ct, \mathrm{id}_i)$ *is the decryption oracle.*
$\mathcal{A}$ *can neither make query* $\mathcal{DO}(ct^*, \mathrm{id}_T^*)$ *nor* $\mathcal{KO}(\mathrm{id}_T^*)$.

mPKG-IBKEM. Next, we introduce a syntax and security notions for mPKG-IBKEM. In mPKG-IBKEM, we suppose that there are a polynomial number of PKGs in the security parameter. Each PKG has a particular master key pair, and each user can obtain decapsulation keys for his/her ID from multiple PKGs. The sender chooses a PKG to encapsulate a session key, and the receiver can decapsulate the ciphertext with the decapsulation key obtained from that PKG.

Definition 2.3 (Syntax of mPKG-IBKEM Schemes). *An mPKG-IBKEM scheme consists of the following four algorithms,* mKEM.KeyGen, mKEM.KeyDer, mKEM.EnCap, *and* mKEM.DeCap:

$(mpk_\iota, msk_\iota) \leftarrow$ mKEM.KeyGen$(1^\lambda, \text{pid}_\iota; r_g)$: *a key generation algorithm which on inputs* 1^λ, *PKG's identity string* pid_ι *and* $r_g \in \mathcal{RS}_G$, *where* λ *is the security parameter and* $\mathcal{RS}_G$ *is a randomness space, outputs master public key and secret key* (mpk_ι, msk_ι).

$dk_{i,\iota} \leftarrow$ mKEM.KeyDer$(mpk_\iota, msk_\iota, \text{id}_i; r_k)$: *a key derivation algorithm which on inputs master public and secret keys* (mpk_ι, msk_ι), *identity string* id_i *and* $r_k \in \mathcal{RS}_K$, *where* $\mathcal{RS}_K$ *is a randomness space, outputs decapsulation key* $dk_{i,\iota}$ *corresponding to* id_i *on PKG* pid_ι.

$(K, ct, \text{pid}_\iota) \leftarrow$ mKEM.EnCap$(mpk_\iota, \text{id}_i, \text{pid}_\iota; r_e)$: *an encapsulation algorithm which on inputs master public key* mpk_ι, *identity string* id_i, *PKG's identity string* pid_ι, *and* $r_e \in \mathcal{RS}_E$, *outputs session key* $K \in \mathcal{KS}$, *ciphertext* $ct \in \mathcal{CS}$, *and* pid_ι, *where* $\mathcal{RS}_E$ *is a randomness space,* $\mathcal{KS}$ *is a session key space, and* $\mathcal{CS}$ *is a ciphertext space.*

$K \leftarrow$ mKEM.DeCap$(mpk_\iota, dk_{i,\iota}, ct, \text{id}_i, \text{pid}_\iota)$: *a decapsulation algorithm which on inputs master public key* mpk_ι, *decapsulation key* $dk_{i,\iota}$, *ciphertext* $ct \in \mathcal{CS}$, *identity string* id_i, *and PKG's identity string* pid_ι, *outputs session key* $K \in \mathcal{KS}$.

Definition 2.4 (IND-{sID/aID}-{sPID/aPID}{CPA/CCA} Security for mPKG-IBKEM). *An mPKG-IBKEM scheme,* Σ, *is* (ρ, ϵ)-IND-id-pid-atk-secure *for mPKG-IBKEM if the following property holds for security parameter* λ; *For any adversary* $\mathcal{A} = (\mathcal{A}_1, \mathcal{A}_2, \mathcal{A}_3)$ *with a time-complexity at most* ρ, $\mathbf{Adv}_\Sigma^{\text{ind-id-pid-atk}}(\mathcal{A}) = |\Pr[r_{g,\alpha} \leftarrow \mathcal{RS}_G; \dots; r_{g,\zeta} \leftarrow \mathcal{RS}_G; (mpk_\alpha, msk_\alpha) \leftarrow$ mKEM.KeyGen$(1^\lambda, \text{pid}_\alpha; r_{g,\alpha}); \dots; (mpk_\zeta, msk_\zeta) \leftarrow$ mKEM.KeyGen$(1^\lambda, \text{pid}_\zeta;$ $r_{g,\zeta}); (\text{OUTPUT}_1, \text{STATE}_1) \leftarrow \mathcal{A}_1^{\mathcal{O}_1(\cdot,\cdot,\cdot),\mathcal{O}'_1(\cdot,\cdot)}(1^\lambda, \text{INPUT}_1); (\text{OUTPUT}_2, \text{STATE}_2) \leftarrow$ $\mathcal{A}_2^{\mathcal{O}_2(\cdot,\cdot,\cdot),\mathcal{O}'_2(\cdot,\cdot)}(1^\lambda, \text{INPUT}_2, \text{STATE}_1); b \leftarrow \{0,1\}; r_e \leftarrow \mathcal{RS}_E; (K_0^*, ct^*, \text{pid}_\tau^*) \leftarrow$ mKEM.EnCap$(mpk_\tau, \text{id}_T^*, \text{pid}_\tau^*; r_e); K_1^* \leftarrow \mathcal{KS}; b' \leftarrow \mathcal{A}_3^{\mathcal{DO}(\cdot,\cdot,\cdot),\mathcal{KO}(\cdot,\cdot)}(\{mpk_\alpha,$ $\dots, mpk_\zeta\}, K_b^*, ct^*, \text{pid}_\tau^*, \text{STATE}_2); b' = b] - 1/2| \leq \epsilon$, *where* $\mathcal{KO}(\text{pid}_\iota, \text{id}_i)$ *is the key derivation oracle,* STATE_i *is state information which* $\mathcal{A}$ *wants to preserve from* $\mathcal{A}_i$ *to* $\mathcal{A}_{i+1}$,

if id = sID *and* pid = sPID *then* $\text{INPUT}_1 = \text{INPUT}_2 = \emptyset$,
$$\text{OUTPUT}_1 = \text{id}_T^*, \text{OUTPUT}_2 = \text{pid}_\tau^*,$$
$$\mathcal{O}_1 = \mathcal{O}'_1 = \emptyset \text{ and } \mathcal{O}_2 = \mathcal{O}'_2 = \emptyset,$$

if id $=$ sID *and* pid $=$ aPID *then* INPUT$_1$ $= \emptyset$, INPUT$_2 = \{mpk_\alpha, \ldots, mpk_\zeta\}$,
$\quad$ OUTPUT$_1$ $=$ id$_T^*$, OUTPUT$_2$ $=$ pid$_\tau^*$,
$\quad \mathcal{O}_1 = \emptyset$, $\mathcal{O}_1' = \emptyset$, $\mathcal{O}_2 = \mathcal{DO}$ *and* $\mathcal{O}_2' = \mathcal{KO}$,
if id $=$ aID *and* pid $=$ sPID *then* INPUT$_1$ $= \emptyset$, INPUT$_2 = \{mpk_\alpha, \ldots, mpk_\zeta\}$,
$\quad$ OUTPUT$_1$ $=$ pid$_\tau^*$, OUTPUT$_2$ $=$ id$_T^*$,
$\quad \mathcal{O}_1 = \emptyset$, $\mathcal{O}_1' = \emptyset$, $\mathcal{O}_2 = \mathcal{DO}$ *and* $\mathcal{O}_2' = \mathcal{KO}$,
if id $=$ aID *and* pid $=$ aPID *then* INPUT$_1$ $=$ INPUT$_2 = \{mpk_\alpha, \ldots, mpk_\zeta\}$,
$\quad$ OUTPUT$_1$ $=$ id$_T^*$, OUTPUT$_2$ $=$ pid$_\tau^*$,
$\quad \mathcal{O}_1 = \mathcal{O}_2 = \mathcal{DO}$ *and* $\mathcal{O}_1' = \mathcal{O}_2' = \mathcal{KO}$,
if atk $=$ CPA *then* $\mathcal{DO}(ct, \text{id}_i, \text{pid}_\iota)$ *outputs* $\perp$, *and*
if atk $=$ CCA *then* $\mathcal{DO}(ct, \text{id}_i, \text{pid}_\iota)$ *is the decryption oracle.*

$\mathcal{A}$ *can neither make query* $\mathcal{DO}(ct^*, \text{id}_T^*, \text{pid}_\tau^*)$ *nor* $\mathcal{KO}(\text{pid}_\tau^*, \text{id}_T^*)$.

2.2 Generic Transformation from sPKG-IBKEM to mPKG-IBKEM

The algorithms in sPKG-IBKEM can be used as the algorithms in mPKG-IBKEM just as they are. Hence, the transformation just replaces terms in sPKG-IBKEM to terms in mPKG-IBKEM. The protocol for an mPKG-IBKEM scheme, $\Sigma' = $ (mKEM.KeyGen, mKEM.KeyDer, mKEM.EnCap, mKEM.DeCap), using an sPKG-IBKEM scheme, $\Sigma = $ (sKEM.KeyGen, sKEM.KeyDer, sKEM.EnCap, sKEM.DeCap), is as follows:

mKEM.KeyGen(1^λ, pid$_\iota$; r_g): Generate $(mpk, msk) \leftarrow$ sKEM.KeyGen(1^λ; r_g),
$\quad$ and output $mpk_\iota = mpk$ and $msk_\iota = msk$ for pid$_\iota$.
mKEM.KeyDer(mpk_ι, msk_ι, id$_i$; r_k): Derive $dk_i \leftarrow$ sKEM.KeyDer(mpk_ι, msk_ι,
$\quad$ id$_i$; r_k), and output $dk_{i,\iota} = dk_i$.
mKEM.EnCap(mpk_ι, id$_i$, pid$_\iota$; r_e): Encapsulate $(K, ct) \leftarrow$ sKEM.EnCap(mpk_ι,
$\quad$ id$_i$, r_e), and output K, ct and pid$_\iota$.
mKEM.DeCap(mpk_ι, $dk_{i,\iota}$, ct, id$_i$, pid$_\iota$): Decapsulate $K \leftarrow$ sKEM.DeCap(mpk_ι,
$\quad$ $dk_{i,\iota}$, ct, id$_i$), and output K.

Security. We show the security of the transformed mPKG-IBKEM based on the security of the underlying sPKG-IBKEM.

The intuitive reason why the security for sPKG is sufficient to the security for mPKG is independence of the key generation procedures of multiple PKGs. Let us consider the case that an adversary breaks the security of mPKG by using information of PKGs other than the target PKG. In this case, we can easily show that the security of sPKG is also broken. Specifically, the adversary in sPKG-IBKEM can generate all master keys other than the target master key because the key generation algorithm does not require any secret information. Hence, the adversary in sPKG-IBKEM has at most the same capacity as the adversary in mPKG-IBKEM. Thus, if the adversary in mPKG-IBKEM can break the security of mPKG by using information of PKGs, then the adversary in sPKG-IBKEM can also break the security of sPKG. Therefore, if sPKG-IBKEM is secure, then mPKG-IBKEM cannot broken by using information of PKGs other than the target PKG because of independence of the key generation procedures.

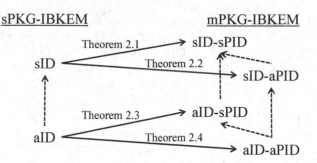

Fig. 1. Implication results for IBKEM

Figure 1 shows our implication results for IBKEM. Note that broken lines mean trivial implications.

Theorem 2.1 (sID-sPID-mPKG from sID-sPKG for IBKEM). *When the underlying sPKG-IBKEM scheme, Σ, satisfies (ρ, ϵ)-IND-sID-atk-security, then the transformed mPKG-IBKEM scheme, Σ', satisfies (ρ', ϵ')-IND-sID-sPID-atk-security, where*

$$\epsilon = \epsilon',$$

$$\rho = \rho' + (N-1)\mathsf{t_{RG}} + (N-1)\mathsf{t_{KG}} + (q_K + q_D)\mathsf{t_{KD}} + q_D\mathsf{t_{DC}},$$

N is the number of PKGs, q_K and q_D are the numbers of queries to $\mathcal{KO}$ and $\mathcal{DO}$, respectively, $\mathsf{t_{RG}}$ is the running time of randomness generation, $\mathsf{t_{KG}}$ is the running time of sKEM.KeyGen, $\mathsf{t_{KD}}$ is the running time of sKEM.KeyDer, and $\mathsf{t_{DC}}$ is the running time of sKEM.DeCap.

Proof. We construct an adversary $\mathcal{A} = (\mathcal{A}_1, \mathcal{A}_2)$ breaking IND-sID-atk-security of Σ by assuming the adversary $\mathcal{A}' = (\mathcal{A}'_1, \mathcal{A}'_2, \mathcal{A}'_3)$ breaking IND-sID-sPID-atk-security of Σ'. Here, we show the case of atk = CCA. The case of atk = CPA can be similarly proved. The construction of $\mathcal{A}$ is as follows:

Procedure of $\mathcal{A}_1$. When $\mathcal{A}_1$ receives 1^λ, $\mathcal{A}_1$ sends 1^λ to $\mathcal{A}'_1$, and receives ($\mathtt{id}_T^*$, STATE$'_1$) from $\mathcal{A}'_1$. Next, $\mathcal{A}_1$ sends $(1^\lambda, \text{STATE}'_1)$ to $\mathcal{A}'_2$, and receives ($\mathtt{pid}_\tau^*$, STATE$'_2$) from $\mathcal{A}'_2$. Then, $\mathcal{A}_1$ sets STATE $= (\text{STATE}'_2, \mathtt{id}_T^*, \mathtt{pid}_\tau^*)$, and outputs ($\mathtt{id}_T^*$, STATE).

Procedure of $\mathcal{A}_2$. When $\mathcal{A}_2$ receives $(mpk, K_b^*, ct^*, \text{STATE})$, parses STATE to STATE $= (\text{STATE}'_2, \mathtt{id}_T^*, \mathtt{pid}_\tau^*)$. $\mathcal{A}_2$ generates $r_{g,\alpha} \leftarrow \mathcal{RS}_G, \ldots, r_{g,\zeta} \leftarrow \mathcal{RS}_G$ and $(mpk_\alpha, msk_\alpha) \leftarrow$ sKEM.KeyGen$(1^\lambda; r_{g,\alpha}), \ldots, (mpk_\zeta, msk_\zeta) \leftarrow$ sKEM.KeyGen$(1^\lambda; r_{g,\zeta})$ except for $\mathtt{pid}_\tau^*$, and sets $mpk_\tau = mpk$. Then, $\mathcal{A}_2$ sends $(\{mpk_\alpha, \ldots, mpk_\zeta\}, K_b^*, ct^*, \text{STATE}'_2)$ to $\mathcal{A}'_3$, and receives b' from $\mathcal{A}'_3$. Finally, $\mathcal{A}_2$ outputs b'.

Simulation of $\mathcal{KO}(\mathtt{id}_i, \mathtt{pid}_\iota)$ by $\mathcal{A}_2$. If $\mathtt{pid}_\iota \neq \mathtt{pid}_\tau^*$, then $\mathcal{A}_2$ generates $r_k \leftarrow \mathcal{RS}_K$, derive $dk_{i,\iota} \leftarrow$ sKEM.KeyDer$(mpk_\iota, msk_\iota, \mathtt{id}_i; r_k)$, and output $dk_{i,\iota}$. Else if $\text{id}_i \neq \text{id}_T^*$, then pose id_i to $\mathcal{KO}$, receives dk_i, and outputs $dk_{i,\tau} = dk_i$. Otherwise, $\mathcal{A}_2$ rejects the query.

Simulation of $\mathcal{DO}(ct, \text{id}_i, \text{pid}_\iota)$ *by* $\mathcal{A}_2$. If $\text{pid}_\iota \neq \text{pid}_\tau^*$, then $\mathcal{A}_2$ generates $r_k \leftarrow \mathcal{RS}_K$, derive $dk_{i,\iota} \leftarrow \text{sKEM.KeyDer}(mpk_\iota, msk_\iota, \text{id}_i; r_k)$, decapsulate $K \leftarrow$ $\text{sKEM.DeCap}(mpk_\iota, dk_{i,\iota}, ct, \text{id}_i)$, and output K. Else if $\text{id}_i \neq \text{id}_T^*$, then pose id_i to $\mathcal{KO}$, receives dk_i, decapsulate $K \leftarrow \text{sKEM.DeCap}(mpk_\iota, dk_i, ct, \text{id}_i)$, and output K. Else if $ct \neq ct^*$, then pose (ct, id_T^*) to $\mathcal{DO}$, receives K, and output K. Otherwise, $\mathcal{A}_2$ rejects the query.

Estimation of advantage of $\mathcal{A}$. $\mathcal{A}$ perfectly simulates the attack environment of $\mathcal{A}'$. Hence, the advantage of $\mathcal{A}$ is $\epsilon = \epsilon'$.

Estimation of running time of $\mathcal{A}$. In addition to ρ', $\mathcal{A}$ runs $(N-1)$ randomness generations, $(N-1)$ master key generations, at most $(q_K + q_D)$ key derivations and at most q_D decapsulations. Hence, the running time ρ of $\mathcal{A}$ is at most $\rho' + (N-1)t_{\text{RG}} + (N-1)t_{\text{KG}} + (q_K + q_D)t_{\text{KD}} + q_D t_{\text{DC}}$.   □

Theorem 2.2 (sID-aPID-mPKG from sID-sPKG for IBKEM). *When the underlying sPKG-IBKEM scheme,* Σ, *satisfies* (ρ, ϵ)-*IND-sID-atk-security, then the transformed mPKG-IBKEM scheme,* Σ', *satisfies* (ρ', ϵ')-*IND-sID-aPID-atk-security, where*

$$\epsilon = \epsilon'/N,$$

$$\rho = \rho' + (N-1)t_{\text{RG}} + (N-1)t_{\text{KG}} + (q_K + q_D)t_{\text{KD}} + q_D t_{\text{DC}},$$

N *is the number of PKGs,* q_K *and* q_D *are the numbers of queries to* $\mathcal{KO}$ *and* $\mathcal{DO}$, *respectively,* t_{RG} *is the running time of randomness generation,* t_{KG} *is the running time of* sKEM.KeyGen, t_{KD} *is the running time of* sKEM.KeyDer, *and* t_{DC} *is the running time of* sKEM.DeCap.

Theorem 2.3 (aID-sPID-mPKG from aID-sPKG for IBKEM). *When the underlying sPKG-IBKEM scheme,* Σ, *satisfies* (ρ, ϵ)-*IND-aID-atk-security, then the transformed mPKG-IBKEM scheme,* Σ', *satisfies* (ρ', ϵ')-*IND-aID-sPID-atk-security, where*

$$\epsilon = \epsilon',$$

$$\rho = \rho' + (N-1)t_{\text{RG}} + (N-1)t_{\text{KG}} + (q_K + q_D)t_{\text{KD}} + q_D t_{\text{DC}},$$

N *is the number of PKGs,* q_K *and* q_D *are the numbers of queries to* $\mathcal{KO}$ *and* $\mathcal{DO}$, *respectively,* t_{RG} *is the running time of randomness generation,* t_{KG} *is the running time of* sKEM.KeyGen, t_{KD} *is the running time of* sKEM.KeyDer, *and* t_{DC} *is the running time of* sKEM.DeCap.

Theorem 2.4 (aID-aPID-mPKG from aID-sPKG for IBKEM). *When the underlying sPKG-IBKEM scheme,* Σ, *satisfies* (ρ, ϵ)-*IND-aID-atk-security, then the transformed mPKG-IBKEM scheme,* Σ', *satisfies* (ρ', ϵ')-*IND-aID-aPID-atk-security, where*

$$\epsilon = \epsilon'/N,$$

$$\rho = \rho' + (N-1)t_{\text{RG}} + (N-1)t_{\text{KG}} + (q_K + q_D)t_{\text{KD}} + q_D t_{\text{DC}},$$

N is the number of PKGs, q_K and q_D are the numbers of queries to $\mathcal{KO}$ and $\mathcal{DO}$, respectively, t_{RG} is the running time of randomness generation, t_{KG} is the running time of sKEM.KeyGen, t_{KD} is the running time of sKEM.KeyDer, and t_{DC} is the running time of sKEM.DeCap.

The above theorems can be proved in a similar way to Theorem 2.1.

3   mPKG Secure IBS from sPKG Secure IBS

In this section, we show that mPKG secure IBS can be generically constructed from sPKG secure IBS.

3.1   Our Model for mPKG-IBS

We propose a security model for mPKG-IBS. As the security model for mPKG-IBKEM, we consider variants according to selective ID (sID) or full adaptive ID (aID), selective PKG's ID (sPID) or full adaptive PKG's ID (aPID), and existentially unforgeable (EUF) or strong existentially unforgeable (sEUF). Hence, we define eight variants of security notions for mPKG-IBS.

sPKG-IBS. First, we recall the syntax and security notions for sPKG-IBS. As IBKEM, we suppose that the global parameter of IBS is already determined outside the master public key if necessary.

Definition 3.1 (Syntax of sPKG-IBS Schemes). *An sPKG-IBS scheme consists of the following 4-tuple* (sSig.KeyGen, sSig.KeyDer, sSig.Sign, sSig.Ver):

- $(mpk, msk) \leftarrow$ sSig.KeyGen$(1^\lambda; r_g)$: *a key generation algorithm which on inputs* 1^λ *and* $r_g \in \mathcal{RS}_G$, *where* λ *is the security parameter and* $\mathcal{RS}_G$ *is a randomness space, outputs master public key and secret key* (mpk, msk).
- $sk_i \leftarrow$ sSig.KeyDer$(mpk, msk, \mathsf{id}_i; r_k)$: *a key derivation algorithm which on inputs master public and secret keys* (mpk, msk), *identity string* id_i *and* $r_k \in \mathcal{RS}_K$, *where* $\mathcal{RS}_K$ *is a randomness space, outputs signing key* sk_i *corresponding to* id_i.
- $\sigma \leftarrow$ sSig.Sign$(mpk, sk_i, m; r_s)$: *a signing algorithm which on inputs master public key* mpk, *signing key* sk_i, *message* m *and* $r_s \in \mathcal{RS}_S$, *outputs signature* $\sigma \in \mathcal{SS}$, *where* $\mathcal{RS}_S$ *is a randomness space, and* $\mathcal{SS}$ *is a signature space.*
- $0/1 \leftarrow$ sSig.Ver$(mpk, \mathsf{id}_i, m, \sigma)$: *a verification algorithm which on inputs master public key* mpk, *identity string* id_i, *message* m, *and signature* σ, *outputs 1 for the valid signature, or 0 for invalid signatures.*

Definition 3.2 ({sID/aID}-{EUF/sEUF}-CMA Security for sPKG-IBS). *A sPKG-IBS scheme,* Σ, *is* (ρ, ϵ)-id-atk-CMA *secure for sPKG-IBS if the following property holds for security parameter* λ; *For any forger* $\mathcal{F} = (\mathcal{F}_1, \mathcal{F}_2)$ *with a time-complexity at most* ρ, $\mathbf{Adv}_\Sigma^{\text{id-atk-cma}}(\mathcal{F}) = \Pr[r_g \leftarrow \mathcal{RS}_G;$ $(mpk, msk) \leftarrow$ sSig.KeyGen$(1^\lambda; r_g)$; (OUTPUT, STATE) $\leftarrow \mathcal{F}_1(1^\lambda)$; $(\mathsf{id}_T^*, m^*,$

$\sigma^*) \leftarrow \mathcal{F}_2^{\mathcal{SO}(\cdot,\cdot),\mathcal{KO}(\cdot)}(mpk, \text{STATE}); 1 \leftarrow \text{sSig.Ver}(mpk, \text{id}_T^*, m^*, \sigma^*)] \leq \epsilon,$
where $\mathcal{KO}(\text{id}_i)$ is the key derivation oracle, $\mathcal{SO}(\text{id}_i, m)$ is the signing oracle, and STATE is state information which $\mathcal{F}$ wants to preserve from $\mathcal{F}_1$ to $\mathcal{F}_2$,

if id = sID then OUTPUT = id_T^* which must be the same as the output of $\mathcal{F}_2$,

if id = aID then OUTPUT = $\perp$,

if atk = EUF then $\mathcal{SO}(\text{id}_T^*, m^*)$ is never posed, and

if atk = sEUF then σ^* is never outputted by query $\mathcal{SO}(\text{id}_T^*, m^*)$.

$\mathcal{F}$ runs in at most ρ steps. $\mathcal{F}$ cannot make query $\mathcal{KO}(\text{id}_T^*)$.

mPKG-IBS. Next, we introduce a syntax and security notions for mPKG-IBS. As mPKG-IBKEM, each user can obtain signing keys for his/her ID from multiple PKGs. The signer chooses a PKG to sign a message, and the verifier can verify the signature with signer's ID.

Definition 3.3 (Syntax of mPKG-IBS Schemes). *An mPKG-IBS scheme consists of the following 4-tuple* (mSig.KeyGen, mSig.KeyDer, mSig.Sign, mSig.Ver):

$(mpk_\iota, msk_\iota) \leftarrow$ mSig.KeyGen$(1^\lambda, \text{pid}_\iota; r_g)$: *a key generation algorithm which on inputs* 1^λ, *PKG's identity string* pid_ι *and* $r_g \in \mathcal{RS}_G$, *where* λ *is the security parameter and* $\mathcal{RS}_G$ *is a randomness space, outputs master public key and private key* (mpk_ι, msk_ι).

$sk_{i,\iota} \leftarrow$ mSig.KeyDer$(mpk_\iota, msk_\iota, \text{id}_i; r_k)$: *a key derivation algorithm which on inputs master public and secret keys* (mpk_ι, msk_ι), *identity string* id_i *and* $r_k \in \mathcal{RS}_K$, *where* $\mathcal{RS}_K$ *is a randomness space, outputs signing key* $sk_{i,\iota}$ *corresponding to* id_i *on PKG* pid_ι.

$(\sigma, \text{pid}_\iota) \leftarrow$ mSig.Sign$(mpk_\iota, sk_{i,\iota}, \text{pid}_\iota, m; r_s)$: *a signing algorithm which on inputs master public key* mpk_ι, *signing key* $sk_{i,\iota}$, *PKG's identity string* pid_ι, *message* m *and* $r_s \in \mathcal{RS}_S$, *outputs signature* $\sigma \in \mathcal{SS}$ *and* pid_ι, *where* $\mathcal{RS}_S$ *is a randomness space, and* $\mathcal{SS}$ *is a signature space.*

$0/1 \leftarrow$ mSig.Ver$(mpk_\iota, \text{id}_i, \text{pid}_\iota, m, \sigma)$: *a verification algorithm which on inputs master public key* mpk_ι, *identity string* id_i, *PKG's identity string* pid_ι, *message* m, *and signature* σ, *outputs 1 for the valid signature, or 0 for invalid signatures.*

Definition 3.4 ({sID/aID}-{sPID/aPID}-{EUF/sEUF}-CMA Security for mPKG-IBS). *An mPKG-IBS scheme,* Σ, *is* (ρ, ϵ)*-id-pid-atk-CMA secure for mPKG-IBS if the following property holds for security parameter* λ; *For any forger* $\mathcal{F} = (\mathcal{F}_1, \mathcal{F}_2)$ *with a time-complexity at most* ρ, $\mathbf{Adv}_\Sigma^{\text{id-pid-atk-cma}}(\mathcal{F}) = \Pr[r_{g,\alpha} \leftarrow \mathcal{RS}_G; \ldots; r_{g,\zeta} \leftarrow \mathcal{RS}_G; (mpk_\alpha, msk_\alpha) \leftarrow$ mSig.KeyGen$(1^\lambda, \text{pid}_\alpha; r_{g,\alpha}); \ldots; (mpk_\zeta, msk_\zeta) \leftarrow$ mSig.KeyGen$(1^\lambda, \text{pid}_\zeta; r_{g,\zeta}); (\text{OUTPUT}, \text{STATE}) \leftarrow \mathcal{F}_1(1^\lambda); (\text{id}_T^*, \text{pid}_\tau^*, m^*, \sigma^*) \leftarrow \mathcal{F}_2^{\mathcal{SO}(\cdot,\cdot,\cdot),\mathcal{KO}(\cdot,\cdot)}(\{mpk_\alpha, \ldots, mpk_\zeta\}, \text{STATE}); 1 \leftarrow$ mSig.Ver$(mpk_\tau, \text{id}_T^*, \text{pid}_\tau^*, m^*, \sigma^*)] \leq \epsilon$, *where* $\mathcal{KO}(\text{pid}_\alpha, \text{id}_i)$ *is the key derivation oracle,* $\mathcal{SO}(\text{pid}_\alpha, \text{id}_i, m)$ *is the signing oracle, and* STATE *is state information which* $\mathcal{F}$ *wants to preserve from* $\mathcal{F}_1$ *to* $\mathcal{F}_2$,

if id = sID *and* pid = sPID *then* OUTPUT = $(\mathrm{id}_T^*, \mathrm{pid}_\tau^*)$
              which must be the same as the output of $\mathcal{F}_2$,
if id = sID *and* pid = aPID *then* OUTPUT = id_T^*
              which must be the same as the output of $\mathcal{F}_2$,
if id = aID *and* pid = sPID *then* OUTPUT = pid_τ^*
              which must be the same as the output of $\mathcal{F}_2$,
if id = aID *and* pid = aPID *then* OUTPUT = $\perp$,
if atk = EUF *then* $\mathcal{SO}(\mathrm{id}_T^*, \mathrm{pid}_\tau^*, m^*)$ *is never posed, and*
if atk = sEUF *then* σ^* *is never outputted by query* $\mathcal{SO}(\mathrm{id}_T^*, \mathrm{pid}_\tau^*, m^*)$.

$\mathcal{F}$ *runs in at most* ρ *steps.* $\mathcal{F}$ *cannot make query* $\mathcal{KO}(\mathrm{id}_T^*, \mathrm{pid}_\tau^*)$.

3.2 Generic Transformation from sPKG-IBS to mPKG-IBS

As IBKEM, the algorithms of sPKG-IBS can be used as the algorithms of mPKG-IBS just as they are. The protocol for an mPKG-IBS scheme, $\Sigma' =$ (mSig.KeyGen, mSig.KeyDer, mSig.Sign, mSig.Ver), using an sPKG-IBS scheme, $\Sigma =$ (sSig.KeyGen, sSig.KeyDer, sSig.Sign, sSig.Ver), is as follows:

mSig.KeyGen(1^λ, pid_ι; r_g): Generate $(mpk, msk) \leftarrow$ sSig.KeyGen(1^λ; r_y), and output $mpk_\iota = mpk$ and $msk_\iota = msk$ for pid_ι.
mSig.KeyDer(mpk_ι, msk_ι, id_i; r_k): Derive $sk_i \leftarrow$ sSig.KeyDer(mpk_ι, msk_ι, id_i; r_k), and output $sk_{i,\iota} = sk_i$.
mSig.Sign(mpk_ι, $sk_{i,\iota}$, pid_ι, m; r_s): Generate $\sigma \leftarrow$ sSig.Sign(mpk_ι, $sk_{i,\iota}$, m; r_s), and output $(\sigma, \mathrm{pid}_\iota)$.
mSig.Ver(mpk_ι, id_i, pid_ι, m, σ): Verify sSig.Ver(mpk_ι, id_i, m, σ), and output the verification result.

Security. We show the security of the transformed mPKG-IBS based on the security of the underlying sPKG-IBS. The intuition is the same as mPKG-IBKEM in Sect. 2.2.

Figure 2 shows our implication results for IBS. Note that broken lines mean trivial implications.

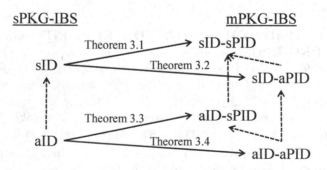

Fig. 2. Implication results for IBS

Theorem 3.1 (sID-sPID-mPKG from sID-sPKG for IBS). *If the underlying sPKG-IBS scheme, Σ, satisfies $(\rho,\ \epsilon)$-sID-atk-CMA security, then the transformed mPKG-IBS scheme, Σ', satisfies $(\rho',\ \epsilon')$-sID-sPID-atk-CMA security, where*

$$\epsilon = \epsilon',$$

$$\rho = \rho' + (N + q_S - 1)\mathsf{t_{RG}} + (N - 1)\mathsf{t_{KG}} + (q_K + q_S)\mathsf{t_{KD}} + q_S\mathsf{t_{Sig}},$$

N is the number of PKGs, q_K and q_S are the numbers of queries to $\mathcal{KO}$ and $\mathcal{SO}$, respectively, $\mathsf{t_{RG}}$ is the running time of randomness generation, $\mathsf{t_{KG}}$ is the running time of $\mathsf{sSig.KeyGen}$, $\mathsf{t_{KD}}$ is the running time of $\mathsf{sSig.KeyDer}$, and $\mathsf{t_{Sig}}$ is the running time of $\mathsf{sSig.Sign}$.

Proof. We construct a forger $\mathcal{F} = (\mathcal{F}_1, \mathcal{F}_2)$ breaking sID-atk-CMA security of Σ by assuming the forger $\mathcal{F}' = (\mathcal{F}_1', \mathcal{F}_2')$ breaking sID-sPID-atk-CMA security of Σ'. Here, we show the case of atk = sEUF. The case of atk = EUF can be similarly proved. The construction of $\mathcal{F}$ is as follows:

Procedure of $\mathcal{F}_1$. When $\mathcal{F}_1$ receives 1^λ, $\mathcal{F}_1$ sends 1^λ to $\mathcal{F}_1'$, and receives $(\mathrm{id}_T^*, \mathrm{pid}_\tau^*, \mathrm{STATE}')$ from $\mathcal{F}_1'$. Then, $\mathcal{F}_1$ sets $\mathrm{STATE} = (\mathrm{STATE}', \mathrm{id}_T^*, \mathrm{pid}_\tau^*)$, and outputs $(\mathrm{id}_T^*, \mathrm{STATE})$.

Procedure of $\mathcal{F}_2$. When $\mathcal{F}_2$ receives (mpk, STATE), parses STATE to $\mathrm{STATE} = (\mathrm{STATE}', \mathrm{id}_T^*, \mathrm{pid}_\tau^*)$. $\mathcal{F}_2$ generates $r_{g,\alpha} \leftarrow \mathcal{RS}_G, \ldots, r_{g,\zeta} \leftarrow \mathcal{RS}_G$ and $(mpk_\alpha, msk_\alpha) \leftarrow \mathsf{sKEM.KeyGen}(1^\lambda; r_{g,\alpha}), \ldots, (mpk_\zeta, msk_\zeta) \leftarrow \mathsf{sKEM.KeyGen}(1^\lambda; r_{g,\zeta})$ except for pid_τ^*, and sets $mpk_\tau = mpk$. Then, $\mathcal{F}_2$ sends $(\{mpk_\alpha, \ldots, mpk_\zeta\}, \mathrm{STATE}')$ to $\mathcal{F}_2'$, and receives $(\mathrm{id}_T^*, \mathrm{pid}_\tau^*, m^*, \sigma^*)$ from $\mathcal{F}_2'$. Finally, if σ^* is not outputted by the simulation of $\mathcal{SO}(\mathrm{id}_T^*, \mathrm{pid}_\tau^*, m^*)$, then $\mathcal{F}_2$ outputs $(\mathrm{id}_T^*, m^*, \sigma^*)$. Otherwise, $\mathcal{F}_2$ halts.

Simulation of $\mathcal{KO}(\mathrm{id}_i, \mathrm{pid}_\iota)$ by $\mathcal{F}_2$. If $\mathrm{pid}_\iota \neq \mathrm{pid}_\tau^*$, then $\mathcal{F}_2$ generates $r_k \leftarrow \mathcal{RS}_K$, derive $sk_{i,\iota} \leftarrow \mathsf{sSig.KeyDer}(mpk_\iota, msk_\iota, \mathrm{id}_i; r_k)$, and output $sk_{i,\iota}$. Else if $\mathrm{id}_i \neq \mathrm{id}_T^*$, then pose id_i to $\mathcal{KO}$, receives sk_i, and outputs $sk_{i,\tau} = sk_i$. Otherwise, $\mathcal{F}_2$ rejects the query.

Simulation of $\mathcal{SO}(\mathrm{id}_i, \mathrm{pid}_\iota, m)$ by $\mathcal{F}_2$. If $\mathrm{pid}_\iota \neq \mathrm{pid}_\tau^*$, then $\mathcal{F}_2$ generates $r_k \leftarrow \mathcal{RS}_K$, derive $sk_{i,\iota} \leftarrow \mathsf{sSig.KeyDer}(mpk_\iota, msk_\iota, \mathrm{id}_i; r_k)$, generate $r_s \leftarrow \mathcal{RS}_S$ and $\sigma \leftarrow \mathsf{sSig.Sign}(mpk_\iota, sk_{i,\iota}, m; r_s)$, and output σ. Else if $\mathrm{id}_i \neq \mathrm{id}_T^*$, then pose id_i to $\mathcal{KO}$, receives sk_i, generate $r_s \leftarrow \mathcal{RS}_S$ and $\sigma \leftarrow \mathsf{sSig.Sign}(mpk_\iota, sk_i, m; r_s)$, and output σ. Otherwise, pose (id_T^*, m) to $\mathcal{SO}$, receives σ, and output σ.

Estimation of advantage of $\mathcal{F}$. $\mathcal{F}$ perfectly simulates the attack environment of $\mathcal{F}'$. Hence, the advantage of $\mathcal{F}$ is $\epsilon = \epsilon'$.

Estimation of running time of $\mathcal{F}$. In addition to ρ', $\mathcal{F}$ runs $(N + q_S - 1)$ randomness generations, $(N - 1)$ master key generations, at most $(q_K + q_S)$ key derivations and at most q_S signature generations. Hence, the running time ρ of $\mathcal{F}$ is at most $\rho' + (N + q_S - 1)\mathsf{t_{RG}} + (N - 1)\mathsf{t_{KG}} + (q_K + q_S)\mathsf{t_{KD}} + q_S\mathsf{t_{Sig}}$. $\qquad\square$

Theorem 3.2 (sID-aPID-mPKG from sID-sPKG for IBS). *If the underlying sPKG-IBS scheme, Σ, satisfies (ρ, ϵ)-sID-atk-CMA security, then the transformed mPKG-IBS scheme, Σ', satisfies (ρ', ϵ')-sID-aPID-atk-CMA security, where*

$$\epsilon = \epsilon'/N,$$

$$\rho = \rho' + (N + q_S - 1)t_{RG} + (N - 1)t_{KG} + (q_K + q_S)t_{KD} + q_S t_{Sig},$$

N is the number of PKGs, q_K and q_S are the numbers of queries to $\mathcal{KO}$ and $\mathcal{SO}$, respectively, t_{RG} is the running time of randomness generation, t_{KG} is the running time of sSig.KeyGen, t_{KD} is the running time of sSig.KeyDer, and t_{Sig} is the running time of sSig.Sign.

Theorem 3.3 (aID-sPID-mPKG from aID-sPKG for IBS). *If the underlying sPKG-IBS scheme, Σ, satisfies (ρ, ϵ)-aID-atk-CMA security, then the transformed mPKG-IBS scheme, Σ', satisfies (ρ', ϵ')-aID-sPID-atk-CMA security, where*

$$\epsilon = \epsilon',$$

$$\rho = \rho' + (N + q_S - 1)t_{RG} + (N - 1)t_{KG} + (q_K + q_S)t_{KD} + q_S t_{Sig},$$

N is the number of PKGs, q_K and q_S are the numbers of queries to $\mathcal{KO}$ and $\mathcal{SO}$, respectively, t_{RG} is the running time of randomness generation, t_{KG} is the running time of sSig.KeyGen, t_{KD} is the running time of sSig.KeyDer, and t_{Sig} is the running time of sSig.Sign.

Theorem 3.4 (aID-aPID-mPKG from aID-sPKG for IBS). *If the underlying sPKG-IBS scheme, Σ, satisfies (ρ, ϵ)-aID-atk-CMA security, then the transformed mPKG-IBS scheme, Σ', satisfies (ρ', ϵ')-aID-aPID-atk-CMA security, where*

$$\epsilon = \epsilon'/N,$$

$$\rho = \rho' + (N + q_S - 1)t_{RG} + (N - 1)t_{KG} + (q_K + q_S)t_{KD} + q_S t_{Sig},$$

N is the number of PKGs, q_K and q_S are the numbers of queries to $\mathcal{KO}$ and $\mathcal{SO}$, respectively, t_{RG} is the running time of randomness generation, t_{KG} is the running time of sSig.KeyGen, t_{KD} is the running time of sSig.KeyDer, and t_{Sig} is the running time of sSig.Sign.

The above theorems can be proved in a similar way to Theorem 3.1.

4   mPKG Secure IBAKE from sPKG Secure IBAKE

In this section, we show that mPKG secure IBAKE can be generically constructed from sPKG secure IBAKE.

4.1   Models for sPKG-IBAKE and mPKG-IBAKE

We recall the id-CK$^+$ model [6] as the security model for sPKG-IBAKE, and propose a new security model, *id(m)-aCK$^+$ model*, as the security model for mPKG-IBAKE. For simplicity, we describe the security models as for two-pass sPKG-/mPKG-IBAKE protocol.

We denote a party as U_i and the identifier of U_i as id_i. For sPKG-IBAKE, there is a single PKG P whose identifier pid. For mPKG-IBAKE, there are multiple PKG; and hence, we denote a PKG as P_ι and the identifier of P_ι as pid_ι.

A PKG, P, for sPKG-IBAKE (resp. each PKG, P_ι, for mPKG-IBAKE) generates a pair of master secret and public keys (mpk, msk) (resp. (mpk_ι, msk_ι)). It is defined as $(mpk, msk) \leftarrow \text{sAKE.KeyGen}(1^\lambda; r_g)$ for sPKG-IBAKE (resp. $(mpk_\iota, msk_\iota) \leftarrow \text{mAKE.KeyGen}(1^\lambda, \text{pid}_\iota; r_g)$ for mPKG-IBAKE), where r_g is randomness.

We outline our model for a two-pass sPKG-/mPKG-IBAKE protocol where parties U_A and U_B exchange ephemeral public keys X_A and X_B. For mPKG-IBAKE, they also exchange the identifiers of their PKGs, i.e., U_A sends (X_A, pid_α) to U_B and U_B sends (X_B, pid_β) to U_A. Finally, they derive a session key. The session key depends on the exchanged ephemeral keys, identifiers of the parties, (identifiers of the PKGs for mPKG-IBAKE,) the static keys corresponding to these identifiers, and the protocol instance that is used.

In the model, each party is a probabilistic polynomial-time Turing machine in security parameter λ and obtains a static private key corresponding to its identifier string from its PKG via a secure and authenticated channel. The static private key is defined as $ssk_i \leftarrow \text{sAKE.KeyDer}(mpk, msk, \text{id}_i; r_k)$ for sPKG-IBAKE (resp. $ssk_{i,\iota} \leftarrow \text{mAKE.KeyDer}(mpk_\iota, msk_\iota, \text{id}_i; r_k)$ for mPKG-IBAKE), where r_k is randomness.

Session. An invocation of a protocol is called *session*. A session is activated via an incoming message in the form of $(\Pi, \mathcal{I}, \text{id}_A, \text{id}_B)$ or $(\Pi, \mathcal{R}, \text{id}_A, \text{id}_B, X_B)$ for sPKG-IBAKE (resp. $(\Pi, \mathcal{I}, \text{id}_A, \text{id}_B, \text{pid}_\alpha, \text{pid}_\beta)$ or $(\Pi, \mathcal{R}, \text{id}_A, \text{id}_B, \text{pid}_\alpha, \text{pid}_\beta, X_B)$ for mPKG-IBAKE), where Π is a protocol identifier. If U_A is activated with $(\Pi, \mathcal{I}, \text{id}_A, \text{id}_B)$ for sPKG-IBAKE (resp. $(\Pi, \mathcal{I}, \text{id}_A, \text{id}_B, \text{pid}_\alpha, \text{pid}_\beta)$ for mPKG-IBAKE), then U_A is the session *initiator*; otherwise, it is the session *responder*. After activation, U_A appends ephemeral public key X_A to the incoming message and sends it as an outgoing response. If U_A is the responder, U_A computes a session key. If U_A is the initiator, U_A that has been successfully activated via $(\Pi, \mathcal{I}, \text{id}_A, \text{id}_B)$ for sPKG-IBAKE (resp. $(\Pi, \mathcal{I}, \text{id}_A, \text{id}_B, \text{pid}_\alpha, \text{pid}_\beta)$ for mPKG-IBAKE), can be further activated via $(\Pi, \mathcal{I}, \text{id}_A, \text{id}_B, X_A, X_B)$ for sPKG-IBAKE (resp. $(\Pi, \mathcal{I}, \text{id}_A, \text{id}_B, \text{pid}_\alpha, \text{pid}_\beta, X_A, X_B)$ for mPKG-IBAKE) to compute a session key.

If U_A is the initiator of a session, the session is identified by either $\text{sid} = (\Pi, \mathcal{I}, \text{id}_A, \text{id}_B, X_A)$ or $\text{sid} = (\Pi, \mathcal{I}, \text{id}_A, \text{id}_B, X_A, X_B)$ for sPKG-IBAKE (resp. $\text{sid} = (\Pi, \mathcal{I}, \text{id}_A, \text{id}_B, \text{pid}_\alpha, \text{pid}_\beta, X_A)$ or $\text{sid} = (\Pi, \mathcal{I}, \text{id}_A, \text{id}_B, \text{pid}_\alpha, \text{pid}_\beta, X_A, X_B)$ for mPKG-IBAKE). If U_B is the responder of a session, the session is identified by $\text{sid} = (\Pi, \mathcal{R}, \text{id}_B, \text{id}_A, X_A, X_B)$ for sPKG-IBAKE (resp. $\text{sid} = (\Pi, \mathcal{R}, \text{id}_B, \text{id}_A, \text{pid}_\beta, \text{pid}_\alpha, X_A, X_B)$ for mPKG-IBAKE). We say that U_A is the *owner* (resp. *peer*) of session sid if the third (resp. fourth) coordinate of session sid is id_A. We say that a session is *completed* if its owner computes a session key. The *matching session* of $(\Pi, \mathcal{I}, \text{id}_A, \text{id}_B, X_A, X_B)$ for sPKG-IBAKE (resp. $(\Pi, \mathcal{I}, \text{id}_A, \text{id}_B, \text{pid}_\alpha, \text{pid}_\beta, X_A, X_B)$ for mPKG-IBAKE) is session $(\Pi, \mathcal{R}, \text{id}_B, \text{id}_A, X_A, X_B)$ for sPKG-IBAKE (resp. $(\Pi, \mathcal{R}, \text{id}_B, \text{id}_A, \text{pid}_\beta, \text{pid}_\alpha, X_A, X_B)$ for mPKG-IBAKE) and vice versa.

The generation of an ephemeral private key by initiator U_A is defined as $x_A \leftarrow \text{sAKE.InitESK}(mpk, \text{id}_A, \text{id}_B, ssk_A)$ for sPKG-IBAKE (resp. $x_A \leftarrow \text{mAKE.InitESK}(mpk_\alpha, \text{id}_A, \text{id}_B, \text{pid}_\alpha, \text{pid}_\beta, ssk_{A,\alpha})$ for mPKG-IBAKE). Also, the generation of an ephemeral private key by responder U_B is defined as $x_B \leftarrow \text{sAKE.ResESK}(mpk, \text{id}_A, \text{id}_B, ssk_B)$ for sPKG-IBAKE (resp. $x_B \leftarrow \text{mAKE.ResESK}(mpk_\beta, \text{id}_A, \text{id}_B, \text{pid}_\alpha, \text{pid}_\beta, ssk_{B,\beta})$ for mPKG-IBAKE).

Based on the ephemeral private key, x_A, the generation of the ephemeral public key by U_A is defined as $X_A \leftarrow \text{sAKE.InitEPK}(mpk, \text{id}_A, \text{id}_B, ssk_A, x_A)$ for sPKG-IBAKE (resp. $X_A \leftarrow \text{mAKE.InitEPK}(mpk_\alpha, \text{id}_A, \text{id}_B, \text{pid}_\alpha, \text{pid}_\beta, ssk_{A,\alpha}, x_A)$ for mPKG-IBAKE). Also, based on the ephemeral private key, x_b, the generation of the ephemeral public key by U_B is defined as $X_B \leftarrow \text{sAKE.ResEPK}(mpk, \text{id}_A, \text{id}_B, ssk_B, x_B, X_A)$ for sPKG-IBAKE (resp. $x_B \leftarrow \text{mAKE.ResEPK}(mpk_\beta, \text{id}_A, \text{id}_B, \text{pid}_\alpha, \text{pid}_\beta, ssk_{B,\beta}, x_B, X_A)$ for mPKG-IBAKE).

The generation of the session key by U_A is defined as $SK \leftarrow \text{sAKE.SesKey}(mpk, \text{id}_A, \text{id}_B, ssk_A, x_A, X_B)$ for sPKG-IBAKE (resp. $SK \leftarrow \text{mAKE.SesKey}(mpk_\alpha, \text{id}_A, \text{id}_B, \text{pid}_\alpha, \text{pid}_\beta, ssk_{A,\alpha}, x_A, X_B)$ for mPKG-IBAKE). The generation of the session key by U_B is also defined in the same manner.

Adversary. Adversary $\mathcal{A}$ is modeled as a probabilistic Turing machine that controls all communications between parties including session activation. Activation is performed via a Send(MESSAGE) query. The MESSAGE has one of the following forms: $(\Pi, \mathcal{I}, \text{id}_A, \text{id}_B)$, $(\Pi, \mathcal{R}, \text{id}_A, \text{id}_B, X_A)$, or $(\Pi, \mathcal{I}, \text{id}_A, \text{id}_B, X_A, X_B)$ for sPKG-IBAKE (resp. $(\Pi, \mathcal{I}, \text{id}_A, \text{id}_B, \text{pid}_\alpha, \text{pid}_\beta)$, $(\Pi, \mathcal{R}, \text{id}_A, \text{id}_B, \text{pid}_\alpha, \text{pid}_\beta, X_A)$, or $(\Pi, \mathcal{I}, \text{id}_A, \text{id}_B, \text{pid}_\alpha, \text{pid}_\beta, X_A, X_B)$ for mPKG-IBAKE). Each party submits its responses to adversary $\mathcal{A}$, who decides the global delivery order. Note that adversary $\mathcal{A}$ does not control the communication between each party and its PKG.

The private information of a party is not accessible to adversary $\mathcal{A}$; however, leakage of private information is obtained via the following adversary queries.

- $\text{SessionKeyReveal(sid)}$: $\mathcal{A}$ obtains the session key for session sid if the session is completed.
- $\text{SessionStateReveal(sid)}$: $\mathcal{A}$ obtains the session state of the owner of session sid if the session is not completed (the session key is not established yet). The session state includes all ephemeral private keys and intermediate computation results except for immediately erased information but does not include the static private key.

- Corrupt(id_i): This query allows $\mathcal{A}$ to obtain all information of the party U_i. If a party is corrupted by a Corrupt(id_i) query issued by $\mathcal{A}$, then we call the party U_i *dishonest*. If not, we call the party *honest*.
- MasterKeyReveal(pid_ι): $\mathcal{A}$ learns the master private key of PKG P_ι. For the sake of convenient queries, when MasterKeyReveal() is called, i.e., called with no argument, the master secret keys of all PKGs are returned.
- NewParty(id_i): This query models malicious insiders. If a party is established by a NewParty(id_i) query issued by $\mathcal{A}$, then we refer to the party as *dishonest*. If not, the party is referred to as *honest*.

For mPKG-IBAKE, a Send query contains pid_α (resp. pid_β), which means that $\mathcal{A}$ specifies the binding between U_A (resp. U_B) and P_α (resp. P_β). $\mathcal{A}$ can obtain all static private keys of U_i on all PKGs via a Corrupt(id_i) query.

Freshness. Our security definition requires the following "freshness" notion.

Definition 4.1 (freshness). *Let* sid^* *be the session identifier of a completed session owned by honest party* U_A *with peer* U_B *who is also honest. If the matching session exists, then let* $\overline{\text{sid}}^*$ *be the session identifier of the matching session of* sid^**. We define* sid^* *to be* fresh *if none of the following conditions hold.*

1. *$\mathcal{A}$ issues* SessionKeyReveal(sid^*) *or* SessionKeyReveal($\overline{\text{sid}}^*$) *if* $\overline{\text{sid}}^*$ *exists.*
2. *$\overline{\text{sid}}^*$ exists and $\mathcal{A}$ makes either of the following queries:*
   - SessionStateReveal(sid^*) *or*
   - SessionStateReveal($\overline{\text{sid}}^*$).
3. *$\overline{\text{sid}}^*$ does not exist and $\mathcal{A}$ makes the following query:*
   - SessionStateReveal(sid^*).

Note that, for mPKG-IBAKE, if adversary $\mathcal{A}$ issues MasterKeyReveal()*, we regard $\mathcal{A}$ as having issued both* Corrupt(id_A) *and* Corrupt(id_B)*. In addition, if $\mathcal{A}$ issues* MasterKeyReveal(P_α) *(resp.* MasterKeyReveal(P_β)*) such that P_α (resp. P_β) is contained in* sid^**, we regard $\mathcal{A}$ as having issued* Corrupt(id_A) *(resp.* Corrupt(id_B)*).*

Security Experiment. Adversary $\mathcal{A}$ starts with common parameters, a set of master public keys together, and a set of honest parties for whom $\mathcal{A}$ adaptively selects identifiers. The adversary makes an arbitrary sequence of the queries described above. During the experiment, $\mathcal{A}$ makes a special query, Test(sid^*), and is given with equal probability either the session key held by session sid^* or a random key. The experiment continues until $\mathcal{A}$ makes a guess regarding whether or not the key is random. The adversary *wins* the game if the test session, sid^*, is *fresh* at the end of execution and if the guess by $\mathcal{A}$ was correct.

Definition 4.2 (id-CK$^+$ security and id(m)-aCK$^+$ security). *The advantage of adversary $\mathcal{A}$ in the experiment with sPKG-IBAKE (resp. mPKG-IBAKE) protocol Π is defined as*

$$\mathbf{Adv}_\Pi^{\{\text{sPKG/mPKG}\}\text{-IBAKE}}(\mathcal{A}) = \Pr[\mathcal{A} \text{ wins}] - \frac{1}{2}.$$

We say that Π is a secure sPKG-IBAKE (resp. mPKG-IBAKE) protocol in the id-CK$^+$ (resp. id(m)-aCK$^+$) model if the following conditions hold.

1. *If two honest parties complete matching sessions, then, they both compute the same session key except with negligible probability in security parameter λ.*
2. *For any probabilistic polynomial-time adversary $\mathcal{A}$, advantage $\mathbf{Adv}_{\Pi}^{\text{sPKG-IBAKE}}(\mathcal{A})$ (resp. $\mathbf{Adv}_{\Pi}^{\text{mPKG-IBAKE}}(\mathcal{A})$) is negligible in security parameter λ for session* sid,
   (a) *if* sid *does not exist, and the static private key of the owner of* sid *is given to $\mathcal{A}$.*
   (b) *if* sid *does not exist, and the ephemeral private key of* sid *is given to $\mathcal{A}$.*
   (c) *if* sid *exists, and the static private key of the owner of* sid *and the ephemeral private key of* sid *are given to $\mathcal{A}$.*
   (d) *if* sid *exists, and the ephemeral private key of* sid *and the ephemeral private key of* sid *are given to $\mathcal{A}$.*
   (e) *if* sid *exists, and the static private key of the owner of* sid *and the static private key of the peer of* sid *are given to $\mathcal{A}$.*
   (f) *if* sid *exists, and the ephemeral private key of* sid *and the static private key of the peer of* sid *are given to $\mathcal{A}$.*

4.2 Generic Transformation from sPKG-IBAKE to mPKG-IBAKE

As IBKEM and IBS, the algorithms of sPKG-IBAKE can be used as the algorithms of mPKG-IBAKE just as they are. The protocol of an mPKG-IBAKE protocol, $\Pi' = $ (mAKE.KeyGen, mAKE.KeyDer, mAKE.InitESK, mAKE.ResESK, mAKE.InitEPK, mAKE.ResEPK, mAKE.SesKey), using an sPKG-IBAKE protocol, $\Pi = $ (sAKE.KeyGen, sAKE.KeyDer, sAKE.InitESK, sAKE.ResESK, sAKE.InitEPK, sAKE.ResEPK, sAKE.SesKey), is as follows:

mAKE.KeyGen(1^λ, pid_ι; r_g): Generate $(mpk, msk) \leftarrow$ sAKE.KeyGen(1^λ; r_g), and output $mpk_\iota = mpk$ and $msk_\iota = msk$ for pid_ι.

mAKE.KeyDer(mpk_ι, msk_ι, id_i; r_k): Derive $ssk_i \leftarrow$ sAKE.KeyDer(mpk_ι, msk_ι, id_i; r_k), and output $ssk_{i,\iota} = ssk_i$.

mAKE.InitESK(mpk_α, id_A, id_B, pid_α, pid_β, $ssk_{A,\alpha}$): Generate a private key as $x_A \leftarrow$ sAKE.InitESK(mpk_α, id_A, id_B, $ssk_{A,\alpha}$), and output x_A.

mAKE.ResESK(mpk_β, id_A, id_B, pid_α, pid_β, $ssk_{B,\beta}$): Generate a private key as $x_B \leftarrow$ sAKE.ResESK(mpk_β, id_A, id_B, $ssk_{B,\beta}$), and output x_B.

mAKE.InitEPK(mpk_α, id_A, id_B, pid_α, pid_β, $ssk_{A,\alpha}$, x_A): Compute the ephemeral public key as $X_A \leftarrow$ sAKE.InitEPK(mpk_α, id_A, id_B, $ssk_{A,\alpha}$, x_A), and output X_A.

mAKE.ResEPK(mpk_β, id_A, id_B, pid_α, pid_β, $ssk_{B,\beta}$, x_B, X_A): Compute the ephemeral public key as $X_B \leftarrow$ sAKE.ResEPK(mpk_β, id_A, id_B, $ssk_{B,\beta}$, x_B, X_A), and output X_B.

mAKE.SesKey(mpk_α, id_A, id_B, pid_α, pid_β, $ssk_{A,\alpha}$, x_A, X_B) **for initiator** U_A: Obtain $SK \leftarrow$ sAKE.SesKey(mpk_α, id_A, id_B, $ssk_{A,\alpha}$, x_A, X_B), and output SK.

mAKE.SesKey(mpk_β, id_A, id_B, pid_α, pid_β, $ssk_{B,\beta}$, x_B, X_A) **for responder** U_B: Obtain $SK \leftarrow$ sAKE.SesKey(mpk_β, id_A, id_B, $ssk_{B,\beta}$, x_B, X_A), and output SK.

Security. We show the id(m)-aCK$^+$ security of the transformed mPKG-IBAKE based on the id-CK$^+$ security of the underlying sPKG-IBAKE. The intuition is the same as mPKG-IBKEM in Sect. 2.2 and mPKG-IBS in Sect. 3.2.

Theorem 4.1 (id(m)-aCK$^+$ Security from id-CK$^+$ Security for IBAKE). *If the underlying sPKG-IBAKE protocol, Π, satisfies the id-CK$^+$ security, then the transformed mPKG-IBAKE protocol, Π', satisfies the id(m)-aCK$^+$ security.*

The proof is shown in the full version.

References

1. Boneh, D., Franklin, M.K.: Identity-based encryption from the Weil pairing. SIAM J. Comput. **32**(3), 586–615 (2003)
2. Chen, L., Kudla, C.: Identity based authenticated key agreement protocols from pairings. In: 16th IEEE Computer Security Foundations Workshop (CSFW-16 2003), pp. 219–233. IEEE Computer Society (2003). http://eprint.iacr.org/2002/184
3. Fiat, A., Shamir, A.: How to prove yourself: practical solutions to identification and signature problems. In: Odlyzko, A.M. (ed.) CRYPTO 1986. LNCS, vol. 263, pp. 186–194. Springer, Heidelberg (1987). https://doi.org/10.1007/3-540-47721-7_12
4. Fujioka, A.: One-round exposure-resilient identity-based authenticated key agreement with multiple private key generators. In: Phan, R.C.-W., Yung, M. (eds.) Mycrypt 2016. LNCS, vol. 10311, pp. 436–460. Springer, Cham (2017). https://doi.org/10.1007/978-3-319-61273-7_21
5. Fujioka, A.: Adaptive security in identity-based authenticated key agreement with multiple private key generators. In: Obana, S., Chida, K. (eds.) IWSEC 2017. LNCS, vol. 10418, pp. 192–211. Springer, Cham (2017). https://doi.org/10.1007/978-3-319-64200-0_12
6. Fujioka, A., Suzuki, K., Xagawa, K., Yoneyama, K.: Strongly secure authenticated key exchange from factoring, codes, and lattices. Des. Codes Cryptogr. **76**(3), 469–504 (2015). A preliminary version is appeared in PKC 2012 (2012)
7. Huang, H., Cao, Z.: An ID-based authenticated key exchange protocol based on bilinear Diffie-Hellman problem. In: Li, W., Susilo, W., Tupakula, U.K., Safavi-Naini, R., Varadharajan, V. (eds.) ASIACCS 2009, pp. 333–342. ACM, New York (2009)
8. Karthikeyan, H., Chakraborty, S., Singh, K., Rangan, C.P.: An efficient multiple PKG compatible identity based key agreement for vehicular networks. IACR Cryptology ePrint Archive 2015, 1012 (2015). A preliminary version was presented as "An Efficient Multiple PKG Compatible Identity Based Key Agreement for Vehicular Networks" in Inscrypt 2015
9. Li, F., Shirase, M., Takagi, T.: Efficient multi-PKG ID-based signcryption for ad hoc networks. In: Yung, M., Liu, P., Lin, D. (eds.) Inscrypt 2008. LNCS, vol. 5487, pp. 289–304. Springer, Heidelberg (2009). https://doi.org/10.1007/978-3-642-01440-6_23
10. Qin, L., Cao, Z., Dong, X.: Multi-receiver identity-based encryption in multiple PKG environment. In: Proceedings of the Global Communications Conference, GLOBECOM 2008, pp. 1862–1866. IEEE (2008)

11. Smart, N.P.: An identity based authenticated key agreement protocol based on the Weil pairing. IACR Cryptology ePrint Archive 2001, 111 (2001). http://eprint.iacr.org/2001/111
12. Wang, S., Cao, Z., Xie, Q., Liu, W.: Practical identity-based encryption in multiple private key generator (PKG) environments. Secur. Commun. Netw. **8**(1), 43–50 (2015)
13. Xu, Z., Ma, R., Liu, S., He, W.: EISM: an efficient ID-based signcryption scheme for multi-PKG multihop wireless networks of mobile hosts. Ad Hoc Sens. Wirel. Netw. **11**(1–2), 93–110 (2011)

Secure Outsourcing of Cryptographic Circuits Manufacturing

Giuseppe Ateniese[1], Aggelos Kiayias[5], Bernardo Magri[3(✉)],
Yiannis Tselekounis[2], and Daniele Venturi[4]

[1] Stevens Institute of Technology, Hoboken, USA
gatenies@stevens.edu
[2] The University of Edinburgh, Edinburgh, UK
ytselekounis@ed.ac.uk
[3] Friedrich-Alexander-Universität Erlangen-Nürnberg, Erlangen, Germany
bernardo.magri@fau.de
[4] Sapienza University of Rome, Rome, Italy
venturi@di.uniroma1.it
[5] University of Edinburgh & IOHK, Edinburgh, UK
akiayias@inf.ed.ac.uk

Abstract. The fabrication process of integrated circuits (ICs) is complex and requires the use of off-shore foundries to lower the costs and to have access to leading-edge manufacturing facilities. Such an outsourcing trend leaves the possibility of inserting malicious circuitry (a.k.a. hardware Trojans) during the fabrication process, causing serious security concerns. Hardware Trojans are very hard and expensive to detect and can disrupt the entire circuit or covertly leak sensitive information via a subliminal channel.

In this paper, we propose a formal model for assessing the security of ICs whose fabrication has been outsourced to an untrusted off-shore manufacturer. Our model captures that the IC specification and design are trusted but the fabrication facility(ies) may be malicious. Our objective is to investigate security in an *ideal sense* and follows a simulation based approach that ensures that Trojans cannot release any sensitive information to the outside. It follows that the Trojans' impact in the overall IC operation, in case they exist, will be negligible up to simulation.

We then establish that such level of security is in fact achievable for the case of a single and of multiple outsourcing facilities. We present two compilers for ICs for the single outsourcing facility case relying on verifiable computation (VC) schemes, and another two compilers for the multiple outsourcing facilities case, one relying on multi-server VC schemes, and the other relying on secure multiparty computation (MPC) protocols with certain suitable properties that are attainable by existing schemes.

A. Kiayias and Y. Tselekounis—Research partly supported by Horizon 2020 project PANORAMIX, No. 653497.

J. Baek et al. (Eds.): ProvSec 2018, LNCS 11192, pp. 75–93, 2018.
https://doi.org/10.1007/978-3-030-01446-9_5

1   Introduction

The fabrication process adopted by the semiconductor industry is fundamentally global, involving several parties that may not be trusted. As a result, integrated circuits (ICs) are vulnerable to so-called hardware Trojans that can compromise or disable critical systems, or covertly leak sensitive information [7]. Analogously to a software Trojan, a hardware Trojan is a *back-door* deliberately added to the circuit to disrupt its operation or disable it when certain events occur. A Trojan can be added to the circuit during the design phase, by some malicious designer, or more often during the manufacturing phase, by some malicious off-shore fabrication facility. A hardware Trojan's objectives may be to modify the functionality of the circuit (e.g., in order to compromise or disable critical systems), modify its specification (e.g., by changing its energy consumption), covertly leak sensitive information (e.g., from a secret memory), or simply disable the entire circuit when instructed to do so [6]. Once the Trojan is inserted into the circuit it can stay active the entire time, or it can be "triggered" by some event such as a special input to the circuit.

Reliably detecting compromised circuit components through testing and reverse engineering appears to be an impossible task given our current technology [9]. Indeed, all non-destructive testing techniques can easily be circumvented by properly obfuscating embedded Trojans. The U.S. military recognized this threat and started two programs, Trust and IRIS, with the intent of developing techniques and metrics to certify ICs going into weapon systems. The main concern is that advanced weapons may appear to work properly but then switch off in combat or when triggered by some special events. Another stated concern is information leakage, where a malicious component is programmed to leak sensitive information [32].

The U.S. military however currently obtains trusted chips through the DOD Trusted Foundry program which is currently managed by the NSA's Trusted Access Program Office (TAPO). Within this program, a trusted design center and foundry are established through an exclusive partnership with IBM for secure semiconductor fabrication and ASIC services, along with the involvement of several Trusted Suppliers which are accredited by an accreditation authority (DMEA). The intent of the Trusted Foundry program is to provide national security and defense programs with access to ICs from trusted sources. However, a report by the U.S. Government Accountability Office (GAO) [25], released in April 2015, found that even though the Trusted Foundry program started in 2004, IBM remained the sole-source supplier for leading-edge technologies meeting the criteria put forth by DOD. GAO's report highlights two main issues: First, it notices that IBM sold its microelectronics fabrication business to a foreign-owned entity (GlobalFoundries). Second, relying on a single source supplier for defense microelectronics hinders competition and thus innovation in this critical area.

1.1   Previous Work

Inspired by the above considerations, in this work we put forward a formal security model for the problem of utilizing off-shore fabrication facilities for IC manufacturing. Our main motivation is that the setting of secure circuit fabrication, while being an extremely important practical problem, almost completely lacks theoretical foundations. We discuss a few remarkable exceptions below.

- Seifert and Bayer [31] introduced a very strong security model for the fabrication of Trojan-resilient circuits, where the produced circuit is required to always have the same output as the original circuit; unfortunately, they show how to achieve their definition only for very limited classes of Trojans (i.e., the adversary is allowed to "corrupt" only a small fraction of the gates in each layer of the IC, and a small fraction of the wires connecting different layers).
- Recently, Wahby et al. [33] introduced a new approach to the problem of defeating hardware Trojans in fabless circuit manufacturing. Their model reflects the fact that IC specification and design are trusted but the fabrication facility is not. Rather than testing or reverse engineering the IC hardware received, which only provides limited security, they consider a class of solutions where the IC's operations are continuously verified.

  In a nutshell, the goal of [33] is to make sure that the produced circuit maintains correctness of the computation, meaning that the output of the circuit is either invalid, or equal to the output of the original circuit. The main drawback is that invalid outputs might be arbitrarily correlated with the secret state of the circuit, which could expose key material in case the produced circuit is a cryptographic circuit. (We will formalize this fact later in the paper.)
- In [14], the authors show how to protect against hardware Trojans using testing-based mechanisms. Their work is based on two existing techniques for Trojan detection, called "input scrambling" and "split manufacturing" [20], for which the authors provide formal models. Hence, they present a generic compiler that transforms any circuit into a new (equivalent) circuit with the following guarantee: Assuming the attacker invokes the circuit q times, and that the device is being tested t times, for $t > q$ uniform on a specific range which is not known to the attacker, the compiled circuit is secure with probability at least $1 - (q/t)^{\ell/2}$, were ℓ is the number of copies of the sub-circuits whose production is outsourced.

  The main limitation is that [14] assumes an a-priori known bound on the number q of interactions between the user and the device; in fact, without such a bound, their construction would require a super-polynomial number of tests. Unfortunately, in many important applications, it is not realistic to assume an upper bound on the value q, and thus it is an important open problem to design a methodology that provides security for an arbitrary polynomial number of interactions between the user/attacker and the device.
- The approach of applying secure distributed computing to defeat hardware Trojans has also been recently explored in [26]. However, this work is more

focused on the implementation aspects of this idea, and moreover it assumes that the possibly malicious circuit components run applications that are developed and signed by a trusted software developer.

1.2 Our Contributions

We put forward a formal framework for assessing security of a circuit whose production has been, in part, outsourced to a set of manufacturers that are not trusted. Our security definition implies that using the produced circuit in the wild leaks no information on its secrets. Additionally, the adversarial model we consider does not assume any a-priori bound on the number of executions, and allows the manufacturer(s) to make arbitrary modifications to the outsourced components. In essence, our security model captures any attack in which the backdoored circuit communicates with the user/attacker through the input/output gates of the produced circuit. (This includes digital and analog Trojans, but not hidden antennas as considered in [14].)

With such a framework in hand, we give several design methodologies that achieve our definition with different tradeoffs in terms of security, efficiency, and underlying assumptions. Thus, our work establishes the theoretical feasibility of utilizing off-shore fabrication facilities for IC manufacturing. A more detailed explanation of our main contributions follows below.

Secure Circuit Fabrication. Let Γ be the original circuit to be produced. Instead of producing Γ directly, we first "compile" it into a different circuit $\widehat{\Gamma}$ using an efficient, possibly randomized, procedure Φ that we call an *outsourcing compiler*. The compiler Φ takes as input a description of Γ and returns a description of $\widehat{\Gamma}$, together with some auxiliary information specifying how $\widehat{\Gamma}$ can be divided into sub-components, and which of these components can be produced off-shore; the remaining components will be instead built in-house. After all components have been produced, the circuit designer re-assembles the circuit $\widehat{\Gamma}$ (by combining the outsourced components and the components built in-house), which is then initialized with some initial secret memory M_1, and used in the wild.

In order to make sense, the above approach needs to satisfy a few important requirements. The first requirement is that Φ needs to be functionality preserving, meaning that the compiled circuit $\widehat{\Gamma}$ should compute the same functionality as the original circuit Γ (for all possible initial memories M_1, and for all possible inputs). The second requirement is that the effort needed to manufacture the trusted sub-components should be (much) less compared to the effort required to manufacture the original circuit Γ. The third requirement is that Φ should be secure, meaning that, under an acceptable assumption about the manufacturers who construct the outsourced components, the produced circuit $\widehat{\Gamma}$ can be safely used in real-life applications.

Our security definition follows the simulation paradigm, and is inspired by similar definitions in the setting of tamper-proof circuit compilers [22]. We refer the reader to Sect. 1.3 for a more detailed comparison between the two approaches. In a nutshell, security of Φ is defined by requiring that whatever an adversary can learn by interacting with the fabricated circuit $\widehat{\Gamma}$ (produced following the steps outlined above), can be simulated given only black-box access to the original circuit Γ. This essentially means that, no matter how the outsourced components are maliciously modified (e.g., by inserting a hardware Trojan), using circuit $\widehat{\Gamma}$ is as secure as using the original circuit Γ, and thus, in particular, does not leak sensitive information on the secret memory. See Sect. 3 for a precise definition.

Case Study I: Single Manufacturer. In Sect. 4, we show how to construct a secure outsourcing compiler that works for *arbitrary* circuits Γ in the setting where *all* outsourcing manufacturers are corrupted. Similarly to [33], our compiler generically leverages a VC scheme for the function $\mathcal{F}$ implemented by Γ. Recent breakthrough research on verifiable computation led to nearly practical schemes that work for any function [10,29]; some schemes additionally preserve the privacy of the inputs on which the function is being computed on [15]. VC schemes satisfying the latter property are called *input-private*.

The main idea of how to use verifiable computation in order to build secure outsourcing compilers is simple enough to describe it here. The fabrication of the chips that perform the entire bulk of computation will be outsourced to the untrusted fabrication facility, whereas the only circuit components that need to be built in-house are: (i) the component corresponding to the algorithm for encoding the inputs (in case of input-private VC), (ii) the component corresponding to the algorithm run by the client in order to verify correctness of the server's computation, and (iii) the component used to generate fresh random coins as needed for computing the function (in case of randomized functions). Thanks to the nature of VC, the size of the components in (i) and (ii) is independent of the size of the original circuit computing the function. As for the component in (iii), we can use any existing (and trusted) circuitry for generating true random numbers (RNG). A good example is the Intel on-chip hardware random number generator which can be accessed through the RDRAND instruction available on all modern processors [19].

Our compiler relies on VC schemes with input-privacy, and achieves our strongest security notion (i.e., no leakage required for the simulation).

Case Study II: Multiple Manufacturers. In Sect. 5, we show how to construct secure outsourcing compilers for arbitrary circuits Γ in the setting where $m \geq 2$ outsourcing manufacturers are available, and a certain unknown subset of them is malicious. This is a strictly stronger assumption compared to the setting of a single manufacturer, nevertheless, as we show, it opens the possibility for more efficient constructions and stronger availability guarantees.

We present an outsourcing compiler utilizing a general client-server secure multiparty computation (MPC) protocol, i.e., a protocol that, for any function, enables a set of clients to privately communicate their inputs to a set of servers that will perform a computation and return the output to a single designated recipient. We stress that many MPC protocols follow this paradigm (e.g., [12]), while others, as we comment later, can be easily adapted to it.

Given such a protocol, the compiler operates in the following way (see also Sect. 5.1). For a given circuit Γ it produces the MPC protocol implementing it, isolates the client and recipient computation for manufacturing in-house, and outsources each of the other components (representing a server in the MPC protocol) to the untrusted manufacturers. The key points of this compiler construction are as follows: (i) The client and recipient computation are typically quite lightweight; the client, in many protocols, simply performs an encryption or a secret-sharing operation, and the recipient a secret-reconstruction protocol; in either case, the computation is independent of the circuit that is outsourced. (ii) There are MPC protocols that can tolerate up to $m - 1$ malicious servers, something we can leverage to argue that if at least one of the outsourcing manufacturer is honest the compiled circuit would be safe for use.

Additional properties of the underlying MPC protocol can also be very valuable by our compiler: for instance, if the underlying MPC protocol supports guaranteed output delivery, we can use this guarantee to argue that the final circuit will be resilient to a certain faulty outsourced sub-component. Moreover, if the underlying protocol satisfies the identifiable abort property, cf. [21], we can enable our compiled circuit to switch-off an outsourced sub-component that is discovered to be faulty (or malicious), thus reducing energy consumption.

1.3   Related Work

Hardware Trojans. Prevention of hardware Trojans in ICs is a common practice that might take place during the design, manufacturing, and post-manufacturing stage [24,30]. However, since it is not always possible to efficiently prevent Trojans insertion, Trojans *detection* has also been vastly explored [9]; once a Trojan is detected, the circuit can be disposed and not used. Common methodologies used to perform Trojans detection vary from invasive ones (that destroy the IC to examine it inside), to non-invasive ones (where the circuit is executed and compared against a trusted copy of the circuit, or against some expected output values). Trojan detection is typically a very expensive and unreliable process, therefore the best practice is usually not to rely on any kind of testing to protect against Trojans. Explicit *countermeasures* against Trojans also exist, where the objective is to guarantee the functionality or security of the circuit even in the presence of some unknown Trojan. For instance, the so-called "data guards" are designed to prevent a Trojan from being activated and/or to access sensitive data [34]. Another approach is the duplication of logic elements and the division of the sensitive data to independent parts of the circuit [27,34].

Tamper-Proof Circuits. Our main security definition shares similarities with analogous definitions in the context of protecting circuits against tampering attacks [11]. The main difference between this setting and the one considered in our paper is that tamper-proof circuit compilers are typically used to protect against fault injection [28] and tampering attacks at run-time; such attacks are usually carried out in an adaptive manner, depending on the outcome of previous attempts. Outsourcing compilers, instead, only protect against (non-adaptive) tampering taking place during the circuit fabrication process. Importantly, the latter restriction allows to obtain security against arbitrary modifications, whereas in circuit tampering one has to consider very restricted attacks (e.g., wire tampering [22] or gate tampering [23]).

Subversion. The above type of non-adaptive tampering is, in fact, reminiscent of the setting of subversion attacks against cryptographic primitives and algorithms. Inspired by the recent revelations of Edward Snowden [18], this line of research recently led to constructing several concrete primitives resisting large classes of subversion attacks [3,8]. In this light, our work could be interpreted as formalizing the security of circuits that might have been subject to subversion during fabrication.

2 Preliminaries

2.1 Notation

For a string x, we denote its length by $|x|$; if S is a set, $|S|$ represents the number of elements in S; for a natural number n, $[n]$ denotes the set $\{1, \ldots, n\}$. When x is chosen randomly in S, we write $x \leftarrow_\$ S$. When $\mathcal{A}$ is an algorithm, we write $y \leftarrow \mathcal{A}(x)$ to denote a run of $\mathcal{A}$ on input x and output y; if $\mathcal{A}$ is randomized, then y is a random variable and $\mathcal{A}(x; r)$ denotes a run of $\mathcal{A}$ on input x and randomness r. An algorithm $\mathcal{A}$ is *probabilistic polynomial-time* (PPT) if $\mathcal{A}$ is randomized and for any input $x, r \in \{0, 1\}^*$ the computation of $\mathcal{A}(x; r)$ terminates in at most poly$(|x|)$ steps. We denote with $\lambda \in \mathbb{N}$ the security parameter. A function $\nu : \mathbb{N} \to [0, 1]$ is negligible in the security parameter (or simply negligible) if it vanishes faster than the inverse of any polynomial in λ, i.e. $\nu(\lambda) = \lambda^{-\omega(1)}$.

The statistical distance between two random variables $\mathbf{Z}$ and $\mathbf{Z}'$ defined over some common set Z is defined as $\Delta(\mathbf{Z}; \mathbf{Z}') = \frac{1}{2} \sum_{z \in Z} |\mathbb{P}[\mathbf{Z} = z] - \mathbb{P}[\mathbf{Z}' = z]|$. For two ensembles $\mathbf{Z} := \{Z_\lambda\}_{\lambda \in \mathbb{N}}$ and $\mathbf{Z}' := \{Z'_\lambda\}_{\lambda \in \mathbb{N}}$, we write $\mathbf{Z} \equiv \mathbf{Z}'$ to denote that the two ensembles are identically distributed. We also write $\mathbf{Z} \approx_c \mathbf{Z}'$ to denote that the ensembles are computationally indistinguishable, i.e. for all PPT distinguishers $\mathcal{D}$ there exists a negligible function $\nu : \mathbb{N} \to [0, 1]$ such that $\Delta^{\mathcal{D}}(\mathbf{Z}; \mathbf{Z}') := |\mathbb{P}[\mathcal{D}(z) = 1 : z \leftarrow_\$ \mathbf{Z}] - \mathbb{P}[\mathcal{D}(z) = 1] : z \leftarrow_\$ \mathbf{Z}'| \leq \nu(\lambda)$.

We rely on the following lemma (which follows directly from the definition of statistical distance):

Lemma 1. *Let $\mathbf{Z}$ and $\mathbf{Z}'$ be a pair of random variables, and W be an event defined over the probability space of $\mathbf{Z}$ and $\mathbf{Z}'$. Then, $\Delta(\mathbf{Z}; \mathbf{Z}') \leq \Delta(\mathbf{Z}; \mathbf{Z}'|\neg W) + \mathbb{P}[W]$.*

2.2 Circuits

A (Boolean) circuit $\Gamma = (V, E)$ is a directed graph. The vertices V are logical gates, and the edges E are wires connecting the gates. For the case of *deterministic* circuits, the gates can be of type AND, XOR and copy, where AND (resp. XOR) have fan-in two and fan-out one, and output the AND (resp. XOR) operation on the input bits; a copy gate, denoted copy, simply forwards the input bit into two output wires. The depth of a circuit is defined as the longest path from an input to an output; the size of a circuit is defined as its total number of gates. Sometimes we explicitly write $\langle \Gamma \rangle$ for the description of the circuit Γ. A circuit is clocked if it evolves in clock cycles (or rounds). The input and output values of the circuit Γ in clock cycle i are denoted by X_i and Y_i, respectively. A circuit is *probabilistic* if it uses internal randomness as part of its logic. We call such probabilistic logic *randomness gates* and denote them with \$. In each clock cycle \$ outputs a fresh random bit. Additionally, a circuit may contain memory gates. Memory gates, which have a single incoming edge and any number of outgoing edges, maintain state: at any clock cycle, a memory gate sends its current state down its outgoing edges and updates it according to the value of its incoming edge. Any cycle in the circuit graph must contain at least one memory gate. The state of all memory gates at clock cycle i is denoted by M_i, with M_1 denoting the initial state. When a circuit is run in state M_i on input X_i, the circuit will output Y_i and the memory gates will be in a new state M_{i+1}. We will denote this by $(Y_i, M_{i+1}) \leftarrow \Gamma[M_i](X_i)$.

3   Secure Circuit Fabrication

In this section we put forward a formal model for assessing security of a (cryptographic) circuit whose production is outsourced to one or more untrusted facilities. We start by recalling the standard notion of connected component of a circuit or graph.

Definition 1. *A circuit $\Gamma' = (V', E')$ is a (connected) component of circuit $\Gamma = (V, E)$ if $V' \subseteq V$, $E' \subseteq E$ and for all $g_1, g_2 \in V'$ we have that $(g_1, g_2) \in E'$ iff $(g_1, g_2) \in E$.*

Next, we introduce the notion of an outsourcing circuit compiler (or simply compiler). In a nutshell, a circuit compiler is an efficient algorithm Φ that takes as input (the description of) a circuit Γ, and outputs (the description of) a compiled circuit $\widehat{\Gamma}$. Additionally, Φ returns a list of sub-components $\widehat{\Gamma}_i$ of $\widehat{\Gamma}$ whose production can be outsourced to one or more external manufacturers, together with the relevant information on how to connect those sub-components with the remaining ones (that need to be built in-house) in order to re-assemble the compiled circuit $\widehat{\Gamma}$.

Definition 2. *Let Γ be an arbitrary circuit. A (ρ, m)-outsourcing compiler Φ is a PPT algorithm $(\widehat{\Gamma}, \mathsf{aux}) \leftarrow \Phi(\Gamma)$, such that the following holds:*

- $\mathsf{aux} := ((\widehat{\Gamma}_1, \ldots, \widehat{\Gamma}_n), \mathcal{M}, (I_1, \ldots, I_m))$, *with $n \in \mathbb{N}$ and $I_j \subseteq [n]$, for $j \in [m]$, mutually disjoint subsets.*
- $(\widehat{\Gamma}_1, \ldots, \widehat{\Gamma}_n)$ *are disjoint (connected) components of $\widehat{\Gamma}$ such that $V = \bigcup_{i \in [n]} V_i$, where $\Gamma_i = (V_i, E_i)$.*

- $\mathcal{M} : V \times V \to \{0,1\}$ is a function such that $\mathcal{M}(v, v') = 1$ iff $v, v' \in V_i, V_j$ for some $i \neq j$ and $(v, v') \in E$.

We call $\rho := \frac{\sum_{i \in [n] \setminus I_1 \cup \ldots \cup I_m} |\widehat{\Gamma}_i|}{|\Gamma|}$ the outsourcing ratio of the compiler.

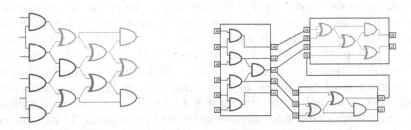

Fig. 1. On the left side we present the description of a (compiled) circuit. On the right side the same circuit is represented as three different components. The mapping function $\mathcal{M}$ establishes the connections between the components.

Intuitively, in the above definition, the outsourcing ratio ρ represents the fraction of the compiled circuit (w.r.t. the original circuit) that should be built in-house. Note that the sub-components $(\widehat{\Gamma}_i)_{i \in [n]}$ "cover" the entire compiled circuit $\widehat{\Gamma}$ (without overlap), and the mapping function $\mathcal{M}$ specifies how to connect the different components in order to reconstruct $\widehat{\Gamma}$. The sets of indexes $I_j \subseteq [n]$ represents the sub-components whose production will be outsourced to manufacturer $j \in [m]$ (Fig. 1).

Correctness of an outsourcing compiler demands that the compiled circuit maintains the same functionality of the original circuit.

Definition 3. *We say that an outsourcing compiler Φ is functionality preserving if for all circuits Γ, for all values of the initial memory M_1, and for any set of public inputs $X_1, \ldots, X_q$, the sequence of outputs $Y_1, \ldots, Y_q$ produced by running the original circuit Γ starting with state M_1 is identical to the sequence of outputs produced by running the transformed circuit $\widehat{\Gamma}$ starting with state M_1 (with all but negligible probability over the randomness of the compiler and the randomness of the original and compiled circuit).*

For randomized functionalities we require the output distributions of the original and the compiled circuits, to be statistically close.

3.1   Security

We define security using the simulation paradigm. Our approach is similar in spirit to previous work on tamper-resilient circuit compilers (see, e.g., [22]). In a nutshell, security is defined by comparing two experiments. In the first experiment, also called the real experiment, the circuit designer compiles the circuit and outsources the production of some of the components in the compiled circuit to a set of m untrusted manufacturers. A subset of size t of the manufacturers are malicious, and controlled by a monolithic adversary $\mathcal{A}$; of course the circuit designer does not know which manufacturers are malicious and which ones are honest. During production, $\mathcal{A}$ is allowed to completely change the outsourced circuit components under its control, whether by adding, removing or changing gates and/or wires. Later, the designer assembles the circuit by re-combining all the components (the outsourced ones and the ones built in-house). Finally, $\mathcal{A}$ can access the assembled circuit in a *black-box* way, that is, it can observe inputs/outputs produced by running the assembled circuit (with some initial memory M_1). In the second experiment, also called the ideal experiment, a simulator is given black-box access to the original circuit (initialized with initial memory M_1). The goal of the simulator is to produce an output distribution which is indistinguishable from the one in the real experiment. In its most general form, our definition allows the simulator to obtain a short leakage on the initial memory. This captures the (reasonable) scenario where the adversary, in the real experiment, could learn at most a short amount of information on the private memory.

Real Experiment. The distribution $\mathbf{Real}_{\mathcal{A},\Phi,\mathcal{C},\Gamma,M_1}(\lambda)$ is parameterized by the adversary $\mathcal{A} = (\mathcal{A}_0, \mathcal{A}_1)$, the set of corrupt manufacturers $\mathcal{C}$, the compiler Φ, and the original circuit Γ with initial memory M_1.

1. $(\widehat{\Gamma}, \mathsf{aux}) \leftarrow \Phi(\Gamma)$: In the first step, the description of the original circuit Γ is given as input to the compiler Φ; the compiler outputs the description of the compiled circuit $\widehat{\Gamma}$ plus the auxiliary information $\mathsf{aux} := ((\widehat{\Gamma}_1, \ldots, \widehat{\Gamma}_n), \mathcal{M}, (I_1, \ldots, I_m))$ which is used to specify how the compiled circuit is split into sub-components, how the different sub-components are connected (via the mapping function $\mathcal{M}$), and the subset of sub-components whose production is outsourced to each manufacturer (in the index sets I_j, for $j \in [m]$).

2. $(\{\widehat{\Gamma}'_i\}_{i \in I}, \tau) \leftarrow \mathcal{A}_0(1^\lambda, \{\langle \widehat{\Gamma}_i \rangle\}_{i \in I}, \langle \Gamma \rangle, \langle \widehat{\Gamma} \rangle)$: The adversary is given as input the description of the components from the index set $I = \cup_{J \in \mathcal{C}} I_j$, the description of the original circuit Γ, the description of the compiled circuit $\widehat{\Gamma}$, and returns the modified components along with some value τ that may contain some auxiliary state information.

3. $\widehat{\Gamma}' := (\widehat{V}', \widehat{E}')$: The compiled circuit $\widehat{\Gamma}'$ is rebuilt by replacing the components $(\widehat{\Gamma}_i)_{i \in I}$ with the modified components $(\widehat{\Gamma}'_i)_{I \in I}$, and by connecting the different components as specified by the mapping function $\mathcal{M}$.

4. $\mathcal{A}_1^{\widehat{\Gamma}'[M_1](\cdot)}(1^\lambda, \tau)$: Adversary $\mathcal{A}_1$, with auxiliary information τ, is given oracle access to the rebuilt circuit $\widehat{\Gamma}'$ with compiled private memory M_1.

Simulation. The distribution $\mathbf{Ideal}_{\mathcal{S},\mathcal{A},\Phi,\mathcal{C},\Gamma,M_1,\ell}(\lambda)$ is parameterized by the simulator $\mathcal{S}$, the adversary $\mathcal{A} = (\mathcal{A}_0, \mathcal{A}_1)$, the compiler Φ, the set of corrupt manufacturers $\mathcal{C}$, the original circuit Γ with initial memory M_1, and some value $\ell \in \mathbb{N}$.

1. $f \leftarrow \mathcal{S}(1^\lambda, \langle \Gamma \rangle, \Phi, \mathcal{A}, \mathcal{C}, \ell)$: Given as input a description of the original circuit, of the compiler and of the adversary, the subset of corrupt manufacturers,

and the parameter $\ell \in \mathbb{N}$, the simulator specifies an arbitrary polynomial-time computable function $f : \{0,1\}^* \to \{0,1\}^\ell$.

2. $\mathcal{S}^{\mathcal{A},\Gamma[M_1](\cdot)}(1^\lambda, L)$: The simulator takes as input leakage $L = f(M_1)$, and is given oracle access to adversary $\mathcal{A} = (\mathcal{A}_0, \mathcal{A}_1)$ and to the original circuit Γ with private memory M_1. We remark that the simulator is restricted to be fully black-box. In particular, $\mathcal{S}$ only accesses the modified sub-components returned by $\mathcal{A}_0$ in a black-box way (i.e., without knowing their description).

Definition 4. *We say that a (ρ, m)-outsourcing circuit compiler Φ is (ℓ, t)-secure if the following conditions are met.*

(i) Non-triviality: *$\rho < 1$, for sufficiently large values of $\lambda \in \mathbb{N}$.*
(ii) Simulatability: *For all $\mathcal{C} \subseteq [m]$ of size at most t and for all PPT adversaries $\mathcal{A}$, for all circuits Γ, there exists a simulator $\mathcal{S}$ with running time $\mathrm{poly}(|\mathcal{A}|, |\Gamma|)$, such that for all initial values of the memory $M_1 \in \{0,1\}^*$,*
$$\{\mathbf{Real}_{\mathcal{A},\Phi,\mathcal{C},\Gamma,M_1}(\lambda)\}_{\lambda \in \mathbb{N}} \approx_c \{\mathbf{Ideal}_{\mathcal{S},\mathcal{A},\Phi,\mathcal{C},\Gamma,M_1,\ell}(\lambda)\}_{\lambda \in \mathbb{N}} .$$

In the above definitions the adversary is allowed to modify each $\widehat{\Gamma}_i$ arbitrarily, i.e., there is no restriction on the edges and nodes of $\widehat{\Gamma}'_i$, as long as the input and output gates enable connectivity with the remaining components. We also allow arbitrary modifications of the circuit memory (cf. Remark 1). Observe that, the above definition is only interesting for small values of ℓ (as, e.g., it becomes trivial in case $\ell = |M_1|$). The non-triviality condition demands that the ratio between the size of the sub-components of the compiled circuit built in-house, and the size of the original circuit, should be less than one. This is necessary, as otherwise a manufacturer could simply produce the entire circuit by itself, without the help of any off-shore facility. Clearly, the smaller ρ is, the better, as this means that a large fraction of the original circuit production can be outsourced.

4 Case Study I: Single Manufacturer

In this section we study secure outsourcing compilers that work for any circuit, in the presence of a *single* malicious manufacturer. In Sect. 4.1 we describe our compiler, that is based on any verifiable computation (VC) scheme (satisfying some properties) for the function computed by the underlying circuit.

A typical VC scheme needs to satisfy some properties that we informally discuss below.

- Correctness: The ProbGen algorithm produces problem instances that allow for a honest server to successfully compute values Σ_Y such that $Y = \mathcal{F}(X)$.
- Soundness: No malicious server can "trick" a client into accepting an incorrect output, i.e, some value Y such that $Y \neq \mathcal{F}(X)$. We require this to hold even in the presence of so-called verification queries [15].
- Inputprivacy: No server can learn the input value X that the function is being computed on.

- Outsourceability: The time to encode the input plus the time to run a verification is smaller than the time to compute the function itself.

The reader is deferred to the full version [2] of this paper for a more thorough treatment of the definitions for VC schemes.

4.1 Compiler Based on Input-Private VC

In this section we construct an outsourcing circuit compiler by using a VC scheme that satisfies the properties of correctness, soundness, input-privacy and outsourceability. Let Γ be a circuit; the idea is to invoke a VC scheme for the function $\mathcal{F}$ corresponding to the functionality computed by Γ. The compiled circuit will consist of four main components $\widehat{\Gamma}_{\mathsf{ProbGen}}$, $\widehat{\Gamma}_{\mathsf{Compute}}$, $\widehat{\Gamma}_{\mathsf{Verify}}$, and $\widehat{\Gamma}_{\$}$. The first three components are the circuit representations of the algorithms ProbGen, Compute and Verify corresponding to the underlying VC scheme; such components hard-wire keys (SK, PK) generated using algorithm KeyGen. The fourth component samples the random coins R_i to be used during each invocation of the circuit. The production of component $\widehat{\Gamma}_{\mathsf{Compute}}$ will then be outsourced to a single untrusted facility, whereas all other components are built in-house (as their implementation needs to be trusted). Notice that the implementation of algorithm KeyGen can be thought of as a pre-processing stage that runs only once (and could be carried out in software).

An important observation is that the size of circuit $\widehat{\Gamma}_{\mathsf{Verify}}$ and $\widehat{\Gamma}_{\mathsf{ProbGen}}$ is independent, and much smaller, than the size of circuit $\widehat{\Gamma}_{\mathsf{Compute}}$. As discussed in the introduction, the size of $\widehat{\Gamma}_{\$}$ can also be considered to be constant (consisting only of a few gates). We describe our first compiler below in more details.

The Compiler $\Phi_{\mathcal{VC}}^1$. Let Γ be a circuit, and $\mathcal{VC} = (\mathsf{KeyGen}, \mathsf{ProbGen}, \mathsf{Compute}, \mathsf{Verify})$ be a VC scheme for the function $\mathcal{F}$ implemented by Γ. Our first compiler is depicted in Fig. 2, and can be described as follows.

1. First run $(SK, PK) \leftarrow \mathsf{KeyGen}(\mathcal{F}, \lambda)$ once, obtaining the pair of keys (SK, PK).
2. Let $\widehat{\Gamma}_{\mathsf{Memory}}$ be a circuit component consisting only of memory gates, as needed by the original circuit Γ, storing the initial value of the private memory M_1.
3. Let $\widehat{\Gamma}_{\$}$ be a circuit outputting random coins $\widehat{R}_i$ (as needed in each invocation of the compiled circuit).
4. Define a component for each function ProbGen, Compute and Verify of the $\mathcal{VC}$ scheme as explained below.
   - $\widehat{\Gamma}_{\mathsf{ProbGen}}$: This component embeds the secret key SK, and it takes three inputs; the input X_i, the (current) private memory M_i, and random coins $\widehat{R}_i := R_i \| R_i'$. It implements function $\mathsf{ProbGen}_{SK}(X_i \| M_i \| R_i; R_i')$, that produces two outputs: an encoding Σ_{X_i, M_i, R_i}, and a verification key VK_{X_i, M_i, R_i}.
   - $\widehat{\Gamma}_{\mathsf{Compute}}$: This component embeds the public key PK, and it takes as input an encoding. It implements the function $\mathsf{Compute}_{PK}(\Sigma_{X_i, M_i, R_i})$, that produces the encoding $\Sigma_{Y_i, M_{i+1}}$ of $(Y_i, M_{i+1}) = \mathcal{F}(X_i, M_i; R_i)$ as output.

– $\widehat{\Gamma}_{\mathsf{Verify}}$: This component embeds the secret key SK, and it takes two inputs; the encoding $\Sigma_{Y_i,M_{i+1}}$ and the verification key VK_{X_i,M_i,R_i}. It implements function $\mathsf{Verify}_S K(VK_{X_i,M_i,R_i}, \Sigma_{Y_i,M_{i+1}})$, to produce the output $Y_i \in \{0,1\}^* \cup \{\bot\}$, and eventually update the circuit private memory to M_{i+1}.

5. The output of $\Phi_{\mathcal{VC}}^1$ is defined as follows. The first output is a (description of the) compiled circuit $\widehat{\Gamma}$ as depicted in Fig. 2. The auxiliary information aux consists of the components $\widehat{\Gamma}_{\mathsf{ProbGen}}, \widehat{\Gamma}_{\mathsf{Compute}}, \widehat{\Gamma}_{\mathsf{Verify}}, \widehat{\Gamma}_{\mathsf{Memory}}$, and $\widehat{\Gamma}_\$$, the mapping function $\mathcal{M}$ that describes the physical connections between such components (i.e., the arrows in Fig. 2), and the index set $I = \{2\}$ specifying the component $\widehat{\Gamma}_{\mathsf{Compute}}$ as a candidate for outsourcing.

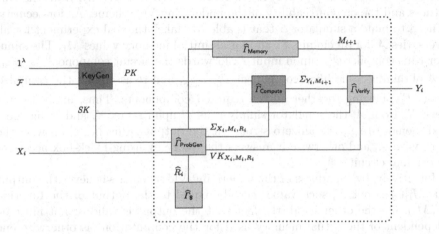

Fig. 2. The description of compilers $\Phi_{\mathcal{VC}}^1$. The green components (i.e., $\widehat{\Gamma}_{\mathsf{ProbGen}}, \widehat{\Gamma}_{\mathsf{Verify}}$, and $\widehat{\Gamma}_\$$) need to be built in-house, while the production of the red component (i.e., $\widehat{\Gamma}_{\mathsf{Compute}}$) can be outsourced; the blue component (i.e., KeyGen) is built only once (not necessarily in hardware). The dotted line depicts the circuit boundaries. The dotted line depicts the circuit boundaries (Color figure online)

Remark 1 (On outsourcing memory gates). In the compiler depicted in Fig. 2, $\widehat{\Gamma}_{\mathsf{Memory}}$ is being built in-house. In order to outsource private memory to a potentially malicious manufacturer we can modify the above compiler as follows: instead of storing in $\widehat{\Gamma}_{\mathsf{Memory}}$ the value M_i in plaintext, we store $C \leftarrow \mathsf{AE}_{SK'}(M_i)$, where C is the encryption of M_i using a symmetric, semantically secure authenticated encryption scheme, with secret key SK'. Moreover, $\widehat{\Gamma}_{\mathsf{ProbGen}}$ is modified such that when receiving the private memory value C, it first decrypts it using SK' and then executes the original circuit $\widehat{\Gamma}_{\mathsf{ProbGen}}$ on the resulting plaintext. We also substitute $\widehat{\Gamma}_{\mathsf{Verify}}$ so that it outputs the encryption of M_{i+1}, under SK'. This modification enables the simulator to execute the circuit using the all-zeros bit-string as the initial memory value, and security follows by the semantic security of the encryption scheme. Finally, whenever the decryption of C gives $\bot$ the circuit output is $\bot$.

The theorem below, whose proof appears in the full version [2] of the paper, states that the compiler from Fig. 2 satisfies our strongest security notion (i.e., Definition 4 with $\ell = 0$), provided that the underlying VC scheme is correct, sound, input-private, and outsourceable.

Theorem 1. *Let Γ be an arbitrary circuit and let $\mathcal{VC}$ be a verifiable computation scheme for the function $\mathcal{F}$ computed by Γ, satisfying the properties of correctness, soundness, input-privacy and outsourceability. Then the compiler $\Phi_{\mathcal{VC}}^1$ is a correct, $(0, 1)$-secure $(o(1), 1)$-outsourcing circuit compiler.*

Proof idea. We give an intuition for the security proof. Correctness of the compiler and the fact that $\rho = o(1)$ follow immediately, respectively, from the correctness and the outsourceability of the underlying VC scheme. As for security, we need to build a simulator $\mathcal{S}$ that is able to "fake" the real experiment for all adversaries $\mathcal{A}$, for all circuits Γ, and for all initial memory values M_1. The simulator runs compiler $\Phi_{\mathcal{VC}}^1$ upon input Γ, forwards the circuit component $\widehat{\Gamma}_{\mathsf{Compute}}$ to $\mathcal{A}$ obtaining a modified component $\widehat{\Gamma}'_{\mathsf{Compute}}$, and re-assembles the compiled circuit $\widehat{\Gamma}'$ plugging together all the required components. Thus, upon input a query X_i from $\mathcal{A}$, the simulator simply runs $\widehat{\Gamma}$ upon input X_i and using some fixed memory (e.g., the all-zero string); if the output is invalid, $\mathcal{S}$ answers the query with $\bot$, and otherwise it answers the query by using black-box access to the original circuit.

Intuitively, by soundness of the underlying VC scheme, whenever the output of $\widehat{\Gamma}[M_i](\cdot)$ is not $\bot$, such value must be equal to the output of the function $\mathcal{F}(\cdot, M_i)$. On the other hand, the fact that the output is valid or not must be independent of the actual memory used for the computation, as otherwise one could break the input-privacy property of the VC scheme. With this in mind, one can show the indistinguishability between the real and the simulated experiments using a hybrid argument.

5   Case Study II: Multiple Manufacturers

In this section we focus on outsourcing compilers in the presence of multiple manufacturers, aiming to improve the efficiency of the resulting circuit at the expense of achieving security in the weaker model where there are $m \geq 2$ manufacturers, a t-fraction of which is malicious (for some threshold $t \leq m - 1$).

Our solution, described in Sect. 5.1, is based on client-server multi-party computation protocols.

5.1   Compiler Based on MPC

In this section we present our compiler based on a client-server multi-party computation (MPC) protocol. The reader is referred to the full version [2] of this paper for a formal definition of client-server MPC.

The compiler $\Phi_{\Pi_{\mathcal{F}}}$. Let Γ be a circuit implementing the function $\mathcal{F}(M_1, \cdot)$, where for any X and $i \in \mathbb{N}$, we have $(Y, M_{i+1}) = \mathcal{F}(M_i, X)$. Let $\Pi_{\mathcal{F}} = (C, S, \mathsf{Enc}, \mathsf{Dec}, \mathsf{Next})$ be an r-round protocol realizing the function $\mathcal{F}$, over a set of m servers with a single client. The compiler produces $(\widehat{\Gamma}, \mathsf{aux}) \leftarrow \Phi_{\Pi_{\mathcal{F}}}(\Gamma)$, where

- $\widehat{\Gamma}$ is the circuit that implements $\Pi_{\mathcal{F}}$ having as a sub-circuit $\widehat{\Gamma}_{\mathsf{Memory}}$, which is a circuit consisting only of memory gates, as needed by the original circuit Γ. During initialization, $\widehat{\Gamma}_{\mathsf{Memory}}$ stores the initial private memory value, M_1.
- $\mathsf{aux} = ((\widehat{\Gamma}_1, \ldots, \widehat{\Gamma}_{m+2}), \mathcal{M}, (I_1, \ldots, I_m))$, where
  - $\widehat{\Gamma}_{m+1} = \widehat{\Gamma}_{\mathsf{Enc}}$ and $\widehat{\Gamma}_{m+2} = \widehat{\Gamma}_{\mathsf{Dec}}$, i.e., the circuits $\widehat{\Gamma}_{m+1}$ and $\widehat{\Gamma}_{m+2}$ implement the encoder, Enc, and the decoder Dec, of $\Pi_{\mathcal{F}}$, respectively.
  - For $i \in [m]$, $\widehat{\Gamma}_i$ is the circuit that implements the code of the i-th server, for the entire execution of $\Pi_{\mathcal{F}}$ (r-rounds). Those circuits can be implemented in a straightforward way using the next message function Next_i.
  - The mapping function $\mathcal{M}$ describes the physical connections between the circuits described above, and I_j, for $j \in [m]$, specifies the components that will be outsourced to the manufacturer with index j. In our case $I_j = \{J\}$.
  - In case the original circuit is randomized, in addition to the components described above, Φ also outputs a circuit $\widehat{\Gamma}_{\$}$ producing random coins R_i (as needed in each invocation of the circuit).

Our construction must be non-trivial (cf. Definition 4), thus the underlying protocol Π must satisfy the following outsourceability property.

Definition 5 (Outsourceability of protocols). *A protocol* $\Pi = (C, S, \mathsf{Enc}, \mathsf{Dec}, \mathsf{Next})$ *that realizes the function* $\mathcal{F}$ *can be outsourced if it satisfies the following condition: The circuit computing the encoding and decoding procedures* $(\mathsf{Enc}, \mathsf{Dec})$ *must be smaller than the circuit computing the function* $\mathcal{F}$.

We prove the following result in the full version [2] of this paper:

Theorem 2. *Let* $\mathcal{F}$ *be any function, and let* $\Pi_{\mathcal{F}}$ *be a* (t, m)-*private MPC protocol for* $\mathcal{F}$, *satisfying the correctness and outsourceability properties. Then, the compiler* $\Phi_{\Pi_{\mathcal{F}}}$ *is a correct,* $(0, t)$-*secure,* $(o(1), m)$-*outsourcing circuit compiler.*

6 Concrete Instantiations

In this section we propose several instantiations for the compilers analyzed in the previous sections, highlighting several possible tradeoffs between security, efficiency, and underlying hardness assumptions (Table 1).

Table 1. Comparing our compilers in terms of security, efficiency, and hardness assumptions. We write s, n, v for the size, number of inputs and number of outputs of the original circuit Γ, respectively; as usual m denotes the number of servers of which up to t might be corrupted (note that $t = m$ corresponds to the case of a single manufacturer). The values s_{in} and s_{out} denote, respectively, for the sizes of the components built in house and the size of the outsourced components; d denotes the number of multiplications in Γ. KoE stands for "Knowledge of Exponent" assumptions, FHE for "Fully-Homomorphic Encryption", OT for "Oblivious Transfer" and SHE for "Somewhat Homomorphic Encryption". The first (colored) row represents the compiler with a single outsourcing facility ($m = 1$), while the remaining rows represent the compiler with multiple outsourcing facilities ($m \geq 2$).

Compiler	Reference	t	s_{in}	s_{out}	No Self-Destruct	Leakage	Assumption
§ 4.1	[15]	–	$O(n + v)$	$O(s \log s)$	✓	0	KoE + FHE
§ 5.1	[13]	$m - 1$	$O(dm)$	$O(sm + m^3)$	✓	0	SHE
	[36]	$m - 1$	$O(dm^2)$	$O(sm^2 \cdot \lambda / \log s)$	✓	0	OT

6.1   Case Study I

The area of verifiable computation has a long history in the cryptographic literature [4,16]. We refer the reader to the excellent survey by Walfish and Blumberg [35] for a thorough introduction. By now, several schemes and models for the problem of outsourcing computation are known (see, among others, [1]). Below, we focus only on single server VC schemes suitable for the single manufacturer compiler.

Input Privacy. For the compiler of Sect. 4.1, we need a VC scheme satisfying both soundness and input-privacy (in the presence of verification queries). The only known schemes meeting these requirements are the ones constructed by Fiore, Gennaro, and Pastro [15].

6.2   Case Study II

We describe below a few possible instantiations for the multiple manufacturers compiler of Sect. 5.

Client-Server MPC. Many MPC protocols satisfy the outsourceability property, as the values that feed the main computation, i.e., the output of the encoder, are independent of the function that is being evaluated, and mostly depend on the number of parties, as in the case of [17] (where the same holds for decoding). An explicit (t, m)-private protocol is given in [12], for $t < m/2$, in which there is a pre-processing phase that can be implemented by the encoder, with running time independent of the function that is being evaluated. The construction uses secure point-to-point and broadcast channels, that can be implemented directly between the components, and besides privacy it also guarantees output delivery.

We can also easily adapt the SPDZ protocol [13] to the client-server setting. The SPDZ protocol requires a pre-processing phase that is performed by the parties, and that will feed the encoder circuit who will perform the actual encoding (which is only a linear operation). The complete protocol requires a linear number of public-key operations in the circuit size s, with the encoder requiring only a linear number of operations in m and the number of multiplications of the original circuit. The efficiency of the pre-processing stage can be further improved [5]. This construction does not guarantee output delivery, but it is secure against adversaries that corrupt up to $m - 1$ sub-components.

References

1. Ananth, P., Chandran, N., Goyal, V., Kanukurthi, B., Ostrovsky, R.: Achieving privacy in verifiable computation with multiple servers – without FHE and without pre-processing. In: Krawczyk, H. (ed.) PKC 2014. LNCS, vol. 8383, pp. 149–166. Springer, Heidelberg (2014). https://doi.org/10.1007/978-3-642-54631-0_9
2. Ateniese, G., Kiayias, A., Magri, B., Tselekounis, Y., Venturi, D.: Secure outsourcing of circuit manufacturing. Cryptology ePrint Archive, Report 2016/527 (2016). https://eprint.iacr.org/2016/527
3. Ateniese, G., Magri, B., Venturi, D.: Subversion-resilient signature schemes. In: ACM CCS, pp. 364–375 (2015)
4. Babai, L., Fortnow, L., Levin, L.A., Szegedy, M.: Checking computations in polylogarithmic time. In: ACM STOC, pp. 21–31 (1991)
5. Baum, C., Damgård, I., Toft, T., Zakarias, R.: Better preprocessing for secure multiparty computation. In: Manulis, M., Sadeghi, A.-R., Schneider, S. (eds.) ACNS 2016. LNCS, vol. 9696, pp. 327–345. Springer, Cham (2016). https://doi.org/10.1007/978-3-319-39555-5_18
6. Beaumont, M., Hopkins, B., Newby, T.: Hardware Trojans—Prevention, detection, countermeasures (a literature review). Technical report. Australian Government Department of Defence, July 2011
7. Becker, G.T., Regazzoni, F., Paar, C., Burleson, W.P.: Stealthy dopant-level hardware Trojans: extended version. J. Cryptogr. Eng. 4(1), 19–31 (2014)
8. Bellare, M., Paterson, K.G., Rogaway, P.: Security of symmetric encryption against mass surveillance. In: Garay, J.A., Gennaro, R. (eds.) CRYPTO 2014. LNCS, vol. 8616, pp. 1–19. Springer, Heidelberg (2014). https://doi.org/10.1007/978-3-662-44371-2_1
9. Bhasin, S., Regazzoni, F.: A survey on hardware Trojan detection techniques. In: IEEE ISCAS, pp. 2021–2024 (2015)
10. Costello, C., et al.: Geppetto: Versatile verifiable computation. In: IEEE Symposium on Security and Privacy, pp. 253–270 (2015)
11. Dachman-Soled, D., Kalai, Y.T.: Securing circuits and protocols against 1/poly(k) tampering rate. In: Lindell, Y. (ed.) TCC 2014. LNCS, vol. 8349, pp. 540–565. Springer, Heidelberg (2014). https://doi.org/10.1007/978-3-642-54242-8_23
12. Damgård, I., Ishai, Y.: Constant-round multiparty computation using a black-box pseudorandom generator. In: Shoup, V. (ed.) CRYPTO 2005. LNCS, vol. 3621, pp. 378–394. Springer, Heidelberg (2005). https://doi.org/10.1007/11535218_23
13. Damgård, I., Pastro, V., Smart, N., Zakarias, S.: Multiparty computation from somewhat homomorphic encryption. In: Safavi-Naini, R., Canetti, R. (eds.) CRYPTO 2012. LNCS, vol. 7417, pp. 643–662. Springer, Heidelberg (2012). https://doi.org/10.1007/978-3-642-32009-5_38

14. Dziembowski, S., Faust, S., Standaert, F.-X.: Private circuits III: hardware Trojan-Resilience via testing amplification. In: ACM CCS, pp. 142–153 (2016)
15. Fiore, D., Gennaro, R., Pastro, V.: Efficiently verifiable computation on encrypted data. In: ACM CCS, pp. 844–855 (2014)
16. Gennaro, R., Gentry, C., Parno, B.: Non-interactive verifiable computing: outsourcing computation to untrusted workers. In: Rabin, T. (ed.) CRYPTO 2010. LNCS, vol. 6223, pp. 465–482. Springer, Heidelberg (2010). https://doi.org/10.1007/978-3-642-14623-7_25
17. Goldreich, O., Micali, S., Wigderson, A.: How to play any mental game or a completeness theorem for protocols with honest majority. In: ACM STOC, pp. 218–229 (1987)
18. Greenwald, G.: No Place to Hide: Edward Snowden, the NSA, and the U.S. Surveillance State. Metropolitan Books, New York (2014)
19. Hamburg, M., Kocher, P., Marson, M.: Analysis of Intel's Ivy Bridge digital random number generator. Technical report. Cryptography Research Inc., March 2012
20. Imeson, F., Emtenan, A., Garg, S., Tripunitara, M.V.: Securing computer hardware using 3D integrated circuit (IC) technology and split manufacturing for obfuscation. In: USENIX Security Symposium, pp. 495–510 (2013)
21. Ishai, Y., Ostrovsky, R., Zikas, V.: Secure multi-party computation with identifiable abort. In: Garay, J.A., Gennaro, R. (eds.) CRYPTO 2014. LNCS, vol. 8617, pp. 369–386. Springer, Heidelberg (2014). https://doi.org/10.1007/978-3-662-44381-1_21
22. Ishai, Y., Prabhakaran, M., Sahai, A., Wagner, D.: Private circuits II: keeping secrets in tamperable circuits. In: Vaudenay, S. (ed.) EUROCRYPT 2006. LNCS, vol. 4004, pp. 308–327. Springer, Heidelberg (2006). https://doi.org/10.1007/11761679_19
23. Kiayias, A., Tselekounis, Y.: Tamper resilient circuits: the adversary at the gates. In: Sako, K., Sarkar, P. (eds.) ASIACRYPT 2013. LNCS, vol. 8270, pp. 161–180. Springer, Heidelberg (2013). https://doi.org/10.1007/978-3-642-42045-0_9
24. Love, E., Jin, Y., Makris, Y.: Enhancing security via provably trustworthy hardware intellectual property. In: IEEE HOST, pp. 12–17 (2011)
25. Mak, M.A.: Trusted defense microelectronics: future access and capabilities are uncertain. Technical report. United States Government Accountability Office, October 2015
26. Mavroudis, V., Cerulli, A., Svenda, P., Cvrcek, D., Klinec, D., Danezis, G.: A touch of evil: high-assurance cryptographic hardware from untrusted components. In: ACM CCS, pp. 1583–1600 (2017)
27. McIntyre, D.R., Wolff, F.G., Papachristou, C.A., Bhunia, S.: Dynamic evaluation of hardware trust. In: IEEE HOST, pp. 108–111 (2009)
28. Otto, M.: Fault attacks and countermeasures. Ph.D. thesis. University of Paderborn, Germany (2006)
29. Parno, B., Howell, J., Gentry, C., Raykova, M.: Pinocchio: nearly practical verifiable computation. In: IEEE Symposium on Security and Privacy, pp. 238–252 (2013)
30. Potkonjak, M.: Synthesis of trustable ICs using untrusted CAD tools. In: DAC, pp. 633–634 (2010)
31. Seifert, J.-P., Bayer, C.: Trojan-resilient circuits, Chap. 14. In: Pathan, A.-S.K. (ed.) Securing Cyber-Physical Systems, pp. 349–370. CRC Press, Boca Raton, London, New York (2015)
32. Sharkey, B.: Trust in integrated circuits program. Technical report. DARPA, March 2007

33. Wahby, R.S., Howald, M., Garg, S.J., Shelat, A., Walfish, M.: Verifiable ASICs. In: IEEE S&P, pp. 759–778 (2016)
34. Waksman, A., Sethumadhavan, S.: Silencing hardware backdoors. In: IEEE Symposium on Security and Privacy, pp. 49–63 (2011)
35. Walfish, M., Blumberg, A.J.: Verifying computations without reexecuting them. Commun. ACM **58**(2), 74–84 (2015)
36. Wang, X., Ranellucci, S., Katz, J.: Global-scale secure multiparty computation. In: ACM CCS (2017)

On the Hardness of Learning Parity with Noise over Rings

Shuoyao Zhao[1,2]($\boxtimes$), Yu Yu[1,2,4]($\boxtimes$), and Jiang Zhang[3]($\boxtimes$)

[1] Department of Computer Science and Engineering, Shanghai Jiao Tong University, Shanghai, China
zhao_sy2016@sjtu.edu.cn, yuyuathk@gmail.com,
[2] National Engineering Laboratory for Wireless Security,
Xi'an University of Posts and Telecommunications, Xi'an, China
[3] State Key Laboratory of Cryptology, P.O. Box 5159, Beijing 100878, China
[4] Westone Cryptologic Research Center, Beijing 100070, China
jiangzhang09@gmail.com

Abstract. Learning Parity with Noise (LPN) represents a notoriously hard problem in learning theory and it is also closely related to the "decoding random linear codes" problem in coding theory. Recently LPN has found many cryptographic applications such as authentication protocols, pseudorandom generators/functions and even advanced tasks including public-key encryption (PKE) schemes and oblivious transfer (OT) protocols. Crypto-systems based on LPN are computationally efficient and parallelizable in concept, thanks to the simple algebraic structure of LPN, but they (especially the public-key ones) are typically inefficient in terms of public-key/ciphertext sizes and/or communication complexity. To mitigate the issue, Heyse et al. (FSE 2012) introduced the ring variant of LPN (Ring-LPN) that enjoys a compact structure and gives rise to significantly more efficient cryptographic schemes. However, unlike its large-modulus analogue Ring-LWE (to which a reduction from ideal lattice problems can be established), no formal asymptotic studies are known for the security of Ring-LPN or its connections to other hardness assumptions.

Informally, we show that for $\mu = 1/n^{0.5-\epsilon}$ and $\delta = \mu\mu'n = o(1)$: assume that the decisional LPN problem of noise rate μ is hard even when its matrix is generated by a random Ring-LPN instance of noise rate μ' (whose matrix is also kept secret in addition to secret and noise), then either Ring-LPN of noise rate δ is hard or public-key cryptography is implied. We remark that the heuristic-based approach to public randomness generation (as used in the assumption) is widely adopted in practice, and the latter statement is less likely because noise rate $\mu = 1/n^{0.5-\epsilon}$ is believed to reside in the minicrypt-only regime for LPN. Therefore, our results constitute non-trivial evidence that Ring-LPN might be as hard as LPN.

Keywords: Learning parity with noise · Ring-LPN · Cryptography

© Springer Nature Switzerland AG 2018
J. Baek et al. (Eds.): ProvSec 2018, LNCS 11192, pp. 94–108, 2018.
https://doi.org/10.1007/978-3-030-01446-9_6

1   Introduction

LEARNING PARITY WITH NOISE. The computational version of learning parity with noise (LPN) assumption with secret size $n \in \mathbb{N}$ and noise rate $0 < \mu < 1/2$ postulates that given any $q = \mathsf{poly}(n)$ samples it is computationally infeasible for any probabilistic polynomial-time (PPT) algorithm to recover the random secret $\mathbf{x} \xleftarrow{\$} \{0,1\}^n$ given $(\mathbf{A}, \mathbf{A} \cdot \mathbf{x} + \mathbf{e})$, where $\mathbf{A}$ is a random $q \times n$ Boolean matrix, $\mathbf{e}$ follows $\mathcal{B}_\mu^q = (\mathcal{B}_\mu)^q$, $\mathcal{B}_\mu$ denotes the Bernoulli distribution with parameter μ (i.e., taking value 1 with probability μ and value 0 otherwise), '$\cdot$' and '$+$' denote (matrix-vector) multiplication and addition modulo 2 respectively. The decisional LPN simply assumes that $(\mathbf{A}, \mathbf{A} \cdot \mathbf{x} + \mathbf{e})$ is pseudorandom, which is known to be polynomially equivalent to its computational version [6,10,32].

HARDNESS OF LPN. The computational LPN problem can be seen as the average-case analogue of the NP-complete problem "decoding random linear codes" [8]. LPN has been also extensively studied in learning theory, and it was shown in [22] that an efficient algorithm for LPN would allow to learn several important function classes such as 2-DNF formulas, juntas, and any function with a sparse Fourier spectrum. Under a constant noise rate, Blum Kalai and Wasserman [11] solved LPN with time/sample complexity $2^{O(n/\log n)}$. Lyubashevsky [36] observed that one can produce almost as many LPN samples as needed using only $q = n^{1+\epsilon}$ LPN samples (of a lower noise rate), which implies a variant of the BKW attack [11] with time complexity $2^{O(n/\log \log n)}$ and sample complexity $n^{1+\epsilon}$. If one is restricted to $q = O(n)$ samples, then the best attack has exponential complexity $2^{O(n)}$ [39]. Quantum algorithms [21] that build upon Grover search may achieve a certain level (up to quadratic) of speedup over classic ones in solving LPN, which does not change the asymptotic order (up to the constant in the exponent) of the complexity of the problem. This makes LPN a promising candidate for "post-quantum cryptography". Furthermore, LPN enjoys simplicity and is more suited for weak-power devices (e.g., RFID tags) than other quantum-secure candidates such as Learning with Errors (LWE) [41] as the many modular additions and multiplications in LWE would be simplified to AND and XOR gates in LPN.

SYMMETRIC-KEY CRYPTOGRAPHY FROM LPN. The first cryptographic application of LPN is lightweight authentication schemes (e.g. [28,31,32], see [1] for a more complete list). Recently, Kiltz et al. [33] and Dodis et al. [18] constructed randomized MACs from LPN, which implies a two-round authentication scheme with man-in-the-middle security. Lyubashevsky and Masny [37] gave a more efficient actively secure three-round authentication scheme from LPN and recently Cash, Kiltz, and Tessaro [15] reduced the round complexity to 2 rounds. Applebaum et al. [5] used LPN to construct efficient symmetric encryption schemes with certain key-dependent message (KDM) security. Jain et al. [30] constructed an efficient perfectly binding string commitment scheme from LPN. We refer to a recent survey [40] about cryptography from the LPN assumption.

PUBLIC-KEY CRYPTOGRAPHY FROM LOW-NOISE LPN. All aforementioned cryptographic applications reside in minicrypt[1] and they rely on the hardness of the standard LPN with constant noise (i.e., μ is a constant independent of secret size n). Alekhnovich [3] constructed the first cryptomania application from the low-noise LPN, in particular, he showed that LPN with noise rate $O(1/\sqrt{n})$ implies CPA secure public-key encryption (PKE) schemes, and more recently Döttling et al. [20] and Kiltz et al. [2] further showed that low-noise LPN alone already suffices for PKE schemes with CCA (and even KDM [19]) security. David et al. [17] showed how to construct universally composable Oblivious Transfer (OT) protocols from low-noise LPN. Under low noise rate $\mu = O(1/\sqrt{n})$, the best attacks [7,9,34,35] solve LPN with time complexity $2^{O(\mu n)}$. To see this, consider an adversary who observes n LPN samples and trivially bets on the noise $\mathbf{e} = 0$, which occurs with probability $(1 - \mu)^n \approx e^{-\mu n}$, and one can trade time for a noticeable success rate.

SECURITY AND EFFICIENCY OF LPN-BASED PKE. It is more convenient to use the "Hermite normal form" of LPN (see Definition 3) where the secret $\mathbf{s}$ is also sampled from $\mathcal{B}_\mu^n$ (instead of from uniform) with equivalent security [5] (see Lemma 1). We depict in Fig. 1 a two-pass protocol by which Alice and Bob agree on a single bit against passive adversaries, which is equivalent to an IND-CPA secure PKE for single bit messages. That is, Alice samples a pair of keys (pk, sk) and sends the public one pk to Bob, and Bob encrypts with pk his message m and returns the ciphertext, which is decrypted with sk to m'. Correctness requires the inner product of two noise vectors sampled from $\mathcal{B}_\mu^{2n}$ to be bounded away from random (see Lemma 5), i.e.,

$$\Pr[m = m'] = \Pr\left[[\mathbf{s}_1^\mathsf{T}, \mathbf{e}_1^\mathsf{T}] \cdot \begin{bmatrix} \mathbf{e} \\ \mathbf{s} \end{bmatrix} = 0\right] \geq 1/2 + 2^{-O(\mu^2 n)},$$

and thus set $\mu = O(1/\sqrt{n})$ to decrypt message with noticeable success probability. However, the low noise rate makes the PKE scheme inefficient in terms of key and ciphertext lengths. Further, the above only serves to show the feasibility by encrypting a single bit (instead of many bits) with noticeable (instead of overwhelming) successful decryption probability. A full-fledge scheme would need to use many repetitions, i.e., $\mathbf{S}_1 \in \{0,1\}^{n \times \ell}$ and $\mathbf{E}_1 \in \{0,1\}^{n \times \ell}$ for $\ell \in \Omega(n)$ (instead of $\mathbf{s}_1^\mathsf{T} \in \{0,1\}^n$ and $\mathbf{e}_1^\mathsf{T} \in \{0,1\}^n$) and an error correction code, which further deteriorate the efficiency. As estimated in [16], an 80-bit secure LPN-based PKE already needs public keys of several megabytes, which is far from practical. Note that one can use heuristic methods [4,12–14] to compress the matrix $\mathbf{A}$, e.g., use a PRG (with seed made public) or a hash function (modelled as a random oracle) to expand a 256-bit random seed to generate as much randomness as needed. But this does not resolve the problem as the other part of public key $\mathbf{b}$ and the ciphertext ($\mathbf{c}_1, \mathbf{c}_2$) cannot be compressed.

---

[1] minicrypt refers to Impagliazzo's [29] hypothetical world where one-way functions exist but public-key cryptography does not, and cryptomania is the more optimistic world where public-key cryptography and multiparty computation are possible.

Noise rate: $\mu = O(1/\sqrt{n})$

Alice		Bob: $m \in \{0,1\}$
$\mathbf{A} \xleftarrow{\$} \{0,1\}^{n \times n}$		$\mathbf{s}_1 \leftarrow \mathcal{B}_\mu^n$
$sk = \mathbf{s} \leftarrow \mathcal{B}_\mu^n$	$pk \overset{\text{def}}{=} (\mathbf{A}, \mathbf{b} \overset{\text{def}}{=} \mathbf{As} + \mathbf{e})$	$\mathbf{e}_1 \leftarrow \mathcal{B}_\mu^n$
$\mathbf{e} \leftarrow \mathcal{B}_\mu^n$	$\xrightarrow{\hspace{5cm}}$	$\mathbf{c}_1 := \mathbf{A}^\mathsf{T}\mathbf{s}_1 + \mathbf{e}_1$
		$\mathbf{c}_2 := \mathbf{s}_1^\mathsf{T} \cdot \mathbf{b} + m$
	ciphertext $= (\mathbf{c}_1, \mathbf{c}_2)$	
$m' := \mathbf{c}_1^\mathsf{T} \cdot \mathbf{s} - \mathbf{c}_2$	$\xleftarrow{\hspace{5cm}}$	

Fig. 1. A two-pass protocol by which Bob transmits a message bit m to Alice with passive security and noticeable correctness (for $\mu = O(1/\sqrt{n})$), where Bob receives $m' = m + (\mathbf{s}_1^\mathsf{T} \cdot \mathbf{e}) + (\mathbf{e}_1^\mathsf{T} \cdot \mathbf{s})$.

RING-LPN. Inspired by Ring-LWE [38], Heyse et al. [25] introduced the ring variant of LPN (Ring-LPN) to improve the efficiency of LPN-based crypto-systems. Informally, the computational (resp., decisional) Ring-LPN assumption postulates that it is hard to recover $\mathbf{s}$ given (resp., distinguish from uniform the following)

$$(\mathbf{a}_1, \cdots, \mathbf{a}_q, \mathbf{a}_1\mathbf{s} + \mathbf{e}_1, \cdots, \mathbf{a}_q\mathbf{s} + \mathbf{e}_q),$$

where $\mathbf{a}_1, \cdots, \mathbf{a}_q \xleftarrow{\$} \{0,1\}^n$ and $\mathbf{s}, \mathbf{e}_1, \cdots, \mathbf{e}_q \xleftarrow{\$} \mathcal{B}_\mu^n$ are treated as elements over a ring $R = \mathbb{F}_2[X]/(g)$ for some carefully chosen polynomial g of degree n. One can compare the above with LPN with $q' = qn$ samples, i.e., the $(qn) \times n$ matrix $\mathbf{A}$ is parsed as square submatrices matrices $\mathbf{A}_1, \cdots, \mathbf{A}_q$, and instead of chosen from uniform each $\mathbf{A}_i$ is succinctly described using a random ring element $\mathbf{a}_i$, i.e., $\mathbf{A}_i = \mathsf{mat}(\mathbf{a}_i)$ such that for every $\mathbf{s} \in \{0,1\}^n$ the product of the two ring elements $\mathbf{a}_i \cdot \mathbf{s}$ always equals to the matrix-vector product $\mathsf{mat}(\mathbf{a}_i) \cdot \mathbf{s}$. As depicted in Fig. 2, this yields very efficient constructions with public-key/ciphertext size $O(n)$, and based on a variant of Ring-LPN, Dåmgard and Park [16] constructed a nearly practical PKE with 128-bit security and 36-kilobyte ciphertext.

SECURITY OF RING-LPN. Unlike its large-modulus analogue Ring-LWE to which reductions are known from ideal lattices [38], Ring-LPN is short of any formal security treatments. When introducing Ring-LPN, the authors of [25] suggested a couple of "judicious" choices[2] for the underlying ring polynomial for which no attacks are known other than generic ones for standard LPN. For example, simply use a polynomial g of degree n that is irreducible over $\mathbb{F}_2$ to enjoy at least the following good properties:

---

[2] Indeed, it is necessary to use "good" polynomials as otherwise there are specific attacks [23,24] utilizing the "bad" structure of the underlying polynomials of Ring-LPN and Ring-LWE.

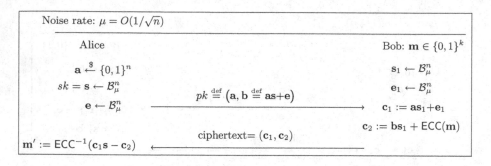

Fig. 2. A two-pass key-agreement protocol (and an IND-CPA public-key encryption scheme) by which Bob transmits a message bit m to Alice with passive security, where $\mu = O(1/\sqrt{n})$ and $(\mathsf{ECC}, \mathsf{ECC}^{-1})$ is the encoding and decoding functions of an error correction code such that Bob receives $m = \mathsf{ECC}^{-1}(\mathsf{ECC}(m) + \mathbf{s}_1\mathbf{e} + \mathbf{se}_1)$ with overwhelming probability, and algebraic operations are carried out over a ring $R = \mathbb{F}_2[X]/(g)$ for some polynomial g of constant weight [16].

1. **Linear independence.** For any non-zero $\mathbf{a} \in R = \mathbb{F}_2[X]/(g)$ with irreducible g, square matrix $\mathbf{A} = \mathsf{mat}(\mathbf{a})$ always has full-rank.[3]
2. **Uniformity.** Every row/column of $\mathbf{A} = \mathsf{mat}(\mathbf{a})$ is uniformly random on its own (i.e., not jointly with others) if the underlying $\mathbf{a}$ is drawn uniformly at random.

However, to our best knowledge, it remains an open problem whether one can establish formal reductions (or non-trivial connections) from LPN to Ring-LPN.

OUR CONTRIBUTIONS. We informally state our main findings as the theorem below.

Theorem 1 (main results, informal). *Let n be the security parameter, let $\mu = \mu(n)$, $\mu' = \mu'(n)$, $\delta = \delta(n)$ and $q = \mathsf{poly}(n)$ such that $\delta = \mu\mu'n = o(1)$. Then, the following hardness assumptions are closely related in certain senses (to be explained below).*

1. *The decisional LPN assumption with noise rate μ.*
2. *The decisional LPN assumption with noise rate μ except that the matrix is generated from a random Ring-LPN instance with noise rate μ', where matrix, secret and noise of Ring-LPN are all kept secret.*
3. *The decisional Ring-LPN assumption with noise rate δ.*

Notice that we essentially aim to show that Assumption 1 is likely to imply Assumption 3, and to this end (inspired by the hybrid argument) we insert an intermediate one Assumption 2, for which we argue that for $i \in \{1,2\}$ Assumption i (hopefully) leads to Assumption $i+1$ either due to heuristic based approaches widely adopted in practice or theoretic barriers of known techniques.

---

[3] Otherwise (i.e., if $\mathbf{A}$ has no full rank), there exists $\mathbf{x} \neq \mathbf{0}$ s.t. $\mathbf{Ax} = \mathbf{ax} = \mathbf{0}$, which is not possible for nonzero elements $\mathbf{a}$ and $\mathbf{x}$ over a field.

ASSUMPTION 1 → ASSUMPTION 2. This implication is immediate if we additionally assume Ring-LPN but then it renders the statement meaningless. However, we argue that this additional assumption may not be necessary as in this case even the matrix of Ring-LPN is kept secret. Furthermore, similar heuristic-based approaches for generating public matrix were also adopted by postquantum public-key cryptographic schemes such as Frodo [14], New Hope [4] and Kyber [12], where either a RO or a PRG (with seed made public) is used to generate as much public randomness as needed without a formal proof in standard model.

ASSUMPTION 2 → ASSUMPTION 3. We give a win-win result (see Lemma 6) that under Assumption 2 we have that either Assumption 3 holds, or otherwise Assumption 2 implies public-key cryptography in a security-preserving manner, which is unlikely for $\mu = \frac{1}{n^{0.5-\epsilon}}$.

HOW TO INTERPRET THE RESULTS. We stress that the above is not a proof that LPN implies Ring-LPN. Instead, it essentially states that, either it is not even secure to use Ring-LPN for generating public randomness for LPN (e.g., when the ring is defined with respect to a "bad" polynomial that introduces vulnerability and results in a malformed matrix), or that for certain meaningful noise rates, e.g., $\mu = 1/n^{2/5}$, $\mu' = 1/n^{3/4}$ and $\delta = 1/n^{3/20}$, LPN of noise rate $\mu = 1/n^{2/5}$ implies either Ring-LPN or public-key cryptography, where the latter is beyond Alekhnovich's $1/\sqrt{n}$ noise regime and thus very unlikely (see discussions in [40, Footnote 4]).

2 Preliminaries

NOTATIONS AND DEFINITIONS. Column vectors are represented by bold lower-case letters (e.g., $\mathbf{s}$), row vectors are denoted as their transpose (e.g., $\mathbf{s}^{\mathsf{T}}$), and matrices are denoted by bold capital letters (e.g., $\mathbf{A}$). $|s|$ refers to the Hamming weight of binary string s. We use $\mathcal{B}_\mu$ to denote the Bernoulli distribution with parameter μ, while $\mathcal{B}_\mu^q$ denotes the concatenation of q independent copies of $\mathcal{B}_\mu$.

$\mathbf{x} \xleftarrow{\$} \mathcal{X}$ refers to drawing $\mathbf{x}$ from set $\mathcal{X}$ uniformly at random, and $\mathbf{x} \leftarrow X$ means drawing $\mathbf{x}$ according to distribution X. We use U_n to denote a uniform distribution over $\{0,1\}^n$ and independent of any other distribution in consideration. For a ring $R = \mathbb{F}_2[X]/(g)$ defined with polynomial g of degree n, $\mathbf{s} \xleftarrow{\$} R$ and $\mathbf{s} \leftarrow \mathcal{B}_\mu^R$ refer to (and are often used interchangeably with) sampling ring element $\mathbf{s}$ according to $\mathbf{s} \xleftarrow{\$} \{0,1\}^n$ and $\mathbf{s} \leftarrow \mathcal{B}_\mu^n$ respectively. For ring element $\mathbf{a}, \mathbf{s} \in R$ we use $\mathsf{mat}(\mathbf{a}) \in \{0,1\}^{n \times n}$ and $\mathsf{vec}(\mathbf{s}) \in \{0,1\}^{n \times 1}$ to denote their respective matrix and (column) vector representations such that $\mathsf{vec}(\mathbf{a} \cdot \mathbf{s}) \equiv \mathsf{mat}(\mathbf{a}) \cdot \mathsf{vec}(\mathbf{s})$, where $\mathsf{vec}(\cdot)$ is often omitted. We use $\log(\cdot)$ to denote the binary logarithm. A function $\mathsf{negl}(\cdot)$ is negligible if for any positive constant N_c we have that $\mathsf{negl}(n) < n^{-N_c}$ for all sufficiently large n.

SAMPLE COMPLEXITY. In general, the polynomial security of LPN and its variants considers adversaries who are not bounded to the number of samples (other than that he is polynomially bounded in running time). However, for more quantitative reductions, we define the variants of LPN with sample complexity bounded by a certain polynomial. Standard (polynomial) security requires that the hardness holds with respect to all polynomials, e.g., we consider the computational LPN problem as hard if for every $q = \mathsf{poly}(n)$ the (n, μ, q)-LPN problem, as defined below, is hard.

Definition 1 (Learning Parity with Noise). *Let n be the security parameter, and let $\mu = \mu(n)$ and $q = \mathsf{poly}(n)$. The decisional LPN problem with secret length n, noise rate $0 < \mu < 1/2$ and sample complexity q, denoted by (n, μ, q)-DLPN, is hard if for every PPT algorithm $\mathcal{D}$*

$$\left| \Pr[\mathcal{D}(\mathbf{A}, \ \mathbf{A} \cdot \mathbf{x} + \mathbf{e}) = 1] - \Pr[\mathcal{D}(\mathbf{A}, \mathbf{r}) = 1] \right| = \mathsf{negl}(n), \tag{1}$$

and the computational LPN problem with the same n and μ and q, denoted by (n, μ, q)-LPN, is hard if for every PPT algorithm $\mathcal{D}$ we have

$$\Pr[\ \mathcal{D}(\mathbf{A}, \ \mathbf{A} \cdot \mathbf{x} + \mathbf{e}) = \mathbf{x}\ ] \ = \ \mathsf{negl}(n), \tag{2}$$

where $q \times n$ matrix $\mathbf{A} \xleftarrow{\$} \{0,1\}^{q \times n}$, $\mathbf{x} \xleftarrow{\$} \{0,1\}^n$, $\mathbf{e} \leftarrow \mathcal{B}_\mu^q$ and $\mathbf{r} \xleftarrow{\$} \{0,1\}^q$.

The ring version of the Learning Parity with Noise (Ring-LPN) problem is defined same as Definition 1 except that algebraic operations are performed between ring elements.

Definition 2 (Ring-LPN). *Let n be the security parameter, and let $\mu = \mu(n)$ and $q = \mathsf{poly}(n)$. The decisional Ring-LPN problem with secret length n, noise rate $0 < \mu < 1/2$ and sample complexity q, denoted by (n, μ, q)-Ring-DLPN, is hard if for every PPT algorithm $\mathcal{D}$ we have*

$$\left| \Pr[\mathcal{D}(\mathbf{a}_1, \cdots, \mathbf{a}_q, \mathbf{a}_1 \cdot \mathbf{x} + \mathbf{e}_1, \cdots, \mathbf{a}_q \cdot \mathbf{x} + \mathbf{e}_q) = 1] - \Pr[\mathcal{D}(\mathbf{a}_1, \cdots, \mathbf{a}_q, \mathbf{r}_1, \cdots, \mathbf{r}_q) = 1] \right|$$
$$\tag{3}$$

equals $\mathsf{negl}(n)$, and the computational Ring-LPN problem with the same n, μ and q, denoted by (n, μ, q)-Ring-LPN, is hard if for every PPT algorithm $\mathcal{D}$ we have

$$\Pr[\mathcal{D}(\mathbf{a}_1, \cdots, \mathbf{a}_q, \mathbf{a}_1 \cdot \mathbf{x} + \mathbf{e}_1, \cdots, \mathbf{a}_q \cdot \mathbf{x} + \mathbf{e}_q) = \mathbf{x}] \ = \ \mathsf{negl}(n), \tag{4}$$

where $\mathbf{a}_1, \cdots, \mathbf{a}_q, \mathbf{x}, \mathbf{r}_1, \cdots, \mathbf{r}_q \xleftarrow{\$} R$ and $\mathbf{e}_1 \cdots, \mathbf{e}_q \leftarrow \mathcal{B}_\mu^R$, '+' and '·' denote additions and multiplications over $R = \mathbb{F}_2[X]/(g)$ for certain polynomial g of degree n respectively.

The (Hermite) normal form of LPN/Ring-LPN is defined the same as the standard counterpart except that the secret is also sampled from the Bernoulli distribution. The normal form is equivalent to the standard form by Lemmas 1 and 2.

Definition 3 (Normal form of LPN/Ring-LPN). *The normal form of computational/decisional LPN (resp., Ring-LPN) problem with secret length n, noise rate $0 < \mu < 1/2$ and sample complexity q, denoted by (n, μ, q)-N-LPN/N-DLPN (resp., (n, μ, q)-N-Ring-LPN/N-Ring-DLPN), is defined same as in Definition 1 (resp., Definition 2) except that $\mathbf{x} \leftarrow \mathcal{B}_\mu^n$ (resp., $\mathbf{x} \leftarrow \mathcal{B}_\mu^R$) instead of from uniform.*

As stated in Lemmas 1 and 2, the standard form of LPN/Ring-LPN is equivalent to its normal form counterpart and thus we can use them almost interchangeably. The reduction [5] easily extends to Ring-LPN [25] although [5] appeared earlier than [25].

Lemma 1 (Standard-to-normal reduction [5]). *Let n be the security parameter, and let $\mu = \mu(n)$ and $q = \mathsf{poly}(n)$. We have the following implications:*

- *$(n, \mu, q+n)$-LPN $\rightarrow$ (n, μ, q)-N-LPN;*
- *$(n, \mu, q+n)$-DLPN $\rightarrow$ (n, μ, q)-N-DLPN;*
- *$(n, \mu, q+1)$-Ring-LPN $\rightarrow$ (n, μ, q)-N-Ring-LPN;*
- *$(n, \mu, q+1)$-Ring-DLPN $\rightarrow$ (n, μ, q)-N-Ring-DLPN.*

Lemma 2 (Normal-to-standard reduction, folklore). *Let n be the security parameter, and let $\mu = \mu(n)$ and $q = \mathsf{poly}(n)$. We have the following implications:*

- *(n, μ, q)-N-LPN $\rightarrow$ (n, μ, q)-LPN;*
- *(n, μ, q)-N-DLPN $\rightarrow$ (n, μ, q)-DLPN;*
- *(n, μ, q)-N-Ring-LPN $\rightarrow$ (n, μ, q)-Ring-LPN;*
- *(n, μ, q)-N-Ring-DLPN $\rightarrow$ (n, μ, q)-Ring-DLPN.*

Computational and decisional LPN are equivalent even for same sample complexity [6].

Lemma 3 (Computational-and-decisional equivalence for LPN [6]). *Let n be the security parameter, and let $\mu = \mu(n)$ and $q = \mathsf{poly}(n)$. We have the following implications:*

- *(n, μ, q)-LPN $\rightarrow$ (n, μ, q)-DLPN $\rightarrow$ (n, μ, q)-LPN;*
- *(n, μ, q)-N-LPN $\rightarrow$ (n, μ, q)-N-DLPN $\rightarrow$ (n, μ, q)-N-LPN.*

Lemma 4 (Decisional-to-computational reduction for Ring-LPN, folklore). *Let n be the security parameter, and let $\mu = \mu(n)$ and $q = \mathsf{poly}(n)$. We have the following implications:*

- *(n, μ, q)-Ring-DLPN $\rightarrow$ (n, μ, q)-Ring-LPN;*
- *(n, μ, q)-N-Ring-DLPN $\rightarrow$ (n, μ, q)-N-Ring-LPN.*

In summary, decisional and computational LPN, whether in standard or normal form, are polynomially equivalent. As for Ring-LPN, a computational-to-decisional reduction remains an open problem. Thus, it would be ideal to establish a connection (or even a reduction) from LPN to decisional Ring-LPN (which in turn implies computational Ring-LPN by Lemma 4). This is the problem we tackle in this paper, for which we make some non-trivial progress.

Lemma 5 (Piling-up lemma). *For $0 < \mu < 1/2$ and random variables E_1, E_2, $\cdots$, E_ℓ that are i.i.d. to $\mathcal{B}_\mu$ we have*

$$\Pr\left[\bigoplus_{i=1}^{\ell} E_i = 0\right] = \frac{1}{2}(1 + (1 - 2\mu)^\ell) = \frac{1}{2}(1 + 2^{-c_\mu \ell}),$$

where $c_\mu = \log\frac{1}{1-2\mu} = 2\mu/\ln 2 + o(\mu)$ due to $\mu = o(1)$ and $e^x = 1 + x + o(x)$ for $|x| = o(1)$.

3   Main Results

Unlike its large-modulus analogue Ring-LWE to which reductions are known from ideal lattices [38], Ring-LPN is short of formal security treatments of any sort, e.g., we do not known how the security of Ring-LPN relates to that of LPN. To fill this gap, below we argue that Ring-LPN may be as nearly secure as the LPN problem (of a slightly lower noise rate) as long as Ring-LPN can serve certain heuristic purposes (for public randomness generation). In particular, we establish the connection by a hybrid of hardness assumptions called Assumptions 1, 2 and 3 respectively. Assumption 1 is LPN (recall that standard LPN and its normal form, either decisional or computational, are all equivalent). Assumption 3 is the normal form of decisional Ring-LPN, which implies (standard or normal) computational/decisional Ring-LPN. We insert Assumption 2 as an intermediate one in between Assumptions 1 and 3, and argue the connections between adjacent ones as below.

Theorem 2 (main results, informal). *Let n be the security parameter, let $\mu = \mu(n)$, $\mu' = \mu'(n)$, $\delta = \delta(n)$ and $q = \mathsf{poly}(n)$ such that $\delta = \mu\mu'n = o(1)$. Then, we consider the following hardness assumptions as closely related (to be explained below).*

1. ***Conservative.*** *(n, μ, nq)-N-DLPN.*
2. ***De facto.*** *(n, μ, nq)-N-DLPN except that the matrix is generated with (n, μ', q)-N-Ring-DLPN. That is, it is computationally infeasible to distinguish between*

$$(\mathbf{B}, \mathbf{Bs} + \mathbf{e}_1) \quad and \quad (\mathbf{B}, \mathbf{r})$$

where $\mathbf{s} \leftarrow \mathcal{B}_\mu^n$, $\mathbf{e}_1 \leftarrow \mathcal{B}_\mu^{nq}$, $\mathbf{r} \xleftarrow{\$} \{0,1\}^{nq}$ and instead of chosen from uniform, we let $\mathbf{B} = \mathbf{A} \cdot \mathbf{X} + \mathbf{E}$ (see matrix visualization below) for $\mathbf{A} \xleftarrow{\$} R^{q\times 1}$, $\mathbf{X} \leftarrow (\mathcal{B}_{\mu'}^R)^{1\times n}$ and $\mathbf{E} \leftarrow (\mathcal{B}_{\mu'}^R)^{q\times n}$.

3. *Idealized.* (n, δ, q)-*N-Ring-DLPN.*

$$
\mathbf{A} \stackrel{\text{def}}{=} \begin{bmatrix} \text{mat}(\mathbf{a}_1) \\ \vdots \\ \text{mat}(\mathbf{a}_q) \end{bmatrix}, \quad \mathbf{X} \stackrel{\text{def}}{=} [\mathbf{x}_1, \cdots, \mathbf{x}_n], \quad \mathbf{E} \stackrel{\text{def}}{=} \begin{bmatrix} e_{11}, e_{12}, \cdots, e_{1n} \\ e_{21}, e_{22}, \cdots, e_{2n} \\ \vdots \quad \vdots \quad \ddots \quad \vdots \\ e_{q1}, e_{q2}, \cdots, e_{qn} \end{bmatrix},
$$

$$
\mathbf{B} := \mathbf{A} \cdot \mathbf{X} + \mathbf{E} = \begin{bmatrix} \mathbf{a}_1\mathbf{x}_1 + e_{11}, \mathbf{a}_1\mathbf{x}_2 + e_{12}, \cdots, \mathbf{a}_1\mathbf{x}_n + e_{1n} \\ \mathbf{a}_2\mathbf{x}_1 + e_{21}, \mathbf{a}_2\mathbf{x}_2 + e_{22}, \cdots, \mathbf{a}_2\mathbf{x}_n + e_{2n} \\ \vdots \quad\quad \vdots \quad\quad \ddots \quad\quad \vdots \\ \mathbf{a}_q\mathbf{x}_1 + e_{q1}, \mathbf{a}_q\mathbf{x}_2 + e_{q2}, \cdots, \mathbf{a}_q\mathbf{x}_n + e_{qn} \end{bmatrix} \in \{0,1\}^{qn \times n}.
$$

Alice		Bob
$\mathbf{a}_1, \cdots, \mathbf{a}_q \stackrel{\$}{\leftarrow} \{0,1\}^n$		$\mathbf{s} \leftarrow \mathcal{B}_\mu^n$
$\mathbf{X} \leftarrow \mathcal{B}_{\mu'}^{n \times n}, \mathbf{E} \leftarrow \mathcal{B}_{\mu'}^{qn \times n}$ $\xrightarrow{\quad \mathbf{B} \quad}$		$\mathbf{e}_1 \leftarrow \mathcal{B}_\mu^{qn}$
$\mathbf{B} := \mathbf{A} \cdot \mathbf{X} + \mathbf{E}$		$m \stackrel{\$}{\leftarrow} \{0,1\}$
		if $m = 1$ then $\mathbf{r} := \mathbf{Bs} + \mathbf{e}_1$
$m' \stackrel{\$}{\leftarrow} \mathcal{D}(\mathbf{A}, \mathbf{r})$ $\xleftarrow{\quad \mathbf{r} \quad}$		else if $m = 0$ then $\mathbf{r} \stackrel{\$}{\leftarrow} \{0,1\}^{qn}$

Fig. 3. A two-pass key agreement protocol that enables Alice and Bob agree on a single key bit, where the passive security is ensured by Assumption 2 and the (noticeable) correctness is guaranteed by any efficient distinguisher $\mathcal{D}$ that falsifies Assumption 3.

Assumption 1 $\rightarrow$ Assumption 2. A reduction can be established if we additionally assume (n, μ', q)-N-Ring-DLPN as $\mathbf{B} = \mathbf{A} \cdot \mathbf{X} + \mathbf{E}$ is an instance of n-fold (n, μ', q)-Ring-LPN by a hybrid argument (but then the statement becomes meaningless). However, we argue that this may not be necessary as the matrix $\mathbf{A}$ can also be a secret and in practice we may not even need pseudorandomness for public matrix. Intuitively, the operations of $\mathbf{A} \cdot \mathbf{X} + \mathbf{E}$ may already destroy the ring structures in $\mathbf{A}$ sufficiently enough in order to safely replace a random matrix in standard LPN. In fact, similar heuristic-based approaches for generating public matrix were also adopted by postquantum public-key cryptographic schemes such as Frodo [14], New Hope [4] and Kyber [12], where either a RO (instantiated by hash functions) or a PRG (with seed made public) is used to generate as much public randomness as needed without a formal proof in standard model.

Lemma 6 (Assumption 2 $\rightarrow$ Assumption 3). *Under assumption 2, i.e., the (n, μ, nq)-LPN problem is hard even when the public matrix is replaced with $\mathbf{B} = \mathbf{A} \cdot \mathbf{X} + \mathbf{E}$, then at least one of the following is true:*

1. *Assumption 3 holds, i.e., the (n, δ, q)-N-Ring-DLPN problem is hard;*
2. *IND-CPA secure PKEs are implied.*

Proof. The idea is to show that if Assumption 3 does not hold then a key agreement protocol depicted in Fig. 3 is implied (for at least infinitely many n's). Under assumption 2, i.e., $(\mathbf{B}, \mathbf{Bs} + \mathbf{e}_1)$ is computationally indistinguishable from $(\mathbf{B}, \mathbf{r} \xleftarrow{\$} \{0,1\}^{nq})$ and thus passive security of the protocol is guaranteed. Further, we observe that

$$\mathbf{Bs} + \mathbf{e}_1 = (\mathbf{AX} + \mathbf{E})\mathbf{s} + \mathbf{e}_1 = \mathbf{A}(\underbrace{\mathbf{Xs}}_{\sim \mathcal{B}_\delta^n}) + (\underbrace{\mathbf{Es} + \mathbf{e}_1}_{\sim \mathcal{B}_\delta^{qn}}),$$

where $0.99\mu n \leq |\mathbf{s}| \leq 1.01\mu n$ except with probability $2^{-\Omega(\mu n)}$ by a Chernoff bound, and conditioned on any fixed s of weight roughly μn, $\mathbf{Xs}$ and $\mathbf{Es} + \mathbf{e}_1$ independently follow $\mathcal{B}_\delta^n$ and $\mathcal{B}_\delta^{qn}$ respectively for δ being the noise rate of taking the XOR sum of μn independent samples from $\mathcal{B}_{\mu'}$, i.e., by Lemma 5 and $e^x \approx 1 + x$ for $|x| = o(1)$ we have

$$\delta \approx \frac{1}{2}(1 - 2^{-\frac{2\mu\mu'n}{\ln 2}}) = \frac{1}{2}(1 - e^{-2\mu\mu'n}) \approx \mu\mu'n.$$

In other words, $(\mathbf{A}, \mathbf{Bs} + \mathbf{e}_1)$ is a random instance of (n, δ, q)-N-Ring-DLPN. If Assumption 3 does not hold, there exist a PPT $\mathcal{D}$ and polynomial $p = \mathsf{poly}(n)$ such that the following holds for at least infinitely many n's:

$$\Pr[\mathcal{D}(\mathbf{A}, \mathbf{Bs} + \mathbf{e}_1) - 1] - \Pr[\mathcal{D}(\mathbf{A}, \mathbf{r} \xleftarrow{\$} \{0,1\}^{nq}) = 1] \geq \frac{1}{p}.$$

This implies that Alice is able to decrypt m with at least noticeable probability:

$$\Pr[m' = m] = \underbrace{\Pr[m = 1]}_{1/2} \cdot \Pr[m' = 1 | m = 1] + \underbrace{\Pr[m = 0]}_{1/2} \cdot \underbrace{\Pr[m' = 0 | m = 0]}_{1 - \Pr[m'=1|m=0]}$$

$$= 1/2 + (\Pr[m' = 1 | m = 1] - \Pr[m' = 1 | m = 0])/2$$

$$= 1/2 + \frac{\Pr[\mathcal{D}(\mathbf{A}, \mathbf{Bs} + \mathbf{e}_1) - 1] - \Pr[\mathcal{D}(\mathbf{A}, \mathbf{r} \xleftarrow{\$} \{0,1\}^{nq}) = 1]}{2}$$

$$\geq 1/2 + \frac{1}{2p}.$$

Using parallel repetition and privacy amplification, it is known [26,27] that any two-round protocol which achieves bit-agreement with noticeable correlation can be turned into a full-fledged two-round key-agreement protocol, which further implies an IND-CPA secure public-key encryption.

In summary, we did not manage to obtain a direct proof, and we believe such a reduction is beyond the reach of conventional techniques. Instead, we establish some weak (but non-trivial) connections. Informally speaking, our results state that either it is not even secure to use Ring-LPN for generating public randomness for LPN (e.g., when the ring is defined with respect to a "bad" polynomial that introduces vulnerability and results in a malformed matrix), or that (n, μ, nq)-LPN may imply either (n, δ, q)-Ring-LPN or public-key encryptions. The latter case is very unlikely, especially for certain parameter settings, e.g., for $\mu = 1/n^{2/5}$, $\mu' = 1/n^{3/4}$ (and thus $\delta \approx 1/n^{3/20}$) it is unlike to build a PKE from LPN of a noise rate $1/n^{2/5}$, which is beyond Alekhnovich's $1/\sqrt{n}$ noise regime, and therefore $(n, 1/n^{3/20}, q)$-N-Ring-DLPN is hard. In fact, even for $\mu \leq 1/\sqrt{n}$ it would be interesting to see any LPN-based PKE that does not follow the Alekhnovich's blueprint in Fig. 1, but a quite exotic one as in Fig. 3. In fact, the only LPN-based PKE beyond the $1/\sqrt{n}$ noise regime [42] has only quasi-polynomial security. This possibility can be ruled out as the PKE in Fig. 3 is roughly as secure as the underlying LPN.

4   Conclusion

We provide some non-trivial evidence that Ring-LPN might be as hard as LPN, assuming the heuristic approach for public randomness generation in practice is secure and utilizing the known infeasible noise regimes for LPN-based public-key cryptography.

Acknowledgments. Yu Yu is supported by the National Natural Science Foundation of China (Grant Nos. 61472249, 61572192) and the National Cryptography Development Fund MMJJ20170209.

Jiang Zhang is supported by the National Natural Science Foundation of China (Grant Nos. 61602046, 61602045, U1536205), and the Young Elite Scientists Sponsorship Program by CAST (2016QNRC001).

References

1. Lightweight protocols: HB and its variations, Sect. 3.1. http://www.ecrypt.eu.org/ecrypt2/documents/D.SYM.5.pdf
2. Krawczyk, H. (ed.): PKC 2014. LNCS, vol. 8383. Springer, Heidelberg (2014). https://doi.org/10.1007/978-3-642-54631-0
3. Alekhnovich, M.: More on average case vs approximation complexity. In: 44th Annual Symposium on Foundations of Computer Science, pp. 298–307. IEEE, Cambridge, October 2003
4. Alkim, E., Ducas, L., Pöppelmann, T., Schwabe, P.: Post-quantum key exchange—A new hope. In: 25th USENIX Security Symposium, USENIX Security 2016, pp. 327–343. USENIX Association, Austin (2016). https://www.usenix.org/conference/usenixsecurity16/technical-sessions/presentation/alkim
5. Applebaum, B., Cash, D., Peikert, C., Sahai, A.: Fast cryptographic primitives and circular-secure encryption based on hard learning problems. In: Halevi, S. (ed.) CRYPTO 2009. LNCS, vol. 5677, pp. 595–618. Springer, Heidelberg (2009). https://doi.org/10.1007/978-3-642-03356-8_35
6. Applebaum, B., Ishai, Y., Kushilevitz, E.: Cryptography with constant input locality. In: Menezes, A. (ed.) CRYPTO 2007. LNCS, vol. 4622, pp. 92–110. Springer, Heidelberg (2007). https://doi.org/10.1007/978-3-540-74143-5_6. http://www.eng.tau.ac.il/ bennyap/pubs/input-locality-full-revised-1.pdf

7. Becker, A., Joux, A., May, A., Meurer, A.: Decoding random binary linear codes in $2^{n/20}$: how $1 + 1 = 0$ improves information set decoding. In: Pointcheval, D., Johansson, T. (eds.) EUROCRYPT 2012. LNCS, vol. 7237, pp. 520–536. Springer, Heidelberg (2012). https://doi.org/10.1007/978-3-642-29011-4_31
8. Berlekamp, E., McEliece, R.J., van Tilborg, H.: On the inherent intractability of certain coding problems. IEEE Trans. Inf. Theory **24**(3), 384–386 (1978)
9. Bernstein, D.J., Lange, T., Peters, C.: Smaller decoding exponents: ball-collision decoding. In: Rogaway, P. (ed.) CRYPTO 2011. LNCS, vol. 6841, pp. 743–760. Springer, Heidelberg (2011). https://doi.org/10.1007/978-3-642-22792-9_42
10. Blum, A., Furst, M., Kearns, M., Lipton, R.J.: Cryptographic primitives based on hard learning problems. In: Stinson, D.R. (ed.) CRYPTO 1993. LNCS, vol. 773, pp. 278–291. Springer, Heidelberg (1994). https://doi.org/10.1007/3-540-48329-2_24
11. Blum, A., Kalai, A., Wasserman, H.: Noise-tolerant learning, the parity problem, and the statistical query model. J. ACM **50**(4), 506–519 (2003)
12. Bos, J., et al.: CRYSTALS – Kyber: a CCA-secure module-lattice-based KEM. Cryptology ePrint Archive, Report 2017/634 (2017). http://eprint.iacr.org/2017/634
13. Bos, J.W., et al.: Frodo: take off the ring! practical, quantum-secure key exchange from LWE. In: Proceedings of the 2016 ACM SIGSAC Conference on Computer and Communications Security, CCS 2016, pp. 1006–1018 (2016)
14. Bos, J.W., Costello, C., Naehrig, M., Stebila, D.: Post-quantum key exchange for the TLS protocol from the ring learning with errors problem. In: 2015 IEEE Symposium on Security and Privacy, SP 2015, pp. 553–570 (2015)
15. Cash, D., Kiltz, E., Tessaro, S.: Two-round man-in-the-middle security from LPN. In: Kushilevitz, E., Malkin, T. (eds.) TCC 2016. LNCS, vol. 9562, pp. 225–248. Springer, Heidelberg (2016). https://doi.org/10.1007/978-3-662-49096-9_10
16. Damgård, I., Park, S.: How practical is public-key encryption based on LPN and ring-LPN? Cryptology ePrint Archive, Report 2012/699 (2012). http://eprint.iacr.org/2012/699
17. David, B., Dowsley, R., Nascimento, A.C.A.: Universally composable oblivious transfer based on a variant of LPN. In: Gritzalis, D., Kiayias, A., Askoxylakis, I. (eds.) CANS 2014. LNCS, vol. 8813, pp. 143–158. Springer, Cham (2014). https://doi.org/10.1007/978-3-319-12280-9_10
18. Dodis, Y., Kiltz, E., Pietrzak, K., Wichs, D.: Message authentication, revisited. In: Pointcheval, D., Johansson, T. (eds.) EUROCRYPT 2012. LNCS, vol. 7237, pp. 355–374. Springer, Heidelberg (2012). https://doi.org/10.1007/978-3-642-29011-4_22
19. Döttling, N.: Low noise LPN: KDM secure public key encryption and sample amplification. In: Katz, J. (ed.) PKC 2015. LNCS, vol. 9020, pp. 604–626. Springer, Heidelberg (2015). https://doi.org/10.1007/978-3-662-46447-2_27
20. Döttling, N., Müller-Quade, J., Nascimento, A.C.A.: IND-CCA secure cryptography based on a variant of the LPN problem. In: Wang, X., Sako, K. (eds.) ASIACRYPT 2012. LNCS, vol. 7658, pp. 485–503. Springer, Heidelberg (2012). https://doi.org/10.1007/978-3-642-34961-4_30
21. Esser, A., Kübler, R., May, A.: LPN decoded. In: Katz, J., Shacham, H. (eds.) CRYPTO 2017. LNCS, vol. 10402, pp. 486–514. Springer, Cham (2017). https://doi.org/10.1007/978-3-319-63715-0_17
22. Feldman, V., Gopalan, P., Khot, S., Ponnuswami, A.K.: New results for learning noisy parities and halfspaces. In: 47th Symposium on Foundations of Computer Science, pp. 563–574. IEEE, Berkeley, 21–24 October 2006

23. Guo, Q., Johansson, T., Löndahl, C.: A new algorithm for solving Ring-LPN with a reducible polynomial. IEEE Trans. Inf. Theory **61**(11), 6204–6212 (2015)
24. Heyse, S.: Post quantum cryptography: implementing alternative public key schemes on embedded devices. Ph.D. thesis. Ruhr-University Bochum (2013). https://www.emsec.rub.de/media/attachments/files/2014/03/thesis-stefan-heyse.pdf
25. Heyse, S., Kiltz, E., Lyubashevsky, V., Paar, C., Pietrzak, K.: Lapin: an efficient authentication protocol based on Ring-LPN. In: Canteaut, A. (ed.) FSE 2012. LNCS, vol. 7549, pp. 346–365. Springer, Heidelberg (2012). https://doi.org/10.1007/978-3-642-34047-5_20
26. Holenstein, T.: Key agreement from weak bit agreement. In: STOC, Baltimore, Maryland, pp. 664–673, 22–24 May 2005
27. Holenstein, T.: Pseudorandom generators from one-way functions: a simple construction for any hardness. In: Halevi, S., Rabin, T. (eds.) TCC 2006. LNCS, vol. 3876, pp. 443–461. Springer, Heidelberg (2006). https://doi.org/10.1007/11681878_23
28. Hopper, N.J., Blum, M.: Secure human identification protocols. In: Boyd, C. (ed.) ASIACRYPT 2001. LNCS, vol. 2248, pp. 52–66. Springer, Heidelberg (2001). https://doi.org/10.1007/3-540-45682-1_4
29. Impagliazzo, R.: A personal view of average-case complexity. In: Structure in Complexity Theory Conference, pp. 134–147 (1995)
30. Jain, A., Krenn, S., Pietrzak, K., Tentes, A.: Commitments and efficient zero-knowledge proofs from learning parity with noise. In: Wang, X., Sako, K. (eds.) ASIACRYPT 2012. LNCS, vol. 7658, pp. 663–680. Springer, Heidelberg (2012). https://doi.org/10.1007/978-3-642-34961-4_40
31. Juels, A., Weis, S.A.: Authenticating pervasive devices with human protocols. In: Shoup, V. (ed.) CRYPTO 2005. LNCS, vol. 3621, pp. 293–308. Springer, Heidelberg (2005). https://doi.org/10.1007/11535218_18
32. Katz, J., Shin, J.S.: Parallel and concurrent security of the HB and HB$^+$ protocols. In: Vaudenay, S. (ed.) EUROCRYPT 2006. LNCS, vol. 4004, pp. 73–87. Springer, Heidelberg (2006). https://doi.org/10.1007/11761679_6
33. Kiltz, E., Pietrzak, K., Cash, D., Jain, A., Venturi, D.: Efficient authentication from hard learning problems. In: Paterson, K.G. (ed.) EUROCRYPT 2011. LNCS, vol. 6632, pp. 7–26. Springer, Heidelberg (2011). https://doi.org/10.1007/978-3-642-20465-4_3
34. Kirchner, P.: Improved generalized birthday attack. Cryptology ePrint Archive, Report 2011/377 (2011). http://eprint.iacr.org/2011/377
35. Kirchner, P., Fouque, P.-A.: An improved BKW algorithm for LWE with applications to cryptography and lattices. In: Gennaro, R., Robshaw, M. (eds.) CRYPTO 2015. LNCS, vol. 9215, pp. 43–62. Springer, Heidelberg (2015). https://doi.org/10.1007/978-3-662-47989-6_3. https://eprint.iacr.org/2015/552.pdf
36. Lyubashevsky, V.: The parity problem in the presence of noise, decoding random linear codes, and the subset sum problem. In: Chekuri, C., Jansen, K., Rolim, J.D.P., Trevisan, L. (eds.) APPROX/RANDOM -2005. LNCS, vol. 3624, pp. 378–389. Springer, Heidelberg (2005). https://doi.org/10.1007/11538462_32
37. Lyubashevsky, V., Masny, D.: Man-in-the-middle secure authentication schemes from LPN and weak PRFs. In: Canetti, R., Garay, J.A. (eds.) CRYPTO 2013. LNCS, vol. 8043, pp. 308–325. Springer, Heidelberg (2013). https://doi.org/10.1007/978-3-642-40084-1_18
38. Lyubashevsky, V., Peikert, C., Regev, O.: On ideal lattices and learning with errors over rings. J. ACM **60**(6), 43:1–43:35 (2013). https://doi.org/10.1145/2535925

39. May, A., Meurer, A., Thomae, E.: Decoding random linear codes in $\tilde{\mathcal{O}}(2^{0.054n})$. In: Lee, D.H., Wang, X. (eds.) ASIACRYPT 2011. LNCS, vol. 7073, pp. 107–124. Springer, Heidelberg (2011). https://doi.org/10.1007/978-3-642-25385-0_6

40. Pietrzak, K.: Cryptography from learning parity with noise. In: Bieliková, M., Friedrich, G., Gottlob, G., Katzenbeisser, S., Turán, G. (eds.) SOFSEM 2012. LNCS, vol. 7147, pp. 99–114. Springer, Heidelberg (2012). https://doi.org/10.1007/978-3-642-27660-6_9

41. Regev, O.: On lattices, learning with errors, random linear codes, and cryptography. In: Gabow, H.N., Fagin, R. (eds.) STOC, pp. 84–93. ACM (2005)

42. Yu, Y., Zhang, J.: Cryptography with auxiliary input and trapdoor from constant-noise LPN. In: Robshaw, M., Katz, J. (eds.) CRYPTO 2016. LNCS, vol. 9814, pp. 214–243. Springer, Heidelberg (2016). https://doi.org/10.1007/978-3-662-53018-4_9

Public Key Encryption

A CCA-Secure Collusion-Resistant Identity-Based Proxy Re-Encryption Scheme

Arinjita Paul[2(✉)], Varshika Srinivasavaradhan[1], S. Sharmila Deva Selvi[2], and C. Pandu Rangan[2]

[1] Thiagarajar College of Engineering, Madurai, India
varshikavaradhan@gmail.com
[2] Theoretical Computer Science Lab, Department of Computer Science and Engineering, Indian Institute of Technology Madras, Chennai, India
{arinjita,sharmila,prangan}@cse.iitm.ac.in

Abstract. Cloud storage enables its users to store confidential information as encrypted files in the cloud. A cloud user (say Alice) can share her encrypted files with another user (say Bob) by availing proxy re-encryption services of the cloud. Proxy Re-Encryption (PRE) is a cryptographic primitive that allows transformation of ciphertexts from Alice to Bob via a semi-trusted proxy, who should not learn anything about the shared message. Typically, the re-encryption rights are enabled only for a bounded, fixed time and malicious parties may want to decrypt or learn messages encrypted for Alice, even beyond that time. The basic security notion of PRE assumes the proxy (cloud) is semi-trusted, which is seemingly insufficient in practical applications. The proxy may want to collude with Bob to obtain the private keys of Alice for later use. Such an attack is called *collusion attack,* allowing colluders to illegally access all encrypted information of Alice in the cloud. Hence, achieving collusion resistance is indispensable to real-world scenarios. Realizing collusion-resistant PRE has been an interesting problem in the ID-based setting. To this end, several attempts have been made to construct a collusion-resistant IB-PRE scheme and we discuss their properties and weaknesses in this paper. We also present a new collusion-resistant IB-PRE scheme that meets the adaptive CCA security under the decisional bilinear Diffie-Hellman hardness assumption in the random oracle model.

Keywords: Identity-based proxy re-encryption · Collusion-resistance Random oracle · Unidirectional · CCA-secure

1 Introduction

Cloud security is imperative in recent years owing to the popularity of cloud data storage and transmission. In order to preserve data privacy, users rely on standard encryption mechanisms that encrypt data using their public keys prior to

© Springer Nature Switzerland AG 2018
J. Baek et al. (Eds.): ProvSec 2018, LNCS 11192, pp. 111–128, 2018.
https://doi.org/10.1007/978-3-030-01446-9_7

cloud storage. Enabling secure data sharing in the cloud calls for fast and secure re-encryption techniques for managing encrypted file systems. Blaze, Bleumer and Strauss [3] introduced the concept of Proxy Re-encryption (PRE) towards an efficient solution that offers delegation of decryption rights without compromising privacy. PRE allows a semi-trusted third party termed proxy to securely divert encrypted files of user A (delegator) to user B (delegatee) without revealing any information about the underlying files to the proxy. In the cloud scenario, the file owner shares a re-encryption key with the proxy (designated server in the cloud) who is assumed semi-trusted. PRE systems are classified as unidirectional and bidirectional based on the direction of delegation. They are also classified as single-hop and multi-hop based on the number of re-encryptions permitted. In this work, we focus on unidirectional and single-hop PRE schemes.

In a single-hop environment, a user A uses the cloud to store encrypted information and further sets the cloud as a proxy to allow re-encryption, thereby maintaining two kinds of encrypted data. The first kind called *first-level ciphertext* is the encrypted data that A would like to share with others. These kinds of data are subject to re-encryption and the cloud performs the conversion as a service upon receiving the re-encryption key (re-key) from user A, re-encrypting towards user B. The second kind called *second-level ciphertext*, is the encrypted data re-encrypted towards A by a user C. Note that the second-level ciphertexts of A cannot be re-encrypted again with the re-key of A, as the PRE scheme is single hop. The re-key is created as a function of the private key of A, the public key of B and possibly some keys associated with the cloud. Hence, it is natural to ask if B and the cloud can collude and acquire the private key of A. To motivate such a collusion, we observe the following two scenarios. Firstly, a malicious user B and a colluding cloud with a re-key may want to obtain the hidden messages in the second-level ciphertexts of A, which can be realized only using the private key of A. Again, the re-encryption rights are enabled for a bounded, fixed period and malicious parties may want to decrypt ciphertexts of A even beyond that period. Such an attack where a colluding cloud and a delegatee B obtains the private key of A is termed *collusion attack*. Preventing collusion attack is one of the major important problems in the context of cloud storage and computing. When the private key of A is obtained, the cloud and user B can cause total damage to user A in every possible way. Such a disclosure could be misused to the detriment of the delegator A such as unauthorized sharing of his confidential files, financial loss and identity theft. This marks collusion-resistance as a crucial property in proxy re-encryption; it achieves re-encryption by placing minimal trust on the proxy. Besides cloud storage, PRE can be applied to secure encrypted electronic mail forwarding, distributed system storage, outsourced filtering of encrypted spam, DRM of apple iTunes among others [1,2,15].

Identity-based PRE was introduced by Green and Ateniese [8] as a solution to the certificate management problem in the PKI based PRE schemes. Of all the properties offered by identity-based proxy re-encryption (IB-PRE), collusion resistance is the most desirable as it preserves the private key of the delegator even during an event of collusion between the proxy and delegatees. This would enable re-encryption in several real-time scenarios, such as secure sharing of files in a cloud with an untrusted server. In this paper, we study IB-PRE in the light of collusion resistance and propose a CCA-secure IB-PRE scheme that achieves the same based on Decisional Bilinear Diffie Hellman (DBDH) assumption and its variants in the random oracle model.

1.1   Related Works and Contribution

In ACNS 2007, Green and Ateniese [8] presented the first two constructions of IB-PRE, one being CPA-secure and the other being CCA-secure using bilinear pairing based on the Decisional Bilinear Diffie-Hellman assumption in the random oracle model. Their scheme is unidirectional, non-interactive, permits multiple re-encryptions but does not offer security against collusion attacks.

In this paper, we address the open problem proposed in [10] to design a non-interactive collusion-resistant IB-PRE scheme. Although several attempts have been made to achieve collusion-resistance in the identity based setting, all existing results are shown to either have some weaknesses or be insecure. In the collusion-resistant IB-PRE scheme given by Wang et al. [18] in the random oracle model, the re-keys are constructed using the master secret key which involves the PKG, making the scheme highly infeasible. Since the PKG is responsible for the generation of private keys, achieving delegation with the involvement of the PKG is trivial but undesirable. In [13], a generic construction for a collusion resistant IB-PRE has been given based on threshold cryptosystem and key-management in IBE. However, their encryption algorithm involves splitting the private keys of the delegator into two components and publishing two public keys corresponding to the private keys. This is equivalent to the PKI setting, as the public keys require certification. Wang *et al.* [19] proposed a collusion-resistant IB-PRE scheme which is CPA-secure for the first-level ciphertext and CCA-secure for the second level ciphertext in the standard model based on the eDBDH assumption. In 2013, Han *et al.* [9] presented a CPA secure collusion-resistant IB-PRE scheme in the standard model based on the DBDH assumption. In 2015, Qiu et al. [12] proposed a collusion-resistant IB-PRE scheme in the standard model. However, in 2016, Zhang et al. [20] showed that the scheme presented in [12] is vulnerable to collusion attacks. They also proposed a new identity-based proxy re-encryption scheme withstanding collusion attack and chosen ciphertext attack in the standard model. Note that both the collusion-resistant PRE schemes [9, 20] make use of the information from the ciphertext components in the process of re-key generation. This clearly forces the user to create a separate delegation key for every ciphertext being translated. In the standard definition of PRE, a re-encryption key is generated only once between two parties (delegator A and delegatee B), irrespective of the number of ciphertexts being translated. But in [9, 20], for every delegation between A and B, A needs to generate a new re-encryption key being delegated from A to B. This enforces the fact that user A needs to be online along with the proxy for converting every ciphertext towards user B. In fact, this is equivalent to the *decrypt-and-then-encrypt* functionality.

Note that making use of the knowledge of information from the ciphertext to generate re-keys is simple and trivial but makes the scheme highly impractical.

In our work, we address the open problem on collusion-resistance in the ID-based setting, affirmatively adhering to the standard definition of PRE. Ever since the problem is proposed, it has remained as a challenging problem. In the recent past, certain attempts have been made but most of them have either major drawbacks or serious flaws as discussed. A summary of IB-PRE schemes is provided in Table 1 in the context of collusion-resistance, alongside our scheme. Our collusion-resistant IB-PRE scheme is based on the IBE scheme of Boneh and Franklin [4] and BLS short signature [5] and satisfies adaptive CCA security based on standard assumptions called the Decisional Diffie-Hellman assumption (DBDH) and its variant (m-DBDH). The proof of CCA security is considered in the random oracle model. The proof of collusion resistance of our scheme is based on modified Computational Diffie Hellman assumption(m-CDH).

Table 1. A summary of IB-PRE schemes in the context of collusion-resistance.

Scheme	Security	Proof model	Delegation process involves	Underlying assumption	Remarks
Wang et al. [18]	CCA	RO	PKG, Delegator	DBDH	PKG involvement for collusion-resistance makes scheme infeasible
Wang et al. [19]	CPA*	Standard	Delegator	eDBDH	Questionable or unproven claims*
Han et al. [9]	CPA	Standard	Ciphertext Components and Delegator	DBDH	Re-key generation involves delegator and ciphertext components for collusion-resistance, standard PRE definition not satisfied
Qiu et al. [12]	CCA	Standard	Delegator	DBDH	Collusion attack reported in [20]
Zhang et al. [20]	CCA	Standard	Ciphertext Components and Delegator	DBDH	Re-key generation involves delegator and ciphertext components for collusion-resistance, standard PRE definition not satisfied
Our scheme	CCA	RO	Delegator	DBDH	Collusion-resistant, adheres to standard PRE definition

*The proof of security in [19] is questionable as simulating the challenge ciphertext solves the discrete log problem, discussed in details in Sect. 5.

2   Preliminaries

2.1   Bilinear Maps

A map $\hat{e} : \mathbb{G}_1 \times \mathbb{G}_1 \to \mathbb{G}_T$ is a bilinear map if it satisfies the following conditions:

1. $\mathbb{G}_1$, $\mathbb{G}_T$ are of the same prime order q.
2. For all a, $b \in \mathbb{Z}_q^*$, $g \in \mathbb{G}_1$, $\hat{e}(g^a, g^b) = \hat{e}(g, g)^{ab}$.
3. The map is non-degenerate, i.e., if $\mathbb{G}_1 = \langle g \rangle$, then $\mathbb{G}_T = \langle \hat{e}(g, g) \rangle$.
4. $\hat{e}$ is efficiently computable.

2.2   Hardness Assumption

We state the computational hardness assumptions that we use to prove the security of our scheme. Let $\mathbb{G}_1$, $\mathbb{G}_T$ be cyclic groups with prime order q and $\hat{e} : \mathbb{G}_1 \times \mathbb{G}_1 \to \mathbb{G}_T$ be an admissible bilinear map.

m-Computational Diffie-Hellman (m-CDH) Assumption [16]: The modified Computational Diffie-Hellman (m-CDH) assumption in $\mathbb{G}_1$ is, given a tuple of elements $(g, g^a, g^b, g^{\frac{1}{b}}, g^{\frac{a}{b}}) \in \mathbb{G}_1{}^5$, where $a, b \in_R \mathbb{Z}_q^*$, there exists no PPT adversary which can compute g^{ab} in $\mathbb{G}_1$, with a non-negligible advantage.

Decisional Bilinear Diffie-Hellman (DBDH) Assumption: The Decisional Bilinear Diffie-Hellman (DBDH) assumption in $\mathbb{G}_1$, $\mathbb{G}_T$ is, given a tuple of elements $(g, g^a, g^b, g^c, T) \in \mathbb{G}_1{}^4 \times \mathbb{G}_T$, where $a, b, c \in_R \mathbb{Z}_q^*$, there exists no PPT adversary which can decide whether $T = \hat{e}(g, g)^{abc}$ or T is a random element in $\mathbb{G}_T$, with a non-negligible advantage.

m-Decisional Bilinear Diffie-Hellman (m-DBDH) Assumption [17]: The modified-Decisional Bilinear Diffie-Hellman (m-DBDH) assumption in $\mathbb{G}_1$, $\mathbb{G}_T$ is, given a tuple of elements $(g, g^a, g^{\frac{1}{a}}, g^{\frac{1}{b}}, g^{\frac{a}{b}}, g^b, g^c, T) \in \mathbb{G}_1{}^7 \times \mathbb{G}_T$, where $a, b, c \in_R \mathbb{Z}_q^*$, there exists no PPT adversary which can decide whether $T = \hat{e}(g, g)^{abc}$ or T is a random element in $\mathbb{G}_T$, with a non-negligible advantage.

3   Definition and Security Model

3.1   Definition

In this section, we describe the syntactical definition of our single-hop unidirectional IB-PRE scheme. An IB-PRE scheme consists of the following algorithms.

- **Setup**(λ): The PKG runs this probabilistic algorithm that takes a security parameter λ as input and outputs the public parameters *params*, which is shared with all the users, and the master secret key *msk* is kept private.
- **KeyGen**(msk, id_i, $params$): This is a probabilistic algorithm run by the PKG which on input of the master secret key *msk* and a user identity $id_i \in \{0,1\}^*$, outputs the private key sk_{id_i} of the user identity id_i, which is securely communicated to the user.
- **ReKeyGen**(sk_{id_i}, id_j, $params$): The delegator runs this probabilistic algorithm and takes as input its private key sk_{id_i} and the public key of the delegatee id_j to generate a re-encryption key $RK_{i \to j}$ from id_i to id_j. The delegator then sends the re-encryption key to the proxy via a secure channel.
- **Encrypt**(m, id_i, $params$): The sender runs the encryption algorithm which takes as input a message $m \in \mathcal{M}$ and an identity id_i under which m is encrypted. It outputs the ciphertext $\mathbb{C}$, which is termed as first-level ciphertext.
- **Decrypt** ($\mathbb{C}$, sk_{id_i}, $params$): The decryption algorithm is a deterministic algorithm run by the delegator. On input of a first-level ciphertext $\mathbb{C}$ and the delegator's private key sk_{id_i}, the algorithm outputs message $m \in \mathcal{M}$ or the error message *"INVALID CIPHERTEXT"*.

- **Re-Encrypt**($\mathbb{C}$, $RK_{i \to j}$, *params*): This is a probabilistic algorithm run by the proxy which takes as input the first-level ciphertext $\mathbb{C}$ and the re-encryption key $RK_{i \to j}$ and outputs the re-encrypted ciphertext $\mathbb{D}$, termed as second-level ciphertext.
- **Re-Decrypt**($\mathbb{D}$, sk_{id_j}, *params*): This is a deterministic algorithm run by the delegatee. On input of the second-level ciphertext $\mathbb{D}$ and the delegatee's private key sk_{id_j}, the algorithm outputs the original message $m \in \mathcal{M}$ or the error message *"INVALID CIPHERTEXT"*.

The consistency of an IB-PRE scheme for any given public parameters *params* and a key pair (id_i, sk_{id_i}), (id_j, sk_{id_j}) is defined as follows:

1. Consistency between encryption and decryption:

$$Decrypt(Encrypt(m, id_i, params), sk_{id_i}, params) = m, \forall m \in \mathcal{M}.$$

2. Consistency between re-encryption and re-decryption:

$$Re - Decrypt(\mathbb{D}, sk_{id_j}, params) = m, \forall m \in \mathcal{M},$$

where $\mathbb{D} \leftarrow Re\text{-}Encrypt(\mathbb{C}, \mathbb{RK}_{i \to j}, params)$, $\mathbb{C} \leftarrow Encrypt(m, id_i, params)$.

3.2   Security Model

In this subsection, we define the security notions of our IB-PRE scheme. In IB-PRE, there are two levels of ciphertexts, the first-level and the second-level ciphertext, and it is crucial to prove the security for both levels [11]. We consider the CK model wherein the adversary $\mathcal{A}$ can adaptively choose public keys for malicious users. $\mathcal{A}$ adaptively queries the oracles listed below, and the challenger $\mathcal{C}$ responds to the queries and simulates an environment running IB-PRE for $\mathcal{A}$.

- **Private Key Extraction Oracle**($\mathcal{O}_{KE}(id_i)$): Given as input an identity id_i, return the corresponding private key sk_{id_i}.
- **Re-Key Generation Oracle**($\mathcal{O}_{RK}(id_i, id_j)$): Given as input (id_i, id_j), return the re-encryption key $RK_{i \to j}$.
- **Re-Encryption Oracle**($\mathcal{O}_{RE}(id_i, id_j, \mathbb{C})$): Given as inputs two identities (id_i, id_j) and a first-level ciphertext $\mathbb{C}$, return the second level ciphertext $\mathbb{D}$.
- **Decryption Oracle**($\mathcal{O}_{DEC}(id_i, \mathbb{C})$): Given as input an identity id_i and a first level ciphertext $\mathbb{C}$ encrypted under id_i, return the message m or *"INVALID CIPHERTEXT"* if the ciphertext is invalid.
- **Re-Decryption Oracle**($\mathcal{O}_{REDEC}(id_j, \mathbb{D})$): Given as input an identity id_j and a second level ciphertext $\mathbb{D}$ re-encrypted under id_j, return the message m or *"INVALID CIPHERTEXT"* if the ciphertext is invalid.

First Level Ciphertext Security: In the first level ciphertext security, an adversary $\mathcal{A}$ is challenged with a first level ciphertext $\mathbb{C}$ encrypted under the target identity id^*. Following is the description of the game template for Chosen Ciphertext Security:

1. **Setup:** The challenger $\mathcal{C}$ takes a security parameter λ and executes the *Setup* algorithm to get the system parameters *params* and returns it to $\mathcal{A}$.
2. **Phase 1:** $\mathcal{A}$ adaptively queries the Private Key Extraction, Re-Key Generation, Re-Encryption, Decryption and Re-Decryption oracles and $\mathcal{C}$ responds to the queries.
3. **Challenge:** When $\mathcal{A}$ decides that Phase 1 is over, it outputs two equal-length plaintexts m_0, $m_1 \in \mathcal{M}$ and a target identity id^* with the following adversarial constraints:
   - The private key of the target identity id^* must not be queried previously.
   - $\mathcal{A}$ must not have queried $\mathcal{O}_{RK}(id^*, d_j)$, such that the private key of id_j is already queried upon.

   On receiving $\{m_0, m_1\}$, $\mathcal{C}$ obtains a random bit $\psi \in \{0, 1\}$ and computes a challenge ciphertext $\mathbb{C}^* = Encrypt(m_\psi, id^*, params)$ and returns $\mathbb{C}^*$ to $\mathcal{A}$.
4. **Phase 2:** $\mathcal{A}$ issues queries as in Phase 1 with the following constraints.
   - The Re-Key Generation query $\mathcal{O}_{RK}(id, id_j)$ is only allowed if the private key of id_j has not been queried previously.
   - If $\mathcal{A}$ issues a Re-Encryption query $\mathcal{O}_{RE}(id_i, id_j, \mathbb{C})$ such that the private key of id_j has been queried upon, $(id_i, \mathbb{C})$ cannot be a challenge derivative (defined next) of $(id^*, \mathbb{C}^*)$.
   - $\mathcal{A}$ can issue a Decryption query $\mathcal{O}_{DEC}(id_i, \mathbb{C})$ or a Re-Decryption query $\mathcal{O}_{REDEC}(id_j, \mathbb{D})$ only if $(id_i, \mathbb{C})$ or $(id_j, \mathbb{D})$ is not a *derivative* of $(id^*, \mathbb{C}^*)$.

Definition 1 (Challenge Derivative). *The challenge derivatives of $(id_i, \mathbb{C})$ in the CCA setting as adopted from [7] are as shown below:*

- *Reflexitivity: $(id_i, \mathbb{C})$ is a challenge derivative of its own.*
- *Derivative by re-encryption: if $\mathbb{D} \leftarrow \mathcal{O}_{RE}(id_i, id_j, \mathbb{C})$, then $(id_j, \mathbb{D})$ is a challenge derivative of $(id_i, \mathbb{C})$.*
- *Derivative by re-key: if $\mathbb{D} \leftarrow Re\text{-}Encrypt(\mathbb{C}, RK_{i \rightarrow j}, params)$, where the re-key $RK_{i \rightarrow j} \leftarrow \mathcal{O}_{RK}(ID_i, ID_j)$, then $(id_j, \mathbb{D})$ is a challenge derivative of $(id_i, \mathbb{C})$.*

5. **Guess:** Finally, $\mathcal{A}$ outputs a guess $\psi' \in \{0, 1\}$.

The advantage of the adversary $\mathcal{A}$ in winning the game is defined as:

$$Adv_{A,first}^{IND-IBPRE-CCA} = 2|Pr[\psi' = \psi] - \frac{1}{2}|$$

where the probability is taken over the coin tosses of the challenger $\mathcal{C}$ and adversary $\mathcal{A}$. The scheme is $IND\text{-}IBPRE\text{-}CCA$ secure for the first level ciphertext against any t-time adversary $\mathcal{A}$ making q_{KE} queries to key extraction oracle, q_{RK} queries to the re-key generation oracle, q_{RE} queries to re-encryption oracle, q_{DEC} queries to decryption oracle, q_{REDEC} queries to re-decryption oracle, if the advantage of $\mathcal{A}$ is: $Adv_{A,first}^{IND-IBPRE-CCA} \leq \epsilon$.

Second Level Ciphertext Security: In the second-level ciphertext security, the adversary $\mathcal{A}$ is challenged with a second level ciphertext $\mathbb{D}^*$ which is a re-encryption of the ciphertext $\mathbb{C}$ under the delegator identity id_i towards target identity id^*, re-encrypted using the re-key $RK_{i \to *}$. $\mathcal{A}$ does not have access to the corresponding first level ciphertext $\mathbb{C}$. The security for the second level ciphertext is unaffected whether the delegator identity id_i is a corrupt user or not. Note that, since a second-level ciphertext cannot be further re-encrypted, $\mathcal{A}$ is allowed to obtain all the re-encryption keys in our security model. This also justifies the removal of the re-encryption oracle from the security model. Following is the description of the game template for Chosen Ciphertext Security:

1. **Setup:** The challenger $\mathcal{C}$ takes a security parameter λ and executes the *Setup* algorithm to get the system parameters *params* and return it to $\mathcal{A}$.
2. **Phase 1:** $\mathcal{A}$ adaptively queries to Private Key Extraction, Re-Key Generation, Decryption and Re-Decryption oracles and $\mathcal{C}$ responds to the queries.
3. **Challenge:** When $\mathcal{A}$ decides that Phase 1 is over, it outputs two equal-length plaintexts $m_0, m_1 \in \mathcal{M}$, a delegator identity id_i and an honest target delegatee identity id^* with the following adversarial constraints:
   - The adversary $\mathcal{A}$ must not have queried $\mathcal{O}_{KE}(id^*)$ at any point in time.
   - The $\mathcal{A}$ must not have queried $\mathcal{O}_{RK}(id_i, id^*)$.
   - $\mathcal{A}$ cannot choose id_i as the delegator if it has already obtained $RK_{i \to *}$.
   On receiving $\{m_0, m_1\}$, $\mathcal{C}$ obtains a random bit $\psi \in \{0, 1\}$ and computes a challenge ciphertext $\mathbb{D}^* = Re\text{-}Encrypt(Encrypt(m_\psi, id_i, params), RK_{i \to *}, params)$ and returns $\mathbb{D}^*$ to $\mathcal{A}$.
4. **Phase 2:** $\mathcal{A}$ issues queries as in Phase 1 with the following constraints:
   - $\mathcal{A}$ cannot issue a Re-Decryption query $\mathcal{O}_{DEC}(id^*, \mathbb{D}^*)$.
   - If sk_{id_i} has been queried previously, $\mathcal{A}$ cannot query $RK_{i \to *}$ to $\mathcal{C}$.
5. **Guess:** Finally, $\mathcal{A}$ outputs a guess $\psi' \in \{0, 1\}$.

The advantage of the adversary $\mathcal{A}$ in winning the game is defined as:

$$Adv_{A,second}^{IND-IBPRE-CCA} = 2|Pr[\psi' = \psi] - \frac{1}{2}|$$

where the probability is over the coin tosses of the challenger $\mathcal{C}$ and adversary $\mathcal{A}$. The scheme is $IND\text{-}IBPRE\text{-}CCA$ secure for the second level ciphertext against a t-time adversary $\mathcal{A}$ making q_{KE} queries to key extraction oracle, q_{RK} queries to the re-key generation oracle, q_{DEC} queries to decryption oracle, q_{REDEC} queries to re-decryption oracle, if the advantage of $\mathcal{A}$ is: $Adv_{A,second}^{IND-IBPRE-CCA} \leq \epsilon$.

Collusion Resistance: Collusion-resistance or delegator secret key (DSK) security prevents a colluding proxy and delegatee to recover the delegator's private key in full [7]. Following is the game template of the security model for collusion resistance as in [6].

- **Setup:** $\mathcal{C}$ takes as input the security parameter λ and runs the *Setup* algorithm to generate and return the system parameters *params* to $\mathcal{A}$.

- **Queries:** $\mathcal{A}$ issues the following queries adaptively to $\mathcal{C}$:
  - Private-Key Extraction Oracle $\mathcal{O}_{KE}(id_i)$: $\mathcal{C}$ runs the KeyGen(msk, id_i, $params$) algorithm to generate the private key sk_{id_i} of identity id_i and returns sk_{id_i} to $\mathcal{A}$.
  - Re-encryption Key Generation Oracle $\mathcal{O}_{RK}(id_i, id_j)$: $\mathcal{C}$ generates and returns the re-encryption key $RK_{i \to j}$ from identity id_i to id_j.
- **Output:** $\mathcal{A}$ returns sk_{i^*} as the private key of an identity id_i^*. $\mathcal{A}$ wins the game if sk_i^* is a valid private key of an identity id_i^* whose private key has not been queried for.

The advantage of $\mathcal{A}$ in attacking the collusion-resistance or delegator secret security of the scheme is defined as $Adv_{\mathcal{A}}^{DSK} = Pr[\mathcal{A}\ wins]$, where the probability is over the random coin tosses of the challenger $\mathcal{C}$ and adversary $\mathcal{A}$. A scheme is defined as (t, ϵ)-DSK secure against a t-time adversary $\mathcal{A}$ making at most q_{KE} key extraction queries and q_{RK} re-encryption key generation queries if the advantage of $\mathcal{A}$ is: $Adv_{\mathcal{A}}^{DSK} \leq \epsilon$.

4   Our Proposed Collusion Resistant IB-PRE Scheme

4.1   Overview of Construction

The starting points of our contruction are the IB-PRE scheme of Green and Ateniese [8] which is based on Boneh and Franklin's IBE scheme [4] and BLS short signature [5]. In the system by Green and Ateniese, the PKG chooses a random element $s \leftarrow \mathbb{Z}_q^*$ as the master secret key and sets the private key for an identity id_i as $H_1(id_i)^s$. Note that the hash functions are used as defined in the IB-PRE scheme in [8]. The original ciphertext of a message $m \in \{0,1\}^n$ is computed by choosing a random element $\sigma \leftarrow \mathbb{G}_T$ and computing $r = H_4(\sigma, m)$. Then the ciphertext components $\mathbb{C}_1 = g^r$, $\mathbb{C}_2 = \sigma \cdot \hat{e}(g^s, H_1(id_i)^r)$ and $\mathbb{C}_3 = m \oplus H_5(\sigma)$ are computed. $S = H_3(id_i || \mathbb{C}_1 || \mathbb{C}_2 || \mathbb{C}_3)^r$ is computed as a BLS signature used during re-encryption/decryption to confirm well-formedness of the ciphertext. Finally $\mathbb{C} = (\mathbb{C}_1, \mathbb{C}_2, \mathbb{C}_3, S)$ is output as the ciphertext of message m. The re-key is generated by picking a random element $N \leftarrow \{0,1\}^n$ and computing $K = \hat{e}(sk_{id_i}, H_1(id_j))$. The re-key $RK_{i \to j} = \langle RK_{i \to j}^1, RK_{i \to j}^2 \rangle = \langle N, H_2(K, id_i, id_j, N) \cdot sk_{id_i} \rangle$ is computed. Now, if the proxy and delegatee collude, $K = \hat{e}(H_1(id_i), sk_{id_j})$ is computed and the private key of the delegator can be recovered by computing $sk_{id_i} = \frac{RK_{i \to j}^2}{H_2(K, id_i, id_j, N)}$.

In order to extend the system proposed by Green and Ateniese to the collusion-resistant setting, we introduce another generator h and two group elements $g_1 = g^\delta$, $h_1 = h^\delta$ to the public parameters. In our attempt, the PKG chooses $s \leftarrow \mathbb{Z}_q^*$ as the master secret key. The re-key is generated by picking $s_1, s_2 \leftarrow \mathbb{Z}_q^*$ and computing $x_{ij} = H_5(\hat{e}(P_{pub_1}, H_1(id_j)_1^s), id_i, id_j)$, where $x_{ij} \in \mathbb{Z}_q^*$ and $P_{pub_1} = g_1^s$. The re-key is computed as $RK_{i \to j} = \langle \mathrm{RK}_{i \to j}^1, \mathrm{RK}_{i \to j}^2, \mathrm{RK}_{i \to j}^3 \rangle = \langle (sk_{id_i})^{-1} \cdot h^{x_{ij} s_2}, h_1^{s_2}, g^{s_1} \rangle$. We construct our re-key in such a way that the private key of the delegator ($sk_{id_i} \in \mathbb{G}_1$) is blinded with a random salt and can only be removed in the target group G_T during decryption of the re-encrypted cipher-texts. The private key sk_{id_i} of delegator can be retrieved from the re-key component $\text{RK}_{i \to j}^1$ only by users with the knowledge of both sk_{id_j} (the delegatee's secret key) and random element s_2 (chosen by delegator). This clearly makes it infeasible to retrieve the private key sk_{id_i} in G_1 from the re-key, which prevents the colluders to recover the delegator's private key and provides collusion-resistance.

4.2   Construction

In this subsection, we present the construction of our collusion-resistant IB-PRE scheme followed by its correctness and security proof. Our IB-PRE scheme consists of the following algorithms:

1. **Setup**(λ): The PKG takes the security parameter λ as input. Let G_1, G_T be groups of prime order q and let g, h be the generators of G_1. The PKG picks $\delta \leftarrow \mathbb{Z}_q^*$ and computes $g_1 = g^\delta$ and $h_1 = h^\delta$. Let $\hat{e} : G_1 \times G_1 \to G_T$ be an admissible bilinear map.

   Five cryptographic hash functions are chosen by PKG as below, which are modelled as random oracles in our security proof:

   $$H_1 : \{0,1\}^* \to G_1$$
   $$H_2 : G_T \times \{0,1\}^n \to \mathbb{Z}_q^*$$
   $$H_3 : G_T \to \{0,1\}^n$$
   $$H_4 : \{0,1\}^* \to G_1$$
   $$H_5 : G_T \times \{0,1\}^* \to \mathbb{Z}_q^*$$

   The PKG selects $s \xleftarrow{\$} \mathbb{Z}_q^*$, computes $P_{pub_1} = g^s$, $P_{pub_2} = g_1^s$ and the master secret key $msk = s$. The message space $\mathcal{M}$ is $\{0,1\}^n$. PKG returns the public parameters $params = (G_1, G_T, g, h, g_1, h_1, P_{pub_1}, P_{pub_2}, \hat{e}, H_1, H_2, H_3, H_4, H_5, n)$.

2. **KeyGen**($msk, id_i, params$): For an identity $id_i \in \{0,1\}^*$, the PKG computes the private key $sk_{id_i} = H_1(id_i)^s$ and sends sk_{id_i} to user id_i in a secure way.

3. **ReKeyGen**($sk_{id_i}, id_j, params$): The user with identity id_i generates a re-encryption key from id_i to user id_j as below:
   - Select $s_1, s_2 \xleftarrow{\$} \mathbb{Z}_q^*$.
   - Compute $x_{ij} = H_5(\hat{e}(P_{pub_1}, H_1(id_j)^{s_1}), id_i, id_j) \in \mathbb{Z}_q^*$.
   - Compute $\text{RK}_{i \to j}^1 = (sk_{id_i})^{-1} \cdot h^{x_{ij} s_2} = H_1(id_i)^{-s} \cdot h^{x_{ij} s_2} \in G_1$.
   - Compute $\text{RK}_{i \to j}^2 = h_1{}^{s_2} \in G_1$.
   - Compute $\text{RK}_{i \to j}^3 = g^{s_1} \in G_1$.

   The delegator id_i sends the re-encryption key $RK_{i \to j} = (RK_{i \to j}^1, RK_{i \to j}^2, RK_{i \to j}^3)$ to the proxy via a secure channel.

4. **Encrypt**($m, id_i, params$): To encrypt the message $m \in \mathcal{M}$ for the user with identity id_i, the sender chooses $\sigma \xleftarrow{\$} G_T$ and computes $r = H_2(\sigma, m)$. The sender then computes the ciphertext $\mathbb{C}$ as below:

- Compute $\mathbb{C}_1 = g^r \in \mathbb{G}_1$.
- Compute $\mathbb{C}_2 = g_1^\tau \in \mathbb{G}_1$.
- Compute $\mathbb{C}_3 = \sigma \cdot \hat{e}(P_{pub_2}, H_1(id_i)^r) \in \mathbb{G}_T$.
- Compute $\mathbb{C}_4 = m \oplus H_3(\sigma) \in \{0,1\}^n$.
- Compute $\mathbb{C}_5 = H_4(id_i\|\mathbb{C}_1\|\mathbb{C}_2\|\mathbb{C}_3\|\mathbb{C}_4)^r \in \mathbb{G}_1$.

The sender returns the first-level ciphertext $\mathbb{C} = (\mathbb{C}_1, \mathbb{C}_2, \mathbb{C}_3, \mathbb{C}_4, \mathbb{C}_5)$.

5. **Decrypt**($\mathbb{C}$, sk_{id_i}, $params$): With input a first level ciphertext $\mathbb{C} = \langle\mathbb{C}_1, \mathbb{C}_2, \mathbb{C}_3, \mathbb{C}_4, \mathbb{C}_5\rangle$, user id_i with his private key sk_{id_i} decrypts as below:
   - Check if both the following conditions hold:

$$\hat{e}(\mathbb{C}_1, g_1) \stackrel{?}{=} \hat{e}(g, \mathbb{C}_2) \tag{1}$$

$$\hat{e}(\mathbb{C}_1, H_4(id_i\|\mathbb{C}_1\|\mathbb{C}_2\|\mathbb{C}_3\|\mathbb{C}_4)) \stackrel{?}{=} \hat{e}(g, \mathbb{C}_5) \tag{2}$$

   If either of the conditions fail, it returns *"INVALID CIPHERTEXT"*.
   - Otherwise, compute σ as below:

$$\sigma = \frac{\mathbb{C}_3}{\hat{e}(\mathbb{C}_2, sk_{id_i})}. \tag{3}$$

   - Compute the message:

$$m = \mathbb{C}_4 \oplus H_3(\sigma), \tag{4}$$

   - Check the following condition:

$$\mathbb{C}_2 \stackrel{?}{=} g_1^{H_2(\sigma, m)}. \tag{5}$$

   If satisfied, it outputs m, else outputs *"INVALID CIPHERTEXT"*.

6. **Re-Encrypt**($\mathbb{C}$, $\mathbb{RK}_{i \to j}$, $params$): The proxy re-encrypts the first-level ciphertext $\mathbb{C}$ to second-level ciphertext $\mathbb{D}$ as below.
   - Check if the following condition holds:

$$\hat{e}(C_1, H_4(id_i\|C_1\|C_2\|C_3\|C_4)) \stackrel{?}{=} \hat{e}(g, C_5). \tag{6}$$

   - If the check fails, return *"INVALID CIPHERTEXT"*.
   - Set $\mathbb{D}_1 = \mathbb{C}_1 = g^r \in \mathbb{G}_1$
   - Set $\mathbb{D}_2 = RK_{i \to j}^3 = g^{s_1} \in \mathbb{G}_1$,
   - Compute $\mathbb{D}_3 = \mathbb{C}_3.\hat{e}(\mathbb{C}_2, RK_{i \to j}^1) = \sigma.\hat{e}(g_1^\tau, h^{x_{ij} s_2}) \in \mathbb{G}_T$,
   - Set $\mathbb{D}_4 = \mathbb{C}_4 = m \oplus H_3(\sigma) \in \{0,1\}^n$,
   - Set $\mathbb{D}_5 = RK_{i \to j}^2 = h_1^{s_2} \in \mathbb{G}_1$.

   The proxy returns the second-level ciphertext $\mathbb{D} = (\mathbb{D}_1, \mathbb{D}_2, \mathbb{D}_3, \mathbb{D}_4, \mathbb{D}_5)$.

7. **Re-Decrypt**($\mathbb{D}$, sk_{id_j}, $params$): With input a second-level ciphertext $\mathbb{D} = (\mathbb{D}_1, \mathbb{D}_2, \mathbb{D}_3, \mathbb{D}_4, \mathbb{D}_5)$, the delegatee id_j performs the following computations:
   - Compute $x_{ij} = H_5(\hat{e}(D_2, sk_{id_j}), id_i, id_j)$ using private key sk_{id_j}.

– Compute σ as below:

$$\sigma = \frac{\mathbb{D}_3}{\hat{e}(\mathbb{D}_1, \mathbb{D}_5)^{x_{ij}}}. \tag{7}$$

– Compute the message m as:

$$m = \mathbb{D}_4 \oplus H_3(\sigma). \tag{8}$$

– Check if the following condition holds:

$$\mathbb{D}_1 \stackrel{?}{=} g^{H_2(\sigma, m)}. \tag{9}$$

If the check holds, it returns m else returns *"INVALID CIPHERTEXT"*.

4.3 Correctness

Our collusion resistant unidirectional IB-PRE scheme is consistent and correct, which can be verified using the following computations:

– Correctness of first-level ciphertext verification from Eq. 6:

$$\begin{aligned}
RHS &= \hat{e}(C_1, H_4(id_i||C_1||C_2||C_3||C_4)) \\
&= \hat{e}(g^r, H_4(id_i||C_1||C_2||C_3||C_4)) \\
&= \hat{e}(g, C_5) \\
&= LHS.
\end{aligned}$$

– Consistency between encryption and decryption from Eq. 3:

$$\begin{aligned}
RHS &= \frac{\mathbb{C}_3}{\hat{e}(\mathbb{C}_2, sk_{id_i})} \\
&= \frac{\sigma \cdot \hat{e}(P_{pub_2}, H_1(id_i)^r)}{\hat{e}(\mathbb{C}_2, sk_{id_i})} \\
&= \frac{\sigma \cdot \hat{e}(g_1{}^s, H_1(id_i)^r)}{\hat{e}(g_1{}^r, H_1(id_i)^s)} \\
&= \sigma \\
&= LHS.
\end{aligned}$$

Using σ in Eq. 4, we get:

$$\begin{aligned}
RHS &= \mathbb{C}_4 \oplus H_3(\sigma) \\
&= m \oplus H_3(\sigma) \oplus H_3(\sigma) \\
&= m \\
&= LHS.
\end{aligned}$$

– Consistency between re-encryption and re-decryption from Eq. 7:

$$RHS = \frac{\mathbb{D}_3}{\hat{e}(\mathbb{D}_1, \mathbb{D}_5)^{x_{ij}}}$$

$$= \frac{\mathbb{C}_3.\hat{e}(\mathbb{C}_1, RK^1_{i \to j})}{\hat{e}(\mathbb{C}_1, RK^2_{i \to j})}$$

$$= \frac{\sigma.\hat{e}(g_1^r, h^{x_{ij} s_2})}{\hat{e}(g^r, h_1^{s_2})^{x_{ij}}}$$

$$= \sigma$$

$$= LHS.$$

Using σ in Eq. 8, we get:

$$RHS = \mathbb{D}_4 \oplus H_3(\sigma)$$

$$= m \oplus H_3(\sigma) \oplus H_3(\sigma)$$

$$= m$$

$$= LHS.$$

Remark 1. Our IB-PRE scheme defines the two levels of ciphertexts as follows. The first level ciphertext $\mathbb{C} = (\mathbb{C}_1, \mathbb{C}_2, \mathbb{C}_3, \mathbb{C}_4, \mathbb{C}_5)$ is generated by the **Encrypt** algorithm, which includes the delegatable ciphertexts encrypted towards the delegator. The second level ciphertext $\mathbb{D} = (\mathbb{D}_1, \mathbb{D}_2, \mathbb{D}_3, \mathbb{D}_4, \mathbb{D}_5)$ is generated by the **Re-Encrypt** algorithm, comprising the re-encrypted ciphertexts that cannot be delegated further in encrypted form. When a user stores her data encrypted in the cloud, the data may belong to any of the two categories.

4.4 Security Proof

Collusion Resistance

Theorem 1. *Our proposed scheme is DSK-secure under the m-CDH assumption. If a DSK adversary $\mathcal{A}$ breaks the DSK security of the given scheme with an advantage ϵ in time t, then there exists a challenger $\mathcal{C}$ who solves the m-CDH problem with advantage ϵ' within time t' where:*

$$\epsilon' \geq \frac{\epsilon}{e(1 + q_{KE})},$$

$$t^* \leq t + O(q_{H_1} + 3q_{RK} + q_{KE})t_{et} + O(q_{RK})t_{bp},$$

where e is the base of natural logarithm, t_{et} denotes the time taken for exponentiation in group $\mathbb{G}_1$ and t_{bp} is the time taken for one bilinear pairing operation.

Proof. Let $\mathcal{A}$ be a p.p.t adversary that has a non-negligible advantage ϵ in breaking the $(t, \epsilon)DSK$ security of the scheme with access to the random oracle H_1. Then, we can construct a polynomial time algorithm $\mathcal{C}$ to solve the m-CDH assumption in $\mathcal{G}_1$ with a non-negligible advantage. Note that the hash functions H_2, H_3, H_4 and H_5 are not modeled as random oracles in the proof. Algorithm $\mathcal{C}$ accepts as input a properly-distributed tuple $\langle \mathbb{G}_1 = \langle g \rangle, g^a, g^b, g^{\frac{1}{b}}, g^{\frac{a}{b}} \rangle$ and outputs the value of g^{ab}. $\mathcal{C}$ plays the DSK game with $\mathcal{A}$ in the following way:

- **Setup:** $\mathcal{C}$ implicitly defines the master secret key $msk = a$ and $\delta = \frac{1}{b}$. It sets $P_{pub_1} = g^a$, $g_1 = g^{\frac{1}{b}}$ and $P_{pub_2} = g^{\frac{a}{b}}$. It picks $\nu \leftarrow \mathbb{Z}_q^*$, computes $h = (g^a)^\nu$ and $h_1 = (g^{\frac{a}{b}})^\nu$ and returns the resulting system parameters $params$ to $\mathcal{A}$.
- **Queries:** $\mathcal{C}$ interacts with $\mathcal{A}$ in the following ways:
  - $H_1(id_i)$ Oracle: $\mathcal{C}$ maintains a list L_{H_1} with tuples of the form $\langle id_i \in \{0,1\}^*, y_i \in \mathbb{Z}_q^*, k_i \in \mathbb{Z}_q^*, \alpha_i \in \{0,1\} \rangle$. If the tuple $\langle id_i, y_i, k_i, \alpha_i \rangle$ already exists in L_{H_1}, retrieve and return the value y_i. Else randomly set $\alpha_i \in \{0,1\}$ such that $Pr[\alpha_i = 0] = \gamma$ which is defined as in the first level ciphertext security. Set the hash value according to the following cases:
    * If $\alpha_i = 0$, select $z_i \leftarrow \mathbb{Z}_q^*$, compute $y_i = g^{z_i}$ and set $H_1(id_i) = y_i$.
    * If $\alpha_i = 1$, select $z_i \leftarrow \mathbb{Z}_q^*$, compute $y = (g^b)^{z_i}$. Set $H_1(id_i) = y_i$.
    Store tuple $\langle id_i, y_i, z_i, \alpha_i \rangle$ in list L_{H_1} and return y_i.
  - Private Key Extraction Oracle $\mathcal{O}_{KE}(id_i)$: $\mathcal{C}$ responds to the key-extraction query of an identity id_i by first checking for a tuple $\langle id_i, y_i, k_i, \alpha_i \rangle$ already exists in L_{H_1}. If $\alpha_i = 1$, abort and return $failure$. Otherwise, return $sk_{id_i} = (g^a)^{z_i}$ as the private key of identity id_i.
  - Re $-$ encryption Key Generation Oracle $\mathcal{O}_{RK}(id_i, id_j)$: $\mathcal{C}$ maintains a list L_{RK} that contains tuples of the form $\langle id_i \in \{0,1\}^*, id_j \in \{0,1\}^*, x_{ij} \in \mathbb{Z}_q^*, RK_{i \rightarrow j}^1 \in \mathbb{G}_1, RK_{i \rightarrow j}^2 \in \mathbb{G}_1, RK_{i \rightarrow j}^3 \in \mathbb{G}_1, s_1 \in \mathbb{Z}_q^*, \bar{s}_2 \in \mathbb{Z}_q^* \rangle$. $\mathcal{C}$ responds to the re-encryption key-generation queries of $\mathcal{A}$ from user id_i to id_j by searching list L_{H_1} for tuples corresponding to id_i and id_j respectively and computing the re-keys as per the following cases:
    * Check if the re-key $RK_{i \rightarrow j}$ exists in L_{RK} by searching for a tuple $\langle id_i, id_j, x_{ij}, RK_{i \rightarrow j}^1, RK_{i \rightarrow j}^2, RK_{i \rightarrow j}^3, s_1, \bar{s}_2 \rangle$. If present, return $RK_{i \rightarrow j}$.
    * If $\alpha_i = 0 \wedge \alpha_j = 0$: generate the re-keys as per **ReKeyGen** protocol.
    * If $\alpha_i = 0 \wedge \alpha_j = 1$: generate the re-keys as per **ReKeyGen** protocol.
    * If $\alpha_i = 1 \wedge \alpha_j = 0$: pick $x_{ij}, s_1, \bar{s}_2 \leftarrow \mathbb{Z}_q^*$. Update list L_{H_5} with the tuple $\langle \hat{e}(g^a, g^{z_j s_1}), id_i, id_j, x_{ij} \rangle$. Implicitly define $s_2 = z_i x_{ij}^{-1} \nu^{-1} b + \bar{s}_2$ and compute the re-key $RK_{i \rightarrow j}$ as follows:
      · Compute $RK_{i \rightarrow j}^1 = (g^a)^{\nu x_{ij} \bar{s}_2}$.
      · Compute $RK_{i \rightarrow j}^2 = (g^a)^{x_{ij}^{-1} z_i} \cdot (g^{\frac{a}{b}})^{\nu \bar{s}_2}$.
      · Compute $RK_{i \rightarrow j}^3 = g^{s_1}$.
    Observe that the re-encryption key $RK_{i \rightarrow j}$ computed is identically distributed as the keys generated by the **ReKeyGen** algorithm in the construction. Infact, we have:
      · $RK_{i \rightarrow j}^1 = (g^a)^{\nu x_{ij} \bar{s}_2} = (g^{bz_i})^{-a} \cdot g^{a\nu x_{ij}(x_{ij}^{-1}\nu^{-1}bz_i + \bar{s}_2)} = H_1(id_i)^{-s} \cdot h^{x_{ij} s_2}$.

$$\cdot \ RK_{i \to j}^2 = (g^a)^{x_{ij}^{-1} z_i} \cdot (g^{\frac{a}{b}})^{\nu \bar{s}_2} = (g^{\frac{a}{b}})^{\nu(z_i x_{ij}^{-1} \nu^{-1} b + \bar{s}_2)} = h_1^{s_2}.$$

∗ If $\alpha_i = 1 \wedge \alpha_j = 1$: generate the re-keys as below:

· Pick $s_1, \bar{s}_2, x_{ij} \leftarrow \mathbb{Z}_q^*$.

· Compute $RK_{i \to j}^1 = (g)^{x_{ij}}$.

· Compute $RK_{i \to j}^2 = g^{\frac{a}{b} \nu s_2} = h_1^{\bar{s}_2}$.

· Compute $RK_{i \to j}^3 = g^{s_1}$.

Update list L_{RK} with the tuple $\langle id_i, id_j, x_{ij}, RK_{i \to j}^1, RK_{i \to j}^2,$ $RK_{i \to j}^3, s_1, \bar{s}_2 \rangle$. Return the re-keys $RK_{i \to j} = (RK_{i \to j}^1, RK_{i \to j}^2, RK_{i \to j}^3)$ to $\mathcal{A}$.

- **Output**: Eventually, $\mathcal{A}$ returns sk_{id^*} as the private key corresponding to the identity id^*, where id^* is honest $(\alpha^* = 1)$. $\mathcal{C}$ recovers the tuple $\langle id^*, y^*, z^*, \alpha^* \rangle$ from list L_{H_1} and returns $(sk_{id^*})^{z^{*-1}}$, where, for an honest identity id^*, $(sk_{id^*})^{z^{*-1}} = (g^{abz^*})^{z^{*-1}} = g^{ab}$ is the solution to the m-CDH problem.

- **Probability Analysis**: We calculate the probability that $\mathcal{C}$ aborts during the simulation. Let $Abort$ denote the event that $\mathcal{C}$ aborts during the game and q_{KE} denote the number of queries made to the key extraction oracle. We note that $\mathcal{C}$ does not abort in the following events:

  - E_1: $\alpha^* = 0$ in the *Private Key Extraction* phase.
  - E_1: $\alpha^* = 1$ in the *Output* phase.

We have $Pr[\neg Abort] \geq \gamma^{q_{KE}}(1 - \gamma)$, which has a maximum value at $\gamma_{OPT} = \frac{q_{KE}}{1 + q_{KE}}$. Using γ_{OPT}, we obtain:

$$Pr[\neg Abort] \geq \frac{1}{e(1 + q_{KE})}.$$

Therefore, the advantage of $\mathcal{C}$ in solving the m-CDH problem is:

$$\epsilon' \geq \epsilon \cdot Pr[\neg Abort]$$
$$\geq \frac{\epsilon}{e(1 + q_{KE})},$$

where, e is the base of the natural logarithm. The running time of $\mathcal{C}$ is:

$$t^* \leq t + O(q_{H_1} + 4q_{RK} + q_{KE})t_{et} + O(q_{RK})t_{bp}.$$

This completes the proof of the theorem.   □

First-Level Ciphertext Security

Theorem 2. *Our proposed scheme is CCA-secure for the first level ciphertext under the DBDH assumption. If an IND-IBPRE-CCA adversary $\mathcal{A}$ breaks the IND-IBPRE-CCA security of the given scheme with an advantage ϵ within time t, then there exists an adversary $\mathcal{C}$ that solves the DBDH problem with an advantage ϵ' within time t' where,*

$$\epsilon' \geq \frac{\epsilon}{e(1 + q_{RK} + q_{KE})},$$

$$t' \leq t + (q_{H_1} + q_{H_2} + q_{H_3} + q_{H_4} + q_{H_5} + q_{KE} + q_{RK} + q_{RE} + q_{DEC}$$
$$+ q_{REDEC})O(1) + (q_{H_1} + q_{H_4} + q_{KE} + 4q_{RK} + 7q_{RE} + 6q_{DEC} + 3q_{REDEC})t_{et}$$
$$+ (q_{RK} + 5q_{RE} + q_{DEC} + 2q_{REDEC})t_{bp},$$

where e is the base of natural logarithm, t_{et} denotes the time taken for exponentiation in group $\mathbb{G}_1$ and t_{bp} denotes the time taken for bilinear pairing operation.

Proof. Due to space constraint, the proof of first-level ciphertext security in given in the full version of the paper [14]. □

Second-Level Ciphertext Security

Theorem 3. *Our proposed scheme is CCA-secure for the second-level ciphertext under the m-DBDH assumption. If an IND-IBPRE-CCA adversary $\mathcal{A}$ breaks the IND-IBPRE-CCA security of the given scheme with a non-negligible advantage, then there exists an adversary $\mathcal{C}$ who solves the m-DBDH problem with an advantage ϵ' within time t' where,*

$$\epsilon' \geq \frac{\epsilon}{e(1 + q_{KE})} - \frac{q_{H_5}}{2^{2n}},$$

$$t' \leq t + (q_{H_1} + q_{H_2} + q_{H_3} + q_{H_4} + q_{H_5} + q_{KE} + q_{RK} + q_{DEC} + q_{REDEC})O(1)$$
$$+ (q_{H_1} + q_{H_4} + 5q_{RK} + 6q_{DEC} + 3q_{REDEC})t_{et} + (q_{RK} + q_{DEC} + 2q_{REDEC})t_{bp},$$

where e is the base of natural logarithm, t_{et} denotes the time taken for exponentiation in group $\mathbb{G}_1$ and t_{bp} denotes the time taken for bilinear pairing operation.

Proof. Due to space constraint, the proof of second-level ciphertext security is given in the full version of the paper [14]. □

5   Discussion on a Collusion-Resistant IB-PRE Scheme in [19]

In the scheme due to Wang *et al.* [19], the first-level ciphertext C_{ID} consists of the following components: $(C_1, C_2, C_3, C_4, C_5, C_6, C_7) = (g^r, (g_2g_3)^r, (g_1^{ID}h)^r,$ SE.Enc$(H_2(e(g_1, g_2))^r), M), H_1(svk)^r, svk, \sigma)$. Note that the hash function H_1 is defined as $H_1 : \mathbb{S} \rightarrow \mathbb{G}$, where $\mathbb{S}$ is the public key space of the one time signature scheme used in the construction. In order to simulate the ciphertext component $C_5 = H_1(svk)^r$ in the Challenge phase, the Challenger must know the value r to form a valid ciphertext component C_5, and when we know such an r, that would solve the discrete log problem with respect to C_1. Also, wellformedness of the ciphertext can be verified using the following check: $e(C_1, H_1(C_6)) \stackrel{?}{=} e(g, C_5)$. Therefore, the challenge ciphertext cannot be simulated without the knowledge of the exponent r, which would lead to solving the discrete log problem.

Another big omission noticed in [19] is that, the private key generation uses a signature scheme whose security is not proven or known. It is quite unlikely that a standard model proof is possible for this signature scheme since the key components d_1 and d_1' are not used as exponents of the generator but used directly as elements of $\mathbb{Z}_p^*$. In fact, there are no known signature schemes in the standard model with the keys used directly.

In light of the above observations, it is impossible to prove the security of the scheme due to Wang *et al.* [19].

6   Conclusion

Though there are several proxy re-encryption (PRE) schemes in the literature constructed in the identity based setting, only one IB-PRE scheme due to Wang *et al.* [19] which is CPA-secure for the first-level ciphertext and CCA-secure for the second-level ciphertext, has reported the collusion resistance property in the standard model and adheres to the standard definition of PRE. However, the scheme is not provably secure, as discussed in our work. Our collusion resistant PRE scheme adheres to the standard definition of PRE, and is shown to be adaptively CCA secure in the random oracle model for both the first-level and second level ciphertexts. Also, the definition of collusion resistance is met wherein the colluders (proxy and the delegatee) cannot obtain the private key components of the delegator. Thus, this paper proposes the *first* provably secure collusion resistant IB-PRE scheme based on the Decisional Bilinear Diffie Hellman (DBDH) assumption and its variants in the random oracle model.

Acknowledgment. The authors would like to thank the anonymous referees for their helpful comments. The authors gratefully acknowledge the partial support of the Ministry of Electronics & Information Technology, Government of India under Project No. CCE/CEP/22/VK&CP/CSE/14-15 on Information Security & Awareness(ISEA) Phase-II.

References

1. Ateniese, G., Fu, K., Green, M., Hohenberger, S.: Improved proxy re-encryption schemes with applications to secure distributed storage. In: NDSS (2005)
2. Ateniese, G., Kevin, F., Green, M., Hohenberger, S.: Improved proxy re-encryption schemes with applications to secure distributed storage. ACM Trans. Inf. Syst. Secur. (TISSEC) **9**(1), 1–30 (2006)
3. Blaze, M., Bleumer, G., Strauss, M.: Divertible protocols and atomic proxy cryptography. In: Nyberg, K. (ed.) EUROCRYPT 1998. LNCS, vol. 1403, pp. 127–144. Springer, Heidelberg (1998). https://doi.org/10.1007/BFb0054122
4. Boneh, D., Franklin, M.: Identity-based encryption from the weil pairing. In: Kilian, J. (ed.) CRYPTO 2001. LNCS, vol. 2139, pp. 213–229. Springer, Heidelberg (2001). https://doi.org/10.1007/3-540-44647-8_13
5. Boneh, D., Lynn, B., Shacham, H.: Short signatures from the weil pairing. J. Cryptol. **17**(4), 297–319 (2004)
6. Chow, S.S.M., Weng, J., Yang, Y., Deng, R.H.: Efficient unidirectional proxy re-encryption. IACR Cryptology ePrint Archive, 2009:189 (2009)

7. Chow, S.S.M., Weng, J., Yang, Y., Deng, R.H.: Efficient unidirectional proxy re-encryption. In: Bernstein, D.J., Lange, T. (eds.) AFRICACRYPT 2010. LNCS, vol. 6055, pp. 316–332. Springer, Heidelberg (2010). https://doi.org/10.1007/978-3-642-12678-9_19

8. Green, M., Ateniese, G.: Identity-based proxy re-encryption. In: Katz, J., Yung, M. (eds.) ACNS 2007. LNCS, vol. 4521, pp. 288–306. Springer, Heidelberg (2007). https://doi.org/10.1007/978-3-540-72738-5_19

9. Han, J., Susilo, W., Mu, Y.: Identity-based data storage in cloud computing. Future Gener. Comput. Syst. **29**(3), 673–681 (2013)

10. Koo, W.K., Hwang, J.Y., Lee, D.H.: Security vulnerability in a non-interactive id-based proxy re-encryption scheme. Inf. Process. Lett. **109**(23), 1260–1262 (2009)

11. Libert, B., Vergnaud, D.: Tracing malicious proxies in proxy re-encryption. In: Galbraith, S.D., Paterson, K.G. (eds.) Pairing 2008. LNCS, vol. 5209, pp. 332–353. Springer, Heidelberg (2008). https://doi.org/10.1007/978-3-540-85538-5_22

12. Qiu, J., Jo, J., Lee, H.: Collusion-resistant identity-based proxy re-encryption without random oracles. Int. J. Secur. Appl. **9**(9), 337–344 (2015)

13. Shao, J., Cao, Z., Liu, P.: SCCR: a generic approach to simultaneously achieve CCA security and collusion-resistance in proxy re-encryption. Secur. Commun. Netw. **4**(2), 122–135 (2011)

14. Srinivasavaradhan, V., Paul, A., Sharmila Deva Selvi, S., Pandu Rangan, C.: A CCA-secure collusion-resistant identity-based proxy re-encryption scheme (full version). Cryptology ePrint Archive, August 2018

15. Smith, T: DVD Jon: buy DRM-less tracks from Apple iTunes (2005). http://www.theregister.co.uk/2005/03/18/itunes pymusique

16. Sree Vivek, S., Sharmila Deva Selvi, S., Radhakishan, V., Pandu Rangan, C.: Efficient conditional proxy re-encryption with chosen ciphertext security. Int. J. Netw. Secur. Appl. **4**(2), 179 (2012)

17. Wang, H., Zeng, P., Choo, K.-K.R.: MDMR-IBE: efficient multiple domain multi-receiver identity-based encryption. Securi. Commun. Netw. **7**(11), 1641–1651 (2014)

18. Wang, L., Wang, L., Mambo, M., Okamoto, E.: New identity-based proxy re-encryption schemes to prevent collusion attacks. In: Joye, M., Miyaji, A., Otsuka, A. (eds.) Pairing 2010. LNCS, vol. 6487, pp. 327–346. Springer, Heidelberg (2010). https://doi.org/10.1007/978-3-642-17455-1_21

19. Wang, X.A., Zhong, W.: A new identity based proxy re-encryption scheme. In: 2010 International Conference on Biomedical Engineering and Computer Science, pp. 1–4, April 2010

20. Zhang, L., Ma, H., Liu, Z., Dong, E.: Security analysis and improvement of a collusion-resistant identity-based proxy re-encryption scheme. In: Barolli, L., Xhafa, F., Yim, K. (eds.) Advances on Broad-Band Wireless Computing, Communication and Applications. LNDECT, vol. 2, pp. 839–846. Springer, Cham (2017). https://doi.org/10.1007/978-3-319-49106-6_86

Multivariate Encryption Schemes Based on the Constrained MQ Problem

Takanori Yasuda[✉]

Okayama University of Science, Okayama, Japan
tyasuda@bme.ous.ac.jp

Abstract. The MQ problem is mathematical in nature and is related to the security of Multivariate Public Key Cryptography (MPKC). In this paper, we introduce *the constrained MQ problem*, which is a new mathematical problem derived from the MQ problem. We also propose an encryption scheme construction method in MPKC, the *pq*-method, whose security is mainly based on the difficulty of solving the constrained MQ problem. We analyze the difficulty level of solving the constrained MQ problem, including different approach from the usual for solving the MQ problem. Furthermore, based on the analysis of the constrained MQ problem, we present secure parameters for the *pq*-method, and implement the practical schemes.

Keywords: Multivariate public key cryptography
Constrained MQ problem · MQ problem · Post-quantum cryptography

1 Introduction

Multivariate Public Key Cryptography (MPKC) [7] is a candidate for post-quantum cryptography. MPKC uses polynomial system as both secret key and public key, and in most cases, their security is mainly based on the difficulty of solving polynomial equations. In particular, the solving problem for quadratic polynomials is called the MQ problem, which is described as follows.

MQ problem: For positive integers m and n, let $\mathcal{F}(\mathbf{x})$ be a polynomial system which consists of m quadratic polynomials over a finite field $\mathbb{F}_q$ of q elements in variables $\mathbf{x} = (x_1, \ldots, x_n)$. Then, find $\mathbf{x}_0 \in \mathbb{F}_q^n$ such that $\mathcal{F}(\mathbf{x}_0) = \mathbf{0}$.

In this paper, we introduce the constrained MQ problem, which is a new mathematical problem derived from the MQ problem. It is described as follows.

Constrained MQ problem: For positive integers m, n and L, let $\mathcal{F}(\mathbf{x})$ be a polynomial system which consists of m quadratic polynomials over $\mathbb{F}_q$ in variables $\mathbf{x} = (x_1, \ldots, x_n)$. Then, find $\mathbf{x}_0 = (x_{0,1}, \ldots, x_{0,n}) \in \mathbb{Z}^n$ such that $\mathcal{F}(\mathbf{x}_0) = \mathbf{0}$ and $-\frac{L}{2} < x_{0,i} \leq \frac{L}{2}$ $(i = 1, \ldots, n)$.

© Springer Nature Switzerland AG 2018
J. Baek et al. (Eds.): ProvSec 2018, LNCS 11192, pp. 129–146, 2018.
https://doi.org/10.1007/978-3-030-01446-9_8

So far, the constrained MQ problem has never been used as a basis of security for encryption scheme. In this paper, encryption schemes whose security is based on the difficulty of solving the constrained MQ problem are proposed for the first time. A solution of the constrained MQ problem is obviously a solution of the (unconstrained) MQ problem. However, since the equation $\mathcal{F}(\mathbf{x}) = \mathbf{0}$ may have solutions outside the constraint domain, a solving algorithm of the (unconstrained) MQ problem may not return a solution of the constrained MQ problem. The difficulty level of solving the constrained MQ problem (of the general type) is analyzed in Sects. 5.1, 5.2 and 5.3.

We are already aware of the encryption schemes in MPKC, Simple Matrix Scheme [28], EFC [27], HFERP [15]. Since HFERP was just proposed, its detailed cryptanalysis will start now. Critical attacks have not yet been reported for Simple Matrix Scheme and EFC; however, the large number of variables that they requires for their security is at the cost of the performance of encryption and decryption. Due to such circumstances, the development of new encryption schemes in MPKC is a critical issue.

In this paper, we propose the pq-method for construction of encryption schemes in MPKC, which is a new method entirely different from any of the previous schemes in MPKC. The pq-method is a converting method from an encryption scheme in MPKC over $\mathbb{F}_p$, where p is a small prime number, to that over $\mathbb{F}_q$, where q is a large prime number. One advantage of the pq-method is that it enhances the security of the original scheme even when the original scheme is insecure. We focus on TTM [19], C^* [18], and Square [5] as they are the previous encryption schemes used in MPKC over $\mathbb{F}_p$. We apply the pq-method to these schemes, and propose three new encryption schemes, namely pq-TM, pq-C^* and pq-Square.

In other words, we explain the pq-method. A regular encryption scheme in MPKC over $\mathbb{F}_p$ is constructed by the following procedure. First, we prepare a multivariate quadratic polynomial system $G_0(\mathbf{x})$ that is (almost) injective and whose inverse can be efficiently computed. Next, we randomly choose two affine transformations T_0, S_0, and define a polynomial function $F_0 = T_0 \circ G_0 \circ S_0$. Now, $F_0(\mathbf{x})$ becomes a trapdoor one-way function, and an encryption scheme with public key $F_0(\mathbf{x})$ is constructed. If $\mathbf{m}$ is a plaintext, the corresponding ciphertext is obtained by $\mathbf{c} = F_0(\mathbf{m})$. This $G_0(\mathbf{x})$ is called the central map of the encryption scheme. On the other hand, the pq-method starts from $G_0(\mathbf{x})$. First, we lift $G_0(\mathbf{x})$ to a polynomial system $\widetilde{G}(\mathbf{x})$ with integer coefficients. Next, another polynomial system $\widetilde{H}_R(\mathbf{x})$ with integer coefficients is prepared, and $G(\mathbf{x})$ is defined by $G(\mathbf{x}) = \widetilde{G}(\mathbf{x}) + \widetilde{H}_R(\mathbf{x})$. The $\widetilde{H}_R(\mathbf{x})$ is appended in order to enhance the security of the scheme constructed by $G_0(\mathbf{x})$. Finally, an affine transformation T over $\mathbb{F}_q$ and a permutation matrix S are chosen randomly, and a polynomial system $F(\mathbf{x})$ is defined by $F = T \circ G \circ S$. We now construct an encryption scheme over $\mathbb{F}_q$ whose public key is $F(\mathbf{x})$. This is a summary of the construction using the pq-method. However, the pq-method requires a constraint on the domain of $F(\mathbf{x})$. In other words, any plaintext $\mathbf{m} = (m_1, \ldots, m_n)$ must satisfy $-\frac{p}{2} < m_i \leq \frac{p}{2}$ ($i = 1, \ldots, n$). Due to the constraint, we can eliminate the part of $T(\widetilde{H}_R(S(\mathbf{m})))$

from a ciphertext $\mathbf{c} = F(\mathbf{m}) = T(G(S(\mathbf{m}))) = T(\widetilde{G}(S(\mathbf{m}))) + T(\widetilde{H}_R(S(\mathbf{m})))$, and thereby the decryption succeeds. According to the constraint, the security of the pq-method is related directly to the constrained MQ problem.

In the security analysis of the pq-method, we also discuss the difficulty of solving the constrained MQ problem. Under the security analysis, we estimate the secure parameters at 128-bit and 192-bit security levels. Moreover, we implement the three encryption schemes constructed by the pq-method for these parameters, and investigate their performance.

This paper is organized in the following manner. In Sect. 2, we discuss a trapdoor one-way function used in the pq-method. We further prove its nature and also describe a computing algorithm of its inverse map. In Sect. 3, the algorithms of key generation, along with encryption and decryption of the pq-method of general type are described. In Sect. 4, we talk about three encryption schemes constructed using the pq-method. In Sect. 5, we analyze the security of the three schemes and discuss the difficulty of solving the constrained MQ problem. Based on the security analysis in Sect. 5, we estimate the secure parameters of the three schemes in Sect. 6. Moreover, the performance of the three schemes is summarized based on our implementation of the schemes. Sect. 7 is the conclusion of this paper.

2   Construction of Multivariate Polynomial Trapdoor Functions

For a positive integer l, we denote the least non-negative remainder of an integer a by $a \bmod l$, and the least absolute remainder of a by $\text{lift}_l(a)$. For $a \in \mathbb{Z}/l\mathbb{Z}$, $a \bmod l$ and $\text{lift}_l(a)$ is defined similarly. I_l is defined by $I_l = (-l/2, l/2] \cap \mathbb{Z}$, then $a \bmod l \in [0, l-1]$ and $\text{lift}_l(a) \in I_l$.

Let $x_1, \ldots, x_n$ be n independent variables and $\mathbf{x} = (x_1, \ldots, x_n)$. Let

$$\widetilde{G}(\mathbf{x}) = (\widetilde{g}_1(\mathbf{x}), \ldots, \widetilde{g}_n(\mathbf{x})) \in \mathbb{Z}[\mathbf{x}]^n,$$
$$\widetilde{H}(\mathbf{x}) = (\widetilde{h}_1(\mathbf{x}), \ldots, \widetilde{h}_n(\mathbf{x})) \in \mathbb{Z}[\mathbf{x}]^n$$

be two polynomial systems with integer coefficients whose absolute values are small. Moreover, we assume that for an odd prime number p, the reduction of $\widetilde{G}(\mathbf{x})$ by p, $\widetilde{G}(\mathbf{x}) \bmod p \in \mathbb{F}_p[\mathbf{x}]^n$ is (almost) injective and its inverse can be computed efficiently. For example, (a lift to $\mathbb{Z}[\mathbf{x}]^n$ of) the central map of an encryption scheme in MPKC satisfies this assumption. Let $M_{\widetilde{G}}, M_{\widetilde{H}}$ be positive integers such that

$$\begin{aligned} M_{\widetilde{G}} &\geq \max_{i=1,\ldots,n}\{|\widetilde{g}_i(a_1, \ldots, a_n)| \mid (a_1, \ldots, a_n) \in I_p^n\}, \\ M_{\widetilde{H}} &\geq \max_{i=1,\ldots,n}\{|\widetilde{h}_i(a_1, \ldots, a_n)| \mid (a_1, \ldots, a_n) \in I_p^n\}. \end{aligned} \tag{1}$$

If $\widetilde{g}_i(\mathbf{x})$ $(i = 1, \ldots, n)$ is expressed as:

$$\widetilde{g}_i(\mathbf{x}) = \sum_{k,l} \alpha_{k,l}^{(i)} x_k x_l + \sum_k \beta_k^{(i)} x_k + \gamma^{(i)} \quad (\alpha_{k,l}^{(i)}, \beta_k^{(i)}, \gamma^{(i)} \in \mathbb{Z}),$$

for example,

$$M_{\widetilde{G}} = \max_{i=1,\ldots,n} \left\{ (\sum_{k,l} |\alpha_{k,l}^{(i)}|) \left(\frac{p-1}{2}\right)^2 + (\sum_k |\beta_k^{(i)}|) \left(\frac{p-1}{2}\right) + |\gamma^{(i)}| \right\}$$

satisfies (1). It is similar for $M_{\widetilde{H}}$.

Taking a (large) prime number q, we choose positive integers $r_1, \ldots, r_n \ (< q)$ such that

$$2M_{\widetilde{G}} < \min_{k=1,\ldots,2M_{\widetilde{H}}} \{|\text{lift}_q(r_i k)|\} \quad (i = 1, \ldots, n), \tag{2}$$

and define $\Lambda_i = \{\text{lift}_q(r_i k) \mid k = 0, \pm 1, \pm 2, \ldots, \pm M_{\widetilde{H}}\}$. To exist the r_i's, q must be sufficiently large. In fact, it is necessary that $q > 4M_{\widetilde{H}} M_{\widetilde{G}}$. Moreover, $r_i > 2M_{\widetilde{G}}$ is also needed.

For $\lambda = r_i k, \lambda' = r_i k' \in \Lambda_i$, from $|k - k'| < 2M_{\widetilde{H}}$ and (2),

$$|\text{lift}_q(\lambda - \lambda')| = |\text{lift}_q(r_i(k - k'))| = |\text{lift}_q(r_i|k - k'|)| > 2M_{\widetilde{G}}.$$

In other words,

$$|\text{lift}_q(\lambda - \lambda')| > 2M_{\widetilde{G}} \quad (\forall \lambda, \lambda' \in \Lambda_i \ (\lambda \neq \lambda')). \tag{3}$$

A polynomial system $G(\mathbf{x})$ is defined by

$$G(\mathbf{x}) = (g_1(\mathbf{x}), \ldots, g_n(\mathbf{x})) = \left(\widetilde{G}(\mathbf{x}) + \widetilde{H}_R(\mathbf{x})\right) \bmod q \in \mathbb{F}_q[\mathbf{x}]^n,$$

$$\text{where} \quad \widetilde{H}_R(\mathbf{x}) = (r_1 \widetilde{h}_1(\mathbf{x}), \ldots, r_n \widetilde{h}_n(\mathbf{x})) \in \mathbb{Z}[\mathbf{x}]^n.$$

Then, $G : \mathbb{Z}^n \to \mathbb{F}_q^n$ becomes a multivariate quadratic polynomial map.

Lemma 1. *For $\widetilde{\mathbf{b}} \in I_p^n$, let $(c_1, \ldots, c_n) \in \mathbb{F}_q^n$ be given by $(c_1, \ldots, c_n) = G(\widetilde{\mathbf{b}})$. Then, for $i = 1, \ldots, n$, there exists a unique $\lambda_i \in \Lambda_i$ such that $|\text{lift}_q(c_i - \lambda_i)| < M_{\widetilde{G}}$. Moreover, when writing $a_i = \text{lift}_q(c_i - \lambda_i)$,*

$$\widetilde{G}(\widetilde{\mathbf{b}}) = (a_1, \ldots, a_n) \quad and \quad \widetilde{H}_R(\widetilde{\mathbf{b}}) \equiv (\lambda_1, \ldots, \lambda_n) \bmod q.$$

Proof. Actually, for the images of $\widetilde{\mathbf{b}}$, $\widetilde{H}_R(\widetilde{\mathbf{b}}) = (\widetilde{\lambda}_1, \ldots, \widetilde{\lambda}_n)$ and $\widetilde{G}(\widetilde{\mathbf{b}}) = (\widetilde{a}_1, \ldots, \widetilde{a}_n)$, we get that for $i = 1, \ldots, n$, $\text{lift}_q(\widetilde{\lambda}_i) \in \Lambda_i$, $\widetilde{a}_i = \text{lift}_q(c_i - \widetilde{\lambda}_i) = \text{lift}_q(c_i - \text{lift}_q(\widetilde{\lambda}_i))$ and $|\text{lift}_q(c_i - \text{lift}_q(\widetilde{\lambda}_i))| = |\widetilde{a}_i| < M_{\widetilde{G}}$ from the property of $M_{\widetilde{H}}, M_{\widetilde{G}}$. The rest of the assertion is sufficient to show that for $\lambda_i' \in \Lambda_i$ such that $\lambda_i' \neq \text{lift}_q(\widetilde{\lambda}_i)$, $|\text{lift}_q(c_i - \lambda_i')| \geq M_{\widetilde{G}}$. This is shown using (3) as follows.

$$|\text{lift}_q(c_i - \lambda_i')| = |\text{lift}_q(c_i - \widetilde{\lambda}_i + \widetilde{\lambda}_i - \lambda_i')| \geq \left||\text{lift}_q(\widetilde{\lambda}_i - \lambda_i')| - |\text{lift}_q(c_i - \widetilde{\lambda}_i)|\right| > M_{\widetilde{G}}. \ \square$$

For any $\mathbf{c} = (c_1, \ldots, c_n) \in G(I_p^n)(\subset \mathbb{F}_q^n)$, the following inference is obtained:

$\widetilde{\mathbf{b}} \in I_p^n$ is a solution of $G(\mathbf{x}) = \mathbf{c}$.
$\Longleftrightarrow \widetilde{\mathbf{b}} \in I_p^n$ is a solution of two equations, $\widetilde{G}(\mathbf{x}) = (a_1, \ldots, a_n)$ and
$\quad \widetilde{H}_R(\mathbf{x}) \equiv (\lambda_1, \ldots, \lambda_n) \bmod q$, which appear in Lemma 1 for $\mathbf{c}$.
$\Longrightarrow \widetilde{\mathbf{b}} \in I_p^n$ is a solution of the equation over $\mathbb{F}_p$, $\widetilde{G}(\mathbf{x}) \equiv (a_1, \ldots, a_n) \bmod p$.

From this, a computing algorithm of $G^{-1}(\mathbf{c}) \in I_p^n$ is obtained as follows:

1. For all $i = 1, \ldots, n$, find a (unique) $\lambda_i \in \Lambda_i$ such that $|\text{lift}_q(c_i - \lambda_i)| < M_{\widetilde{G}}$, and set $\widetilde{c}_i = \text{lift}_q(c_i - \lambda_i) \in \mathbb{Z}$.
2. Solve the equation over $\mathbb{F}_p$, $\widetilde{G}(\mathbf{x}) \equiv (\widetilde{c}_1, \ldots, \widetilde{c}_n) \bmod p$. (We can solve this by the assumption for $\widetilde{G}(\mathbf{x})$.) The solution is denoted by $\mathbf{b} = (b_1, \ldots, b_n) \in \mathbb{F}_p^n$.
3. $G^{-1}(\mathbf{c}) = \text{lift}_p(\mathbf{b}) = (\text{lift}_p(b_1), \ldots, \text{lift}_p(b_n))$.

3 Key Generation, Encryption and Decryption of pq-Method

The polynomial system $G(\mathbf{x})$ described in the previous section can be applied to construction of encryption scheme in MPKC. By choosing an affine transformation T on $\mathbb{F}_q^n$ and a permutation matrix S randomly, we define $F(\mathbf{x})$ by $F = T \circ G \circ S$. Here, S is regarded as a linear transformation on $\mathbb{Z}^n$. We can then construct an encryption scheme whose public key is $F(\mathbf{x})$. The following are the algorithms for key generation, encryption and decryption method for this encryption scheme.

- **Key Generation Algorithm**
  Let p be an odd prime number, n a positive integer, and $l_{\widetilde{H}}$ a positive odd integer.
  1. Take a multivariate quadratic polynomial system $\widetilde{G}(\mathbf{x}) \in \mathbb{Z}[\mathbf{x}]^n$ such that $\widetilde{G}(\mathbf{x}) \bmod p$ is (almost) injective and its inverse can be computed efficiently.
  2. Choose a multivariate quadratic polynomial system $\widetilde{H}(\mathbf{x}) = (\widetilde{h}_1(\mathbf{x}), \ldots, \widetilde{h}_n(\mathbf{x})) \in \mathbb{Z}[\mathbf{x}]^n$ whose coefficients are randomly sampled from $I_{l_{\widetilde{H}}}$.
  3. Compute $M_{\widetilde{G}}, M_{\widetilde{H}}$ satisfying (1), and choose an odd prime number q such that $q > 4M_{\widetilde{H}}M_{\widetilde{G}}$.
  4. Choose $(M_{\widetilde{G}} <) r_1, \ldots, r_n \ (< q)$ such that

  $$2M_{\widetilde{G}} < \min_{k=1,\ldots,2M_{\widetilde{H}}}\{|\text{lift}_q(r_i k)|\} \quad (i = 1, \ldots, n).$$

  Unless such $r_1, \ldots, r_n$ are obtained, restart from Step 3 and reselect q.
  5. Compute $\widetilde{H}_R(\mathbf{x}) = (r_1\widetilde{h}_1(\mathbf{x}), \ldots, r_n\widetilde{h}_n(\mathbf{x})) \in \mathbb{Z}[\mathbf{x}]^n$, and
  $$G(\mathbf{x}) = (g_1(\mathbf{x}), \ldots, g_n(\mathbf{x})) = \left(\widetilde{G}(\mathbf{x}) + \widetilde{H}_R(\mathbf{x})\right) \bmod q \in \mathbb{F}_q[\mathbf{x}]^n.$$
  6. Choose an affine transformation T on $\mathbb{F}_q^n$ and a permutation matrix S of size n randomly.
  7. Compute $F = T \circ G \circ S : \mathbb{Z}^n \to \mathbb{F}_q^n$.
  The secret key consists of $\widetilde{G}(\mathbf{x}) \bmod p, \{r_1, \ldots, r_n\}, T, S$, and the public key consists of p and $F(\mathbf{x})$.
- **Encryption Algorithm**
  Let $\mathbf{m} \in I_p^n$ be a plaintext.
  1. Compute $\mathbf{c} = F(\mathbf{m}) \in \mathbb{F}_q^n$.
  Now, $\mathbf{c}$ is the ciphertext corresponding to $\mathbf{m}$.
- **Decryption Algorithm**
  Let $\mathbf{c} \in \mathbb{F}_q^n$ be a ciphertext.

$\underline{1}$. Compute $\mathbf{c}' = (c_1', \ldots, c_n') = T^{-1}(\mathbf{c})$.

$\underline{2}$. For all $i = 1, \ldots, n$, find a (unique) $\lambda_i \in \Lambda_i$ satisfying $|\mathrm{lift}_q(c_i' - \lambda_i)| < M_{\widetilde{G}}$ and set $\widetilde{c}_i = \mathrm{lift}_q(c_i' - \lambda_i) \in \mathbb{Z}$.

$\underline{3}$. Solve the equation over $\mathbb{F}_p$, $\widetilde{G}(\mathbf{x}) \equiv (\widetilde{c}_1, \ldots, \widetilde{c}_n) \bmod p$. The solution is denoted by $\widetilde{\mathbf{b}} \in I_p^n$. ($\widetilde{\mathbf{b}}$ is computable by the assumption for $\widetilde{G}(\mathbf{x})$.)

$\underline{4}$. Compute $\mathbf{a} = S^{-1}(\widetilde{\mathbf{b}})$.

Now, $\mathbf{a}$ coincides with the plaintext $\mathbf{m}$.

4   Encryption Schemes Constructed by pq-Method

In the previous section, while discussing the pq-method, $\widetilde{G}(\mathbf{x})$ is expressed as a general form and its concrete construction is not given. In this section, three types of $\widetilde{G}(\mathbf{x})$ are exemplified from the central map of previous encryption schemes used in MPKC, and subsequently, three encryption scheme, pq-TM, pq-C^* and pq-Square are proposed.

4.1 pq-TM

pq-TM is an encryption scheme that uses a triangular map. Similar to TTM [19, 20], several other encryption schemes in MPKC using a triangular map have already been proposed [11, 26, 29] and analyzed [6, 8, 13, 14, 21, 24] in several papers. From these study, we know that the rank attack works well with the schemes using a triangular map.

In pq-TM, the following is adopted as $\widetilde{G}(\mathbf{x})$. Let $l_{\widetilde{G},1}, l_{\widetilde{G},2}$ be positive odd integers. $\widetilde{G}_1(\mathbf{x}) = (\phi_1(\mathbf{x}), \ldots, \phi_n(\mathbf{x}))$, $\widetilde{G}_2(\mathbf{x}) = (\psi_1(\mathbf{x}), \ldots, \psi_n(\mathbf{x})) \in \mathbb{Z}[\mathbf{x}]^n$ are taken randomly in the following form: for any $i = 1, \ldots, n$,

$$\phi_i(\mathbf{x}) = \sum_{0 \le k \le l < i} \alpha_{k,l}^{(i)} x_k x_l + \sum_{0 \le k < i} \beta_k^{(i)} x_k + x_i + \gamma^{(i)} \quad (\alpha_{k,l}^{(i)}, \beta_k^{(i)}, \gamma^{(i)} \in I_{l_{\widetilde{G},1}}),$$

$$\psi_i(\mathbf{x}) = \sum_{\substack{0 \le k \le l \le n, \\ k \ge i \text{ or } l \ge i}} {\alpha'}_{k,l}^{(i)} x_k x_l + \sum_{i < k \le n} {\beta'}_k^{(i)} x_k \quad ({\alpha'}_{k,l}^{(i)}, {\beta'}_k^{(i)} \in I_{l_{\widetilde{G},2}}).$$

$\psi_i(\mathbf{x})$ is a polynomial replenishing the terms that do not appear in $\phi_i(\mathbf{x})$. We define $\widetilde{G}(\mathbf{x})$ by $\widetilde{G}(\mathbf{x}) = \widetilde{G}_1(\mathbf{x}) + p\widetilde{G}_2(\mathbf{x})$. Remember that $\widetilde{G}(\mathbf{x}) \equiv \widetilde{G}_1(\mathbf{x}) \bmod p$ by the definition of $\widetilde{G}(\mathbf{x})$. $\widetilde{G}(\mathbf{x}) \bmod p : \mathbb{F}_p^n \to \mathbb{F}_p^n$ is injective, in fact, the inverse image $\mathbf{b} = (b_1, \ldots, b_n) \in \mathbb{F}_p^n$ of $\mathbf{c} = (c_1, \ldots, c_n) \in \mathbb{F}_p^n$ is obtained as follows:

$\underline{1}$. For $i = 1, \ldots, n$ in this order, the following is executed.

$$b_i = c_i - \left(\sum_{0 \le k \le l < i} \alpha_{k,l}^{(i)} b_k b_l + \sum_{0 \le k < i} \beta_k^{(i)} b_k + \gamma^{(i)} \right).$$

The reason why $\widetilde{G}_2(\mathbf{x})$ is used in the definition of $\widetilde{G}(\mathbf{x})$ consists in the security. This is discussed in Sect. 5.4.

4.2 $pq\text{-}C^*$

$pq\text{-}C^*$ uses the central map of the scheme C^* as $\widetilde{G}(\mathbf{x})$ mod p. C^* was initially proposed by Matsumoto and Imai [18], however, it was broken by Patarin [25]. It is known that the Kipnis-Shamir attack [17] and the direct attack [7] also work efficiently for C^*.

Let us explain $\widetilde{G}(\mathbf{x})$ used in $pq\text{-}C^*$. Let $h(t) \in \mathbb{F}_p[t]$ be a monic irreducible polynomial of degree n, and $K = \mathbb{F}_p[t]/(h(x))$ be an extension field of $\mathbb{F}_p$ of degree n. The $\mathbb{F}_p$-isomorphism $\rho : K \to \mathbb{F}_p^n$ is defined by

$$\rho(a_0 + a_1 t + \cdots + a_{n-1} t^{n-1}) = (a_0, a_1, \ldots, a_{n-1}) \quad (a_0, \ldots, a_{n-1} \in \mathbb{F}_p).$$

Choose θ such that $0 < \theta < n$, let integers κ and α be defined by $\kappa = \gcd(p^\theta + 1, p^n - 1)$ and $\kappa = \alpha(p^\theta + 1)$ mod $p^n - 1$. A polynomial $\check{G}(X)$ over K in one variable is defined by $\check{G}(X) = X^{p^\theta + 1}$, and $\check{G}_0(\mathbf{x}) : \mathbb{F}_p^n \to \mathbb{F}_p^n$ is given by $\check{G}_0 = \rho \circ \check{G} \circ \rho^{-1}$. Then, $\check{G}_0(\mathbf{x})$ becomes a homogeneous quadratic polynomial system. $\widetilde{G}(\mathbf{x}) \in \mathbb{Z}[\mathbf{x}]$ is defined as satisfying that its all coefficients belong to I_p and $\widetilde{G}(\mathbf{x}) \equiv \check{G}_0(\mathbf{x})$ mod p. Then, $\widetilde{G}(\mathbf{x})$ mod p ($= \check{G}_0(\mathbf{x})$) is almost injective, and the inverse image $\mathbf{b} = (b_1, \ldots, b_n) \in \mathbb{F}_p^n$ of $\mathbf{c} = (c_1, \ldots, c_n) \in \mathbb{F}_p^n$ is obtained as follows:

1. Compute $\mathbf{w} = \rho^{-1}(\mathbf{c})$.
2. Compute $\mathbf{v} = \mathbf{w}^\alpha$.
3. Compute a solution $\mathbf{u}$ of the equation $X^\kappa = \mathbf{v}$ (using a solver such as the Berlekamp algorithm).
4. Compute $\mathbf{b} = \rho(\mathbf{u})$.

In $pq\text{-}C^*$, T is not chosen as an affine transformation, but as a linear transformation. Thereby, $F(\mathbf{x})$ becomes a homogeneous quadratic polynomial system.

4.3 $pq\text{-}$Square

$pq\text{-}$Square uses the central map of the scheme, Square as $\widetilde{G}(\mathbf{x})$ mod p. Square was proposed by Clough et al. [5], however, it was broken using the differential attack by Billet et al. [3].

Let us explain $\widetilde{G}(\mathbf{x})$ used in $pq\text{-}$Square. Similarly for $pq\text{-}C^*$, let $h(t) \in \mathbb{F}_p[t]$ be a monic irreducible polynomial of degree n, and $K = \mathbb{F}_p[t]/(h(x))$ an extension field of $\mathbb{F}_p$ of degree n. The $\mathbb{F}_p$-isomorphism $\rho : K \to \mathbb{F}_p^n$ is defined similar to the case of $pq\text{-}C^*$. A polynomial $\check{G}(X)$ over K in one variable is defined by $\check{G}(X) = X^2$, and $\check{G}_1(\mathbf{x}) : \mathbb{F}_p^n \to \mathbb{F}_p^n$ is given by $\check{G}_1 = \rho \circ \check{G} \circ \rho^{-1}$. Then, $\check{G}_1(\mathbf{x})$ becomes a homogeneous quadratic polynomial system. $\widetilde{G}_1(\mathbf{x}) \in \mathbb{Z}[\mathbf{x}]$ is defined to be satisfying as all its coefficients belong to I_p and $\widetilde{G}_1(\mathbf{x}) \equiv \check{G}_1(\mathbf{x})$ mod p. Let $l_{\widetilde{G},2}$ be a positive odd integer. A homogeneous quadratic polynomial system $\widetilde{G}_2(\mathbf{x}) = (\psi_1(\mathbf{x}), \ldots, \psi_n(\mathbf{x})) \in \mathbb{Z}[\mathbf{x}]^n$ is taken randomly, for $i = 1, \ldots, n$, in the form,

$$\psi_i(\mathbf{x}) = \sum_{\substack{0 \le k \le l \le n, \\ k+l < n}} \alpha'^{(i)}_{k,l} x_k x_l \qquad (\alpha'^{(i)}_{k,l} \in I_{l_{\tilde{G},2}}).$$

$\widetilde{G}(\mathbf{x})$ is defined by $\widetilde{G}(\mathbf{x}) = \widetilde{G}_1(\mathbf{x}) + p\,\widetilde{G}_2(\mathbf{x})$. Then, $\widetilde{G}(\mathbf{x}) \bmod p \ (= \check{G}_1(\mathbf{x}))$ is almost injective (exactly, two-to-one), and the inverse image $\mathbf{b} = (b_1, \ldots, b_n) \in \mathbb{F}_p^n$ of $\mathbf{c} = (c_1, \ldots, c_n) \in \mathbb{F}_p^n$ is obtained as follows:

1. Compute $\mathbf{w} = \rho^{-1}(\mathbf{c})$.
2. Compute a solution $\mathbf{u}$ of the equation $X^2 = \mathbf{w}$ (using a square root algorithm such as the Tonelli-Shanks algorithm).
3. Compute $\mathbf{b} = \rho(\mathbf{u})$.

In pq-Square, similar to pq-C^*, T is not chosen as an affine transformation, but as a linear transformation. Then, $F(\mathbf{x})$ becomes a homogeneous quadratic polynomial system.

Remark 1. (1) Any coefficient of the terms $x_k x_l$ $(k+l < n)$ of each component of $\widetilde{G}_1(\mathbf{x})$ is either 0 or 1. Therefore, in order to increase the number of candidates of the coefficient, $\widetilde{G}_2(\mathbf{x})$ is appended. This is necessary for security, and its reason is discussed in Sect. 5.4.

(2) In case of a scheme in "big field" system such as C^* and Square, the equivalence class of the public key itself remains unchanged even if a monic irreducible polynomial $h(t)$ is exchanged. However, in the case of pq-C^* and pq-Square, different equivalence classes of public key are obtained when $h(t)$ is exchanged because the action of reduction modulo p cannot be realized by the arithmetic operation of $\mathbb{F}_q$. Therefore, many equivalence classes of public key can be created by exchanging $h(t)$.

5   Security Analysis of pq-Method

The security of the pq-method is mainly based on the difficulty of solving the constrained MQ problem.

Constrained MQ problem: For positive integers m, n and L, let $\mathcal{F}(\mathbf{x})$ be a polynomial system which consists of m quadratic polynomials over $\mathbb{F}_q$ in variables $\mathbf{x} = (x_1, \ldots, x_n)$. Then, find $\mathbf{x}_0 \in I_L^n$ such that $\mathcal{F}(\mathbf{x}_0) = \mathbf{0}$.

In this section, fixing a ciphertext $\mathbf{c} \in \mathbb{F}_q^n$, we consider a polynomial system $\mathcal{F}(\mathbf{x}) = F(\mathbf{x}) - \mathbf{c}$ for a public key $F(\mathbf{x})$ constructed by the pq-method. For this $\mathcal{F}(\mathbf{x})$, we obtain the plaintext corresponding to $\mathbf{c}$ by solving the constrained MQ problem where $L = p$.

5.1   Constrained MQ Problem

A solution of the constrained MQ problem is also a solution for the general MQ problem. Therefore, attacks against the general MQ problem are applicable to the constrained MQ problem. Such attacks are considered in Sect. 5.3; however here, we observe a peculiar attack against the constrained MQ problem.

For $\mathcal{F}(\mathbf{x}) = (\hat{f}_1(\mathbf{x}), \ldots, \hat{f}_n(\mathbf{x}))$, each component $\hat{f}_i(\mathbf{x})$ has $\frac{n(n+1)}{2} + n + 1 = \frac{(n+1)(n+2)}{2}$ terms. This number is denoted by s_0. Determining an order of these terms, a vector $\mathbf{a}_i \in \mathbb{Z}^{s_0}$ is defined as the vector of coefficients lifted to integers from the coefficients of $\hat{f}_i(\mathbf{x})$. The q-ary lattice generated by $\mathbf{a}_1, \ldots, \mathbf{a}_n$ is denoted by $\mathcal{A}$. By solving the Shortest Independent Vector Problem (SIVP) for $\mathcal{A}$, n linearly independent short vectors $\mathbf{b}_1, \ldots, \mathbf{b}_n \in \mathbb{Z}^{s_0}$ in $\mathcal{A}$ are obtained. The polynomial over $\mathbb{Z}$ corresponding to the vector $\mathbf{b}_i$ is denoted by $\hat{h}_i(\mathbf{x})$, and let $\mathcal{H}(\mathbf{x}) = (\hat{h}_1(\mathbf{x}), \ldots, \hat{h}_n(\mathbf{x}))$. Then, the problem of solving the equation $\mathcal{F}(\mathbf{x}) = \mathbf{0}$ is reduced to the problem of solving the equation $\mathcal{H}(\mathbf{x}) \equiv \mathbf{0}$ mod q. Here, let us assume that for a solution $\mathbf{x}_0$ of the constrained MQ problem,

$$|\hat{h}_i(\mathbf{x}_0)| < \frac{q-1}{2} \quad (i = 1, \ldots, n) \tag{4}$$

are satisfied. Then, $\mathbf{x}_0$ is not only a solution of $\mathcal{H}(\mathbf{x}) \equiv \mathbf{0}$ mod q, but also a solution of the equation over $\mathbb{Z}$, $\mathcal{H}(\mathbf{x}) = \mathbf{0}$.

Solving the equation $\mathcal{H}(\mathbf{x}) = 0$ can be carried out efficiently by combining methods to solve approximately nonlinear equations over the real number field with the fact that $\mathbf{x}_0$ has integer components. Method to solve approximately $\mathcal{H}(\mathbf{x}) = 0$, includes the Levenberg-Marquardt method [16], and also optimization technique [2,23] for $\|\mathcal{H}(\mathbf{x})\|_2^2$ where $\| \cdot \|_2$ is the usual Euclid norm.

First, let us consider the possibility that $\mathcal{H}(\mathbf{x})$ satisfies (4) for a general constrained MQ problem. Since $\mathrm{vol}(\mathcal{A}) = q^{s_0-n}$, according to the Gaussian heuristic [22], it is expected that

$$\|\mathbf{b}_i\|_2 \approx \sqrt{\frac{s_0}{2\pi e}} q^{1-\frac{n}{s_0}} \quad (i = 1, \ldots, n).$$

Here, e is Napier's constant. Simply, assuming that $\sqrt{\frac{s_0}{2\pi e}}$ components of $\mathbf{b}_i$ are close to q, the probability satisfying (4) will be negligible if s_0 is sufficiently large.

Next, consider the case of a constrained MQ problem obtained by the pq-method. $\widetilde{G}(\mathbf{x}), \widetilde{H}(\mathbf{x})$ have small coefficients, but, the distribution of $r_1, \ldots, r_n$ is close to the uniform distribution on $[2M_{\widetilde{G}}, q - 2M_{\widetilde{G}} - 1]$. Therefore, considering $G(\mathbf{x})$ defined as, a coefficient of the components of $G(\mathbf{x})$ behaves as chosen randomly in $[M_{\widetilde{G}}, q - M_{\widetilde{G}} - 1]$. Since $M_{\widetilde{G}}$ is small as compared to q, similarly for a general constrained MQ problem, the probability of satisfying (4) must be negligible. This argument implies that the part $\widetilde{H}_R(\mathbf{x})$ is indispensable while defining $G(\mathbf{x})$.

5.2   Exhaustive Search

For the ciphertext $\mathbf{c}$, the solution $\mathbf{x}_0$ of $F(\mathbf{x}) = \mathbf{c}$ on I_p^n coincides with the plaintext. In the case of pq-C^* and pq-Square, $-\mathbf{x}_0$ is also a solution of $F(\mathbf{x}) = \mathbf{c}$ because $F(\mathbf{x})$ is homogeneous quadratic. Therefore, the complexity of the exhaustive search is given by $\mathcal{O}(p^n/2)$. In case of pq-TM, if the linear part $L(\mathbf{x})$ of $F(\mathbf{x})$ is regular, by changing $F(\mathbf{x})$ by $L^{-1} \circ F(\mathbf{x})$, it can be assumed that the linear part of $F(\mathbf{x})$ is the identity map. Instead of the equation $F(\mathbf{x}) = \mathbf{c}$, consider the inequality

$$\|F(\mathbf{x}) - \mathbf{x} - \mathbf{c}\|_\infty \leq p, \tag{5}$$

and find a solution of this inequality using the exhaustive search. Here, $\| \cdot \|_\infty$ represents the supremum norm (= the maximum of the absolute values of components). Since $\pm\mathbf{x}_0$ are all solutions of (5), the complexity also becomes $\mathcal{O}(p^n/2)$.

5.3   Algebraic Attack

The algebraic attack uses algebraic equation solvers such as XL [4] and Gröbner basis techniques [9,10] for solving the general MQ problem. The complexity of the algebraic attack can be calculated by the complexity of the hybrid approach [1] of computing the Gröbner basis and exhaustive search. In [1], while conducting the exhaustive search, all the elements in a finite field are substituted for several variables, but, in the pq-method, the part of the finite field must be changed into I_p.

For $k = 0, 1, \ldots, n$, we randomly choose $(v_{n-k+1}, v_{n-k+2}, \ldots, v_n) \in I_p^{\ k}$. We denote the polynomial system in $n - k$ variables obtained by substituting $(x_{n-k+1}, \ldots, x_n) = (v_{n-k+1}, \ldots, v_n)$ for $\mathcal{F}(\mathbf{x})$ by $\mathcal{F}_k(\mathbf{x}^{(k)})$. Here, $\mathbf{x}^{(k)} = (x_1, \ldots, x_{n-k})$. Note that $\mathcal{F}_0(\mathbf{x}^{(0)})$ is same as $\mathcal{F}(\mathbf{x})$.

For $\mathcal{F}_k(\mathbf{x}^{(k)}) = (\hat{f}_1(\mathbf{x}^{(k)}), \ldots, \hat{f}_n(\mathbf{x}^{(k)}))$, the homogeneous quadratic part of $\hat{f}_i(\mathbf{x}^{(k)})$ $(i = 1, \ldots, n)$ is denoted by $\hat{f}_i^h(\mathbf{x}^{(k)})$, and the homogeneous ideal $J^{(k)}$ of $\mathbb{F}_q[\mathbf{x}^{(k)}]$ is defined by

$$J^{(k)} = \langle \hat{f}_1^h(\mathbf{x}^{(k)}), \ldots, \hat{f}_n^h(\mathbf{x}^{(k)}) \rangle.$$

For $d \geq 0$, let $\mathbb{F}_q[\mathbf{x}^{(k)}]_d$ denote the subspace of $\mathbb{F}_q[\mathbf{x}^{(k)}]$ consisting of homogeneous polynomials of degree d, and $J_d^{(k)} = J^{(k)} \cap \mathbb{F}_q[\mathbf{x}^{(k)}]_d$. The Hilbert series of the quotient ring $\mathbb{F}_q[\mathbf{x}^{(k)}]/J^{(k)}$ is defined by

$$\mathrm{HS}_{\mathbb{F}_q[\mathbf{x}^{(k)}]/J^{(k)}}(t) = \sum_{d=0}^{\infty} \dim_{\mathbb{F}_q}(\mathbb{F}_q[\mathbf{x}^{(k)}]_d/J_d^{(k)})\, t^d \in \mathbb{Z}[[t]].$$

If the Krull-dimension of $J^{(k)}$ is zero, $\mathrm{HS}_{\mathbb{F}_q[\mathbf{x}^{(k)}]/J^{(k)}}(t)$ becomes a polynomial. Then, the degree of regularity, $d_{\mathrm{reg}}(k)$ is defined by $d_{\mathrm{reg}}(k) = \deg(\mathrm{HS}_{\mathbb{F}_q[\mathbf{x}^{(k)}]/J^{(k)}}(t)) + 1$. For any $S(t) \in \mathbb{Z}[[t]]$, the power series obtained by truncating $S(t)$ at its first non positive coefficient is denoted by $[S(t)]_+ \in \mathbb{Z}_{>0}[[t]]$. If

$$\mathrm{HS}_{\mathbb{F}_q[\mathbf{x}^{(k)}]/J^{(k)}}(t) = \left[\frac{(1-t^2)^n}{(1-t)^{n-k}} \right]_+ \tag{6}$$

is satisfied, $\mathcal{F}_k(\mathbf{x}^{(k)})$ is said to be semi-regular. When $k = 0$ and $\mathcal{F}_k(\mathbf{x}^{(k)})$ is semi-regular, it is simply called regular.

Under the preceding preparation, the complexity of the algebraic attack is described as follows [1]:

$$\min_{0 \leq k \leq n} \mathcal{O}\left(p^k \left(\frac{n - k + d_{\mathrm{reg}}(k) - 1}{d_{\mathrm{reg}}(k)} \right)^\omega \right). \tag{7}$$

Here, $2 \leq \omega \leq 3$ is the linear algebra constant of solving a linear system. Tables 1, 2 and 3 show the experimental result of computing the degree of regularity of $\mathcal{F}(\mathbf{x})$ for the three encryption schemes. For each parameter, 100 samples are experimented using MAGMA. As a result, for all cases, we got that $d_{\mathrm{reg}}(0) = n + 1$, or, $\mathcal{F}(\mathbf{x})$ is regular.

Based on the experimental result, we assume that $\mathcal{F}(\mathbf{x})$ is regular for any other parameter. When $\mathcal{F}(\mathbf{x})$ is regular, for $k = 1, \ldots, n$ and random substitution for k variables, the possibility that $\mathcal{F}_k(\mathbf{x}^{(k)})$ is semi-regular is high from the point of view of the Fröberg conjecture [12]. Therefore, by assuming that all $\mathcal{F}_k(\mathbf{x}^{(k)})$ are semi-regular, the complexity (7) of the algebraic attack can be computed using the value of the degree of regularity obtained by the Eq. (6).

5.4   Key Recovery Attack

Once an adversary knows the linear transformation part of the affine transformation T, he or she can calculate $G(\mathbf{x})$ from the public key, and can compute $r_1, \ldots, r_n, \widetilde{G}(\mathbf{x}), \widetilde{H}(\mathbf{x})$ easily from $G(\mathbf{x})$; hence, the secret information necessary for decryption become known. Therefore, let us now consider an attack to discover the linear transformation part T_1 of T.

Let $l_{\widetilde{G}}$ be defined by

$$l_{\widetilde{G}} = \begin{cases} \min\{l_{\widetilde{G},1}, l_{\widetilde{G},2}\} & \text{if } pq\text{-TM}, \\ p & \text{if } pq\text{-}C^*, \\ \min\{p, l_{\widetilde{G},2}\} & \text{if } pq\text{-Square}. \end{cases}$$

Table 1. Degree of regularity of pq-TM

Bit length of q	n	$d_{\mathrm{reg}}(0)$
22 bits	10	11
22 bits	11	12
23 bits	12	13
23 bits	13	14
24 bits	14	15

Table 2. Degree of regularity of pq-C^*

Bit length of q	n	$d_{\mathrm{reg}}(0)$
19 bits	10	11
20 bits	11	12
20 bits	12	13
21 bits	13	14
21 bits	14	15

Table 3. Degree of regularity of pq-Square

Bit length of q	n	$d_{\mathrm{reg}}(0)$
21 bits	10	11
21 bits	11	12
22 bits	12	13
22 bits	13	14
23 bits	14	15

An adversary who knows r_j for some j can compute the j-th row vector of T_1^{-1} by the following procedure.

1. Choose an integer u such that $n < u \leq \frac{(n+2)(n+1)}{2}$, and a (ordered) set M consisting of u monomials of degree less than or equal to 2.
2. For $F(\mathbf{x}) = (f_1(\mathbf{x}), \ldots, f_n(\mathbf{x}))$ and $i = 1, \ldots, n$, compute a vector $\mathbf{a}_i \in \mathbb{Z}^u$ of coefficients lifted to integers from coefficients of $f_i(\mathbf{x})$ with respect to M. The q-ary lattice of $\mathbb{Z}^u$ generated by $\mathbf{a}_1, \ldots, \mathbf{a}_n$ is denoted by $\mathcal{A}$.
3. Choose $\mathbf{b} = (b_1, \ldots, b_u) \in I_{l_{\tilde{A}}}^u$ randomly.
4. Search the vector $\mathbf{a}$ in $\mathcal{A}$ closest to $r_j\mathbf{b}$. If $\|r_j\mathbf{b} - \mathbf{a}\|_\infty < l_{\tilde{G}}/2$ is satisfied, output the coefficient vector $(c_1, \ldots, c_n)$ of the linear combination $\mathbf{a} \equiv c_1\mathbf{a}_1 + \cdots + c_n\mathbf{a}_n \bmod q$, and terminate. Otherwise, go back to Step 3.

The reason why u is chosen as $u > n$ in Step 1 is because otherwise, the lattice $\mathcal{A}$ coincides with the trivial lattice $\mathbb{Z}^u$. Again, in the case that u is close to n, the above algorithm may fail to output the j-th row vector of T_1^{-1}. Since $\mathbf{b}$ satisfying the inequality in Step 4 exists uniquely, even if we estimate the cost of searching the closest vector to be 1, the complexity of the preceding algorithm becomes $\mathcal{O}(l_{\widetilde{H}}^u)$, which is larger than $\mathcal{O}(l_{\widetilde{H}}^n)$.

If the vector $\mathbf{g} \in \mathbb{Z}^u$ of coefficients lifted to integers from coefficients of $\widetilde{g}_j(\mathbf{x})$ with respect to M coincides with $\mathbf{0}$, then $\mathbf{b}$ satisfying the inequality in Step 4 can be found by computing the shortest vector of $\mathcal{A}$. Therefore, in this case, the complexity of the algorithm is reduced dramatically. To prevent this, we must ensure that $\mathbf{g}$ is never equal to $\mathbf{0}$. In the case of pq-C^*, the construction of $\widetilde{G}(\mathbf{x})$ ensures that $\mathbf{g}$ is not equal to $\mathbf{0}$. In the case of pq-TM and pq-Square, since a replenishing polynomial $\widetilde{G}_2(\mathbf{x})$ of $\widetilde{G}_1(\mathbf{x})$ is appended in the construction of $\widetilde{G}(\mathbf{x})$, $\mathbf{g}$ becomes non-zero.

Moreover, the above attack can exchange the roll of $\widetilde{G}(\mathbf{x})$ and $\widetilde{H}(\mathbf{x})$. Namely, if the above algorithm is changed by $l_{\widetilde{G}} \leftrightarrow l_{\widetilde{H}}, r_i \rightarrow 1/r_i$, it will work as an attack. The complexity of this attack is $\mathcal{O}(l_{\widetilde{G}}^u)(> \mathcal{O}(l_{\widetilde{G}}^n))$.

5.5   Attack Against pq-TM

In pq-TM, a triangular map $\widetilde{G}_1(\mathbf{x}) = (\phi_1(\mathbf{x}), \ldots, \phi_n(\mathbf{x}))$ is used. While writing the homogeneous quadratic part of each $\phi_i(\mathbf{x})$ for $\phi_i^h(\mathbf{x})$, we have

$$\phi_1^h(\mathbf{x}) = 0,$$
$$\phi_2^h(\mathbf{x}) \in \mathbb{Z}[x_1],$$
$$\phi_3^h(\mathbf{x}) \in \mathbb{Z}[x_1, x_2],$$
$$\phi_4^h(\mathbf{x}) \in \mathbb{Z}[x_1, x_2, x_3],$$
$$\vdots$$

Most schemes in MPKC that use a triangular map as the secret key, such as TTM, were broken using the above structure of triangular map [13].

In pq-TM, to $\widetilde{G}_1(\mathbf{x})$, a polynomial $p\widetilde{G}_2(\mathbf{x})$ is appended, therefore, it is designed not to have any special structure as above. Moreover, since a polynomial $\widetilde{H}_R(\mathbf{x})$ is also appended, it is difficult to extract the part $\widetilde{G}(\mathbf{x})$ from $G(\mathbf{x})$. Therefore, the application of the rank attack as seen in [13] is impossible.

5.6   Attack Against pq-C^* and pq-Square

C^* and Square use a special polynomial with one variable over the extension field K as the central map. This is same for pq-C^* and pq-Square. The linearization equation attack [25] and the Kipnis-Shamir attack [17] which are attacks against C^*, and the differential attack [3] which is an attack against Square, make use of the algebraic structure of the extension field K.

Whereas, in the case of pq-C^* and pq-Square, K is used for the construction of $\check{G}_0(\mathbf{x})$ and $\check{G}_1(\mathbf{x})$. However, other than these polynomials, $G(\mathbf{x})$ can also be constructed by appending polynomials such as $\widetilde{H}_R(\mathbf{x})$ that have no relation with K. Therefore, properties of K are not reflected in $G(\mathbf{x})$, and the linearization equation attack, the Kipnis-Shamir attack and the differential attack cannot be applied to pq-C^* and pq-Square.

6   Selection of Parameters and Implementation

6.1   Selection of Parameters

Based on the security analysis in the previous section, we present secure parameters. Hereafter, we assume that $l_{\widetilde{H}} = p$, and both $l_{\widetilde{G},1}$ and $l_{\widetilde{G},2}$ appearing in pq-TM or pq-Square are equal to p. The complexity (7) of the algebraic attack is estimated using $\omega = 2$. The complexity of the attack in Sect. 5.4 is estimated by $\mathcal{O}(p^n)$. Then, all of pq-TM, pq-C^* and pq-Square have the correspondence of the security levels with the parameters (p, n) as Table 4.

Table 4. Security level and parameters

Security level	(p, n)
128 bits	$(3, 91), (5, 71), (7, 65)$
192 bits	$(3, 140), (5, 110), (7, 99)$

6.2   Implementation

We explain our implementation for searching λ_i in Step 2 in the decryption algorithm in Sect. 3. Let μ be an integer such that $0 \leq \mu \leq 2M_{\widetilde{H}}$, and

$$\Lambda_i'(\mu) = \{\mathrm{lift}_q(r_i k) \mid k = 0, 1, 2, \ldots, \mu\}.$$

This set is computed and sorted in the usual order in the process of the key generation. In our implementation, λ_i is found as follows:

1. Search $\lambda' \in \Lambda_i'(\mu)$ such that $|\mathrm{lift}_q(|c_i'| - \lambda')| < M_{\widetilde{G}}$ using the binary search. If λ' is found, go to Step 3.
2. For $k = \mu+1, \mu+2, \ldots$ in this order, find k such that $|\mathrm{lift}_q(|c_i'| - r_i k)| < M_{\widetilde{G}}$. Set $\lambda' = r_i k$.
3. Determine $\lambda = \pm\lambda'$ by $c_i \cdot \lambda \geq 0$, and output λ.

The binary search is executed efficiently in $\mathcal{O}(\log \mu)$ time. However, as μ gets larger, the secret key size becomes larger.

We implemented pq-TM, pq-C^* and pq-Square with secure parameters given in Table 4 using Intel Core i7-6700, 3.4GHz. We used C++ programming language with g++ compiler. As an algorithm of the binary search, lower_bound in <algorithm> library was used. The experiment is carried out for three kinds of μ. One is $\mu = 0$, another is $\mu = 2M_{\widetilde{H}}$, and the other is about twice of the average of the evaluation of $H(\mathbf{x})$. The following is the experimental result.

128-bit security level

– pq-TM

p	n	q	PK (bytes)	Enc.(μs)	μ	SK (bytes)	Dec.(μs)
					0	60, 697	210
3	91	27 bits	1, 285, 625	619	200	125, 443	183
					2, 930	995, 585	215
					0	44, 410	102
5	71	33 bits	748, 588	288	800	278, 710	103
					12, 900	3, 827, 184	115
					0	37, 269	136
7	65	36 bits	627, 412	144	2, 000	622, 269	115
					34, 500	10, 099, 561	130

– pq-C^*

p	n	q	PK (bytes)	Enc.(μs)	μ	SK (bytes)	Dec.(μs)
					0	27, 231	2, 286
3	91	26 bits	1, 238, 009	634	200	86, 381	2, 275
					2, 850	876, 921	2, 582
					0	19, 196	1, 184
5	71	30 bits	680, 535	284	800	232, 196	1, 208
					12, 600	3, 377, 141	1, 286
					0	17, 720	1, 177
7	65	33 bits	575, 128	155	2, 000	553, 970	1, 131
					34, 200	9, 165, 877	1, 146

– pq-Square

p	n	q	PK (bytes)	Enc.(μs)	μ	SK (bytes)	Dec.(μs)
					0	28, 278	1, 526
3	91	27 bits	1, 285, 625	627	200	89, 703	1, 522
					2, 900	905, 734	1, 525
					0	20, 474	896
5	71	32 bits	725, 904	290	800	247, 674	872
					12, 700	3, 594, 330	886
					0	18, 793	856
7	65	35 bits	609, 984	152	2, 000	587, 543	842
					34, 300	9, 706, 027	858

192-bit security level

– pq-TM

p	n	q	PK (bytes)	Enc.(μs)	μ	SK (bytes)	Dec.(μs)
3	140	30 bits	5,181,750	2,520	0	190,820	530
					300	348,320	508
					6,800	3,764,495	534
5	110	35 bits	2,938,031	1,578	0	138,888	313
					1,400	812,638	313
					30,200	14,625,476	322
7	99	38 bits	2,327,737	888	0	109,518	290
					3,200	1,614,318	285
					78,500	36,820,055	311

– pq-C^*

p	n	q	PK (bytes)	Enc.(μs)	μ	SK (bytes)	Dec.(μs)
3	140	28 bits	4,836,300	2,392	0	69,125	7,046
					300	216,125	6,949
					6,700	3,355,065	7,088
5	110	33 bits	2,770,143	1,534	0	50,407	3,774
					1,400	685,657	3,743
					29,900	13,595,752	3,750
7	99	36 bits	2,205,225	865	0	44,587	3,262
					3,200	1,470,187	3,110
					78,000	34,835,018	3,139

– pq-Square

p	n	q	PK (bytes)	Enc.(μs)	μ	SK (bytes)	Dec.(μs)
3	140	29 bits	5,009,025	2,432	0	74,060	4,835
					300	223,842	4,575
					6,680	3,463,722	4,596
5	110	34 bits	2,854,087	1,544	0	51,933	2,573
					1,400	706,433	2,502
					29,800	14,011,483	2,543
7	99	37 bits	2,266,481	844	0	47,062	2,389
					3,200	1,511,024	2,377
					78,000	35,790,294	2,388

7 Conclusion

We have introduced the constrained MQ problem as a new mathematical problem to be used as a security assumption for encryption schemes in MPKC.

We have also proposed the pq-method, as a construction method of encryption schemes in MPKC whose security is mainly based on the constrained MQ problem. In this paper, three encryption schemes using the pq-method are presented. On the other hand, the pq-method can be regarded as a kind of modifier of encryption scheme in MPKC. Therefore, the pq-method is also applicable to any encryption scheme in MPKC other than our proposals.

The constrained MQ problem itself is an interesting problem and should be analyzed by various approach. We expect that the constrained MQ problem will be discussed well and be applied to many scheme constructions.

Acknowledgement. This work was supported by JSPS Grant-in-Aid for Scientific Research(C), KAKENHI Grant Number JP17K00197.

References

1. Bettale, L., Faugère, J.-C., Perret, L.: Hybrid approach for solving multivariate systems over finite fields. J. Math. Cryptol. **3**(3), 177–197 (2009)
2. Bertsekas, D.P.: Nonlinear Programming, 3rd edn. Athena Scientific, Belmont (2016)
3. Billet, O., Macario-Rat, G.: Cryptanalysis of the square cryptosystems. In: Matsui, M. (ed.) ASIACRYPT 2009. LNCS, vol. 5912, pp. 451–468. Springer, Heidelberg (2009). https://doi.org/10.1007/978-3-642-10366-7_27
4. Yang, B.-Y., Chen, J.-M.: All in the XL family: theory and practice. In: Park, C., Chee, S. (eds.) ICISC 2004. LNCS, vol. 3506, pp. 67–86. Springer, Heidelberg (2005). https://doi.org/10.1007/11496618_7
5. Clough, C., Baena, J., Ding, J., Yang, B.-Y., Chen, M.: Square, a new multivariate encryption scheme. In: Fischlin, M. (ed.) CT-RSA 2009. LNCS, vol. 5473, pp. 252–264. Springer, Heidelberg (2009). https://doi.org/10.1007/978-3-642-00862-7_17
6. Coppersmith, D., Stern, J., Vaudenay, S.: The security of the birational permutation signature schemes. J. Cryptogr. **10**(3), 207–221 (1997)
7. Ding, J., Gower, J.E., Schmidt, D.S.: Multivariate Public Key Cryptosystems. Advances in Information Security, vol. 25. Springer, Heidelberg (2006). https://doi.org/10.1007/978-0-387-36946-4
8. Ding, J., Schmidt, D.: The new implementation schemes of the TTM cryptosystem are not secure. Progress Comput. Sci. Appl. Log. **23**, 113–127 (2004)
9. Faugère, J.-C.: A new efficient algorithm for computing Gröbner bases (F4). J. Pure Appl. Algebra **139**, 61–88 (1999)
10. Faugère, J.-C.: A new efficient algorithm for computing Gröbner bases without reduction to zero (F5). In: Proceedings of ISSAC 2002, pp. 75–83. ACM Press (2002)
11. Fell, H.J., Diffie, W.: Analysis of a public key approach based on polynomial substitution. In: Williams, H.C. (ed.) CRYPTO 1985. LNCS, vol. 218, pp. 340–349. Springer, Heidelberg (1986). https://doi.org/10.1007/3-540-39799-X_24
12. Fröberg, R.: An inequality for Hilbert series of graded algebras. Mathematica Scandinavica **56**, 117–144 (1985)
13. Goubin, L., Courtois, N.T.: Cryptanalysis of the TTM cryptosystem. In: Okamoto, T. (ed.) ASIACRYPT 2000. LNCS, vol. 1976, pp. 44–57. Springer, Heidelberg (2000). https://doi.org/10.1007/3-540-44448-3_4

14. Hassegawa, S., Kaneko, T.: An attacking method for a public key cryptosystem based on the difficulty of solving a system of non-linear equations. In: Proceedings of 10th SITA, JA5-3 (1987). (in Japanese)

15. Ikematsu, Y., Perlner, R., Smith-Tone, D., Takagi, T., Vates, J.: HFERP - a new multivariate encryption scheme. In: Lange, T., Steinwandt, R. (eds.) PQCrypto 2018. LNCS, vol. 10786, pp. 396–416. Springer, Cham (2018). https://doi.org/10. 1007/978-3-319-79063-3_19

16. Kanzowa, C., Yamashita, N., Fukushima, M.: Levenberg-Marquardt methods with strong local convergence properties for solving nonlinear equations with convex constraints. J. Comput. Appl. Math. **172**(2), 375–397 (2004)

17. Kipnis, A., Shamir, A.: Cryptanalysis of the HFE public key cryptosystem by relinearization. In: Wiener, M. (ed.) CRYPTO 1999. LNCS, vol. 1666, pp. 19–30. Springer, Heidelberg (1999). https://doi.org/10.1007/3-540-48405-1_2

18. Matsumoto, T., Imai, H.: Public quadratic polynomial-tuples for efficient signature-verification and message-encryption. In: Barstow, D., et al. (eds.) EUROCRYPT 1988. LNCS, vol. 330, pp. 419–453. Springer, Heidelberg (1988). https://doi.org/ 10.1007/3-540-45961-8_39

19. Moh, T.-T.: A fast public key system with signature and master key functions. Commun. Algebra **27**(5), 2207–2222 (1999)

20. Moh, T.-T.: A fast public key system with signature and master Key functions. In: Proceedings of CrypTEC 1999, pp. 63–69 (1999)

21. Moh, T.-T., Chen, J.-M.: On the Goubin-Courtois attack on TTM. Cryptology ePrint Archive (2001). http://eprint.iacr.org/2001/072

22. Nguyen, P.Q.: Hermite's constant and lattice algorithms. In: Nguyen, P., Vallée, B. (eds.) The LLL Algorithm. ISC, pp. 19–69. Springer, Heidelberg (2009). https:// doi.org/10.1007/978-3-642-02295-1_2

23. Nocedal, J., Wright, S.J.: Numerical Optimization, 2nd edn. Springer, Heidelberg (2006). https://doi.org/10.1007/978-0-387-40065-5

24. Okamoto, E., Nakamura, K.: Evaluation of public key cryptosystems proposed recently. In: Proceedings of 1986's Symposium of Cryptography and Information Security, vol. D1 (1986). (in Japanese)

25. Patarin, J.: Cryptanalysis of the matsumoto and imai public key scheme of Eurocrypt 88. In: Coppersmith, D. (ed.) CRYPTO 1995. LNCS, vol. 963, pp. 248–261. Springer, Heidelberg (1995). https://doi.org/10.1007/3-540-44750-4_20

26. Shamir, A.: Efficient signature schemes based on birational permutations. In: Stinson, D.R. (ed.) CRYPTO 1993. LNCS, vol. 773, pp. 1–12. Springer, Heidelberg (1994). https://doi.org/10.1007/3-540-48329-2_1

27. Szepieniec, A., Ding, J., Preneel, B.: Extension field cancellation: a new central trapdoor for multivariate quadratic systems. In: Takagi, T. (ed.) PQCrypto 2016. LNCS, vol. 9606, pp. 182–196. Springer, Cham (2016). https://doi.org/10.1007/ 978-3-319-29360-8_12

28. Tao, C., Diene, A., Tang, S., Ding, J.: Simple matrix scheme for encryption. In: Gaborit, P. (ed.) PQCrypto 2013. LNCS, vol. 7932, pp. 231–242. Springer, Heidelberg (2013). https://doi.org/10.1007/978-3-642-38616-9_16

29. Tsujii, S., Itoh, T., Fujioka, A., Kurosawa, K., Matsumoto, T.: Public-key cryptosystem based on the difficulty of solving a system of nonlinear equations. IEEE Xplore Electron. Lett. **23**(11), 558–560 (1987)

Token-Based Multi-input Functional Encryption

Nuttapong Attrapadung[1], Goichiro Hanaoka[1], Takato Hirano[2],
Yutaka Kawai[2(✉)], Yoshihiro Koseki[2], and Jacob C. N. Schuldt[1]

[1] National Institute of Advanced Industrial Science and Technology (AIST),
Tokyo, Japan
[2] Mitsubishi Electric Corporation, Tokyo, Japan
Kawai.Yutaka@da.MitsubishiElectric.co.jp

Abstract. In this paper, we put forward the notion of a token-based
multi-input functional encryption (token-based MIFE) scheme – a notion
intended to give encryptors a mechanism to control the decryption of
encrypted messages, by extending the encryption and decryption algorithms to additionally use tokens. The basic idea is that a decryptor
must hold an appropriate decryption token in addition to his secrete
key, to be able to decrypt. This type of scheme can address security concerns potentially arising in applications of functional encryption aimed
at addressing the problem of privacy preserving data analysis. We firstly
formalize token-based MIFE, and then provide two basic schemes based
on an ordinary MIFE scheme and a public key encryption scheme and a
pseudorandom function (PRF), respectively. Lastly, we extend the latter
construction to allow decryption tokens to be restricted to specified set
of encryptions, even if all encryptions have been done using the same
encryption token. This is achieved by using a constrained PRF.

1 Introduction

1.1 Background and Motivation

Nowadays, large amounts of data is constantly being collected, and data analysis has become an indispensable tool for extracting value from this data. However, central data collection and processing, which is typically at the heart of
the data collection, potentially leads to security or privacy issues, as the storage and processing provider, such as a cloud environment, is often not fully
trusted to keep the data or the extracted information private. This is especially
a concern, if the collected data contains sensitive information. As a potential
solution, homomorphic encryption (HE) and functional encryption (FE) have
attracted attention. Especially, multi-key homomorphic encryption (MKHE) or
multi-input functional encryption (MIFE) is expected to be suitable for the case
where the data is collected by different entities and will be processed by an entity
which is not fully trusted. Recently, MIFE for inner products has been studied [BLR+14, ARW16, LL16, KLM+16, ABDP15, DOT18] since the inner product operation frequently appears in various statistical computation.

© Springer Nature Switzerland AG 2018
J. Baek et al. (Eds.): ProvSec 2018, LNCS 11192, pp. 147–164, 2018.
https://doi.org/10.1007/978-3-030-01446-9_9

Let us consider the following data analysis scenario using HE or FE. A data analyst wants to analyze users' data stored on a cloud server, but is only trusted with the result of the analysis, and not the individual data of the users. In order to achieve this securely, users might encrypt their own data by using the HE or FE public key of the data analyst, and the store the ciphertexts in the cloud. Here, we refer to each user's ciphertext stored in the cloud as the *original ciphertext*. In the HE case, the data analyst might request the cloud to perform homomorphic evaluations of the original ciphertexts corresponding to the desired analysis, and will then be able to obtain the result by decrypting the evaluated ciphertext using his own (master) secret key. In the FE case, the data analyst can obtain the result of the data analysis by merely decrypting the original ciphertext(s) under his own secret key which embeds a function corresponding to the desired analysis.

The above approach might seem to be a secure way for the analyst to obtain the desired result. However, this might not be the case in all scenarios. For example, in the HE case, the analyst might be able to instruct the cloud environment to do a different type of processing or to limit the data which is being processed such that additional details regarding the data of individual users are leaked. In the extreme case, the analyst gains access to the original ciphertexts, in which case he can directly obtain the data of the individual users. In the FE case, analysts will often be required to have access to many different keys implementing various functions, and decrypting the user data with all of these will potentially leak unintended information regarding the user data. Furthermore, and perhaps more importantly, a different analysts holding a key corresponding to a different function might gain access the original ciphertexts and decrypt these using his key. As the data was intended for the original analyst holding a key for the original function, this might lead to unintended data leaks. This problem might be amplified if the key of one data analyst is compromised, as this will put all existing and future data at risk. Hence, in these scenarios, additional security measures might be warranted.

1.2 Our Contributions

In this paper, we attempt to address the above described problem, and focus on reducing the power of the master or user secret key. We propose a new encryption primitive, called *token-based* encryption, which provides the encryptor with additional means to control the decryption possible with the user secret key or the master secret key. Our token-based multi-input functional encryption (token-based MIFE) uses tokens both in the encryption and decryption processes, in addition to secret keys. Roughly speaking, in token-based MIFE, both an appropriate decryption token and the secret key are required to decrypt, and as the encryptors control the tokens, this provides an additional mechanism to address the above discussed issues. The purpose of this paper it to formalize token-based MIFE.

Token-Based MIFE. In this paper, we focus on multi-input functional encryption in the private key setting [GGG+14, BLR+14, ARW16, LL16, BKS16,

KLM+16, ABDP15, DOT18]. In token-based MIFE, we introduce new parameters – encryption tokens etk and decryption tokens dtk – which are output by a token generation algorithm GenToken. Informally speaking, token-based MIFE scheme is similar to ordinary MIFE scheme, except that (1) an encryption token etk is added to the input of encryption algorithm Enc, and (2) decryption algorithm Dec takes as input a decryption token in addition to the user secret key (and ciphertext). The encryption and decryption tokens are intended to be generated by the users encrypting the data in question, and the generation can be done independently of the key generation server holding the master secret key. Furthermore, new tokens can be generated as frequently as desired, which allow the user to partition the data they encrypt. By only distributing the relevant decryption tokens to the relevant decryption servers/analysts, the users can control what part of the data is accessible. For example, by encrypting data for two different analysts using different tokens, the user can ensure that one analyst cannot access data intended for the other.

In principle, users could generate a new set of tokens for each encryption done, which would correspond to a very fine-grained partitioning. However, the overhead of generating and managing tokens might make this undesirable. Furthermore, at the time of encryption, it might not be clear how the data should be partitioned. To address this, we additionally consider the ability to restrict decryption tokens to only work for a specified set of encryptions, even if all encryptions have been done using the same encryption token.

Specific Token-Based MIFE Schemes. In this paper, we present three specific token-based MIFE schemes. Firstly, we construct a simple scheme by combining a MIFE scheme and an ordinary public key encryption (PKE) scheme. In this scheme, the encryption and decryption tokens etk and dtk correspond to a public and private key of the PKE scheme, and encryptions simply correspond to double encryptions, using the MIFE scheme as the inner encryption. This scheme allows the entity generating the tokens, e.g. a chosen user, to broadcast the encryption token to the other users over a public channel.

The second token-based MIFE is constructed from a pseudorandom function (PRF) and a MIFE scheme. In this scheme, the ciphertexts of the underlying MIFE scheme are masked with masks generated using the PRF. However, to ensure security, the scheme is required to be stateful. In contrast to the first scheme, the token generation can be run in a distributed manner in the sense that each user can run the corresponding part of the token generation independently of the other users, but is then required to send the generated part of the decryption token to the decryption server.

Lastly, the third construction is an extension of the second one using a constrained PRF as opposed to an ordinary one. This allows the scheme to support decryption token restriction. Furthermore, using the GGM tree-based PRF [GGM84] as a constrained PRF, allows an efficient instantiation.

1.3　Paper Organization

The rest of the paper is organized as follows: In Sect. 2 we review the cryptographic preliminaries. In Sect. 3, we introduce the formal syntax and security definitions of token-based MIFE. In Sect. 4, we show our specific *stateless* scheme and it's security. In Sects. 5 and 6, we show our specific efficient *stateful* schemes and their security.

2　Preliminaries

In the following, we introduce the notion used in the paper, as well as the primitives our constructions are based on. In addition to the primitives in this section, we make use of a standard public key encryption scheme, which is defined in Appendix A.

2.1　Notation

Throughout the paper we will use $\lambda \in \mathbb{N}$ to denote the security parameter and will sometimes suppress the dependency on λ, when λ is clear from the context. We denote by $y \leftarrow x$ the assignment of y to x, and by $s \leftarrow S$ we denote the selection of an element s uniformly at random from the set S. The notation $[n]$ represents the set $\{1, 2, \ldots, n\}$, and for $n_1 < n_2$, $[n_1; n_2]$ represents the set $\{n_1, n_1 + 1, \ldots, n_2\}$. For an algorithm $\mathcal{A}$, we denote by $y \leftarrow \mathcal{A}(x)$ that A is run with input x, and that the output is assigned to y.

2.2　Pseudorandom Function

A pseudorandom function (PRF) $F : \mathcal{K} \times \mathcal{D} \to \mathcal{R}$ with keyspace $\mathcal{K}$, domain $\mathcal{D}$, and range $\mathcal{R}$, is given by the following two algorithms.

F.KeyGen(1^λ) This is the key generation algorithm which, on input the security parameter 1^λ, returns a key $k \in \mathcal{K}$.

F.Eval(k, x) This is the evaluation algorithm which, given key $k \in \mathcal{K}$ and input $x \in D$, returns an output value $y \in R$.

Security is defined via the security game shown in Fig. 1.

Definition 1. *Let the advantage of an adversary $\mathcal{A}$ playing the security game in Fig. 1 with respect to a pseudorandom function $F =$ (KeyGen, Eval) be defined as*

$$\mathrm{Adv}_{F,\mathcal{A}}^{\mathrm{PRF}}(\lambda) = 2 \left| \mathrm{Pr}[\mathrm{PRF}_{\mathcal{A}}^{F}(\lambda) \Rightarrow 1] - \frac{1}{2} \right|.$$

F is said to be secure if for all PPT adversaries $\mathcal{A}$, $\mathrm{Adv}_{F,\mathcal{A}}^{\mathrm{PRF}}(\lambda)$ is negligible in the security parameter λ.

$\mathrm{PRF}_{\mathcal{A}}^{\mathrm{F}}(\lambda):$
$k \leftarrow \mathsf{F.KeyGen}(1^{\lambda})$
$b \leftarrow_{\$} \{0, 1\}$
$\mathcal{F} \leftarrow \emptyset$
$b' \leftarrow \mathcal{A}^{\mathrm{EVAL}}(1^{\lambda})$
return $(b = b')$

proc. $\mathrm{EVAL}(x):$
if $b = 1$
    $y \leftarrow \mathsf{F.Eval}(k, x)$
else
    if $\mathcal{F}[x] = \bot$, then $\mathcal{F}[x] \leftarrow_{\$} R$
    $y \leftarrow \mathcal{F}[x]$
return y

Fig. 1. Game defining security of a pseudorandom function.

$\mathrm{PRF}_{\mathcal{A}}^{\mathrm{F}}(\lambda):$
$(S, st) \leftarrow \mathcal{A}(1^{\lambda})$
$k \leftarrow \mathsf{F.KeyGen}(1^{\lambda})$
$k_S \leftarrow \mathsf{F.Constrain}(k, S)$
$b \leftarrow_{\$} \{0, 1\}$
$\mathcal{F} \leftarrow \emptyset$
$b' \leftarrow \mathcal{A}^{\mathrm{EVAL}}(st, k_S)$
return $(b = b')$

proc. $\mathrm{EVAL}(x):$
if $x \in S$ return $\bot$
if $b = 1$
    $y \leftarrow \mathsf{F.Eval}(k, x)$
else
    if $\mathcal{F}[x] = \bot$, then $\mathcal{F}[x] \leftarrow_{\$} R$
    $y \leftarrow \mathcal{F}[x]$
return y

Fig. 2. Game defining security of a constrained pseudorandom function.

Constrained Pseudorandom Function. A constrained PRF is an extension of an ordinary PRF that allows PRF keys to be constrained to only be usable for certain inputs. Specifically, besides the algorithms KeyGen and Eval defined for an ordinary PRF, a constrained PRF additionally includes the following algorithm:

Constrain(k, S) Given a key $k \in \mathcal{K}$ and a set $S \subset \mathcal{D}$, this constraining algorithm returns a constrained key k_S.

For correctness, it is required that for all security parameters λ, all keys $k \leftarrow$ KeyGen(1^{λ}), all sets $S \subset \mathcal{D}$, all constrained keys $k_S \leftarrow$ Puncture(k, S), it holds that

$$\mathsf{Eval}(k_S, x) = \begin{cases} \mathsf{Eval}(k, x) & \text{if } x \in S \\ \bot & \text{otherwise} \end{cases}$$

We define (selective) security for a constrained PRF F via the game shown in Fig. 2.

Definition 2. *Let the advantage of an adversary $\mathcal{A}$ playing the security game in Fig. 1 with respect to a pseudorandom function $F = (\mathsf{KeyGen}, \mathsf{Eval})$ be defined as*

$$\mathrm{Adv}_{F, \mathcal{A}}^{\mathrm{PRF}}(\lambda) = 2 \left| \Pr[\mathrm{PRF}_{\mathcal{A}}^{F}(\lambda) \Rightarrow 1] - \frac{1}{2} \right|.$$

F is said to be secure if for all PPT adversaries $\mathcal{A}$, $\mathrm{Adv}_{F, \mathcal{A}}^{\mathrm{PRF}}(\lambda)$ is negligible in the security parameter λ.

Note the the above defined security notion for a constrained PRF is slightly weaker than the notion considered by [BW13], as the adversary is only given access to a challenge evaluation oracle returning real or random values, as opposed to both an ordinary evaluation oracle alway returning $\mathtt{Eval}(k, x)$ and a challenge evaluation oracle which can be evaluated on distinct inputs. However, the above defined notion is sufficient to guarantee security for in our construction based on a constrained PRF.

2.3   Symmetric-Key Multi-input Functional Encryption

A symmetric-key multi-input functional encryption (MIFE) scheme $\mathtt{M}$ for a function f is given by the following algorithms [BLR+14].

$\mathtt{Setup}(1^\lambda)$ Given the security parameter λ, this setup algorithm returns public parameters mpk and a private master key msk.

$\mathtt{KeyGen}(msk, y)$ Given msk and value y, this key generation algorithm returns a secret key sk_y.

$\mathtt{Enc}(msk, x)$ Given the master key msk, an index i, and a message x_i, this encryption algorithm returns a ciphertext c_i.

$\mathtt{Dec}(sk_y, c_1, \ldots, c_n)$ Given sk_y and ciphertexts $(c_1, \ldots, c_n)$ encrypting message vectors $x_1, \ldots, x_n$, this decryption algorithm returns either $f(x_1, \ldots, x_n, y)$ or the error symbol $\perp$.

Correctness is defined in the obvious way. Adaptive security of a MIFE scheme $\mathtt{M}$ is defined via the following security game.

$\mathrm{IND}^\beta_{\mathtt{M},\mathcal{A}}(\lambda)$:	proc. $\mathrm{KEYGEN}(y)$:
$(mpk, msk) \leftarrow \mathtt{Setup}(1^\lambda)$	$sk_y \leftarrow \mathtt{KeyGen}(msk, y)$
$b \leftarrow \mathcal{A}^{\mathrm{KEYGEN}, \mathrm{ENC}}(mpk)$	return sk_y
return b	
	proc. $\mathrm{ENC}(i, x_i^0, x_i^1)$:
	$c \leftarrow \mathtt{Enc}(msk, i, x_i^\beta)$
	return c

In the above game it is required that for all $j_1, \ldots, j_n \in [Q_1] \times \cdots \times [Q_n]$, where for all $i \in [n]$, Q_i denotes the number of encryption queries for index i, $\mathcal{A}$ only makes queries y to KEYGEN satisfying

$$f(x_1^{j_1,0}, \ldots, x_n^{j_n,0}, y) = f(x_1^{j_1,1}, \ldots, x_n^{j_n,1}, y)$$

where $(x_i^{j,0}, x_i^{j,1})$ denotes the values submitted by $\mathcal{A}$ in its jth query to ENC for index i.

Definition 3. *A scheme MIFE $\mathtt{M}$ is said to be IND secure, if for all PPT algorithms $\mathcal{A}$, the advantage*

$$\mathtt{Adv}^{\mathtt{IND}}_{\mathtt{M},\mathcal{A}}(\lambda) = \left| \Pr[IND^0_{\mathtt{M},\mathcal{A}}(\lambda) \Rightarrow 1] - \Pr[IND^1_{\mathtt{M},\mathcal{A}}(\lambda) \Rightarrow 1] \right|$$

is negligible in the security parameter λ.

3   Token-Based MIFE

3.1   Functionality

A token-based MIFE extends the functionality of an ordinary MIFE as defined in Sect. 2.3, by including an additional algorithm GenToken which, on input the parameters mpk of the scheme, generates encryption tokens $etk_1, \ldots, etk_n$ and a decryption token dtk. Each user i will then use encryption token etk_i as an additional input to the encryption algorithm, while the decryption server will use dtk as an additional input to the decryption algorithm. For simplicity, we will in our formalization consider a setup in which the evaluation of the functionality f implemented by the token-based MIFE is done over values $x_1, \ldots, x_n$ where x_i is encrypted by user i using encryption token etk_i. Lastly, our formalization considers token-based MIFE schemes supporting restricting decryption tokens to only work for specific ciphertexts. This is captured via the Restrict algorithm, which takes as input a decryption token dtk and a set S consisting of index pairs (i, j) referring to the jth encryption of the ith input, and outputs a decryption token dtk_S that only works for ciphertexts specified by S.

More formally, a token-based MIFE scheme for functionality $f : \mathcal{X}_1 \times \ldots \times \mathcal{X}_n \times \mathcal{Y} \to \mathcal{R}$ and a class $\mathcal{S} \subseteq 2^{[n] \times \mathbb{N}}$ of supported restriction sets, is given by the following algorithms.

Setup (1^λ) Given the security parameter λ, this setup algorithm returns a secret master key msk and public parameters mpk.

KeyGen (msk, y) Given msk and value y, this key generation algorithm returns a secret key sk_y.

GenToken (mpk) Given the public parameters mpk, this token generation algorithm returns encryption tokens $etk_1, \ldots, etk_u$ and a decryption token dtk.

Enc (msk, i, etk_i, x_i) Given the master key msk, a slot index i, a corresponding encryption token etk_i, and a message x_i, this encryption algorithm returns a ciphertext c_i and an updated encryption token etk_i'.

Restrict (dtk, S) Given dtk and a set S of index pairs, each pair $(i, j) \in S$ referring to the jth ciphertext encrypted for slot i, this algorithm returns a restricted decryption token dtk_S.

Dec$(dtk, sk_y, c_1, \ldots, c_n)$ Given dtk, sk_y, and ciphertexts $c_1, \ldots, c_n$ encrypting messages $x_1, \ldots, x_n$, this decryption algorithm returns either $f(x_1, \ldots, x_n, y)$ or the error symbol $\perp$.

Stateful/Stateless Schemes. Note that the above definition allows the encryption algorithm Enc to be stateful in the sense that, in addition to the ciphertext c, Enc returns an updated encryption token etk_i'. The premise is that user i will use the updated token etk_i' (as opposed to the old encryption token etk_i) in the following encryption. We refer to this type of scheme as a *stateful* scheme. However, we will additionally consider *stateless* schemes in which the encryption token is not updated, that is, for $(c_i, etk_i') \leftarrow \text{Enc}(msk, i, etk_i, x_i)$ it holds that $etk_i' = etk_i$ regardless of the other inputs msk, i, and x_i.

Support for Decryption Token Restriction. While the above definition allows decryption tokens to be restricted via the `Restrict` algorithm, we will also consider scheme that essentially do not support this. In this case, we simply set the supported class of restriction sets $\mathcal{S}$ to be $\emptyset$ and let `Restrict` return an empty string. In particular note that for a stateless scheme, the input to the encryption algorithm besides x_i will remain the same, which implies that decryption tokens cannot be meaningfully restricted, assuming the ability to decrypt is independent of x_i. Hence, we will only consider decryption token restriction for stateful schemes.

Correctness for Stateless Schemes. For a token-based MIFE scheme T for function f, we require that for all security parameters λ, any input $x_1, \ldots, x_n \in \mathcal{X}$, any $y \in \mathcal{Y}$, any $(mpk, msk) \leftarrow \mathtt{T.Setup}(1^\lambda)$, any $sk_y \leftarrow \mathtt{T.KeyGen}(msk, y)$, any $(etk_1, \ldots, etk_u, dtk) \leftarrow \mathtt{T.GenToken}(mpk)$, any $i \in [n]$, and any $c_i \leftarrow \mathtt{T.Enc}(msk, i, etk_i, x_i)$, it holds that

$$\mathtt{T.Dec}(sk_y, dtk, c_1, \ldots, c_n) = f(x_1, \ldots, x_n, y).$$

Correctness for Stateful Schemes. For a token-based MIFE scheme T for function f, we require that for all security parameters λ, any set of n values $s_1, \ldots, s_n$ polynomial in λ, any set of $n(s_1 + \cdots + s_n)$ inputs, namely, $x_1^{(1)}, \ldots, x_1^{(s_1)} \in \mathcal{X}_1; \ldots; x_1^{(n)}, \ldots, x_n^{(s_n)} \in \mathcal{X}_n$, any $y \in \mathcal{Y}$, any $(mpk, msk) \leftarrow \mathtt{T.Setup}(1^\lambda)$, any $sk_y \leftarrow \mathtt{T.KeyGen}(msk, y)$, any set of encryption/decryption tokens $(etk_1, \ldots, etk_u, dtk) \leftarrow \mathtt{T.GenToken}(mpk)$, any set of ciphertexts $(c_1^{(j_1)}, \ldots, c_n^{(j_n)})$ obtained by, for each $i \in [n]$, iteratively computing $(c_i^{(j)}, etk_i^{(j+1)}) \leftarrow \mathtt{T.Enc}(msk, i, etk_i^{(j)}, x_i^{(j)})$, $j \in [s_i]$, where $etk_i^{(1)} = etk_i$, it holds that

$$\mathtt{T.Dec}(sk_y, dtk, c_1^{(s_1)}, \ldots, c_n^{(s_n)}) = f(x_1^{(s_1)}, \ldots, x_n^{(s_n)}, y)$$

and for all sets $S \in \mathcal{S}$ for which $(1, j_1), \ldots, (n, j_n) \in S$, and all $dtk_S \leftarrow \mathtt{T.Restrict}(dtk, S)$, it likewise holds that

$$\mathtt{T.Dec}(sk_y, dtk_S, c_1^{(s_1)}, \ldots, c_n^{(s_n)}) = f(x_1^{(s_1)}, \ldots, x_n^{(s_n)}, y)$$

Remark 1. Note that correctness for stateless schemes is in fact captured as a special case of correctness for stateful schemes. However, we explicitly included the former for readability, since it is simpler than the latter.

3.2   Security

FE-IND Security. Firstly, we consider security against a malicious decryption server who attempts to derive additional information regarding plaintexts x_i beyond what is revealed by $f(x_1, \ldots, x_n, y)$ obtained in an honest decryption. This is captured by the security notion functional encryption indistinguishability (FE-IND) defined via the following game for a scheme T. In the game, the adversary will be given an unrestricted decryption token, a key generation oracles, as well as a (stateful) challenge encryption oracle. The FE-IND notion mirrors the IND notion defined for an ordinary MIFE (see Sect. 2.3).

FE-IND$_{T,\mathcal{A}}^{\beta}(\lambda)$:

$(mpk, msk) \leftarrow \mathtt{Setup}(1^\lambda)$

$(etk_1, \ldots, etk_n, dtk) \leftarrow \mathtt{GenToken}(mpk)$

$b \leftarrow \mathcal{A}^{\mathrm{KeyGen,Enc}}(mpk, dtk)$

return b

proc. $\mathrm{KeyGen}(y)$:

return $sk_y \leftarrow \mathtt{KeyGen}(msk, y)$

proc. $\mathrm{Enc}(i, x_i^0, x_i^1)$:

$(c, etk_i') \leftarrow \mathtt{Enc}(msk, etk_i, i, x_i^\beta)$

$etk_i \leftarrow etk_i'$

return c

In the above game it is required that for all $j_1, \ldots, j_n \in [Q_1] \times \cdots \times [Q_n]$, where for all $i \in [n]$, Q_i denotes the number of encryption queries for index i, $\mathcal{A}$ only makes queries y to KeyGen satisfying

$$f(x_1^{j,0}, \ldots, x_n^{j,0}, y) = f(x_1^{j,1}, \ldots, x_n^{j,1}, y)$$

where $(x_i^{j,0}, x_i^{j,1})$ denotes the values submitted by $\mathcal{A}$ in its jth query to Enc for index i.

Definition 4. *A scheme token-based MIFE T is said to be **FE-IND** secure, if for all PPT algorithms $\mathcal{A}$, the advantage*

$$\mathrm{Adv}_{T,\mathcal{A}}^{\mathrm{FE-IND}}(\lambda) = \left| \Pr[FE - IND_{T,\mathcal{A}}^0(\lambda) \Rightarrow 1] - \Pr[FE - IND_{T,\mathcal{A}}^1(\lambda) \Rightarrow 1] \right|$$

is negligible in the security parameter λ.

TK-IND Security. We additionally consider security against a malicious decryption server who attempts to learn any information regarding plaintexts x_i without possessing the appropriate decryption token. This is captured by the security notion token-based indistinguishability (TK-IND) defined via the following game for scheme T. Note that in the security game, the adversary $\mathcal{A}$ is given the master secret key msk as input, and hence captures a malicious decryption server colluding with the key generation server. Furthermore, $\mathcal{A}$ is given a restricted decryption token dtk_S for a set S of his own choice, but is required to submit challenge queries that are not covered by S. This captures that dtk_S does not leak information that would assist decryption of ciphertexts not covered by S. Note that our notion is selective in terms of the choice of S, as $\mathcal{A}$ is required to commit to S before interacting with the challenge encryption oracle. Lastly note that for a scheme not supporting decryption token restriction, the `Restrict` algorithm is implicitly defined to always return an empty string, which implies that $\mathcal{A}$ would only receive msk as input.

TK-IND$_{T,\mathcal{A}}^{\beta}(\lambda)$:

$(mpk, msk) \leftarrow \mathtt{Setup}(1^\lambda)$

$(S, st) \leftarrow \mathcal{A}(mpk, msk)$

$(etk_1, \ldots, etk_l, dtk) \leftarrow \mathtt{GenToken}(mpk)$

$j_1, \ldots, j_n \leftarrow 0$

$dtk_S \leftarrow \mathtt{Restrict}(dtk, S)$

$b \leftarrow \mathcal{A}^{\mathrm{Enc}}(st, dtk_S)$

return b

proc. $\mathrm{Enc}(i, x_i^0, x_i^1)$:

if $(i, j_i) \in S$

    return $\bot$

$(c, etk_i') \leftarrow \mathtt{Enc}(msk, etk_i, i, x_i^\beta)$

$j_i \leftarrow j_i + 1$

$etk_i \leftarrow etk_i'$

return c

Definition 5. *A token-based MIFE scheme T is said to be TK-IND secure, if for all PPT algorithms $\mathcal{A}$, the advantage*

$$\text{Adv}_{T,\mathcal{A}}^{\text{TK-IND}}(\lambda) = \left| \Pr[TK - IND_{T,\mathcal{A}}^0(\lambda) \Rightarrow 1] - \Pr[TK - IND_{T,\mathcal{A}}^1(\lambda) \Rightarrow 1] \right|$$

is negligible in the security parameter λ.

Besides the above, we consider a slightly stronger security notion which captures schemes in which the encryption tokens are broadcast to the users over a public channel. We will refer to this notion as public token-based indistinguishability (pTK-IND). More specifically, we denote by pTK-IND a security game identical to the TK-IND game defined above, except that in the second invocation of the adversary $\mathcal{A}$, $etk_1, \ldots, etk_n$ will be given as input to $\mathcal{A}$ in addition to st and dtk_S. Based on this game, pTK-IND security is defined as follows.

Definition 6. *A token-based MIFE scheme T is said to be pTK-IND secure, if for all PPT algorithms $\mathcal{A}$, the advantage*

$$\text{Adv}_{T,\mathcal{A}}^{\text{pTK-IND}}(\lambda) = \left| \Pr[pTK - IND_{T,\mathcal{A}}^0(\lambda) \Rightarrow 1] - \Pr[pTK - IND_{T,\mathcal{A}}^1(\lambda) \Rightarrow 1] \right|$$

is negligible in the security parameter λ.

4   A Stateless Scheme

We will now present a simple stateless token-based MIFE scheme based on a standard MIFE scheme and a public key encryption scheme. The construction uses a single public key for the encryption tokens, and simply constructs a double encryption of messages, using the public key encryption as the outer layer. This leads to a scheme in which e.g. a chosen user can generate the encryption/decryption tokens on behalf of all users, and then simply broadcast the encryption token to the remaining users (as well as provide the decryption token to the decryption server fi/when appropriate). However, as this is a stateless scheme, it will not support decryption token restriction.

Concretely, we construct a token-based MIFE scheme T for function f using an ordinary public-key encryption scheme $\text{PKE} = (\text{KeyGen}, \text{Enc}, \text{Dec})$ and a multi-input functional encryption scheme $\text{M} = (\text{Setup}, \text{KeyGen}, \text{Enc}, \text{Dec})$ for f as follows.

Setup (1^λ) Return $(mpk, msk) \leftarrow \text{M.Setup}(1^\lambda)$.
KeyGen (msk, y) Return $sk_y \leftarrow \text{M.KeyGen}(msk, y)$.
GenToken (λ) Compute $(pk, sk) \leftarrow \text{PKE.KeyGen}(1^\lambda)$, set $etk_1 = \cdots = etk_l \leftarrow pk$ and $dtk \leftarrow sk$. Finally return $(etk_1, \ldots, etk_l, dtk)$.
Enc (msk, i, etk_i, x_i) Compute $c' \leftarrow \text{M.Enc}(msk, i, x_i)$; $c \leftarrow \text{PKE.Enc}(etk_i, c')$. Return (c, u).
Dec $(dtk, sk_y, c_1, \ldots, c_n)$ For each $i \in [n]$, compute $c_i' \leftarrow \text{PKE.Dec}(dtk, c_i)$. Return $\text{M.Dec}(sk_y, c_1', \ldots, c_n')$.

4.1   Security

The security of the above construction is established via the following two theorems. The corresponding proofs can be found in Appendix B.

Theorem 1. *Assume the MIFE scheme M is IND secure. Then the above scheme T is FE-IND secure. Specifically, for every PPT adversary $\mathcal{A}$ against the FE-IND security of T, there exists a PPT adversary $\mathcal{B}$ against the IND security of M such that* $\mathrm{Adv}_{T,\mathcal{A}}^{\mathrm{FE-IND}} \leq \mathrm{Adv}_{M,\mathcal{B}}^{\mathrm{IND}}$.

Theorem 2. *Assume PKE is IND-CPA secure. Then the above scheme T is pTK-IND secure. Specifically, for every PPT adversary $\mathcal{A}$ against the pTK-IND security of T, there exists a PPT adversary $\mathcal{B}$ against the IND-CPA security of PKE such that* $\mathrm{Adv}_{T,\mathcal{A}}^{\mathrm{TK-IND}} \leq n \cdot \mathrm{Adv}_{PKE,\mathcal{B}}^{\mathrm{IND-CPA}}$.

5   A Stateful Scheme

We will now present a stateful token-based MIFE scheme based on a standard MIFE scheme and a PRF. Compared to the stateless scheme in the previous section, the computational overhead of making the MIFE scheme token-based is much lower, as a PRF can be implemented much more efficiently compared to a PKE. Furthermore, the scheme allows the GenToken algorithm to be computed in a distributed manner; each user will be able to independently generate his own encryption token etk_i and the corresponding part of the decryption token dtk_i. For the decryption server to be able to decrypt, it is then required that each user sends dtk_i to the server, which will then form the full decryption token $dtk = (dtk_1, \ldots, dtk_n)$. Like the stateless scheme, the construction idea is simple; the ciphertexts of the MIFE are simply masked with a mask generated using the PRF evaluated. To guarantee security, the scheme must be stateful, as it must be ensured that the same mask is never used twice.

Concretely, we construct a token-based MIFE scheme T using a PRF PRF = {KeyGen, Eval} with range $\{0,1\}^l$, and a MIFE scheme M = {Setup, KeyGen, Enc, Dec} with ciphertext space $\mathcal{C} \subset \{0,1\}^l$ as follows.

Setup (1^λ) Return $(mpk, msk) \leftarrow \mathrm{M.Setup}(1^\lambda)$.

KeyGen (msk, y) Return $sk_y \leftarrow \mathrm{M.KeyGen}(msk, y)$.

GenToken (λ) For $i \in [n]$ compute $k_i \leftarrow \mathrm{PRF.KeyGen}(1^\lambda)$, and set $etk_i \leftarrow (k_i, 0)$. Finally set $dtk \leftarrow (k_1, \ldots, k_n)$, and return $(etk_1, \ldots, etk_n, dtk)$.

Enc (msk, i, etk, x_i) Parse $etk \rightarrow (k, j)$, and compute $m \leftarrow \mathrm{PRF.Eval}(k, j)$. Then compute $c' \leftarrow \mathrm{M.Enc}(msk, i, x_i)$, and set $c \leftarrow (c' \oplus m, j)$, $j' \leftarrow j + 1$, and $etk' \leftarrow (k, u, j')$. Finally return (c, etk').

Dec $(dtk, sk_y, c_1, \ldots, c_n)$ Parse $dtk \rightarrow (k_1, \ldots, k_l)$ and $c_i \rightarrow (c'_i, j_i)$ for $i \in [n]$. For each $i \in [n]$, compute $m_i \leftarrow \mathrm{PRF.Eval}(k_i, j_i)$ and $c''_i \leftarrow c'_i \oplus m_i$. Finally return $z \leftarrow \mathrm{M.Dec}(sk'_y, c''_1, \ldots, c''_n)$.

5.1 Security

The security of the above construction is established via the following two theorems.

Theorem 3. *Assume the MIFE scheme M is IND secure. Then the above scheme T is FE-IND secure. Specifically, for every PPT adversary $\mathcal{A}$ against the FE-IND security of T, there exists a PPT adversary $\mathcal{B}$ against the IND security of M such that $\mathrm{Adv}_{T,\mathcal{A}}^{\mathrm{TK-IND}} \leq \mathrm{Adv}_{M,\mathcal{B}}^{\mathrm{IND}}$.*

Proof. The proof is a simple and straightforward reduction. Given adversary $\mathcal{A}$ against the FE-IND security of T, we construct adversary $\mathcal{B}$ against the IND security of M as follows.

Initially, $\mathcal{B}$ is given parameters mpk which $\mathcal{B}$ simply forwards to $\mathcal{A}$. Furthermore, $\mathcal{B}$ will compute PRF keys $k_i \leftarrow \mathrm{P.KeyGen}(1^\lambda)$ and set variables $j_i \leftarrow 0$ for $i \in [n]$. When $\mathcal{A}$ submits a key generation query y, $\mathcal{B}$ simply forwards y to his own KEYGEN oracle, and returns the response sk_y to $\mathcal{A}$. When $\mathcal{A}$ makes an encryption query (u, i, x_i^0, x_i^1), $\mathcal{B}$ forwards (i, x_i^0, x_i^1) to his own ENC oracle to obtain ciphertext c'. Then $\mathcal{B}$ computes $m \leftarrow \mathrm{P.Eval}(k_i, j_i)$, sets $c \leftarrow (c' \oplus m, j_i)$ and $j_i \leftarrow j_i + 1$, and lastly returns c to $\mathcal{A}$. Eventually $\mathcal{A}$ will terminate with output b, which $\mathcal{B}$ forwards as his own output.

By inspection, it should be clear that $\mathcal{B}$ provides a perfect simulation of the FE-IND game for $\mathcal{A}$, and that $\mathcal{B}$ wins the IND game for M (i.e. correctly guesses the challenge bit β) whenever $\mathcal{A}$ wins the FE-IND game for T. Hence the theorem follows.

Theorem 4. *Assume the PRF P is secure. Then the above scheme T is TK-IND secure. Specifically, for every PPT adversary $\mathcal{A}$ against the TK-IND security of T, there exists a PPT adversaries $\mathcal{B}_1, \ldots, \mathcal{B}_l$ against the PRF security of P such that $\mathrm{Adv}_{T,\mathcal{A}}^{\mathrm{TK-IND}} \leq \mathrm{Adv}_{P,\mathcal{B}_1}^{\mathrm{PRF}} + \ldots + \mathrm{Adv}_{P,\mathcal{B}_{2l}}^{\mathrm{PRF}}$.*

Proof. The proof is a series of simple game hops, firstly replacing the output of the PRF P with random values for each user, then changing the challenge bit β used by the encryption oracle, and finally replacing the output of P back to the real values. Note that since the scheme does not support decryption token restrictions, the restricted decryption token dtk_S will correspond to $\perp$ regardless of the set S, and we can ignore this input to $\mathcal{A}$ (as well as S output by $\mathcal{A}$).

More concretely, let G_0 denote the $TK-IND_{T,\mathcal{A}}^0$ game, and let G_t, $t \in [n]$, denote modifications of this game in which the encryption done in response to encryption queries (i, x_i^0, x_i^1), is modified as follows: if $i \leq t$, set $m \leftarrow \{0,1\}^t$, otherwise set $m \leftarrow \mathrm{P.Eval}(k_i, j_i)$. Furthermore, let G_{n+1} denote a modification of G_n in which the encryption oracle uses $\beta = 1$. Finally, let G_t for $t \in [n+2; 2n+1]$ denote modifications of G_{n+1} corresponding to reversing the changes introduced in games $G_1, \ldots, G_n$ i.e. the random masks m used in the response to encryption queries are replaced with $m \leftarrow \mathrm{P.Eval}(k_i, j_i)$ for each user i in turn, starting from user 1. It should be clear the game G_{2n+1} is identical to $\mathrm{TK-IND}_{T,\mathcal{A}}^1$.

Via a simple reduction, we bound the difference between the probability that $\mathcal{A}$ outputs 1 in game G_t and in game G_{t+1}, $t \in \{0, \ldots, n-1\}$, with $\mathrm{Adv}_{P,\mathcal{B}_t}^{\mathrm{PRF}}$ for a

PPT algorithm $\mathcal{B}_t$. Specifically, $\mathcal{B}_t$ is constructed as follows. Initially, $\mathcal{B}_t$ generates $(mpk, msk) \leftarrow \text{M.Setup}(1^\lambda)$, sets $j_1, \ldots, j_n \leftarrow 0$, computes $k_i \leftarrow \text{P.KeyGen}(1^\lambda)$ for all $i \neq t$ and $i \in [n]$, and forwards (mpk, msk) to $\mathcal{A}$ (note that (k_i, j_i) corresponds to the encryption token etk_i for user i). For encryption queries (i, x_i^0, x_i^1) where $i \leq t$, $\mathcal{B}_t$ responds by using a randomly chosen mask $m_i \leftarrow \{0, 1\}^l$. For queries where $i > t+1$, $\mathcal{B}_t$ responds using $m_i \leftarrow \text{P.Eval}(k_u, i||j)$ and updating $j_i \leftarrow j_i + 1$. However, for queries where $i = t + 1$, $\mathcal{B}_t$ forwards j_i to his own Eval oracle to obtain m_i, and sets $j_i \leftarrow j_i + 1$. Finally, when $\mathcal{A}$ returns a bit b', $\mathcal{B}_t$ forwards this as his own output.

From the above description, it should be clear that $\mathcal{B}_t$ provides a perfect simulation of game G_t for $\mathcal{A}$ if the challenge bit β in the PRF security game played by $\mathcal{B}_t$ is 0. On the other hand, if $\beta = 1$, $\mathcal{B}_t$ provides a perfect simulation of game G_{t+1}. Hence, it directly follows that $|\Pr[G_t \Rightarrow 1] - \Pr[G_{t+1} \Rightarrow]| \leq \text{Adv}_{\text{P},\mathcal{B}_t}^{\text{PRF}}$, $t \in [0; l - 1]$. Furthermore, since in game G_n and G_{n+1}, the masks used in the response to encryption queries are picked uniformly at random, the distributions of $(m_i \oplus c_i', j_i)$ in the two games are identical, even though c_i' encrypts x_i^0 in game G_n and x_i^1 in game G_{n+1}. Finally, using an identical argument to the above, it follows that $|\Pr[G_i \Rightarrow 1] - \Pr[G_{i+1} \Rightarrow]| \leq \text{Adv}_{\text{P},\mathcal{B}_i}^{\text{PRF}}$, $i \in [l + 1; 2l + 1]$.

Combining the above bounds, we obtain

$$\text{Adv}_{\text{T},\mathcal{A}}^{\text{TK-IND}} = |\Pr[TK - IND_{\text{T},\mathcal{A}}^0 \Rightarrow 1] - TK - IND_{\text{T},\mathcal{A}}^1 \Rightarrow 1]|$$

$$\leq \sum_{t=0}^{2l} |\Pr[G_t \Rightarrow 1] - \Pr[G_{t+1} \Rightarrow 1]|$$

$$\leq \text{Adv}_{\text{P},\mathcal{B}_0}^{\text{PRF}} + \ldots + \text{Adv}_{\text{P},\mathcal{B}_{l-1}}^{\text{PRF}} + \text{Adv}_{\text{P},\mathcal{B}_{l+1}}^{\text{PRF}} + \ldots + \text{Adv}_{\text{P},\mathcal{B}_{2l}}^{\text{PRF}}$$

$\square$

6   A Stateful Scheme Supporting Decryption Tokens Restriction

We will now present an extension of the scheme from Sect. 5 that allows restricting decryption tokens. First observe that the stateful scheme from Sect. 5 actually supports a simple form of decryption token restriction. Specifically, note that the decryption server is required to recover the masks m_i to be able to decrypt, which is possible as the decryption token dtk contains the PRF keys k_i used to generate these. To restrict dtk to only be usable for a set of ciphertext specified by a given set S, e.g. $S = \{(1, j_1), \ldots, (n, j_n)\}$, it is possible to simply use the relevant masks as a restricted decryption token i.e. $dtk_S = \{m_i = \text{Eval}(k_i, j_i)\}_{i \in [n]}$. It is not difficult to see that security for ciphertexts not described by S will be preserved. However, the disadvantage of this solution is that the size of the decryption token will equal the size of S.

To obtain a more efficient solution, we will make use of a constrained PRF to limit the ability of the decryption server to only be able to generate the masks required to decrypt the ciphertexts described by S. By choosing an appropriate instantiation of the constrained PRF, the size of the decryption token can be reduced. We discuss the details of the instantiation below.

The scheme rT is based on a MIFE $M = \{\texttt{Setup}, \texttt{KeyGen}, \texttt{Enc}, \texttt{Dec}\}$ and a constrained PRF $cP = \{\texttt{KeyGen}, \texttt{Eval}, \texttt{Restrict}\}$. The algorithms rT.Setup, rT.KeyGen, rT.GenToken, rT.Enc, and rT.Dec are identical to the stateless scheme T in Sect. 4, but for clarity, all algorithms are described below.

Setup (1^λ) Return $(mpk, msk) \leftarrow \texttt{M.Setup}(1^\lambda)$.
KeyGen (msk, y) Return $sk_y \leftarrow \texttt{M.KeyGen}(msk, y)$.
GenToken (λ) For $i \in [n]$ compute $k_i \leftarrow \texttt{cP.KeyGen}(1^\lambda)$, and set $etk_i \leftarrow (k_i, 0)$.
   Finally set $dtk \leftarrow (k_1, \ldots, k_n)$, and return $(etk_1, \ldots, etk_n, dtk)$.
Enc (msk, i, etk, x_i) Parse $etk \to (k, j)$, and compute $m \leftarrow \texttt{cP.Eval}(k, j)$. Then
   compute $c' \leftarrow \texttt{M.Enc}(msk, i, x_i)$, and set $c \leftarrow (c' \oplus m, j)$, $j' \leftarrow j + 1$, and
   $etk' \leftarrow (k, u, j')$. Finally return (c, etk').
Restrict (dtk, S) Parse $dtk \to (k_1, \ldots, k_n)$ and let $S_i = \{j | (i, j) \in S\}$. Set
   $k_i' \leftarrow \texttt{cP.Restrict}(k_i, S_i)$ for $i \in [n]$, and return $dtk_S \leftarrow (k_1', \ldots, k_n')$.
Dec $(dtk, sk_y, c_1, \ldots, c_n)$ Parse $dtk \to (k_1, \ldots, k_l)$ and $c_i \to (c_i', j_i)$ for $i \in [n]$.
   For each $i \in [n]$, compute $m_i \leftarrow \texttt{cP.Eval}(k_i, j_i)$ and $c_i'' \leftarrow c_i' \oplus m_i$. Finally
   return $z \leftarrow \texttt{M.Dec}(sk_y', c_1'', \ldots, c_n'')$.

It is relatively straightforward to confirm that the scheme is correct.

6.1   Security

Theorem 5. *Assume the MIFE scheme M is IND secure. Then the above scheme rT is FE-IND secure. Specifically, for every PPT adversary $\mathcal{A}$ against the FE-IND security of rT, there exists a PPT adversary $\mathcal{B}$ against the IND security of M such that* $\texttt{Adv}_{rT,\mathcal{A}}^{\text{TK-IND}} \leq \texttt{Adv}_{M,\mathcal{B}}^{\text{IND}}$.

The proof of the above theorem is identical to the proof of Theorem 3

Theorem 6. *Assume the PRF P is secure. Then the above scheme T is TK-IND secure. Specifically, for every PPT adversary $\mathcal{A}$ against the TK-IND security of T, there exists a PPT adversaries $\mathcal{B}_1, \ldots, \mathcal{B}_l$ against the PRF security of P such that* $\texttt{Adv}_{T,\mathcal{A}}^{\text{TK-IND}} \leq \texttt{Adv}_{P,\mathcal{B}_1}^{\text{cPRF}} + \ldots + \texttt{Adv}_{P,\mathcal{B}_{2l}}^{\text{cPRF}}$.

(*Proof Sketch*). The proof is almost identical to the proof of Theorem 4, so we will just highlight the differences. In fact, the only difference is that the adversary $\mathcal{A}$ will have to be given a correctly formed restricted decryption token dtk_S corresponding to the set S output by $\mathcal{A}$. Following the description of the scheme, this implies that in all games G_t, $i \in [2l + 1]$, $\mathcal{A}$ will be given $dtk_S = (k_{S_1}, \ldots, k_{S_n})$, where $S_i = \{j | (i, j) \in S\}$ and $k_{S_i} \leftarrow \texttt{cP.Restrict}(dtk, S_i)$. Note that the adversary $\mathcal{B}_t$ constructed to bound the difference between games G_t and G_{t+1}, for $t \in 0, \ldots, l - 1$, will have access to all keys k_i for $i \neq t + 1$ $i \in [n]$, and can hence directly compute $k_{S_i} \leftarrow \texttt{P.Constrain}(k_i, S_i)$. Furthermore, $\mathcal{B}_t$ will initially be given S and can derive $S_{t+1} = \{j | (t + 1, j) \in S\}$, and since $\mathcal{B}_t$ will be interacting in the security game of the constrained PRF cP, $\mathcal{B}_t$ will be able to submit this as the initial step, and obtain $k_{S_{t+1}} \leftarrow$ cP.Restrict(k_{t+1}, S_{t+1}) for the challenge key k_{t+1}. The remaining part of the simulation is exactly as in the proof of Theorem 4, and a an identical bound on the advantage of $\mathcal{A}$ is obtained. $\square$

6.2 Efficient Instantiation of a Constrained PRF

As also observed in several other works [BW13, BGI14, KPTZ13], a selective secure constrained PRF can be obtained directly from the GGM tree-based construction of a PRF [GGM84]. More precisely, the secret key k_s at an internal node associated with the string s in the tree, allows the PRF to be evaluated on strings with the prefix s i.e. k_s is a constrained key for the set of strings with prefix s. Using this construction in combination with the above token-based MIFE, leads to restricted decryption tokens dtk_S consisting of PRF keys k_s such that all values j in the set S is captured by a prefix s, but no value $j' \in S$ is. This construction is particularly efficient when the values j in S are consecutive values.

A   Public Key Encryption

A public key encryption (PKE) scheme PKE is defined by three algorithms with the following functionality:

PKE.KeyGen(1^λ) This is the key generations algorithm, which on input the security parameter 1^λ, returns a public/private key pair (pk, sk).

PKE.Enc(par, pk, m) This is the encryption algorithm, which on input a public key pk and a message m, returns an encryption c of m under pk.

PKE.Dec(par, sk, c) This is the decryption algorithm, which on input a private key sk and a ciphertext c, returns either a message m or the error symbol $\perp$.

We require that a PKE scheme satisfies *perfect correctness*, that is, for all λ, all $(pk, sk) \leftarrow$ PKE.KeyGen(1^λ), and all m, it holds that PKE.Dec$(sk,$ PKE.Enc$(pk, m)) = m$.

$$
\begin{aligned}
&\text{IND-CPA}^{\text{PKE}}_{\mathcal{A}}(\lambda): \\
&\overline{(pk^*, sk^*) \leftarrow \text{PKE.KeyGen}(1^\lambda)} \\
&b \leftarrow_{\$} \{0, 1\}; \\
&(m_0, m_1, st) \leftarrow \mathcal{A}^{(}pk^*) \\
&c^* \leftarrow \text{PKE.Enc}(pk^*, m_b) \\
&b' \leftarrow \mathcal{A}(st, c^*) \\
&\text{return } (b = b')
\end{aligned}
$$

Fig. 3. Game defining indistinguishability under chosen plaintext attacks (IND-CPA) for a PKE scheme.

The standard IND-CPA security notion for PKE scheme is defined via the game shown in Fig. 3.

Definition 7. *Let the advantage of an adversary A playing the IND-CPA game with respect to a PKE scheme PKE, be defined as:*

$$\mathrm{Adv}_{PKE,A}^{IND-CPA}(\lambda) = 2 \left| \Pr[IND\text{-}CPA_A^{PKE}(\lambda) \Rightarrow 1] - \frac{1}{2} \right|.$$

A scheme PKE is said to be IND-CPA secure, if for all PPT adversaries A, $\mathrm{Adv}_{PKE,A}^{IND-CPA}(\lambda)$ is negligible in the security parameter λ.

B Security Proofs for Stateless Scheme

Theorem 7. *Assume the MIFE scheme M is IND secure. Then the above scheme T is FE-IND secure. Specifically, for every PPT adversary A against the FE-IND security of T, there exists a PPT adversary B against the IND security of M such that $\mathrm{Adv}_{T,A}^{FE-IND} \leq \mathrm{Adv}_{M,B}^{IND}$.*

Proof. The proof is a simple and straightforward reduction. Given adversary A against the FE-IND security of T, we construct adversary B against the IND security of M as follows.

Initially, B is given parameters mpk which B simply forwards to A. Furthermore, B will compute $(pk, sk) \leftarrow$ PKE.KeyGen(1^λ). When A submits a key generation query y, B simply forwards y to his own KEYGEN oracle, and returns the response sk_y to A. When A makes an encryption query (i, x_i^0, x_i^1), B forwards (i, x_i^0, x_i^1) to his own ENC oracle to obtain ciphertext c'. Then B computes $c \leftarrow$ PKE.Enc(pk, c'), and returns c to A. Eventually A will terminate with output b', which B forwards as his own output.

By inspection, it should be clear that B provides a perfect simulation of the FE-IND game for A, and that B wins the IND game for M (i.e. correctly guesses the challenge bit b) whenever A wins the FE-IND game for T. Hence the theorem follows.

Theorem 8. *Assume PKE is IND-CPA secure. Then the above scheme T is pTK-IND secure. Specifically, for every PPT adversary A against the pTK-IND security of T, there exists a PPT adversary B against the IND-CPA security of PKE such that $\mathrm{Adv}_{T,A}^{TK-IND} \leq n \cdot \mathrm{Adv}_{PKE,B}^{IND-CPA}$.*

Proof. Again, the proof is a simple and straightforward reduction. In the following, we will for convenience make use of the standard extension of IND-CPA security to the multi-challenge setting.

Given adversary A against the TK-IND security of T, we construct adversary B against the IND-CPA security of PKE as follows.

Initially, B is given parameters pk. B computes $(mpk, msk) \leftarrow$ M.Setup(1^λ). and forwards (mpk, msk) to A. When A submits a key generation query y, B simply computes $sk_y \leftarrow$ M.KeyGen(msk, y) and returns sk_y to A. When A makes an encryption query (i, x_i^0, x_i^1), B computes $c_i'^{(0)} \leftarrow$ M.Enc(msk, i, x_i^0) and $c_i'^{(1)} \leftarrow$ M.Enc(msk, i, x_i^1). B then submits $(c_1'^{(0)}, c_1'^{(1)}), \ldots, (c_n'^{(0)}, c_n'^{(1)})$ to the multi-challenge IND-CPA challenge oracle to obtain the challenge vector $(c_1, \ldots, c_n)$. $\mathcal{B}$ then returns it to $\mathcal{A}$. Eventually $\mathcal{A}$ will terminate with output b', which $\mathcal{B}$ forwards as his own output.

By inspection, it should be clear that $\mathcal{B}$ provides a perfect simulation of the TK-IND game for $\mathcal{A}$, and that $\mathcal{B}$ wins the multi-challange IND-CPA game for M (i.e. correctly guesses the challenge bit b) whenever $\mathcal{A}$ wins the TK-IND game for T. Furthermore, since the multi-challenge IND-CPA security reduces to the normal IND-CPA security with reduction n, the number of challenges, the theorem follows. □

References

[ABDP15] Abdalla, M., Bourse, F., De Caro, A., Pointcheval, D.: Simple functional encryption schemes for inner products. Cryptology ePrint Archive, Report 2015/017 (2015). http://eprint.iacr.org/2015/017

[ARW16] Abdalla, M., Raykova, M., Wee, H.: Multi-input inner-product functional encryption from pairings. Cryptology ePrint Archive, Report 2016/425 (2016). http://eprint.iacr.org/2016/425

[BGI14] Boyle, E., Goldwasser, S., Ivan, I.: Functional signatures and pseudorandom functions. In: Krawczyk, H. (ed.) PKC 2014. LNCS, vol. 8383, pp. 501–519. Springer, Heidelberg (2014). https://doi.org/10.1007/978-3-642-54631-0_29

[BKS16] Brakerski, Z., Komargodski, I., Segev, G.: Multi-input functional encryption in the private-key setting: stronger security from weaker assumptions. In: Fischlin, M., Coron, J.-S. (eds.) EUROCRYPT 2016. LNCS, vol. 9666, pp. 852–880. Springer, Heidelberg (2016). https://doi.org/10.1007/978-3-662-49896-5_30

[BLR+14] Boneh, D., Lewi, K., Raykova, M., Sahai, A., Zhandry, M., Zimmerman, J.: Semantically secure order-revealing encryption: multi-input functional encryption without obfuscation. Cryptology ePrint Archive, Report 2014/834 (2014). http://eprint.iacr.org/2014/834

[BW13] Boneh, D., Waters, B.: Constrained pseudorandom functions and their applications. In: Sako, K., Sarkar, P. (eds.) ASIACRYPT 2013. LNCS, vol. 8270, pp. 280–300. Springer, Heidelberg (2013). https://doi.org/10.1007/978-3-642-42045-0_15

[DOT18] Datta, P., Okamoto, T., Tomida, J.: Full-hiding (Unbounded) multi-input inner product functional encryption from the k-linear assumption. In: Abdalla, M., Dahab, R. (eds.) PKC 2018. LNCS, vol. 10770, pp. 245–277. Springer, Cham (2018). https://doi.org/10.1007/978-3-319-76581-5_9

[GGG+14] Goldwasser, S., et al.: Multi-input functional encryption. In: Nguyen, P.Q., Oswald, E. (eds.) EUROCRYPT 2014. LNCS, vol. 8441, pp. 578–602. Springer, Heidelberg (2014). https://doi.org/10.1007/978-3-642-55220-5_32

[GGM84] Goldreich, O., Goldwasser, S., Micali, S.: How to construct random functions (extended abstract). In: 25th FOCS, pp. 464–479. IEEE Computer Society Press, October 1984

[KLM+16] Kim, S., Lewi, K., Mandal, A., Montgomery, H., Roy, A., Wu, D.J.: Function-hiding inner product encryption is practical. Cryptology ePrint Archive, Report 2016/440 (2016). http://eprint.iacr.org/2016/440

[KPTZ13] Kiayias, A., Papadopoulos, S., Triandopoulos, N., Zacharias, T.: Delegatable pseudorandom functions and applications. In: Sadeghi, A.-R., Gligor, V.D., Yung, M. (eds.) ACM CCS 13, pp. 669–684. ACM Press, November 2013

[LL16] Lee, K., Lee, D.H.: Two-input functional encryption for inner products from bilinear maps. Cryptology ePrint Archive, Report 2016/432 (2016). http://eprint.iacr.org/2016/432

On the CCA2 Security of McEliece
in the Standard Model

Edoardo Persichetti[(✉)]

Florida Atlantic University, Boca Raton, USA
epersichetti@fau.edu

Abstract. In this paper we study public-key encryption schemes based on error-correcting codes that are IND-CCA2 secure in the standard model. In particular, we analyze a protocol due to Dowsley, Müller-Quade and Nascimento, based on a work of Rosen and Segev. The original formulation of the protocol contained some ambiguities and incongruences, which we point out and correct; moreover, the protocol deviates substantially from the work it is based on. We then present a construction which resembles more closely the original Rosen-Segev framework, and show how this can be instantiated with the McEliece scheme.

1 Introduction

The McEliece cryptosystem [11] is the first scheme based on coding theory problems and it makes use of error-correcting codes (binary Goppa codes in the original proposal). Persichetti [15] has shown that it is possible to produce a very efficient CCA2-secure scheme in the random oracle model; it is however of interest to study systems that are secure in the standard model.

Rosen and Segev in [16] gave a general approach for CCA2 security in the standard model incorporating tools like lossy trapdoor functions and one-time signature schemes. This general protocol can be applied directly to many different hard problems such as Quadratic Residuosity, Composite Residuosity, the d-linear Assumption and the Syndrome Decoding Problem, as shown in [6]. Dowsley et al. [3] have attempted to adopt the Rosen-Segev approach to the McEliece framework. To do this, a new structure called k-repetition PKE is introduced, as well as a number of differences in the key generation, encryption and decryption processes. It is claimed that the scheme has IND-CCA2 security in the standard model, but some ambiguities in the constructions were present which undermined this claim. These have been addressed in subsequent works: in a follow-up paper [2], the authors, with the addition of Döttling, present a corrected version of the scheme of [3]. The paper was published in 2012, around the same time an earlier version of this work [14] was released. It is therefore safe to assume the results were obtained independently.

Mathew et al. [10] introduced an alternative construction for code-based IND-CCA2 secure PKE in the standard model, which is more efficient than the proposals studied in this work. However, their construction is based on the

© Springer Nature Switzerland AG 2018
J. Baek et al. (Eds.): ProvSec 2018, LNCS 11192, pp. 165–181, 2018.
https://doi.org/10.1007/978-3-030-01446-9_10

Niederreiter scheme [12]. Finally, in an independent work [19], Yoshida, Morozov and Tanaka proved that it is possible to obtain Key Privacy for both the Rosen-Segev scheme and the Dowsley et al. scheme. This is an alternative security notion that aims at guaranteeing the non-malleability of public keys, rather than ciphertexts. For this reason, it is also known as Anonymity or Indistinguishability of Keys (IK). Note that this notion was proved to hold for code-based schemes in the random oracle model, again in [15].

In this paper we analyze in detail the construction of [3], since we believe it introduced an interesting alternative to the Rosen-Segev approach. First of all, we make some observations, point out the ambiguities of the description of the scheme, and discuss the fixes of [2,14]. For the sake of completeness, we provide a correct formulation together with a proof of security. Finally, we show how to get a CCA2-secure encryption scheme based on the McEliece assumptions using the original Rosen-Segev approach.

2   Preliminaries

We will summarize here all the objects we are going to work with in the paper.

Formally, we define a Public-Key Encryption scheme (PKE) to be formed by the 6-tuple $(\mathsf{K}, \mathsf{P}, \mathsf{C}, \mathsf{KeyGen}, \mathsf{Enc}, \mathsf{Dec})$, defined as follows:

- K: The pair $(\mathsf{K}_{\mathsf{publ}}, \mathsf{K}_{\mathsf{priv}})$, respectively the public key and private key spaces.
- P: The set of messages to be encrypted, or *plaintext space*.
- C: The set of the messages transmitted over the channel, or *ciphertext space*.
- KeyGen: A probabilistic key generation algorithm that takes as input a security parameter 1^δ and outputs a public key $\mathsf{pk} \in \mathsf{K}_{\mathsf{publ}}$ and a private key $\mathsf{sk} \in \mathsf{K}_{\mathsf{priv}}$.
- Enc: A (possibly probabilistic) encryption algorithm that receives as input a public key $\mathsf{pk} \in \mathsf{K}_{\mathsf{publ}}$ and a plaintext $\phi \in \mathsf{P}$ and returns a ciphertext $\psi \in \mathsf{C}$.
- Dec: A deterministic decryption algorithm that receives as input a private key $\mathsf{sk} \in \mathsf{K}_{\mathsf{priv}}$ and a ciphertext $\psi \in \mathsf{C}$ and outputs a plaintext $\phi \in \mathsf{P}$ or the failure symbol $\perp$.

Similarly, we define a Signature scheme (SS) as a 6-tuple $(\mathsf{K}, \mathsf{M}, \Sigma, \mathsf{KeyGen}, \mathsf{Sign}, \mathsf{Ver})$, defined as follows:

- K: The pair $(\mathsf{K}_{\mathsf{sign}}, \mathsf{K}_{\mathsf{ver}})$, respectively the signing key and verification key spaces.
- M: The set of documents to be signed, or *message space*.
- Σ: The set of the signatures to be transmitted with the messages, or *signature space*.
- KeyGen: A probabilistic key generation algorithm that takes as input a security parameter 1^δ and outputs a signing key $\mathsf{sgk} \in \mathsf{K}_{\mathsf{sign}}$ and a verification key $\mathsf{vk} \in \mathsf{K}_{\mathsf{ver}}$.
- Sign: A (possibly probabilistic) signing algorithm that receives as input a signing key $\mathsf{sgk} \in \mathsf{K}_{\mathsf{sign}}$ and a message $\mu \in \mathsf{M}$ and returns a signature $\sigma \in \Sigma$.

– Ver: A deterministic decryption algorithm that receives as input a verification key vk $\in K_{ver}$, a message $\mu \in M$ and a signature $\sigma \in \Sigma$ and outputs 1, if the signature is recognized as valid, or 0 otherwise.

2.1 Security Notions

Here we refresh the security notions which will be addressed in this work.

Definition 1 (IND). *An adversary $\mathcal{A}$ for the indistinguishability (IND) property is a two-stage polynomial-time algorithm. In the first stage, $\mathcal{A}$ takes as input a public key pk $\in K_{publ}$, then outputs two arbitrary plaintexts ϕ_0, ϕ_1. In the second stage, it receives a ciphertext $\psi^* = Enc_{pk}(\phi_b)$, for $b \in \{0,1\}$, and returns a bit b^*. The adversary succeeds if $b^* = b$. More precisely, we define the advantage of $\mathcal{A}$ against PKE as*

$$Adv_{\mathcal{A}}(\lambda) = Pr[b^* = b] - \frac{1}{2}. \tag{1}$$

Indistinguishability can be achieved in various attack models. In the strongest model (that of interest to us), called CCA2, the adversary is allowed to make use of a decryption oracle during the game, with the only exception that it is not allowed to ask for the decryption of the challenge ciphertext.

Definition 2 (IND-CCA2). *The attack game for IND-CCA2 (or active attack) proceeds as follows:*

– *Query a key generation oracle to obtain a public key pk.*
– *Make a sequence of calls to a decryption oracle, submitting any string ψ of the proper length (not necessarily an element of C). The oracle will respond with $Dec_{sk}(\psi)$.*
– *Choose $\phi_0, \phi_1 \in P$ and submit them to an encryption oracle. The oracle will choose a random $b \in \{0,1\}$ and reply with the "challenge" ciphertext $\psi^* = Enc_{pk}(\phi_b)$.*
– *Keep performing decryption queries. If the submitted ciphertext is $\psi = \psi^*$, return $\bot$.*
– *Output $b^* \in \{0,1\}$.*

We say that a PKE has Indistinguishability against Adaptive Chosen Ciphertext Attacks (IND-CCA2) *if the advantage Adv_{CCA2} of any IND adversary $\mathcal{A}$ in the CCA2 attack model is negligible.*

There are many notions of security for signature schemes; the one we present here is what we need for the Rosen-Segev scheme.

Definition 3 (One-Time Strong Unforgeability). *We define an adversary $\mathcal{A}$ as a polynomial-time algorithm that acts as follows:*

– *Query a key generation oracle to obtain a verification key vk.*
– *Choose a message $\mu \in M$ and submit it to a signing oracle. The oracle will reply with $\sigma = Sign_{sgk}(\mu)$.*

– *Output a pair* (μ^*, σ^*).

The adversary succeeds if $Ver_{vk}(\mu^*, \sigma^*) = 1$ and $(\mu^*, \sigma^*) \neq (\mu, \sigma)$. We say that a signature scheme is One-Time Strongly Unforgeable *if the probability of success of any adversary* $\mathcal{A}$ *is negligible in the security parameter, i.e.*

$$Pr[vk \leftarrow K_{ver} : Ver_{vk}(\mathcal{A}(vk, Sign_{sgk}(\mu))) = 1] \in negl(\lambda). \qquad (2)$$

Note that in this scenario the adversary is only allowed to ask for the signature of a **single** message (hence the One-Time), so this is a relatively weak security assumption.

Definition 4 (Hard-Core Predicate). *Let* f *be a one-way function and* h *be a predicate, i.e. a function whose output is a single bit. Define an adversary* $\mathcal{A}$ *to be a probabilistic polynomial-time algorithm that, on input* $f(x)$, *tries to compute* $h(x)$, *i.e.* $\mathcal{A}(f(x)) = b \in \{0, 1\}$. *The predicate* h *is a* Hard-Core Predicate *of the function* f *if the probability* $Pr[b = h(x)] - \frac{1}{2}$ *is negligible for all random choices of* x.

2.2 The McEliece Cryptosystem

The McEliece cryptosystem, based on coding theory, was introduced in 1978 by McEliece [11] and, for an appropriate choice of parameters, it is still unbroken. In the original proposal, binary Goppa codes are used as a basis for the construction. We give here a more general and modern description extending the scheme to generic finite fields $\mathbb{F}_q$ and introducing a few little optimizations. The input parameters are the code length n, the code dimension k and the error-correction capacity w.

– Setup: Choose a code family and fix public parameters n, k, w.
– K_{publ}: The set of $k \times n$ matrices over $\mathbb{F}_q$.
– K_{priv}: The set[1] of "code descriptions" for the chosen code family.
– P: The vector space $\mathbb{F}_q^k$.
– C: The vector space $\mathbb{F}_q^n$.
– KeyGen: Sample a random generator matrix G for a code of the chosen family. Compute the "scrambled" generator matrix $\hat{G}$, then publish the public key $\hat{G} \in K_{publ}$ and store the private key $\Gamma \in K_{priv}$.
– Enc: On input a public key $\hat{G} \in K_{publ}$ and a plaintext $m \in P$, sample a random error vector e of weight w in $\mathbb{F}_q^n$ and return the ciphertext $\psi = m\hat{G} + e \in C$.
– Dec: On input the private key $\Gamma \in K_{priv}$ and a ciphertext $\psi \in C$, apply the decoding algorithm D_Γ to it. If the decoding succeeds, return the resulting plaintext $\phi = m$. Otherwise, output $\perp$.

---

[1] For instance for Goppa codes, this is given by the support $\alpha_1, \ldots, \alpha_n \in \mathbb{F}_{q^m}$ and the Goppa polynomial g.

Remark 1. In the original McEliece proposal the scrambling process was accomplished using an invertible matrix S and a permutation matrix P, and $\hat{G}$ was obtained as SGP. This is rather outdated and unpractical; moreover, it can introduce vulnerabilities to the scheme as per the work of Strenzke et al. (for example [17,18]). A still secure (Biswas and Sendrier, [1]), but much simpler description would be to take the public key $\hat{G}$ to be just the systematic form of G.

The security of the McEliece scheme relies on two computational assumptions.

Assumption 1 (Indistinguishability). *The matrix $\hat{G}$ output by KeyGen is computationally indistinguishable from a uniformly chosen matrix of the same size.*

Assumption 2 (Decoding hardness). *Decoding a random linear code with parameters n, k, w is hard.*

It is immediately clear that the following corollary is true.

Corollary 1. *Given that both the above assumptions hold, the McEliece cryptosystem is one-way secure under passive attacks.*

Remark 2. In a recent paper [4], Faugère et al. presented a distinguisher for instances of the McEliece cryptosystem that make use of high-rate Goppa codes. While the distinguisher works only in a special case and doesn't affect security for the general scheme, it is still recommended to avoid such insecure choices.

As we mentioned in the introduction, it is possible to easily obtain CCA2 security for the McEliece cryptosystem in the Random Oracle Model using either standard conversions (as in [7,8]) or the dedicated paradigm of [15]. We therefore consider only the issue of achieving such a security level in the Standard Model.

2.3   Computable Functions and Correlated Products

We define here the notion of security under correlated products for a collection of functions. Formally, we describe a collection of *efficiently computable functions* as a pair of algorithms $\mathcal{F} = (\mathsf{G}, \mathsf{F})$ where G is a generation algorithm that samples the description f of a function and $\mathsf{F}(f, x)$ is an evaluation algorithm that evaluates the function f on a given input x. We then define a k-wise product as follows:

Definition 5. *Let $\mathcal{F} = (\mathsf{G}, \mathsf{F})$ be a collection of efficiently computable functions and k be an integer. The k-wise product $\mathcal{F}_k$ is a pair of algorithms $(\mathsf{G}_k, \mathsf{F}_k)$ such that:*

- *G_k is a generation algorithm that independently samples k functions from $\mathcal{F}$ by invoking k times the algorithm G and returns a tuple $(f_1, \ldots, f_k)$.*

– F_k is an evaluation algorithm that receives as input a sequence of functions $(f_1, \ldots, f_k)$ and a sequence of points $(x_1, \ldots, x_k)$ and invokes F to evaluate each function on the corresponding point, i.e.

$$F_k(f_1, \ldots, f_k, x_1, \ldots, x_k) = (F(f_1, x_1), \ldots, F(f_k, x_k)).$$

A trapdoor one-way function is then an efficiently computable function that, given the image of a uniform chosen input, is easy to invert with the use of a certain trapdoor td but hard to invert otherwise; i.e. there exists an algorithm F^{-1} such that $F^{-1}(\mathsf{td}, F(f, x)) = x$.

We may think to extend the notion to the case where the input is given according to a certain distribution, that is, there exists a correlation between the points $x_1, \ldots, x_k$.

Definition 6. *Let $\mathcal{F} = (G, F)$ be a collection of efficiently computable functions with domain D and $\mathcal{C}_k$ be a distribution of points in $D_1 \times \cdots \times D_k$. We say that $\mathcal{F}$ is secure under a $\mathcal{C}_k$-correlated product if $\mathcal{F}_k$ is one-way with respect to the input distribution $\mathcal{C}_k$.*

In the special case where the input distribution $\mathcal{C}_k$ is exactly the uniform k-repetition distribution (that is, k copies of the same input $x \in D$) we simply speak about *one-wayness under k-correlated inputs*. Rosen and Segev in [16] showed that a collection of lossy trapdoor functions for an appropriate choice of parameters can be used to construct a collection of functions that is one-way under k-correlated inputs. Their work is summarized in the next section.

3   The Rosen-Segev Scheme

The computational assumption underlying the scheme is that there exists a collection of functions $\mathcal{F} = (G, F)$ which is secure under k-correlated inputs. The scheme makes use of a strongly-unforgeable signature scheme and of a hard-core predicate h for the collection $\mathcal{F}_k$.

$\mathsf{KeyGen}^{\mathrm{RS}}$: Invoke G for 2k times independently and obtain the descriptions of functions $(f_1^0, f_1^1, \ldots, f_k^0, f_k^1)$ and the corresponding trapdoors $(\mathsf{td}_1^0, \mathsf{td}_1^1, \ldots, \mathsf{td}_k^0, \mathsf{td}_k^1)$. The former is distributed as the public key pk, while the latter is the private key sk.

$\mathsf{Enc}^{\mathrm{RS}}$: To encrypt a plaintext $m \in \{0, 1\}$ with the public key pk, sample a key from a strongly-unforgeable one-time signature scheme, say $(\mathsf{vk}, \mathsf{sgk})$ and a random $x \in \{0, 1\}^N$. Write vk_i for the i-th bit of vk and let h be a hard-core predicate, then:

– $c_i = F(f_i^{\mathsf{vk}_i}, x)$ for $i = 1, \ldots, k$.
– $y = m \oplus h(f_1^{\mathsf{vk}_1}, \ldots, f_k^{\mathsf{vk}_k}, x)$.
– $\sigma = \mathsf{Sign}_{\mathsf{sgk}}^{\mathrm{SS}}(c_1, \ldots, c_k, y)$.

It is assumed that $\mathsf{vk} \in \{0,1\}^k$: if not, it is enough to apply a universal one-way hash function to obtain the desired length.

Finally, output the ciphertext $\psi = (\mathsf{vk}, c_1, \ldots, c_k, y, \sigma)$.

Dec^{RS}: Upon receipt of a ciphertext ψ:

- Verify the signature; if $\mathsf{Ver}^{SS}_{\mathsf{vk}}((c_1, \ldots, c_k, y), \sigma) = 0$ output $\perp$.
- Otherwise compute $x_i = \mathsf{F}^{-1}(\mathsf{td}_i^{\mathsf{vk}_i}, c_i)$ for $i = 1, \ldots, k$.
- If $x_1 = \cdots = x_k$ then set $m = y \oplus h(f_1^{\mathsf{vk}_1}, \ldots, f_k^{\mathsf{vk}_k}, x_1)$ and return the plaintext m, otherwise output $\perp$.

The security of the scheme is summarized in the next theorem, which was proved in [16].

Theorem 1. *Assuming that $\mathcal{F}$ is secure under k-correlated inputs, and that the signature scheme is one-time strongly unforgeable, the above encryption scheme is IND-CCA2-secure.*

The proof consists of a standard argument, divided in two parts. The first part shows that if an adversary exists capable to break the CCA2 security of the scheme, it can be converted to an adversary able to forge the signature scheme. In the second part, assuming that the forgery doesn't occur, an adversary is built that contradicts the security of the hard-core predicate. Due to space constraints, we don't present the proof here, but we refer the reader to [16] for more details.

4   Previous Proposals

It would be natural to describe the McEliece encryption process as a function $f_G(x, y) = xG + y$. However, this function is clearly not secure under correlated inputs. Let us assume $\mathbb{F}_q$ has characteristic 2 like in the original McEliece scheme. Then, given two evaluations $f_{G_1}(x, y) = xG_1 + y$ and $f_{G_2}(x, y) = xG_2 + y$, an attacker could simply sum the outputs together and, since the error vector cancels out, obtain $x(G_1 + G_2)$, from which it is easy to recover x. The problem is that, since we are defining a function, there is no randomness anymore, whereas McEliece requires a random error vector in order to be secure under k-correlated inputs. A mapping that incorporates a random element would in fact give a different result for multiple encryptions of the same plaintext and so would not have a unique image.

We now present two schemes that have been proposed to deal with the matter.

4.1   Syndrome Decoding

This construction was presented in [6] and is based on the Niederreiter cryptosystem [12]. Since this relies on the properties of the parity-check matrix rather than the generator matrix, it is often considered the "dual" cryptosystem and the computational assumptions for the security change accordingly.

The Niederreiter trapdoor function can be described as the family $\mathcal{N} = (\mathsf{G}, \mathsf{F})$ in the following way:

Generation: On input n, k the algorithm G generates a random parity-check matrix H for an $[n, k]$-linear code with an efficient decoding algorithm over $\mathbb{F}_q$, then computes its systematic form $\hat{H}$. The algorithm returns the public key $\hat{H}$ and the private key Γ.

Evaluation: On input $\hat{H}, e$, where e is a string of fixed weight w in $\mathbb{F}_q^n$, the algorithm F computes $\psi = \hat{H}e$ and returns the ciphertext ψ.

It is possible to invert F using the trapdoor: on input Γ and ψ, simply decode to obtain e using the decoding algorithm connected to Γ. The function is proved to be one-way under k-correlated inputs in [6, Theorem 6.2] if k is chosen such that the Niederreiter assumptions hold for n and $(n - k)$k, and it is intended to be used in the general Rosen-Segev framework.

4.2   k-Repetition PKE

Dowsley, Müller-Quade and Nascimento [3] propose a scheme that resembles the Rosen-Segev protocol trying to apply it to the McEliece cryptosystem. Despite the authors' claim that this is the "direct translation" of [16], this is not exactly the case.

Among other differences, the main discrepancy is that the scheme doesn't rely on a collection of functions but instead defines a structure called *k-repetition Public-Key Encryption* (PKE_k). This is essentially an application of k samples of the PKE to the same input, in which the decryption algorithm also includes a verification step on the k outputs. The encryption step produces a signature directly on the McEliece ciphertexts instead of introducing a random vector x as in the original scheme. This means that it is necessary to use an IND-CPA secure variant of McEliece's cryptosystem to achieve CCA2 security. For this task, the authors propose to use the "Randomized McEliece" variant by Nojima et al. [13]. This variant uses, as the name says, additional randomness, in the form of a random string. The string is sampled from a randomness set R with elements of length k_2, and then concatenated to the plaintext so that the resulting string has length k and can be encoded as normal. We briefly recall the scheme below.

- Setup: Fix public system parameters $q, n, k, w \in \mathbb{N}$ such that $k = k_1 + k_2$.
- $\mathsf{K_{publ}}$: The set of $k \times n$ matrices over $\mathbb{F}_q$.
- $\mathsf{K_{priv}}$: The set of "code descriptions" for the chosen code family.
- P: The vector space $\mathbb{F}_q^{k_1}$.
- R: The vector space $\mathbb{F}_q^{k_2}$.
- C: The vector space $\mathbb{F}_q^n$.
- KeyGen: Sample a random generator matrix G for a code of the chosen family. Compute the "scrambled" generator matrix $\hat{G}$, then publish the public key $\hat{G} \in \mathsf{K_{publ}}$ and store the private key $\Gamma \in \mathsf{K_{priv}}$.

- Enc: On input a public key $\hat{G} \in \mathsf{K}_{\mathsf{publ}}$, a plaintext $m \in \mathsf{P}$ and a random string $r \in \mathsf{R}$, sample a random error vector e of weight w in $\mathbb{F}_q^n$ and return the ciphertext $\psi = (r|m)\hat{G} + e \in \mathsf{C}$.
- Dec: On input the private key $\Gamma \in \mathsf{K}_{\mathsf{priv}}$ and a ciphertext $\psi \in \mathsf{C}$, apply the decoding algorithm D_Γ to it. If the decoding succeeds, parse the result as $(r|m)$ and return the plaintext $\phi = m$. Otherwise, output $\perp$.

Remark 3. It is clear that, as already mentioned by the authors in [13], the IND-CPA security of the randomized McEliece scheme is not absolute, but depends on the choice of the sizes of the message m and randomness r in the encryption procedure $(r|m)\hat{G} + e$. In the context of a CPA attack game, in fact, this ciphertext is subject to general decoding attacks with partial information about the plaintext. As illustrated in [13, Table 1], if the randomness r is not large enough, the IND-CPA security of the scheme can be easily broken.

We now present the scheme described in [3]. Note that, in the paper, this is presented as a general scheme, applicable to any IND-CPA secure PKE which is secure and verifiable under k-correlated inputs.

$\mathsf{KeyGen}^{\mathrm{DMQN}}$: Invoke $\mathsf{KeyGen}^{\mathrm{PKE}}$ for $2k$ times independently and obtain the collection of public keys $(\mathsf{pk}_1^0, \mathsf{pk}_1^1, \ldots, \mathsf{pk}_k^0, \mathsf{pk}_k^1)$ and the corresponding private keys $(\mathsf{sk}_1^0, \mathsf{sk}_1^1, \ldots, \mathsf{sk}_k^0, \mathsf{sk}_k^1)$, then run the key generation algorithm for the signature scheme to obtain a key $(\mathsf{vk}^*, \mathsf{sgk}^*)$. Publish the public key $\mathsf{pk} = (\mathsf{pk}_1^0, \mathsf{pk}_1^1, \ldots, \mathsf{pk}_k^0, \mathsf{pk}_k^1)$ and choose the private key accordingly to vk^*, i.e. $\mathsf{sk} = (\mathsf{vk}^*, \mathsf{sk}_1^{1-\mathsf{vk}_1^*}, \ldots, \mathsf{sk}_k^{1-\mathsf{vk}_k^*})$.

$\mathsf{Enc}^{\mathrm{DMQN}}$: To encrypt a plaintext m with the public key pk, sample another, different key $(\mathsf{vk}, \mathsf{sgk})$ from the signature scheme, then:

- $c_i = \mathsf{Enc}^{\mathrm{PKE}}_{\mathsf{pk}_i^{\mathsf{vk}_i}}(m)$ for $i = 1, \ldots, k$.
- $\sigma = \mathsf{Sign}^{\mathrm{SS}}_{\mathsf{sgk}}(c_1, \ldots, c_k)$.
- Output the ciphertext $\psi = (\mathsf{vk}, c_1, \ldots, c_k, \sigma)$.

$\mathsf{Dec}^{\mathrm{DMQN}}$: Upon receipt of a ciphertext ψ:

- If $\mathsf{vk} = \mathsf{vk}^*$ or $\mathsf{Ver}^{\mathrm{SS}}_{\mathsf{vk}}((c_1, \ldots, c_k), \sigma) = 0$ output $\perp$.
- Otherwise compute $m = \mathsf{Dec}^{\mathrm{PKE}}_{\mathsf{sk}_i^{\mathsf{vk}_i}}(c_i)$ for some i such that $\mathsf{vk}_i \neq \mathsf{vk}_i^*$.
- Verify that $c_i = \mathsf{Enc}^{\mathrm{PKE}}_{\mathsf{pk}_i^{\mathsf{vk}_i}}(m)$ for all $i = 1, \ldots, k$. If the verification is successful return the plaintext m, otherwise output $\perp$.

Since we know that $\mathsf{vk} \neq \mathsf{vk}^*$, there is at least one position in which they differ, hence the decryption process is well defined.

Remark 4. Note that, even though the encryption process is not deterministic, for McEliece encryption it is still possible to perform the check in the last step of $\mathsf{Dec}^{\mathrm{DMQN}}$. It is in fact enough to check the Hamming weight of $c_i - m\hat{G}_i$ where $\hat{G}_i$ is the generator matrix corresponding to the public key $\mathsf{pk}_i^{\mathsf{vk}_i}$. This is not clearly stated by the authors along with the description of the general scheme, but it is mentioned later on in [3, Theorem 3] for the particular case of the randomized McEliece.

The above specification of the scheme appears to be ambiguous. In fact, even assuming that the underlying encryption scheme is IND-CPA secure, the encryption step is described simply as $\mathsf{Enc}^{\mathrm{PKE}}_{\mathsf{pk}_i^{\mathsf{vk}_i}}(m)$ for $i = 1, \ldots, \mathsf{k}$, without indicating explicitly the role of the randomness. In [3, Section 4] some remarks are made about the security and there is the suggestion that the scheme in use be the randomized McEliece scheme from [13]; however, precise details on how this should be instantiated are missing. One could in general think at the k encryptions as $c_i = \mathsf{Enc}^{\mathrm{PKE}}_{\mathsf{pk}_i^{\mathsf{vk}_i}}(m, r_i) = (r_i|m)\hat{G}_i + e_i$. In this case, since we check the Hamming weight of $c_i - (r_i|m)\hat{G}_i$, the check would obviously fail unless $r_1 = \cdots = r_\mathsf{k} = r$.

Remark 5. The KeyGen algorithm is slightly different from the Rosen-Segev case. In particular, 2k keys are generated, then a random verification key vk^* is chosen and half of the private keys (the ones corresponding to vk^*) are discarded. This also implies that decryption only works when $\mathsf{vk} \neq \mathsf{vk}^*$. This technique is used in the context of the proof of Theorem 1, specifically in the second part while constructing an efficient distinguisher for the hard-core predicate. While, as we will see in the following, this is necessary for the proof (both for the original paper and for the proposed scheme), it is certainly a redundant requirement in the KeyGen process.

In light of the previous observations, we describe below a corrected description of the three algorithms composing the scheme:

$\mathsf{KeyGen}^{\mathrm{DMQN}}$: Invoke $\mathsf{KeyGen}^{\mathrm{PKE}}$ for 2k times independently and obtain the collection of public keys $(\mathsf{pk}_1^0, \mathsf{pk}_1^1, \ldots, \mathsf{pk}_\mathsf{k}^0, \mathsf{pk}_\mathsf{k}^1)$ and the corresponding private keys $(\mathsf{sk}_1^0, \mathsf{sk}_1^1, \ldots, \mathsf{sk}_\mathsf{k}^0, \mathsf{sk}_\mathsf{k}^1)$. The former is distributed as the public key pk, while the latter is the private key sk.

$\mathsf{Enc}^{\mathrm{DMQN}}$: To encrypt a plaintext m with the public key pk, sample a key $(\mathsf{vk}, \mathsf{sgk})$ from the signature scheme *and a randomness* r, then:

- $c_i = \mathsf{Enc}^{\mathrm{PKE}}_{\mathsf{pk}_i^{\mathsf{vk}_i}}(m, r)^2$ for $i = 1, \ldots, \mathsf{k}$.
- $\sigma = \mathsf{Sign}^{\mathrm{SS}}_{\mathsf{sgk}}(c_1, \ldots, c_\mathsf{k})$.
- Output the ciphertext $\psi = (\mathsf{vk}, c_1, \ldots, c_\mathsf{k}, \sigma)$.

$\mathsf{Dec}^{\mathrm{DMQN}}$: Upon receipt of a ciphertext ψ:

- If $\mathsf{Ver}^{\mathrm{SS}}_{\mathsf{vk}}((c_1, \ldots, c_\mathsf{k}), \sigma) = 0$ output $\bot$.
- Otherwise compute $(m, r) = \mathsf{Dec}^{\mathrm{PKE}}_{\mathsf{sk}_i^{\mathsf{vk}_i}}(c_i)$ for some i.
- Verify that $c_i = \mathsf{Enc}^{\mathrm{PKE}}_{\mathsf{pk}_i^{\mathsf{vk}_i}}(m, r)$ for all $i = 1, \ldots, \mathsf{k}$. If the verification is successful return the plaintext m, otherwise output $\bot$.

---

[2] Note that the randomness we are expliciting here is the one necessary to realize the IND-CPA security of PKE, hence Enc is still a randomized algorithm. In particular, for the McEliece instantiation we would have $c_i = (r|m)\hat{G}_i + e_i$.

The original construction is proved to be CCA2-secure in [3, Theorem 1]. We have constructed our own arguments for security, but due to space limitations, these have been moved to Appendix A.

Remark 6. The follow-up paper of [2] also includes a modified version that allows to encrypt correlated inputs. Note that, however, this is still not a "direct translation" of the Rosen-Segev scheme. Moreover, improvements such as encrypting correlated inputs are not necessarily relevant when public-key encryption is used to exchange a single symmetric key (e.g. as a Key Encapsulation Mechanism, or KEM), which is (or should be) its main purpose. Therefore, in the next section, we propose a version that is simpler, and much closer to [16].

5   A Direct Translation of McEliece

We now explain how to realize the Rosen-Segev scheme using McEliece. The construction arises naturally if we want to be as close as possible to the original McEliece formulation. We hence follow the usual approach of the McEliece cryptosystem, that is to choose a different random error vector every time we call the evaluation algorithm; this implies that we are not using functions anymore. The construction is proved to be secure under k-correlated inputs in Theorem 2. It proceeds as follows:

Describe McEliece as a pair $\mathsf{McE} = (\mathsf{G}, \mathsf{F})$ composed by two algorithms: G is a generation algorithm that samples a description, and F is an evaluation algorithm that provides the evaluation on a given input.

Generation: On input n, k the algorithm G generates a random generator matrix G for an $[n, k]$-linear code with an efficient decoding algorithm over $\mathbb{F}_q$, computes the "scrambled" generator matrix $\hat{G}$, then publishes the public key $\hat{G}$ and stores the private key Γ.

Evaluation: On input $\hat{G}, m$ the algorithm F generates a random error vector e of fixed weight w in $\mathbb{F}_q^n$, computes $\psi = m\hat{G} + e$ and outputs the ciphertext ψ.

It is possible to invert F using the trapdoor: on input Γ and ψ, simply decode to obtain e using the decoding algorithm connected to Γ, then retrieve m using linear algebra.

We claim that this encryption process is secure under k-correlated inputs. First, we need a technical lemma.

Lemma 1. *If Assumption 2 holds for parameters $\hat{n}, k$ and $\hat{w}$, then the ensembles* $\{(G, mG + e) : G \in \mathbb{F}_q^{k \times \hat{n}}, m \in \mathbb{F}_q^k, e \in \mathcal{W}_{\hat{n}, \hat{w}}\}$ *and* $\{(G, y) : G \in \mathbb{F}_q^{k \times \hat{n}}, y \xleftarrow{R} \mathbb{F}_q^{\hat{n}}\}$ *are computationally indistinguishable.*

Proof. Consider the problem of distinguishing the ensembles $\{(H, He^T) : H \in \mathbb{F}_q^{(\hat{n}-k) \times \hat{n}}, e \in \mathcal{W}_{\hat{n}, \hat{w}}\}$ and $\{(H, y) : H \in \mathbb{F}_q^{(\hat{n}-k) \times \hat{n}}, y \xleftarrow{R} \mathbb{F}_q^{\hat{n}-k}\}$ as in [5] and suppose $\mathcal{A}$ is a probabilistic polynomial-time algorithm that is able to distinguish the ensembles described above. In particular, say $\mathcal{A}$ outputs 1 if the challenge ensemble is of the form $(G, mG + e)$ and 0 otherwise. We show how to construct an adversary $\mathcal{A}'$ that solves the above problem.

Let (H, z) be the received input, where z is either He^T for a certain error vector $e \in \mathcal{W}_{\hat{n}, \hat{w}}$ or a random vector of $\mathbb{F}_q^{\hat{n}-k}$. By linear algebra, is easy to find a vector $x \in \mathbb{F}_q^{\hat{n}}$ with $\mathsf{wt}(x) \geq \hat{w}$ such that $z = Hx^T$. Submit $(\tilde{G}, x)$ to $\mathcal{A}$, where $\tilde{G}$ is the generator matrix associated to H. Now, if $z = He^T$ we can write $x = \tilde{m}\tilde{G} + e$; in this case, in fact, we have $Hx^T = z = He^T \implies H(x - e)^T = 0$ and clearly this implies that $(x - e)^T$ is a codeword. Then $\mathcal{A}$ will output 1 and so will $\mathcal{A}'$. Otherwise, $\mathcal{A}$ will output 0 and so will $\mathcal{A}'$. In both cases, $\mathcal{A}'$ is able to distinguish correctly and this terminates the proof.   □

Note that this was proved in [5] for the syndrome decoding (Niederreiter) case. We know [9] that the two formulations are equivalent; in particular, any adversary able to distinguish the above ensembles can be used to build an adversary for the Niederreiter case.

The security of the construction is proved in the following theorem, which closely follows the proof of [6, Theorem 6.2].

Theorem 2. *Fix an integer k. If the parameters n, k, w are chosen such that decoding a random linear code with parameters nk, k and wk is hard, then the above encryption process is secure under k-correlated inputs.*

Proof. Let $\mathcal{A}$ be an adversary for the one-wayness under k-correlated inputs. We define the advantage of $\mathcal{A}$ to be

$$\mathsf{Adv}_{\mathcal{A}}(\lambda) = \Pr[\mathcal{A}(\hat{G}_1, \ldots, \hat{G}_k, \mathsf{F}(\hat{G}_1, m), \ldots, \mathsf{F}(\hat{G}_k, m)) = m]$$

where $\hat{G}_1, \ldots, \hat{G}_k$ are k independent public keys generated by G.

We assume the indistinguishability assumption holds: we can then exchange all the matrices $\hat{G}_i$ with uniform matrices U_i with a negligible advantage for the attacker. Now, let's define the $k \times nk$ matrix U by concatenating the rows of the matrices U_i, i.e. $U = (U_1 | \ldots | U_k)$. We assume that the distributions $(U_1, \ldots, U_k, \mathsf{F}(U_1, m), \ldots, \mathsf{F}(U_k, m))$ and $(U, \mathsf{F}(U, m))$ are interchangeable without a significant advantage for the attacker. Note that in the latter the error vector used will have length nk and weight wk. A formal argument for this indistinguishability assumption will be provided below.

We now invoke Lemma 1 with $\hat{n} = nk$ and $\hat{w} = wk$. Hence

$$\mathsf{Adv}_{\mathcal{A}}(\lambda) = \Pr[\mathcal{A}(U, \mathsf{F}(U, m)) = m] - \Pr[\mathcal{A}(U, y) = m] \in \mathsf{negl}(n)$$

and since this last one is of course negligible, we conclude the proof.   □

An indistinguishability assumption on error vectors Similarly to what happens for the IND-CPA security of the McEliece variant (as pointed out in Remark 3), also in this case the security we are trying to achieve is not absolute, but depends on a suitable choice of parameters. The assumption in this case is that we can replace the vector $(mU_1 + e_1 | \ldots | mU_k + e_k)$ with the vector $mU + e$, where $U = (U_1 | \ldots | U_k)$ and e is a random error vector of weight wk; in other words, we would like to argue that $e' = (e_1| \ldots |e_k)$ is indistinguishable from e. Note that $\mathsf{wt}(e') = \mathsf{wt}(e)$ but while the distribution of the error positions on e is truly pseudorandom, e' is formed by k blocks of weight w each. It is plausible that the number of vectors of this kind (that we denote $\#_{e'}$) is not too small compared to the total of error vectors with same length and weight. Unfortunately, the only estimate we can provide is not of help:

$$\frac{\#_{e'}}{|\mathcal{W}_{nk,wk}|} = \frac{\binom{n}{w}^k}{\binom{nk}{wk}} \geq \frac{\left(\frac{n}{w}\right)^{wk}}{\left(\frac{ne}{w}\right)^{wk}} = \frac{1}{e^{wk}}. \tag{3}$$

However, the bound is not tight, and experimental evidence indicates that this ratio is much bigger.

It is possible to implement the Rosen-Segev scheme using the choice of F and G that we described above. We present the details below.

$\mathsf{KeyGen}^{\mathrm{P}}$: Invoke G for 2k times independently and obtain the collections of public keys $\mathsf{pk} = (\mathsf{pk}_1^0, \mathsf{pk}_1^1, \ldots, \mathsf{pk}_k^0, \mathsf{pk}_k^1)$ and private keys $\mathsf{sk} = (\mathsf{sk}_1^0, \mathsf{sk}_1^1, \ldots, \mathsf{sk}_k^0, \mathsf{sk}_k^1)$, where $\mathsf{pk}_j^i = (\hat{G}_j)^i$ and $\mathsf{sk}_j^i = (S, P, \Gamma)_j^i$ as above.

$\mathsf{Enc}^{\mathrm{P}}$: To encrypt a plaintext m with the public key pk, sample a key $(\mathsf{vk}, \mathsf{sgk})$ and a random $x \in \{0,1\}^k$, then:

- $c_i = \mathsf{F}(\mathsf{pk}_i^{\mathsf{vk}_i}, x)$ for $i = 1, \ldots, k$.
- $y = m \oplus h(\mathsf{pk}_1^{\mathsf{vk}_1}, \ldots, \mathsf{pk}_k^{\mathsf{vk}_k}, x)$.
- $\sigma = \mathsf{Sign}_{\mathsf{sgk}}^{\mathrm{SS}}(c_1, \ldots, c_k, y)$.

where vk_i represents the i-th bit of vk. The ciphertext is $\psi = (\mathsf{vk}, c_1, \ldots, c_k, y, \sigma)$.

$\mathsf{Dec}^{\mathrm{P}}$: Upon receipt of a ciphertext ψ:

- Verify the signature; if $\mathsf{Ver}_{\mathsf{vk}}^{\mathrm{SS}}((c_1, \ldots, c_k, y), \sigma) = 0$ output $\bot$.
- Otherwise compute $x_i = \mathsf{F}^{-1}(\mathsf{sk}_i^{\mathsf{vk}_i}, c_i)$ for $i = 1, \ldots, k$.[3]
- If $x_1 = \cdots = x_k$ then set $m = y \oplus h(\mathsf{pk}_1^{\mathsf{vk}_1}, \ldots, \mathsf{pk}_k^{\mathsf{vk}_k}, x_1)$ and return the plaintext m, otherwise output $\bot$.

For simplicity, as in the original construction, we can assume m to be a single bit, in which case h describes a hard-core predicate for McEliece. However, the protocol extends easily to multiple bits plaintexts: as suggested in [16], to encrypt a polynomial number T of bits, it is enough to replace the hard-core predicate h with a hard-core *function* $h' : \{0,1\}^* \rightarrow \{0,1\}^T$.

The security is summarized in the following corollary.

Corollary 2. *The above encryption scheme is IND-CCA2 secure in the standard model.*

---

[3] By analogy with the Rosen-Segev scheme. Clearly in practice it would be much more efficient, rather than decoding k ciphertexts, to just decode one and then re-encode and test as in [3, Theorem 3].

Proof. By Theorem 2, the collection of McEliece encryption schemes McE is k-correlation secure. Then this is analogous to Theorem 1, noting that the same argument applies when $\mathcal{F} = $ McE, i.e. f describes a randomized algorithm rather than a function. The proof uses the same steps as in Theorem 3, with the exception that in our case Lemma 3 is proved by constructing an adversary $\mathcal{A}'$ that works as a predictor for the hard-core predicate h.   □

6 Conclusions

The scheme of Dowsley et al. [3] is a first proposal to translate the Rosen-Segev protocol to the McEliece setting. However, the construction is ambiguous, as we have shown in Sect. 4, and features some strange and unnecessary modifications such as "forgetting" half the private keys, or forbidding ciphertexts to feature the verification key vk*. The original Rosen-Segev scheme has no such requirements.

The scheme was subsequently fixed in the follow-up joint work with Döttling [2], but still deviates substantially from the original Rosen-Segev framework. We therefore present a construction that, instead, follows more closely the original framework. We provide a choice of algorithms F and G, based on the McEliece cryptosystem, that can be used directly into the Rosen-Segev scheme. We then show that our construction is IND-CCA2 secure following the original security arguments of Rosen and Segev.

A Security Arguments for the Corrected Scheme

Theorem 3. *Assuming that PKE_k is IND-CPA secure and verifiable under k-correlated inputs, and that the signature scheme is one-time strongly unforgeable, the above encryption scheme is IND-CCA2-secure.*

Let $\mathcal{A}$ be an IND-CCA2 adversary. During the attack game, $\mathcal{A}$ submits m_0, m_1 and gets back the challenge ciphertext $\psi^* = (\text{vk}^*, c_1^*, \ldots, c_k^*, \sigma^*)$. Indicate with Forge the event that, for one of $\mathcal{A}$'s decryption queries $\psi = (\text{vk}, c_1, \ldots, c_k, \sigma)$, it holds $\text{vk} = \text{vk}^*$ and $\text{Ver}_{\text{vk}}^{\text{SS}}((c_1, \ldots, c_k), \sigma) = 1$. The theorem is proved by means of the two following lemmas.

Lemma 2. *Pr[Forge] is negligible.*

Proof. Assume that there exists an adversary $\mathcal{A}$ for which Pr[Forge] is not negligible. We build an adversary $\mathcal{A}'$ that breaks the security of the one-time strongly unforgeable scheme. $\mathcal{A}'$ works as follows:

Key Generation: Invoke $\text{KeyGen}^{\text{DMQN}}$ as above and return pk to $\mathcal{A}$.

Decryption Queries: Upon a decryption query $\psi = (\text{vk}, c_1, \ldots, c_k, \sigma)$:

1. If $\text{vk} = \text{vk}^*$ and $\text{Ver}_{\text{vk}}^{\text{SS}}((c_1, \ldots, c_k), \sigma) = 1$ output $\perp$ and halt.
2. Otherwise, decrypt normally using Dec^{DMQN}.

Challenge Queries: Upon a challenge query m_0, m_1:

1. Choose random $b \in \{0, 1\}$.
2. Use $\mathsf{Enc}^{\mathrm{DMQN}}$ to compute $c_i^* = \mathsf{Enc}_{\mathsf{pk}_i^{\mathsf{vk}_i^*}}(m_b, r)$ for $i = 1, \ldots, \mathsf{k}$.
3. Obtain the signature σ^* on $(c_1^*, \ldots, c_{\mathsf{k}}^*)$ with respect to vk^{*}[4].
4. Return the challenge ciphertext $\psi^* = (\mathsf{vk}^*, c_1^*, \ldots, c_{\mathsf{k}}^*, \sigma^*)$.

Note that, if Forge doesn't occur, the simulation of the CCA2 interaction is perfect. Therefore, the probability that $\mathcal{A}'$ breaks the security of the one-time signature scheme is exactly $\Pr[\mathsf{Forge}]$. The one-time strong unforgeability implies that this probability is negligible. □

Lemma 3. $\left| \Pr[b = b^* \wedge \neg \mathsf{Forge}] - \frac{1}{2} \right|$ *is negligible.*

Proof. Assume that there exists an adversary $\mathcal{A}$ for which $\left| \Pr[b = b^* \wedge \neg \mathsf{Forge}] - \frac{1}{2} \right|$ is not negligible. We build an adversary $\mathcal{A}'$ that breaks the IND-CPA security of PKE_{k}. $\mathcal{A}'$ works as follows:

Key Generation: On input the public key $(\mathsf{pk}_1, \ldots, \mathsf{pk}_{\mathsf{k}})$ for PKE_{k}:

1. Execute $\mathsf{KeyGen}^{\mathrm{SS}}$ and obtain a key $(\mathsf{vk}^*, \mathsf{sgk}^*)$.
2. Set $\mathsf{pk}_i^{\mathsf{vk}^*} = \mathsf{pk}_i$ for $i = 1, \ldots, \mathsf{k}$.
3. Run $\mathsf{KeyGen}^{\mathrm{PKE}}$ for k times and denote the resulting public keys by $(\mathsf{pk}_1^{1-\mathsf{vk}_1^*}, \ldots, \mathsf{pk}_{\mathsf{k}}^{1-\mathsf{vk}_{\mathsf{k}}^*})$ and private keys by $(\mathsf{sk}_1^{1-\mathsf{vk}_1^*}, \ldots, \mathsf{sk}_{\mathsf{k}}^{1-\mathsf{vk}_{\mathsf{k}}^*})$.
4. Return the public key $\mathsf{pk} = (\mathsf{pk}_1^0, \mathsf{pk}_1^1, \ldots, \mathsf{pk}_{\mathsf{k}}^0, \mathsf{pk}_{\mathsf{k}}^1)$ to $\mathcal{A}$.

Decryption Queries: Upon a decryption query from $\mathcal{A}$:

1. If Forge occurs output $\perp$ and halt.
2. Otherwise, there will be some i such that $\mathsf{vk}_i \neq \mathsf{vk}_i^*$. Decrypt normally using $\mathsf{Dec}^{\mathrm{DMQN}}$ with the key $\mathsf{sk}_i^{\mathsf{vk}_i}$ previously generated.

Challenge Queries: Upon a challenge query m_0, m_1:

1. Send m_0, m_1 to the challenge oracle for the IND-CPA game of $\mathcal{A}'$ and obtain the corresponding challenge ciphertext $(c_1^*, \ldots, c_{\mathsf{k}}^*)$.
2. Sign $(c_1^*, \ldots, c_{\mathsf{k}}^*)$ using sgk^* to get the signature σ^*.
3. Return the challenge ciphertext $\psi^* = (\mathsf{vk}^*, c_1^*, \ldots, c_{\mathsf{k}}^*, \sigma^*)$.

Output: When $\mathcal{A}$ outputs b^* also $\mathcal{A}'$ outputs b^*.

As long as Forge doesn't occur, it is clear that the IND-CPA advantage of $\mathcal{A}'$ against PKE_{k} is the same as the IND-CCA2 advantage of $\mathcal{A}$ against the above scheme. Since we are assuming the IND-CPA security of PKE_{k}, we have the IND-CCA2 security as desired. □

---

[4] Remember that in the one-time strong unforgeability game the adversary is allowed to ask to a signing oracle for the signature on one message.

References

1. Biswas, B., Sendrier, N.: McEliece cryptosystem implementation: theory and practice. In: Buchmann, J., Ding, J. (eds.) PQCrypto 2008. LNCS, vol. 5299, pp. 47–62. Springer, Heidelberg (2008). https://doi.org/10.1007/978-3-540-88403-3_4
2. Döttling, N., Dowsley, R., Müller-Quade, J., Nascimento, A.C.: A CCA2 secure variant of the McEliece cryptosystem. IEEE Trans. Inf. Theory **58**(10), 6672–6680 (2012)
3. Dowsley, R., Müller-Quade, J., Nascimento, A.C.A.: A CCA2 secure public key encryption scheme based on the mceliece assumptions in the standard model. In: Fischlin, M. (ed.) CT-RSA 2009. LNCS, vol. 5473, pp. 240–251. Springer, Heidelberg (2009). https://doi.org/10.1007/978-3-642-00862-7_16
4. Faugère, J.-C., Gauthier-Umaña, V., Otmani, A., Perret, L., Tillich, J.-P.: A distinguisher for high rate McEliece cryptosystems. In: 2011 IEEE Information Theory Workshop (ITW), pp. 282–286, October 2011
5. Fischer, J.-B., Stern, J.: An efficient pseudo-random generator provably as secure as syndrome decoding. In: Maurer, U. (ed.) EUROCRYPT 1996. LNCS, vol. 1070, pp. 245–255. Springer, Heidelberg (1996). https://doi.org/10.1007/3-540-68339-9_22
6. Freeman, D.M., Goldreich, O., Kiltz, E., Rosen, A., Segev, G.: More constructions of lossy and correlation-secure trapdoor functions. In: Nguyen, P.Q., Pointcheval, D. (eds.) PKC 2010. LNCS, vol. 6056, pp. 279–295. Springer, Heidelberg (2010). https://doi.org/10.1007/978-3-642-13013-7_17
7. Fujisaki, E., Okamoto, T.: Secure integration of asymmetric and symmetric encryption schemes. In: Wiener, M. (ed.) CRYPTO 1999. LNCS, vol. 1666, pp. 537–554. Springer, Heidelberg (1999). https://doi.org/10.1007/3-540-48405-1_34
8. Kobara, K., Imai, H.: Semantically secure McEliece public-key cryptosystems - conversions for McEliece PKC. In: Kim, K. (ed.) PKC 2001. LNCS, vol. 1992, pp. 19–35. Springer, Heidelberg (2001). https://doi.org/10.1007/3-540-44586-2_2
9. Li, Y.X., Deng, R.H., Wang, X.M.: On the equivalence of McEliece's and Niederreiter's public-key cryptosystems. IEEE Trans. Inf. Theory **40**(1), 271–273 (1994)
10. Preetha Mathew, K., Vasant, S., Venkatesan, S., Pandu Rangan, C.: An efficient IND-CCA2 secure variant of the niederreiter encryption scheme in the standard model. In: Susilo, W., Mu, Y., Seberry, J. (eds.) ACISP 2012. LNCS, vol. 7372, pp. 166–179. Springer, Heidelberg (2012). https://doi.org/10.1007/978-3-642-31448-3_13
11. McEliece, R.J.: A public-key cryptosystem based on algebraic coding theory. Deep Space Netw. Progress Rep. **44**, 114–116 (1978)
12. Niederreiter, H.: Knapsack-type cryptosystems and algebraic coding theory. Prob. Control Inf. Theory **15**(2), 159–166 (1986)
13. Nojima, R., Imai, H., Kobara, K., Morozov, K.: Semantic security for the McEliece cryptosystem without random oracles. Des. Codes Cryptogr. **49**(1–3), 289–305 (2008)
14. Persichetti, E.: On a CCA2-secure variant of McEliece in the standard model. IACR Cryptology ePrint Archive 2012:268 (2012)
15. Persichetti, E.: Secure and anonymous hybrid encryption from coding theory. In: Gaborit, P. (ed.) PQCrypto 2013. LNCS, vol. 7932, pp. 174–187. Springer, Heidelberg (2013). https://doi.org/10.1007/978-3-642-38616-9_12
16. Rosen, A., Segev, G.: Chosen-ciphertext security via correlated products. In: Reingold, O. (ed.) TCC 2009. LNCS, vol. 5444, pp. 419–436. Springer, Heidelberg (2009). https://doi.org/10.1007/978-3-642-00457-5_25

17. Strenzke, F.: A timing attack against the secret permutation in the McEliece PKC. In: Sendrier, N. (ed.) PQCrypto 2010. LNCS, vol. 6061, pp. 95–107. Springer, Heidelberg (2010). https://doi.org/10.1007/978-3-642-12929-2_8
18. Strenzke, F., Tews, E., Molter, H.G., Overbeck, R., Shoufan, A.: Side channels in the McEliece PKC. In: Buchmann, J., Ding, J. (eds.) PQCrypto 2008. LNCS, vol. 5299, pp. 216–229. Springer, Heidelberg (2008). https://doi.org/10.1007/978-3-540-88403-3_15
19. Yoshida, Y., Morozov, K., Tanaka, K.: CCA2 key-privacy for code-based encryption in the standard model. In: Lange, T., Takagi, T. (eds.) PQCrypto 2017. LNCS, vol. 10346, pp. 35–50. Springer, Cham (2017). https://doi.org/10.1007/978-3-319-59879-6_3

Efficient Attribute-Based Encryption
with Blackbox Traceability

Shengmin Xu[1,2]([✉]), Guomin Yang[1], Yi Mu[4], and Ximeng Liu[2,3]

[1] Institute of Cybersecurity and Cryptology, School of Computing and Information
Technology, University of Wollongong, Wollongong, Australia
{sx914,gyang}@uow.edu.au
[2] School of Information Systems, Singapore Management University,
Singapore, Singapore
snbnix@gmail.com
[3] College of Mathematics and Computer Science,
Fuzhou University, Fuzhou, Fujian, China
[4] Fujian Provincial Key Laboratory of Network Security and Cryptology,
Fujian Normal University, Fuzhou, China
ymu.ieee@gmail.com

Abstract. Traitor tracing scheme can be used to identify a decryption
key is illegally used in public-key encryption. In CCS'13, Liu et al. proposed an attribute-based traitor tracing (ABTT) scheme with blackbox
traceability which can trace decryption keys embedded in a decryption
blackbox/device rather than tracing a well-formed decryption key. However, the existing ABTT schemes with blackbox traceability are based
on composite order group and the size of the decryption key depends
on the policies and the number of system users. In this paper, we revisit
blackbox ABTT and introduce a new primitive called attribute-based set
encryption (ABSE) based on key-policy ABE (KP-ABE) and identity-
based set encryption (IBSE), which allows aggregation of multiple related
policies and reduce the decryption key size in ABTT to be irrelevant to
the number of system users. We present a generic construction of the
ABTT scheme from our proposed ABSE scheme and fingerprint code
based on the Boneh-Naor paradigm in CCS'08. We then give a concrete
construction of the ABSE scheme which can be proven secure in the random oracle model under the decisional BDH assumption and a variant
of q-BDHE assumption.

Keywords: Public-key cryptosystems · Attribute-based encryption
Blackbox traceability

1 Introduction

Public-key encryption is the most fundamental primitive of public-key cryptography. However, the traditional public-key infrastructure (PKI) suffers from
the certificate management problem. To overcome this drawback, identity-based

© Springer Nature Switzerland AG 2018
J. Baek et al. (Eds.): ProvSec 2018, LNCS 11192, pp. 182–200, 2018.
https://doi.org/10.1007/978-3-030-01446-9_11

encryption (IBE) has been proposed, and it provides a new paradigm for public-key encryption [3]. IBE uses the identity string (e.g., email or IP address) of a user as the public key of that user. The sender using an IBE does not need to look up the public keys and the corresponding certificates of the receiver. However, IBE cannot efficiently handle data sharing among multiple users. To address this issue, attribute-based encryption (ABE) was introduced [3] to provide fine-grained access control. However, encryption schemes supporting multiple valid decryptors suffer the problem of decryption key re-distribution. A malicious user might have an intention to leak the decryption key or some decryption privileges by giving the decryption key or decryption blackbox/device to other unauthorized users for financial gain or for some other incentives.

To address this problem, traitor tracing scheme [4] was proposed to identify the traitor who violates the copyright restrictions. A traitor tracing scheme comprises an encryption key, a tracing key and n decryption keys, where n is the number of system users. Each legitimate user is given a unique decryption key that can decrypt any properly encrypted message. The tracing key can trace at least one user decryption used to construct the decryption blackbox/device. A traitor tracing scheme is said to be t-collusion resistant if the tracing is still successful against t colluded users. In this paper, we investigate the traitor tracing scheme in the ABE setting.

ABE with traitor tracing (ABTT) has been studied in the literature [9–11,14]. There are two levels of traceability depending on the way of tracing traitors. Level one is whitebox traceability [10,14], by which given a well-formed decryption key as input, a tracing algorithm can find out user who owns this decryption key. Level two is blackbox traceability [9,11], by which given a decryption blackbox/device, which the decryption key and even decryption algorithm could be hidden, the tracing algorithm, which treats the decryption blackbox as an oracle, can still find out the malicious user whose key has been used in constructing the decryption blackbox.

In this paper, we present a new construction of ABTT based on a new primitive called attribute-based set encryption (ABSE) inspired by KP-ABE [16] and IBSE [7]. We then describe our ABTT scheme from our proposed ABSE scheme and fingerprint code [4] to provide the efficient traitor tracing mechanism in the ABE setting. Our ABSE scheme is provably secure in the random oracle model under the decisional BDH assumption and a variant of q-BDHE assumption. Compared with the previous ABTT schemes, our ABTT scheme only requires the prime order group and the size of the decryption key only depends on the access policies as traditional KP-ABE rather than both the access policies and the number of system users.

1.1   Related Work

Sahai and Waters [16] introduced ABE that allows users to selectively share their encrypted data at a fine-grained level. To enrich expressiveness of access control policies, Goyal et al. [6] and Bethencourt et al. [2] then proposed key-policy and ciphertext-policy ABE schemes, respectively. In KP-ABE schemes, attribute sets are used to annotate ciphertexts, and private keys are associated with access structures that specify which ciphertexts the user will be entitled to decrypt. Ciphertext-policy ABE (CP-ABE) proceeds in a dual way, by assigning attribute sets to private keys and letting senders specify an access policy that receivers' attribute sets should comply with. However, the seminal works [2,6,16] of ABE schemes suffer some common problems, such as the size of the key and the ciphertext are linear to the attribute set and security proofs are under the selective model. Attrapadung et al. [1] proposed the first constant-size ABE and Lewko et al. [8] provided first fully secure ABE with dual encryption system [17], respectively. Unfortunately, the above schemes must define the attribute universe at setup phase or have to sacrifice the security by deploying the random oracle to scale up the attribute universe. Rouselakis and Waters [15] proposed large universe ABE schemes with selective security that can overcome this problem.

The concept of whitebox ABTT was introduced by Liu et al. [10] to identify the traitors who violate the copyright restrictions in the ABE setting. However, Liu et al.'s work must define the attribute universe at setup phase and cannot support the large attribute universe. To overcome this drawback, several ABTT [14,18] schemes were proposed to support the large universe. Liu et al. [9,11] introduced blackbox ABTT to solve a practical problem that the decryption key may not be a well-formed key and it may be embedded in a decryption blackbox/device. However, the decryption key in the proposed scheme is in the order of $O(|\mathcal{S}| + \sqrt{n})$, where $|\mathcal{S}|$ represents the number of attributes in the attribute set $\mathcal{S}$ and n is the number of system users. After that, some other works [12,13,19,20] have been proposed to improve efficiency, functionality or security. Unfortunately, the above schemes require the composite order group or large decryption key size depending on the number of system users.

1.2 Contribution

In this paper, we proposed an efficient blackbox ABTT scheme. Compared to previous ABTT schemes, our scheme provides the blackbox traceability based on prime order group and decryption key only relates to the access policies as the traditional ABE rather than both the access policies and the number of system users. Note that most of the previous blackbox ABTT schemes are based on Boneh et al.' traitor tracing scheme [5], which requires the decryption key in the order of $O(\sqrt{n})$, where n is the number of system users.

Our approach utilizes fingerprint codes to realize the traitor tracing mechanism. However, the trivial solution needs $O(n)$ private keys by appending a unique index from fingerprint codes as the user identifier at the end of each access policy. Suppose the ith user has an access structure $\mathbb{A} = (\mathbb{M}, \rho)$ with the matrix $\mathbb{M}$ of size $d \times l$ and mapping function ρ mapping each row in the matrix to the attribute universe. The trivial solution requires to extend each row j in the matrix to a set of policies for tracing traitors in blackbox, e.g., the jth row policy $(\mathbb{M}_j, \rho(j))$ extends to a set of policies

$$(\mathbb{M}_j, \rho(j)\|1\|w_1^{(i)}), (\mathbb{M}_j, \rho(j)\|2\|w_2^{(i)}), \ldots, (\mathbb{M}_j, \rho(j)\|\ell\|w_\ell^{(i)}), \tag{1}$$

where ℓ denotes the size of codeword in fingerprint codes and $w_k^{(i)}$ represents the kth position codeword for the ith user. It is obvious that the trivial solution requires the policy size of $\ell \times d \times l$ eventually.

To reduce the size of the decryption key, we introduce a new cryptographic primitive called attribute-based set encryption (ABSE). Roughly speaking, our ABSE compresses the decryption key for set of policies as shown in Eq. (1) to two policies

$$(\mathbb{M}_j, \rho(j)\|\mathcal{S}_0\|0) \text{ and } (\mathbb{M}_j, \rho(j)\|\mathcal{S}_1\|1)$$

with $O(1)$ size for each row in the access policy, where $\mathcal{S}_b$ represents a set of indices recording all positions $j \in [\ell]$ s.t. $w_j^{(i)} = b$ ($w_j^{(i)}$ representing j^{th} position in the codeword for the ith user). Finally, the decryption key has the policy size of $d \times l$ as the traditional ABE system.

We provide a generic construction of ABTT from fingerprint codes and ABSE under the prime order group, and it is provably secure based on the underlying fingerprint code and ABSE. The ABSE scheme instantiated in this paper is provably secure in random oracle model based on the decisional BDH assumption and a variant of q-BDHE assumption.

1.3   Outline

We introduce some preliminaries in Sect. 2 and provide the generic construction of the ABTT scheme and its proof in Sect. 3. In Sect. 4, we provide the concrete construction of ABSE scheme and its formal proof. We then summarize this paper in Sect. 5.

2   Preliminaries

2.1   Notations

Let $\mathbb{N}$ denote the set of all natural numbers, and for $n \in \mathbb{N}$, we define $[n] := \{1, \ldots, n\}$. If a and b are strings, then $|a|$ denotes the bit-length of a, $a\|b$ denotes the concatenation of a and b. Let $\vec{u} := (u_1, u_2, \ldots, u_\ell)$ denote a vector of dimension ℓ in $\mathbb{Z}_p$. Let the Greek character λ denote a security parameter. A function $\epsilon(\lambda) : \mathbb{N} \to [0, 1]$ is said to be negligible if for all positive polynomials $p(\lambda)$ and all sufficiently large $\lambda \in \mathbb{N}$, we have $\epsilon(\lambda) < 1/p(\lambda)$. To simplify, ϵ is used to represent negligible.

2.2   Bilinear Map

Let $\mathbb{G}$ and $\mathbb{G}_T$ be two cyclic multiplicative groups of prime order p and g be a generator of $\mathbb{G}$. The map $e : \mathbb{G} \times \mathbb{G} \to \mathbb{G}_T$ is said to be an admissible bilinear pairing if the following properties hold true.

- Bilinearity: for all $u, v \in \mathbb{G}$ and $a, b \in \mathbb{Z}_p$, $e(u^a, v^b) = e(u, v)^{ab}$.
- Non-degeneration: $e(g, g) \neq 1$.
- Computability: it is efficient to compute $e(u, v)$ for any $u, v \in \mathbb{G}$.

2.3   Decisional Bilinear Diffie-Hellman Assumption

Let $a, b, c, z \in \mathbb{Z}_p$ be chosen at random and g be a generator of $\mathbb{G}$. The decisional Bilinear Diffie-Hellman (BDH) assumption [16] is that no probabilistic time algorithm can distinguish the tuple $(g^a, g^b, g^c, e(g,g)^{abc})$ from the tuple $(g^a, g^b, g^c, e(g,g)^z)$ with a non-negligible advantage over random guess.

2.4   Modified q-Biliner Diffie-Hellman Exponent Assumption

Let $a \in \mathbb{Z}_p$ be chosen at random and g be a generator of $\mathbb{G}$. The modified q-Bilinear Diffie-Hellman Exponent (q-BDHE) [7] is that giving the terms $g, g^{(a)}$, $g^{(a^2)}, \ldots, g^{a^q}, g^{(a^{2q+2})}, g^{(a^{2q+3})}, \ldots, g^{(a^{3q+1})} \in \mathbb{G}^{2q+1}$, no probabilistic time algorithm can output the term $e(g,g)^{a^{2q+1}}$ with a non-negligible advantage.

2.5   Access Structure and Monotone Span Program

We recall the definition of access structures and monotone span program, as defined in [6].

Definition 1 (Access Structure). *Let $\{P_1, \ldots, P_n\}$ be a set of parties. A collection $\mathbb{A} \subseteq 2^{\{P_1, \ldots, P_n\}}$ is monotone if $\forall B, C$: if $B \in \mathbb{A}$ and $B \subseteq C$, then $C \subseteq \mathbb{A}$. A monotone access structure is a monotone collection $\mathbb{A}$ of non-empty subsets of $\{P_1, \ldots, P_n\}$, i.e., $\mathbb{A} \subseteq 2^{\{P_1, \ldots, P_n\}} \setminus \{\emptyset\}$. The sets in $\mathbb{A}$ are called authorized sets, and the sets not in $\mathbb{A}$ are called unauthorized sets.*

Definition 2 (Monotone Span Program (MSP)). *Let $\mathcal{K}$ be a field and $\{x_1, \ldots, x_n\}$ be a set of variables. A MSP over $\mathcal{K}$ is labeled matrix $\tilde{M}(\mathbb{M}, \rho)$ where $\mathbb{M}$ is a matrix over $\mathcal{K}$, and ρ is a labeling of the rows of $\mathbb{M}$ by literals from $\{x_1, \ldots, x_n\}$ (every row is labeled by one literal). A MSP accepts or rejects an input by the following criterion. For every input set $\mathcal{S}$ if literals, define the submatrix $\mathbb{M}_{\mathcal{S}}$ of $\mathbb{M}$ consisting of those rows whose labels are in S, i.e., rows labeled by some i such that $i \in \mathcal{S}$. The MSP $\tilde{M}$ accepts $\mathcal{S}$ of and only if $\vec{1} \in \mathrm{span}(\mathbb{M}_{\mathcal{S}})$, i.e., some linear combination of the rows of $\mathbb{M}_{\mathcal{S}}$ given the all-one vector $\vec{1}$. The MSP $\tilde{M}$ computes a boolean function $f_{\mathbb{M}}$ if it accepts exactly those input $\mathcal{S}$ where $f_{\mathbb{M}}(\mathcal{S}) = 1$. The size of $\tilde{M}$ is the number of rows in $\mathbb{M}$.*

In the rest of paper, we define $\mathbb{M}$ as a matrix with $d \times l$ elements, where d is a dynamic value depending on the access policy $\mathbb{A}$. $\mathbb{M}_i$ stands for the ith row of the matrix $\mathbb{M}$ and is a vector size of l. In our proposed scheme, each row of the matrix $\mathbb{M}$ maps to different attributes. For simply the notation, let $\mathbb{A}(\mathcal{S}) = 1$ indicate the attribute set $\mathcal{S}$ satisfies the access policy $\mathbb{A}$ and $\mathbb{A}(\mathcal{S}) = 0$ denote the attribute set $\mathcal{S}$ does not satisfy the access policy $\mathbb{A}$.

2.6   Fingerprint Code

The fingerprint code [4] is defined as follows.

- Let $\bar{w} \in \{0,1\}^{\ell}$ be an ℓ-bit codeword. We write $\bar{w} = w_1 w_2 \cdots w_{\ell}$ and assume w_i is the ith bit of $\bar{w}$.
- Let $\mathbb{W} = \{\bar{w}^{(1)}, \bar{w}^{(2)}, \cdots, \bar{w}^{(n)}\}$ codewords in $\{0,1\}^{\ell}$. We say that a codeword $\bar{w} = w_1 w_2 \cdots w_{\ell}$ is feasible for the set $\mathbb{W}$, if for all $i \in [\ell]$ there exists a $j \in [n]$ such that the ith bit of $\bar{w}^{(j)}$, denoted by $w_i^{(j)}$, is equal to w_i.
- Let $F(\mathbb{W})$ be a feasible set of $\mathbb{W}$, it includes all codewords that are feasible for $\mathbb{W}$.

Definition 3 (Fingerprint Code). *Let $\mathcal{FC}$ denote a fingerprint code and it consists of two algorithms defined as follows.*

$\mathcal{FC}.\mathsf{Gen}(n, t, \lambda) \rightarrow (\Gamma, tk)$. *On input the number of codewords n, the collusion bound t and a security parameter λ, the generation algorithm outputs a codebook Γ containing n codewords $\{\bar{w}^{(1)}, \bar{w}^{(2)}, \cdots, \bar{w}^{(n)}\}$ in $\{0,1\}^{\ell}$ with length $\ell = \ell(n, t, \lambda)$ and a tracing key tk.*

$\mathcal{FC}.\mathsf{Trace}(\bar{w}^*, tk) \rightarrow \mathbb{S}$. *On input a codeword $\bar{w}^* \in \{0,1\}^{\ell}$ and the tracing key tk, the tracing algorithm outputs a subset $\mathbb{S} \subseteq [n]$. Informally, let $\mathbb{W}$ be a subset of Γ, if $\bar{w}^* \in F(\mathbb{W})$, we have that the output set $\mathbb{S}$ is a subset of $\mathbb{W}$.*

Definition 4 (Security Model of Fingerprint Code). *The security definition of a fingerprint code from the following experiment:*

$$\mathbf{Exp}_{\mathcal{FC}, \mathcal{A}}(n, t, \lambda)$$
$$(\Gamma, tk) \leftarrow \mathcal{FC}.\mathsf{Gen}(n, t, \lambda);$$
$$\bar{w}^* \leftarrow \mathcal{A}^{\mathcal{O}(\cdot)}(n, t);$$
$$\textit{If } \mathcal{FC}.\mathsf{Trace}(\bar{w}^*, tk) \not\subseteq \emptyset \textit{ return 1 else return 0.}$$

$\mathcal{O}(\cdot)$ *is a oracle that allows the adversary queries the index $\mathbb{I} \subseteq [n]$ with $|\mathbb{I}| \leq t$, the challenger responds by returning the codewords $\mathbb{W} = \{\bar{w}_i\}_{i \in \mathbb{I}}$ to the adversary. Note that the challenge codeword $\bar{w}^*$ is not belongs to the returning codeword set $\mathbb{W}$, such that $\bar{w}^* \notin \mathbb{W}$.*

A fingerprint code is t-collusion resistant if for all adversaries, all n, t satisfying $n \geq t$, all $\mathbb{I}$ satisfying $\mathbb{I} \subseteq [n]$ and $|\mathbb{I}| \leq t$, we have that the advantage of the adversary in the above game $\mathbf{Adv}_{\mathcal{FC}, \mathcal{A}}$ is negligible:

$$\mathbf{Adv}_{\mathcal{FC}, \mathcal{A}}(n, t, \lambda) = \left| \Pr[\mathbf{Exp}_{\mathcal{FC}, \mathcal{A}}(n, t, \lambda) = 1] \right|.$$

2.7 Attribute-Based Encryption with Traitor Tracing

We refine the definition and security model in [9,11]. It is worth to notice that the augmented ABTT scheme is considered in the previous works since the encryption algorithm needs an additional index for labeling users, which works as an identifier that allows another user to identify the malicious users. In our proposed scheme, we use fingerprint codes as a different tracing method, thus our scheme does not need to consider augmented ABTT.

Definition 5 (Attribute-Based Encryption with Traitor Tracing). *Let $\mathcal{ABTT}$ denote an ABTT scheme and an ABTT scheme with the attribute set Ω that supports policies $\mathcal{P}$ with the message space $\mathcal{M}$ consists of five algorithms as follows.*

$\mathcal{ABTT}$.Setup$(n, t, \lambda) \rightarrow (pp, msk, tk)$. *The probabilistic setup algorithm takes the number of system users n, the collusion bound t and a security parameter λ as input, and outputs the public parameter pp, the master secret key msk and the tracing key tk.*

$\mathcal{ABTT}$.KeyGen$(msk, \mathbb{A}) \rightarrow sk_{\mathbb{A}}$. *The probabilistic key generation algorithm takes the master secret key msk and the an access structure $\mathbb{A} \in \mathcal{P}$ as input, and outputs the secret key $sk_{\mathbb{A}}$.*

$\mathcal{ABTT}$.Enc$(pp, m, \mathcal{S}) \rightarrow ct_{\mathcal{S}}$. *The probabilistic encryption algorithm takes the public parameter pp, a message $m \in \mathcal{M}$ and an attribute set $\mathcal{S} \subseteq \Omega$ as input, and outputs the ciphertext $ct_{\mathcal{S}}$.*

$\mathcal{ABTT}$.Dec$(sk_{\mathbb{A}}, ct_{\mathcal{S}}) \rightarrow m$. *The deterministic decryption algorithm takes the secret key $sk_{\mathbb{A}}$ and the ciphertext $ct_{\mathcal{S}}$ as input, and outputs a message $m \in \mathcal{M}$.*

$\mathcal{ABTT}$.Trace$^{\mathcal{PD}}(tk) \rightarrow \mathbb{S}$. *The deterministic tracing algorithm is an oracle algorithm takes is given as input the tracing key tk. The tracing algorithm queries the pirate decoders $\mathcal{PD}$ as a blackbox oracle. It outputs a set of traitors $\mathbb{S}$ which is a subset of $[n]$.*

Next, we define the security of the traitor tracing scheme in terms of the following games, called selective indistinguishability under chosen plaintext attack (sIND-CPA) and traceability against t-collusion attack.

Definition 6 (sIND-CPA   in Attribute-Based Encryption with Traitor Tracing). *The security definition of an ABTT scheme for message hiding is based on the following experiment:*

$$\text{Exp}_{\mathcal{ABTT}, \mathcal{A}}^{\text{sIND-CPA}}(n, t, \lambda)$$
$$\mathcal{S}^* \leftarrow \mathcal{A}(n, t, \lambda);$$
$$(pp, msk, tk) \leftarrow \mathcal{ABTT}.\text{Setup}(n, t, \lambda);$$
$$(m_0, m_1) \leftarrow \mathcal{A}^{\mathcal{O}_{\mathcal{ABTT}.\text{KeyGen}}(\cdot)}(pp);$$
$$b \leftarrow \{0, 1\};$$
$$ct_{\mathcal{S}^*} \leftarrow \mathcal{ABTT}.\text{Enc}(pp, m_b, \mathcal{S}^*);$$
$$b' \leftarrow \mathcal{A}^{\mathcal{O}_{\mathcal{ABTT}.\text{KeyGen}}(\cdot)}(ct_{\mathcal{S}^*});$$
$$\text{If } b = b' \text{ return } 1 \text{ else return } 0.$$

$\mathcal{O}_{\mathcal{ABTT}.\text{KeyGen}}(\cdot)$ *represents the key generation oracle that allows the adversary to query an access structure $\mathbb{A} \in \mathcal{P}$ except $\mathbb{A}(\mathcal{S}^*) = 1$, and it returns the secret key $sk_{\mathbb{A}}$ by running $\mathcal{ABTT}.\text{KeyGen}(msk, \mathbb{A})$.*

An *ABTT* scheme is said to be sIND-CPA *secure if for any probabilistic polynomial time adversary* $\mathcal{A}$, *the following advantage is negligible:*

$$\mathbf{Adv}_{ABTT,\mathcal{A}}^{\text{sIND-CPA}}(n,t,\lambda) = \left| \Pr[\mathbf{Exp}_{ABTT,\mathcal{A}}^{\text{sIND-CPA}}(n,t,\lambda) = 1] - 1/2 \right|.$$

Definition 7 (Traceability against t-collusion Attack in Attribute-Based Encryption with Traitor Tracing). *The security definition of an ABTT scheme for traceability is based on the following experiment:*

$$\mathbf{Exp}_{ABTT,\mathcal{A}}^{\text{Trace}}(n,t,\lambda)$$
$$\mathcal{S}^* \leftarrow \mathcal{A}(n,t,\lambda);$$
$$(pp, msk, tk) \leftarrow ABTT.\text{Setup}(n,t,\lambda);$$
$$\mathcal{PD} \leftarrow \mathcal{A}^{\mathcal{O}_{ABTT.\text{KeyGen}}(\cdot)}(pp);$$
$$\mathbb{S} \leftarrow ABTT.\text{Trace}^{\mathcal{PD}}(tk);$$
$$\text{If } \Pr[\mathcal{PD}(ABTT.\text{Enc}(pp, m, \mathcal{S}^*)) = m] = 1 \text{ and}$$
$$\mathbb{S} \subseteq \emptyset \text{ or } \mathbb{S} \nsubseteq \mathbb{I} \text{ return } 1 \text{ else return } 0.$$

$\mathcal{O}_{ABTT.\text{KeyGen}}(\cdot)$ *represents the key generation oracle that allows the adversary to query a set of the indices* $\mathbb{I} \subseteq [n]$ ($|\mathbb{I}| \leq t$), *and it runs* $ABTT.\text{KeyGen}(msk, \mathbb{A})$ *to all* $i \in \mathbb{I}$ *and* $\mathbb{A}(\mathcal{S}^*) = 0$, *and then returns the secret key* $\{sk_i\}_{i \in \mathbb{I}}$. *Notice that the adversary cannot adaptively query this oracle since this oracle only runs once before the challenge phase.*

An *ABTT* scheme is said to be t-collusion resistant *if for any probabilistic polynomial time adversary* $\mathcal{A}$, *the following advantage is negligible:*

$$\mathbf{Adv}_{ABTT,\mathcal{A}}^{\text{Trace}}(n,t,\lambda) = \Pr[\mathbf{Exp}_{ABTT,\mathcal{A}}^{\text{Trace}}(n,t,\lambda) = 1].$$

2.8   Attribute-Based Set Encryption

An IBSE scheme [7] was introduced to improve the efficiency of identity-based traitor tracing scheme by reducing the size of private key and ciphertext. We refined the definition and security model in the IBE setting to the ABE setting. It is worth to notice that the following algorithms have some elements in the definition of fingerprint code as given Sect. 2.6.

Definition 8 (Attribute-Based Set Encryption). *Let* $ABSE$ *be an ABSE scheme and an ABSE scheme with the attribute set* Ω *that supports the policies* $\mathcal{P}$ *and the message space* $\mathcal{M}$ *consists of four algorithms as follows.*

$ABSE.\text{Setup}(n, \lambda) \rightarrow (pp, msk)$. *The probabilistic setup algorithm takes the number* n *and a security parameter* λ *as input, and outputs the public parameter* pp *and the master secret key* msk.

$ABSE.\text{KeyGen}(msk, \mathbb{A}, b, \mathcal{L}) \rightarrow sk_{\mathbb{A}}$. *The probabilistic key generation algorithm takes the master secret key* msk *and the access structure* $\mathbb{A} \in \mathcal{P}$, *a bit* $b \in \{0, 1\}$ *and a list of indices* $\mathcal{L}$ ($|\mathcal{L}| \leq \ell$ *and* $\mathcal{L}$ *represents all indices* $j \in [\ell]$ *s.t.* $w_j^{(i)} = b$, where $w_j^{(i)}$ representing j^{th} position in the codeword for the ith user) as input, and outputs the private key $sk_\mathbb{A}$.

$ABSE.\text{Enc}(pp, m, S, b, \ell, \tau) \rightarrow ct_S$. The probabilistic encryption algorithm takes the public parameter pp, the message $m \in \mathcal{M}$, an attribute set S, a bit $b \in \{0, 1\}$, a number ℓ representing the size of each codeword and a number τ ($\tau \leq \ell$ which represents the position in the codeword and will be used to form the attribute $A\|\tau\|b$ for all $A \in S$) as input, and outputs a ciphertext ct_S.

$ABSE.\text{Dec}(sk_\mathbb{A}, ct_S, b) \rightarrow m$. The deterministic decryption algorithm takes the secret key $sk_\mathbb{A}$, the ciphertext ct_S and a bit $b \in \{0, 1\}$ as input, and outputs a message $m \in \mathcal{M}$.

Next, we describe the security of selective indistinguishability under chosen plaintext attack in the random oracle model (sIND-CPA security) for the ABSE setting.

Definition 9 (sIND-CPA in Attribute-Based Set Encryption). *The security definition of an ABSE scheme is based on the following experiment:*

$$\mathbf{Exp}_{ABSE,\mathcal{A}}^{\text{sIND-CPA}}(n, \lambda)$$
$$S^* \leftarrow \mathcal{A}(n, \lambda);$$
$$(pp, msk) \leftarrow ABSE.\text{Setup}(n, \lambda);$$
$$(m_0, m_1, b, \tau) \leftarrow \mathcal{A}^{\mathcal{O}}(pp);$$
$$c \leftarrow \{0, 1\};$$
$$ct_{S^*} \leftarrow ABSE.\text{Enc}(pp, m_c, S^*, b, \ell, \tau);$$
$$c' \leftarrow \mathcal{A}^{\mathcal{O}}(ct_{S^*});$$
$$\text{If } c = c' \text{ return } 1 \text{ else return } 0.$$

In the random oracle setting $\mathcal{O}$ *represent a set of oracles,* $\{\mathcal{O}_{ABSE.\text{KeyGen}}(\cdot, \cdot, \cdot), \mathcal{O}_H(\cdot)\}$, *and the details are given in below.*

- $\mathcal{O}_{ABSE.\text{KeyGen}}(\cdot, \cdot, \cdot)$ *is the key generation oracle that allows the adversary to query on the access structure* $\mathbb{A}$ *(expect* $\mathbb{A}(S^*) = 1$*), a bit* b *and a set of indices* $\mathcal{L}$*, and the challenger runs the* $ABSE.\text{KeyGen}(msk, \mathbb{A}, b, \mathcal{L})$ *algorithm and returns the secret key* $sk_\mathbb{A}$ *to the adversary.*
- *In random oracle model, we provide the oracle* $\mathcal{O}_H(\cdot)$ *that allows the adversary to query on the message* s*, if* s *has been queried, it will output the same has output; otherwise, it outputs a random hash output. Note that, we may provide multiple hash oracles in the random oracle model.*

An ABSE scheme is said to be sIND-CPA *secure if for any probabilistic polynomial time adversary* $\mathcal{A}$*, the following advantage is negligible:*

$$\mathbf{Adv}_{ABSE,\mathcal{A}}^{\text{sIND-CPA}}(n, \lambda) = \left| \Pr[\mathbf{Exp}_{ABSE,\mathcal{A}}^{\text{sIND-CPA}}(n, \lambda) = 1] - 1/2 \right|.$$

3 Attribute-Based Encryption with Traitor Tracing

3.1 Generic Construction

Let $\mathcal{FC} = (\mathsf{Gen}, \mathsf{Trace})$ be an fingerprint code and $\mathcal{ABSE} = (\mathsf{Setup}, \mathsf{KeyGen}, \mathsf{Enc}, \mathsf{Dec})$ be an ABSE scheme. Our ABTT is described as follows.

$\mathcal{ABTT}.\mathsf{Setup}(n, t, \lambda) \to (pp, msk, tk)$. Let $\ell = \ell(n, t, \lambda)$ be the length of codeword in the fingerprint code. The setup algorithm runs

$$\mathcal{FC}.\mathsf{Gen}(n, t, \lambda) \to (\Gamma, tk),$$
$$\mathcal{ABSE}.\mathsf{Setup}(n, \lambda) \to (pp_0, msk_0).$$
$$\mathcal{ABSE}.\mathsf{Setup}(n, \lambda) \to (pp_1, msk_1).$$

The public parameter is $pp = (\Gamma, pp_0, pp_1)$ and the master secret key is $msk = (msk_0, msk_1)$.

$\mathcal{ABTT}.\mathsf{KeyGen}(msk, \mathbb{A}) \to sk_{\mathbb{A}}$. For the ith user, this algorithm assigns the ith codeword $\bar{w}^{(i)}$ to this user and initializes two empty lists $\mathcal{L}_0$ and $\mathcal{L}_1$. For $j \in [\ell]$, the algorithm derives the ciphertext $sk_{\mathbb{A}}$ as: If $w_j^{(i)} = 0$,

$$\mathcal{L}_0 \leftarrow \mathcal{L}_0 \cup \{j\};$$

otherwise,

$$\mathcal{L}_1 \leftarrow \mathcal{L}_1 \cup \{j\}.$$

The key generation algorithm runs

$$\mathcal{ABSE}.\mathsf{KeyGen}(msk_0, \mathbb{A}, 0, \mathcal{L}_0) \to sk_{\mathbb{A}}^{(0)},$$
$$\mathcal{ABSE}.\mathsf{KeyGen}(msk_1, \mathbb{A}, 1, \mathcal{L}_1) \to sk_{\mathbb{A}}^{(1)}.$$

Finally, it returns the secret key $sk_{\mathbb{A}} = (sk_{\mathbb{A}}^{(0)}, sk_{\mathbb{A}}^{(1)})$ for the access structure $\mathbb{A}$.

$\mathcal{ABTT}.\mathsf{Enc}(pp, m, \mathcal{S}) \to ct_{\mathcal{S}}$. The encryption algorithm randomly pick $\tau \in \mathbb{Z}_p$ ($\tau \leq \ell$). Then, it runs

$$\mathcal{ABSE}.\mathsf{Enc}(pp_0, m, \mathcal{S}, 0, \tau) \to ct_{\mathcal{S}}^{(0)},$$
$$\mathcal{ABSE}.\mathsf{Enc}(pp_1, m, \mathcal{S}, 1, \tau) \to ct_{\mathcal{S}}^{(1)}.$$

The ciphertext is $ct_{\mathcal{S}} = (\tau, ct_{\mathcal{S}}^{(0)}, ct_{\mathcal{S}}^{(1)})$.

$\mathcal{ABTT}.\mathsf{Dec}(sk_{\mathbb{A}}, ct_{\mathcal{S}}) \to m$. For the ith user, the decryption algorithm runs as follows. If $w_\tau^{(i)} = 0$, it runs

$$\mathcal{ABSE}.\mathsf{Dec}(sk_{\mathbb{A}}^{(0)}, ct_{\mathcal{S}}^{(0)}, 0) \to m;$$

otherwise, it runs

$$\mathcal{ABSE}.\mathsf{Dec}(sk_{\mathbb{A}}^{(1)}, ct_{\mathcal{S}}^{(1)}, 1) \to m.$$

$\mathcal{ABTT}.\text{Trace}^{\mathcal{PD}}(tk) \rightarrow \mathbb{S}$. Suppose the pirate decoder $\mathcal{PD}$ claims to be able to decrypt any message $m \in \mathcal{M}$ under the access structure $\mathbb{A}$: For all $j \in [\ell]$, the tracing algorithm randomly chooses a message $m_j \neq 0$, and derives the ciphertext under the attribute set $\mathcal{S}$ with $\mathbb{A}(\mathcal{S}) = 1$ by running

$$\mathcal{ABSE}.\text{Enc}(pp_0, m_j, \mathcal{S}, 0, \ell, j) \rightarrow ct_{\mathcal{S}}^{(0)},$$
$$\mathcal{ABSE}.\text{Enc}(pp_1, 0, \mathcal{S}, 1, \ell, j) \rightarrow ct_{\mathcal{S}}^{(1)}.$$

It then sends the ciphertext $ct_{\mathbb{A}} = (j, ct_{\mathcal{S}}^{(0)}, ct_{\mathcal{S}}^{(1)})$ to $\mathcal{PD}$. Let the return from $\mathcal{PD}$ be m_j'. Define the bit w_j^* as

$$w_j^* = \begin{cases} 0 & \text{if } m_j' = m_j, \text{ and} \\ 1 & \text{otherwise.} \end{cases}$$

It outputs the ℓ-bit codeword $\bar{w}^* = w_1^* w_2^* \cdots w_\ell^*$ and returns a set of traitors $\mathbb{S} \subseteq [n]$ by running

$$\mathcal{FC}.\text{Trace}(\bar{w}^*, tk) \rightarrow \mathbb{S}.$$

3.2 Security Analysis

Our ABTT scheme above is extended from the public-key traitor tracing scheme [4]. We do not change their paradigm, but replace the public-key encryption scheme in [4] with ABSE. The following theorem shows that our ABTT scheme is secure.

Theorem 1. *Given an attribute-based set encryption scheme $\mathcal{ABSE} = (\text{Setup},$ $\text{KeyGen}, \text{Enc}, \text{Dec})$, which is sIND-CPA secure and fingerprint codes $\mathcal{FC} = (\text{Gen},$ $\text{Trace})$, which is t-collusion resistant, our $\mathcal{ABTT} = (\text{Setup}, \text{KeyGen}, \text{Enc}, \text{Dec},$ $\text{Trace})$ is a t-collusion resistant attribute-based traitor tracing scheme. Particularly, using the notion in Sect. 2, for all $t > 0, n > t$, and all polynomial time adversaries attacking ABTT, there exist polynomial adversaries attacking ABSE or fingerprint code such that*

$$\mathbf{Adv}_{\mathcal{ABTT},\mathcal{A}}^{\text{sIND-CPA}}(n, t, \lambda) \leq 2\ell \cdot \mathbf{Adv}_{\mathcal{ABSE},\mathcal{A}}^{\text{sIND-CPA}}(n, t),$$
$$\mathbf{Adv}_{\mathcal{ABTT},\mathcal{A}}^{\text{Trace}}(n, t, \lambda) \leq \mathbf{Adv}_{\mathcal{FC},\mathcal{A}}(n, t, \lambda) + \ell \cdot (\mathbf{Adv}_{\mathcal{ABSE},\mathcal{A}}^{\text{sIND-CPA}}(n, t) + 1/|\mathcal{M}|).$$

where ℓ denotes the bit length of codeword and $\mathcal{M}$ denotes the message space.

The proof of Theorem 1 is very similar to the proof of Theorem 1 in [4]. We detail the proof in the full version of this paper[1].

---

[1] Please contact the authors for it.

4 The Proposed Attribute-Based Set Encryption

4.1 Our Construction

An ABSE scheme with the attribute set Ω that supports policies $\mathcal{P}$ with message space Ω is described as follows.

$\mathcal{ABSE}$.Setup$(n, \lambda) \rightarrow (pp, msk)$. The setup algorithm takes the number of system users n and the security parameter λ as input. It first generates the bilinear groups $(g, p, \mathbb{G}, \mathbb{G}_T, e)$ by running the bilinear group generator $\mathcal{G}(\lambda)$. The algorithm randomly chooses the terms $\alpha, \beta \in \mathbb{Z}_p$ and $h \in \mathbb{G}$, then the algorithm computes the terms $h_1, h_2, g_1, g_2, \ldots, g_n$ as:

$$h_1 = g^\alpha, h_2 = h^\beta, g_1 = g^{(\beta)}, g_2 = g^{(\beta^2)}, \ldots, g_n = g^{(\beta^n)}.$$

It picks three collusion-resistant hash functions H_1, H_2 and H_3 at random:

$$H_1 : \Omega \rightarrow \mathbb{G}, \quad H_2 : \{0,1\}^* \rightarrow \mathbb{Z}_p, \quad H_3 : \mathbb{G}_T \rightarrow \mathcal{M}.$$

The public parameter pp and the master secret key msk are

$$pp = (p, \mathbb{G}, \mathbb{G}_T, e, g, g_1, \ldots, g_n, h, h_1, h_2, H_1, H_2, H_3), \quad msk = (\alpha, \beta).$$

$\mathcal{ABSE}$.KeyGen$(msk, \mathbb{A}, b, \mathcal{L}) \rightarrow sk_\mathbb{A}$. The key generation algorithm takes the master secret key msk, an access structure $\mathbb{A} = (\mathbb{M}, \rho) \in \mathcal{P}$, a bit $b \in \{0,1\}$ and a index list $\mathcal{L}$ ($|\mathcal{L}| \leq n$) as input, where $\mathbb{M}$ is a matrix of the size $d \times l$ in $\mathbb{Z}_p$ and $\rho : [d] \rightarrow \Omega$ is a mapping function. Let $\vec{u}$ be a random l dimensional vector over $\mathbb{Z}_p$ and $\vec{1} \cdot \vec{u} = \alpha$. For each row i in the matrix $\mathbb{M}$, it randomly chooses $r_i \in \mathbb{Z}_p$ and computes the terms $K_i^{(0)}, K_i^{(1)}$ and $K_i^{(2)}$ as:

$$K_i^{(0)} = h^{\mathbb{M}_i \vec{u}_i} H_1(\rho(i))^{r_i}, \quad K_i^{(1)} = g^{r_i}, \quad K_i^{(2)} = h^{\sum_{j \in \mathcal{L}} \frac{1}{\beta - H_2(\rho(i)\|j\|b)}}.$$

The secret key $sk_\mathbb{A}$ is

$$sk_\mathbb{A} = \{K_i^{(0)}, K_i^{(1)}, K_i^{(2)}\}_{i \in [d]}.$$

$\mathcal{ABSE}$.Enc$(pp, m, \mathcal{S}, b, \ell, \tau) \rightarrow ct_\mathcal{S}$. The encryption algorithm takes the public parameter pp, the message $m \in \mathcal{M}$, an attribute set $\mathcal{S} = (A_1, A_2, \ldots, A_k)$, a random bit $b \in \{0,1\}$, and a number $\ell \in \mathbb{Z}_p$ and a number $\tau \in \mathbb{Z}_p$ ($\tau \leq \ell$) as input. It randomly chooses a message $m' \in \mathcal{M}$, and derives the message m'' as:

$$m'' = m \oplus m'.$$

It chooses a random exponent $s \in \mathbb{Z}_p$ and computes the terms $C^{(0)}$ and $C^{(1)}$ as:

$$C^{(0)} = m' \cdot e(h, h_1)^s, \quad C^{(1)} = g^s.$$

For all $i \in [k]$, it computes the terms $C_i^{(2)}, C_i^{(3)}, C_i^{(4)}$ and $C_i^{(5)}$ as:

$$C_i^{(2)} = H_1(A_i)^s,$$

$$C_i^{(3)} = \left(g^{\prod_{j=1}^{\ell} \beta - H_2(A_i\|j\|b)} \right)^{s'},$$

$$C_i^{(4)} = \left(h^{\beta - H_2(A_i\|\tau\|b)} \right)^{s'},$$

$$C_i^{(5)} = m'' \oplus H_3 \left(e \left(g^{\frac{\prod_{j=1}^{\ell} \beta - H_2(A_i\|j\|b)}{\beta - H_2(A_i\|\tau\|b)}}, h \right)^{s'} \right).$$

The ciphertext $ct_{\mathcal{S}}$ is

$$ct_{\mathcal{S}} = (\tau, C^{(0)}, C^{(1)}, \{C_i^{(2)}, C_i^{(3)}, C_i^{(4)}, C_i^{(5)}\}_{i \in [k]}).$$

$\mathcal{ABSE}.\mathsf{Dec}(sk_{\mathbb{A}}, ct_{\mathcal{S}}, b) \to m$. The decryption algorithm takes the secret key $sk_{\mathbb{A}}$, the ciphertext $ct_{\mathcal{S}}$ and a bit $b \in \{0,1\}$ as input. It takes the vector $\vec{w}$ s.t. $\sum_{\rho(i) \in \mathcal{S}} \mathbb{M}_i w_i = \vec{1}$ and recovers the message m' by computing:

$$C^{(0)} \cdot \prod_{\rho(i) \in \mathcal{S}} \left(\frac{e(K_i^{(1)}, C_i^{(2)})}{e(K_i^{(0)}, C^{(1)})} \right)$$

$$= m' \cdot e(h, h_1)^s \cdot \prod_{\rho(i) \in \mathcal{S}} \left(\frac{e(g^{r_i}, H_1(\rho(i))^s)}{e(h^{\mathbb{M}_i \vec{u}_i} H_1(\rho(i))^{r_i}, g^s)} \right)$$

$$= m'.$$

It randomly chooses $A_i \in \mathcal{S}$ and recovers the message m'' as: Let the polynomial function $f(a)$ be

$$f(a) = \prod_{j=1}^{\ell} (a - H_2(A_i\|j\|b)) \cdot \left(\sum_{j \in \mathcal{L}} \frac{1}{a - H_2(A_i\|\tau\|b)} \right)$$

$$= \frac{\prod_{j=1}^{\ell} (a - H_2(A_i\|j\|b))}{a - H_2(A_i\|\tau\|b)} + (a - H_2(A_i\|\tau\|b)) \cdot \left(\sum_{j=0}^{\ell-2} f_j a^j \right),$$

where f_j is the coefficient of a^j. The algorithm derives the message m'' by computing:

$$C_i^{(5)} \oplus H_3 \left(e(C_i^{(3)}, K_i^{(2)}) \cdot e \left(C_i^{(4)}, \prod_{j=1}^{\ell-2} g_j^{f_j} \cdot g^{f_0} \right)^{-1} \right)$$

$$= m'' \oplus H_3 \left(e \left(g^{\frac{\prod_{j=1}^{\ell} \beta - H_2(A_i\|j\|b)}{\beta - H_2(A_i\|\tau\|b)}}, h \right)^{s'} \right) \oplus H_3 \left(e \left(g^{\frac{\prod_{j=1}^{\ell} \beta - H_2(A_i\|j\|b)}{\beta - H_2(A_i\|\tau\|b)}}, h \right)^{s'} \right)$$

$$= m''.$$

The returning message m is $m = m' \oplus m''$.

4.2   Security Proof

We prove the security of our ABSE in the selective security model based on the decisional BDH assumption and the modified q-BDHE assumption.

Theorem 2. *Suppose the hash functions H_1, H_2, H_3 are three random oracles. Let q_{H_1}, q_{H_2} and q_{H_3} be the query number to the oracle H_1, H_2 and H_3, respectively. Assuming the decisional BDH assumption is ϵ_{BDH}-hard, and the modified q-BDHE is $\epsilon_{q\text{-}\mathsf{BDHE}}$-hard, our ABSE scheme is $(q_{H_2}, q_{H_3}, \epsilon)$-secure under selective IND-CPA model under the ABSE setting. We have*

$$\mathbf{Adv}_{ABSE,\mathcal{A}}^{\mathsf{sIND\text{-}CPA}} \leq 1/2 \cdot (\epsilon_{\mathsf{BDH}} + 1/(q_{H_2}q_{H_3}) \cdot \epsilon_{q\text{-}\mathsf{BDHE}}).$$

Proof. Suppose there exist a probabilistic polynomial time adversary $\mathcal{A}$ that can break our ABSE scheme in the selective security model with a non-negligible advantage. We can build an algorithm $\mathcal{B}$ that can have a non-negligible advantage to break the decisional BDH problem or the modified q-BDHE problem.

Init. $\mathcal{B}$ runs $\mathcal{A}$. $\mathcal{A}$ chooses the challenge attribute set $\mathcal{S}^*$ and sends $\mathcal{S}^*$ to $\mathcal{B}$. $\mathcal{B}$ randomly chooses a bit $\hat{c} \in \{0, 1\}$.

If $\hat{c} = 0$, $\mathcal{B}$ is giving the terms $(A = g^a, B = g^b, C = g^c, Z)$ and the aim of $\mathcal{B}$ is to distinguish Z is $e(g, g)^{abc}$ or a random value.

If $\hat{c} = 1$, $\mathcal{B}$ is giving the terms $g, g^{(a)}, g^{(a^2)}, \ldots, g^{a^q}, g^{(a^{2q+2})}, g^{(a^{2q+3})},$ $\ldots, g^{(a^{3q+1})} \in \mathbb{G}^{2q+1}$ and the aim of $\mathcal{B}$ is to output $e(g, g)^{(a^{2q+1})}$.

Setup. $\mathcal{B}$ generates the public parameters pp to $\mathcal{A}$.

If $\hat{c} = 0$, $\mathcal{B}$ assigns the public parameter $h = B$ and $h_1 = A$ and chooses random value $\beta \in \mathbb{Z}_p$ to derive the rest of public elements:

$$h_2 = h^\beta, g_1 = g^{(\beta)}, g_2 = g^{(\beta^2)}, \ldots, g_n = g^{(\beta^n)}.$$

$\mathcal{B}$ then randomly chooses two collusion-resistant function $H_2 : \{0, 1\}^* \to \mathbb{Z}_p$ and $H_3 : \mathbb{G}_T \to \mathcal{M}$, and forwards the public parameter as:

$$pp = (p, \mathbb{G}, \mathbb{G}_T, e, g, g_1, \ldots, g_n, h, h_1, h_2, H_2, H_3)$$

except the hash function H_1 to $\mathcal{A}$, where H_1 works as a random oracle in the rest of reduction.

If $\hat{c} = 1$, $\mathcal{B}$ randomly picks a random value $\alpha \in \mathbb{Z}_p$ and sets $h_1 = g^\alpha$. Next, $\mathcal{B}$ randomly chooses $\{I_1, I_2, \ldots, I_{q_{H_2}}\}$ from $\mathbb{Z}_p$, and picks a random $i^* \in [q_{H_2}]$. Let $F(x) \in \mathbb{Z}_p[x]$ be a $(q_{H_2} - 1)$-degree polynomial function as:

$$F(x) = b \prod_{i=1, i \neq i^*}^{q_{H_2}} (x - I_i) = F_{q_{H_2}-1} x^{q_{H_2}-1} + \cdots + F_2 x^2 + F_1 x + F_0.$$

It sets $g_i = g^{(a^i)}$ for all $i \in [\ell]$ and computes $h = g^{F(a)}$ and $h_2 = g^{aF(a)}$ from the challenge input and $F(x)$. $\mathcal{B}$ then randomly chooses a collusion-resistant hash function $H_1 : \Omega \to \mathbb{G}$, and forwards the public parameter pp as

$$pp = (p, \mathbb{G}, \mathbb{G}_T, e, g, g_1, \ldots, g_n, h, h_1, h_2, H_1)$$

except the two hash functions to $\mathcal{A}$, and sets H_1 and H_2 as random oracles.

Hash Queries. If $\hat{c} = 0$, $\mathcal{A}$ can query the random oracle H_1 at any time; otherwise, $\mathcal{A}$ can query the random oracles H_2 and H_3 at any time.

$\mathcal{O}_{H_1}(\cdot)$. For any query on A to the random oracle H_1, $\mathcal{B}$ maintains a list $\mathcal{L}_{H_1}$ and responds as follows. If A is not in the list, the algorithm responds depended on S^*. If $A \in S^*$, the algorithm sets $r = 0$ and randomly picks $r' \in \mathbb{Z}_p$. If $A \notin S^*$, the algorithm randomly chooses $r, r' \in \mathbb{Z}_p$. The algorithm returns $H_1(A) = h^r g^{r'}$ to $\mathcal{A}$, and adding (A, r, r') to $\mathcal{L}_{H_1}$. Otherwise, there has been already a tuple (A, r, r') in the list and the algorithm responds with $H_1(A) = h^r g^{r'}$.

$\mathcal{O}_{H_2}(\cdot)$. For any query on A to the random oracle H_2, $\mathcal{B}$ maintains a list $\mathcal{L}_{H_2}$ and responds as follows. If there has been already a tuple (A, I) in the list $\mathcal{L}_{H_2}$, the algorithm responds with $H_2(A) = I$. Otherwise, let A be the ith distinct query. $\mathcal{B}$ responds by returning $H_2(A) = I_i$ to $\mathcal{A}$, and adding (A, I_i) to $\mathcal{L}_{H_2}$.

$\mathcal{O}_{H_3}$. For a random query on R to the random oracle H_3, $\mathcal{B}$ maintains a list $\mathcal{L}_{H_3}$ and responds as follows. If R is not in the list, the algorithm responds by randomly choosing a different $Y \in \mathbb{Z}_p$, returning $H_3(R) = Y$ to $\mathcal{A}$, and adding (R, Y) to $\mathcal{L}_{H_3}$. Otherwise, there has been already a tuple (R, Y) in the list and the algorithm responds with $H_2(R) = Y$.

Phase 1. $\mathcal{A}$ queries the key generation oracle $\mathcal{O}_{\mathcal{ABSE}.\mathsf{KeyGen}}(\cdot, \cdot, \cdot)$. For the query on access structure $\mathbb{A} = (\mathbb{M}, \rho)$, a bit b and a number ℓ from $\mathcal{A}$, $\mathcal{B}$ responds as: If $\hat{c} = 0$, according to the proposition 1 in [6], we have

$$\mathbb{M}_i \vec{u} = \vec{v} + \frac{ab - \vec{v}}{h} \cdot \vec{w} = \alpha \mu_1 + \mu_2,$$

where the coefficients $\mu_1 = \mathbb{M}_i \vec{w} \cdot h^{-1}$ and $\mu_2 = \mathbb{M}_i(h\vec{v} - \vec{v}\vec{w})$ are computable. For all $i \in [d]$, the algorithm fetches $(\rho(i), r, r')$ and computes the terms $K_i^{(0)}$ and $K_i^{(1)}$ as:

If $\rho(i) \in S^*$, the algorithm randomly chooses $r_i \in \mathbb{Z}_p$ and sets

$$K_i^{(0)} = h^{\mathbb{M}_i \vec{u}_i} H_3(\rho(i))^{r_i}, \quad K_i^{(1)} = g^{r_i}, \quad K_i^{(2)} = h^{\sum_{j=1}^{\ell} \frac{1}{\beta - H_2(\rho(i)\|j\|b)}}.$$

If $\rho(i) \notin S^*$, the algorithm randomly chooses $r_i' \in \mathbb{Z}_p$ and sets

$$K_i^{(0)} = h_1^{\frac{-\mu_1 \cdot r'}{r}} g_2^{\mu_2} H_3(\rho(i))^{r_i'}, \quad K_i^{(1)} = g^{r_i'} h_1^{\frac{-\mu_1}{r}}, \quad K_i^{(2)} = h^{\sum_{j=1}^{\ell} \frac{1}{\beta - H_2(\rho(i)\|j\|b)}}.$$

If $\hat{c} = 1$, it computes the terms $\{K_i^{(0)}, K_i^{(1)}\}_{i \in [d]}$ as our proposed scheme. For all $i \in [d]$, let the response for $\rho(i)\|j\|b$ in the list $\mathcal{L}_{H_2}$ be $(\rho(i)\|j\|b, I_j)$ for all $j \in [\ell]$. If $I_j = I^*$ holds for any $i \in [\ell]$, the algorithm aborts the simulation. When $I_j \neq I^*$ holds for $j \in [\ell]$, we have that $H_2(\rho(i)\|1\|b), H_2(\rho(i)\|2\|b), \ldots, H_2(\rho(i)\|\ell\|b)$ are all the roots of $F(x)$. Then, we deduce that

$$F_{\rho(i)}(x) = F(x) \cdot \left(\sum_{j=1}^{\ell} \frac{1}{x - H_2(\rho(i)\|j\|b)} \right)$$

is a $(q_{H_2} - 2)$-degree at most polynomial function, and $\mathcal{B}$ can compute

$$K_i^{(2)} = h^{\sum_{j=1}^{\ell} \frac{1}{\beta - H_2(\rho(i)\|j\|b)}} = g^{F(\beta) \cdot \left(\sum_{j=1}^{\ell} \frac{1}{\beta - H_2(\rho(i)\|j\|b)} \right)} = g^{F_{\rho(i)}(a)}$$

from $F_{\rho(i)}(x)$ and $g, g^{(a)}, \ldots, g^{(a^q)}$, and $K_i^{(2)}$ is a valid secret key component.

Finally, $\mathcal{B}$ returns the secret key $sk_A = \{K_i^{(0)}, K_i^{(1)}, K_i^{(2)}\}_{i \in [d]}$ to $\mathcal{A}$.

Challenge. $\mathcal{A}$ will submit two challenge message (m_0, m_1, b, τ) to $\mathcal{B}$. $\mathcal{B}$ flips a fair binary coin $\bar{c}$.

If $\hat{c} = 0$, $\mathcal{B}$ randomly chooses $m' \in \mathbb{M}$ and sets $m'' = m_{\bar{c}} \oplus m'$, then computes the terms $C^{(0)}, C^{(1)}, C^{(2)}$ as:

$$C = m' \cdot Z, \quad C^{(1)} = C, \quad \forall A_i \in \mathcal{S}^* : C_i^{(2)} = C^{r'}.$$

If $Z = e(g, g)^{abc}$. Then the ciphertext is:

$$C = m' \cdot e(g, g)^{abc}, \quad C^{(1)} = g^c, \quad \forall A_i \in \mathcal{S}^* : C_i^{(2)} = H_3(A_i)^c.$$

The rest of ciphertext $(\tau, \{C_i^{(3)}, C_i^{(4)}, C_i^{(5)}\}_{A_i \in \mathcal{S}^*})$ are generated as our proposed scheme.

If $\hat{c} = 1$, $\mathcal{B}$ randomly chooses $m' \in \mathbb{M}$ and sets $m'' = m_{\bar{c}} \oplus m'$, then computes the terms $C^{(0)}, C^{(1)}, C_i^{(2)}$ as our proposed scheme. For each attribute $\rho(i)$ in $\mathcal{S}$, $\mathcal{B}$ works as follows:

If $\mathcal{B}$ cannot find the tuple $(\rho(i)\|\tau\|b, I^*) \in \mathcal{L}_{H_2}$ satisfies $I^* \neq I_\tau$, abort; otherwise, the algorithm randomly chooses $C_i^{(5)*} \in \{0,1\}^\ell$. Let

$$F'(x) = \frac{\sum_{j=1}^{\ell} \frac{1}{\beta - H_2(\rho(i)\|j\|b)}}{x - I^*}$$

be an $(n-1)$-degree polynomial function. The algorithm randomly chooses $r' \in \mathbb{Z}_p$ and computes the challenge ciphertext $(C_i^{(3)}, C_i^{(4)}, C_i^{(5)})$ by

$$C_i^{(3)} = g^{r'(a^{2q+2} - I^{*2q+2})F'(a)}, \quad C_i^{(4)} = g^{r'(a^{2q+2} - I^{*2q+2})F(a)}, \quad C_i^{(5)} = C_i^{(5)*}.$$

where $C_i^{(3)}$ and $C_i^{(4)}$ are computable from $F'(x)$ and $F(x)$ and the challenge input. Let the randomness r be

$$r = r' \cdot \frac{a^{2q+2} - I^{*2q+2}}{a - I^*},$$

which is also universally random in $\mathbb{Z}_p$. We have the challenge ciphertext is equivalent to

$$C_i^{(3)} = \left(g^{\sum_{j=1}^{\ell} \frac{1}{\beta - H_2(\rho(i)\|j\|b)}} \right)^r, \quad C_i^{(4)} = \left(h^{\beta - H_2(\rho(i)\|\tau\|b)} \right)^r, \quad C_i^{(5)} = C_i^{(5)*}.$$

According to our setting, there must exist a hash query on $e\left(g^{\frac{\sum_{j=1}^{\ell} \frac{1}{\beta - H_2(\rho(i)\|j\|b)}}{\beta - H_2(\rho(i)\|\tau\|b)}}, h \right)^r$ to the random oracle H_3 in order to decrypt the message in the challenge ciphertext.

$$m'' = H_3 \left(e \left(g^{\frac{\sum_{j=1}^{\ell} \frac{1}{\beta - H_2(\rho(i)\|j\|b)}}{\beta - H_2(\rho(i)\|\tau\|b)}}, h \right) \right) \cdot C_i^{(5)*}.$$

Phase 2. Phase 2 is same as Phase 1.

Guess. If $\hat{c} = 0$, $\mathcal{A}$ will submit a guess $\bar{c}'$. If $\bar{c} = \bar{c}'$, $\mathcal{B}$ will output 0 to indicate that is was given a valid BDH-tuple otherwise it will output 1 to indicate it was given a random 4-tuple.

If $\hat{c} = 1$, $\mathcal{A}$ returns a guess $\bar{c}'$. Let $F''(x)$ be the $(2q + n + q_{H_1} - 1)$-degree polynomial function

$$F''(x) = r' \cdot \frac{x^{2q+2} - I^{*2q+2}}{x - I^*} \cdot F'(x) \cdot F(x)$$

and F_i'' be the coefficient of x^i in $F''(x)$. We have that $e \left(g^{\frac{\sum_{j=1}^{\ell} \frac{1}{\beta - H_2(\rho(i)\|j\|b)}}{\beta - H_2(\rho(i)\|\tau\|b)}}, h \right)^r$
$= e(g, g)^{F''(a)}$. It is easy to verify that F_{2q+1}'' is equal to $r'F'(I^*)F(I^*)$ which is non-zero, and that $e(g, g)^{F'' \cdot a^i}$ for all $i \neq 2q + 1$ are computable from the challenge input. $\mathcal{B}$ picks a random tuple (R, Y) from the list $\mathcal{L}_{H_3}$ and computes

$$\left(R \cdot \prod_{i=1, i \neq 2q+1}^{2q+n+q_{H_2}-1} e(g, g)^{-F_i'' \cdot a^i} \right)^{\frac{1}{r'F'(I^*)F(I^*)}} = e(g, g)^{a^{2q+1}}$$

as the solution to the modified q-BDHE problem.

When $\hat{c} = 0$, if $\mathcal{B}$ output 0 ($\bar{c} = \bar{c}'$), the generation of public parameters and secret keys is identical to that of the actual scheme. In the case where outputs 1 ($\bar{c} \neq \bar{c}'$), $\mathcal{A}$ gains no information about $\bar{c}$. Therefore, the probability of guessing successful is $1/2$. In the case where outputs 0, $\mathcal{A}$ sees an encryption of $m_{\bar{c}}$. The advantage in this situation is ϵ_{BDH} by definition. Hence, the advantage is ϵ_{BDH}.

When $\hat{c} = 1$, we need to consider of three events. The first event is $\mathcal{B}$ can generate i^{th} key generation query on the challenge attribute. The second event is $\mathcal{B}$ does not abort in the challenge phase. Hence, we have the overall abort in the guess phase $1/q_{H_2}$. The last one is $\mathcal{B}$ may not query $e(g, g)^{F''(a)}$ to the random oracle $\mathcal{O}_{H_3}$, and the probability of choosing a correct randomness R_i is $1/q_{H_3}$. The advantage in this situation is $(1/(q_{H_2}q_{H_3}))\epsilon_{\mathsf{q\text{-}BDHE}}$. Therefore, the advantage of $\mathcal{A}$ breaking the game is $(1/(q_{H_2}q_{H_3}))\epsilon_{\mathsf{q\text{-}BDHE}}$

We have the advantage when $\hat{c} = 0$ and $\hat{c} = 1$, respectively. Hence, the above probability analysis does not consider $\mathcal{B}$ guessing $\hat{c}$ correctly, and the probability of $\mathcal{B}$ guessing $\hat{c}$ successful is $1/2$. Therefore, the overall advantage is

$$\mathbf{Adv}_{ABSE, \mathcal{A}}^{\mathsf{sIND\text{-}CPA}} = 1/2 \cdot (\epsilon_{\mathsf{BDH}} + 1/(q_{H_2}q_{H_3}) \cdot \epsilon_{\mathsf{q\text{-}BDHE}}).$$

5 Conclusion

We introduced the attribute-based traitor tracing scheme based on the finger-print code in blackbox setting. The size of the secret key relates to the size of policies as the normal attribute-based encryption scheme rather than the previous blackbox attribute-based traitor tracing schemes depend on both the number of the user in the system and the size of policies. It saves both secure storage and bandwidth for ABTT applications. We also introduced a new primitive of attribute-based set encryption for reducing the multi-attribute scenarios. Our proposed ABSE scheme is provably secure in the random oracle under the decisional BDH assumption and the modified q-BDHE assumption.

References

1. Attrapadung, N., Herranz, J., Laguillaumie, F., Libert, B., de Panafieu, E., Ràfols, C.: Attribute-based encryption schemes with constant-size ciphertexts. Theor. Comput. Sci. **422**, 15–38 (2012)
2. Bethencourt, J., Sahai, A., Waters, B.: Ciphertext-policy attribute-based encryption. In: IEEE Symposium on Security and Privacy, pp. 321–334 (2007)
3. Boneh, D., Franklin, M.: Identity-based encryption from the weil pairing. In: Kilian, J. (ed.) CRYPTO 2001. LNCS, vol. 2139, pp. 213–229. Springer, Heidelberg (2001). https://doi.org/10.1007/3-540-44647-8_13
4. Boneh, D., Naor, M.: Traitor tracing with constant size ciphertext. In: CCS, pp. 501–510 (2008)
5. Boneh, D., Sahai, A., Waters, B.: Fully collusion resistant traitor tracing with short ciphertexts and private keys. In: Vaudenay, S. (ed.) EUROCRYPT 2006. LNCS, vol. 4004, pp. 573–592. Springer, Heidelberg (2006). https://doi.org/10.1007/11761679_34
6. Goyal, V., Pandey, O., Sahai, A., Waters, B.: Attribute-based encryption for fine-grained access control of encrypted data. In: CCS, pp. 89–98 (2006)
7. Guo, F., Mu, Y., Susilo, W.: Identity-based traitor tracing with short private key and short ciphertext. In: Foresti, S., Yung, M., Martinelli, F. (eds.) ESORICS 2012. LNCS, vol. 7459, pp. 609–626. Springer, Heidelberg (2012). https://doi.org/10.1007/978-3-642-33167-1_35
8. Lewko, A., Okamoto, T., Sahai, A., Takashima, K., Waters, B.: Fully secure functional encryption: attribute-based encryption and (hierarchical) inner product encryption. In: Gilbert, H. (ed.) EUROCRYPT 2010. LNCS, vol. 6110, pp. 62–91. Springer, Heidelberg (2010). https://doi.org/10.1007/978-3-642-13190-5_4
9. Liu, Z., Cao, Z., Wong, D.S.: Blackbox traceable CP-ABE: how to catch people leaking their keys by selling decryption devices on eBay. In: Sadeghi, A.-R., Gligor, V.D., Yung, M. (eds.) 2013 ACM SIGSAC Conference on Computer and Communications Security, CCS 2013, Berlin, Germany, 4–8 November 2013, pp. 475–486. ACM (2013)
10. Liu, Z., Cao, Z., Wong, D.S.: White-box traceable ciphertext-policy attribute-based encryption supporting any monotone access structures. IEEE Trans. Inf. Forensics Secur. **8**(1), 76–88 (2013)
11. Liu, Z., Cao, Z., Wong, D.S.: Traceable CP-ABE: how to trace decryption devices found in the wild. IEEE Trans. Inf. Forensics Secur. **10**(1), 55–68 (2015)

12. Liu, Z., Wong, D.S.: Practical attribute-based encryption: traitor tracing, revocation and large universe. Comput. J. **59**(7), 983–1004 (2016)
13. Ning, J., Dong, X., Cao, Z., Wei, L.: Accountable authority ciphertext-policy attribute-based encryption with white-box traceability and public auditing in the cloud. In: Pernul, G., Ryan, P.Y.A., Weippl, E. (eds.) ESORICS 2015. LNCS, vol. 9327, pp. 270–289. Springer, Cham (2015). https://doi.org/10.1007/978-3-319-24177-7_14
14. Ning, J., Dong, X., Cao, Z., Wei, L., Lin, X.: White-box traceable ciphertext-policy attribute-based encryption supporting flexible attributes. IEEE Trans. Inf. Forensics Secur. **10**(6), 1274–1288 (2015)
15. Rouselakis, Y., Waters, B.: Practical constructions and new proof methods for large universe attribute-based encryption. In: CCS, pp. 463–474 (2013)
16. Sahai, A., Waters, B.: Fuzzy identity-based encryption. In: Cramer, R. (ed.) EUROCRYPT 2005. LNCS, vol. 3494, pp. 457–473. Springer, Heidelberg (2005). https://doi.org/10.1007/11426639_27
17. Waters, B.: Dual system encryption: realizing fully secure IBE and HIBE under simple assumptions. In: Halevi, S. (ed.) CRYPTO 2009. LNCS, vol. 5677, pp. 619–636. Springer, Heidelberg (2009). https://doi.org/10.1007/978-3-642-03356-8_36
18. Yu, G., Cao, Z., Zeng, G., Han, W.: Accountable ciphertext-policy attribute-based encryption scheme supporting public verifiability and nonrepudiation. In: Chen, L., Han, J. (eds.) ProvSec 2016. LNCS, vol. 10005, pp. 3–18. Springer, Cham (2016). https://doi.org/10.1007/978-3-319-47422-9_1
19. Yu, G., Ma, X., Cao, Z., Zhu, W., Zeng, J.: Accountable multi-authority ciphertext-policy attribute-based encryption without key escrow and key abuse. In: CSS, pp. 337–351 (2017)
20. Zhang, Y., Li, J., Zheng, D., Chen, X., Li, H.: Accountable large-universe attribute-based encryption supporting any monotone access structures. In: Liu, J.K.K., Steinfeld, R. (eds.) ACISP 2016. LNCS, vol. 9722, pp. 509–524. Springer, Cham (2016). https://doi.org/10.1007/978-3-319-40253-6_31

Digital Signature

A Code-Based Linkable Ring Signature Scheme

Pedro Branco and Paulo Mateus[✉]

SQIG - Instituto de Telecomunicações, Department of Mathematics,
IST-Universidade de Lisboa, Lisbon, Portugal
pmat@math.ist.utl.pt

Abstract. Linkable ring signature schemes are cryptographic primitives which have important applications in *e-voting* and *e-cash*. They are ring signature schemes with the extra property that, if the same user signs two messages, a verifier knows they were signed by the same user. In this work, we present a new linkable ring signature scheme. The security of our proposal is based on the hardness of the syndrome decoding problem. To construct it, we use a variant of Stern's protocol and apply the Fiat-Shamir transform to it. We prove that the scheme has the usual properties for a linkable ring signature scheme: unforgeability, signer anonymity, non-slanderability and linkability.

Keywords: Linkable ring signature scheme · Code-based cryptography

1 Introduction

With the advent of the quantum computer, most of the standard asymmetric cryptography is threatened since Shor's algorithm is able to solve both discrete logarithm and factorization problems [28]. As a consequence of this fact, the development of post-quantum cryptographic primitives is crucial for the future. Among the most important cryptographic primitives are digital signature schemes. They have the same legal value of a physical signature and can be used in a wide range of applications such as authentication for a secure access to a website, non-repudiation of contracts, validating transactions (as in the Bitcoin system and other cryptocurrencies system) or e-voting. However, post-quantum (in particular, code-based) digital signature schemes are still very inefficient for applications and there are a lot of signature types for which there is no code-based variant.

Linkable ring signature schemes [24] are a special type of ring signature schemes that allow linkability, i.e., that allow two different signatures to be linked to the same signer in a ring. Their applications to *e-voting*, *e-cash* and cryptocurrencies are well known [27,31]. But, until now, there was no construction of this primitive based on coding theory.

In this work, we present the first linkable ring signature scheme whose security is based on a hard problem in coding theory, the syndrome decoding problem.

© Springer Nature Switzerland AG 2018
J. Baek et al. (Eds.): ProvSec 2018, LNCS 11192, pp. 203–219, 2018.
https://doi.org/10.1007/978-3-030-01446-9_12

Until this moment, most of the linkable ring signature schemes had their security based on the discrete logarithm problem, which makes them useless for the post-quantum era. Since our construction is based on a well-known code-based hard problem, it is conjecture to be robust against quantum attacks and thus, suitable for the post-quantum world.

1.1 Previous Work

Ring Signatures. Ring signature schemes are a special type of digital signature [26]. They allow for a user in a group to sign a message in name of the group while preserving its anonymity. They can be seen as a particular case of group signature scheme [13], where a member of a group can sign messages in name of the group such that a verifier cannot know who signed the message but the anonymity can be revoked by a group manager.

In some applications, one may be interested in knowing if two ring signatures were issued by the same user in the ring. This can be done trivially using a group signature scheme. The problem is that, in group signature schemes, anonymity only exists as long as the group manager wants. Sometimes we may wish to preserve the anonymity of a signer in a ring and give the verifier the chance to know if two signatures were issued by the same user. This is the motivation for creating linkable ring signature schemes.

Linkable Ring Signatures. Linkable ring signatures [24] are ring signature schemes where it is possible to determine when two different messages were signed by the same group user. They have important applications in *e-cash* and *e-voting* [31]. At the moment, most of the existing signature schemes are based on the discrete logarithm problem [7,23–25,31,32]. Therefore their security is threatened: Shor's algorithm [28] solves the discrete logarithm problem and, thus, it breaks all of these linkable ring signature schemes. Very recently two different lattice-based linkable ring signature schemes were presented [8,30], which are conjectured to be secure against quantum adversaries.

Code-Based Signatures. The first signature scheme based on coding theory appeared in 2001 [14] and, in the last years, there was a huge development of post-quantum signatures and, in particular, of code-based signature schemes. The first code-based ring signature scheme appeared in 2007 [34]. After that, many other variants were proposed like threshold ring signatures schemes [3,16], undeniable signature schemes [2] or group signature schemes [4,5,18]. But, as far as the authors know, this is the first proposal for a linkable ring signatures scheme based on coding theory.

The signature schemes of [14,34] use trapdoors and, for this reason, their security is based on both the Syndrome Decoding problem and on the Goppa Distinguisher problem [14]. The latter can be solved when Goppa codes are used with high rates [19] and hence, we have to increase their security parameters, making them impractical in real-life applications. To overcome this problem, we use the Fiat-Shamir transform (following [3,16]) to obtain linkable ring signature scheme with more practical key sizes.

1.2   Our Contribution

In this paper, we give the first construction of a linkable ring signature scheme whose security is based on a hard problem in coding theory. We also give a variant of the proposed linkable ring signature scheme that provides the usual security properties of existential unforgeability, anonymity and linkability.

To construct our proposal, we use a variant of Stern's protocol and then we apply the Fiat-Shamir transform to it. Signatures can be linked to each other by a vector $\mathbf{r}$ that is the syndrome of the secret key of the signer by a random matrix $\tilde{\mathbf{H}}$.

1.3   Organization of the Paper

We begin the paper by introducing some notation and preliminary results. In Sect. 3 we present both linkable ring signature schemes, one that achieves security in the classical setting and a variant that achieves security in the quantum setting. The proof of security for both schemes is given in Sect. 4. Finally, we conclude this work by proposing parameters for the scheme and analyzing its signature and key size.

2   Notation and Preliminaries

If $\mathcal{A}$ is an algorithm, $y \leftarrow \mathcal{A}(x)$ denotes the result of running $\mathcal{A}$ on input x and outputting y and $\mathcal{A}^{\mathcal{O}}$ denotes $\mathcal{A}$ running with access to oracle $\mathcal{O}$. If S is a finite set, then $x \leftarrow_\$ S$ means that x is chosen uniformly at random from S. A negligible function $\mathsf{negl}(n)$ is a function such that $\mathsf{negl}(n) < 1/\mathsf{poly}(n)$ for every polynomial $\mathsf{poly}(n)$ and sufficiently large n. We denote $\Pr[A \mid B_1, \ldots, B_n]$ the probability of event A after events $B_1, \ldots, B_n$ happened sequentially.

2.1   Linkable Ring Signature

In this section, we give the definition of a linkable ring signature scheme and present the security model we adopt. By *linked* signatures we mean that they were signed by the same user in the ring.

Definition 1. A *linkable ring signature scheme* is a tuple of algorithms (KeyGen, Sign, Ver, Link) where:

- (pk, sk) ← KeyGen(1^κ) is a probabilistic polynomial-time (PPT) algorithm that receives as input the security parameter κ and outputs a pair of public and secret keys (pk, sk).
- $\sigma \leftarrow$ Sign($1^\kappa, \overline{\mathbf{pk}}, M, \mathsf{sk}$) is a PPT algorithm that receives as input a security parameter κ, a list of public keys $\overline{\mathbf{pk}}$ of size N (where the public key corresponding to sk is included), a message M to be signed and a secret key sk. It outputs a signature σ.

- $b \leftarrow \mathsf{Ver}\left(1^{\kappa}, \overline{\mathbf{pk}}, M, \sigma\right)$ is a deterministic polynomial-time algorithm that receives as input a security parameter κ, a list of public keys $\overline{\mathbf{pk}}$ of size N, a message M and a signature σ and outputs a bit $b \in \{0, 1\}$ corresponding to whether the signature σ is a valid one ($b = 1$) or not ($b = 0$).
- $b \leftarrow \mathsf{Link}(1^{\kappa}, \overline{\mathbf{pk}}, M_1, \sigma_1, M_2, \sigma_2)$ is a deterministic polynomial-time algorithm that takes as input a list of public keys $\overline{\mathbf{pk}}$ two messages M_1 and M_2 and two signatures σ_1 and σ_2 such that $\mathsf{Ver}\left(1^n, \overline{\mathbf{pk}}, M_1, \sigma_1\right) = 1$ and $\mathsf{Ver}(1^n, \overline{\mathbf{pk}}, M_2, \sigma_2) = 1$. It outputs $b = 1$ for linked signatures and $b = 0$ otherwise.

The security model we adopt is based on [7, 25]. In order for a linkable ring signature scheme to be secure, it must be existential unforgeable, anonymous, non-slanderable and linkable. Existential unforgeability prevents an adversary from forging a signature in name of a group if it does not have a public key in this group, for any message M, while anonymity certifies that an adversary is incapable of knowing who inside the group has signed a given message. Non-slanderability (firstly introduced in [31] and formalized in [7]) prevents an adversary from creating a signature that is linked to a second signature issued by other user. Linkability guarantees that a user cannot create two valid signatures that are not linked.

In the following, let $\overline{\mathbf{pk}} = \{\mathsf{pk}_1, \ldots, \mathsf{pk}_N\}$ be the set of public keys of the users in the ring and $L \subseteq \overline{\mathbf{pk}}$. $\mathsf{Sign}(\cdot, \mathsf{sk})$ is a signing oracle that receives queries of the form $(\overline{\mathbf{pk}}, M)$, and outputs $\sigma \leftarrow \mathsf{Sign}(1^{\kappa}, \overline{\mathbf{pk}}, M, \mathsf{sk}_i)$, for any $i \in \{1, \ldots, N\}$, and $\mathsf{Co}(\cdot)$ be a corruption oracle that receives queries of the for pk and outputs the corresponding secret key sk.

Existential Unforgeability. Consider the following game:

$$
\begin{array}{ll}
\hline
\textbf{Game}_{\mathcal{A}}^{\mathrm{unf}}(\kappa, N) : \\
\hline
1: & (\mathsf{pk}_i, \mathsf{sk}_i) \leftarrow \mathsf{KeyGen}(1^{\kappa}) \quad i = 1, \ldots, N \\
2: & (L, M, \sigma) \leftarrow \mathcal{A}^{\mathsf{Sign}(\cdot, \mathsf{sk}_i), \mathsf{Co}(\cdot)}(\overline{\mathbf{pk}}) \\
3: & b \leftarrow \mathsf{Ver}\left(1^{\kappa}, L, M, \sigma\right) \\
4: & \textbf{return } b \\
\hline
\end{array}
$$

where (L, M) was not asked $\mathsf{Sign}(\cdot, \mathsf{sk})$ and $\mathcal{A}$ only queried $\mathsf{Co}(\cdot)$ for $\mathsf{pk} \notin L$. We define

$$\mathsf{Adv}_{\mathcal{A}}^{\mathrm{unf}}(\kappa, N) := \Pr[b = 1].$$

If for all PPT adversaries $\mathcal{A}$ we have that $\mathsf{Adv}_{\mathcal{A}}^{\mathrm{unf}}(\kappa, N) \leq \mathsf{negl}(\kappa, N)$ then the linkable ring signature scheme is existentially unforgeable. This is called unforgeability with respect to insider corruption in [9] and it is the strongest level of unforgeability that a ring signature can achieve.

Anonymity. Consider the following game:

$$
\begin{array}{|l|}
\hline
\mathsf{Game}_{\mathcal{A}}^{\mathrm{anon}}(\kappa, N): \\
\hline
1: \quad (\mathsf{pk}_i, \mathsf{sk}_i) \leftarrow \mathsf{KeyGen}(1^\kappa) \quad i = 0, 1 \\
2: \quad b \leftarrow_\$ \{0, 1\} \\
3: \quad b' \leftarrow \mathcal{A}^{\mathsf{Sign}(\cdot, \mathsf{sk}_b), \mathsf{Sign}(\cdot, \mathsf{sk}_0), \mathsf{Sign}(\cdot, \mathsf{sk}_1)}(\mathsf{pk}_0, \mathsf{pk}_1) \\
4: \quad \textbf{return } b' \\
\hline
\end{array}
$$

where the adversary is not allowed to ask queries with different L to $\mathsf{Sign}(\cdot, \mathsf{sk}_b)$ nor to ask queries with the same L to both $\mathsf{Sign}(\cdot, \mathsf{sk}_b)$ and $\mathsf{Sign}(\cdot, \mathsf{sk}_0)$ or to both $\mathsf{Sign}(\cdot, \mathsf{sk}_b)$ and $\mathsf{Sign}(\cdot, \mathsf{sk}_1)$. We do not allow this to happen to avoid the trivial attacks. We define
$$
\mathsf{Adv}_{\mathcal{A}}^{\mathrm{anon}}(\kappa, N) := \Pr[b = b'] - \frac{1}{2}.
$$
If for all PPT adversaries $\mathcal{A}$ we have $\mathsf{Adv}_{\mathcal{A}}^{\mathrm{anon}}(\kappa, N) \leq \mathsf{negl}(\kappa, N)$ then the linkable ring signature scheme is anonymous. This definition is equivalent to the definition of anonymity with respect to adversarially-chosen keys in [9], as it is stated in [21].

Non-slanderability. Consider the following game:

$$
\begin{array}{|l|}
\hline
\mathsf{Game}_{\mathcal{A}}^{\mathrm{nsla}}(\kappa, N): \\
\hline
1: \quad (\mathsf{pk}_i, \mathsf{sk}_i) \leftarrow \mathsf{KeyGen}(1^\kappa), \quad i = 1, \ldots N \\
2: \quad (L, \mathsf{pk}_1, M_1) \leftarrow \mathcal{A}^{\mathsf{Sign}(\cdot, \mathsf{sk}_i)}(\overline{\mathbf{pk}}) \\
3: \quad \sigma_1 \leftarrow \mathsf{Sign}(1^\kappa, L, M_1, \mathsf{sk}_1) \\
4: \quad (\mathsf{pk}_2, M_2, \sigma_2) \leftarrow \mathcal{A}^{\mathsf{Sign}(\cdot, \mathsf{sk}_i)}(\overline{\mathbf{pk}}, L, \mathsf{sk}_2, \mathsf{pk}_1, M_1, \sigma_1) \\
5: \quad b \leftarrow \mathsf{Link}(1^\kappa, L, M_1, \sigma_1, M_2, \sigma_2) \\
6: \quad \textbf{return } b \\
\hline
\end{array}
$$

where $\mathsf{pk}_1, \mathsf{pk}_2 \in L$, $\mathsf{pk}_1 \neq \mathsf{pk}_2$ and both pairs $(L, M_1), \sigma_1$ and $(L, M_2), \sigma_2$ were not asked to nor replied by $\mathsf{Sign}(\cdot, \mathsf{sk}_i)$. We define
$$
\mathsf{Adv}_{\mathcal{A}}^{\mathrm{nsl}}(\kappa, N) := \Pr[b = 1].
$$

If for all PPT adversaries $\mathcal{A}$ we have $\mathsf{Adv}_{\mathcal{A}}^{\mathrm{nsl}}(\kappa, N) \leq \mathsf{negl}(\kappa, N)$ then the linkable ring signature scheme has non-slanderability.

Linkability. Consider the game:

$$
\begin{array}{|l|}
\hline
\mathsf{Game}_{\mathcal{A}}^{\mathrm{link}}(\kappa, N): \\
\hline
1: \quad (\mathsf{pk}_i, \mathsf{sk}_i) \leftarrow \mathsf{KeyGen}(1^\kappa), \quad i = 1, \ldots, N \\
2: \quad \mathsf{pk} \leftarrow \mathcal{A}^{\mathsf{Sign}(\cdot, \mathsf{sk}_i)}(\overline{\mathbf{pk}}) \\
3: \quad (L, M_1, \sigma_1, M_2, \sigma_2) \leftarrow \mathcal{A}^{\mathsf{Sign}(\cdot, \mathsf{sk}_i)}(\overline{\mathbf{pk}}, \mathsf{pk}) \\
4: \quad b \leftarrow 1 - \mathsf{Link}(1^\kappa, L, M_1, \sigma_1, M_2, \sigma_2) \\
5: \quad \textbf{return } b \\
\hline
\end{array}
$$

where $\mathsf{Ver}(1^\kappa, L, M_1, \sigma_1) = 1$, $\mathsf{Ver}(1^\kappa, L, M_2, \sigma_2) = 1$ and both pairs (L, M_1), σ_1 and (L, M_2), σ_2 were not asked to nor replied by $\mathsf{Sign}(\cdot, \mathsf{sk}_i)$. We define

$$\mathsf{Adv}_{\mathcal{A}}^{\mathsf{link}}(\kappa, L) := \Pr[b = 1].$$

If for all PPT adversaries $\mathcal{A}$ we have that $\mathsf{Adv}_{\mathcal{A}}^{\mathsf{link}}(\kappa, L) \leq \mathsf{negl}(\kappa, N)$ then the linkable ring signature scheme has linkability.

2.2 Sigma Protocols

Due to the lack of space, we review very briefly some basic concepts on sigma protocols and on the Fiat-Shamir transform. For a more detailed review, see [17]. A sigma protocol $(\mathcal{P}, \mathcal{V})$ is a three-round protocol between a prover $\mathcal{P}$ and a verifier $\mathcal{V}$ where the prover tries to convince the verifier about the validity of some statement. A proof of knowledge (PoK) is a particular case of a sigma protocol. Here, the prover $\mathcal{P}$ convinces the verifier $\mathcal{V}$, not only about the veracity of the statement but also that $\mathcal{P}$ has a witness for it. The three rounds of any sigma protocol are the commitment (com) by the prover, the challenge (ch) by the verifier and the response ($resp$) by the prover. A transcript ($com, ch, resp$) is said to be valid if the verifier accepts it as a valid proof.

A sigma protocol must have the following properties: (i) completeness, which guarantees that the verifier will accept the proof with high probability if the prover has the secret; (ii) special soundness, which ensures that there is an extractor such that, given two valid transcripts ($com, ch, resp$) and ($com, ch', resp'$) where $ch \neq ch'$, then it can extract the secret; and (iii) honest-verifier zero-knowledge (HVZK) which ensures that no information is gained by the verifier by just looking at the proof. This is usually proven by showing the existence of a simulator that can generate transcripts that are computationally indistinguishable from transcripts generated by the interaction between the prover and the verifier.

As usual, we denote a relation of size n in $X \times W$ by R_n. Given $x \in X$ (which is public information) and $w \in W$ (usually called the witness), it can be computed whether $R_n(x, w) = 1$. We define the set $L_R = \{x \in X : \exists w \in W \text{ s.t. } R_n(x, w) = 1\}$.

The following definitions are taken from [33] and they will be useful to argue post-quantum security of the Fiat-Shamir transform.

A sigma protocol $(\mathcal{P}, \mathcal{V})$ is said to be *statistically sound* if

$$\Pr\left[1 \leftarrow \mathcal{V} \wedge x \notin L_{R_n} \mid (x, com) \leftarrow \mathcal{A}_1, ch \leftarrow_\$ \{0,1\}^l, resp \leftarrow \mathcal{A}_2\right] \leq \mathsf{negl}(n),$$

where $\mathcal{A}_2$ takes (ch) as input and $\mathcal{V}$ takes the transcript ($com, ch, resp$). The sigma protocol $(\mathcal{P}, \mathcal{V})$ is said to have *unpredictable commitments* if for all (x, w) such that $R_n(x, w) = 1$ we have that

$$\Pr\left[com = com' \mid com \leftarrow \mathcal{P}(x, w), com' \leftarrow \mathcal{P}(x, w)\right] \leq \mathsf{negl}(n).$$

Let $\mathcal{K}$ be a (possibly quantum) polynomial-time algorithm. We call $\mathcal{K}$ a *hard instance generator* for some relation R_n of size n if, for all PPT adversaries $\mathcal{A}$ and $(x, w) \leftarrow \mathcal{K}$ such that $R_n(x, w) = 1$ we have

$$\Pr[R(x, w') = 1 \mid w' \leftarrow \mathcal{A}(x)] \leq \mathsf{negl}(n).$$

Definition 2 ([33]). We call $\mathcal{K}$ a *dual-mode hard instance generator* if there is a PPT algorithm $\mathcal{K}^*$ such that

$$\Pr[1 \leftarrow \mathcal{A}(x) \mid (x, w) \leftarrow \mathcal{K}] - \Pr[1 \leftarrow \mathcal{A}(x) \mid x \leftarrow \mathcal{K}^*] \leq \mathsf{negl}(n)$$

and

$$\Pr[x \in L_{R_n} \mid x \leftarrow \mathcal{K}^*] \leq \mathsf{negl}(n).$$

Informally, a dual-mode hard instance generator is a hard instance generator where, not only it is hard to find witnesses for a word x, but also it is hard to distinguish if there is a witness w for this word x.

2.3 Fiat-Shamir Transform

The Fiat-Shamir transform [20] is a generic method to convert any PoK protocol that is complete, special sound and HVZK into a signature scheme. The security of the Fiat-Shamir transform is proven to be secure both in the random oracle model (ROM) [1] and in the quantum random oracle model (QROM) [33], under certain conditions.

The idea behind the Fiat-Shamir transform is that the prover is able to simulate the challenge that is usually sent by the verifier. Since this challenge should be chosen uniformly at random, the prover sets the challenge according to a cryptographic hash function depending on the message to be signed and on the commitment chosen previously by the prover. More precisely, given a proof of knowledge $(\mathcal{P}, \mathcal{V})$, the prover computes *com*, then sets $ch = h(com, M)$ where h is a cryptographic hash function and M is the message to be signed. Finally, it computes *resp* such that $(com, ch, resp)$ is a valid transcript. The signature of M is $(com, resp)$. For someone to verify the validity of the signature, one just has to compute $ch = h(com, M)$ and then check that $(com, ch, resp)$ is a valid transcript.

The following result guarantees the security of the Fiat-Shamir transform in the classical setting.

Theorem 1 ([1]). *Suppose that $(\mathcal{P}, \mathcal{V})$ is a sigma protocol that is complete, special sound and HVZK. Then the signature scheme obtained by applying the Fiat-Shamir transform is secure in the ROM.*

However, in the quantum setting, where an adversary can perform quantum computations in the quantum random oracle model (QROM [11]), the Fiat-Shamir transformation seems to be insecure, or, at least, it is not secure in some cases [6]. Fortunately, Unruh gave sufficient conditions for the Fiat-Shamir transform to be secure in the quantum setting [33].

Theorem 2 ([33]). *Let $\mathcal{K}$ be a dual-mode hard instance generator for some relation R. Let $(\mathcal{P}, \mathcal{V})$ be a sigma protocol for the relation R that is complete, statistical sound, HVZK and has unpredictable commitments. Then the signature scheme obtained by applying the Fiat-Shamir transformation to $(\mathcal{P}, \mathcal{V})$ is secure in the QROM.*

We will use the Fiat-Shamir transform to construct a linkable ring scheme and we will use Theorem 1 to prove its security in the ROM. Theorem 2 gives the basis to prove security in the QROM.

2.4   Hard Problems in Coding Theory

We present the Syndrome Decoding (SD) problem, which is proven to be NP-complete [10].

Problem 1 (Syndrome Decoding - Decision Version). *Given a binary matrix $\mathbf{H} \in \{0,1\}^{(n-k)\times n}$, a vector $\mathbf{s} \in \{0,1\}^{n-k}$, and an integer $t \geq 0$ determine whether there exists $\mathbf{e}$ such that $w(\mathbf{e}) \leq t$ and $\mathbf{H}\mathbf{e}^T = \mathbf{s}^T$.*

The following problem is a generalization of the SD problem. We will call this problem the General Syndrome Decoding (GDS) problem.

Problem 2 (General Syndrome Decoding). *Given binary matrices $\mathbf{H}, \mathbf{G} \in \{0,1\}^{(n-k)\times n}$, vectors $\mathbf{s}, \mathbf{r} \in \{0,1\}^{n-k}$, and an integer $t \geq 0$ determine whether there exists $\mathbf{e}$ such that $w(\mathbf{e}) \leq t$, $\mathbf{H}\mathbf{e}^T = \mathbf{s}^T$ and $\mathbf{G}\mathbf{e}^T = \mathbf{r}^T$.*

It is easy to see that SD can be reduced to the GSD problem. More precisely, we have that $(\mathbf{H}, \mathbf{s}, t) \in \text{SD}$ iff $(\mathbf{H}, \mathbf{s}, \mathbf{H}, \mathbf{s}, t) \in \text{GSD}$, which gives a Karp reduction of SD to GSD. In other words, the SD problem is the diagonal of GSD. Moreover, since the SD problem is NP-complete, we conclude that the SD problem and the GSD problem are equivalent. Furthermore, observe that the reduction presented is tight. Hence, the parameters for which the SD problem is infeasible also make the GSD problem infeasible.

Note that it is trivial to conceive an algorithm that satisfies the conditions of a dual-mode hard instance generator that creates instances of the SD problem, in the sense of Definition 2: one just has to choose a random matrix and a random error vector and then compute the syndrome of the error vector. The matrix, the syndrome and the weight of the error vector form an instance of the SD problem. The same applies to the GSD problem.

We present a variant of Stern's protocol [29] based on the hardness of the GSD problem. In this variant, the prover is able to prove that it has the solution for an instance of the GSD problem. That is, given $(\mathbf{H}, \mathbf{s}, \mathbf{G}, \mathbf{r}, t)$, it proves that it has an error vector $\mathbf{e}$ such that $\mathbf{H}\mathbf{e}^T = \mathbf{s}$, $\mathbf{G}\mathbf{e}^T = \mathbf{r}^T$ and $w(\mathbf{e}) \leq t$. The protocol is presented in Algorithm 1. We will call it the GStern's protocol.

As in the original Stern's protocol, when $b = 1$, $\mathcal{V}$ can check that c_1 was honestly computed by computing $\mathbf{H}(\mathbf{y} + \mathbf{e}) + \mathbf{s} = \mathbf{H}\mathbf{y}$ and $\mathbf{G}(\mathbf{y} + \mathbf{e}) + \mathbf{r} = \mathbf{G}\mathbf{y}$. Also, the verifier can check that the same error vector $\mathbf{e}$ that was used to compute both the syndrome vectors $\mathbf{s}$ and $\mathbf{r}$. The next lemma states that GStern's protocol has the usual properties of completeness, special soundness and HVZK.

Algorithm 1. GStern's protocol

1. **Public information:** $\mathbf{H}, \mathbf{G} \in \{0,1\}^{n \times n-k}$ and $\mathbf{s}, \mathbf{r} \in \{0,1\}^{n-k}$.
2. **Secret information:** $\mathbf{e} \in \{0,1\}^n$ such that $\mathbf{He}^T = \mathbf{s}^T$, $\mathbf{Ge}^T = \mathbf{r}^T$ and $w(\mathbf{e}) = t$.
3. **Prover's commitment:**
   - Chooses $\mathbf{y} \leftarrow_\$ \{0,1\}^n$ and a permutation δ;
   - Computes $c_1 = h(\delta, \mathbf{Hy}^T, \mathbf{Gy}^T)$, $c_2 = h(\delta(\mathbf{y}))$ and $c_3 = h(\delta(\mathbf{y} + \mathbf{e}))$;
   - $\mathcal{P}$ sends c_1, c_2 and c_3.
4. **Verifier's challenge:** $\mathcal{V}$ sends $b \leftarrow_\$ \{0,1,2\}$.
5. **Prover's answer:**
   - If $b = 0$, $\mathcal{P}$ reveals $\mathbf{y}, \delta$;
   - If $b = 1$, $\mathcal{P}$ reveals $\mathbf{y} + \mathbf{e}, \delta$;
   - If $b = 2$, $\mathcal{P}$ reveals $\delta(\mathbf{y}), \delta(\mathbf{e})$.
6. **Verifier's verification:**
   - If $b = 0$, $\mathcal{V}$ checks if $h(\delta, \mathbf{Hy}^T, \mathbf{Gy}^T) = c_1$ and $h(\delta(\mathbf{y})) = c_2$;
   - If $b = 1$, $\mathcal{V}$ checks if $h(\delta, \mathbf{H}(\mathbf{y}+\mathbf{e})^T + \mathbf{s}^T, \mathbf{G}(\mathbf{y}+\mathbf{e})^T + \mathbf{r}^T) = c_1$ and $h(\delta(\mathbf{y} + \mathbf{e})) = c_3$;
   - If $b = 2$, $\mathcal{V}$ checks if $h(\delta(\mathbf{y})) = c_2$, $h(\delta(\mathbf{y}) + \delta(\mathbf{e})) = c_3$ and $w(\delta(\mathbf{e})) = t$.

Lemma 1. *The protocol presented in Algorithm 1 is complete, special sound and HVZK.*

Proof. The proof is similar to the proofs of completeness, special soundness and HVZK for Stern's protocol, presented in [29]. □

Next we present in Algorithm 2 a variant of the above protocol that enables a prover to prove the knowledge of the solution of an instance of the problem without revealing which one it is. It is based on the generic construction in [15] and on the previous proof of knowledge. In this new protocol, given N instances of the GSD problem, the prover is able to prove that it has a solution for one of these instances, without revealing to the verifier which one is it. More precisely, given $(\mathbf{H}_1, \mathbf{s}_1, \mathbf{G}_1, \mathbf{r}_1, t_1), \ldots, (\mathbf{H}_N, \mathbf{s}_N, \mathbf{G}_N, \mathbf{r}_N, t_N)$, the prover proves the knowledge of an error vector $\mathbf{e}$ such that $\mathbf{H}_i \mathbf{e}^T = \mathbf{s}_i$, $\mathbf{G}_i \mathbf{e}^T = \mathbf{r}_i^T$ and $w(\mathbf{e}) \leq t_i$, for some $i \in \{1, \ldots N\}$ unknown to the verifier. Here, *com* corresponds to the prover's commitment, *ch* to the challenge by the verifier, *resp* the response of the prover and (*com, ch, resp*) to a transcript according to the previous protocol. The protocol presented in Algorithm 2 will be called $\binom{N}{1}$-GStern's protocol.

The protocol is proven to be a proof of knowledge that is complete, special sound and HVZK [15].

Based on the results of [33], for the GStern's protocol to be secure in the post-quantum setting it needs to achieve statistical soundness.

To this end, we need to introduce the concept of perfectly binding commitment schemes. First, we present the definition of commitment scheme. A *commitment scheme* is a protocol between two parties, the committer and the receiver, that has two phases: the commitment phase where the committer commits to a value, and the opening phase where the committer opens her commitment. A commitment scheme should be *hiding*, meaning that the receiver should not

---

Algorithm 2. $\binom{N}{1}$-GStern's protocol

1. **Public information:** $\mathbf{H}, \mathbf{G} \in \{0,1\}^{n \times n-k}$, $\mathbf{s}_1, \ldots, \mathbf{s}_N, \mathbf{r}_1, \ldots, \mathbf{r}_N \in \{0,1\}^{n-k}$ and $t \in \mathbb{Z}$.
2. **Secret information:** $\mathbf{e} \in \{0,1\}^n$ such that $w(\mathbf{e}) = t$, $\mathbf{He}^T = \mathbf{s}_i^T$ and $\mathbf{Ge}^T = \mathbf{r}_i^T$ for some i.
3. **Prover's commitment:**
   - $\mathcal{P}^*$ simulates transcripts $(com_j, ch_j, resp_j)$ using the simulator $\mathcal{S}$ for GStern's protocol for $j \neq i$;
   - $\mathcal{P}^*$ computes com_i according to GStern's protocol;
   - $\mathcal{P}^*$ sends $com_1, \ldots, com_n$;
4. **Verifier's challenge:** $\mathcal{V}$ sends $b \leftarrow_{\$} C$.
5. **Prover's answer:**
   - $\mathcal{P}$ computes $ch_i = b + \sum_{j \neq i} ch_j$;
   - $\mathcal{P}$ chooses $resp_i$, according to com_i and ch_i;
   - Sends $(com_j, ch_j, resp_j)$ for every j;
6. **Verifier's verification:**
   - $\mathcal{V}$ checks that $(com_j, ch_j, resp_j)$ is valid for every j according to GStern's protocol;
   - $\mathcal{V}$ checks that $b = \sum_j ch_j$;
   - If all the previous conditions hold, $\mathcal{V}$ accepts.

---

be able to know the committer's commitment before the opening phase; and it should be *binding*, meaning that the committer should not be able to open a different message from the one she has committed before. By a *perfectly binding commitment scheme* (PBCS) we mean a commitment scheme for which the user that commits cannot change its commitment even if it has unlimited computational power. In this work, we use a post-quantum PBCS as a black-box, although it is known that PBCS exist in the post-quantum setting (see, for instance [22], that is proven to be secure under the LPN problem, the dual and equivalent version of the SD problem). In our construction, any commitment scheme can be used as long as it is *perfectly binding and computationally hiding against quantum attacks*.

As we show in the next result, to construct a variant of GStern's protocol that achieves statistical soundness, it is enough to replace the hash function h used to create the commitments, in the Prover's commitment phase, by a perfectly binding commitment scheme. We will call it the PQ GStern's protocol. Observe that this is still a complete and HVZK protocol.

Lemma 2. *PQ GStern's protocol is statistically sound.*

Proof. First, note that, if Com is a PBCS, then $\mathsf{Com}(x_1) \neq \mathsf{Com}(x_2)$ for $x_1 \neq x_2$ except with negligible probability. If this happens with non-negligible probability, then the user who is committing could send $\mathsf{Com}(x_1)$ and then reveal x_2 with non-negligible probability, contradicting the fact that Com is perfectly binding.

Suppose that there is an algorithm $\mathcal{A}$ (not necessarily running in polynomial-time) that breaks the statistical soundness of PQ Stern's protocol. Then $\mathcal{A}$ is able to find $\mathbf{H}$, $\mathbf{s}$, $\mathbf{G}$, $\mathbf{r}$ and t, for which there is no $\mathbf{e}$ such that $w(\mathbf{e}) = t$, $\mathbf{He}^T = \mathbf{s}$ and $\mathbf{Ge}^T = \mathbf{r}^T$, and com such that it is able to answer correctly to any challenge with non-negligible probability. This implies that either $\mathcal{A}$ is able to break the special soundness of the protocol (note that, since there is no witness for the instance $(\mathbf{H}, \mathbf{s}.\mathbf{G}, \mathbf{r}, t)$ then the adversary must build its commitments according to some strategy since, if it follows the protocol, it will be caught) or it is able to break the PBCS. The first event happens with probability as close to zero as we want and the second event also happens with negligible probability. In both cases, we reach a contradiction. □

Recall that a sigma protocol is said to have unpredictable commitments if the probability of getting the same value when running twice the commitment phase of the sigma protocol is negligible, as it was defined in 2.2.

Lemma 3. *PQ GStern's protocol has unpredictable commitments.*

Proof. Again, recall that $\mathsf{Com}(x_1) \neq \mathsf{Com}(x_2)$ for $x_1 \neq x_2$ except with negligible probability, when Com is a PBCS.

Now consider GStern's protocol. For two commitments made in different executions of the protocol to be equal, the prover would have to choose uniformly at random two vectors y and z of length n and two permutations δ and γ over $1, \ldots, n$ such that

1. $(\delta, \mathbf{Hy}^T, \mathbf{Gy}^T) = (\gamma, \mathbf{Hz}^T, \mathbf{Gz}^T)$
2. $\delta(\mathbf{y}) = \gamma(\mathbf{z})$
3. $\delta(\mathbf{y} + \mathbf{e}) = \gamma(\mathbf{z} + \mathbf{e})$.

By 1. we conclude that $\delta = \gamma$ in order for the commitments to be equal. But the probability of this happening is $1/n!$. This is enough to prove the lemma, since we have that

$$\Pr[com = com' \mid com \leftarrow \mathcal{P}(1^n, x, w), com' \leftarrow \mathcal{P}(1^n, x, w)] \leq 1/n!$$

which is, of course, negligible in n. □

To finish this section, note that the same technique can be applied to $\binom{N}{1}$-GStern's protocol in order to obtain new a sigma protocol that yield statistical soundness. It is obvious that $\binom{N}{1}$-GStern's protocol also has unpredictable commitments. We will call PQ $\binom{N}{1}$-GStern's protocol to this new version.

3   A Linkable Ring Signature Scheme

We present the new linkable ring signature scheme in Algorithm 3. To obtain the signature scheme we apply the Fiat-Shamir transform to $\binom{N}{1}$-GStern protocol. More precisely, the signer creates an instance $\mathcal{I} = (\mathbf{H}, \mathbf{s}, \widetilde{\mathbf{H}}, \mathbf{r})$ using its secret key and where the matrix $\widetilde{\mathbf{H}}$ is obtained via a cryptographic hash function and $\mathbf{r}$ is the syndrome of its secret key by $\widetilde{\mathbf{H}}$. Then, it applies the Fiat-Shamir transform to $\binom{N}{1}$-GStern's protocol on input $(\mathbf{H}, \bar{\mathbf{s}}, \widetilde{\mathbf{H}}, \bar{\mathbf{r}})$ where $\bar{\mathbf{s}} = (\mathbf{s}_1, \ldots \mathbf{s}_N)$ are the public keys of the members in the ring and $\bar{\mathbf{r}} = (\mathbf{r}, \ldots, \mathbf{r})$. On the one hand, the verifier will not be able to check which user computed $\mathbf{r}$, due to the hardness of the SD problem. On the other hand, $\mathbf{r}$ will be part of every signature issued by this user with respect to the same ring. So, these signatures can be linked by a verifier. In the following, let g and f be two different cryptographic hash functions and consider a ring with N users with public keys $\overline{\mathbf{pk}} = (\mathsf{pk}_1, \ldots, \mathsf{pk}_N)$.

Algorithm 3. A new linkable ring signature scheme

1. **Parameters:** $n, k, t \in \mathbb{N}$ such that $n > k$, $\mathbf{H} \leftarrow_\$ \{0,1\}^{n \times (n-k)}$
2. **Key Generation:** Each user $\mathcal{P}_i$:
   - Chooses $\mathbf{e}_i \leftarrow_\$ \{0,1\}^n$ such that $w(\mathbf{e}) = t$;
   - Computes $\mathbf{s}_i^T = \mathbf{H}\mathbf{e}_i^T$.

   Public key of user $\mathcal{P}_i$: $\mathbf{H}, \mathbf{s}_i, t$.

   Secret key of user $\mathcal{P}_i$: $\mathbf{e}_i$ such that $w(\mathbf{e}) = t$ and $\mathbf{H}\mathbf{e}_i^T = \mathbf{s}_i^T$.
3. **Sign:** To sign message M, user $\mathcal{P}_i$:
   - Computes matrix $g(\overline{\mathbf{pk}}) = \widetilde{\mathbf{H}}$ and $\widetilde{\mathbf{H}}\mathbf{e}_i^T = \mathbf{r}^T$;
   - Applies the Fiat-Shamir transform to $\binom{N}{1}$-GStern's protocol on input $(\mathbf{H}, \bar{\mathbf{s}}, \widetilde{\mathbf{H}}, \bar{\mathbf{r}})$ where $\bar{\mathbf{s}} = (\mathbf{s}_1, \ldots, \mathbf{s}_N)$ and $\bar{\mathbf{r}} = (\mathbf{r}, \ldots, \mathbf{r})$:
     - Computes the commitments Com according to $\binom{N}{1}$-GStern's protocol;
     - Simulates the verifier's challenge Ch as $f(Com, M)$;
     - Computes the corresponding responses $Resp$ according to step 5 of $\binom{N}{1}$-GStern's protocol;
     - Outputs the transcript $T = (Com, Ch, Resp)$.
   - Outputs the signature $(\overline{\mathbf{pk}}, M, \sigma)$ where $\sigma = (\mathbf{r}, Com, Resp)$.
4. **Verify:** To verify, the verifier:
   - Computes $Ch = f(Com, M)$;
   - Computes $\widetilde{\mathbf{H}} = g(\overline{\mathbf{pk}})$;
   - Verifies that $T = (Com, Ch, Resp)$ is a valid transcript, according to $\binom{N}{1}$-GStern's protocol and input $(\mathbf{H}, \bar{\mathbf{s}}, \widetilde{\mathbf{H}}, \bar{\mathbf{r}})$.
5. **Link:** Given two signatures $(\overline{\mathbf{pk}}, M, \sigma)$ and $(\overline{\mathbf{pk}}, M', \sigma')$ where $\sigma = (\mathbf{r}, Com, Resp)$ and $\sigma' = (\mathbf{r}', Com', Resp')$ and such that $\mathsf{Ver}(\overline{\mathbf{pk}}, M, \sigma) = 1$ and $\mathsf{Ver}(\overline{\mathbf{pk}}, M', \sigma') = 1$, the verifier:
   - Checks if $\mathbf{r} = \mathbf{r}'$;
   - Outputs 1 if it is equal; else, outputs 0.

---

4 Security of the Scheme

In this section we present the results concerning the security of the proposed scheme. We prove that the scheme has the usual properties for a linkable ring signature scheme: existential unforgeability, anonymity, non-slanderability and linkability. The proofs are presented in the extended version of the paper.

Existential Unforgeability. Existential unforgeability in the classical setting is a direct consequence of the fact that the signature is obtained from a sigma protocol that is complete, special sound and HVZK and Theorem 1. The post-quantum security of the proposed PQ linkable ring signature scheme is guaranteed by the fact that the sigma protocol used in the Fiat-Shamir transform is complete, statistically sound, HVZK and has unpredictable commitments.

Theorem 3. *Assume that the GSD problem is hard. The linkable ring signature scheme proposed is existentially unforgeable in the ROM.*

Anonymity. In order to prove anonymity for the linkable ring signature scheme, we reduce the GSD problem to that of breaking anonymity. In this proof, we assume that we are able to break the anonymity of the scheme, and construct an algorithm that solves the GSD problem. However, we have to know beforehand some non-null coordinates of the error vector, namely we assume that $t/2$ positions are known. This is required because we know how the algorithm that breaks the anonymity behaves when it is given two valid public key or when it is given two random values as public keys. However, we do not know how it behaves when it is given one valid public key and one random value as public key. Moreover, given a tuple $(\mathbf{H}, \mathbf{s}, \mathbf{G}, \mathbf{r}, t)$, we do not know if this represents a valid public key of the cryptosystem or if it is a random tuple. However, if we know part of the secret, we are able to construct another tuple $(\mathbf{H}, \mathbf{s}', \mathbf{G}, \mathbf{r}', t)$ that is a GSD tuple if $(\mathbf{H}, \mathbf{s}, \mathbf{G}, \mathbf{r}, t)$ is a GSD tuple or that is a random tuple if $(\mathbf{H}, \mathbf{s}, \mathbf{G}, \mathbf{r}, t)$ is a random tuple. The fact that $t/2$ positions are known does not threat the security proof since the GSD problem is still computationally hard. We just have to increase the parameters to maintain the same level of security.

Theorem 4. *Assume that the GSD problem knowing $t/2$ positions of the error vector is hard. The proposed linkable ring signature scheme has anonymity in the ROM.*

Non-slanderability. To argue that our proposal has the non-slanderability property, we prove that it is infeasible for an adversary to frame another user in the ring. That is, given a message and a signature produced by some user, it is infeasible for an adversary to create a signature for another message that is linked to the first one.

Theorem 5. *Assume that the GSD problem is hard. The linkable ring signature scheme is non-slanderable in the ROM.*

Linkability. Linkability prevents a user from signing two messages that are not linked. To show that the proposed linkable ring signature scheme has linkability, we must prove that it is infeasible for an adversary with access to at most one secret key to create signatures that are not linked.

Theorem 6. *Assume that the GSD problem is hard. The linkable ring signature scheme is linkable in the ROM.*

5   Parameters and Key Size

To conclude, we propose parameters for the scheme and analyze its signature and key size. For the cheating probability of GStern's protocol to be approximately 2^{-80}, it has to be iterated 140 times. Recall that anonymity for our linkable ring signature scheme is proven when knowing $t/2$ positions of the error vector. Hence, to yield the standard security of approximately 80 bits for signature schemes according to the best known attack [12], we consider a code with $n = 1268$, $k = n/2$ and $t = 130$. Note that a code with these parameters has a security of at least 80 bits even when knowing $t/2$ positions of the error vector. This is necessary to maintain the anonymity of the scheme.

Size of the Sigma Protocol. Using a cryptographic hash function with a security of 128 bits, each round of GStern's protocol has approximately 2270 bits of exchange information. Let N be the number of users in the ring. Since $\binom{N}{1}$-GStern's protocol is just the previous protocol repeated N times, then $\binom{N}{1}$-GStern's protocol has $2270N$ bits of exchange information in each round.

Signature Size. To estimate the size of a signature, notice that the signature is a transcript of $\binom{N}{1}$-GStern's protocol repeated 140 times plus the size of a vector **r**, in order to guarantee the usual level of security for signature schemes, which is about 80 bits of security. Hence, the signature size is approximately $317\,800N$ bits , where N is the number of users in the ring. In other words, the signature size is approximately $39N$ kBytes. For example, for a ring with $N = 100$ users, the signature size is approximately 4 MBytes.

Public Key Size. The public key of the ring is composed by $(\mathbf{H}, \mathbf{s}_1, \ldots, \mathbf{s}_N)$. Therefore, the total size of the public key is approximately $803917 + 634N$ bits, which is linear in the number of users in the ring. For each user, the public key is of size $803917 + 634$ bits and a secret key of size 1268 bits.

Comparison with Lattice-Based Linkable Ring Signature Schemes. The signature size of our proposal is slightly bigger than the signature size of the schemes in [8,30] (around 4 times bigger for the same number of users in the ring). The public key size is roughly the same as the scheme in [8] and it is ten times bigger than the one presented in [30], for a ring with 10 users. The secret key size of our proposal is much smaller than both schemes [8,30] (it is 50 times smaller than [8] and 6 times smaller than [30]).

6   Discussion and Conclusion

Linkable ring signature schemes have become important in today's world mainly because of their importance in e-voting schemes and in cryptocurrencies. In this paper we presented the first code-based linkable ring signature scheme. To achieve this, we applied the Fiat-Shamir transform to a variant of Stern's protocol.

A candidate for post-quantum linkable ring signature scheme can be obtained by applying the Fiat-Shamir transform to the PQ $\binom{N}{1}$-GStern protocol (that is, the post-quantum version of Algorithm 2) in a similar way as presented in Algorithm 3. It is easy to extend the the proofs of Theorem 3 (existential unforgeability), Theorem 5 (non-slanderability) and Theorem 6 (linkability) for such ring signature scheme in the QROM. But it is now straightforward to extend the result of Theorem 4 (anonymity). We leave as an open problem the case where an adversary can make queries in superposition to the random oracle, as usual for other post-quantum signature schemes, e.g. [4,8]. Although this case was not addressed yet by the community, it is strongly believed that there is no efficient quantum attack on the anonymity for these schemes.

Finally, the protocol we described outputs signatures and keys which are too long for some applications (as it is usual for code-based cryptographic schemes). Still, we think that there is room for improvement. For example, in some applications, the public matrix $\mathbf{H}$ can be divided among the several users in the ring since $\mathbf{H}$ is part of the public key of every user. This would reduce the key size for each user.

Acknowledgments. The authors acknowledge the anonymous referees that contributed to the readability and improvement of the final manuscript. The first author thanks the support from DP-PMI and FCT (Portugal) through the grant PD/BD/135181/2017. The authors thank IT, namely via SQIG and the FCT projects number PEst-OE/EEI/LA0008/2013 and Confident PTDC/EEI-CTP/4503/2014. The authors also thank the H2020 SPARTA project under SU-ICT-03.

References

1. Abdalla, M., An, J.H., Bellare, M., Namprempre, C.: From identification to signatures via the fiat-shamir transform: minimizing assumptions for security and forward-security. In: Knudsen, L.R. (ed.) EUROCRYPT 2002. LNCS, vol. 2332, pp. 418–433. Springer, Heidelberg (2002). https://doi.org/10.1007/3-540-46035-7_28
2. Aguilar-Melchor, C., Bettaieb, S., Gaborit, P., Schrek, J.: A code-based undeniable signature scheme. In: Stam, M. (ed.) IMACC 2013. LNCS, vol. 8308, pp. 99–119. Springer, Heidelberg (2013). https://doi.org/10.1007/978-3-642-45239-0_7
3. Aguilar Melchor, C., Cayrel, P.L., Gaborit, P., Laguillaumie, F.: A new efficient threshold ring signature scheme based on coding theory. IEEE Trans. Inf. Theor. **57**(7), 4833–4842 (2011)
4. Alamélou, Q., Blazy, O., Cauchie, S., Gaborit, P.: A practical group signature scheme based on rank metric. In: Duquesne, S., Petkova-Nikova, S. (eds.) WAIFI 2016. LNCS, vol. 10064, pp. 258–275. Springer, Cham (2016). https://doi.org/10.1007/978-3-319-55227-9_18
5. Alamélou, Q., Blazy, O., Cauchie, S., Gaborit, P.: A code-based group signature scheme. Des. Codes Crypt. **82**(1), 469–493 (2017). https://doi.org/10.1007/s10623-016-0276-6
6. Ambainis, A., Rosmanis, A., Unruh, D.: Quantum attacks on classical proof systems: the hardness of quantum rewinding. In: Proceedings of the 2014 IEEE 55th Annual Symposium on Foundations of Computer Science, FOCS 2014, pp. 474–483. IEEE Computer Society, Washington (2014). http://dx.doi.org/10.1109/FOCS.2014.57

7. Au, M.H., Chow, S.S.M., Susilo, W., Tsang, P.P.: Short linkable ring signatures revisited. In: Atzeni, A.S., Lioy, A. (eds.) EuroPKI 2006. LNCS, vol. 4043, pp. 101–115. Springer, Heidelberg (2006). https://doi.org/10.1007/11774716_9

8. Baum, C., Lin, H., Oechsner, S.: Towards practical lattice-based one-time linkable ring signatures. Cryptology ePrint Archive, Report 2018/107 (2018). https://eprint.iacr.org/2018/107

9. Bender, A., Katz, J., Morselli, R.: Ring signatures: stronger definitions, and constructions without random oracles. In: Halevi, S., Rabin, T. (eds.) TCC 2006. LNCS, vol. 3876, pp. 60–79. Springer, Heidelberg (2006). https://doi.org/10.1007/11681878_4

10. Berlekamp, E.R., McEliece, R.J., van Tilborg, H.: On the inherent intractability of certain coding problems (corresp.). IEEE Trans. Inf. Theor. **24**(3), 384–386 (1978)

11. Boneh, D., Dagdelen, Ö., Fischlin, M., Lehmann, A., Schaffner, C., Zhandry, M.: Random Oracles in a quantum world. In: Lee, D.H., Wang, X. (eds.) ASIACRYPT 2011. LNCS, vol. 7073, pp. 41–69. Springer, Heidelberg (2011). https://doi.org/10.1007/978-3-642-25385-0_3

12. Canteaut, A., Chabaud, F.: A new algorithm for finding minimum-weight words in a linear code: application to McEliece's cryptosystem and to narrow-sense BCH codes of length 511. IEEE Trans. Inf. Theor. **44**(1), 367–378 (1998)

13. Chaum, D., van Heyst, E.: Group signatures. In: Davies, D.W. (ed.) EUROCRYPT 1991. LNCS, vol. 547, pp. 257–265. Springer, Heidelberg (1991). https://doi.org/10.1007/3-540-46416-6_22

14. Courtois, N.T., Finiasz, M., Sendrier, N.: How to achieve a McEliece-based digital signature scheme. In: Boyd, C. (ed.) ASIACRYPT 2001. LNCS, vol. 2248, pp. 157–174. Springer, Heidelberg (2001). https://doi.org/10.1007/3-540-45682-1_10

15. Cramer, R., Damgård, I., Schoenmakers, B.: Proofs of partial knowledge and simplified design of witness hiding protocols. In: Desmedt, Y.G. (ed.) CRYPTO 1994. LNCS, vol. 839, pp. 174–187. Springer, Heidelberg (1994). https://doi.org/10.1007/3-540-48658-5_19

16. Dallot, L., Vergnaud, D.: Provably secure code-based threshold ring signatures. In: Parker, M.G. (ed.) IMACC 2009. LNCS, vol. 5921, pp. 222–235. Springer, Heidelberg (2009). https://doi.org/10.1007/978-3-642-10868-6_13

17. Damgård, I.: On σ-protocols. Lecture Notes, University of Aarhus, Department for Computer Science (2002)

18. Ezerman, M.F., Lee, H.T., Ling, S., Nguyen, K., Wang, H.: A provably secure group signature scheme from code-based assumptions. In: Iwata, T., Cheon, J.H. (eds.) ASIACRYPT 2015. LNCS, vol. 9452, pp. 260–285. Springer, Heidelberg (2015). https://doi.org/10.1007/978-3-662-48797-6_12

19. Faugre, J., Gauthier-Umaa, V., Otmani, A., Perret, L., Tillich, J.: A distinguisher for high-rate mceliece cryptosystems. IEEE Trans. Inf. Theor. **59**(10), 6830–6844 (2013)

20. Fiat, A., Shamir, A.: How to prove yourself: practical solutions to identification and signature problems. In: Odlyzko, A.M. (ed.) CRYPTO 1986. LNCS, vol. 263, pp. 186–194. Springer, Heidelberg (1987). https://doi.org/10.1007/3-540-47721-7_12

21. Fujisaki, E., Suzuki, K.: Traceable ring signature. In: Okamoto, T., Wang, X. (eds.) PKC 2007. LNCS, vol. 4450, pp. 181–200. Springer, Heidelberg (2007). https://doi.org/10.1007/978-3-540-71677-8_13

22. Jain, A., Krenn, S., Pietrzak, K., Tentes, A.: Commitments and efficient zero-knowledge proofs from learning parity with noise. In: Wang, X., Sako, K. (eds.) ASIACRYPT 2012. LNCS, vol. 7658, pp. 663–680. Springer, Heidelberg (2012). https://doi.org/10.1007/978-3-642-34961-4_40

23. Liu, J.K., Au, M.H., Susilo, W., Zhou, J.: Linkable ring signature with unconditional anonymity. IEEE Trans. Knowl. Data Eng. **26**(1), 157–165 (2014)
24. Liu, J.K., Wei, V.K., Wong, D.S.: Linkable spontaneous anonymous group signature for Ad Hoc groups. In: Wang, H., Pieprzyk, J., Varadharajan, V. (eds.) ACISP 2004. LNCS, vol. 3108, pp. 325–335. Springer, Heidelberg (2004). https://doi.org/10.1007/978-3-540-27800-9_28
25. Liu, J.K., Wong, D.S.: Linkable ring signatures: security models and new schemes. In: Gervasi, O., Gavrilova, M.L., Kumar, V., Laganà, A., Lee, H.P., Mun, Y., Taniar, D., Tan, C.J.K. (eds.) ICCSA 2005. LNCS, vol. 3481, pp. 614–623. Springer, Heidelberg (2005). https://doi.org/10.1007/11424826_65
26. Rivest, R.L., Shamir, A., Tauman, Y.: How to leak a secret. In: Boyd, C. (ed.) ASIACRYPT 2001. LNCS, vol. 2248, pp. 552–565. Springer, Heidelberg (2001). https://doi.org/10.1007/3-540-45682-1_32
27. van Saberhagen, N.: Cryptonote v 2.0 (2013)
28. Shor, P.W.: Polynomial-time algorithms for prime factorization and discrete logarithms on a quantum computer. SIAM J. Comput. **26**(5), 1484–1509 (1997). https://doi.org/10.1137/S0097539795293172
29. Stern, J.: A new identification scheme based on syndrome decoding. In: Stinson, D.R. (ed.) CRYPTO 1993. LNCS, vol. 773, pp. 13–21. Springer, Heidelberg (1994). https://doi.org/10.1007/3-540-48329-2_2
30. Torres, W.A., et al.: Post-quantum one-time linkable ring signature and application to ring confidential transactions in blockchain (lattice ringCT v1.0). Cryptology ePrint Archive, Report 2018/379 (2018). https://eprint.iacr.org/2018/379
31. Tsang, P.P., Wei, V.K.: Short linkable ring signatures for e-voting, e-cash and attestation. In: Deng, R.H., Bao, F., Pang, H.H., Zhou, J. (eds.) ISPEC 2005. LNCS, vol. 3439, pp. 48–60. Springer, Heidelberg (2005). https://doi.org/10.1007/978-3-540-31979-5_5
32. Tsang, P.P., Wei, V.K., Chan, T.K., Au, M.H., Liu, J.K., Wong, D.S.: Separable linkable threshold ring signatures. In: Canteaut, A., Viswanathan, K. (eds.) INDOCRYPT 2004. LNCS, vol. 3348, pp. 384–398. Springer, Heidelberg (2004). https://doi.org/10.1007/978-3-540-30556-9_30
33. Unruh, D.: Post-quantum security of Fiat-Shamir. In: Takagi, T., Peyrin, T. (eds.) ASIACRYPT 2017. LNCS, vol. 10624, pp. 65–95. Springer, Cham (2017). https://doi.org/10.1007/978-3-319-70694-8_3
34. Zheng, D., Li, X., Chen, K.: Code-based ring signature scheme. Int. J. Netw. Secur. **5**(2), 154–157 (2007)

Towards Static Assumption Based Cryptosystem in Pairing Setting: Further Applications of DéjàQ and Dual-Form Signature (Extended Abstract)

Sanjit Chatterjee and R. Kabaleeshwaran[✉]

Department of Computer Science and Automation, Indian Institute of Science,
Bangalore, India
{sanjit,kabaleeshwar}@iisc.ac.in

Abstract. A large number of parameterized complexity assumptions have been introduced in the bilinear pairing setting to design novel cryptosystems and an important question is whether such "q-type" assumptions can be replaced by some static one. Recently Ghadafi and Groth captured several such parameterized assumptions in the pairing setting in a family called bilinear target assumption (BTA). We apply the DéjàQ techniques for all q-type assumptions in the BTA family. In this process, first we formalize the notion of extended adaptive parameter-hiding property and use it in the Chase-Meiklejohn's DéjàQ framework to reduce those q-type assumptions from subgroup hiding assumption in the asymmetric composite-order pairing. In addition, we extend the BTA family further into BTA1 and BTA2 and study the relation between different BTA variants. We also discuss the inapplicability of DéjàQ techniques on the q-type assumptions that belong to BTA1 or BTA2 family. We then provide one further application of Gerbush et al.'s dual-form signature techniques to remove the dependence on a q-type assumption for which existing DéjàQ techniques are not applicable. This results in a variant of Abe et al.'s structure-preserving signature with security based on a static assumption in composite order setting.

Keywords: Bilinear target assumption · q-type assumption
DejaQ technique · Dual form signature technique

1 Introduction

Rapid development of pairing-based cryptography has witnessed an enormous number of complexity assumptions. The thrust for new complexity assumptions become somewhat unavoidable due to the role they play in the security reduction of many novel construction of cryptographic protocols. For example, Boneh and Boyen [5] introduced strong Diffie-Hellman (SDH) assumption to propose a

© Springer Nature Switzerland AG 2018
J. Baek et al. (Eds.): ProvSec 2018, LNCS 11192, pp. 220–238, 2018.
https://doi.org/10.1007/978-3-030-01446-9_13

signature scheme in the standard model and Abe et al. [2] introduced a tailor-made assumption (later called as q-AGHO assumption) to prove the security of their structure preserving signature scheme.

Parameterized Assumptions. This type of non-static q-type assumptions have been extensively used in the security argument of pairing-based protocols. For example, the q-SDH assumption and its variants q-hidden SDH (HSDH), q-asymmetric hidden SDH (ADHSDH), (q, ℓ)-Poly-SDH, q-2 variable SDH (2SDH) are used in various signature schemes [5,8,16,27]. The parameter q is typically related to the number of (signing) oracle queries given to the adversary in the security game. However, parameterized assumptions do have some implication on concrete security and may require larger size for the underlying groups. Also it is observed that the parameterized assumption becomes stronger as these parameters grow. In particular Cheon [15] proved that for q-SDH assumption, the secret information (say x) can be recovered using $O(\sqrt{p/q})$ group operations, where p is the underlying group order. Jao and Yoshida [24] proved that q-SDH assumption is equivalent to Boneh-Boyen signature and also showed that given access to a sufficient number of signing oracle queries, an adversary can recover the secret signing key much faster than solving the discrete log problem. Hence, it's relevant to investigate whether for a particular cryptosystem one can remove the dependency on parameterized assumption. Two prominent approaches in this direction are DéjàQ [11,12] and dual-form signature techniques [19].

BTA. Boneh, Boyen and Goh [6] introduced the Uber assumption family which captures many complexity assumptions under it. Boyen [9] informally suggested to extend the Uber assumption family to those assumptions with (a) flexible challenge terms, (b) rational polynomial exponents in both problem instance and challenge terms, (c) composite-order group of known or unknown factorization. Recently, Ghadafi and Groth [22] focused on the first two points above in the context of non-interactive computational assumptions. In the bilinear pairing setting, they formulated the bilinear target assumption (BTA) family. In the BTA family, the exponent of both problem instance and challenge terms are represented using rational polynomials and all the polynomial coefficients are given explicitly as $\mathbb{Z}_p$ elements, where p is the group order. The challenge terms are determined by the adversary's input, whose exponents are represented as coefficients of a rational polynomial. However there are many tailor-made assumptions that are not captured by this BTA family. Some examples are (q, ℓ)-Poly-SDH [8], q-AGHO [2], q-simultaneous flexible pairing (SFP) [1] etc.

In this work we focus on q-type assumptions that belong to BTA family for which no reduction is known from subgroup hiding (SGH) assumption. Examples of such assumptions are generalized q-co-SDH [17] and Boneh-Boyen computational Diffie-Hellman (BB-CDH) assumption [3].

DéjàQ. Our main approach is to use the DéjàQ framework. The seminal work of Chase and Meiklejohn [12] showed that certain parameterized assumptions are implied by SGH assumption in the asymmetric composite-order pairing. In particular, they gave a reduction from SGH to certain q-type assumptions such as decisional q-type assumptions which are one sided (for example, exponent q-SDH assumption) and computational q-type assumptions which are two sided (q-Diffie-Hellman inversion assumption). Also they gave a reduction for q-SDH from SGH assumption, which is having flexible challenge term. However they were not able to give a reduction for those q-type assumptions where challenge terms belong to the target group G_T in the bilinear pairing setting (for example, q-DDHE assumption). This is solved by Chase et al.'s [11] extended framework. Their technique treats the generators of different groups using separate ways in the asymmetric composite-order pairing. In particular separate generators are used to answer separate types of queries and because of the access to additional randomness, these generators are indistinguishable by the bounded adversary. In 2015, Wee [29] came up with similar approach at protocol level instead of assumption level, but in the symmetric composite-order pairing setting.

Dual-Form Signatures. Our second approach for removing dependence on parameterized assumption is to utilize Gerbush et al.'s [19] dual-form signature techniques. For example, we consider the Abe et al.'s structure-preserving signature scheme [2] which is used as a building block in other cryptosystems [20, 21]. The security of Abe et al.'s structure-preserving signature is proved under q-AGHO assumption. We observe that the existing DéjàQ technique is not applicable to reduce this q-AGHO assumption to SGH assumption. Hence we construct a dual-form of Abe et al.'s structure-preserving signature scheme and prove its security under SGH assumption. The dual-form signature technique may change the scheme construction slightly from the original, as it introduces some additional randomness in the construction to argue security based on static assumption. For example, in the full version of this paper [13], we construct the dual-form of Boyen-Waters [10] group signature scheme under static assumption instead of the originally used q-HSDH assumption.

1.1 Our Contribution

1. We extend the BTA family further (in Sect. 3.2) to capture the assumptions (q, ℓ)-Poly-SDH, q-AGHO, q-SFP and q-HSDH, which are not covered under BTA family [22]. Also we investigate the relation among these new variants in Sect. 3.3.
2. We formalize the extended adaptive parameter-hiding property (in Sect. 4.1). Then we use it in the Chase-Meiklejohn's DéjàQ framework to give a reduction from subgroup hiding assumption to all the q-type assumptions that belong to BTA family (in Sect. 4.2). As a consequence, we can prove the security of Fuchsbauer et al.'s set commitment scheme [17] under subgroup hiding assumption, instead of generalized q-co-SDH and q-co-DL assumptions used in the original proof.
3. We construct the dual-form variant of Abe et al.'s structure-preserving signature scheme in Sect. 5.1 whose security is proved under subgroup hiding assumption instead of q-AGHO assumption. Similarly, in the full version [13], we construct the dual-form variant of Boyen-Waters group signature scheme

whose security is proved under subgroup hiding assumption instead of q-HSDH assumption.

2 Preliminaries

2.1 Notation

Let X denote the vector representation of m monomials $(X_1, \ldots, X_m)$. Let $q(X) = \sum a_{k_1, \ldots, k_m} X_1^{k_1} \cdots X_m^{k_m}$ be the multivariate polynomial of degree $d \geq 0$ with m variables, where the summation is taken over all $k_i \in [0, d]$ such that $\sum_{i=1}^{m} k_i \leq d$. The polynomial $q(X)$ is represented using the coefficients $(a_{k_1, \ldots, k_m})_{\substack{k_i \in [0,d] \\ \sum_i k_i \leq d}}$. We denote $q(x)$ to be the polynomial $q(X)$ which is evaluated at $X = x$, for $x \in \mathbb{Z}_p^m$, for some prime p. We also denote $x \xleftarrow{\$} G$ to be the element x which is chosen uniformly at random from the group G. Similarly, for any randomized algorithm A, $y \xleftarrow{\$} A(x)$ denotes the algorithm A which takes the value x from the appropriate domain and outputs y uniformly at random. For any function f, $f.\mathcal{D}$ denotes the domain of f. For any $n \in \mathbb{N}$, we denote $[1, n]$ to be the collection of all natural numbers that lies between 1 and n. Throughout this paper, λ denotes the security parameter.

2.2 Definitions

We first begin by recalling the definition of a bilinear group generator from [12].

Definition 1. *A bilinear group generator $\mathcal{G}$ is a probabilistic polynomial time (PPT) algorithm which takes the security parameter λ as input and outputs (N, G, H, G_T, e, μ), where N is either prime or composite, G, H and G_T are the groups such that $|G| = |H| = k_1 N$ and $|G_T| = k_2 N$ for $k_1, k_2 \in \mathbb{N}$, all the elements of G, H, G_T are of order atmost N and $e : G \times H \longrightarrow G_T$ is a bilinear map and it satisfies, (i) Bilinearity: For all $g, g' \in G$ and $h, h' \in H$, one has $e(g \cdot g', h \cdot h') = e(g, h) \cdot e(g, h') \cdot e(g', h) \cdot e(g', h')$, (ii) Non degeneracy: If a fixed $g \in G$ satisfies $e(g, h) = 1$ for all $h \in H$, then $g = 1$ and similarly for elements of H and (iii) Computability: The map e is efficiently computable. The additional information μ is optional and defined as follows. Whenever G and H are prime-order cyclic groups, then μ contains their respective generators g and h. Whenever the groups G and H are decomposed into its cyclic subgroups $G_1, \ldots, G_n$ and $H_1, \ldots, H_n$ respectively, then μ contains the description of these subgroups and/or their generators.*

The bilinear group generator $\mathcal{G}$ is said to be composite-order (resp. prime-order), if N is composite (resp. prime). In this paper we use both prime-order and composite-order bilinear group generator simultaneously. Hence for ease of readability, we use the following notation to differentiate between these two settings. In the prime-order setting, we denote $\mathbb{G}_1 = G$, $\mathbb{G}_2 = H$, $\mathbb{G}_T = G_T$ and we could obtain only trivial subgroups, hence μ contains the generators g and h of the respective groups $\mathbb{G}_1$ and $\mathbb{G}_2$. In the composite-order setting, we decompose the groups $G \cong G_1 \oplus \ldots \oplus G_n$ and $H \cong H_1 \oplus \ldots \oplus H_n$ for $N = p_1 \ldots p_n$ with μ containing required subgroup information i.e., μ contains $\{g_i, h_i\}_{i=1}^n$, where g_i (resp. h_i) is the generator of the subgroup G_i (resp. H_i).

Now we define the subgroup hiding assumption in the composite-order pairing setting and one can see that it is equivalent to the definition given by [12].

Definition 2. *Consider a composite-order bilinear group generator $\mathcal{G}$ which takes λ as input and outputs (N, G, H, G_T, e, μ). $\mathcal{G}$ is said to satisfy the subgroup hiding assumption in G for subgroup G_1 with respect to μ, if for every PPT adversary $\mathcal{A}$ the following advantage is negligible in the security parameters,*

$$Adv_{\mathcal{A}}^{SGH_G} = \left| Pr[\mathcal{A}(N, G, x, \mu) = 1 : x \in G] - Pr[\mathcal{A}(N, G, x, \mu) = 1 : x \in G_1] \right|$$

where $g_1 \in \mu$. Similarly we can define the subgroup hiding (SGH) assumption in H.

From the above definition it is clear that the choice of μ might make the subgroup hiding easy. In the above definition, if μ contains h_2 then one can easily decide whether the given element x is from the subgroup G_1 or from the group G, by checking $e(x, h_2) \stackrel{?}{=} 1$. Without loss of generality we assume that μ does not contain such elements which make the SGH easy.

In this paper we will be using several computational parameterized (q-type) assumptions which are given in the full version [13].

3   Bilinear Target Assumption and Its Extension

Boneh et al. [6] introduced Uber assumption (we call it classical Uber) and argued its security in the generic group model. However Boyen [9, Sect. 6] informally suggested to capture the Uber assumptions which have (a) challenge terms with adversary's input and (b) rational polynomial representation in the exponent. In 2017, Ghadafi and Groth [22] formalized an assumption family which captures the above features in both cyclic group setting and in the bilinear group setting of prime-order. The first assumption type is said to be target assumption family. Whereas the second type is known as bilinear target assumption (BTA) family and here we focus on this assumption family.

In this section we recall the definition of BTA family [22]. We identify some of the concrete computational assumptions which satisfy Boyen's (a) and (b), but will not fall under this BTA family. Hence we extend the BTA definition to capture such computational assumptions. We also look at the possible relation among the BTA family and its extension.

First, we fix some notation which will be used in this section. Let us denote the generator of the groups $\mathbb{G}_1$, $\mathbb{G}_2$ and $\mathbb{G}_T$ by $[1]_1$, $[1]_2$ and $[1]_T$ respectively. Hence $[a]_1$ denote the group element having discrete logarithm of a with respect to its generator $[1]_1$ in $\mathbb{G}_1$. Similarly we denote $[a]_2$ (resp. $[a]_T$) for the group element in $\mathbb{G}_2$ (resp. $\mathbb{G}_T$). The group operation $[a]_1 \cdot [b]_1$ is denoted as $[a+b]_1$ in $\mathbb{G}_1$. For the other groups $\mathbb{G}_2$ and $\mathbb{G}_T$, we follow the similar notation. The pairing operation is denoted as $e([a]_1, [b]_2) = [ab]_T$.

3.1   Definition

We fix some notation to define the BTA assumption. As we know that the BTA is a family of computational assumptions which are defined in the cyclic group of prime order p. Hence any group element can be written as its discrete logarithm value exponentiated with a fixed random generator of that group. Ghadafi and Groth [22] represented those exponent values using some multivariate rational polynomials of bounded degree. Let X be the indeterminate with m variables and $a(X)$, $b(X)$ denote the multivariate polynomials of degree $d \geq 0$ over $\mathbb{Z}_p$. For randomly chosen x from $\mathbb{Z}_p^m$ such that $b(x) \neq 0$, we denote $\left[\frac{a(x)}{b(x)}\right]_j$ be the group element from $\mathbb{G}_j$ having exponent which is represented using the rational polynomial $\frac{a(X)}{b(X)}$ evaluated at $X = x$, for $j \in \{1, 2, T\}$. Since the polynomials are represented using the coefficients, we denote that $[a(X)]_i$ (resp. $[b(X)]_i$) be the coefficient representation of the polynomial $a(X)$ (resp. $b(X)$) in the group $\mathbb{G}_i$, for $i, j \in \{1, 2, T\}$.

   In the BTA assumption [22] exponent of both problem instance and challenge term are represented using rational polynomials and all the polynomial coefficients are given explicitly as $\mathbb{Z}_p$ elements. More formally we define as follows.

Assumption 1 BTA. *Let $\Theta = (p, \mathbb{G}_1, \mathbb{G}_2, \mathbb{G}_T, e)$ be the output of a bilinear group generator $\mathcal{G}$ on the input λ. For $\iota \in \{1, 2, T\}$, $\mathcal{G}$ is said to satisfy bilinear target assumption [22] in $\mathbb{G}_\iota$, if for every PPT adversary $\mathcal{A}$, the advantage as defined below. Let $Adv_{\mathcal{A}}^{BTA_{\mathbb{G}_\iota}} := Pr[\mathcal{A}(\Gamma) \xrightarrow{\$} \Delta : \Delta$ satisfies **cond** 1] and it is negligible in the security parameters, where the problem instance Γ is defined as*

$$\Gamma = \left(\Theta, \left\{ \left\{ \left[\frac{a_i^{(j)}(x)}{b_i^{(j)}(x)} \right]_j, \frac{a_i^{(j)}(X)}{b_i^{(j)}(X)} \right\}_{i=1}^{n_j} \right\}_{j \in \{1,2,T\}}, pub \right)$$

and the challenge term Δ is defined as

$$\Delta = \left(\left[\frac{r(x)}{s(x)} \right]_\iota, r(X), s(X), sol \right).$$

The condition **cond** *1 is defined as,*

$$r(X) \prod_{i=1}^{n_\iota} b_i^{(\iota)}(X) \notin Span\left(\left\{ s(X) a_i^{(\iota)}(X) \prod_{l \neq i} b_l^{(\iota)}(X) \right\}_{i=1}^{n_\iota} \right). \tag{1}$$

The condition from Eq. 1 is used to avoid the trivial attacks due to generic group operations. The above defined BTA assumption is parameterized with (d, m, n_1, n_2, n_T), where d denotes the degree of polynomials (from both problem instance and challenge terms[1]) and m denotes the number of indeterminates in X and for $j \in \{1, 2, T\}$, n_j denotes the total number of elements from $\mathbb{G}_j$ which are present in the problem instance. Once the parameter is clear from the context, for simplicity we ignore this parameter. In the above definition, pub contains all the coefficients of the polynomials presented in the problem instance and sol contains some additional information in order to validate the challenge term. The secret vector x that is used in the assumption should not be given explicitly as part of the problem instance.

Example 1. *We recall the generalized q-co-SDH problem [17] defined in Table 1 of [13]: given the instance $\left(\{[1]_j, \{[x^i]_j\}_{i=1}^{q}\}_{j=1}^{2} \right)$ compute $\left(r(X), s(X), \left[\frac{r(x)}{s(x)} \right]_1 \right)$ such that $0 \leq deg\ r(X) < deg\ s(X) \leq q$. Note that this assumption is same as q-bilinear simple fractional assumption (BSFrac) [22] defined in $\mathbb{G}_1$. We represent the exponent values as a polynomial in X which is evaluated at $X = x$. Hardness of this problem ensures that the challenge term satisfies Eq. 1. Thus the generalized q-co-SDH assumption belongs to BTA family with $d = q$, $m = 1$, $n_1 = n_2 = q + 1$, $n_T = 0$.* □

Similarly it is easy to check that the assumptions such as q-Diffie-Hellman inversion (DHI), q-Diffie-Hellman exponent (DHE) q-modified SDH (mSDH), q-modified double SDH (mDSDH) and BB-CDH (see Table 1 of [13]) are examples for BTA family, since all the polynomial coefficients of both problem instance and challenge term are given explicitly.

3.2   BTA Extension

Recall that in the BTA definition all the polynomial coefficients in both problem instance and challenge term are given explicitly. However there are many assumptions in which not all the polynomial coefficients from problem instance and challenge terms are given explicitly. Some examples of such assumptions are q-HSDH, q-SFP, q-Triple Diffie-Hellman (TDH), q-simultaneous pairing (SP). See the complete list of such assumptions in Table 1 of [13].

Before defining the variants of BTA we observe that we could extend Ghadafi and Groth's BTA definition by including more number of challenge terms, in particular polynomial number of terms. However one can see that this extension is equivalent to the original BTA assumption.

First we motivate the definition of BTA1 with a concrete assumption. Recall that, Abe et al. [2] defined a variant of q-AGHO assumption (see Table 1 of [13]).

Example 2. *We recall the q-AGHO' problem defined in Table 1 of [13]: given $\left([1]_1, [1]_2, [w]_2, [x]_2, [y]_2, \left\{ [x - a_i w - r_i y]_1, [a_i]_1, [r_i]_1, [a_i^{-1}]_2 \right\}_{i=1}^{q} \right)$ compute $([x - $*

---

[1] For BTA in $\mathbb{G}_T$, the degree of the challenge term polynomials are bounded by $2d$, as given the d degree polynomials in both source groups, one can use the pairing to compute the product of these polynomials in $\mathbb{G}_T$.

$a^*w - r^*y]_1, [a^*]_1, [r^*]_1, [(a^*)^{-1}]_2)$. *As in Example 1, the exponent values are represented using polynomials in W, X and Y which are evaluated at $W = w$, $X = x$ and $Y = y$. The exponent values such as a_i, r_i from the instance and a^*, r^* from the challenge terms are the coefficients of the polynomials. In this assumption, none of the polynomial coefficients are given explicitly rather given as the exponent of the source group element. Here the parameters can be computed with $d = 1$, $m = 3$, $n_1 = 3q+1$, $n_2 = q+4$, $n_{c_1} = 3$, $n_{c_2} = 1$ and $n_T = n_{c_T} = 0$, where n_{c_j} denotes the total number of challenge terms in $\mathbb{G}_j$, for $j \in \{1, 2, T\}$.* □

From the above example, we define a new family of BTA variant called BTA1, in which not all the polynomial coefficients in both problem instance and challenge terms are given explicitly, rather given in the exponent of some source group element. In this paper we focus on the BTA1 family defined only in the source groups, since all the known instances of the parameterized assumptions described in Table 1 of [13] are defined in the source groups.

Assumption 2 BTA1. *Let $\Theta = (p, \mathbb{G}_1, \mathbb{G}_2, \mathbb{G}_T, e) \xleftarrow{\$} \mathcal{G}(\lambda)$. For $\iota \in [1, 2]$, $\mathcal{G}$ is said to satisfy bilinear target assumption-1 (BTA1) in $\mathbb{G}_\iota$, if for every PPT adversary $\mathcal{A}$, the advantage as defined below. Let*

$$Adv_\mathcal{A}^{BTA1_{\mathbb{G}_\iota}} := Pr[\mathcal{A}(\Gamma) \xrightarrow{\$} \Delta : \Delta \text{ satisfies either } \textbf{cond } 2 \text{ or } \textbf{cond } 3]$$

and it is negligible in λ, where

$$\Gamma = \left(\Theta, \left\{ \left\{ \left[\frac{a_i^{(j)}(\boldsymbol{x})}{b_i^{(j)}(\boldsymbol{x})} \right]_j, \left(\left\{ \left[a_i^{(j)}(\boldsymbol{X}) \right]_{j_a} \right\}_{j_a=1}^2 \text{ or } a_i^{(j)}(\boldsymbol{X}) \right), \right. \right. \right.$$
$$\left. \left. \left. \left(\left\{ \left[b_i^{(j)}(\boldsymbol{X}) \right]_{j_b} \right\}_{j_b=1}^2 \text{ or } b_i^{(j)}(\boldsymbol{X}) \right) \right\}_{i=1}^{n_j} \right\}_{j \in \{1,2,T\}}, \textbf{pub} \right),$$

$$\Delta = \left(\left\{ \left[\frac{r_t^{(\iota)}(\boldsymbol{x})}{s_t^{(\iota)}(\boldsymbol{x})} \right]_\iota, \left(\left\{ \left[r_t^{(\iota)}(\boldsymbol{X}) \right]_{\iota_r} \right\}_{\iota_r=1}^2 \text{ or } r_t^{(\iota)}(\boldsymbol{X}) \right), \right. \right.$$
$$\left. \left. \left(\left\{ \left[s_t^{(\iota)}(\boldsymbol{X}) \right]_{\iota_s} \right\}_{\iota_s=1}^2 \text{ or } s_t^{(\iota)}(\boldsymbol{X}) \right) \right\}_{t=1}^{n_{c_\iota}}, \textbf{sol} \right).$$

The condition $\textbf{cond } 2$ states that, there exists $t \in [1, n_{c_\iota}]$ with atleast one of the following condition should satisfy, either $\left[r_t^{(\iota)}(\boldsymbol{X}) \right]_\iota$ or $\left[s_t^{(\iota)}(\boldsymbol{X}) \right]_\iota$ or $\left[\frac{r_t^{(\iota)}(\boldsymbol{X})}{s_t^{(\iota)}(\boldsymbol{X})} \right]_\iota$

$$\notin Span\left(\left\{ \left[\frac{a_i^{(\iota)}(\boldsymbol{X})}{b_i^{(\iota)}(\boldsymbol{X})} \right]_\iota \right\}_{i=1}^{n_\iota}, \left\{ \left[a_{i_1}^{(\iota_1)}(\boldsymbol{X}) \right]_\iota, \left[b_{i_2}^{(\iota_2)}(\boldsymbol{X}) \right]_\iota \right\}_{\substack{\iota_1, \iota_2 \in \{1,2\} \\ i_1, i_2 \in [1,n_1] \cup [1,n_2]}} \right). \quad (2)$$

Also the condition **cond** 3 states that, for $\varsigma = 3 - \iota$, either $\left[r_t^{(\varsigma)}(\boldsymbol{X})\right]_\varsigma$ or $\left[s_t^{(\varsigma)}(\boldsymbol{X})\right]_\varsigma$

$$\notin Span\left(\left\{\left[\frac{a_i^{(\varsigma)}(\boldsymbol{X})}{b_i^{(\varsigma)}(\boldsymbol{X})}\right]_\varsigma\right\}_{i=1}^{n_\varsigma}, \left\{\left[a_{i_1}^{(\iota_1)}(\boldsymbol{X})\right]_\varsigma, \left[b_{i_2}^{(\iota_2)}(\boldsymbol{X})\right]_\varsigma\right\}_{\substack{\iota_1,\iota_2\in\{1,2\}\\i_1,i_2\in[1,n_1]\cup[1,n_2]}}\right). \quad (3)$$

The above defined BTA1 family is parameterized with $(d, m, n_1, n_2, n_T, n_{c_1}, n_{c_2}, n_{c_T})$, where n_{c_j} denotes the total number of challenge terms from $\mathbb{G}_j$, for $j \in \{1, 2, T\}$ and the remaining parameters are defined as in BTA family. The condition from Eqs. 2 and 3 are used to avoid the trivial attacks due to generic group operation. As some of the challenge terms are given in the exponent instead of as $\mathbb{Z}_p$ element, this will be more flexible to mount some trivial attacks due to generic group operations. As a concrete example, we explain this attack for the variant of q-SDH assumption described in the following remark.

Remark 1. *We consider the q-2SDH$_S$ problem [27]: given $\left(\left\{[1]_j, [x]_j, [y]_j\right\}_{j=1}^2, \left\{[a_i]_1, [a_i]_2, b_i, \left[\frac{y+b_i}{x+a_i}\right]_j\right\}_{i=1}^q\right)$ compute $\left(\left[\frac{y+d}{x+c}\right]_1, [c]_1, [c]_2, d\right)$, for $d \neq b_i$. As in Example 1, we represent the exponent values as polynomials in X and Y which are evaluated at $X = x$ and $Y = y$. One can solve this problem by computing $\left[\frac{y+d}{x+c}\right]_1 = [y]_1 [d]_1, [c]_1 = [1-x]_1$ and $[c]_2 = [1-x]_2$, for $d \xleftarrow{\$} \mathbb{Z}_p$ with $d \neq b_i$, for all $i \in [1, q]$. This attack is captured using **cond** 2 and **cond** 3.*

From the definition of BTA1, it is easy to see that assumptions such as q-HSDH, q-ADHSDH, q-SFP and q-AGHO (defined in Table 1 of [13]) belong to BTA1 family, since not all the polynomial coefficients in both problem instance and challenge terms are given explicitly.

Now consider the BB-HSDH assumption [3] in which all the polynomial coefficients of the problem instance are given explicitly, whereas all the polynomial coefficients of the challenge terms are given in the exponent of both source groups. Thus BB-HSDH assumption will not fall under BTA1 family. This motivate us to define another variant of BTA family, called BTA2. There are many assumptions such as q-TDH, q-SP, (q, ℓ, ℓ')-Pluri-SDH and (q, ℓ)-Poly-SDH (see Table 1 of [13]) that fall in this family.

Assumption 3 BTA2. *Let $\Theta = (p, \mathbb{G}_1, \mathbb{G}_2, \mathbb{G}_T, e) \xleftarrow{\$} \mathcal{G}(\lambda)$. For $\iota \in [1, 2]$, $\mathcal{G}$ is said to satisfy bilinear target assumption-2 (BTA2) in $\mathbb{G}_\iota$, if for every PPT adversary $\mathcal{A}$, the advantage as defined below. Let*

$$Adv_{\mathcal{A}}^{BTA2_{\mathbb{G}_\iota}} := Pr[\mathcal{A}(\Gamma) \xrightarrow{\$} \Delta : \Delta \text{ satisfies either } \textbf{cond } 2 \text{ or } \textbf{cond } 3]$$

and it is negligible in λ, where

$$\Gamma = \left(\Theta, \left\{\left\{\left[\frac{a_i^{(j)}(\boldsymbol{x})}{b_i^{(j)}(\boldsymbol{x})}\right]_j, a_i^{(j)}(\boldsymbol{X}), b_i^{(j)}(\boldsymbol{X})\right\}_{i=1}^{n_j}\right\}_{j\in\{1,2,T\}}, pub\right),$$

$$\Delta = \left(\left\{ \left[\frac{r_t^{(\iota)}(\boldsymbol{x})}{s_t^{(\iota)}(\boldsymbol{x})} \right]_\iota, \left(\left\{ \left[r_t^{(\iota)}(\boldsymbol{X}) \right]_{\iota_r} \right\}_{\iota_r=1}^2 \; or \; r_t^{(\iota)}(\boldsymbol{X}) \right), \right.$$

$$\left. \left(\left\{ \left[s_t^{(\iota)}(\boldsymbol{X}) \right]_{\iota_s} \right\}_{\iota_s=1}^2 \; or \; s_t^{(\iota)}(\boldsymbol{X}) \right) \right\}_{t=1}^{n_{c_\iota}}, \; sol \right).$$

The conditions for this assumption remains same as in BTA1.

Similar to BTA1, BTA2 family is parameterized with $(d, m, n_1, n_2, n_T, n_{c_1}, n_{c_2}, n_{c_T})$. Conditions **cond** 2 and **cond** 3 ensure that trivial attacks due to generic group operation can be avoided. In order to better understand the importance of the conditions **cond** 2 and **cond** 3, consider the following problem. Given $\left(\left\{ [1]_j, [x]_j \right\}_{j=1}^2, \left\{ \left[\frac{1}{x+a_i} \right]_1, a_i \right\}_{i=1}^q \right)$ whether we can compute the challenge terms $\left(\left[\frac{1}{x+a} \right]_1, [a]_1, [a]_2 \right)$ or not. Similar to Remark 1, one can solve this problem using generic group operation.

Also we observe that there are assumptions in which challenge terms do not output all the polynomial coefficients even in the exponent of a group element. As a concrete example we describe the (q, ℓ)-Poly-SDH assumption [8] and we show that it belongs to BTA2 family.

Example 3. *Refer to the (q, ℓ)-Poly-SDH problem defined in [13]: given the instance $\left([1]_1, [1]_2, \; \left\{ [x_i]_1, [x_i]_2 \right\}_{i=1}^\ell, \; \left\{ \left[\frac{1}{x_i+c_{ij}} \right]_1, \; c_{ij} \right\}_{i,j=1}^{\ell,q} \right)$ compute $\left(\left\{ \left[\frac{\gamma_i}{x_i+c_i} \right]_1, c_i \right\}_{i=1}^\ell \right)$ such that $\sum_{i=1}^\ell \gamma_i = 1$. As similar to previous examples, the exponent values which are having terms like x_i are represented as polynomials in $\{X_i\}_{i=1}^\ell$ that are evaluated at $X_i = x_i$ and all the remaining exponent values are the coefficients of the polynomials. In this assumption, none of the numerator's polynomial coefficients of the challenge terms (i.e., γ_i) are given explicitly. However the condition $\sum_{i=1}^\ell \gamma_i = 1$ is included as part of sol, which ensure the wellformedness of the challenge terms by $\prod_{i=1}^\ell e\left(\left[\frac{\gamma_i}{x_i+c_i} \right]_1, [x_i]_2 [c_i]_2 \right) \stackrel{?}{=} e([1]_1, [1]_2)$. The hardness of this assumption [8] requires that it also satisfy the Eqs. 2 and 3. Thus (q, ℓ)-Poly-SDH assumption belongs to BTA2 family.* $\qquad \square$

3.3 Relation Among BTA Variants

We briefly discuss the relation among newly defined variants of BTA assumption. Since BTA is a family of assumptions, Ghadafi and Groth [22] used the following notion to prove the reduction between two families $\mathcal{F}_1$ and $\mathcal{F}_2$. For any assumption $\mathcal{P}_1$ in $\mathcal{F}_1$, there exists an assumption $\mathcal{P}_2$ in $\mathcal{F}_2$ such that $\mathcal{P}_2$ implies $\mathcal{P}_1$, which ensures that the assumption family $\mathcal{F}_2$ reduces to $\mathcal{F}_1$. Using this reduction, we prove that the assumptions in BTA2 family could be a possible candidate Uber assumption as compared to the assumptions in BTA and BTA1 families. We emphasize that while describing BTA and its variants we use both assumption and family interchangeably.

Lemma 1. *(i) For any (d, m, n_1, n_2, n_T)-BTA assumption, there exists $(d, m, n_1, n_2, n_T, n_{c_1}, n_{c_2}, n_{c_T})$-BTA2 assumption such that BTA2 implies BTA. (ii) For any $(d, m, n_1, n_2, n_T, n_{c_1}, n_{c_2}, n_{c_T})$-BTA1 assumption, there exists $(d, m, n_1, n_2, n_T, n_{c_1}, n_{c_2}, n_{c_T})$-BTA2 assumption such that BTA2 implies BTA1.*

Proof of this lemma can be found in the full version [13].

However it's still an open problem whether such implications will also hold in the other directions. The source of the difficulty for proving that BTA is reducible to BTA1 and BTA is reducible to BTA2 (resp. BTA1 is reducible to BTA and BTA1 is reducible to BTA2) is computing the discrete logarithm for the challenge terms (resp. problem instance) in the appropriate groups.

4   BTA in DéjàQ Framework

In this section we prove that subgroup hiding implies all the q-type assumptions that belong to bilinear target assumption (BTA) family. Recall that Chase-Mciklejohn's [12] DéjàQ framework ensures the reduction from SGH to q-SDH and q-generalized Diffie-Hellman exponent (q-GDHE) assumptions. However they did not consider the assumptions such as generalized q-co-SDH, q-mDSDH and BB-CDH. We notice that generalized q-co-SDH assumption was used to prove the security of Fuchsbauer et al.'s set commitment scheme [17]. To the best of our knowledge no prior work proved that generalized q-co-SDH assumption is implied by SGH assumption. Hence it is worth investigating whether SGH assumption implies the parameterized assumptions that belong to BTA family.

First we formalize the extended adaptive parameter-hiding property and use this property in Chase-Meiklejohn's DéjàQ techniques [12]. We also discuss the apparent inapplicability of the existing DéjàQ techniques for the concrete q-type assumptions that fall in either BTA1 or BTA2 family.

4.1   Extended Adaptive Parameter-Hiding Property

Parameter-hiding [25] is a property which ensures that the elements in one subgroup do not reveal anything about related elements in other subgroups. Chinese Remainder Theorem (CRT) ensures the same in the composite-order pairing setting. Lewko [25] informally used parameter-hiding property to convert Lewko-Waters IBE scheme from composite-order to prime-order pairing. In 2014, Chase and Meiklejohn [12] defined parameter-hiding property for any polynomial function in the composite-order setting and used it to prove SGH implies decisional q-type assumption which are one-sided,[2] such as exponent q-SDH assumption [30]. Also, they defined *extended parameter-hiding* property and used it to prove SGH implies the computational q-type assumptions which are two-sided, such as q-SDH assumption. Informally, extended parameter hiding property says that

---

[2] We say that the BTA assumption defined in the asymmetric pairing setting is one-sided, if the secret vector x associated with the polynomial representation occurs in exactly one of the source groups. Otherwise we say that the assumption is two-sided.

the distributions $\{g_1^{f(x)} g_2^{f(x)}\}$ and $\{g_1^{f(x)} g_2^{f(x')}\}$ are identical, even if some auxiliary informations are given in the exponent of h_1. The other definition by Chase and Meiklejohn is the *adaptive parameter-hiding* property. Informally, this property ensures that any unbounded adversary who makes only polynomial number of queries cannot statistically distinguish between the distributions $\{g_1^{f(x)} g_2^{f(x)}\}$ and $\{g_1^{f(x)} g_2^{f'(x)}\}$, for any f, f' from the family of functions $\mathcal{F}$. In particular, they have used this property for rational polynomial function of the form $\frac{1}{x+c}$ with c being chosen by the adversary.

Now we consider the computational q-type assumptions that belong to BTA family which are two-sided in which all the polynomial coefficients of the challenge terms are chosen by the adversary. Hence it is natural to use the adaptive parameter-hiding property along with some auxiliary information. We note that this idea has been already noted by Chase and Meiklejohn [12, footnote 2] to prove SGH implies q-SDH assumption. Similarly we can use the adaptive parameter-hiding property for the computational q-type assumptions which are one-sided. Now we formally define the extended adaptive parameter-hiding property for any function as follows.

Definition 3. *Let $\mathcal{G}$ be a bilinear group generator and functions f, f' are chosen at random from a family of functions $\mathcal{F}$. Let Aux denote the auxiliary information. Let $\mathcal{O}(\cdot)$ be the oracle that returns $g_1^{f(\cdot)} g_2^{f(\cdot)}$ if the input is in the domain $f.\mathcal{D}$ and 1 otherwise. Similarly, let $\mathcal{O}'(\cdot)$ be the oracle that returns $g_1^{f(\cdot)} g_2^{f'(\cdot)}$ if the input is in the domain $f.\mathcal{D} \cap f'.\mathcal{D}$ and 1 otherwise. Let $\Theta = (N, G, H, G_T, e, \mu) \xleftarrow{\$} \mathcal{G}(\lambda),$[3] where $\mu = \{g_1, g_2\}$, $g_1 \in G_1$, $g_2 \in G_2$ and $G \cong G_1 \oplus G_2$. We say that $\mathcal{G}$ satisfies extended adaptive parameter-hiding with respect to $\mathcal{F}$ and Aux, if the oracles $\mathcal{O}$ and $\mathcal{O}'$ are statistically indistinguishable and if they are given with auxiliary information Aux and queried polynomially many times. In other words, for any unbounded adversary $\mathcal{A}$ that makes $poly(\lambda)$ queries, there exists a negligible function $\nu(\cdot)$ such that*

$$\left| Pr[f \xleftarrow{\$} \mathcal{F} : \mathcal{A}^{\mathcal{O}(\cdot)}(\Theta, Aux) = 1] - Pr[f, f' \xleftarrow{\$} \mathcal{F} : \mathcal{A}^{\mathcal{O}'(\cdot)}(\Theta, Aux) = 1] \right| < \nu(\cdot).$$

We emphasize that the above definition is applicable for any function, in particular it can be applied for rational polynomial functions in the following way. Consider the functions f and f' which take rational polynomial coefficients as input and evaluate on some random vectors x and x' from $\mathbb{Z}_N^m$, i.e., the function f is defined as $f(r(X), s(X)) := \frac{r(x)}{s(x)}$ and f' is defined as $f'(r(X), s(X)) := \frac{r(x')}{s(x')}$, where $r(X)$ and $s(X)$ denote the coefficient representation of the polynomials of degree d (defined over $\mathbb{Z}_N$) with m many monomials. We know that in the BTA family, given the instance, adversary chooses some random coefficients which determine the challenge term. Hence we can apply the extended adaptive parameter-hiding property for this rational polynomials. Also we consider the

---

[3] Even if $N = p_1 \ldots p_n$, we decompose G using two of its subgroups G_1 and G_2 such that G_1 (resp. G_2) is a subgroup of order $p_1 \ldots p_{n-1}$ (resp. p_n).

auxiliary information as $\mathsf{Aux} = \{h_1^{\zeta^{(j)}(\boldsymbol{x})}\}_{j=2,T}$ for BTA assumption defined in G, where $\zeta^{(j)}(\boldsymbol{x}) \in \left\{ \frac{a_i^{(j)}(\boldsymbol{x})}{b_i^{(j)}(\boldsymbol{x})} \right\}_{i=1}^{n_j}$.

4.2 SGH Implies BTA

In this section we prove that all the q-type assumptions that belong to BTA family defined in composite-order pairing setting can be reduced from SGH assumption. This reduction uses the extended adaptive parameter-hiding property (Definition 3). As mentioned earlier, instead of polynomial function of the form $f(\boldsymbol{X})$, we apply this property for rational polynomial function of the form $\frac{f_1(\boldsymbol{X})}{f_2(\boldsymbol{X})}$.

For the q-type assumption that belongs to BTA family, it is guaranteed from the BTA definition that atleast one of the parameter from $\{n_1, n_2, n_T\}$ can be written as some function of q, where $q = poly(\lambda)$. Now we consider the BTA assumption defined in G. As a concrete example, we consider generalized q-co-SDH assumption described in Example 1 that belongs to BTA family with $n_1 = n_2 = q + 1$ and $n_T = 0$. Now, without loss of generality, it is sufficient to consider the BTA assumption defined in G with n_1 being expressed as some function of q. For the BTA assumption with n_2 being expressed as some function of q can be handled as follows. Consider a BTA problem instance (say $\mathcal{P}_1$) defined in G where n_1 and n_T are some constants but n_2 is expressed as some function of q (say $n_2(q)$). First one can construct a stronger problem (say $\mathcal{P}_2$) from $\mathcal{P}_1$ by including all its $n_2(q)$ many exponents of H component to the exponent of G. Then we can apply our DéjàQ framework on $\mathcal{P}_2$ assumption. This guarantees that SGH is reducible to $\mathcal{P}_1$ via $\mathcal{P}_2$ assumption. Similarly we can handle the BTA assumption with n_T being some function of q.

Now we proceed with Chase-Meiklejohn's DéjàQ framework along with extended adaptive parameter-hiding property on BTA assumption with n_1 being expressed as some function of q. First we define a variant of BTA assumption, which will be useful while proving SGH implies BTA assumption.

Assumption 4. *Let* $\Theta = (N, G, H, G_T, e, \mu) \xleftarrow{\$} \mathcal{G}(\lambda)$ *with* $\mu = \{G_1, G_2\}$. $\mathcal{G}$ *is said to satisfy a variant of bilinear target assumption (vBTA) in* G, *if for every PPT adversary* $\mathcal{A}$ *and for all* $\ell = poly(\lambda)$, *the following advantage is negligible in* λ, $Adv_{\mathcal{A}}^{vBTA_G} := Pr[\mathcal{A}(\Gamma) \xleftarrow{\$} \Delta]$,[4] *where*

---

[4] As similar to BTA assumption, hardness of Assumption 4 ensures that the instance and challenge terms should satisfy certain linearly independent condition that corresponds to Eq. 1. However we directly prove the hardness of Assumption 4 in Corollary 1. This guarantees that the above condition automatically satisfies and hence we do not need to explicitly state such condition here.

$$\Gamma = \left(\Theta, g_1 g_2^{\sum_{i=1}^{\ell} r_i}, h_1, \left\{ g_1^{\frac{a_i^{(1)}(x)}{b_i^{(1)}(x)}} g_2^{\sum_{j=1}^{\ell} r_j \frac{a_i^{(1)}(x_j)}{b_i^{(1)}(x_j)}} \right\}_{i=1}^{n_1}, \left\{ h_1^{\frac{a_i^{(2)}(x)}{b_i^{(2)}(x)}} \right\}_{i=1}^{n_2}, \right.$$

$$\left. \left\{ e(g_1, h_1)^{\frac{a_i^{(T)}(x)}{b_i^{(T)}(x)}} \right\}_{i=1}^{n_T}, \left\{ \left\{ \frac{a_i^{(\iota)}(X)}{b_i^{(\iota)}(X)} \right\}_{i=1}^{n_\iota} \right\}_{\iota \in \{1,2,T\}}, pub \right),$$

for $g_1 \xleftarrow{\$} G_1$, $g_2 \xleftarrow{\$} G_2 \setminus \{1\}$ and $r_j \xleftarrow{\$} \mathbb{Z}_N$, $x, x_j \xleftarrow{\$} \mathbb{Z}_N^m$, for all $j \in [1, \ell]$ and the output Δ is $\left(g_1^{\frac{r(x)}{s(x)}} g_2^{\sum_{j=1}^{\ell} r_j \frac{r(x_j)}{s(x_j)}}, r(X), s(X), sol \right)$.

Now we prove that BTA assumption (Assumption 1) defined in G is implied by Assumption 4 using subgroup hiding assumption and extended adaptive parameter-hiding property.

Theorem 1. *For a bilinear group generator $\mathcal{G}(\lambda) \xrightarrow{\$} (N, G, H, G_T, e, \mu)$, consider $\mathcal{G}$ satisfies (d, m, n_1, n_2, n_T) bilinear target assumption in G. Suppose that $\mathcal{G}$ satisfies the following, (i) subgroup hiding assumption for subgroup G_1 with respect to $\mu = \{g_2, h_1\}$ and for subgroup H_1 with respect to $\mu = \{g_1\}$ and (ii) extended adaptive parameter-hiding with respect to*

$$\mathcal{F} = \left\{ \left\{ \frac{a_i^{(1)}(x)}{b_i^{(1)}(x)} \right\}_{i=1}^{n_1}, \frac{r(x)}{s(x)} \right\} \text{ and } \mathsf{Aux} = \{h_1^{\zeta}\}_{\zeta \in} \left\{ \left\{ \frac{a_j^{(2)}(x)}{b_j^{(2)}(x)} \right\}_{i=1}^{n_2}, \left\{ \frac{a_j^{(T)}(x)}{b_j^{(T)}(x)} \right\}_{i=1}^{n_T} \right\}$$

for any $h_1 \in H_1$ and if G_2 is of prime-order, then the BTA assumption is implied by the Assumption 4.

Proof Sketch. The detailed proof can be found in the full version [13]. Here we give the proof sketch and it uses the hybrid argument using a sequence of games. The intuitive idea as follows, consider the BTA assumption defined over composite-order bilinear groups, first translate all the elements from the group of composite-order to its subgroup of order p_1. Thus the elements of G and H are shifted to subgroups G_1 and H_1 and this shifting goes unnoticed under subgroup hiding in G and H respectively. Notice that the challenge term of BTA belongs to the group G, as BTA is defined in G. Since the exponent of the group elements are interpreted as rational polynomials that are evaluated at some secret vector x, the translation of elements from G_1 into G_2 retains the same polynomial evaluation as its shadow copy in the exponent of G_2. This transition is unnoticed under subgroup hiding in G. Now the shadow copy of the rational polynomials that corresponds to the subgroup G_2's exponents are evaluated using different secret vector x_1 and is statistically indistinguishable to its previous state. This transition is achieved by using the extended adaptive parameter-hiding property defined in Definition 3. We repeat the above procedure polynomial many times (say ℓ) and thus prove the theorem. $\square$

In order to prove the hardness of Assumption 4, it is sufficient to take ℓ to be $n_1 + 2$ in the following Corollary 1. This implies that SGH is reducible to BTA assumption.

Corollary 1. *For a bilinear group generator $\mathcal{G}(\lambda) \xrightarrow{\$} (N, G, H, G_T, e, \mu)$, $\mathcal{G}$ satisfies (d, m, n_1, n_2, n_T)-BTA assumption in G, if (i) $N = p_1 \ldots p_n$ for distinct primes $p_1, \ldots, p_n \in \Omega(2^\lambda)$ and $\mathcal{G}$ satisfies the following, (ii) subgroup hiding for subgroup G_1 with respect to $\mu = \{g_2, h_1\}$ and for subgroup H_1 with respect to $\mu = \{g_1\}$, (iii) extended adaptive parameter-hiding with respect to class $\mathcal{F}$ and Aux which are defined as in Theorem 1 and (iv) the polynomials in $\mathcal{F}$ are linearly independent and have maximum degree poly(λ).*

Proof. From the requirements (ii) and (iii), Theorem 1 tells us that BTA assumption is implied by the Assumption 4. In order to prove this corollary, it is sufficient to prove that the advantage as defined in Assumption 4 is negligible in the security parameter. Now for the sake of simplicity we assume that g_1 and $\boldsymbol{x}$ are public. Hence adversary can compute the G_1 component of any challenge term, which boils down to computing $g_2^{\sum_{j=1}^{\ell} r_j \frac{r(\boldsymbol{x}_j)}{s(\boldsymbol{x}_j)}}$. Also note that the auxiliary information Aux doesn't provide any advantage in computing the above element, since they operate on different groups with completely independent set of variables. Consider the following matrix from the G_2 component of Assumption 4,

$$
V = \begin{pmatrix}
1 & \frac{a_1^{(1)}(\boldsymbol{x}_1)}{b_1^{(1)}(\boldsymbol{x}_1)} & \cdots & \frac{a_{n_1}^{(1)}(\boldsymbol{x}_1)}{b_{n_1}^{(1)}(\boldsymbol{x}_1)} & \frac{r(\boldsymbol{x}_1)}{s(\boldsymbol{x}_1)} \\
\vdots & \vdots & \ddots & \vdots & \vdots \\
1 & \frac{a_1^{(1)}(\boldsymbol{x}_\ell)}{b_1^{(1)}(\boldsymbol{x}_\ell)} & \cdots & \frac{a_{n_1}^{(1)}(\boldsymbol{x}_\ell)}{b_{n_1}^{(1)}(\boldsymbol{x}_\ell)} & \frac{r(\boldsymbol{x}_\ell)}{s(\boldsymbol{x}_\ell)}
\end{pmatrix}.
$$

Here we set ℓ as $n_1 + 2$. Including the requirement (iv), [12, Lemma 4.1] ensures that the above matrix V is nonsingular. For randomly chosen vector $\boldsymbol{r}$ from $\mathbb{Z}_N^{n_1+2}$ (it was chosen during the simulation, see the full version [13]), we define $\boldsymbol{y} = \boldsymbol{r} \cdot V$. Thus from this matrix relation, the first $n_1 + 1$ elements are given to $\mathcal{A}$ and his goal is to compute the last element of $\boldsymbol{y}$. Since V is invertible and $\boldsymbol{r}$ is chosen uniformly at random from $\mathbb{Z}_N^{n_1+2}$, then the vector $\boldsymbol{y}$ is uniformly at random from $\mathbb{Z}_N^{n_1+2}$. In particular the last element of $\boldsymbol{y}$ is uniformly distributed. Hence probability of computing such challenge term is negligible in the security parameter. $\qquad\square$

In the full version [13], we show that the SGH assumption implies all the q-type assumptions that belong to BTA family defined in G_T. From the definition of BTA1 and BTA2, the polynomial coefficient of the challenge terms and problem instance are not given explicitly. Hence one cannot apply the existing DéjàQ framework. The detailed explanation can be found in the full version [13].

5   Dual-Form Signature Variants

Here we consider two protocols whose security is proved under q-type assumptions that belong to either BTA1 or BTA2 family. The first one is Abe et al.'s

[2] structure-preserving signature (SPS) scheme which is proven secure under q-AGHO assumption. We apply the dual-form signature techniques of Gerbush et al.'s [19] to construct a dual-form SPS scheme where security is based on some static assumption. The detailed construction is described in Sect. 5.1. The second one is Boyen-Waters [10] group signature scheme which is secure under q-HSDH assumption. We describe the dual-form variant of Boyen-Waters group signature scheme in the full version [13].

5.1 Dual-Form Abe et al.'s Structure-Preserving Signature Scheme

Structure-preserving signature (SPS) is used as a building block to construct several cryptographic primitives such as group signature, blind signature, anonymous credentials etc. SPS is a special type of signature scheme where the message, public key and signature components belong to the underlying bilinear groups and the signature is verified using pairing product equations over the public key, the message and the signature.

Gerbush et al. introduced dual-form signature [19] which is defined using two signing algorithms, namely Sign_A and Sign_B that will respectively return two forms of signature and both will verify under the same public key. The security definition categorizes the forgeries into two types, Type I and Type II which typically correspond to the signatures returned by Sign_A and Sign_B respectively. See the full version [13] for the definition of dual-form signature, structure preserving signature schemes and their security.

Informally, we directly instantiate the original Abe et al.'s SPS scheme [2] in the asymmetric composite-order pairing and using dual-form signature techniques we prove its security under static assumption. Without loss of generality, in the following we assume that the signer chooses the message M from the group G. However the same techniques can be extended for the message vectors from either or both of the source groups G and H. Let $\Theta := (N = p_1 p_2, G, H, G_T, e, \mu = \{g_1', g_2', h_1'\}) \overset{\$}{\leftarrow} \mathcal{G}(\lambda)$, where g_i' (resp. h_1') is a random element from the p_i-order (resp. p_1-order) subgroup G_i (resp. H_1) of G (resp. H) and pairing is defined as $e : G \times H \to G_T$, for $i \in [1, 2]$. We instantiate the dual-form SPS scheme using the above mentioned bilinear group generator $\mathcal{G}$. In this construction, the public key and signatures returned by Sign_A algorithm reside in the subgroup of order p_1, whereas the signature returned by Sign_B algorithm resides in the group of order N. The dual-form SPS scheme consists of four PPT algorithms, which are defined as follows.

KeyGen(Θ). Choose g_i (resp. h_1) uniformly at random from G_i (resp. H_1). Choose w, x, y_1, y_2 uniformly at random from $\mathbb{Z}_N$ and compute $W = h_1^w, X = h_1^x, Y_1 = h_1^{y_1}$ and $Y_2 = h_1^{y_2}$. Return the secret key $SK = (w, x, y_1, y_2, g_2)$ and public key $PK = (g_1, h_1, W, X, Y_1, Y_2)$.

$\mathrm{Sign}_A(SK, M)$. Choose r (resp. a) uniformly at random from $\mathbb{Z}_N$ (resp. $\mathbb{Z}_N^*$). Compute $A = g_1^a, D = h_1^{1/a}, B = g_1^{x-aw-ry_1} M^{-y_2}$ and $R = g_1^r$. Return the signature $\sigma = (A, D, B, R)$ along with the message M.

$\text{Sign}_B(SK, M)$. Choose $r, \gamma_1, \gamma_2, \gamma_3$ (resp. a) uniformly at random from $\mathbb{Z}_N$ (resp. $\mathbb{Z}_N^*$). Compute $A = g_1^a g_2^{\gamma_1}$, $D = h_1^{1/a}$, $B = g_1^{x - aw - ry_1} M^{-y_2} g_2^{\gamma_2}$ and $R = g_1^r g_2^{\gamma_3}$. Return the signature $\sigma = (A, D, B, R)$ along with the message M.

$\text{Verify}(PK, M, \sigma)$. Parse the signature and check $A, B, R \overset{?}{\in} G, D \overset{?}{\in} H_1$.[5] If any of the above checks fail to hold, then abort, else check

$$e(R, h_1) \neq 1, \ e(A, D) \overset{?}{=} e(g_1, h_1)$$
$$e(B, h_1)e(A, W)e(R, Y_1)e(M, Y_2) \overset{?}{=} e(g_1, X). \tag{4}$$

If all the above relations hold then return *accept*, otherwise return *reject*.

The signature returned by both Sign_A and Sign_B algorithms can be verified using Eq. 4. It is easy to check the correctness of the scheme from Eq. 4. Similar to Abe et al.'s [2] SPS scheme, we prove the above dual-form SPS scheme is secure in the sense of strongly unforgeable. The detailed proof can be found in the full version [13].

References

1. Abe, M., Fuchsbauer, G., Groth, J., Haralambiev, K., Ohkubo, M.: Structure-preserving signatures and commitments to group elements. In: Rabin, T. (ed.) CRYPTO 2010. LNCS, vol. 6223, pp. 209–236. Springer, Heidelberg (2010). https://doi.org/10.1007/978-3-642-14623-7_12
2. Abe, M., Groth, J., Haralambiev, K., Ohkubo, M.: Optimal structure-preserving signatures in asymmetric bilinear groups. In: Rogaway, P. (ed.) CRYPTO 2011. LNCS, vol. 6841, pp. 649–666. Springer, Heidelberg (2011). https://doi.org/10.1007/978-3-642-22792-9_37
3. Belenkiy, M., Camenisch, J., Chase, M., Kohlweiss, M., Lysyanskaya, A., Shacham, H.: Randomizable proofs and delegatable anonymous credentials. In: Halevi, S. (ed.) CRYPTO 2009. LNCS, vol. 5677, pp. 108–125. Springer, Heidelberg (2009). https://doi.org/10.1007/978-3-642-03356-8_7
4. Belenkiy, M., Chase, M., Kohlweiss, M., Lysyanskaya, A.: P-signatures and non-interactive anonymous credentials. In: Canetti, R. (ed.) TCC 2008. LNCS, vol. 4948, pp. 356–374. Springer, Heidelberg (2008). https://doi.org/10.1007/978-3-540-78524-8_20
5. Boneh, D., Boyen, X.: Short signatures without random oracles. In: Cachin, C., Camenisch, J.L. (eds.) EUROCRYPT 2004. LNCS, vol. 3027, pp. 56–73. Springer, Heidelberg (2004). https://doi.org/10.1007/978-3-540-24676-3_4
6. Boneh, D., Boyen, X., Goh, E.-J.: Hierarchical identity based encryption with constant size ciphertext. In: Cramer, R. (ed.) EUROCRYPT 2005. LNCS, vol. 3494, pp. 440–456. Springer, Heidelberg (2005). https://doi.org/10.1007/11426639_26
7. Boneh, D., Gentry, C., Waters, B.: Collusion resistant broadcast encryption with short ciphertexts and private keys. In: Shoup, V. (ed.) CRYPTO 2005. LNCS, vol. 3621, pp. 258–275. Springer, Heidelberg (2005). https://doi.org/10.1007/11535218_16

---

[5] First we check A (resp. D) belongs to G (resp. H) by verifying $A^N = 1_G$ (resp. $D^N = 1_H$). Then the pairing equation $e(A, D) = e(g_1, h_1)$ ensures that D indeed belongs to subgroup H_1.

8. Boyen, X.: Mesh signatures. In: Naor, M. (ed.) EUROCRYPT 2007. LNCS, vol. 4515, pp. 210–227. Springer, Heidelberg (2007). https://doi.org/10.1007/978-3-540-72540-4_12

9. Boyen, X.: The uber-assumption family. In: Galbraith, S.D., Paterson, K.G. (eds.) Pairing 2008. LNCS, vol. 5209, pp. 39–56. Springer, Heidelberg (2008). https://doi.org/10.1007/978-3-540-85538-5_3

10. Boyen, X., Waters, B.: Full-domain subgroup hiding and constant-size group signatures. In: Okamoto, T., Wang, X. (eds.) PKC 2007. LNCS, vol. 4450, pp. 1–15. Springer, Heidelberg (2007). https://doi.org/10.1007/978-3-540-71677-8_1

11. Chase, M., Maller, M., Meiklejohn, S.: Déjà Q all over again: tighter and broader reductions of q-type assumptions. In: Cheon, J.H., Takagi, T. (eds.) ASIACRYPT 2016. LNCS, vol. 10032, pp. 655–681. Springer, Heidelberg (2016). https://doi.org/10.1007/978-3-662-53890-6_22

12. Chase, M., Meiklejohn, S.: Déjà Q: using dual systems to revisit q-type assumptions. In: Nguyen, P.Q., Oswald, E. (eds.) EUROCRYPT 2014. LNCS, vol. 8441, pp. 622–639. Springer, Heidelberg (2014). https://doi.org/10.1007/978-3-642-55220-5_34

13. Chatterjee, S., Kabaleeshwaran, R.: Towards static assumption based cryptosystem in pairing setting: further applications of DéjàQ and dual-form signature. IACR Cryptology ePrint Archive 2018/738 (2018)

14. Chatterjee, S., Menezes, A.: On cryptographic protocols employing asymmetric pairings - the role of Ψ revisited. Discrete Appl. Math. 159(13), 1311–1322 (2011)

15. Cheon, J.H.: Security analysis of the strong Diffie-Hellman problem. In: Vaudenay, S. (ed.) EUROCRYPT 2006. LNCS, vol. 4004, pp. 1–11. Springer, Heidelberg (2006). https://doi.org/10.1007/11761679_1

16. Fuchsbauer, G.: Automorphic signatures in bilinear groups and an application to round-optimal blind signatures. IACR Cryptology ePrint Archive 2009/320 (2009)

17. Fuchsbauer, G., Hanser, C., Slamanig, D.: Structure-preserving signatures on equivalence classes and constant-size anonymous credentials. IACR Cryptology ePrint Archive 2014/944 (2014)

18. Fuchsbauer, G., Pointcheval, D., Vergnaud, D.: Transferable constant-size fair e-cash. In: Garay, J.A., Miyaji, A., Otsuka, A. (eds.) CANS 2009. LNCS, vol. 5888, pp. 226–247. Springer, Heidelberg (2009). https://doi.org/10.1007/978-3-642-10433-6_15

19. Gerbush, M., Lewko, A., O'Neill, A., Waters, B.: Dual form signatures: an approach for proving security from static assumptions. In: Wang, X., Sako, K. (eds.) ASIACRYPT 2012. LNCS, vol. 7658, pp. 25–42. Springer, Heidelberg (2012). https://doi.org/10.1007/978-3-642-34961-4_4

20. Ghadafi, E.: Efficient distributed tag-based encryption and its application to group signatures with efficient distributed traceability. In: Aranha, D.F., Menezes, A. (eds.) LATINCRYPT 2014. LNCS, vol. 8895, pp. 327–347. Springer, Cham (2015). https://doi.org/10.1007/978-3-319-16295-9_18

21. Ghadafi, E.: Stronger security notions for decentralized traceable attribute-based signatures and more efficient constructions. In: Nyberg, K. (ed.) CT-RSA 2015. LNCS, vol. 9048, pp. 391–409. Springer, Cham (2015). https://doi.org/10.1007/978-3-319-16715-2_21

22. Ghadafi, E., Groth, J.: Towards a classification of non-interactive computational assumptions in cyclic groups. In: Takagi, T., Peyrin, T. (eds.) ASIACRYPT 2017. LNCS, vol. 10625, pp. 66–96. Springer, Cham (2017). https://doi.org/10.1007/978-3-319-70697-9_3

23. Groth, J., Lu, S.: A non-interactive shuffle with pairing based verifiability. In: Kurosawa, K. (ed.) ASIACRYPT 2007. LNCS, vol. 4833, pp. 51–67. Springer, Heidelberg (2007). https://doi.org/10.1007/978-3-540-76900-2_4
24. Jao, D., Yoshida, K.: Boneh-Boyen signatures and the strong Diffie-Hellman problem. In: Shacham, H., Waters, B. (eds.) Pairing 2009. LNCS, vol. 5671, pp. 1–16. Springer, Heidelberg (2009). https://doi.org/10.1007/978-3-642-03298-1_1
25. Lewko, A.: Tools for simulating features of composite order bilinear groups in the prime order setting. In: Pointcheval, D., Johansson, T. (eds.) EUROCRYPT 2012. LNCS, vol. 7237, pp. 318–335. Springer, Heidelberg (2012). https://doi.org/10.1007/978-3-642-29011-4_20
26. Mitsunari, S., Sakai, R., Kasahara, M.: A new traitor tracing. IEICE Trans. Fundam. Electron. Commun. Comput. Sci. 85(2), 481–484 (2002)
27. Okamoto, T.: Efficient blind and partially blind signatures without random oracles. In: Halevi, S., Rabin, T. (eds.) TCC 2006. LNCS, vol. 3876, pp. 80–99. Springer, Heidelberg (2006). https://doi.org/10.1007/11681878_5
28. Okamoto, T.: Efficient blind and partially blind signatures without random oracles. IACR Cryptology ePrint Archive 2006/102 (2006)
29. Wee, H.: Déjà Q: encore! Un petit IBE. IACR Cryptology ePrint Archive 2015/1064 (2015)
30. Zhang, F., Safavi-Naini, R., Susilo, W.: An efficient signature scheme from bilinear pairings and its applications. In: Bao, F., Deng, R., Zhou, J. (eds.) PKC 2004. LNCS, vol. 2947, pp. 277–290. Springer, Heidelberg (2004). https://doi.org/10.1007/978-3-540-24632-9_20

Digital Signatures from the Middle-Product LWE

Ryo Hiromasa[✉]

Mitsubishi Electric, Kanagawa, Japan
Hiromasa.Ryo@aj.MitsubishiElectric.co.jp

Abstract. We construct digital signatures secure in the quantum random oracle model (QROM) under the middle-product learning with errors problem, which is recently proposed by Roşca et al. (CRYPTO 2017) and shown by Roşca et al. (EUROCRYPT 2018) that it can be reduced from the worst-case hardness of ideal lattice problems for a large class of polynomial rings. The previous signatures secure under the lattice problems not specified in a certain ring is based on the short integer solution (SIS) problems for bounded-degree polynomials (Lyubashevsky, ASIACRYPT 2016). The standard path to construct efficient signatures secure in the QROM (Kiltz et al., EUROCRYPT 2018) requires hardness of a decision problem, but the SIS problems for polynomial rings are not known to have search-to-decision reductions. Our signatures are the first efficient signatures *secure in the QROM* under the *worst-case hardness* of ideal lattice problems for *many rings*.

Keywords: Lattices-based cryptography · Digital signatures
Middle-product learning with errors

1 Introduction

Lattice-based cryptography takes very much attention in the post-quantum era. Besides that the lattice-based cryptography has resilience to quantum computers, they have many attracting features for practical use-cases. One of such features is that breaking a lattice-based cryptosystems leads to solve the worst-case instance of an underlying lattice problem.

Almost provably secure lattice-based cryptosystems are shown to be secure under two problems: the short integer solution (SIS) problem of [2] and the learning with errors (LWE) problem of [22]. Infeasibility of the both problems is guaranteed by the worst-case hardness of a lattice problem: solving a randomly chosen instance of these problems leads to find a short vector in any lattices with non-negligible probability. This worst-case hardness guarantee helps us to choose an exact secure parameter for cryptographic schemes whose security is proven under the hardness of these problems.

The security of efficient lattice-based cryptosystems (such as [4,6,11]) are often based on the hardness of ring- or module-LWE [17,20]. It was known that

© Springer Nature Switzerland AG 2018
J. Baek et al. (Eds.): ProvSec 2018, LNCS 11192, pp. 239–257, 2018.
https://doi.org/10.1007/978-3-030-01446-9_14

solving a ring-LWE problem leads to approximate a short vector in ideal lattices corresponding to a certain cyclotomic polynomial [20,21]. There are some attacks [8–10] that use the structure of an underlying integer ring for the cyclotomic polynomial to solve the lattice problem. In particular, Cramer et al. [10] showed that efficient quantum algorithms can approximate a short vector with subexponential factor in ideal lattices for cyclotomic polynomials. The module-LWE was also known to have the worst-case hardness guarantee of a problem over module lattices. Albrecht et al. [3] showed that the module-LWE can be reduced to the ring-LWE for a large modulus (whose size depends on the rank of the underlying module). Therefore, breaking a specific ideal lattice problem for cyclotomic polynomials means that the cryptographic scheme constructed on the hardness of the ring- or module-LWE problem may be broken by adversaries.

It may be hopeful that lattice-based cryptographic schemes meet security guarantee not regarding to a specific polynomial rings. There are two works that hardness of SIS- and LWE-like assumptions can be ensured under a large class of polynomials. In the SIS-case, Lyubashevsky [19] proposed the signature scheme whose security is proven under the Ring-SIS problem not parametrized by a certain polynomial: the problem can be reduced from every SIS problems in polynomial rings with some bounded degree. Also on the LWE-case, Roşca et al. [23] showed that the middle-product LWE (MPLWE) problem can be reduced from the polynomial LWE problems for polynomials with bounded degree and expansion factor, where solving the polynomial LWE leads to approximate a short vectors in ideal lattices for any modulus and many polynomial rings [21,24]. The hardness of solving the MPLWE problem is a base of the Titanium public-key encryption [26], which is the one of NIST submissions for post-quantum cryptography.

For security against a quantum adversary, we also need to consider the case where a quantum adversary may execute offline cryptographic primitives such as hash functions on arbitrary superposition. The security model that maintain such situations is the quantum random oracle model (QROM). A standard path to construct efficient signatures secure in the QROM is the generic transformation of [16], which showed that Fiat-Shamir transformed signatures from a lossy identification scheme [1,15] can be secure in the quantum random oracle model. The lossy identification is usually constructed under the hardness of a decision problem. To construct lossy identification secure under a lattice assumption not regarding a specific ring in the QROM, we may first consider to use the decision variant of the Ring-SIS problem. As well as the search Ring-SIS can be reduced from every search SIS problem for bounded degree polynomials [19], the decision variant of that problem is reduced from every decision SIS for such polynomials. While the search version of the SIS can be guaranteed by the worst-case hardness of lattice problems for the polynomial ring, the decision SIS does not have any worst-case hardness guarantee because we do not know any search-to-decision reduction of the SIS for polynomial rings.

Therefore, the ultimate goal of achieving quantum security for lattice-based signatures is to build the signature scheme so that its security is based on the *worst-case hardness* of ideal lattice problems for a *large family of polynomial rings* in the *QROM*.

1.1 Our Result

In this paper, we construct digital signatures secure in the QROM under the MPLWE problem. The MPLWE problem is recently proposed by Roşca et al. [23], and shown that it has the worst-case hardness guarantee of ideal lattice problems for many polynomial rings [24]. Our signatures are obtained by adapting [16]'s transformation, which is a quantumly secure variant of the Fiat-Shamir transformation [13], to the lossy identification constructed under the MPLWE. The resulting signature scheme from our identification scheme can be seen as an MPLWE variant of Dilithium-QROM in [16], so the [5,11]-like compression technique for the MPLWE setting is applied to our signatures.

2 Preliminaries

We denote the set of natural numbers by $\mathbb{N}$, and the set of integers by $\mathbb{Z}$. In this paper, we use the standard interval notations: for any integers $a, b \in \mathbb{Z}$, the notation (a, b) (or $[a, b]$) means the set $\{x \in \mathbb{Z}$ s.t. $a < x < b\}$ (or $\{x \in \mathbb{Z}$ s.t. $a \leq x \leq b\}$, respectively). For any positive integer $d > 0$, we abuse an interval notation $[d]$ to represent the set $\{1, 2, \ldots, d\}$. Let S be a set and $\mathcal{P}$ be a probability distribution over S. Then, $a \xleftarrow{\$} S$ means that $a \in S$ is chosen uniformly at random from S, and $b \xleftarrow{\$} \mathcal{P}$ means that $b \in S$ is sampled from $\mathcal{P}$. The notation $\mathsf{negl}(\lambda)$ represents the set of negligible functions for $\lambda \in \mathbb{N}$.

2.1 Identification Schemes

A (canonical) identification scheme is a two-party three-move protocol between a prover and verifier. The prover first sends a message w called commitment, and the verifier chooses a uniformly random challenge c from a set $\mathcal{C}$. When given a response z from the prover, the verifier makes a deterministic decision.

Definition 1 (Canonical Identification Schemes). *A (canonical) identification scheme* ID *is defined as the triple of the following algorithms* ID := (IGen, P, V)

- *The instance generation algorithm* IGen *takes as input a security parameter* λ, *and outputs a public and secret key* (pk, sk). *Suppose that the public key* pk *defines the commitment, challenge, and response set:* $\mathcal{W}$, $\mathcal{C}$, *and* $\mathcal{Z}$, *respectively.*
- *The prover algorithm* P *is split into two algorithms* P = (P₁, P₂) *where* P₁ *takes as input secret key* sk, *and outputs a commitment* $w \in \mathcal{W}$ *and state information* st; P₂ *takes as input a secret key* sk, *commitment* $w \in \mathcal{W}$, *challenge* $c \in \mathcal{C}$, *and state* st, *and outputs a response* $z \in \mathcal{Z}$.

– *The Verifier algorithm* V *takes a public key* pk, *and transcript of the conversation between the prover and verifier,* (w, c, z), *and outputs* 1 *or* 0.

A transcript is a tuple of three elements $(w, c, z) \in \mathcal{W} \times \mathcal{C} \times \mathcal{Z}$. The transcript (w, c, z) is valid if $V(pk, w, c, z) = 1$.

Definition 2 (Transcript). *A transcript algorithm* Tr, *which takes as input a secret key* sk *and outputs a honestly generated transcript (i.e., a result of real interaction of a prover and verifier)* $(w, c, z) \in \mathcal{W} \times \mathcal{C} \times \mathcal{Z}$, *is defined as*

– $(w, \mathsf{st}) \xleftarrow{\$} \mathsf{P}_1(\mathsf{sk})$
– $c \xleftarrow{\$} \mathcal{C}$
– $z \xleftarrow{\$} \mathsf{P}_2(\mathsf{sk}, w, c, \mathsf{st})$
– *if* $z = \perp$ *then return* $(\perp, \perp, \perp)$
– *return* (w, c, z)

Correctness of the identification schemes is defined as all transcripts output by Tr and not including $\perp$ are valid, and $\perp$ is output by Tr with smaller probability than the given correctness error.

Definition 3 (Correctness). *Identification scheme* ID *is* ϵ_c-*correct if for all* $(\mathsf{pk}, \mathsf{sk}) \in \mathsf{IGen}(1^\lambda)$, *the following holds*

– *All possible transcripts* (w, c, z) *satisfying* $z \neq \perp$ *are valid, namely, for all* $(w, \mathsf{st}) \in \mathsf{P}_1(\mathsf{sk})$, *all* $c \in \mathcal{C}$, *and all* $z \in \mathsf{P}_2(\mathsf{sk}, q, c, \mathsf{st})$ *with* $z \neq \perp$, *we have* $V(\mathsf{pk}, w, c, z) = 1$.
– *The probability that a honestly generated transcript* (w, c, z) *contains* $z = \perp$ *is bounded by* ϵ_c, *that is,*

$$\Pr\left[z = \perp : (w, , c, z) \xleftarrow{\$} \mathsf{Tr}(\mathsf{sk})\right] \leq \epsilon_c.$$

No Abort Honest-Verifier Zero-Knowledge property [18] defined below is a weak variant of honest-verifier zero-knowledge property where transcripts of the protocol are required to be publicly simulatable, conditioned on $z \neq \perp$.

Definition 4 (No Abort Honest-Verifier Zero-Knowledge). *A canonical identification scheme* ID *is* ϵ_{ZK}-*perfect* naHVZK *(non-abort honest-verifier zero-knowledge) if there exist an algorithm* S *that given only the public key* pk, *outputs* (w, c, z) *such that the following holds:*

– *The statistical distance between the distribution of* $(w^*, c^*, z^*) \xleftarrow{\$} \mathsf{S}(\mathsf{pk})$ *and a real transcript* $(w, c, z) \xleftarrow{\$} \mathsf{Tr}(\mathsf{sk})$ *is at most* ϵ_{ZK}.
– *The distribution of* c^* *from the simulator* S *is uniformly random in* $\mathcal{C}$.

We define a notion of min-entropy for identification schemes, which says the probability that the most likely value of commitments output by the prover occurs, given an honestly-generated key pair.

Definition 5 (Min-Entropy). *We say that the identification scheme* ID *has* α*-bits of min-entropy if*

$$\Pr\left[H_{\min}(w : (w, \mathsf{st}) \xleftarrow{\$} P_1(\mathsf{sk})) \geq \alpha : (\mathsf{pk}, \mathsf{sk}) \xleftarrow{\$} \mathsf{IGen}(1^\lambda) \right] \geq 1 - 2^{-\alpha},$$

where for a probability distribution $\mathcal{D}$*,* $H_{\min}(w : w \xleftarrow{\$} \mathcal{D}) \geq \alpha$ *means that the most likely value of* w *chosen from* $\mathcal{D}$ *occurs with probability* $2^{-\alpha}$*.*

The lossy identification scheme is an identification scheme whose public key is indistinguishable from a special key called lossy key, on which a malicious prover cannot impersonate the verifier.

Definition 6 (Lossy Identification Schemes [1]). *An identification scheme* ID $=$ (IGen, P, V) *is lossy if there exists a lossy key generation algorithm* LossyIGen *that takes as input a security parameter* λ *and returns a lossy public key* $\mathsf{pk}_{\mathsf{ls}}$ *with the following properties:*

- *Lossy-Key Indistinguishability: The lossy key* $\mathsf{pk}_{\mathsf{ls}}$ *is indistinguishable from the real public key* pk *generated by the instance generation algorithm* IGen. *The advantage of a quantum adversary* $\mathcal{A}$ *in distinguishing between the lossy and public keys is defined by*

$$\mathsf{Adv}_{\mathcal{A}}^{\mathsf{LOSSY-IND}}(\lambda) := \left| \begin{array}{l} \Pr\left[\mathcal{A}(\mathsf{pk}_{\mathsf{ls}}) \to 1 : \mathsf{pk}_{\mathsf{ls}} \xleftarrow{\$} \mathsf{LossyIGen}(1^\lambda) \right] \\ - \Pr\left[\mathcal{A}(\mathsf{pk}) \to 1 : (\mathsf{pk}, \mathsf{sk}) \xleftarrow{\$} \mathsf{IGen}(1^\lambda) \right] \end{array} \right|.$$

- *Lossy Soundness: The identification scheme is* ϵ_{ls}*-sound if the probability that the unbounded adversary* $\mathcal{A}$ *with the lossy key successfully impersonate in the interaction with the honest verifier is negligible:*

$$\Pr\left[\mathsf{V}(\mathsf{pk}_{\mathsf{ls}}, w^*, c^*, z^*) \to 1 : \begin{array}{l} \mathsf{pk}_{\mathsf{ls}} \xleftarrow{\$} \mathsf{LossyIGen}(1^\lambda); \\ (w^*, \mathsf{st}) \xleftarrow{\$} \mathcal{A}(\mathsf{pk}_{\mathsf{ls}}); \\ c^* \xleftarrow{\$} \mathcal{C}; z^* \xleftarrow{\$} \mathcal{A}(\mathsf{st}, c^*) \end{array} \right] = \mathsf{negl}(\lambda)$$

2.2   Middle-Product Learning with Errors

We present the definition of the middle-product learning with errors (MPLWE) problem first introduced in [23]. We denote by $R^{<k}$ (or $R_q^{<k}$) the set of polynomials of coefficients in $\mathbb{Z}$ (or $\mathbb{Z}_q$ respectively) with degree at most $k - 1 > 0$. We write the ℓ_∞ norm and ℓ_2 norm for a polynomial r by $\|r\|_\infty$ and $\|r\|_2$, respectively, and, we use $S_\alpha^{<k}$ for $\alpha \in \mathbb{N}$ to denote the set of all elements w such that $\|w\|_\infty \leq \alpha$. For a polynomial $r := r_0 + r_1 x + \cdots + r_{k-1} x^{k-1} \in R^{<k}$ (or $r \in S^{<k}$), we use the notations $\mathbf{r} = (r_0, r_1, \ldots, r_{k-1})$ and $\bar{\mathbf{r}} = (r_{k-1}, r_{k-2}, \ldots, r_0)$. For a vector $\mathbf{r} \in R^k$, $\mathbf{r}[i; j]$ $(0 < i < j < k)$ denotes the vector with the coefficients from the i-th element through the j-th element of $\mathbf{r}$.

The middle-product of polynomials is used to accelerate computation in polynomial rings [14, 25]. Here we introduce the middle-product of two polynomials.

Definition 7 (Middle-Product). *Let* d_a, d_b, d, k *be integers such that* $d_a + d_b - 1 = d + 2k$. *The middle product* $\odot_d : R^{<d_a} \times R^{<d_b} \to R^{<d}$ *is the following map:*

$$(a, b) \mapsto a \odot_d b = \left\lfloor \frac{a \cdot b \bmod x^{k+d}}{x^k} \right\rfloor.$$

We use the notation $\odot_d$ *for every* d_a, d_b *such that* $d_a + d_b - 1 - d$ *is non-negative and even.*

The middle-product can instead be represented by a product between a Toeplitz matrix and vector, which can be computed in quasi-linear time.

Definition 8 (Toeplitz matrix). *For any* $d, k > 0$, *and* $a \in R^{<k}$, *we let* $\mathsf{Toep}^{d,k}(a)$ *denote the matrix in* $R^{d \times (k+d-1)}$ *whose i-th row, for* $i = 1, \ldots, d$, *is given by the coefficients of* $x^{i-1} \cdot a$.

Lemma 1 (Lemma 3.2 of [23]). *Let* $d, k > 0$. *Let* $r \in R^{<k+1}$, $a \in R^{<k+d}$, *and* $b := r \odot_d a$. *Then*

$$\bar{\mathbf{b}} = \mathsf{Toep}^{d,k+1}(r) \cdot \bar{\mathbf{a}}.$$

The above representation can be re-written as the following form by an easy deformation.

Corollary 1. *Let* $d, k > 0$. *Let* $r \in R^{<k+1}$, $a \in R^{<k+d}$, *and* $b := r \odot_d a$. *Then*

$$\mathbf{b} = \mathbf{A}\bar{\mathbf{r}},$$

where

$$\mathbf{A} = \left[\mathbf{a}[1; k+1] \parallel \mathbf{a}[2; k+2] \parallel \cdots \parallel \mathbf{a}[d; k+d]\right]^T$$

For polynomials with compatible dimensions, middle-product and polynomial product have the following property like associativity.

Lemma 2 (Lemma 3.3 of [23]). *Let* $d, k, n > 0$. *For all* $r \in R^{<k+1}$, $a \in R^{<n}$, $s \in R^{<n+d+k-1}$, *we have* $r \odot_d (a \odot_{d+k} s) = (r \cdot a) \odot_d s$.

On polynomials with the same dimensions of the above lemma, we can easily see that middle-product is *partially-commutative* from the commutative-property of polynomial products.

Corollary 2. *For the same* $r \in R^{<k+1}$, $a \in R^{<n}$, $s \in R^{<n+d+k-1}$ *in Lemma 2, we have* $r \odot_d (a \odot_{d+k} s) = a \odot_d (r \odot_{d+n-1} s)$.

Proof. From Lemma 2, it holds that

$$\begin{aligned} r \odot_d (a \odot_{d+k} s) &= (r \cdot a) \odot_d s \\ &= (a \cdot r) \odot_d s \\ &= a \odot_d (r \odot_{d+n-1} s). \end{aligned}$$

$\square$

Here we define the decision variant of the MPLWE problem [23], which is the problem to distinguish elements sampled from the MPLWE distribution and uniform distribution. The decision MPLWE assumption states that the MPLWE problem is infeasible for any efficient (classical or quantum) adversary.

Definition 9 (MPLWE Distribution). *Let $n, d > 0$, $q \geq 2$, and χ be a distribution over $\mathbb{Z}$. For $s \in R_q^{<n+d-1}$, we define the distribution $\mathsf{MPLWE}_{q,n,d,\chi}(s)$ over $R_q^{<n} \times R_q^{<d}$ as the one obtained by: sample $a \xleftarrow{\$} R_q^{<n}$, $e \xleftarrow{\$} \chi^{<d}$, and returning $(a, b := a \odot_d s + e)$.*

Definition 10 ((Decision) MPLWE Problem). *Let $n, d > 0$, $q \geq 2$, and χ be a distribution over $R^{<d}$. The (decision) $\mathsf{MPLWE}_{n,d,q,\chi}$ problem consists in distinguishing between arbitrary many samples from $\mathsf{MPLWE}_{n,d,q,\chi}(s)$ and the same number of samples from the uniform distribution over $R_q^{<n} \times R_q^{<d}$. For an adversary $\mathcal{A}$, the advantage of $\mathcal{A}$ for the $\mathsf{MPLWE}_{n,d,q,\chi}(s)$ problem is defined as*

$$\mathsf{Adv}_{\mathcal{A}}^{\mathsf{MPLWE}_{n,d,q,\chi}}(\lambda) := \left| \begin{array}{l} \Pr\left[1 \leftarrow \mathcal{A}(a, t) : (a, t) \xleftarrow{\$} \mathsf{MPLWE}_{n,d,q,\chi}(s)\right] \\ - \Pr\left[1 \leftarrow \mathcal{A}(a, t) : (a, t) \xleftarrow{\$} R_q^{<n} \times R_q^{<d}\right] \end{array} \right|,$$

where the probabilities are taken over $s \xleftarrow{\$} \chi$ and randomness of the adversary. The $\mathsf{MPLWE}_{n,d,q,\chi}$ assumption states that for any PPT algorithm it is infeasible to solve the $\mathsf{MPLWE}_{n,d,q,\chi}$ problem, namely $\mathsf{Adv}_{\mathcal{A}}^{\mathsf{MPLWE}}(\lambda) = \mathsf{negl}(\lambda)$.

The MPLWE problem can be reduced from the polynomial LWE problem for polynomials with bounded degree and expansion factor, and the polynomial LWE problem is known to be reducible from the worst-case hardness of approximating short vectors on ideal lattices [24]. To ready for introducing the reduction to the MPLWE problem, we now define the polynomial LWE problem and the expansion factor of polynomials.

Definition 11 (Polynomial LWE Problem PLWE). *Let $q > 0$ and f be a polynomial of degree $n > 0$. Let $R := \mathbb{Z}[x]/(f)$ and $R_q := R/qR$ be polynomial rings, and χ be a distribution over R. The $\mathsf{PLWE}_{q,\chi}^{(f)}$ problem is to distinguish the following two distribution:*

- *Sample $a \xleftarrow{\$} R_q$, $s \xleftarrow{\$} R_q$, and $e \xleftarrow{\$} \chi$, and output $(a, b := as + e) \in R_q^2$,*
- *Sample uniformly random elements $(a, b) \xleftarrow{\$} R_q^2$.*

Definition 12 (Expansion Factor). *The expansion factor of polynomial f with degree n is defined as $\max_{g \in \mathbb{Z}^{<2n-1}[x] \setminus \{0\}} \{\|g \bmod f\|_\infty / \|g\|_\infty\}$.*

The reduction of the following theorem supports Gaussian distribution, but we can immediately switch the distribution to some bounded uniform distribution. For $n, s > 0$, we denote by $D_{n,s}$ a Gaussian distribution over $\mathbb{Z}^n$ with parameter s.

Theorem 1 (Theorem 3.6 of [23]). *Let $n, d > 0$, $q \geq 2$, and $\alpha \in (0,1)$. For $S > 0$, we let $\mathcal{F}(S, d, n)$ denote the set of polynomial $f \in \mathbb{Z}[x]$ that are monic, have constant coefficient coprime with q, have degree $m \in [d, n]$ and whose expansion factor is less than S. Then there exists a PPT reduction from* $\mathsf{PLWE}_{q, D_{m, \alpha \cdot q}}^{(f)}$ *for any $f \in \mathcal{F}(S, d, n)$ to* $\mathsf{MPLWE}_{q, n, d, D_{d, \alpha' \cdot q}}$ *with $\alpha' = \alpha d S$.*

3   Lossy Identification from MPLWE

In this section, we give the construction of the lossy identification scheme $\mathsf{ID}_{\mathsf{MPLWE}}$ whose security is based on the MPLWE problem. Our identification can be seen as an MPLWE-analogue of the identification scheme for Dilithium-QROM [16]. The construction of the signatures obtained by applying the transformation of [16] to our identification is shown in Appendix A.

3.1   Supporting Algorithms

<u>Notations.</u> We first give the notational definitions of special modular reductions and a function with related to Boolean statements. For any integer r and any even (or odd) integer $\alpha > 0$, let $r' = r \bmod^{\pm} \alpha$ be the unique element $r' \in (-\alpha/2, \alpha/2]$ (or $r' \in [-(\alpha-1)/2, (\alpha-1)/2]$) such that $r' \equiv r \pmod{\alpha}$, and let $r' = r \bmod^{+} \alpha$ be the unique integer $r' \in [0, \alpha)$ such that $r' \equiv r \pmod{\alpha}$. Also, we denote by $[\![B]\!]$ the bit that is 1 if the Boolean statement B is true, and 0 otherwise.

<u>Algorithm Description.</u> Here we describe the supporting algorithms used in [11] to compress protocol messages of our identification scheme. The algorithms are defined over the integers, but can easily be generalized to the case over polynomials (or also vectors) via coefficient-wise application.

- $\mathsf{Power2Round}_q(r, d)$: Compute $r := r \bmod^{+} q$ and then set $r_0 := r \bmod^{\pm} 2^d$. Output $(r - r_0)/2^d$.
- $\mathsf{Decompose}_q(r, \alpha)$: Compute $r := r \bmod^{+} q$ and $r_0 := r \bmod^{\pm} \alpha$. If $r - r_0 = q - 1$ then set $r_1 := 0$ and $r_0 := r_0 - 1$, else set $r_1 := (r - r_0)/\alpha$. Output (r_1, r_0).
- $\mathsf{HighBits}_q(r, \alpha)$: Compute $(r_0, r_1) := \mathsf{Decompose}_q(r, \alpha)$ and output r_1.
- $\mathsf{LowBits}_q(r, \alpha)$: Compute $(r_0, r_1) := \mathsf{Decompose}_q(r, \alpha)$ and output r_0.
- $\mathsf{UseHint}_q(h, r, \alpha)$: Set $m := (q - 1)/\alpha$ and compute $(r_0, r_1) := \mathsf{Decompose}_q(r, \alpha)$. If $h = 1$ and $r_0 > 0$, then output $(r_1 + 1) \bmod^{+} m$. If $h = 1$ and $r_0 \leq 0$, then output $(r_1 - 1) \bmod^{+} m$.
- $\mathsf{MakeHint}_q(z, r, \alpha)$: Set $r_1 := \mathsf{HighBits}_q(r, \alpha)$ and $v_1 := \mathsf{HighBits}_q(r + z, \alpha)$, and outputs $[\![r_1 \neq v_1]\!]$.

The following two lemmas are useful facts that the above three supporting algorithms UseHint, MakeHint, and HighBits satisfy.

Lemma 3 (from [11,16]). *Suppose that q and α are positive integers satisfying $q > 2\alpha$, $q \equiv 1 \pmod{\alpha}$, and α even. Let r and z be elements in $R_q^{<n}$ where $\|z\|_\infty \le \alpha/2$ and let $\mathbf{h}, \mathbf{h}'$ be binary vectors. Then the $\mathsf{HighBits}_q$, $\mathsf{MakeHint}_q$ and $\mathsf{UseHint}_q$ algorithms satisfy the following properties:*

- $\mathsf{UseHint}_q(\mathsf{MakeHint}_q(z, r, \alpha), r, \alpha) = \mathsf{HighBits}_q(r + z, \alpha)$
- *Let* $\mathbf{v}_1 := \mathsf{UseHint}_q(\mathbf{h}, r, \alpha)$. *Then* $\|r - \mathbf{v}_1 \cdot \alpha\|_\infty \le \alpha + 1$.
- *For any* $\mathbf{h}, \mathbf{h}'$, *if* $\mathsf{UseHint}_q(\mathbf{h}, r, \alpha) = \mathsf{UseHint}_q(\mathbf{h}', r, \alpha)$, *then* $\mathbf{h} = \mathbf{h}'$.

Lemma 4 (from [11,16]). *If* $\|s\|_\infty \le \beta$ *and* $\|\mathsf{LowBits}_q(r, \alpha)\|_\infty < \alpha/2 - \beta$, *then*

$$\mathsf{HighBits}_q(r, \alpha) = \mathsf{HighBits}_q(r + s, \alpha)$$

3.2 Construction of $\mathsf{ID}_{\mathsf{MPLWE}}$

Our lossy identification scheme $\mathsf{ID}_{\mathsf{MPLWE}}$ consists of the following three algorithms, $\mathsf{ID}_{\mathsf{MPLWE}} = \{\mathsf{IGen}, \mathsf{P}, \mathsf{V}\}$. As similar with [5,11], our identification uses uniform samplings rather than Gaussian samplings to get resilience against side-channel analysis (e.g., [7,12]). Because of the uniform sampling, our identification scheme equips compression mechanisms to reduce size of protocol messages especially the response.

In the following, we use the extendable output function $\mathsf{Sam}(\cdot)$, which is modeled as a random oracle and used to expand a λ-bit random seed $\rho \in \{0,1\}^\lambda$. Let $\mathcal{C}$ be the challenge set of polynomials of ℓ_∞ norm 1, and of ℓ_2 norm bounded so that their polynomials have λ-bits of min entropy.

- <u>Instance Generation IGen.</u> The instance generation algorithm IGen takes as input a security parameter λ, and sets $n = n(\lambda)$, $d = d(\lambda)$, $k = k(\lambda)$, and $q = q(\lambda)$. The algorithm chooses a random seed $\rho \xleftarrow{\$} \{0,1\}^\lambda$, and compute $a := \mathsf{Sam}(\rho) \in R_q^{<n}$. It samples $s_1 \xleftarrow{\$} S_\alpha^{<n+d+k-1}$ and $s_2 \xleftarrow{\$} S_\alpha^{<d+k}$ uniformly at random. The algorithm computes $t := a \odot_{d+k} s_1 + s_2 \in R_q^{<d+k}$. Then it generates $t_1 := \mathsf{Power2Round}_q(t, \delta)$ and $t_0 := t - t_1 \cdot 2^\delta \in R^{<d+k}$. The algorithm IGen outputs $\mathsf{sk} := (\rho, s_1, s_2, t_0)$ and $\mathsf{pk} := (\rho, t_0, t_1)$.
- <u>Prover P.</u> The prover algorithm consists of two algorithms, $\mathsf{P} = (\mathsf{P}_1, \mathsf{P}_2)$. The first prover algorithm P_1 takes as input a secret key $\mathsf{sk} = (\rho, s_1, s_2, t_0)$. The algorithm P_1 first construct $a := \mathsf{Sam}(\rho)$. Then P_1 samples $y \xleftarrow{\$} S_\beta^{<n+d+1}$, and computes $w := a \odot_d y \in R_q^{<d}$ and $w_1 := \mathsf{HighBits}_q(w, 2\beta')$. It sets state information $\mathsf{st} := (w, y)$ and sends a commitment w_1 to the verifier.
  The second prover algorithm P_2 takes as input a secret key $\mathsf{sk} = (s_1, s_2)$, challenge c sent from the verifier, and state $\mathsf{st} = (w, y)$ from P_1. The algorithm computes $z := c \odot_{n+d-1} s_1 + y \in R^{<n+d-1}$. If $\|z\|_\infty \ge \gamma$ or $\|\mathsf{LowBits}_q(w - c \odot_d s_2, 2\beta')\|_\infty \ge \gamma'$ then set $(z, h) := (\perp, \perp)$, else set $h := \mathsf{MakeHint}_q(-c \odot_d t_0, w - c \odot_d s_2 + c \odot_d t_0, 2\beta')$. Finally P_2 outputs a response (z, h) to V.
- <u>Verifier V.</u> The verifier algorithm V accepts if $\|z\|_\infty < \gamma$ and $w_1 = \mathsf{UseHint}_q(h, a \odot_d z - c \odot_d t_1 \cdot 2^\delta)$, rejects otherwise.

3.3 Proofs

We show some properties of our $\mathsf{ID}_{\mathsf{MPLWE}}$: naHVZK property, correctness, min-entropy of commitments, lossy-key indistinguishability and lossy soundness. The proofs of this section are almost according to [16].

<u>Non Abort Honest Verifier Zero-Knowledge.</u> We show that our identification scheme $\mathsf{ID}_{\mathsf{MPLWE}}$ is perfectly naHVZK, i.e., the probability distribution of the output of the transcript algorithm Tr that takes as input a secret key is exactly the same as that of the naHVZK simulator S that is given only the public key.

Lemma 5 (Non Abort Honest Verifier Zero-Knowledge). *The identification scheme* $\mathsf{ID}_{\mathsf{MPLWE}}$ *is perfectly* naHVZK *if* $(k+1)\alpha \le \beta - \gamma$.

Proof. We first give the constructions of the algorithm Tr that outputs an honestly generated transcript of our identification protocol and its simulator S:

- $\mathsf{Tr}(\mathsf{sk})$: Generate $a := \mathsf{Sam}(\rho)$. Sample $y \xleftarrow{\$} S_\beta^{<n+d-1}$ uniformly at random, compute $w := a \odot_d y \in R_q^{<d}$, and $w_1 :- \mathsf{HighBits}_q(w, 2\beta')$. Choose $c \xleftarrow{\$} \mathcal{C}$ at random, and compute $z := c \odot_{n+d-1} s_1 + y \in R^{<n+d-1}$. If $\|z\|_\infty \ge \gamma$, then return $\perp$. Also, if $\|\mathsf{LowBits}_q(w - c \odot_d s_2, 2\beta')\|_\infty \ge \gamma'$, then return $\perp$. Compute $h := \mathsf{MakeHint}_q(-c \odot_d t_0, w - c \odot_d s_2 + c \odot_d t_0, 2\beta')$, and output $(c, (z, h))$.
- $\mathsf{S}(\mathsf{pk})$: Compute $a := \mathsf{Sam}(\rho)$. Output $\perp$ with probability $1 - (|S_\gamma^{<n+d-1}|/|S_\beta^{<n+d-1}|)$. Sample $z \xleftarrow{\$} S_\gamma^{<n+d-1}$ and $c \xleftarrow{\$} \mathcal{C}$ uniformly at random. Return $\perp$ if $\|\mathsf{LowBits}_q(a \odot_d z - c \odot_d t, 2\beta')\|_\infty \ge \gamma'$. Compute $h := \mathsf{MakeHint}_q(-c \odot_d t_0, a \odot_d z - c \odot_d t + c \odot_d t_0, 2\beta')$, and output $(c, (z, h))$.

Let $(s_1, s_2) \in S_{\alpha_1}^{<n+d+k-1} \times S_{\alpha_2}^{<d+k}$ be any polynomials satisfying $t = a \odot_{d+k} s_1 + s_2 \in R_q^{<d+k}$. For any $z \in S_\gamma^{<n+d-1}$ and $c \in \mathcal{C}$, it holds that

$$\Pr\left[z = c \odot_{n+d-1} s_1 + y : y \xleftarrow{\$} S_\beta^{<n+d-1}\right] = \Pr\left[y = z - c \odot_{n+d-1} s_1 : y \xleftarrow{\$} S_\beta^{<n+d-1}\right].$$

Since we have $z - c \odot_{n+d-1} s_1 \in S_\beta^{<n+d-1}$ because of $\|c \odot_{n+d-1} s_1\|_\infty \le \beta - \gamma$, it holds that

$$\Pr\left[y = z - c \odot_{n+d-1} s_1 : y \xleftarrow{\$} S_\beta^{<n+d-1}\right] = \frac{1}{\left|S_\beta^{<n+d-1}\right|}.$$

Thus every $z \in S_\gamma^{<n+d-1}$ occurs in an equal probability. The probability that the algorithm Tr generates $z \in S_\gamma^{<n+d-1}$ and does not return $\perp$ is $|S_\gamma^{<n+d-1}|/|S_\beta^{<n+d-1}|$. Hence, Tr outputs either $\perp$ except with probability $|S_\gamma^{<n+d-1}|/|S_\beta^{<n+d-1}|$, or (c, z) is distributed uniformly over $\mathcal{C} \times S_\gamma^{<n+d-1}$. This is the same distribution as the outputs of the simulator S.

To conclude the prove of this lemma, we show that the final process of Tr is the same as that of S. From Corollary 2, it holds that

$$w - c \odot_d s_2 = a \odot_d y - c \odot_d s_2$$
$$= a \odot_d (z - c \odot_{n+d-1} s_1) - c \odot_d s_2$$
$$= a \odot_d z - c \odot_d (a \odot_{d+k} s_1) - c \odot_d s_2$$
$$= a \odot_d z - c \odot_d t$$

$\square$

Correctness. To check that well-formed transcript of our identification scheme is accepted by the verifier V with high probability, in the following lemma, we estimate the probability that the reject symbol $\perp$ is not sent from the prover P, and the probability that the verifier V accepts when P does not send $\perp$ to V.

Lemma 6 (Correctness). *If* $\|c \odot_d s_2\|_\infty < (k+1)\alpha$, *the identification scheme* $\mathsf{ID}_{\mathsf{MPLWE}}$ *is* ϵ_c-*correct, where*

$$\epsilon_c < \left(\frac{2\gamma + 1}{2\beta + 1}\right)^{n+d-1} \left(\frac{2\gamma' + 1}{2\beta' - 1}\right)^d$$

Proof. We first estimate the probability that the simulator S described in the above outputs $\perp$, since our identification scheme is perfectly naHVZK (i.e., the distribution of protocol messages is exactly the same as that of Tr, and so is $\mathsf{ID}_{\mathsf{MPLWE}}$).

The probability that S does not output $\perp$ before sampling z and c is

$$\frac{|S_\gamma^{<n+d-1}|}{|S_\beta^{<n+d-1}|} = \left(\frac{2\gamma + 1}{2\beta + 1}\right)^{n+d-1}.$$

If we heuristically assume that for uniformly random $z \xleftarrow{\$} S_\gamma^{<n+d-1}$, the distribution of $a \odot_d z - c \odot_d t \in R_{2\beta'}^{<d}$ is approximately uniform, then the probability that S outputs $\perp$ in his last step is

$$\Pr[\|\mathsf{LowBits}_q(a \odot_d z - c \odot_d t, 2\beta')\|_\infty < \gamma' : z \xleftarrow{\$} S_\gamma^{<n+d-1}] < \left(\frac{2\gamma' + 1}{2\beta' - 1}\right)^d.$$

To complete the proof of this lemma, we only show that the verification algorithm V will always accept if $(z, h) \neq (\perp, \perp)$. Suppose that V receives $(z, h) \neq (\perp, \perp)$. Then the check $\|z\|_\infty < \gamma$ of V will always pass, since the prover always outputs $(z, h) = (\perp, \perp)$ if $\|z\|_\infty \geq \gamma$. From the proof of Lemma 5, we know that

$$w - c \odot_d s_2 = a \odot_d z - c \odot_d t$$
$$= a \odot_d z - c \odot_d t_0 - c \odot_d t_1 \cdot 2^\delta,$$

so it holds that

$$h = \mathsf{MakeHint}_q(-c \odot_d t_0, w - c \odot_d s_2 + c \odot_d t_0, 2\beta')$$
$$= \mathsf{MakeHint}_q(-c \odot_d t_0, a \odot_d z - c \odot_d t_1 \cdot 2^\delta, 2\beta').$$

By $\|c \odot_d t_0\|_\infty < \beta'$ and Lemma 3, we have

$$\mathsf{UseHint}_q(h, a \odot_d z - c \odot_d t_1 \cdot 2^\delta, 2\beta')$$
$$= \mathsf{HighBits}_q(a \odot_d z - c \odot_d t_0 - c \odot_d t_1 \cdot 2^\delta, 2\beta')$$
$$= \mathsf{HighBits}_q(w - c \odot_d s_2, 2\beta').$$

Since $\|c \odot_d s_2\|_\infty < (k+1)\alpha$, and the prover always outputs $(\perp, \perp)$ if $\|\mathsf{LowBits}_q(w - c\odot_d s_2, 2\beta')\|_\infty \geq \gamma'$ (so we have $\|\mathsf{LowBits}_q(w - c\odot_d s_2, 2\beta')\|_\infty < \gamma'$ from supposing that the prover does not output $(\perp, \perp)$), by Lemma 4 it holds that

$$\mathsf{HighBits}_q(w - c \odot_s s_2, 2\beta') = \mathsf{HighBits}_q(w, 2\beta') = w_1.$$

From the above, the verifier can correctly computes $w_1 = \mathsf{UseHint}_q(h, a \odot_d z - c \odot_d t_1 \cdot 2^\delta, 2\beta')$, and so accept a honest prover. $\qquad\square$

Min-Entropy. The following lemma says that it is difficult for a malicious verifier to guess a internal state of the prover when a commitment is given.

Lemma 7 (Min-Entropy of Commitments). *If q is prime, then the identification scheme $\mathsf{ID}_{\mathsf{MPLWE}}$ has*

$$\alpha \geq \min\left\{\log\left(\frac{q^d}{((4\beta+1)^{d+n-1}(4\beta'+1)^d)}\right), (d+n-1)\cdot\log(2\beta+1)\right\}$$

bits of min-entropy.

Proof. We first estimate the probability

$$\mathsf{p} := \Pr\left[\begin{array}{l}\exists y \neq y' \in S_\beta^{<d+n-1} \\ \text{s.t. } \mathsf{HighBits}_q(a \odot_d y, 2\beta') = \mathsf{HighBits}_q(a \odot_d y', 2\beta')\end{array} : a \xleftarrow{\$} R_q^{<n}\right].$$

If we define $(w_0, w_1) := \mathsf{Decompose}_q(a \odot_d y, 2\beta')$ and $(w_0', w_1') := \mathsf{Decompose}_q(a \odot_d y', 2\beta')$, then from $\mathsf{HighBits}_q(a \odot_d y, 2\beta') = \mathsf{HighBits}_q(a \odot_d y', 2\beta')$, we have $a \odot_d y = w_1 \cdot 2\beta' + w_0$ and $a \odot_d y' = w_1' \cdot 2\beta' + w_0'$ for $w_1 = w_1'$ and $\|w_0\|_\infty, \|w_0'\|_\infty \leq \beta'$. Let $\hat{y} := y - y'$ and $\hat{w}_0 := w_0 - w_0'$, then the above implies $a \odot_d \hat{y} = \hat{w}_0$ with $\|\hat{y}\|_\infty < 2\beta$ and $\|\hat{w}_0\| < 2\beta'$. By Corollary 1 we have

$$a \odot_d \hat{y} = \begin{bmatrix} \hat{y}_1 & \hat{y}_2 & \cdots & \hat{y}_n \\ \hat{y}_2 & \hat{y}_3 & \cdots & \hat{y}_{n+1} \\ & & \vdots & \\ \hat{y}_d & \hat{y}_{d+1} & \cdots & \hat{y}_{d+n-1} \end{bmatrix}\begin{bmatrix} a_n \\ a_{n-1} \\ \vdots \\ a_1 \end{bmatrix}.$$

Since it holds that $a_i \equiv (\hat{w}_{0,i} - \sum_{j\in[n]\setminus\{i\}} a_j \cdot \hat{y}_{i+n-j})/\hat{y}_n \pmod{q}$ for any $i \in [d]$, and all the a_i's are independently and identically sampled from the uniform distribution over $R_q^{<n}$, we have

$$\Pr[a \odot_d \hat{y} = \hat{w}_0 : a \xleftarrow{\$} R_q^{<n}] < \frac{1}{q^d}.$$

Then it holds that

$$\mathsf{p} < \sum_{\hat{y} \in S_{2\beta}^{<d+n-1}, \hat{w}_0 \in R_{2\beta'}^{<d}} \Pr[a \odot_d \hat{y} = \hat{w}_0 : a \xleftarrow{\$} R_q^{<n}] < \frac{(4\beta+1)^{d+n-1}(4\beta'+1)^d}{q^d}.$$

Therefore, in the probability at most $1 - ((4\beta+1)^{d+n-1}(4\beta'+1)^d/q^d)$ over the randomness of $a \xleftarrow{\$} R_q^{<n}$, each w occurs with the probability at most $(2\beta + 1)^{-(d+n-1)}$. □

Lossy Identification. Here we first give the construction of a lossy key generation algorithm, which just outputs an uniformly random element in the same domain as the public key of our lossy identification scheme.

- LossyIGen(1^λ): Sample a random seed $\rho \xleftarrow{\$} \{0,1\}^\lambda$, and choose $t \xleftarrow{\$} R_q^{<d+k}$ uniformly at random. Set $t_0 := \mathsf{Power2Round}(t, \delta)$ and $t_1 := t - t_0 \cdot 2^\delta$. Output a lossy key $\mathsf{pk}_{\mathsf{ls}} := (\rho, t_0, t_1)$.

To prove that our construction $\mathsf{ID}_{\mathsf{MPLWE}}$ is a lossy identification scheme, we show that our identification scheme $\mathsf{ID}_{\mathsf{MPLWE}}$ satisfies two properties of lossy identifications: lossy-key indistinguishability and lossy soundness. In the following, we prove that the lossy key is (computationally) indistinguishable from the real public key under the MPLWE assumption.

Lemma 8 (Lossy-key Indistinguishability). *Under the* MPLWE *assumption, the identification scheme is lossy-key indistinguishable. Namely, for any PPT adversary $\mathcal{A}_1$ for the lossy ID scheme $\mathsf{ID}_{\mathsf{MPLWE}}$, there exists an PPT adversary $\mathcal{A}_2$ for the decision* MPLWE *problem such that*

$$\mathsf{Adv}_{\mathcal{A}_1}^{\mathsf{LOSSY-IND}}(\lambda) = \mathsf{Adv}_{\mathcal{A}_2}^{\mathsf{MPLWE}}(\lambda).$$

Proof. Since the public key of $\mathsf{ID}_{\mathsf{MPLWE}}$ is just an MPLWE instance, probability of distinguishing an MPLWE instance from a uniformly random element is equal to the winning probability of an adversary in the lossy-key indistinguishability game. Particularly, it holds that

$$\mathsf{Adv}_{\mathcal{A}_1}^{\mathsf{LOSSY-IND}}(\lambda) = \mathsf{Adv}_{\mathcal{A}_2}^{\mathsf{MPLWE}}(\lambda).$$

From the MPLWE assumption, we have $\mathsf{Adv}_{\mathcal{A}}^{\mathsf{LOSSY-IND}}(\lambda) = \mathsf{negl}(\lambda)$ for any PPT algorithm $\mathcal{A}$. □

Now we prove that our identification scheme is lossy sound, namely the probability that an adversarial prover with lossy key can impersonate the verifier is negligible in a security parameter.

Lemma 9 (Lossy Soundness). *If q is prime and $2^\delta \leq (4\gamma+1)^{n-1}$, then the identification scheme $\mathsf{ID}_{\mathsf{MPLWE}}$ is ϵ_{ls}-lossy, where*

$$\epsilon_{ls} < \frac{(4\gamma+1)^{d+n-1}(8\beta'+5)^d|\mathcal{C}|^2}{q^d}.$$

Proof. We first formalize the lossy impersonation game where a malicious prover only with a lossy key try to impersonate a verifier.

1. $\mathsf{pk}_{\mathsf{ls}} := (\rho, t_0, t_1) \xleftarrow{\$} \mathsf{LossyIGen}(1^\lambda)$.
2. $(w_1, \mathsf{st}) \xleftarrow{\$} \mathcal{A}(\mathsf{pk}_{\mathsf{ls}})$
3. $c \xleftarrow{\$} \mathcal{C}$
4. $(z, h) \xleftarrow{\$} \mathcal{A}(\mathsf{st}, c)$
5. Return $[\![w_1 = \mathsf{UseHint}_q(h, a \odot_d z - c \odot_d t_1 \cdot 2^\delta, 2\beta')]\!]$ and $[\![\|z\|_\infty < \gamma]\!]$

Suppose that for some $w_1 \in R_q^{<d}$, there exist two $c \neq c' \in \mathcal{C}$ and two $(z, h), (z', h') \in S_\gamma^{<n+d-1} \times \{0, 1\}$ such that an unbounded adversary $\mathcal{A}$ that is given c and output $(z, h), (z', h')$ wins the impersonation game. Then the following two equations holds:

$$w_1 = \mathsf{UseHint}_q(h, a \odot_d z - c \odot_d t_1 \cdot 2^\delta, 2\beta'),$$
$$w_1 = \mathsf{UseHint}_q(h, a \odot_d z' - c' \odot_d t_1 \cdot 2^\delta, 2\beta').$$

We know from Lemma 3 that the above two equations leads

$$\|a \odot_d z - c \odot_d t_1 \cdot 2^\delta - w_1 \cdot 2\beta'\|_\infty \leq 2\beta' + 1,$$
$$\|a \odot_d z' - c' \odot_d t_1 \cdot 2^\delta - w_1 \cdot 2\beta'\|_\infty \leq 2\beta' + 1.$$

By the triangular inequality, they imply that

$$\|a \odot_d (z - z') - (c - c') \odot_d t_1 \cdot 2^\delta\|_\infty \leq 4\beta' + 2.$$

Let $\hat{z}_1 := z - z' \in S_{2\gamma}^{<n+d-1}$ and $\hat{c} := c - c' \in [-2, 1]^{<k+1}$. Then the above inequation can be rewritten as

$$a \odot_d \hat{z}_1 + \hat{z}_2 = \hat{c} \odot_d t_1 \cdot 2^\delta,$$

for some $\hat{z}_2 \in S_{4\beta'+2}^{<d}$.

We need to estimate the probability that the above equation is satisfied. By taking the two cases where $z_1 = 0$ or not, we consider the following probability p:

$$\mathsf{p} := \Pr\left[\begin{array}{c|c} \exists (z_1, z_2, c) \in S_{2\gamma}^{<d+n-1} \times S_{4\beta'+2}^{<d} \times S^{<k+1} \backslash \{0\} & a \xleftarrow{\$} R_q^{<n}; t \xleftarrow{\$} R_q^{<d+k}; \\ \text{s.t. } a \odot_d z_1 + z_2 = c \odot_d t_1 \cdot 2^\delta & t_1 := \mathsf{Power2Round}_q(t, \delta) \end{array}\right].$$

Case 1. Here we will manage the case where $z_1 = 0$, namely, we estimate the probability

$$\mathsf{p}_1 := \Pr\left[\begin{array}{c|c} \exists (z_2, c) \in S_{4\beta'+2}^{<d} \times S^{<k+1} \backslash \{0\} & t \xleftarrow{\$} R_q^{<d+k}; \\ \text{s.t. } z_2 = c \odot_d t_1 \cdot 2^\delta & t_1 := \mathsf{Power2Round}_q(t, \delta) \end{array}\right].$$

By the union bound, p_1 is re-written as

$$p_1 < \sum_{z_2,c} \Pr\left[z_2 = c \odot_d t_1 \cdot 2^\delta : \begin{array}{l} t \xleftarrow{\$} R_q^{<d+k}; \\ t_1 := \mathsf{Power2Round}_q(t,\delta) \end{array}\right]$$

$$\leq \sum_{z_2,c} \Pr\left[c \odot_d t_1 = 2^{-\delta}(z_2) : \begin{array}{l} t \xleftarrow{\$} R_q^{<d+k}; \\ t_1 := \mathsf{Power2Round}_q(t,\delta) \end{array}\right],$$

where from Corollary 1 it holds that

$$c \odot_d t_1 = \begin{bmatrix} t_{1,1} & t_{1,2} & \cdots & t_{1,k+1} \\ t_{1,2} & t_{1,3} & \cdots & t_{1,k+2} \\ & & \vdots & \\ t_{1,d} & t_{1,d+1} & \cdots & t_{1,d+k} \end{bmatrix} \begin{bmatrix} c_{k+1} \\ c_k \\ \vdots \\ :c_1 \end{bmatrix}.$$

Without loss of generality, we can suppose that the first element of the vector $\bar{c}$ is not 0. So it holds that for any $i \in [d]$,

$$t_{1,i} = c_{k+1}^{-1} \cdot \left\{ 2^{-\delta}\left(z_2[i] - \sum_{j\in[r]} t_{1,i+j} \cdot c_{k+1-j}\right) \right\}.$$

Since the most frequent value of coefficients of t_1 occurs with probability at most $2^\delta/q$, we have

$$p_1 < \sum_{z_2 \in S_{4\beta'+2}^{<d}, c \in S^{<k+1}\setminus\{0\}} \left(\frac{2^\delta}{q}\right)^d < \frac{(8\beta'+5)^d |\mathcal{C}|^2 (2^\delta)^d}{q^d}.$$

<u>Case 2.</u> We will take the case where $z_1 \neq 0$ by estimating the probability

$$p_2 := \Pr\left[\begin{array}{l} \exists(z_1,z_2,c) \in S_{2\gamma}^{<d+n-1}\setminus\{0\} \times S_{4\beta'+2}^{<d} \times S^{<k+1}\setminus\{0\} \\ \text{s.t. } a \odot_d z_1 + z_2 = c \odot_d t_1 \cdot 2^\delta \end{array} : \begin{array}{l} a \xleftarrow{\$} R_q^{<n}; t \xleftarrow{\$} R_q^{<d+k}; \\ t_1 := \mathsf{Power2Round}_q(t,\delta) \end{array}\right].$$

By the union bound and the similar argument with Lemma 7, the probability p_2 is rewritten as

$$p_2 < \sum_{z_1 \in S_{2\gamma}^{<n+d-1}\setminus\{0\}, z_2 \in S_{4\beta'+2}^{<d}, c \in S^{<k+1}\setminus\{0\}} \Pr\left[a \odot_d z_1 = c \odot_d t_1 \cdot 2^\delta - z_2 : a \xleftarrow{\$} R_q^{<n}\right]$$

$$< \sum_{z_1 \in S_{2\gamma}^{<n+d-1}\setminus\{0\}, z_2 \in S_{4\beta'+2}^{<d}, c \in S^{<k+1}\setminus\{0\}} \frac{1}{q^d}$$

$$< \frac{(4\gamma+1)^{n+d-1}(8\beta'+5)^d |\mathcal{C}|^2}{q^d}.$$

By combining the above two cases and from the assumption that $2^\delta \leq (4\gamma + 1)^{n-1}$, we can obtain the probability bound in the statement of this lemma. $\square$

A   Digital Signatures from the MPLWE

A.1   Digital Signatures

We first introduce the definition of digital signatures and pseudorandom functions.

Definition 13. *A digital signature scheme consists of a triple of polynomial-time algorithms* $\Sigma := \{\text{Keygen}, \text{Sign}, \text{Verify}\}$ *with the following syntax:*

- $\text{KeyGen}(1^\lambda)$: *given a security parameter* λ, *outputs secret and public keys* (sk, pk).
- $\text{Sign}_{\text{sk}}(\mu \in \{0,1\}^*)$: *given a secret key* sk *and message* μ, *outputs a signature* σ.
- $\text{Verify}_{\text{pk}}(\mu, \sigma)$: *given a public key* pk, *message* μ, *and signature* σ, *outputs 1 if* σ *is a valid signature of* μ, *and 0 otherwise.*

The signature scheme has correctness error γ *if for all* $(\text{pk}, \text{sk}) \in \text{KeyGen}(1^\lambda)$ *and all message* $\mu \in \{0,1\}^*$, *it holds that* $\Pr[\text{Verify}_{\text{pk}}(\mu, \text{Sign}_{\text{sk}}(\mu)) - 0] \leq \gamma$.

Let $\mathcal{O}^{\text{Sign}}$ *be an oracle that outputs a signature for a queried message, and* $\mathcal{M}$ *be the set of queried messages to* $\mathcal{O}^{\text{Sign}}$. *The advantage of an algorithm* $\mathcal{F}$ *is defined as*

$$\text{Adv}_{\Sigma, \mathcal{F}}^{\text{EUF-CMA}}(\lambda) := \Pr\left[\begin{array}{l} \text{Verify}_{\text{pk}}(\mu^*, \sigma^*) = 1 \\ \wedge \mu^* \notin \mathcal{M} \end{array} : \begin{array}{l} (\text{pk}, \text{sk}) \xleftarrow{\$} \text{KeyGen}(1^\lambda); \\ (\mu^*, \sigma^*) \xleftarrow{\$} \mathcal{F}^{\mathcal{O}^{\text{Sign}}}(\text{pk}) \end{array}\right].$$

The signature scheme Σ *is called* EUF-CMA *secure if* $\text{Adv}_{\Sigma, \mathcal{F}}^{\text{EUF-CMA}}(\lambda) = \text{negl}(\lambda)$ *for any PPT adversary* $\mathcal{F}$.

Definition 14 (Pseudorandom Function). *For a security parameter* λ, *let* $n = n(\lambda)$ *and* $k = k(\lambda)$ *be integers, and* $\mathcal{K}$ *be a finite key space. The advantage of a map* $\text{PRF} : \mathcal{K} \times \{0,1\}^n \to \{0,1\}^k$ *for an adversary* $\mathcal{D}$ *is defined as*

$$\text{Adv}_{\text{PRF}, \mathcal{D}}^{\text{PR}}(\lambda) := \left| \Pr[\mathcal{D}^{\text{PRF}_K(\cdot)}(1^\lambda) \to 1; K \xleftarrow{\$} \mathcal{K}] - \Pr[\mathcal{D}^{\text{RF}(\cdot)}(1^\lambda) \to 1] \right|,$$

where $\text{RF} : \{0,1\}^n \to \{0,1\}^k$ *be a random function. The map* PRF *is called a pseudorandom function if* $\text{Adv}_{\text{PRF}, \mathcal{D}}^{\text{PR}}(\lambda) = \text{negl}(\lambda)$.

The following signatures Σ_{DFS}, obtained from the deterministic variant of Fiat-Shamir transformation for the (canonical) identification, is a triple of key generation, signing, and verification algorithm, but we omit the description of the key generation, since it is the same as the instance generation algorithm of the underlying identification. Let $H : \{0,1\}^* \to R^{<k+1}$ be a hash function implemented by the random oracle, $\text{PRF}_K(\cdot)$ be a pseudorandom function with key K, and κ_m be a positive integer.

- $\mathsf{Sign}_{\mathsf{sk},K}(\mu \in \{0,1\}^*)$: Set $\kappa := 0$. Repeat the followings while $z = \perp$ and $\kappa \leq \kappa_m$: set $\kappa := \kappa + 1$; compute $(w,\mathsf{st}) := \mathsf{P}_1(\mathsf{sk}; \mathsf{PRF}_K(0 \parallel \mu \parallel \kappa))$; set $c := H(w\|\mu)$; compute $z := \mathsf{P}_2(\mathsf{sk}, w, c, \mathsf{st}; \mathsf{PRF}_K(1\|\mu\|\kappa))$. If $z = \perp$ then return $\sigma := \perp$, else return $\sigma := (w, z)$.
- $\mathsf{Verify}_{\mathsf{pk}}(\mu, \sigma)$: Parse $\sigma = (w, z)$, and return $\mathsf{V}(\mathsf{pk}, w, c, z) \in \{0,1\}$ for $c := H(w\|\mu)$.

In [16], Kiltz et al. showed quantum security of the signatures obtained from the (deterministic) Fiat-Shamir transformation for a lossy identification scheme.

Theorem 2 (Adapted from Theorem 3.1 of [16]). *Assume the identification scheme* ID *is lossy key indistinguishable,* ϵ_{ls}*-lossy sound,* ϵ_{ZK}*-perfect naHVZK, and has an* α*-bits of min entropy. For any quantum* $\mathsf{EUF\text{-}CMA}$ *adversary* $\mathcal{F}$ *that issues at most* q_H *queries to the quantum random oracle* $|H\rangle$*, and* q_S *classical queries to the signing oracle, there exists a quantum adversary* $\mathcal{A}$ *against* ID *and a quantum adversary* $\mathcal{D}$ *against* PRF *such that*

$$\mathsf{Adv}^{\mathsf{EUF\text{-}CMA}}_{\Sigma_{\mathsf{DFS}},\mathcal{F}}(\lambda) \leq \mathsf{Adv}^{\mathsf{LOSSY\text{-}IND}}_{\mathsf{ID},\mathcal{A}}(\lambda) + 8(q_H+1)^2 \cdot \epsilon_{\mathsf{ls}} + \mathsf{Adv}^{\mathsf{PR}}_{\mathsf{PRF},\mathcal{D}}(\lambda) + 2^{-\alpha+1} + \kappa_m q_S \epsilon_{\mathsf{ZK}}.$$

A.2   Fiat-Shamir Transformed Signatures from $\mathsf{ID}_{\mathsf{MPLWE}}$

We here give a construction of the signatures from our identification scheme $\mathsf{ID}_{\mathsf{MPLWE}}$ described in Sect. 3.2. The signatures are obtained by applying the transformation of [16] to $\mathsf{ID}_{\mathsf{MPLWE}}$. The resulting signature scheme can be seen as an MPLWE variant of Dilithium-QROM [16].

The (deterministic) Fiat-Shamir transformed signature scheme Σ_{MPLWE} consists of the following three algorithms:

- $\mathsf{KeyGen}(1^\lambda)$: Generate $(\mathsf{pk}, \mathsf{sk}) \xleftarrow{\$} \mathsf{IGen}(1^\lambda)$.
- $\mathsf{Sign}_{\mathsf{sk},K}(\mu \in \{0,1\}^*)$: Parse $\mathsf{sk} = (\rho, s_1, s_2, t_0)$, set $\kappa := 0$, and recover $a := \mathsf{Sam}(\rho)$. Repeat the followings while $(z, h) = (\perp, \perp)$ and $\kappa \leq \kappa_m$: set $\kappa := \kappa + 1$; compute $y := \mathsf{PRF}_K(\mu \parallel \kappa)$; compute $w := a \odot_d y \in R_q^{<d}$ and $w_1 := \mathsf{HighBits}_q(w, 2\beta')$; set $c := H(w_1 \parallel \mu)$; compute $z := c \odot_{n+d-1} s_1 + y \in R^{<n+d-1}$; if $\|z\|_\infty \geq \gamma$ or $\|\mathsf{LowBits}_q(w - c \odot_d s_2, 2\beta')\|_\infty \geq \gamma'$ then set $(z, h) := (\perp, \perp)$, else set $h := \mathsf{MakeHint}_q(-c \odot_d t_0, w - c \odot_d s_2 + c \odot_d t_0, 2\beta')$. Output $\sigma := (h, z, c)$.
- $\mathsf{Verify}_{\mathsf{pk}}(\mu, \sigma)$: Parse $\sigma = (h, z, c)$. Generate $a = \mathsf{Sam}(\rho)$ and compute $w_1' := \mathsf{UseHint}_q(h, a \odot_d z - c \odot_d t_1 \cdot 2^\delta, 2\beta')$. Output 1 if $\|z\|_\infty < \gamma$ and $c = H(w_1' \parallel \mu)$ holds, 0 otherwise.

From Theorem 2 and the lemmas proven in Sect. 3, the Fiat-Shamir Transformed signatures from our identification scheme $\mathsf{ID}_{\mathsf{MPLWE}}$ is EUF-CMA secure in the QROM.

Corollary 3. *If the decision MPLWE assumption holds, and the function PRF is pseudorandom against quantum adversaries, then the signature scheme* Σ_{MPLWE} *is EUF-CMA secure in the QROM. In particular, for any quantum adversary* $\mathcal{F}$

against EUF-CMA *security for the signature scheme* Σ_{MPLWE} *that issues at most* q_H *queries to the quantum random oracle* $|H\rangle$, *and* q_S *classical queries to the signing oracle, there exists a quantum adversary* $\mathcal{A}$ *of* MPLWE *assumption and a quantum adversary* $\mathcal{D}$ *against* PRF *such that*

$$\mathsf{Adv}^{\mathsf{EUF\text{-}CMA}}_{\Sigma_{\mathsf{MPLWE}},\mathcal{F}}(\lambda) \leq \mathsf{Adv}^{\mathsf{MPLWE}}_{\mathcal{A}}(\lambda) + 8(q_H + 1)^2 \cdot \epsilon_{\mathsf{ls}} + \mathsf{Adv}^{\mathsf{PR}}_{\mathsf{PRF},\mathcal{D}}(\lambda) + 2^{-\alpha+1}.$$

References

1. Abdalla, M., Fouque, P.-A., Lyubashevsky, V., Tibouchi, M.: Tightly-secure signatures from lossy identification schemes. In: Pointcheval, D., Johansson, T. (eds.) EUROCRYPT 2012. LNCS, vol. 7237, pp. 572–590. Springer, Heidelberg (2012). https://doi.org/10.1007/978-3-642-29011-4_34

2. Ajtai, M.: Generating hard instances of lattice problems. In: STOC, pp. 99–108 (1996)

3. Albrecht, M.R., Deo, A.: Large modulus ring-LWE $\geq$ Module-LWE. In: Takagi, T., Peyrin, T. (eds.) ASIACRYPT 2017. LNCS, vol. 10624, pp. 267–296. Springer, Cham (2017). https://doi.org/10.1007/978-3-319-70694-8_10

4. Alkim, E., Ducas, L., Pöppelmann, T., Schwabe, P.: Post-quantum key exchange - a new hope. In: USENIX, pp. 327–343 (2016)

5. Bai, S., Galbraith, S.D.: An improved compression technique for signatures based on learning with errors. In: Benaloh, J. (ed.) CT-RSA 2014. LNCS, vol. 8366, pp. 28–47. Springer, Cham (2014). https://doi.org/10.1007/978-3-319-04852-9_2

6. Bos, J.W., et al.: CRYSTALS - Kyber: a CCA-secure module-lattice-based KEM. In: EURO S&P (2018). https://eprint.iacr.org/2017/634

7. Groot Bruinderink, L., Hülsing, A., Lange, T., Yarom, Y.: Flush, gauss, and reload – a cache attack on the BLISS lattice-based signature scheme. In: Gierlichs, B., Poschmann, A.Y. (eds.) CHES 2016. LNCS, vol. 9813, pp. 323–345. Springer, Heidelberg (2016). https://doi.org/10.1007/978-3-662-53140-2_16

8. Campbell, P., Groves, M., Shepherd, D.: SOLILOQUY: a cautionary tale. In: ETSI 2nd Quantum-Safe Crypto Workshop, pp. 1–9 (2014)

9. Cramer, R., Ducas, L., Peikert, C., Regev, O.: Recovering short generators of principal ideals in cyclotomic rings. In: Fischlin, M., Coron, J.-S. (eds.) EUROCRYPT 2016. LNCS, vol. 9666, pp. 559–585. Springer, Heidelberg (2016). https://doi.org/10.1007/978-3-662-49896-5_20

10. Cramer, R., Ducas, L., Wesolowski, B.: Short stickelberger class relations and application to ideal-SVP. In: Coron, J.-S., Nielsen, J.B. (eds.) EUROCRYPT 2017. LNCS, vol. 10210, pp. 324–348. Springer, Cham (2017). https://doi.org/10.1007/978-3-319-56620-7_12

11. Ducas, L., et al.: CRYSTALS - dilithium: a lattice-based digital signature scheme. In: CHES, pp. 238–268 (2018)

12. Espitau, T., Fouque, P.A., Gérard, B., Tibouchi, M.: Side-channel attacks on bliss lattice-based signatures - exploiting branch tracing against strong swan and electromagnetic emanations in microcontrollers. In: CCS, pp. 1857–1874 (2017)

13. Fiat, A., Shamir, A.: How to prove yourself: practical solutions to identification and signature problems. In: Odlyzko, A.M. (ed.) CRYPTO 1986. LNCS, vol. 263, pp. 186–194. Springer, Heidelberg (1987). https://doi.org/10.1007/3-540-47721-7_12

14. Hanrot, G., Quercia, M., Zimmermann, P.: The middle product algorithm I. Appl. Algebra Eng. Commun. Comput. **14**(6), 415–438 (2004)

15. Katz, J., Wang, N.: Efficiency improvements for signature schemes with tight security reductions. In: CCS, pp. 155–164 (2003)
16. Kiltz, E., Lyubashevsky, V., Schaffner, C.: A concrete treatment of fiat-shamir signatures in the quantum random-oracle model. In: Nielsen, J.B., Rijmen, V. (eds.) EUROCRYPT 2018. LNCS, vol. 10822, pp. 552–586. Springer, Cham (2018). https://doi.org/10.1007/978-3-319-78372-7_18
17. Langlois, A., Stehlé, D.: Worst-case to average-case reductions for module lattices. Des. Codes Cryptogr. **75**, 565–599 (2015)
18. Lyubashevsky, V.: Fiat-shamir with aborts: applications to lattice and factoring-based signatures. In: Matsui, M. (ed.) ASIACRYPT 2009. LNCS, vol. 5912, pp. 598–616. Springer, Heidelberg (2009). https://doi.org/10.1007/978-3-642-10366-7_35
19. Lyubashevsky, V.: Digital signatures based on the hardness of ideal lattice problems in all rings. In: Cheon, J.H., Takagi, T. (eds.) ASIACRYPT 2016. LNCS, vol. 10032, pp. 196–214. Springer, Heidelberg (2016). https://doi.org/10.1007/978-3-662-53890-6_7
20. Lyubashevsky, V., Peikert, C., Regev, O.: On ideal lattices and learning with errors over rings. In: Gilbert, H. (ed.) EUROCRYPT 2010. LNCS, vol. 6110, pp. 1–23. Springer, Heidelberg (2010). https://doi.org/10.1007/978-3-642-13190-5_1
21. Peikert, C., Regev, O., Stephens-Davidowitz, N.: Pseudorandomness of Ring-LWE for any ring and modulus. In: STOC, pp. 461–473 (2017)
22. Regev, O.: On lattices, learning with errors, random linear codes, and cryptography. In: STOC, pp. 84–93 (2005)
23. Roşca, M., Sakzad, A., Stehlé, D., Steinfeld, R.: Middle-product learning with errors. In: Katz, J., Shacham, H. (eds.) CRYPTO 2017. LNCS, vol. 10403, pp. 283–297. Springer, Cham (2017). https://doi.org/10.1007/978-3-319-63697-9_10
24. Rosca, M., Stehlé, D., Wallet, A.: On the ring-LWE and polynomial-LWE problems. In: Nielsen, J.B., Rijmen, V. (eds.) EUROCRYPT 2018. LNCS, vol. 10820, pp. 146–173. Springer, Cham (2018). https://doi.org/10.1007/978-3-319-78381-9_6
25. Shoup, V.: Efficient computation of minimal polynomials in algebraic extensions of finite fields. In: ISSAC, pp. 53–58 (1999)
26. Steinfeld, R., Sakzad, A., Zhao, R.K.: Titanium: post-quantum public-key encryption and KEM algorithms. Technical report, National Institution of Standards and Technology (2017). http://users.monash.edu.au/~rste/Titanium_NISTSub.pdf

Generic Double-Authentication Preventing Signatures and a Post-quantum Instantiation

David Derler[1], Sebastian Ramacher[1(✉)], and Daniel Slamanig[2]

[1] IAIK, Graz University of Technology, Graz, Austria
cryptsec@derler.info, sebastian.ramacher@tugraz.at
[2] AIT Austrian Institute of Technology GmbH, Vienna, Austria
daniel.slamanig@ait.ac.at

Abstract. Double-authentication preventing signatures (DAPS) are a variant of digital signatures which have received considerable attention recently (Derler et al. EuroS&P 2018, Poettering AFRICACRYPT 2018). They are unforgeable signatures in the usual sense and sign messages that are composed of an address and a payload. Their distinguishing feature is the property that signatures on *two different* payloads with respect to the *same* address allow to publicly extract the secret signing key. Thus, they are a means to disincentivize double-signing and are a useful tool in various applications.

DAPS are known in the factoring, the discrete logarithm and the lattice setting. The majority of the constructions are ad-hoc. Only recently, Derler et al. (EuroS&P 2018) presented the first generic construction that allows to extend *any* discrete logarithm based secure signature scheme to DAPS. However, their scheme has the drawback that the number of potential addresses (the address space) used for signing is polynomially bounded (and in fact small) as the size of secret and public keys of the resulting DAPS are linear in the address space. In this paper we overcome this limitation and present a generic construction of DAPS with constant size keys and signatures. Our techniques are not tailored to a specific algebraic setting and in particular allow us to construct the first DAPS without structured hardness assumptions, i.e., from symmetric key primitives, yielding a candidate for post-quantum secure DAPS.

Keywords: Digital signatures
Double-authentication prevention · Shamir secret sharing
Provable-security · Generic construction
Exponential size address space

The full version of this paper is available as IACR Cryptology ePrint Archive Report. All authors have been supported by EU H2020 project PRISMACLOUD, grant agreement n°644962.

J. Baek et al. (Eds.): ProvSec 2018, LNCS 11192, pp. 258–276, 2018.
https://doi.org/10.1007/978-3-030-01446-9_15

1   Introduction

Digital signatures are an important cryptographic primitive used to provide strong integrity and authenticity guarantees for digital messages. Among many other applications, they are used to issue digital certificates for public keys within public-key infrastructures, to guarantee the origin of executable code, to sign digital documents such as PDF documents (in a legally binding way), as well as in major cryptographic protocols such as TLS. Recently, signatures also emerged to be a cornerstone of distributed cryptocurrencies such as Bitcoin, i.e., are used to bind coins to users (by means of public keys) and to sign transactions.

Double-authentication preventing signatures (DAPS) are a variant of digital signatures used to sign messages of the form $m = (a, p)$ with a being the so called address and p the payload. They provide unforgeability guarantees in the sense of conventional signatures but have the special property that signing two different payloads $p \neq p'$ using the same address a allows to publicly extract the secret signing key from the respective signatures. In the literature, various compelling applications for DAPS have been proposed. Those applications include penalizing double spending attacks in cryptocurrencies [27] or penalizing certification authorities for issuing two certificates with respect to the same domain name, but for two different public keys [25], for example. In this work we purely focus on DAPS constructions and we refer the reader to [25,26] for a comparison with other types of self-enforcing digital signatures.

Currently, DAPS are known in the factoring [6,25,26], the discrete logarithm [16,24,27] and the lattice setting [10]. The majority of the constructions (the only exception being [16]) are ad-hoc. Unfortunately, such an approach yields very specific constructions, whose security may not be well understood. Having generic DAPS constructions, in contrast, yields much more flexibility, as it allows to plug in building blocks whose security is well understood. In addition, this yields simplicity and modularity in the security analysis. Only recently, Derler et al. (EuroS&P 2018) presented the first generic construction that allows to extend *any* discrete logarithm based EUF-CMA secure signatures scheme to DAPS. However, their scheme has the drawback that the number of potential addresses (the address space) used for signing is polynomially bounded (and in fact small) as the size of secret and the public keys of the resulting DAPS are linear in the address space. We ask whether we can come up with a generic construction without this drawback.

Somewhat orthogonal to the motivational discussion above, our work is also driven by the question whether it is possible to construct DAPS without relying on structured hardness assumptions, i.e., solely from symmetric key primitives (following up on a very recent line of work [9,12,15,22]). This is interesting, because symmetric key primitives are conjectured to remain secure in the advent of sufficiently powerful quantum computers. Such quantum computers would break all discrete log and RSA based public key cryptosystems [30].

1.1 Existing DAPS Constructions

DAPS have been introduced by Poettering and Stebila [25,26] in a factoring-based setting. Ruffing, Kate and Schröder later introduced the notion of account-able assertions (AS) in [27], being a related but weaker primitive than DAPS. In addition they present one AS that also is a DAPS (RKS henceforth). The RKS construction is based on Merkle tress and chameleon hash functions in the discrete logarithm setting. Very recently, Bellare, Poettering and Stebila [6] proposed new factoring-based DAPS from trapdoor identification-schemes using an adaption and extension of a transform from [5]. Their two transforms applied to the Guillou-Quisquater (GQ) [20] and Micali-Reyzin (MR) [23] identification scheme yield signing and verification times as well as signature sizes comparable (or slightly above) standard RSA signatures. Boneh et al. [10] propose constructions of DAPS from lattices. They consider DAPS as a special case of what they call predicate-authentication-preventing signatures (PAPS). In PAPS one considers a k-ary predicate on the message space and given any k valid signatures that satisfy the predicate reveal the signing key. Consequently, DAPS are PAPS for a specific 2-ary predicate. Derler, Ramacher and Slamanig (DRS henceforth) in [16] recently provided the first black-box construction of DAPS from digital signatures schemes and demonstrate how this approach can be used to construct N-times-authentication-preventing signatures (NAPS) (a notion called k-way DAPS in [10]). In addition, they introduced weaker extraction notions, where the focus of the extraction is on the signing key of the underlying signature scheme only. A drawback of their work is that the constructions have $O(n)$ secret and public key size where n is the size of the address space. So their constructions are only suitable for small message spaces. In a follow up work Poettering [24], also focusing on DAPS for small address spaces, showed how for a certain class of signature schemes (obtained via Fiat-Shamir from certain identification schemes), the DRS approach can be improved by reducing the signature size by a factor of five and the size of the secret key from $O(n)$ to $O(1)$. However, this comes at the cost of no longer being able to do a black-box reduction to the underlying signature scheme. In Table 1 we provide a comparison of existing DAPS approaches with the ones presented in this paper regarding address space, extraction capabilities, algebraic setting as well as their characteristic as either being tailored to a specific setting or generic.

1.2 Contribution

Our contributions can be summarized as follows:

- We propose a generic DAPS, respectively NAPS, construction building upon DRS' secret-sharing approach, which resolves the address-space limitation in the DRS construction, and, in particular, supports an exponentially large address space. This improvement is achieved by deriving the coefficients of the secret sharing polynomial from the address using a carefully chosen pseudorandom function with an output domain being compatible with the secret

Table 1. Overview of DAPS constructions

Approach	Address space	Extraction	Setting	Generic
[25,26]	Exponential	DSE	Factoring	×
[27]	Exponential	DSE	DLOG	×
[6]	Exponential	DSE	Factoring	×
[10]	Exponential	DSE	Lattices	×
[16]	Small	wDSE*	DLOG	✓
[24]	Small	DSE	DLOG	×
Construction 1	Exponential	wDSE	Symmetric	✓
Construction 2	Exponential	DSE	Any	✓

key space of the underlying signature scheme. Consequently, the overhead in the public-key reduces to a constant factor. Like the DRS approach, our generic approach satisfies a relaxed notion of extractability. Interestingly, we can instantiate this construction solely from symmetric-key primitives, yielding a candidate for post-quantum secure DAPS/NAPS.

- While the aforementioned construction thus closes an important gap in the literature, the signature sizes are somewhat large compared to signatures in the discrete log or RSA setting. To this end, we additionally follow a different direction which basically targets the extension of any digital signature scheme (such as ECDSA or EdDSA, for example) to a DAPS. Essentially, we present a compiler which uses an arbitrary DAPS scheme to extend any given signature scheme to a DAPS. While this might sound somewhat odd at first sight, we want to stress that all existing DAPS which have compact keys and exponentially large address space are ad-hoc constructions, whereas practical applications most likely will use standardized signature schemes. Using our construction it is possible to generically bring extraction to any signature scheme. Hence we obtain more efficient DAPS being compatible with standardized signature schemes such as ECDSA or EdDSA.

2   Preliminaries

In this section we firstly present a formal model for the security of signature and DAPS schemes, recall non-interactive zero-knowledge proof systems and Shamir's secret sharing.

2.1   Digital Signature Schemes

Subsequently we formally recall the notion of digital signature schemes.

Definition 1 (Signature Scheme). *A signature scheme* Σ *is a triple* (KGen_Σ, Sign_Σ, Verify_Σ) *of PPT algorithms, which are defined as follows:*

$\mathsf{KGen}_\Sigma(1^\kappa)$: *This algorithm takes a security parameter κ as input and outputs a secret (signing) key sk_Σ and a public (verification) key pk_Σ with associated message space $\mathcal{M}$ (we may omit to make the message space $\mathcal{M}$ explicit).*

$\mathsf{Sign}_\Sigma(\mathsf{sk}_\Sigma, m)$: *This algorithm takes a secret key sk_Σ and a message $m \in \mathcal{M}$ as input and outputs a signature σ.*

$\mathsf{Verify}_\Sigma(\mathsf{pk}_\Sigma, m, \sigma)$: *This algorithm takes a public key pk_Σ, a message $m \in \mathcal{M}$ and a signature σ as input and outputs a bit $b \in \{0,1\}$.*

We require a signature scheme to be correct and to provide existential unforgeability under adaptively chosen message attacks (EUF-CMA security). For correctness we require that for all $\kappa \in \mathbb{N}$, for all $(\mathsf{sk}_\Sigma, \mathsf{pk}_\Sigma) \leftarrow \mathsf{KGen}_\Sigma(1^\kappa)$ and for all $m \in \mathcal{M}$ it holds that

$$\Pr\left[\mathsf{Verify}_\Sigma(\mathsf{pk}_\Sigma, m, \mathsf{Sign}_\Sigma(\mathsf{sk}_\Sigma, m)) = 1\right] = 1.$$

Definition 2 (EUF-CMA). *For a PPT adversary $\mathcal{A}$, we define the advantage function in the sense of EUF-CMA as*

$$\mathsf{Adv}_{\mathcal{A},\Sigma}^{\mathsf{EUF\text{-}CMA}}(\kappa) = \Pr\left[\mathsf{Exp}_{\mathcal{A},\Sigma}^{\mathsf{EUF\text{-}CMA}}(\kappa) = 1\right]$$

where the corresponding experiment is depicted in Fig. 1. If for all PPT adversaries $\mathcal{A}$ there is a negligible function $\varepsilon(\cdot)$ such that

$$\mathsf{Adv}_{\mathcal{A},\Sigma}^{\mathsf{EUF\text{-}CMA}}(\kappa) \leq \varepsilon(\kappa)$$

we say that Σ is EUF-CMA secure.

$\mathsf{Exp}_{\mathcal{A},\Sigma}^{\mathsf{EUF\text{-}CMA}}(\kappa)$:
$(\mathsf{sk}_\Sigma, \mathsf{pk}_\Sigma) \leftarrow \mathsf{KGen}_\Sigma(1^\kappa)$
$\mathcal{Q} \leftarrow \emptyset$
$(m^*, \sigma^*) \leftarrow \mathcal{A}^{\mathsf{Sign}_\Sigma'(\mathsf{sk}_\Sigma, \cdot)}(\mathsf{pk})$
    where oracle Sign_Σ' on input m:
        $\sigma \leftarrow \mathsf{Sign}_\Sigma(\mathsf{sk}_\Sigma, m), \mathcal{Q} \leftarrow \mathcal{Q} \cup \{m\}$
        return σ
return 1, if $\mathsf{Verify}_\Sigma(\mathsf{pk}_\Sigma, m^*, \sigma^*) = 1 \wedge m^* \notin \mathcal{Q}$
return 0

Fig. 1. EUF-CMA security.

2.2 Double-Authentication-Preventing Signatures

Double-authentication-preventing signatures (DAPS) are signature schemes being capable of signing messages from a message space $\mathcal{M}$ of the form $\mathsf{A} \times \mathsf{P}$. Each message $m = (a, p) \in \mathcal{M}$ thereby consists of an address a in address space A and a payload p from payload space P. In addition to the algorithms provided by conventional signature schemes, a DAPS scheme provides a fourth algorithm $\mathsf{Ex_D}$ that extracts the secret key from signatures on two colliding messages, i.e., two different messages sharing the same address. Formally, a pair of colliding messages is defined as follows:

Definition 3 (Colliding Messages). *We call two messages $m_1 = (a_1, p_1)$ and $m_2 = (a_2, p_2)$ colliding if $a_1 = a_2$, but $p_1 \neq p_2$.*

Below, we now formally define DAPS following [25, 26].

Definition 4 (DAPS). *A double-authentication-preventing signature scheme DAPS is a tuple $(\mathsf{KGen_D}, \mathsf{Sign_D}, \mathsf{Verify_D}, \mathsf{Ex_D})$ of PPT algorithms, which are defined as follows:*

$\mathsf{KGen_D}(1^\kappa)$: *This algorithm takes a security parameter κ as input and outputs a secret (signing) key $\mathsf{sk_D}$ and a public (verification) key $\mathsf{pk_D}$ with associated message space $\mathcal{M}$ (we may omit to make the message space $\mathcal{M}$ explicit).*

$\mathsf{Sign_D}(\mathsf{sk_D}, m)$: *This algorithm takes a secret key $\mathsf{sk_D}$ and a message $m \in \mathcal{M}$ as input and outputs a signature σ.*

$\mathsf{Verify_D}(\mathsf{pk_D}, m, \sigma)$: *This algorithm takes a public key $\mathsf{pk_D}$, a message $m \in \mathcal{M}$ and a signature σ as input and outputs a bit $b \in \{0, 1\}$.*

$\mathsf{Ex_D}(\mathsf{pk_D}, m_1, m_2, \sigma_1, \sigma_2)$: *This algorithm takes a public key $\mathsf{pk_D}$, two colliding messages m_1 and m_2 and signatures σ_1 for m_1 and σ_2 for m_2 as inputs and outputs a secret key $\mathsf{sk_D}$.*

Note that the algorithms $\mathsf{KGen_D}$, $\mathsf{Sign_D}$, and $\mathsf{Verify_D}$ match the definition of the algorithms of a conventional signature scheme. For DAPS one requires a restricted but otherwise standard notion of unforgeability [25,26], where adversaries can adaptively query signatures for messages but only on distinct addresses. Figure 2 details the unforgeability security experiment.

Definition 5 (EUF-CMA [25]). *For a PPT adversary $\mathcal{A}$, we define the advantage function in the sense of EUF-CMA as*

$$\mathsf{Adv}_{\mathcal{A},\mathsf{DAPS}}^{\mathsf{EUF\text{-}CMA}}(\kappa) = \Pr\left[\mathsf{Exp}_{\mathcal{A},\mathsf{DAPS}}^{\mathsf{EUF\text{-}CMA}}(\kappa) = 1\right]$$

where the corresponding experiment is depicted in Fig. 2. If for all PPT adversaries $\mathcal{A}$ there is a negligible function $\varepsilon(\cdot)$ such that

$$\mathsf{Adv}_{\mathcal{A},\mathsf{DAPS}}^{\mathsf{EUF\text{-}CMA}}(\kappa) \leq \varepsilon(\kappa)$$

we say that DAPS is EUF-CMA secure.

The interesting property of a DAPS scheme is the notion of double-signature extractability (DSE). It requires that whenever one obtains signatures on two colliding messages, one should be able to extract the signing key using the extraction algorithm $\mathsf{Ex_D}$. We present the security definition denoted as DSE in Fig. 3. Thereby, we consider the common notion which requires extraction to work if the key pair has been generated honestly. In this game, the adversary is given a

$\mathsf{Exp}_{\mathcal{A},\mathsf{DAPS}}^{\mathsf{EUF\text{-}CMA}}(\kappa):$
  $(\mathsf{sk}_D, \mathsf{pk}_D) \leftarrow \mathsf{KGen}_D(1^\kappa)$
  $\mathcal{Q} \leftarrow \emptyset, \mathcal{R} \leftarrow \emptyset$
  $(m^*, \sigma^*) \leftarrow \mathcal{A}^{\mathsf{Sign}_D'(\mathsf{sk}_D, \cdot)}(\mathsf{pk}_\Sigma)$
    where oracle Sign_D' on input m:
      $(a, p) \leftarrow m$
      if $a \in \mathcal{R}$, return $\perp$
      $\sigma \leftarrow \mathsf{Sign}_D(\mathsf{sk}_D, m), \mathcal{Q} \leftarrow \mathcal{Q} \cup \{m\}, \mathcal{R} \leftarrow \mathcal{R} \cup \{a\}$
      return σ
  return 1, if $\mathsf{Verify}_D(\mathsf{pk}_D, m^*, \sigma^*) = 1 \wedge m^* \notin \mathcal{Q}$
  return 0

Fig. 2. EUF-CMA security for DAPS.

key pair and outputs two colliding messages and corresponding signatures. The adversary wins the game if the key produced by Ex_D is different from the signing key, although extraction should have succeeded, i.e., the messages were colliding and their signatures were valid.

Definition 6 (DSE [25]). *For a PPT adversary $\mathcal{A}$, we define the advantage function in the sense of double-signature extraction (DSE) as*

$$\mathsf{Adv}_{\mathcal{A},\mathsf{DAPS}}^{\mathsf{DSE}}(\kappa) = \Pr\left[\mathsf{Exp}_{\mathcal{A},\mathsf{DAPS}}^{\mathsf{DSE}}(\kappa) = 1\right]$$

where the corresponding experiment is depicted in Fig. 3. If for all PPT adversaries $\mathcal{A}$ there is a negligible function $\varepsilon(\cdot)$ such that

$$\mathsf{Adv}_{\mathcal{A},\mathsf{DAPS}}^{\mathsf{DSE}}(\kappa) \leq \varepsilon(\kappa),$$

then DAPS *provides* DSE.

$\mathsf{Exp}_{\mathcal{A},\mathsf{DAPS}}^{\mathsf{DSE}}(\kappa):$
  $(\mathsf{sk}_D, \mathsf{pk}_D) \leftarrow \mathsf{KGen}_D(1^\kappa)$
  $(m_1, m_2, \sigma_1, \sigma_2) \leftarrow \mathcal{A}(\mathsf{sk}_D, \mathsf{pk}_D)$
  return 0, if m_1 and m_2 are not colliding
  return 0, if $\mathsf{Verify}_D(\mathsf{pk}_D, m_i, \sigma_i) = 0$ for any $i \in [2]$
  $\mathsf{sk}_D' \leftarrow \mathsf{Ex}_D(\mathsf{pk}_D, m_1, m_2, \sigma_1, \sigma_2)$
  return 1, if $\mathsf{sk}_D' \neq \mathsf{sk}_D$
  return 0

Fig. 3. DSE security for DAPS.

In the full version we recall the strong variant of extractability under malicious keys (denoted as DSE*), where the adversary is allowed to generate the key arbitrarily. The DSE* notion is very interesting from a theoretical perspective, but no practically efficient DAPS construction can achieve this notion so far.

DRS in [16] argue that when DAPS are constructed by extending a conventional signature scheme Σ, extraction of the part of the signing key corresponding to Σ is already sufficient to disincentivizes double-authentication for many applications. Hence, Derler et al. [16] defined two weaker double-signature extraction notions that cover extraction of the signing key of the underlying signature scheme for honestly and maliciously generated DAPS keys. The security games for weak double-signature extraction (wDSE) and weak double-signature extraction under malicious keys (wDSE*) are depicted in Figs. 4 and 5. DSE and DSE* imply their weaker counterparts and wDSE* implies wDSE.

Definition 7 $(T \in \{\mathsf{wDSE}, \mathsf{wDSE}^*\})$. *For a PPT adversary $\mathcal{A}$, we define the advantage function in the sense of weak double-signature extraction ($T = \mathsf{wDSE}$) and weak double-signature extraction under malicious keys ($T = \mathsf{wDSE}^*$), as*

$$\mathsf{Adv}^T_{\mathcal{A},\mathsf{DAPS}}(\kappa) = \Pr\left[\mathsf{Exp}^T_{\mathcal{A},\mathsf{DAPS}}(\kappa) = 1\right]$$

where the corresponding experiments are depicted in Figs. 4 and 5 respectively. If for all PPT adversaries $\mathcal{A}$ there is a negligible function $\varepsilon(\cdot)$ such that

$$\mathsf{Adv}^T_{\mathcal{A},\mathsf{DAPS}}(\kappa) \leq \varepsilon(\kappa),$$

then DAPS *provides T.*

$\mathsf{Exp}^{\mathsf{wDSE}}_{\mathcal{A},\mathsf{DAPS}}(\kappa)$:
  $(\mathsf{sk}_\mathsf{D}, \mathsf{pk}_\mathsf{D}) \leftarrow \mathsf{KGen}_\mathsf{D}(1^\kappa)$ with $\mathsf{sk}_\mathsf{D} = (\mathsf{sk}_\Sigma, \ldots)$
  $(m_1, m_2, \sigma_1, \sigma_2) \leftarrow \mathcal{A}(\mathsf{sk}_\mathsf{D}, \mathsf{pk}_\mathsf{D})$
  return 0, if m_1 and m_2 are not colliding
  return 0, if $\mathsf{Verify}_\mathsf{D}(\mathsf{pk}_\mathsf{D}, m_i, \sigma_i) = 0$ for any $i \in [2]$
  $\mathsf{sk}'_\mathsf{D} \leftarrow \mathsf{Ex}_\mathsf{D}(\mathsf{pk}_\mathsf{D}, m_1, m_2, \sigma_1, \sigma_2)$ where $\mathsf{sk}'_\mathsf{D} = (\mathsf{sk}'_\Sigma, \ldots)$
  return 1, if $\mathsf{sk}'_\Sigma \neq \mathsf{sk}_\Sigma$
  return 0

Fig. 4. wDSE security for DAPS.

$\mathsf{Exp}^{\mathsf{wDSE}^*}_{\mathcal{A},\mathsf{DAPS}}(\kappa)$:
  $(\mathsf{pk}_\mathsf{D}, m_1, m_2, \sigma_1, \sigma_2) \leftarrow \mathcal{A}(1^\kappa)$ where $\mathsf{pk}_\mathsf{D} = (\mathsf{pk}_\Sigma, \ldots)$
  return 0, if m_1 and m_2 are not colliding
  return 0, if $\mathsf{Verify}_\mathsf{D}(\mathsf{pk}_\mathsf{D}, m_i, \sigma_i) = 0$ for any $i \in [2]$
  $\mathsf{sk}'_\mathsf{D} \leftarrow \mathsf{Ex}_\mathsf{D}(\mathsf{pk}_\mathsf{D}, m_1, m_2, \sigma_1, \sigma_2)$ where $\mathsf{sk}'_\mathsf{D} = (\mathsf{sk}'_\Sigma, \ldots)$
  return 1, if sk'_Σ is not the secret key corresponding to pk_Σ
  return 0

Fig. 5. wDSE* security for DAPS.

Finally, for our constructions we may sometimes require a very mild additional property of DAPS which we call *verifiability of secret keys*. Informally it requires that there is an additional efficient algorithm VKey which, given a key pair, outputs 1 if the given secret key is the key corresponding to the given public key. Formally we define verifiability of keys as follows:

Definition 8 (Verifiability of Keys). *We say that a DAPS scheme* DAPS = $(KGen_D, Sign_D, Verify_D, Ex_D)$ *provides verifiability of keys, if it provides an additional efficient algorithm* VKey *so that for all* $\kappa \in \mathbb{N}$, *for all* (sk, pk) *it holds that*

$$VKey(sk, pk) = 1 \implies (sk, pk) \in KGen_D(1^\kappa).$$

2.3 Non-interactive ZK Proof Systems (NIZK)

We recall a standard definition of non-interactive zero-knowledge proof systems. Let $L \subseteq X$ be an **NP**-language with associated witness relation R so that $L = \{x \mid \exists w : R(x, w) = 1\}$.

Definition 9 (Non-Interactive Zero-Knowledge Proof System). *A non-interactive proof system* Π *is a tuple of algorithms* (Setup$_\Pi$, Proof$_\Pi$, Verify$_\Pi$), *which are defined as follows:*

Setup$_\Pi(1^\kappa)$: *This algorithm takes a security parameter* κ *as input, and outputs a common reference string* crs.

Proof$_\Pi$(crs, x, w) : *This algorithm takes a common reference string* crs, *a statement* x, *and a witness* w *as input, and outputs a proof* π.

Verify$_\Pi$(crs, x, π) : *This algorithm takes a common reference string* crs, *a statement* x, *and a proof* π *as input, and outputs a bit* $b \in \{0, 1\}$.

From a non-interactive zero-knowledge proof system we require *completeness*, *soundness* and *adaptive zero-knowledge* and *simulation-sound extractability*. In the full version we recall formal definitions of those properties.

NIZK from Σ-protocols. A Σ-protocol for language L is an interactive three move protocol between a prover and a verifier, where the prover proves knowledge of a witness w to the statement $x \in L$. We recall the formal definition of Σ-protocols in the full version. One can obtain a non-interactive proof system with the above properties by applying the Fiat-Shamir transform [17] to any Σ-protocol where the min-entropy μ of the commitment a sent in the first message of the Σ-protocol is so that $2^{-\mu}$ is negligible in the security parameter κ and its challenge space C is exponentially large in the security parameter. Essentially, the transform removes the interaction between the prover and the verifier by using a hash function H (modelled as a random oracle) to obtain the challenge. That is, the algorithm Challenge obtains the challenge as $H(a, x)$. Due to the lack of space we postpone a formal presentation to the full version.

Efficient NIZK Proof Systems for General Circuits. Over the last few years NIZK proof systems for general circuits have seen significant progress improving their overall efficiency. Based on the MPC-in-the-head paradigm by Ishai et al. [21], ZKBoo [19] and the optimized version ZKB++ [12] are zero-knowledge proof systems covering languages over arbitrary circuits. They roughly work as follows: The prover simulates all parties of a multiparty computation (MPC) protocol implementing the joint evaluation of some function, say $y = \text{SHA-3}(x)$, and computes commitments to the states of all players. The verifier then randomly corrupts a subset of the players and checks whether those players performed the computation correctly. Following the same paradigm, Katz et al. [22] recently proposed to use a MPC protocol with a preprocessing phase, which allows to significantly reduce the proof sizes. This proof system, denoted as KKW, allows one to choose a larger number of players then in the case of ZKBoo and ZKB++, where larger numbers lead to smaller proofs. For all three proof systems, the number of binary multiplication gates is the main factor influencing the proof size, as the proof size grows linearly with the number of those gates.

Finally, Ames et al. [4] introduced Ligero, which offers proofs of logarithmic size in the number of multiplication gates if the circuit is represented using a prime field. When considering binary circuits, the number of addition respectively XOR gates has also to be accounted for in the proof size. But, as noted by Katz et al. in [22], especially for large circuits with more than 100,000 gates Ligero beats ZKBoo, ZKB++ and KKW in term of proof size.

2.4 Shamir's Secret Sharing

Shamir's (k, ℓ)-threshold secret sharing [29] is a secret sharing scheme which allows to information-theoretically share a secret s among a set of ℓ parties so that any collection of at least k shares allow to reconstruct s. Let s be the constant term of an otherwise randomly chosen $k - 1$ degree polynomial

$$f(X) = \rho_{k-1}X^{k-1} + \cdots + \rho_1 X + s$$

over a finite field $\mathbb{F}$. A share is computed as $f(i)$ for party i, $1 \leq i \leq \ell$. Let $\mathcal{S}$ be any set of cardinality at least k of these ℓ shares and let $I_\mathcal{S}$ be the set of indices corresponding to shares in $\mathcal{S}$. Using Lagrange interpolation one can then can reconstruct the secret s by computing $s = f(0)$ as

$$s = \sum_{j \in I_\mathcal{S}} \lambda_j f(j) \quad \text{with} \quad \lambda_j = \prod_{i \in I_\mathcal{S} \backslash \{j\}} \frac{j}{j - i}.$$

As long as only $k - 1$ or less shares are available the secret s is information-theoretically hidden.

3   DAPS Without Structured Hardness Assumptions

For our first construction we follow the basic idea of Derler et al. [16] and build DAPS by including secret shares of the signing key in the signatures. To resolve the address space limitation of their approach, however, we derive the coefficients

---

KGen$_D$(1^κ): Fix a signature scheme $\Sigma = (\text{KGen}_\Sigma, \text{Sign}_\Sigma, \text{Verify}_\Sigma)$, a value-key-binding
    PRF $\mathcal{F} : \mathcal{S} \times D \to \mathsf{R}$ with respect to $\beta \in D$. Let $\text{sk}_{\text{PRF}} \overset{R}{\leftarrow} \mathcal{S}$, and crs $\leftarrow \text{Setup}_\Pi(1^\kappa)$.
    Let $c = \mathcal{F}(\text{sk}_{\text{PRF}}, \beta)$. Set $\text{sk}_D \leftarrow (\text{sk}_\Sigma, \text{sk}_{\text{PRF}})$, $\text{pk}_D \leftarrow (\text{pk}_\Sigma, \text{crs}, \beta, c)$.
Sign$_D$(sk_D, m): Parse sk_D as $(\text{sk}_\Sigma, \text{sk}_{\text{PRF}})$ and m as (a, p).
    1. $\rho \leftarrow \mathcal{F}(\text{sk}_{\text{PRF}}, a)$
    2. $z \leftarrow \rho p + \text{sk}_\Sigma$
    3. $\pi \leftarrow \text{Proof}_\Pi(\text{crs}, (\text{pk}_\Sigma, \beta, c, a, z, m), (\text{sk}_\Sigma, \text{sk}_{\text{PRF}}, \rho))$
    4. Return (z, π).
Verify$_D$(pk_D, m, σ): Parse pk_D as $(\text{pk}_\Sigma, \text{crs}, \beta, c)$, m as (a, p) and σ as (z, π).
    1. Return $\text{Verify}_\Pi(\text{crs}, (\text{pk}_\Sigma, \beta, c, a, z, m), \pi)$.
Ex$_D$($\text{pk}_D, m_1, m_2, \sigma_1, \sigma_2$): Parse σ_i as $(z_i, \cdot)$, m_i as (a_i, p_i).
    1. If m_1 and m_2 are not colliding, return $\bot$
    2. if $\text{Verify}_D(\text{pk}_D, m_i, \sigma_i) = 0$ for any i, return $\bot$
    3. let $\text{sk}_\Sigma \leftarrow \frac{z_1 p_2 - z_2 p_1}{p_2 - p_1}$
    4. return sk_Σ

Scheme 1. Generic DAPS from Σ.

of the sharing polynomial using a pseudorandom function (PRF). By then additionally proving the correct evaluation of the PRF, it is no longer necessary to store encrypted versions of the coefficients in the public key. The only issue which remains, is to additionally prove consistency with respect to a "commitment" to the PRF secret key contained in the public key (we commit to it using a fixed-value key-binding PRF as defined in Appendix A). To bind the message to the proof, we use a signature-of-knowledge style methodology [14].

More precisely, we start from a one-way function $f : S \to P$, which we use to define the relation between public and secret keys, i.e., so that $\text{pk}_\Sigma = f(\text{sk}_\Sigma)$. In addition we carefully choose a PRF $\mathcal{F}$, which maps to the secret key space S. At the core of our DAPS construction we use a NIZK proof to prove consistency of the secret signing key, as well as the correctness of the secret sharing. For this proof we define an language L with associated witness relation R in the following way:

$$((\text{pk}_\Sigma, \beta, c, a, z), (\text{sk}_\Sigma, \text{sk}_{\text{PRF}}, \rho)) \in R \Longleftrightarrow$$
$$\rho = \mathcal{F}(\text{sk}_{\text{PRF}}, a) \ \wedge \ z = \rho p + \text{sk}_\Sigma \ \wedge \ c = \mathcal{F}(\text{sk}_{\text{PRF}}, \beta) \ \wedge \ \text{pk}_\Sigma = f(\text{sk}_\Sigma)$$

In this statement we cover three aspects: First, we prove that the polynomial for Shamir's secret sharing is derived from the address and that the secret share is correctly calculated. Second, we prove the relation between the secret and public key of the signature scheme. Third, we "commit" to the PRF secret key using a fixed-value key-binding PRF. The full scheme is depicted in Scheme 1.

It is important to note that the PRF needs to be compatible with the signature scheme, in the sense that secret-key space of Σ, i.e., S, and R match. For simplicity, we assume that $\mathsf{R} = S$. Additionally, the domain and codomain of the PRF also define the message space of the DAPS. In the following theorem we prove that Scheme 1 is an EUF-CMA-secure DAPS.

Theorem 1. *If the NIZK proof system Π is simulation-sound extractable, $\mathcal{F}$ is a PRF, and f is an OWF, then Scheme 1 provides* **EUF-CMA** *security.*

Proof We prove this theorem using a sequence of games. We denote the winning event of game G_i as S_i. We let Q_{Σ} be the number of signing oracle queries.

Game 0: The original game.

Game 1: As before, but we modify KGen_D as follows:

$\mathsf{KGen}_\mathsf{D}(1^\kappa)$: As before, but let $\boxed{(\mathsf{crs}, \tau) \leftarrow \mathcal{S}_{1,\Pi}(1^\kappa)}$ and store $\boxed{\tau}$.

Transition $0 \Rightarrow 1$: Both games are indistinguishable under adaptive zero-knowledge of the proof system, i.e. $|\Pr[S_0] - \Pr[S_1]| \leq \mathsf{Adv}_{\mathcal{A},\mathsf{S},\Pi}^{\mathsf{Sim}}(\kappa)$.

Game 2: As Game 1, but we modify Sign_D as follows:

$\mathsf{Sign}_\mathsf{D}(\mathsf{sk}, m)$: As before, but let $\boxed{\pi \leftarrow \mathcal{S}_{2,\Pi}(\mathsf{crs}, \tau, (\mathsf{pk}_\Sigma, \beta, c, a, z, m))}$.

Transition $1 \Rightarrow 2$: Both games are indistinguishable under adaptive zero-knowledge of the proof system, i.e. $|\Pr[S_1] - \Pr[S_2]| \leq \mathsf{Adv}_{\mathcal{A},\mathsf{S},\Pi}^{\mathsf{ZK}}(\kappa)$.

Game 3: As before, but we modify KGen_D and Sign_D as follows.

$\mathsf{KGen}_\mathsf{D}(1^\kappa)$: As before, but let $\boxed{c \xleftarrow{R} \mathsf{R}}$.

$\mathsf{Sign}_\mathsf{D}(\mathsf{sk}_\mathsf{D}, m)$: As before, but let $\boxed{\rho \xleftarrow{R} \mathsf{R}}$.

Transition $2 \Rightarrow 3$: We engage with a PRF challenger $\mathcal{C}$ against $\mathcal{F}$. We modify Sign_D as follows:

$\mathsf{KGen}_\mathsf{D}(1^\kappa)$: As before, but let $\boxed{c \xleftarrow{R} \mathcal{C}(\beta)}$.

$\mathsf{Sign}_\mathsf{D}(\mathsf{sk}_\mathsf{D}, m)$: As before, but let $\boxed{\rho \xleftarrow{R} \mathcal{C}(a)}$.

Thus an adversary distinguishing the two games also distinguishes the PRF from a random function, i.e. $|\Pr[S_4] - \Pr[S_3]| \leq \mathsf{Adv}_{\mathcal{D},F}(\kappa)$.

Game 4: As before, but we modify Sign_D as follows.

$\mathsf{Sign}_\mathsf{D}(\mathsf{sk}_\mathsf{D}, m)$: As before, but track all (a, ρ) pairs in $\mathcal{Q}$.

We abort if there exists $(a_1, \rho), (a_2, \rho) \in \mathcal{Q}$ such that $a_1 \neq a_2$.

Transition $3 \Rightarrow 4$: Both games proceed identically, unless the abort event happens. The probability of the abort event is bounded by $1/|\mathsf{R}|$, i.e. $|\Pr[S_5] - \Pr[S_4]| \leq Q_{\Sigma}/|\mathsf{R}|$.

Game 5: As before, but we modify Sign_D as follows.

$\mathsf{Sign}_\mathsf{D}(\mathsf{sk}_\mathsf{D}, m)$: As before, but let $\boxed{z \xleftarrow{R} \mathsf{R}}$.

Transition $4 \Rightarrow 5$: This change is conceptional. Note that ρ is uniformly random and not revealed, and thus z is uniformly random.

Game 6: As before, but we modify KGen_D as follows:

$\mathsf{KGen}_\mathsf{D}(1^\kappa)$: As before, but let $\boxed{(\mathsf{crs}, \tau, \xi) \leftarrow \mathcal{E}_{1,\Pi}(1^\kappa)}$ and store $\boxed{(\tau, \xi)}$.

Transition $5 \Rightarrow 6$: Both games are indistinguishable under simulation-sound extractability of the proof system, i.e. $|\Pr[S_6] - \Pr[S_5]| \leq \mathsf{Adv}_{\mathcal{A},\mathcal{E},\Pi}^{\mathsf{Ext}_1}(\kappa)$.

Game 7: As before, but we now use the extractor to obtain $\mathsf{sk}_\Sigma^* \leftarrow \mathcal{E}_{2,\Pi}(\mathsf{crs}, \xi, (\mathsf{pk}_\Sigma, \beta, c, a, z, m), \pi)$ and abort in case the extraction fails.

Transition $6 \Rightarrow 7$: Both games proceed identically, unless we abort. The probability of that happening is bounded by the simulation-sound extractablity of the proof system, i.e. $|\Pr[S_7] - \Pr[S_6]| \leq \mathsf{Adv}_{\mathcal{A},\mathcal{E},\Pi}^{\mathsf{Ext}_2}(\kappa)$.

Reduction. Now we are ready to present a reduction which engages with an OWF challenger $\mathcal{C}$. In particular, we obtain a challenge and embed it in the public key, i.e.

$\mathsf{KGen_D}(1^\kappa)$: As before, but $\boxed{\mathsf{pk}_\Sigma \leftarrow \mathcal{C}}$.

Once the adversary returns a forgery, we extract sk_Σ^* and forward the solution to the OWF challenger. Hence $\Pr[S_7] \leq \mathsf{Adv}_{\mathcal{A},f}^{\mathsf{OWF}}(\kappa)$, which concludes the proof.

$\square$

We now show that Scheme 1 also provides wDSE security. We note that in the proof of Theorem 2 we do not need to simulate proofs, so a weaker extraction notion would suffice. The proof of Theorem 1, however, already requires simulation-sound extractability which is why we directly resort to simulation-sound extractability.

Theorem 2. *If the NIZK proof system Π is simulation-sound extractable and the PRF $\mathcal{F}$ is computationally fixed-value-key-binding, then Scheme 1 provides wDSE security.*

Proof We prove this theorem using a sequence of games. We denote the winning event of game G_i as S_i. Let $m_1, m_2, \sigma_1, \sigma_2$ denote the output of $\mathcal{A}$. For simplicity we write $m_j = (a, p_j)$, $\sigma_j = (z_j, \pi_j)$ for $j \in [2]$. Now, we have proofs attesting that $z_j = \rho p_j + \mathsf{sk}_\Sigma$ for $j \in [2]$.

Game 0: The original game.
Game 1: As before, but we modify $\mathsf{KGen_D}$ as follows:
   $\mathsf{KGen_D}(1^\kappa)$: As before, but let $\boxed{(\mathsf{crs}, \tau) \leftarrow \mathcal{S}_{1,\Pi}(1^\kappa)}$ and store $\boxed{\tau}$.
Transition $0 \Rightarrow 1$: Both games are indistinguishable under adaptive zero-knowledge of the proof system, i.e. $|\Pr[S_0] - \Pr[S_1]| \leq \mathsf{Adv}_{\mathcal{A},\mathcal{S},\Pi}^{\mathsf{Sim}}(\kappa)$.
Game 2: As before, but we modify $\mathsf{KGen_D}$ as follows:
   $\mathsf{KGen_D}(1^\kappa)$: As before, but let $\boxed{(\mathsf{crs}, \tau, \xi) \leftarrow \mathcal{E}_{1,\Pi}(1^\kappa)}$ and store $\boxed{\xi}$.
Transition $1 \Rightarrow 2$: Both games are indistinguishable under simulation-sound extractability of the proof system, i.e. $|\Pr[S_2] - \Pr[S_1]| \leq \mathsf{Adv}_{\Sigma,\mathcal{E},\Pi}^{\mathsf{Ext}_1}(\kappa)$.
Game 3: As before, but we now use the extractor to obtain $(\mathsf{sk}_{\Sigma,j}^*, \mathsf{sk}_{\mathsf{PRF},j}^*) \leftarrow \mathcal{E}_{2,\Pi}(\mathsf{crs}, \xi, (\mathsf{pk}_\Sigma, \beta, c, a, z_j, m_j), \pi)$ for $j \in [2]$ and abort if the extraction fails.
Transition $2 \Rightarrow 3$: Both games proceed identically, unless we abort. The probability of that happening is bounded by the simulation-sound extractablity of the proof system, i.e. $|\Pr[S_3] - \Pr[S_2]| \leq 2 \cdot \mathsf{Adv}_{\mathcal{A},\mathcal{E},\Pi}^{\mathsf{Ext}_2}(\kappa)$.
Game 4:] As before, but we abort if $\mathsf{sk}_{\mathsf{PRF}} \neq \mathsf{sk}_{\mathsf{PRF},j}^*$ for any $j \in [2]$.
Transition $3 \Rightarrow 4$: Both games proceed identically, unless we abort. Let $j \in [2]$ be such that $\mathsf{sk}_{\mathsf{PRF}} \neq \mathsf{sk}_{\mathsf{PRF},j}^*$. We bound the abort probability using $\mathcal{F}$. Let $\mathcal{C}$ be a computational fixed-value-key-binding challenger. We modify $\mathsf{KGen_D}$ as follows:
   $\mathsf{KGen_D}(1^\kappa)$: As before, but let $\boxed{(\mathsf{sk}_{\mathsf{PRF}}, \beta)} \leftarrow \mathcal{C}$.
   Then we have that $\mathcal{F}(\mathsf{sk}_{\mathsf{PRF}}, \beta) = \mathcal{F}(\mathsf{sk}_{\mathsf{PRF},j}^*, \beta)$, hence we forward $\mathsf{sk}_{\mathsf{PRF},j}^*$ to $\mathcal{C}$. Thus we built an adversary $\mathcal{B}$ against fixed-value-key-binding of $\mathcal{F}$, i.e. $|\Pr[S_4] - \Pr[S_3]| \leq \mathsf{Adv}_{\mathcal{B},\mathcal{F}}^{\mathsf{cFKVB}}(\kappa) = \varepsilon(\kappa)$.

As we have now ensured that the correct PRF secret key was used to generate ρ from a, sk_Σ is now uniquely determined via the secret sharing. Thus the adversary can no longer win, i.e. $\Pr[S_4] = 0$. $\qquad\square$

Extension to NAPS. Following the ideas outlined in [16], Scheme 1 can be extended to an N-time authentication-preventing signature scheme by changing the sharing polynomial $\rho X + \mathsf{sk}_\Sigma$ to a polynomial of degree $N - 1$ with coefficients $\rho_1, \ldots, \rho_{N-1}$ obtained from the PRF via $\rho_i = \mathcal{F}(\mathsf{sk}_{\mathsf{PRF}}, a\|i)$.

Instantiations. The requirement on the signature scheme are very weak, yet finding a suitable combination of primitives can be difficult. Thus we discuss some possible instantiations. One candidate scheme on top of which the DAPS extension can be applied is Picnic [12,13]. In Picnic the public key pk_Σ is the image of the secret key sk_Σ under a one-way function built from LowMC [2, 3]. Signatures are then generated by proving this relation using a NIZK from ZKB++ made non-interactive. In this case it is straight forward to use the block cipher LowMC (denoted by $\mathcal{E}$) as PRF by setting $\mathcal{F}(s, x) = \mathcal{E}(s, x) \oplus x$. We argue that this PRF can also be considered a computational fixed-value-key-binding PRF, since it is reasonable to assume that finding a new key which maps one particular input to one particular output is no easier than generic key search. Furthermore, when increasing the block size of LowMC relative to the key size, the existence of second key mapping to the same output becomes increasingly unlikely.

The circuit for the secret sharing can either be implemented using a binary circuit realizing the required arithmetic, or, more efficiently, by computing the sharing bit-wise. For the latter, we consider ρ, p and sk_Σ as n bit values, and compute secret shares $z_i = \rho_i p_i + \mathsf{sk}_{\Sigma,i}$ for each bit $i \in [n]$. Thus only n ANDs are required to implemented the secret sharing. All in all Picnic signatures can be easily extended to a DAPS without requiring extensive changes. We also note that the Fiat-Shamir transformed ZKB++ is in fact simulation-sound extractable NIZK proof systems as confirmed in [15]. Using the signature size formulas, we can estimate DAPS signatures sizes at around 408 KB, meaning there is a overhead of 293 KB compared to Picnic signatures requiring roughly 115 KB in the ROM targeting 256 bit classical security. Analogously to the QROM security of Picnic, Unruh's transform [31–33] can be used to obtain QROM security for the DAPS construction.

Also hash-based signatures such as SPHINCS [8] are well suited for this construction. Similar to the case of Picnic, the PRF can be instantiated using LowMC. However, the consistency proof is more expensive, as computing the public key requires multiple evaluations of hash functions.

Relying on Structured Hardness Assumptions. The situation is different for signature schemes relying on structured hardness assumptions, e.g., those in the discrete logarithm setting such as Schnorr signatures [28], ECDSA and EdDSA [7]. While they would fulfill the requirement for the secret-key-to-public-key relation, i.e., here working in a group $\mathbb{G}$ with generator g the OWF is of the form $f(x) := g^x$, the problem is finding an efficient NIZK proof system to prove statements over $\mathbb{Z}_p$ and in a prime order group $\mathbb{G}$ simultaneously. Furthermore the NIZK proof system would also need to support statements over binary circuits for the PRF evaluation. Recently, Agrawal et al. [1] made progress in this direction, enabling non-interactive proofs of composite statements for relations over multiple groups and binary circuits. Using these techniques to construct DAPS is an interesting open problem.

4   Extending Any Signature Scheme Using DAPS

Finally, we follow a different direction for our second approach. Here we start from an already existing DAPS and use it to extend *any* unforgeable signature scheme to a DAPS. Interestingly, both the unforgeability and extraction follow in a black-box way from the signature scheme and the underlying DAPS, respectively. In this construction, the secret key consists of the secret keys of the underlying DAPS and signature scheme. To guarantee extraction of the full secret key, we apply the technique of Bellare et al. [6] and encrypt the key of the signature scheme using a one-time pad derived from the secret key of the DAPS scheme. The public key then consists of that encrypted key and the public keys of the underlying DAPS and signature scheme. However, for extraction of maliciously generated keys, i.e., DSE*-security, this means that public keys need to be extended with a NIZK proof that the encryption was performed correctly. For the sake of simplicity, we thus concentrate on the DSE security of the scheme. We present the compiler in Scheme 2.

$\mathsf{KGen_D}(1^\kappa)$: Fix some signature scheme $\Sigma = (\mathsf{KGen_\Sigma}, \mathsf{Sign_\Sigma}, \mathsf{Verify_\Sigma})$ and some DAPS $\mathsf{DAPS} = (\mathsf{KGen_D}, \mathsf{Sign_D}, \mathsf{Verify_D}, \mathsf{Ex_D})$ with verifiability of keys. Let $(\mathsf{sk_\Sigma}, \mathsf{pk_\Sigma}) \leftarrow \Sigma.\mathsf{KGen_\Sigma}(1^\kappa)$, $(\mathsf{sk}, \mathsf{pk}) \leftarrow \mathsf{DAPS}.\mathsf{KGen_D}(1^\kappa)$, $Y \leftarrow \mathsf{sk_\Sigma} \oplus H(\mathsf{sk})$, and return $(\mathsf{sk_D}, \mathsf{pk_D}) := ((\mathsf{sk_\Sigma}, \mathsf{sk}), (\mathsf{pk_\Sigma}, \mathsf{pk}, Y))$.

$\mathsf{Sign_D}(\mathsf{sk_D}, m)$: Parse $\mathsf{sk_D}$ as $(\mathsf{sk_\Sigma}, \mathsf{sk})$.
    1. $\sigma_0 \leftarrow \Sigma.\mathsf{Sign_\Sigma}(\mathsf{sk_\Sigma}, m)$
    2. $\sigma_1 \leftarrow \mathsf{DAPS}.\mathsf{Sign_D}(\mathsf{sk}, m)$
    3. Return $\sigma = (\sigma_0, \sigma_1)$

$\mathsf{Verify_D}(\mathsf{pk_D}, m, \sigma)$: Parse $\mathsf{pk_D}$ as $(\mathsf{pk_\Sigma}, \mathsf{pk}, \cdot)$, and return 1 if all of the following checks hold and 0 otherwise:
    – $\Sigma.\mathsf{Verify_\Sigma}(\mathsf{pk}, (a, p)) = 1$
    – $\mathsf{DAPS}.\mathsf{Verify_D}(\mathsf{pk_D}, (a, p)) = 1$

$\mathsf{Ex_D}(\mathsf{pk_D}, m_1, m_2, \sigma_1, \sigma_2)$: Parse $\mathsf{pk_D}$ as $(\mathsf{pk_\Sigma}, \mathsf{pk}, Y)$, obtain $\mathsf{sk} \leftarrow \mathsf{DAPS}.\mathsf{Ex_D}(\mathsf{pk}, m_1, m_2, \sigma_1, \sigma_2)$ and $\mathsf{sk_\Sigma} \leftarrow Y \oplus H(\mathsf{sk})$, and return $\mathsf{sk_D} = (\mathsf{sk_\Sigma}, \mathsf{sk})$.

Scheme 2. Black-Box Extension of any Signature Scheme to DAPS.

In the following theorem we formally state that the DAPS construction in Scheme 2 yields an EUF-CMA-secure DAPS.

Theorem 3. *If Σ is unforgeable,* DAPS *is unforgeable and provides verifiability of keys, then the DAPS construction in Scheme 2 is unforgeable in the ROM.*

The theorem above is proven in the full version. Additionally, Scheme 1 provides DSE-security if the underlying DAPS provides it as well.

Theorem 4. *If* DAPS *provides* DSE-*security, then the construction of DAPS in Scheme 2 provides* DSE-*security as well.*

The theorem above is proven in the full version.

5   Conclusion

In this work, we close two important gaps in the literature on DAPS. First, we present a generic DAPS construction, which, in contrast to [16], does not come with the drawback of a polynomially bounded address space. Our construction only relies on assumptions related to symmetric key primitives, which is why we also obtain a candidate for a post-quantum DAPS construction. Second, we also present an alternative generic construction of DAPS which basically shows how to bring DAPS features to any signature scheme. This is of particular practical importance, as it allows to extend arbitrary signature schemes with double signature extraction features. As our compiler works by using an arbitrary DAPS scheme to extend a given signature scheme in a black-box way, this yields more efficient DAPS than previously known for standardized and widely used signature schemes such as ECDSA or EdDSA.

A   One-Way Functions and Pseudorandom Function Families

We recall the definitions of one-way functions and pseudorandom function (families).

Definition 10 (OWF). *Let $f : S \to P$ be a function. For a PPT adversary $\mathcal{A}$ we define the advantage function as*

$$\mathsf{Adv}^{\mathsf{OWF}}_{\mathcal{A},f}(\kappa) = \Pr\left[x \xleftarrow{R} S, x^* \leftarrow \mathcal{A}(1^\kappa, f(x)) : f(x) = f(\mathcal{A}^*)\right].$$

The function f is one-way function (OWF) if it is efficiently computable and for all PPT adversaries $\mathcal{A}$ there exists a negligible function $\varepsilon(\cdot)$ such that

$$\mathsf{Adv}^{\mathsf{OWF}}_{\mathcal{A},f}(\kappa) \le \varepsilon(\kappa).$$

Definition 11 (PRF). *Let $\mathcal{F} : S \times D \to R$ be a family of functions and let Γ be the set of all functions $D \to R$. For a PPT distinguisher $\mathcal{D}$ we define the advantage function as*

$$\mathsf{Adv}^{\mathsf{PRF}}_{\mathcal{D},\mathcal{F}}(\kappa) = \left|\Pr\left[s \xleftarrow{R} S, \mathcal{D}^{\mathcal{F}(s,\cdot)}(1^\kappa)\right] - \Pr[f \xleftarrow{R} \Gamma, \mathcal{D}^{f(\cdot)}(1^\kappa)]\right|.$$

$\mathcal{F}$ is a pseudorandom function (family) if it is efficiently computable and for all PPT distinguishers $\mathcal{D}$ there exists a negligible function $\varepsilon(\cdot)$ such that

$$\mathsf{Adv}^{\mathsf{PRF}}_{\mathcal{D},\mathcal{F}}(\kappa) \leq \varepsilon(\kappa).$$

Below, we provide a slightly stronger variant of a definition of a notion introduced in [11,18].

Definition 12 (Fixed-Value-Key-Binding PRF). *A PRF family $\mathcal{F} : \mathcal{S} \times D \to \mathsf{R}$ and a $\beta \in D$, is fixed-value-key-binding if for all adversaries $\mathcal{A}$*

$$\Pr\left[s \xleftarrow{R} \mathcal{S}, s' \leftarrow \mathcal{A}(s,\beta) : \mathcal{F}(s,\beta) = \mathcal{F}(s',\beta) \wedge s \neq s' \right] = 0.$$

Moreover, we present a relaxed (computational) version of the above definition.

Definition 13 (Computational Fixed-Value-Key-Binding PRF). *For a PRF family $\mathcal{F} : \mathcal{S} \times D \to \mathsf{R}$ and a $\beta \in D$, we define the advantage function of a PPT adversary $\mathcal{A}$ as*

$$\mathsf{Adv}^{\mathsf{cFKVB}}_{\mathcal{A},\mathcal{F}}(\kappa) = \Pr\left[s \xleftarrow{R} \mathcal{S}, s' \leftarrow \mathcal{A}(1^{\kappa},s,\beta) : \mathcal{F}(s,\beta) = \mathcal{F}(s',\beta) \wedge s \neq s' \right].$$

$\mathcal{F}$ is computationally fixed-value-key-binding if for all PPT adversaries there exists as negligible function $\varepsilon(\cdot)$ such that

$$\mathsf{Adv}^{\mathsf{cFKVB}}_{\mathcal{A},\mathcal{F}}(\kappa) = \varepsilon(\kappa).$$

References

1. Agrawal, S., Ganesh, C., Mohassel, P.: Non-interactive zero-knowledge proofs for composite statements. In: Shacham, H., Boldyreva, A. (eds.) CRYPTO 2018. LNCS, vol. 10993, pp. 643–673. Springer, Cham (2018). https://doi.org/10.1007/978-3-319-96878-0_22

2. Albrecht, M.R., Rechberger, C., Schneider, T., Tiessen, T., Zohner, M.: Ciphers for MPC and FHE. In: Oswald, E., Fischlin, M. (eds.) EUROCRYPT 2015. LNCS, vol. 9056, pp. 430–454. Springer, Heidelberg (2015). https://doi.org/10.1007/978-3-662-46800-5_17

3. Albrecht, M.R., Rechberger, C., Schneider, T., Tiessen, T., Zohner, M.: Ciphers for MPC and FHE. IACR Cryptology ePrint Archive 2016/687 (2016)

4. Ames, S., Hazay, C., Ishai, Y., Venkitasubramaniam, M.: Ligero: lightweight sublinear arguments without a trusted setup. In: CCS, pp. 2087–2104. ACM (2017)

5. Bellare, M., Poettering, B., Stebila, D.: From identification to signatures, tightly: a framework and generic transforms. In: Cheon, J.H., Takagi, T. (eds.) ASIACRYPT 2016. LNCS, vol. 10032, pp. 435–464. Springer, Heidelberg (2016). https://doi.org/10.1007/978-3-662-53890-6_15

6. Bellare, M., Poettering, B., Stebila, D.: Deterring certificate subversion: efficient double-authentication-preventing signatures. In: Fehr, S. (ed.) PKC 2017. LNCS, vol. 10175, pp. 121–151. Springer, Heidelberg (2017). https://doi.org/10.1007/978-3-662-54388-7_5

7. Bernstein, D.J., Duif, N., Lange, T., Schwabe, P., Yang, B.: High-speed high-security signatures. J. Cryptographic. Eng. **2**(2), 77–89 (2012)

8. Bernstein, D.J., et al.: SPHINCS: practical stateless hash-based signatures. In: Oswald, E., Fischlin, M. (eds.) EUROCRYPT 2015. LNCS, vol. 9056, pp. 368–397. Springer, Heidelberg (2015). https://doi.org/10.1007/978-3-662-46800-5_15

9. Boneh, D., Eskandarian, S., Fisch, B.: Post-quantum group signatures from symmetric primitives. IACR Cryptology ePrint Archive 2018/261 (2018)

10. Boneh, D., Kim, S., Nikolaenko, V.: Lattice-based DAPS and generalizations: self-enforcement in signature schemes. In: Gollmann, D., Miyaji, A., Kikuchi, H. (eds.) ACNS 2017. LNCS, vol. 10355, pp. 457–477. Springer, Cham (2017). https://doi.org/10.1007/978-3-319-61204-1_23

11. Canetti, R., Micciancio, D., Reingold, O.: Perfectly one-way probabilistic hash functions (preliminary version). In: STOC, pp. 131–140. ACM (1998)

12. Chase, M., et al.: Post-quantum zero-knowledge and signatures from symmetric-key primitives. In: CCS, pp. 1825–1842. ACM (2017)

13. Chase, M., et al.: The Picnic Signature Algorithm Specification (2017). https://github.com/Microsoft/Picnic/blob/master/spec.pdf

14. Chase, M., Lysyanskaya, A.: On signatures of knowledge. In: Dwork, C. (ed.) CRYPTO 2006. LNCS, vol. 4117, pp. 78–96. Springer, Heidelberg (2006). https://doi.org/10.1007/11818175_5

15. Derler, D., Ramacher, S., Slamanig, D.: Post-quantum zero-knowledge proofs for accumulators with applications to ring signatures from symmetric-key primitives. In: Lange, T., Steinwandt, R. (eds.) PQCrypto 2018. LNCS, vol. 10786, pp. 419–440. Springer, Cham (2018). https://doi.org/10.1007/978-3-319-79063-3_20

16. Derler, D., Ramacher, S., Slamanig, D.: Short double- and n-times-authentication-preventing signatures from ECDSA and more. In: EuroS&P, pp. 273–287. IEEE (2018)

17. Fiat, A., Shamir, A.: How to prove yourself: practical solutions to identification and signature problems. In: Odlyzko, A.M. (ed.) CRYPTO 1986. LNCS, vol. 263, pp. 186–194. Springer, Heidelberg (1987). https://doi.org/10.1007/3-540-47721-7_12

18. Fischlin, M.: Pseudorandom function tribe ensembles based on one-way permutations: improvements and applications. In: Stern, J. (ed.) EUROCRYPT 1999. LNCS, vol. 1592, pp. 432–445. Springer, Heidelberg (1999). https://doi.org/10.1007/3-540-48910-X_30

19. Giacomelli, I., Madsen, J., Orlandi, C.: ZKBoo: faster zero-knowledge for Boolean circuits. In: USENIX Security Symposium, pp. 1069–1083. USENIX Association (2016)

20. Guillou, L.C., Quisquater, J.-J.: A "Paradoxical" indentity-based signature scheme resulting from zero-knowledge. In: Goldwasser, S. (ed.) CRYPTO 1988. LNCS, vol. 403, pp. 216–231. Springer, New York (1990). https://doi.org/10.1007/0-387-34799-2_16

21. Ishai, Y., Kushilevitz, E., Ostrovsky, R., Sahai, A.: Zero-knowledge proofs from secure multiparty computation. SIAM J. Comput. 39(3), 1121–1152 (2009)

22. Katz, J., Kolesnikov, V., Wang, X.: Improved non-interactive zero knowledge with applications to post-quantum signatures. IACR Cryptology ePrint Archive 2018/475 (2018)

23. Micali, S., Reyzin, L.: Improving the exact security of digital signature schemes. J. Cryptol. 15(1), 1–18 (2002)

24. Poettering, B.: Shorter double-authentication preventing signatures for small address spaces. In: Joux, A., Nitaj, A., Rachidi, T. (eds.) AFRICACRYPT 2018. LNCS, vol. 10831, pp. 344–361. Springer, Cham (2018). https://doi.org/10.1007/978-3-319-89339-6_19

25. Poettering, B., Stebila, D.: Double-authentication-preventing signatures. In: Kutyłowski, M., Vaidya, J. (eds.) ESORICS 2014. LNCS, vol. 8712, pp. 436–453. Springer, Cham (2014). https://doi.org/10.1007/978-3-319-11203-9_25
26. Poettering, B., Stebila, D.: Double-authentication-preventing signatures. Int. J. Inf. Sec. **16**(1), 1–22 (2017)
27. Ruffing, T., Kate, A., Schröder, D.: Liar, liar, coins on fire! Penalizing equivocation by loss of bitcoins. In: ACM Conference on Computer and Communications Security, pp. 219–230. ACM (2015)
28. Schnorr, C.P.: Efficient identification and signatures for smart cards. In: Brassard, G. (ed.) CRYPTO 1989. LNCS, vol. 435, pp. 239–252. Springer, New York (1990). https://doi.org/10.1007/0-387-34805-0_22
29. Shamir, A.: How to share a secret. Commun. ACM **22**(11), 612–613 (1979)
30. Shor, P.W.: Polynomial-time algorithms for prime factorization and discrete logarithms on a quantum computer. SIAM J. Comput. **26**(5), 1484–1509 (1997)
31. Unruh, D.: Quantum proofs of knowledge. In: Pointcheval, D., Johansson, T. (eds.) EUROCRYPT 2012. LNCS, vol. 7237, pp. 135–152. Springer, Heidelberg (2012). https://doi.org/10.1007/978-3-642-29011-4_10
32. Unruh, D.: Non-interactive zero-knowledge proofs in the quantum random oracle model. In: Oswald, E., Fischlin, M. (eds.) EUROCRYPT 2015. LNCS, vol. 9057, pp. 755–784. Springer, Heidelberg (2015). https://doi.org/10.1007/978-3-662-46803-6_25
33. Unruh, D.: Computationally binding quantum commitments. In: Fischlin, M., Coron, J.-S. (eds.) EUROCRYPT 2016. LNCS, vol. 9666, pp. 497–527. Springer, Heidelberg (2016). https://doi.org/10.1007/978-3-662-49896-5_18

A Simpler Construction of Identity-Based Ring Signatures from Lattices

Gongming Zhao and Miaomiao Tian[✉]

School of Computer Science and Technology, Anhui University, Hefei, China
mtian@ahu.edu.cn

Abstract. Ring signature is an attractive cryptographic primitive that has been widely used in many fields because of its anonymity. Traditional ring signatures rely on the public key infrastructure and require lots of digital certificates. To eliminate the digital certificates, Zhang and Kim (Asiacrypt'02) introduced the concept of identity-based ring signatures. So far, however there is few identity-based ring signatures built on lattice-related assumptions and they are not efficient enough for applications. In this paper we present a new identity-based ring signature scheme from lattices. Compared with the existing counterparts, our scheme has the advantages of higher computational efficiency and lower storage overhead. We prove the security of our construction in the random oracle model under the short integer solution assumption.

Keywords: Ring signature · Identity-based cryptography · Lattice

1 Introduction

Digital signature is one of the fundamental primitives of modern cryptography and has been widely used in almost all aspects of daily-life. However, ordinary digital signatures are not of anonymity—a verifier could recognize the signer of a signature, and thus they may not be usable in some specific applications, e.g., electronic voting. In 2001, Rivest et al. [28] first introduced the concept of ring signature, which enables a signer to sign a message on behalf of a signer-included-group (called a ring) and an outsider cannot distinguish the signer from the other group members. In contrast to the similar notion of group signature [9], there is no group establishment process as well as the revocation mechanism in ring signatures. Thanks to its simplicity and full anonymity, ring signature has received a plenty of attention from the cryptographic community (see, e.g., [1,5,10,12,17,24,29,33]).

Traditional ring signatures are built on the Public Key Infrastructure (PKI) and hence require lots of digital certificates to bind users' random public keys with their real identities. This undoubtedly increases the storage and computation overhead of users, and leads to the certificate management problem. To eliminate the certificate management problem, Zhang and Kim [34] adopted the advantages of identity-based cryptography [30] to ring signatures and presented

© Springer Nature Switzerland AG 2018
J. Baek et al. (Eds.): ProvSec 2018, LNCS 11192, pp. 277–291, 2018.
https://doi.org/10.1007/978-3-030-01446-9_16

the concept of identity-based ring signatures. In an identity-based cryptosystem, a user no longer needs a public key certificate, but instead sets its identity (such as an email address) as an public key. Therefore, identity-based ring signatures are more efficient than their PKI-based counterparts.

Since the pioneering work of Zhang and Kim [34], many new identity-based ring signature schemes have been published, e.g., [3,11,16,18]. However, those schemes are all based on traditional number theory assumptions that are easy for quantum algorithms [31]. With the rapid development of quantum computers, it is increasingly important to find alternatives that can resist quantum attacks. Wang [32] recently proposed two identity-based ring signature schemes with and without random oracles from lattices. Due to the fact that there is no efficient algorithm for some lattice problems, the two schemes are conjectured to be quantum-secure. Besides, lattice problems also enjoy the average-to-worst reduction [2]. In a nutshell, Wang's identity-based ring signatures undertake the "hash-and-sign" methodology of [15] and form rings using the lattice basis delegation mechanism of [8]. Therefore, they need some tanglesome preimage sampling algorithms [8,15] to generate signatures, and the delegation mechanism [8] would also increase their signature sizes. Moreover, we note that the identity-based ring signatures in [32] miss security proofs.

Our Contribution. In this paper, we propose a new identity-based ring signature scheme from lattices. Compared with Wang's ones [32], our scheme has the advantages of higher computational efficiency and lower storage overhead. Specifically, we use the rejection sampling algorithm of [13] instead of the preimage sampling algorithm to generate signatures. In addition, we also discard the lattice trapdoor delegation mechanism [8] to produce rings. We formally prove the security of our scheme in the random oracle model under the standard short integer solution assumption. We stress that our scheme can be transformed into the ideal lattices [22] to further reduce its storage overhead. Moreover, we also note that our scheme can be further improved by replacing the discrete Gaussians in rejection sampling algorithms with the rounded Gaussians [19].

Overview of Our Scheme. Now we briefly sketch our identity-based ring signature scheme. In our scheme, the master public key is a matrix $\mathbf{A} \in \mathbb{Z}_{2q}^{n \times m}$ and the master secret key is a relevant $\mathbf{G}$-trapdoor $\mathbf{R} \in \mathbb{Z}^{\bar{m} \times nk}$ with $m = \bar{m} + nk$. Different from the traditional lattice trapdoors in e.g. [8,15], the $\mathbf{G}$-trapdoor (introduced in [25]) is smaller than a lattice basis. We set the public matrix of a user with identity ID_i as $\mathbf{A}_i = [\mathbf{A}|H_1(ID_i)] \in \mathbb{Z}_{2q}^{n \times (m+nk)}$ where $H_1 : \{0,1\}^* \rightarrow \mathbb{Z}_{2q}^{n \times nk}$ is a collision-resistant hash function, and let the user's secret key be a small matrix $\mathbf{S}_i \in \mathbb{Z}^{(m+nk) \times n}$ satisfying $\mathbf{A}_i \mathbf{S}_i = q\mathbf{I}_n \mod 2q$, where $\mathbf{I}_n$ is an identity matrix with order n. We can generate the secret key $\mathbf{S}_i$ lightly using the $\mathbf{G}$-trapdoor $\mathbf{R}$. To sign a message μ on a ring R with l identities, the signer $ID_s \in R$ first picks l vectors $\mathbf{y}_j$'s from the Gaussian distribution D_σ^{m+nk} and computes $\mathbf{c} = H_2(\sum \mathbf{A}_j \mathbf{y}_j, R, \mu)$, where H_2 is a secure hash function and $\mathbf{A}_j$'s are the public matrices corresponding to all identities in R. Then for all $j \neq s$, let $\mathbf{z}_j = \mathbf{y}_j$. If $j = s$, the signer chooses a random bit $b \in \{0, 1\}$ and calculates $\mathbf{z}_s = (-1)^b \mathbf{S}_s \mathbf{c} + \mathbf{y}_s$. The candidate ring signature is $(\{\mathbf{z}_j\}, \mathbf{c}, R)$.

It is not difficult to see that the candidate ring signature is related to the signer's secret key $\mathbf{S}_s$. To obtain a secure signature scheme, we apply the rejection sampling technique [13,21] to make the distribution of the outputted ring signatures independent of the secret key $\mathbf{S}_s$. Roughly speaking, the rejection sampling technique is used to ensure the real distribution of signatures is statistically close to the ideal distribution that we want. Assume f and g are two probability distributions and $M \in \mathbb{R}$ is a positive constant such that $f(x) \leq Mg(x)$ for all $x \in \mathbb{R}$. If we sample an element x from distribution g and output it with probability $f(x)/(Mg(x))$, then the resulting distribution of x will follow f and the expected number of repetitions required to output a sample is M.

Related Work. The rejection sampling algorithm was first proposed in 2012 by Lyubashevsky [21], which is very efficient since it just requires simple matrix-vector multiplications and outputs results according to some distributions. As an application, Melchor et al. [24] showed how to design a lattice ring signature scheme using the rejection sampling algorithm of [21]. Later, Ducas et al. [13] improved the Lyubashevsky's algorithm using the bimodal discrete Gaussian distributions instead of the standard discrete Gaussian distributions. Very recently, Hülsing et al. [19] showed that the discrete Gaussians used in [13] can be replaced by rounded Gaussians.

The existing lattice-based signature schemes mostly rely on the "hash-and-sign" methodology of [15]. Their signatures essentially are preimages of some message-associated images. The preimages are generated using the preimage sampling algorithm of [15] with a lattice basis as the secret key (also called trapdoor). In 2012, Micciancio and Peikert [25] improved the preimage sampling algorithm of [15] and proposed the concepts of primitive matrices and **G**-trapdoors. The generations of primitive matrices and **G**-trapdoors are very simple, and the preimage sampling algorithm built on them can be executed quickly and efficiently. Since then, some improvements and schemes on [25] were successively proposed (e.g., [6,7,14,20,23,27]).

Paper Organization. The rest of this paper is organized as follows. Section 2 reviews the definition of identity-based ring signatures and some preliminaries about lattices. Section 3 presents our identity-based ring signature scheme and its security proofs. Besides, we also analyze the efficiency of our scheme in this section. Finally, Sect. 4 concludes this paper.

2 Preliminaries

Notations. Throughout this paper, the security parameter is a positive integer n. For any positive integer d, we define $[d]$ as the set $\{1, 2, \ldots, d\}$. We denote the number of elements in a set S by $|S|$. We represent vectors by bold lower case letters and matrices by bold upper case letters. Unless otherwise indicated, all vectors are viewed as column. We use $\mathbf{v}^t$ (resp. $\mathbf{A}^t$) to denote the transpose of $\mathbf{v}$ (resp. $\mathbf{A}$). Let the i-th component of a vector $\mathbf{v}$ be v_i. We define the l_p-norm of $\mathbf{v}$ as $\|\mathbf{v}\|_p = (\sum_i |v_i|^p)^{1/p}$ for any integer $p > 0$. For convenience, we will omit the subscript for the l_2-norm. For a matrix $\mathbf{A} = [\mathbf{a}_1, \ldots, \mathbf{a}_m]$, $\tilde{\mathbf{A}}$ denotes its Gram-Schmidt orthogonalization and define $\|\mathbf{A}\|_p = \max_i \|\mathbf{a}_i\|_p$ for any integer $p > 0$. The concatenation of $\mathbf{A}$ and $\mathbf{B}$ is written as $[\mathbf{A}|\mathbf{B}]$. Let S_w^n be the set of binary vectors of length n with Hamming weight w (i.e. the number of non-zero elements in the vector is w). Define the largest singular value of $\mathbf{A}$ as $s_1(\mathbf{A}) = \max_{\mathbf{u}} \|\mathbf{A}\mathbf{u}\|$, where the maximum is taken over all unit vectors $\mathbf{u}$.

For a distribution D, we denote by $x \xleftarrow{\$} D$ that x is sampled randomly according to D. For a set S, we denote by $x \xleftarrow{\$} S$ that x is sampled uniformly at random from S. We say that the function $\mathsf{negl}(n)$ is negligible meaning that it is smaller than all polynomial fractions for sufficiently large n. We say that an event happens with overwhelming probability if it happens with probability at least $1 - \mathsf{negl}(n)$.

Let X and Y be two random variables over a finite domain D. We define their statistical distance as $\Delta(X, Y) = \frac{1}{2} \sum_{x \in D} |\Pr[X = x] - \Pr[Y = x]|$. We say X and Y are statistically indistinguishable if $\Delta(X, Y) < \mathsf{negl}(n)$.

2.1 Identity-Based Ring Signatures

Definition 1 (Syntax). *An identity-based ring signature scheme consists of the following four polynomial-time algorithms:*

- *Setup(1^n): On input a security parameter n, it outputs the public parameter PP and the master secret key MSK.*
- *Extract(PP, ID, MSK): On input the public parameter PP, a user identity $ID \in \{0, 1\}^*$ and the master secret key MSK, it generates a secret key SK_{ID} corresponding to the identity.*
- *RSign(PP, μ, ID, R, SK_{ID}): On input the public parameter PP, a message μ, a ring R, an identity $ID \in R$ and the corresponding secret key SK_{ID}, it outputs a ring signature Sig.*
- *RVerify(PP, μ, Sig, R): On input the public parameter PP, a message μ, a ring R and a signature Sig, it returns 1 if the signature is valid; otherwise, it returns 0.*

Correctness. We require that an identity-based ring signature scheme must satisfy the standard consistency. That is, for all message μ, ring R and $ID \in R$, let $(PP, MSK) \leftarrow$ Setup(1^n), $SK_{ID} \leftarrow$ Extract(PP, ID, MSK) and Sig $\leftarrow$ RSign(PP, μ, ID, R, SK_{ID}), then RVerify(PP, μ, Sig, R) will output 1 with overwhelming probability. Like PKI-based ring signature schemes, a secure identity-based ring signature scheme should also satisfy both anonymity and unforgeability [5].

Definition 2 (Anonymity). *An identity-based ring signature scheme is anonymous if the advantage of any polynomial-time adversary in the following game is negligible. The game is played between a challenger $\mathcal{C}$ and an adversary $\mathcal{A}$.*

Setup. Given a security parameter n, the challenger $\mathcal{C}$ runs the algorithm Setup to generate the public parameter PP and the master secret key MSK. Then $\mathcal{C}$ sends both PP and MSK to the adversary $\mathcal{A}$.

Challenge. The adversary $\mathcal{A}$ submits a signing query to the challenger $\mathcal{C}$ on a message μ, a ring R and two identities $ID_b \in R$ for $b \in \{0, 1\}$. The challenger $\mathcal{C}$ picks a random $b \in \{0, 1\}$ and returns a ring signature Sig $\leftarrow$ RSign$(PP, \mu, ID_b, R, SK_{ID_b})$.

Guess. The adversary $\mathcal{A}$ outputs a guess b' of b.

The advantage of $\mathcal{A}$ in this game is defined as $|\Pr[b' = b] - 1/2|$.

Definition 3 (Unforgeability). *An identity-based ring signature scheme is unforgetable under adaptive chosen-identity and chosen-message attacks if for any polynomial-time adversary $\mathcal{A}$ the probability that $\mathcal{A}$ wins the following game is negligible. The game is also played between a challenger $\mathcal{C}$ and adversary $\mathcal{A}$.*

Setup: Given a security parameter n, the challenger $\mathcal{C}$ runs the algorithm Setup to generate the public parameter PP and the master secret key MSK. Then $\mathcal{C}$ sends PP to the adversary $\mathcal{A}$.

Extract query: The adversary $\mathcal{A}$ submits an identity $ID \in \{0, 1\}^*$ adaptively. The challenger $\mathcal{C}$ runs the algorithm Extract to obtain a secret key SK_{ID} corresponding to ID and then sends it to $\mathcal{A}$.

Sign query: The adversary $\mathcal{A}$ submits a message μ, a ring R and an identity $ID \in R$ adaptively. The challenger $\mathcal{C}$ runs the algorithm RSign and then forwards its result to $\mathcal{A}$.

Forgery: The adversary $\mathcal{A}$ finally outputs a ring signature Sig* on the message μ^* and ring R^*. $\mathcal{A}$ wins the game if RVerify$(PP, \mu^*, \text{Sig}^*, R^*) = 1$, (μ^*, R^*) has never been submitted to **Sign query** and all identities in R^* have never been input to **Extract query** either.

2.2 Lattices

Definition 4. *Given a matrix $\mathbf{B} \in \mathbb{R}^{m \times m}$ that contains a set of linearly independent m-dimensional vectors $\mathbf{b}_1, \dots, \mathbf{b}_m$, the m-dimensional full-rank lattice Λ generated by $\mathbf{B}$ is defined as the linear combination of vectors $\mathbf{b}_1, \dots, \mathbf{b}_m$,*

$$\Lambda = \mathcal{L}(\mathbf{B}) = \{\mathbf{Bc} = \sum c_i \mathbf{b}_i : \mathbf{c} \in \mathbb{Z}^m\}.$$

We call the matrix $\mathbf{B}$ in the above a basis of the lattice $\mathcal{L}(\mathbf{B})$. In this paper, we are only interested in the following lattices.

Definition 5. *For positive integers q and m, a matrix $\mathbf{A} \in \mathbb{Z}_q^{n \times m}$ and a vector $\mathbf{u} \in \mathbb{Z}_q^n$, define:*

$$\Lambda^{\perp}(\mathbf{A}) = \{\mathbf{e} \in \mathbb{Z}^m \ s.t. \ \mathbf{Ae} = \mathbf{0} \pmod q\},$$

$$\Lambda^{\mathbf{u}}(\mathbf{A}) = \{\mathbf{e} \in \mathbb{Z}^m \ s.t. \ \mathbf{Ae} = \mathbf{u} \pmod q\}.$$

We can observe that if $\mathbf{v} \in \Lambda^{\mathbf{u}}(\mathbf{A})$ then we have $\Lambda^{\mathbf{u}}(\mathbf{A}) = \Lambda^{\perp}(\mathbf{A}) + \mathbf{v}$ clearly, that is, $\Lambda^{\mathbf{u}}(\mathbf{A})$ is a coset of $\Lambda^{\perp}(\mathbf{A})$.

2.3 Hardness Assumption

The security of our scheme relies on the hardness of the short integer solution (SIS) problem [2].

Definition 6 (SIS$_{q,m,\beta}$ Problem). *Given positive integers q, m, $\boldsymbol{A} \in \mathbb{Z}_q^{n \times m}$ and $\beta \in \mathbb{R}^+$, the SIS$_{q,m,\beta}$ problem is to find a vector $\mathbf{e} \in \mathbb{Z}^m \backslash \{\mathbf{0}\}$ satisfying $\mathbf{Ae} = \mathbf{0} \pmod q$ and $\|\mathbf{e}\| \leq \beta$.*

For the hardness of the SIS$_{q,m,\beta}$ problem, Micciancio and Regev [26] have shown that, for any polynomial-bounded $m, \beta = \mathsf{poly}(n)$ and any prime $q \geq \beta \cdot \omega(\sqrt{n \log n})$, solving the SIS$_{q,n,m,\beta}$ problem on the average is as hard as approximating some intractable lattice problems in the worst case.

2.4 Discrete Gaussians

For any $\sigma > 0$ and $\mathbf{x} \in \mathbb{R}^m$, the Gaussian function over $\mathbb{R}^m$ centered at some $\mathbf{v} \in \mathbb{R}^m$ with parameter σ is defined as

$$\rho_{\mathbf{v},\sigma}(\mathbf{x}) = \exp(-\pi \|\mathbf{x} - \mathbf{v}\|^2 / \sigma^2).$$

For any $\sigma > 0$ and m-dimensional lattice $\Lambda \subseteq \mathbb{Z}^m$, the discrete Gaussian distribution over Λ centered at some $\mathbf{v} \in \mathbb{Z}^m$ with parameter σ is defined as

$$\forall \mathbf{x} \in \Lambda, D_{\Lambda,\mathbf{v},\sigma}(\mathbf{x}) = \rho_{\mathbf{v},\sigma}(\mathbf{x}) / \rho_{\mathbf{v},\sigma}(\Lambda),$$

where $\rho_{\mathbf{v},\sigma}(\Lambda) = \sum_{\mathbf{z} \in \Lambda} \rho_{\mathbf{v},\sigma}(\mathbf{z})$.

For notation convenience, we may omit the parameter $\mathbf{v}$ (resp. σ) if $\mathbf{v} = \mathbf{0}$ (resp. $\sigma = 1$) in the following. When the lattice is $\mathbb{Z}^m$, we denote the discrete Gaussian distribution $D_{\mathbb{Z}^m,\mathbf{v},\sigma}$ by $D_{\mathbf{v},\sigma}^m$.

The discrete Gaussian distribution has following useful properties:

Lemma 1 ([26]). *Let n, q be any positive integers and $m \geq 2n \log q$. Given a matrix $\mathbf{A} \in \mathbb{Z}_q^{n \times m}$, a basis $\mathbf{B}$ of $\Lambda^\perp(\mathbf{A})$ and a vector $\mathbf{u} \in \mathbb{Z}_q^n$, if the gaussian parameter $\sigma \geq \|\tilde{\mathbf{B}}\| \cdot \omega(\sqrt{\log n})$, then for any $\mathbf{x} \xleftarrow{\$} D_{\Lambda^{\mathbf{u}}(\mathbf{A}),\sigma}$, we have $\|\mathbf{x}\| \leq \sigma\sqrt{m}$ with overwhelming probability.*

Lemma 2 ([21]). *For any positive $k, \sigma \in \mathbb{R}$ and any vector $\mathbf{v} \in \mathbb{Z}^m$, we have*

1. *$Pr[|z| > k\sigma; z \xleftarrow{\$} D_\sigma^1] \leq 2e^{\frac{-k^2}{2}}$.*
2. *$Pr[\|\mathbf{z}\| > k\sigma\sqrt{m}; \mathbf{z} \xleftarrow{\$} D_\sigma^m] < k^m e^{\frac{m}{2}(1-k^2)}$.*
3. *If $\sigma \geq 3$, then $D_\sigma^m(\mathbf{z}) \leq 2^{-m}$.*
4. *$Pr[D_\sigma^m(\mathbf{z}) / D_{\mathbf{v},\sigma}^m(\mathbf{z}) = O(1); \mathbf{z} \xleftarrow{\$} D_\sigma^m] = 1 - 2^{-\omega(\log m)}$ for $\sigma = \omega(\|\mathbf{v}\|\sqrt{\log m})$.*

2.5 Primitive Matrix

In this subsection, we will recall the primitive matrix $\mathbf{G}$ introduced in [25]. The primitive matrix $\mathbf{G}$ is a matrix with special structure. It is usually generated by the vector $\mathbf{g}^t = (1, 2, 4, \ldots, 2^{k-1}) \in \mathbb{Z}_q^k$ for $k = \lceil \log q \rceil$ and $\mathbf{G}$ is defined as

$$\mathbf{G} = \mathbf{I}_n \otimes \mathbf{g}^t \in \mathbb{Z}_q^{n \times nk},$$

where $\mathbf{I}_n \in \mathbb{Z}^{n \times n}$ is the identity matrix with order n and $\otimes$ denotes the tensor product. That is,

$$\mathbf{G} = \begin{bmatrix} \mathbf{g}^t & & & \\ & \mathbf{g}^t & & \\ & & \ddots & \\ & & & \mathbf{g}^t \end{bmatrix} \in \mathbb{Z}_q^{n \times nk}.$$

The vector $\mathbf{g}$ defines a k-dimensional lattice $\Lambda^{\perp}(\mathbf{g}^t)$. Let $\mathbf{S}_k \in \mathbb{Z}^{k \times k}$ be a basis of $\Lambda^{\perp}(\mathbf{g}^t)$, i.e., $\mathbf{g}^t \cdot \mathbf{S}_k = \mathbf{0} \in \mathbb{Z}_q^k$. Then $\mathbf{S} = \mathbf{I}_n \otimes \mathbf{S}_k \in \mathbb{Z}^{nk \times nk}$ is the basis of $\Lambda^{\perp}(\mathbf{G})$, and we have

$$\mathbf{S}_k = \begin{bmatrix} 2 & & & & q_0 \\ -1 & 2 & & & q_1 \\ & -1 & \ddots & & \vdots \\ & & & 2 & q_{k-2} \\ & & & -1 & q_{k-1} \end{bmatrix} \in \mathbb{Z}^{k \times k}, \ \mathbf{S} = \begin{bmatrix} \mathbf{S}_k & & & \\ & \mathbf{S}_k & & \\ & & \ddots & \\ & & & \mathbf{S}_k \\ & & & & \mathbf{S}_k \end{bmatrix} \in \mathbb{Z}^{nk \times nk},$$

where $(q_0, q_1, \ldots, q_{k-1})$ is the binary expansion of $q = \sum_i 2^i \cdot q_i$.

We can easily compute a vector $\mathbf{x}$ such that $\mathbf{Gx} = \mathbf{u} \bmod q$ for any $\mathbf{u} \in \mathbb{Z}_q^n$. By Lemma 1, we know that $\mathbf{x}$ can be small.

Next, we give a formal definition of $\mathbf{G}$-trapdoors which will play an important role in our scheme.

Definition 7. *Given a matrix $\mathbf{A} \in \mathbb{Z}_q^{n \times m}$ and the primitive matrix $\mathbf{G} \in \mathbb{Z}_q^{n \times nk}$ for some positive integers q, m, k. Let $\mathbf{H} \in \mathbb{Z}_q^{n \times n}$ be some invertible matrix. The $\mathbf{G}$-trapdoor for $\mathbf{A}$ with tag $\mathbf{H}$ is a matrix $\mathbf{R}$ such that $\mathbf{A} \begin{bmatrix} \mathbf{R} \\ \mathbf{I} \end{bmatrix} = \mathbf{HG} \pmod{q}$. The quality of the trapdoor $\mathbf{R}$ is measured by $s_1(\mathbf{R})$.*

Lemma 3 ([25]). *Let $D_\sigma^{n \times m}$ be a discrete Gaussian distribution with parameter σ. For any $\mathbf{X} \xleftarrow{\$} D_\sigma^{n \times m}$, we have $s_1(\mathbf{X}) \leq \sigma \cdot O(\sqrt{n} + \sqrt{m})$ except with negligible probability.*

The motivation behind the usage of primitive matrices is that it's easy to be produced and takes up little storage. In addition, the preimage sampling algorithm and the trapdoor delegation algorithm derived from primitive matrices are also quite efficient.

Theorem 1 ([25]). *For any integers $q \geq 2, k = \lceil \log q \rceil$, there is a primitive matrix $\mathbf{G} \in \mathbb{Z}_q^{n \times nk}$ such that*

- *The lattice $\Lambda^{\perp}(\mathbf{G})$ has a known basis $\mathbf{S} \in \mathbb{Z}^{nk \times nk}$ with $\|\tilde{\mathbf{S}}\| \leq \sqrt{5}$ and $\|\mathbf{S}\| \leq \max\{\sqrt{5}, \sqrt{k}\}$.*
- *Both $\mathbf{G}$ and $\mathbf{S}$ require little storage. In particular, they are sparse (with only $O(nk)$ nonzero entries) and highly structured.*
- *Preimage sampling for $f_{\mathbf{G}}(\mathbf{x}) = \mathbf{G}\mathbf{x} \pmod{q}$ with Gaussian parameter $\sigma \geq \|\tilde{\mathbf{S}}\| \cdot \omega(\sqrt{\log n})$ can be performed in quasilinear time.*

Now we recall several useful algorithms related with primitive matrices and G-trapdoors. Their details can be found in [25].

GenTrap($\bar{\mathbf{A}}, \mathbf{H}$): Let $q \geq 2, \bar{m} \geq 1$ be integers and $k = \lceil \log q \rceil$. Given an uniformly random matrix $\bar{\mathbf{A}} \in \mathbb{Z}_q^{n \times \bar{m}}$ and an invertible matrix $\mathbf{H} \in \mathbb{Z}_q^{n \times n}$, the polynomial time algorithm **GenTrap($\bar{\mathbf{A}}, \mathbf{H}$)** will output a random matrix $\mathbf{A} = [\bar{\mathbf{A}}|\mathbf{H}\mathbf{G} - \bar{\mathbf{A}}\mathbf{R}]$ and a G-trapdoor $\mathbf{R} \sim D_{\sigma}^{\bar{m} \times nk}$ with tag $\mathbf{H}$, where $\sigma = \omega(\sqrt{\log n})$.

SampleD ($\mathbf{A}, \mathbf{R}, \mathbf{H}, \mathbf{u}, \sigma$): Let $q \geq 2, m = O(n \log q)$ be integers and $k = \lceil \log q \rceil$. Given a matrix $\mathbf{A} \in \mathbb{Z}_q^{n \times m}$, a G-trapdoor $\mathbf{R} \in \mathbb{Z}^{m \times nk}$ with tag $\mathbf{H}$ and a vector $\mathbf{u} \in \mathbb{Z}_q^n$. Let $\mathbf{A}' = \mathbf{H}\mathbf{G} - \mathbf{A}\mathbf{R} \in \mathbb{Z}_q^{n \times nk}$ and Gaussian parameter $\sigma \geq s_1(\mathbf{R}) \cdot \omega(\sqrt{\log n})$. The polynomial time algorithm **SampleD($\mathbf{A}, \mathbf{R}, \mathbf{H}, \mathbf{u}, \sigma$)** will output a vector $\mathbf{e} \in \mathbb{Z}^{m+nk}$ sampled from a distribution that is statistically close to $D_{\Lambda^{\mathbf{u}}([\mathbf{A}|\mathbf{A}']), \sigma}$.

DelTrap($\mathbf{A}, \mathbf{A}_1, \mathbf{R}, \mathbf{H}, \sigma$): Let $q \geq 2, m = O(n \log q)$ be integers and $k = \lceil \log q \rceil$. Given a matrix $\mathbf{A} \in \mathbb{Z}_q^{n \times m}$ along with a G-trapdoor $\mathbf{R} \in \mathbb{Z}^{(m-nk) \times nk}$, a new matrix $\mathbf{A}_1 \in \mathbb{Z}_q^{n \times nk}$, an invertible matrix $\mathbf{H} \in \mathbb{Z}_q^{n \times n}$ and a Gaussian parameter $\sigma \geq s_1(\mathbf{R}) \cdot \omega(\sqrt{\log n})$, the polynomial time algorithm **DelTrap($\mathbf{A}, \mathbf{A}_1, \mathbf{R}, \mathbf{H}, \sigma$)** will output a G-trapdoor $\mathbf{R}' \in \mathbb{Z}^{m \times nk}$ for matrix $[\mathbf{A}|\mathbf{A}_1]$ with tag $\mathbf{H}$.

In the rest of the paper, we will set $\mathbf{H} = \mathbf{I}_n$ and omit it for simplicity.

2.6 Rejection Sampling

As mentioned before, the rejection sampling technique used in this paper is to ensure the real distribution of signatures is statistically close to the ideal distribution that we want. We will use the technique to make the distribution of outputted signatures independent of users' secret keys in our scheme.

Lemma 4 ([21], Rejection Sampling). *Let m be a positive integer and V be an arbitrary set. Let f and g_v be probability distributions over $\mathbb{Z}^m$ where g_v is a family of probability distributions indexed by $v \in V$ with the property that*

$$\exists M \in \mathbb{R}^+ \quad s.t. \quad Mg_v(\mathbf{z}) \geq f(\mathbf{z}) \quad \text{for all } v \in V, \ \mathbf{z} \xleftarrow{\$} f.$$

Then the distributions of the following two algorithms are statistically indistinguishable (within statistical distance $\frac{2^{-\omega(\log m)}}{M}$):

1. *$v \xleftarrow{\$} V$, $\mathbf{z} \xleftarrow{\$} g_v$, output $(\mathbf{z}, v)$ with probability $\min(\frac{f(\mathbf{z})}{Mg_v(\mathbf{z})}, 1)$.*
2. *$v \xleftarrow{\$} V$, $\mathbf{z} \xleftarrow{\$} f$, output $(\mathbf{z}, v)$ with probability $1/M$.*

3   Our Identity-Based Ring Signature Scheme

3.1   Description

Our scheme works as follows:

Setup: Given a security parameter n, pick integers $q \geq 2$, $m = O(n \log q)$, $\bar{m} \geq 1$, $w \geq 3$ and $k = \lceil \log 2q \rceil$, and a fixed positive real $M < 3$. Let $m = \bar{m} + nk$. Select two hash functions $H_1 : \{0,1\}^* \to \mathbb{Z}_{2q}^{n \times nk}$ and $H_2 : \{0,1\}^* \to S_w^n$. Choose an uniformly random matrix $\bar{\mathbf{A}} \in \mathbb{Z}_{2q}^{n \times \bar{m}}$, run the algorithm $\mathbf{GenTrap}(\bar{\mathbf{A}})$ to generate a matrix $\mathbf{A} \in \mathbb{Z}_{2q}^{n \times m}$ along with a G-trapdoor $\mathbf{R} \sim D_{\sigma_1}^{\bar{m} \times nk}$. The system public parameter is $(\mathbf{A}, H_1, H_2)$ and the master secret key is $\mathbf{R}$.

Extract: Given an identity $ID_i \in \{0,1\}^*$, do:
 1. Let $\mathbf{Q}_i = H_1(ID_i)$ and $\mathbf{A}_i = [\mathbf{A}|\mathbf{Q}_i]$;
 2. Run the algorithm $\mathbf{DelTrap}(\mathbf{A}, \mathbf{Q}_i, \mathbf{R}, \sigma_2)$ to generate the G-trapdoor $\mathbf{R}_i$ for $\mathbf{A}_i$;
 3. Run the algorithm $\mathbf{SampleD}(\mathbf{A}_i, \mathbf{R}_i, \mathbf{u}_t, \sigma_3)$ repeatedly to generate a short matrix $\mathbf{S}_i$ such that $\mathbf{A}_i\mathbf{S}_i = q\mathbf{I}_n \bmod 2q$, where $\mathbf{u}_t$ is the t-th column of $q\mathbf{I}_n$ for $t \in [n]$;
 4. Output the secret key $SK_{ID_i} = \mathbf{S}_i \in \mathbb{Z}^{(m+nk) \times n}$.

RSign: Given a message μ, a ring $R = (ID_1, ID_2, \ldots, ID_l)$, an identity $ID_s \in R$ and a corresponding secret key SK_{ID_s}, do:
 1. For each identity $ID_j \in R$, choose a vector $\mathbf{y}_j \xleftarrow{\$} D_\sigma^{m+nk}$;
 2. Calculate $\mathbf{c} = H_2(\sum_{j \in [l]} \mathbf{A}_j\mathbf{y}_j, R, \mu)$;
 3. For all $j \in [l] \backslash \{s\}$, let $\mathbf{z}_j = \mathbf{y}_j$;
 4. Choose a random bit $b \in \{0,1\}$, calculate $\mathbf{z}_s = (-1)^b\mathbf{S}_s\mathbf{c} + \mathbf{y}_s$ and output $\mathbf{z}_s$ with probability

$$1 \Big/ \left(M \exp\left(-\frac{\|\mathbf{S}_s\mathbf{c}\|^2}{2\sigma^2} \right) \cosh\left(\frac{\langle \mathbf{z}_s, \mathbf{S}_s\mathbf{c} \rangle}{\sigma^2} \right) \right);$$

 5. Output the ring signature $\mathsf{Sig} = (\{\mathbf{z}_j\}_{j \in [l]}, \mathbf{c}, R)$.
Verify: Given a message μ, a ring $R = (ID_1, \ldots, ID_l)$ and a signature $\mathsf{Sig} = (\{\mathbf{z}_j\}_{j \in [l]}, \mathbf{c}, R)$, the algorithm outputs 1 if the following conditions hold:
 1. For all $j \in [l]$, $\|\mathbf{z}_j\| \leq \eta\sigma\sqrt{m+nk}$, where $1.1 \leq \eta \leq 1.4$;
 2. $\mathbf{c} = H_2(\sum_{j=1}^l \mathbf{A}_j\mathbf{z}_j + q\mathbf{c} \bmod 2q, R, \mu)$.

3.2   Parameters and Correctness

In order to generate a matrix $\mathbf{A} \in \mathbb{Z}_{2q}^{n \times m}$ and its G-trapdoor $\mathbf{R} \sim D_{\sigma_1}^{\bar{m} \times nk}$, we set integers $q \geq 2, k = \lceil \log 2q \rceil$ and $\bar{m} \geq 2n \log 2q$. For sampling preimages of $f_\mathbf{G}(\mathbf{x}) = \mathbf{Gx} \pmod{q}$, the Gaussian parameter in the algorithm $\mathbf{GenTrap}$ should be set as $\sigma_1 \geq \|\tilde{\mathbf{S}}\| \cdot \omega(\sqrt{\log n}) = \sqrt{5} \cdot \omega(\sqrt{\log n})$ by Theorem 1. From Lemma 3, we know $s_1(\mathbf{R}) \leq \sigma_1 \cdot (\sqrt{\bar{m}} + \sqrt{nk}) = O(\sqrt{n \log 2q}) \cdot \omega(\sqrt{\log n})$. The Gaussian parameter σ_2 for delegating the G-trapdoor $\mathbf{R}_i$ should be set as $\sigma_2 \geq$

$s_1(\mathbf{R}) \cdot \|\tilde{\mathbf{S}}\| \cdot \omega(\sqrt{\log n}) = O(\sqrt{n \log 2q}) \cdot \omega(\log n)$ according to the algorithm **Del-Trap**. Thus we have $s_1(\mathbf{R}_i) \leq \sigma_2 \cdot O(\sqrt{m} + \sqrt{nk}) = O(n \log 2q) \cdot \omega(\log n)$. To sample a secret key $\mathbf{S}_i$, we set $\sigma_3 \geq s_1(\mathbf{R}_i) \cdot \|\tilde{\mathbf{S}}\| \cdot \omega(\sqrt{\log n}) = O(n \log 2q) \cdot \omega(\log^{3/2} n)$ according to the algorithm **SampleD**. Finally, we set $\sigma = w\sigma_3\sqrt{m + nk}$ to make $p_{\mathbf{z}_s} \leq 1$ (defined later) so that the rejection sampling works.

For a signature $\mathsf{Sig} = (\{\mathbf{z}_j\}_{j \in [l]}, \mathbf{c}, R)$ generated by the algorithm RSign, we know that all $\mathbf{z}_j$'s are distributed according to the distribution $f = D_\sigma^{m+nk}$ except $\mathbf{z}_s$ that satisfies the distribution $g_{\mathbf{S}_s\mathbf{c}} = \frac{1}{2}D_{\mathbf{S}_s\mathbf{c},\sigma}^{m+nk} + \frac{1}{2}D_{-\mathbf{S}_s\mathbf{c},\sigma}^{m+nk}$ before performing rejection sampling. By Lemma 4, to get the distribution of $f = D_\sigma^{m+nk}$, we can output $\mathbf{z}_s$ with probability

$$p_{\mathbf{z}_s} = \frac{f(\mathbf{z}_s)}{Mg_{\mathbf{S}_s\mathbf{c}}(\mathbf{z}_s)} = 1 \Big/ \left(M \exp\left(-\frac{\|\mathbf{S}_s\mathbf{c}\|^2}{2\sigma^2}\right) \cosh\left(\frac{\langle \mathbf{z}_s, \mathbf{S}_s\mathbf{c}\rangle}{\sigma^2}\right) \right).$$

From Lemma 2, we have that $\|\mathbf{z}_j\| \leq \eta\sigma\sqrt{m + nk}$ with overwhelming probability. In addition, we know

$$\begin{aligned}
\textstyle\sum_{j \in [l]} \mathbf{A}_j\mathbf{z}_j + q\mathbf{c} &= \textstyle\sum_{j \in [l] \setminus \{s\}} \mathbf{A}_j\mathbf{y}_j + \mathbf{A}_s((-1)^b\mathbf{S}_s\mathbf{c} + \mathbf{y}_s) + q\mathbf{c} \pmod{2q} \\
&= \textstyle\sum_{j \in [l] \setminus \{s\}} \mathbf{A}_j\mathbf{y}_j + \mathbf{A}_s\mathbf{y}_s + ((-1)^b\mathbf{A}_s\mathbf{S}_s)\mathbf{c} + q\mathbf{c} \pmod{2q} \\
&= \textstyle\sum_{j \in [l]} \mathbf{A}_j\mathbf{y}_j + (-1)^b q\mathbf{c} + q\mathbf{c} \pmod{2q} \\
&= \textstyle\sum_{j \in [l]} \mathbf{A}_j\mathbf{y}_j \pmod{2q}
\end{aligned}$$

Therefore, we can obtain that $\mathbf{c} = H_2(\sum_{j=1}^{l} \mathbf{A}_j\mathbf{z}_j + q\mathbf{c} \bmod 2q, R, \mu)$.

3.3   Security

Theorem 2. *Our identity-based ring signature scheme is secure in the random oracle model under the SIS assumption.*

We prove the theorem using the following two lemmas.

Lemma 5. *Our identity-based ring signature scheme satisfies anonymity.*

Proof. The anonymity is straightforward. Assume there are two signers each with an identity ID_b for $b \in \{1,2\}$. We denote $\mathsf{Sig}_b = (\{\mathbf{z}_j^b\}_{j \in [l]}, \mathbf{c}^b, R)$ as the ring signature on ring $R = (ID_1, ID_2, \ldots, ID_l)$ and message μ generated by the signer ID_b. Since all $\mathbf{z}_j^b$ for both $b \in \{1,2\}$ and $j \in [l]$ are distributed close to D_σ^{m+nk} by construction and by Lemmas 2 and 4. Thus, the two signatures $\mathsf{Sig}_1, \mathsf{Sig}_2$ on the same message and ring but generated by two different signers would also be statistically close. This concludes the proof.

Lemma 6. *If there is a polynomial-time adversary $\mathcal{A}$ who can break our identity-based ring signature scheme with non-negligible probability, then there exists a polynomial-time algorithm $\mathcal{C}$ who can solve the SIS problem with non-negligible probability.*

Proof. Given a security parameter n, integers $q \geq 2$, $m = O(n \log q)$, $w \geq 3$ and $k = \lceil \log 2q \rceil$. The simulation works as follows:

- **Setup:** The algorithm $\mathcal{C}$ first picks two collision-resistant hash functions $H_1 : \{0,1\}^* \rightarrow \mathbb{Z}_{2q}^{n \times nk}, H_2 : \{0,1\}^* \rightarrow S_w^n$ and chooses an uniformly random matrix $\mathbf{A} \in \mathbb{Z}_{2q}^{n \times m}$. Assume the adversary $\mathcal{A}$ can make at most s queries to the signing oracle, h queries to the random oracle H_2 and e queries to the secret key extraction oracle. Let the maximum number of identities in the system be d. Then the algorithm $\mathcal{C}$ chooses $\mathbf{c}_1, \ldots, \mathbf{c}_t \xleftarrow{\$} S_w^n$ for $t = s + h$ and random $\mathbf{B}_1, \ldots, \mathbf{B}_d \in \mathbb{Z}_{2q}^{n \times nk}$. Finally, $\mathcal{C}$ sends the public parameter $PP = (\mathbf{A}, H_1, H_2)$ to the adversary $\mathcal{A}$. Here H_1 and H_2 will be viewed as random oracles controlled by $\mathcal{C}$. The SIS problem is to find a non-zero short $\mathbf{x}$ such that $[\mathbf{A}|\mathbf{B}_1| \ldots |\mathbf{B}_d]\mathbf{x} = \mathbf{0} \mod q$.
- **Query:** The adversary $\mathcal{A}$ could make the following types of queries.
  - H_1 query: The adversary $\mathcal{A}$ sends an identity ID_i to $\mathcal{C}$. Then $\mathcal{C}$ retrieves the list L_1, an initially empty list with tuples like $(ID_i, \mathbf{Q}_i, \mathbf{R}_i, \mathbf{A}_i, j)$. If ID_i already appears in the list L_1, $\mathcal{C}$ simply returns $\mathbf{Q}_i$. Otherwise, $\mathcal{C}$ selects a matrix $\mathbf{R}_i \sim D_{\sigma_1}^{m \times nk}$ randomly and selects an unused matrix $\mathbf{B}_k$ from the set $\{\mathbf{B}_1, \ldots, \mathbf{B}_d\}$, then returns $\mathbf{Q}_i = \mathbf{G} - \mathbf{A}\mathbf{R}_i$ with probability $\delta = \frac{e}{e+d}$ and returns $\mathbf{Q}_i = \mathbf{B}_k$ with probability $1 - \delta$. Finally, $\mathcal{C}$ inserts the tuple $(ID_i, \mathbf{Q}_i, \mathbf{R}_i, \mathbf{A}_i, j)$ into the list L_1, where $\mathbf{A}_i = [\mathbf{A}|\mathbf{Q}_i]$, and $j = 1$ if $\mathbf{Q}_i = \mathbf{G} - \mathbf{A}\mathbf{R}_i$, otherwise $j = 2$ and $\mathbf{R}_i = \perp$.
  - H_2 query: The adversary $\mathcal{A}$ sends a message μ and ring $R = (ID_1, \ldots, ID_l)$ to $\mathcal{C}$. $\mathcal{C}$ retrieves the list L_2, an initially empty list with tuples like $(\mu, R, \mathbf{c})$. If $\mathcal{C}$ finds a match, $\mathcal{C}$ simply returns $\mathbf{c}$. Otherwise, $\mathcal{C}$ replies the query by selecting an unused $\mathbf{c}_i$ from the set $\{\mathbf{c}_1, \ldots, \mathbf{c}_t\}$ and gives it back to the adversary $\mathcal{A}$. Then $\mathcal{C}$ adds the tuple $(\mu, R, \mathbf{c})$ to the list L_2.
  - Extract query: The adversary $\mathcal{A}$ submits an identity ID_i adaptively. $\mathcal{C}$ retrieves the list L_3, an initially empty list with tuples like $(ID_i, \mathbf{S}_i)$. If ID_i has already appeared in the list L_3, then $\mathcal{C}$ returns $\mathbf{S}_i$. Otherwise, $\mathcal{C}$ retrieves the list L_1 and finds the tuple $(ID_i, \mathbf{Q}_i, \mathbf{R}_i, \mathbf{A}_i, j)$. If $j = 1$, then $\mathcal{C}$ runs the algorithm **SampleD** with $\mathbf{R}_i$ to generate a secret key $\mathbf{S}_i$ and adds the tuple $(ID_i, \mathbf{S}_i)$ to the list L_3. If $j = 2$, $\mathcal{C}$ will abort. We can see that in the simulation $\mathcal{C}$ doesn't abort in this step with probability at least δ^e.
  - Sign query: The adversary $\mathcal{A}$ submits a message μ, a ring R and an identity $ID_i \in R$. Then challenger $\mathcal{C}$ retrieves the list L_4, an initially empty list with tuples like $(ID_i, R, \mu, \{\mathbf{z}_j\}, \mathbf{c})$. If this query has been submitted before, $\mathcal{C}$ finds a match and replies with $(\{\mathbf{z}_j\}, \mathbf{c})$. Otherwise, $\mathcal{C}$ chooses random $\mathbf{z}_j \xleftarrow{\$} D_\sigma^{m+nk}$ and an unused $\mathbf{c}_i$, sets $\mathbf{c} = \mathbf{c}_i$ and programs the random oracle $H_2(\sum \mathbf{A}_j \mathbf{z}_j + q\mathbf{c} \mod 2q, R, \mu) = \mathbf{c}$. Finally, $\mathcal{C}$ returns $(\{\mathbf{z}_j\}, \mathbf{c})$ to $\mathcal{A}$ and inserts the tuple $(ID_i, R, \mu, \{\mathbf{z}_j\}, \mathbf{c})$ into L_4.
- **Forgery:** The adversary $\mathcal{A}$ eventually outputs a valid forgery $(\{\mathbf{z}_j^*\}, \mathbf{c}^*)$ on the message μ^* and ring R^* with non-negligible probability ϵ. And $\mathcal{A}$ has not made any sign queries on (μ^*, R^*) and extract queries on any $ID_i \in R^*$.

If there is an identity in R^* such that the corresponding $\mathbf{Q}_i$ is not selected from the set $\{\mathbf{B}_1, \ldots, \mathbf{B}_d\}$, then $\mathcal{C}$ will abort. We know that in the simulation $\mathcal{C}$ doesn't abort in this step with probability at least $(1 - \delta)^d$.

If H_2 and signing oracle have not been queried, then $\mathcal{A}$ can produce $\mathbf{c}^*$ such that $\mathbf{c}^* = H_2(\sum \mathbf{A}_j \mathbf{z}_j^* + q\mathbf{c}^* \bmod 2q, R^*, \mu^*)$ only with probability $1/|S_w^n|$. So, with probability at least $1 - 1/|S_w^n|$, $\mathbf{c}^*$ is one of the elements in the set $\{\mathbf{c}_1, \ldots, \mathbf{c}_t\}$. Hence, we know the probability that $\mathcal{A}$ outputs a valid forgery and $\mathbf{c}^*$ is in the set $\{\mathbf{c}_1, \ldots, \mathbf{c}_t\}$ is at least $\epsilon - 1/|S_w^n|$.

Assume that $\mathbf{c}^* = \mathbf{c}_i$ where $\mathbf{c}_i$ is a response of $\mathcal{C}$ to a query on H_2 made by $\mathcal{A}$. Now we repeat the above process. According to the General Forking Lemma of [4], we can obtain a new valid signature $(\{\mathbf{z}_j'\}, \mathbf{c}')$ on the message μ^* and ring R^* such that $\mathbf{c}' \neq \mathbf{c}^*$ with non-negligible probability. Moreover, we know $\sum \mathbf{A}_j \mathbf{z}_j^* + q\mathbf{c}_i = \sum \mathbf{A}_j \mathbf{z}_j' + q\mathbf{c}_i' \bmod 2q$. Let $\mathbf{z}_j = \mathbf{z}_j^* - \mathbf{z}_j' = (\mathbf{z}_{j1}^t, \mathbf{z}_{j2}^t)^t$. We have

$$\sum_{j=1}^{l} \mathbf{A}_j \mathbf{z}_j = [\mathbf{A}|\mathbf{Q}_1|\mathbf{Q}_2|...|\mathbf{Q}_l](\mathbf{z}_{11}^t + \mathbf{z}_{21}^t + ... + \mathbf{z}_{l1}^t, \mathbf{z}_{12}^t, \mathbf{z}_{22}^t, \ldots, \mathbf{z}_{l2}^t)^t.$$

Let $\mathbf{F} = [\mathbf{A}|\mathbf{Q}_1|\mathbf{Q}_2|...|\mathbf{Q}_l]$ and $\mathbf{v} = (\mathbf{z}_{11}^t + \mathbf{z}_{21}^t + ... + \mathbf{z}_{l1}^t, \mathbf{z}_{12}^t, \mathbf{z}_{22}^t, \ldots, \mathbf{z}_{l2}^t)^t$. We can obtain $\mathbf{Fv} = q(\mathbf{c}' - \mathbf{c}^*) \bmod 2q$. Since $\mathbf{c}' - \mathbf{c}^* \neq \mathbf{0} \bmod 2$, we know that $\mathbf{v} \neq \mathbf{0}$ $\bmod 2q$. Furthermore, we also have $\mathbf{v} \neq \mathbf{0} \bmod q$ with high probability. So, we know $\mathbf{Fv} = \mathbf{0} \bmod q$. Since the matrices $\mathbf{Q}_i$ are chosen from the set $\{\mathbf{B}_1, \ldots, \mathbf{B}_d\}$, a non-zero short vector $\mathbf{u}$ can be obtained by padding 0 at the appropriate positions of the vector $\mathbf{v}$ such that $\mathbf{F}'\mathbf{u} = \mathbf{0} \bmod q$ where $\mathbf{F}' = [\mathbf{A}|\mathbf{B}_1|...|\mathbf{B}_d]$. Therefore, we obtain a solution of the SIS problem.

3.4 Efficiency

In Table 1, we compare the efficiency of our scheme and Wang's schemes [32], where ℓ is the length of messages in [32] and l is the size of the ring used in signatures. We can see that compared with [32], our scheme has less storage overhead than Wang's ones.

In addition, we can see that our scheme is also more efficient than Wang's ones in terms of computational costs. The notations T_{EB} and T_{RB} denote the costs of the algorithms **ExtBasis** and **RandBasis** used in [32] respectively. And T_{SP} and T_{SD} denote the costs of the algorithms **SamplePre** and **SampleD** respectively. Let T_{DT} denote the cost of the algorithm **DelTrap** and T_{SM} denote the cost of a scalar multiplication. We omit the costs of hashing and addition operations. From Table 1, we can see that the signature generation process in our scheme only involves simple operations while it involves the preimage sampling algorithm in Wang's schemes. The secret key extraction algorithm in our scheme will run **SampleD** about n-times, it is faster than the algorithm **RandBasis** used in Wang's schemes. Therefore, our scheme is more efficient in terms of both storage and computational overhead.

Table 1. Comparison of several schemes.

Scheme	[32] Sect. 4.1	[32] Sect. 4.2	Our scheme
PP size	$O(n^2 \log q)$	$O(\ell n^2 \log q)$	$O(n^2 \log q)$
SK size	$O(n^2 \log^2 q)$	$O(n^2 \log^2 q)$	$O(n^2 \log q)$
Sig size	$O(ln \log q)$	$O(ln \log q)$	$O(ln \log q)$
Extract cost	$O(T_{EB} + T_{RB})$	$O(T_{EB} + T_{RB})$	$O(T_{DT} + nT_{SD})$
RSign cost	$O(T_{SP} + ln^2 \log q T_{SM})$	$O(T_{SP} + ln^2 \log q T_{SM})$	$O(ln^2 \log q T_{SM})$
ROM	Yes	No	Yes

4 Conclusion

In this paper, we have proposed a new identity-based ring signature scheme from lattices and proved its security in the random oracle model under the SIS assumption. Comparisons show that our scheme is more efficient than Wang's ones [32] in terms of both storage and computational overhead.

Acknowledgements. We thank the anonymous reviewers for helpful comments. This work is supported by the National Natural Science Foundation of China under Grant 61502443.

References

1. Abe, M., Ohkubo, M., Suzuki, K.: 1-out-of-n signatures from a variety of keys. In: Zheng, Y. (ed.) ASIACRYPT 2002. LNCS, vol. 2501, pp. 415–432. Springer, Heidelberg (2002). https://doi.org/10.1007/3-540-36178-2_26
2. Ajtai, M.: Generating hard instances of lattice problems. In Annual ACM Symposium on Theory of Computing, pp. 99–108. ACM (1996)
3. Au, M.H., Liu, J.K., Yuen, T.H., Wong, D.S.: ID-Based ring signature scheme secure in the standard model. In: Yoshiura, H., Sakurai, K., Rannenberg, K., Murayama, Y., Kawamura, S. (eds.) IWSEC 2006. LNCS, vol. 4266, pp. 1–16. Springer, Heidelberg (2006). https://doi.org/10.1007/11908739_1
4. Bellare, M., Neven, G.: Multi-signatures in the plain public-key model and a general forking lemma. In: ACM Conference on Computer and Communications Security, pp. 390–399. ACM (2006)
5. Bender, A., Katz, J., Morselli, R.: Ring signatures: stronger definitions, and constructions without random oracles. In: Halevi, S., Rabin, T. (eds.) TCC 2006. LNCS, vol. 3876, pp. 60–79. Springer, Heidelberg (2006). https://doi.org/10.1007/11681878_4
6. Boyen, X., Li, Q.: Towards tightly secure lattice short signature and id-based encryption. In: Cheon, J.H., Takagi, T. (eds.) ASIACRYPT 2016. LNCS, vol. 10032, pp. 404–434. Springer, Heidelberg (2016). https://doi.org/10.1007/978-3-662-53890-6_14
7. Boyen, X., Li, Q.: All-but-many lossy trapdoor functions from lattices and applications. In: Katz, J., Shacham, H. (eds.) CRYPTO 2017. LNCS, vol. 10403, pp. 298–331. Springer, Cham (2017). https://doi.org/10.1007/978-3-319-63697-9_11

8. Cash, D., Hofheinz, D., Kiltz, E., Peikert, C.: Bonsai trees, or how to delegate a lattice basis. In: Gilbert, H. (ed.) EUROCRYPT 2010. LNCS, vol. 6110, pp. 523–552. Springer, Heidelberg (2010). https://doi.org/10.1007/978-3-642-13190-5_27

9. Chaum, D., van Heyst, E.: Group signatures. In: Davies, D.W. (ed.) EUROCRYPT 1991. LNCS, vol. 547, pp. 257–265. Springer, Heidelberg (1991). https://doi.org/10.1007/3-540-46416-6_22

10. Chow, S.S., Wei, V.K., Liu, J.K., Yuen, T.H.: Ring signatures without random oracles. In: ACM Symposium on Information, Computer and Communications Security, pp. 297–302. ACM (2006)

11. Chow, S.S.M., Yiu, S.-M., Hui, L.C.K.: Efficient identity based ring signature. In: Ioannidis, J., Keromytis, A., Yung, M. (eds.) ACNS 2005. LNCS, vol. 3531, pp. 499–512. Springer, Heidelberg (2005). https://doi.org/10.1007/11496137_34

12. Dodis, Y., Kiayias, A., Nicolosi, A., Shoup, V.: Anonymous identification in *Ad Hoc* groups. In: Cachin, C., Camenisch, J.L. (eds.) EUROCRYPT 2004. LNCS, vol. 3027, pp. 609–626. Springer, Heidelberg (2004). https://doi.org/10.1007/978-3-540-24676-3_36

13. Ducas, L., Durmus, A., Lepoint, T., Lyubashevsky, V.: Lattice signatures and bimodal Gaussians. In: Canetti, R., Garay, J.A. (eds.) CRYPTO 2013. LNCS, vol. 8042, pp. 40–56. Springer, Heidelberg (2013). https://doi.org/10.1007/978-3-642-40041-4_3

14. Genise, N., Micciancio, D.: Faster Gaussian sampling for trapdoor lattices with arbitrary modulus. IACR Cryptology ePrint Archive 2017:308 (2017)

15. Gentry, C., Peikert, C., Vaikuntanathan, V.: Trapdoors for hard lattices and new cryptographic constructions. In: Annual ACM Symposium on Theory of Computing, pp. 197–206. ACM (2008)

16. Herranz, J.: Identity-based ring signatures from RSA. Theoret. Comput. Sci. **389**(1–2), 100–117 (2007)

17. Herranz, J., Sáez, G.: Forking lemmas for ring signature schemes. In: Johansson, T., Maitra, S. (eds.) INDOCRYPT 2003. LNCS, vol. 2904, pp. 266–279. Springer, Heidelberg (2003). https://doi.org/10.1007/978-3-540-24582-7_20

18. Herranz, J., Sáez, G.: New identity-based ring signature schemes. In: Lopez, J., Qing, S., Okamoto, E. (eds.) ICICS 2004. LNCS, vol. 3269, pp. 27–39. Springer, Heidelberg (2004). https://doi.org/10.1007/978-3-540-30191-2_3

19. Hülsing, A., Lange, T., Smeets, K.: Rounded Gaussians. In: Abdalla, M., Dahab, R. (eds.) PKC 2018. LNCS, vol. 10770, pp. 728–757. Springer, Cham (2018). https://doi.org/10.1007/978-3-319-76581-5_25

20. Libert, B., Sakzad, A., Stehlé, D., Steinfeld, R.: All-but-many lossy trapdoor functions and selective opening chosen-ciphertext security from LWE. In: Katz, J., Shacham, H. (eds.) CRYPTO 2017. LNCS, vol. 10403, pp. 332–364. Springer, Cham (2017). https://doi.org/10.1007/978-3-319-63697-9_12

21. Lyubashevsky, V.: Lattice signatures without trapdoors. In: Pointcheval, D., Johansson, T. (eds.) EUROCRYPT 2012. LNCS, vol. 7237, pp. 738–755. Springer, Heidelberg (2012). https://doi.org/10.1007/978-3-642-29011-4_43

22. Lyubashevsky, V., Peikert, C., Regev, O.: On ideal lattices and learning with errors over rings. In: Gilbert, H. (ed.) EUROCRYPT 2010. LNCS, vol. 6110, pp. 1–23. Springer, Heidelberg (2010). https://doi.org/10.1007/978-3-642-13190-5_1

23. Lyubashevsky, V., Wichs, D.: Simple lattice trapdoor sampling from a broad class of distributions. In: Katz, J. (ed.) PKC 2015. LNCS, vol. 9020, pp. 716–730. Springer, Heidelberg (2015). https://doi.org/10.1007/978-3-662-46447-2_32

24. Aguilar Melchor, C., Bettaieb, S., Boyen, X., Fousse, L., Gaborit, P.: Adapting Lyubashevsky's signature schemes to the ring signature setting. In: Youssef, A., Nitaj, A., Hassanien, A.E. (eds.) AFRICACRYPT 2013. LNCS, vol. 7918, pp. 1–25. Springer, Heidelberg (2013). https://doi.org/10.1007/978-3-642-38553-7_1
25. Micciancio, D., Peikert, C.: Trapdoors for lattices: simpler, tighter, faster, smaller. In: Pointcheval, D., Johansson, T. (eds.) EUROCRYPT 2012. LNCS, vol. 7237, pp. 700–718. Springer, Heidelberg (2012). https://doi.org/10.1007/978-3-642-29011-4_41
26. Micciancio, D., Regev, O.: Worst-case to average-case reductions based on Gaussian measures. SIAM J. Comput. $37(1)$, 267–302 (2007)
27. Micciancio, D., Walter, M.: Gaussian sampling over the integers: efficient, generic, constant-time. In: Katz, J., Shacham, H. (eds.) CRYPTO 2017. LNCS, vol. 10402, pp. 455–485. Springer, Cham (2017). https://doi.org/10.1007/978-3-319-63715-0_16
28. Rivest, R.L., Shamir, A., Tauman, Y.: How to leak a secret. In: Boyd, C. (ed.) ASIACRYPT 2001. LNCS, vol. 2248, pp. 552–565. Springer, Heidelberg (2001). https://doi.org/10.1007/3-540-45682-1_32
29. Shacham, H., Waters, B.: Efficient ring signatures without random oracles. In: Okamoto, T., Wang, X. (eds.) PKC 2007. LNCS, vol. 4450, pp. 166–180. Springer, Heidelberg (2007). https://doi.org/10.1007/978-3-540-71677-8_12
30. Shamir, A.: Identity-based cryptosystems and signature schemes. In: Blakley, G.R., Chaum, D. (eds.) CRYPTO 1984. LNCS, vol. 196, pp. 47–53. Springer, Heidelberg (1985). https://doi.org/10.1007/3-540-39568-7_5
31. Shor, P.W.: Polynomial-time algorithms for prime factorization and discrete logarithms on a quantum computer. SIAM J. Comput. $26(5)$, 1484–1509 (1997)
32. Wang, J.: Identity-based ring signature from lattice basis delegation (2010). https://eprint.iacr.org/2010/378
33. Wang, J., Sun, B.: Ring signature schemes from lattice basis delegation. In: Qing, S., Susilo, W., Wang, G., Liu, D. (eds.) ICICS 2011. LNCS, vol. 7043, pp. 15–28. Springer, Heidelberg (2011). https://doi.org/10.1007/978-3-642-25243-3_2
34. Zhang, F., Kim, K.: ID-Based blind signature and ring signature from pairings. In: Zheng, Y. (ed.) ASIACRYPT 2002. LNCS, vol. 2501, pp. 533–547. Springer, Heidelberg (2002). https://doi.org/10.1007/3-540-36178-2_33

Symmetric Key Cryptography

Generic Construction of Sequential Aggregate MACs from Any MACs

Shingo Sato[1], Shoichi Hirose[2], and Junji Shikata[1]($\boxtimes$)

[1] Graduate School of Environment and Information Sciences,
Yokohama National University, Yokohama, Japan
sato-shingo-cz@ynu.jp, shikata@ynu.ac.jp
[2] Faculty of Engineering, University of Fukui, Fukui, Japan
hrs_shch@u-fukui.ac.jp

Abstract. The aggregate message authentication code (aggregate MAC) is a cryptographic primitive which can compress MAC tags on multiple messages into a short aggregate MAC tag. Furthermore, the sequential aggregate MAC can check not only the validity of multiple messages but also the (sequential) order of messages. In this paper, we introduce a new model of sequential aggregate MACs where an aggregation algorithm generates a sequential aggregate tag depending only on any multiple and independent MAC tags with no secret-key, and we formally define security in this model. We also propose a generic construction of sequential aggregate MACs starting from various MACs without changing the structure of the MACs. This property is useful to make the existing networks more efficient by combining the aggregation algorithm with various MAC schemes already existing in the networks.

Keywords: Message authentication · MAC · Aggregate MAC
Sequential aggregate MAC

1 Introduction

The message authentication code (MAC) is one of the most fundamental cryptographic primitives. Furthermore, Katz and Lindell [8] proposed the aggregate MAC that can compress multiple MAC tags on multiple messages generated by different signers into a single aggregate tag. The advantage of the aggregate MAC lies in that the size of an aggregate tag is much smaller than total sizes of MAC tags, and hence it will be useful in applications in mobile networks or IoT (Internet of Things) networks where many devices sending messages are connected. The model and security of aggregate MACs were introduced by Katz and Lindell [8], and they proposed the simple construction satisfying the security by using exclusive-or of MAC tags.

Furthermore, there is another line of research about compressing MAC tags, called the sequential aggregate MACs. In sequential aggregate MACs, we can check not only the validity of multiple messages (like the aggregate MACs) but

© Springer Nature Switzerland AG 2018
J. Baek et al. (Eds.): ProvSec 2018, LNCS 11192, pp. 295–312, 2018.
https://doi.org/10.1007/978-3-030-01446-9_17

also the (sequential) order of messages. This property is required in applications including networks of resource-constrained devices such as IoT networks and mobile ad-hoc networks (MANET). Eikemeier et al. [5] formally defined the model and security for sequential aggregate MACs. They also introduced history-freeness which is a property depending only on a local message of each sender and the prior aggregate tag (aggregate-so-far tag), and they proposed history-free sequential aggregate MAC schemes. Ma and Tsudik [9] gave a simple construction by using hash functions for sequential aggregate MACs with forward security, however, they did not give a formal security proof to show that their construction met the security. Hence, Hirose and Kuwakado [6] formally defined the forward security in sequential aggregate MACs, and proposed a construction satisfying the security property with a formal security proof. Tomita et al. [10] gave a model of sequential aggregate authentication codes in the information-theoretic security setting, and they proposed constructions along with their model. The model in [10] focuses the one-time information-theoretic security which is different from those of [5,6,9].

Our motivation is to make the existing networks using MACs more efficient than the present state of affairs, however, it is not realistic to replace the currently existing network protocols with other ones entirely in general. Instead, we consider to simply embed a new node for improvement of efficiency (by aggregating MAC-tags sequentially) into the existing network without changing input-formats or structures of the existing MACs in the networks. In this paper, we call such a node an *aggregate node* whose role is to sequentially compress any multiple MAC-tags into a short tag without managing secret keys. The prior work for sequential aggregate MACs [5,6,9] does not satisfy our targeted property, namely, the prior work needs a new system setting (e.g., changing composition of MACs or setting an aggregate algorithm with a secret-key) or needs to change input-formats of the underlying MAC schemes (e.g., additional information with the local message would be required as input of MACs).

In this paper, we introduce a new model of sequential aggregate MACs where an aggregation algorithm generates a sequential aggregate tag depending only on multiple and independent MAC tags without any secret-key, and we formally define security in this model in Sect. 3. Our model and security are quite different from those of previous works. In addition, we propose two generic constructions of sequential aggregate MACs, called SAMAC1 and SAMAC2, starting from any MAC schemes (e.g., HMAC [2,3] and CMAC [1]) in Sect. 4.1, and we formally prove that our constructions meet the security in Sect. 4.2. We also show an application of our sequential aggregate MACs in Sect. 5: we consider a case where a device transmits long data by data-partitioning in a wireless network. Furthermore, it is shown in Sect. 6 that we can transform our construction into history-free sequential aggregate MACs [5]. Hence, ours can also be used as the prior sequential aggregate MACs.

To clarify the (dis)advantage of our constructions, we compare ours (i.e., SAMAC1 and SAMAC2) and the existing ones (i.e., MT [9], EFG+ [5], and HK [6]) in terms of *universal applicability*, *security*, and *efficiency* in Tables 1,

2 and 3, where we do not compare TWS [10] with others, since the security of TWS is information-theoretic and quite different from others. In the following, we explain differences among them by using Tables 1, 2 and 3.

(i) **Universal Applicability.** We consider applicability of embedding an *aggregate node* into the existing MAC protocols without changing the input-formats or network connections of underlying MACs. We also consider whether an aggregate algorithm can be executed without secret keys. Table 1 summarizes information about this. In previous works [5,6], each sender has to use not only a local message but also an aggregate-so-far tag to generate an aggregate tag, which means that we need to change the input-formats or structure of the underlying MACs. In addition, the constructions in [5,6,9] require other primitives except for MACs, such as a collision-resistant hash function [9], a pseudorandom permutation [5], or a pseudorandom generator [6]. On the other hand, our two constructions, SAMAC1 and SAMAC2, need not to change the input-formats or network connections of underlying MACs, and can generate an aggregate tag from MAC-tags without a secret key. While SAMAC1 requires only a MAC as a primitive, SAMAC2 needs a cryptographic hash function in addition to a MAC.

(ii) **Security.** We summarize provable security in Table 2. We note that a security proof of MT is not given, while other ones have provable security. We also note that the security proof of SAMAC2 is given in the random oracle model (ROM) while the security of HK, EFG+, and SAMAC1 are proved in the standard model (i.e., without random oracles).

(iii) **Efficiency.** Table 3 shows efficiency for the constructions. The number of function-calls, denoted by #Func.-call, shows how many times the required primitives are invoked in generating an aggregate tag. The number of function-calls in our constructions is smaller than those of the existing ones, which indicates that communication among senders and an aggregation node in our constructions is more efficient. Parallel computation in Table 3 means whether we can compute an aggregate tag in parallel. Although MT, HK, and EFG+ need to transmit an aggregate tag in a sequential way from a sender to another sender due to the order of messages, ours can compute an aggregate tag in parallel since each sender can compute a MAC-tag in parallel and then an aggregation node aggregates them into an aggregate tag following the order of messages. Parallel computability leads to less time complexity and avoids delay of sending messages in a network. Time complexity in Table 3 means the number of operations required for computing an aggregate tag. Our constructions do not need to compute MAC-tags N times owing to parallel computation of MAC-tags, while we need $(N - 1)$ matrix multiplications in SAMAC1. It is not easy to strictly compare time complexity of SAMAC1 with those of MT, HK, and EFG+, since quite different operations are used. Anyway, we can say that our second construction SAMAC2 is best in time complexity since its time complexity does not depend on N. All of the constructions have the same bit-length of aggregate tags. The reduction loss being small implies that the gap between the resulting constructions and the underlying MACs in the security proof is small. From this viewpoint, SAMAC1 and SAMAC2 are superior to HK and EFG+. In total, we see that SAMAC2 is best among all ones in terms of efficiency.

(iv) **Summary.** In order to make the existing networks using MACs more efficient with slight change, universal applicability shown in Table 1 is important in a real world. In addition, we require provable security for the constructions, and we desire more efficiency than the current situation of the network that is our goal in this paper. From the viewpoints, we consider SAMAC2 is superior to others, though the security proof is given in the random oracle model. It is interesting to consider SAMAC1 as well in the standard model, and it is also interesting in versatility since it can be transformed into a history-free sequential aggregate MAC in the model of [5] without changing the input-formats of the MAC or adding any other primitive except for the MAC.

Table 1. Universal Applicability: CRH means a collision-resistant hash function, PRP means a pseudorandom permutation, PRG means a pseudorandom generator, and HF is a cryptographic hash function. MAC's input means the input-format required for the underlying MAC, m is a message, e is the end-marker in a time period, and $\tilde{\tau}$ is a previous aggregate tag.

Construction	Keyless aggregation	Primitive	MAC's input
MT [9]	✓	MAC and CRH	m
HK [6]		MAC and PRG	$m\|e\|\tilde{\tau}$
EFG+ [5]		MAC and PRP	m
SAMAC1	✓	MAC	m
SAMAC2	✓	MAC and HF	m

Table 2. Security: UF means unforgeability. ROM means the random oracle model, and Standard Model means the model without any random oracles.

Construction	Security level	Provable security	Standard model
MT [9]	Forward UF		n/a
HK [6]	Forward UF	✓	✓
EFG+ [5]	UF	✓	✓
SAMAC1	UF	✓	✓
SAMAC2	UF	✓	ROM

Table 3. Efficiency: Let N be the number of senders, let q be the number of queries to the tagging oracle, and let L be the maximum number of ID/message pairs in submitted queries. #Func.-call means the number that primitives are invoked in generating an aggregate tag. For a primitive $P \in \{\mathsf{MAC}, \mathsf{CRH}, \mathsf{PRG}, \mathsf{PRP}, \mathsf{HF}\}$, T_P means time complexity for computing P, and T_{MUL} means time complexity for computing multiplication of two matrices. Agg.-tag size means bit-length of aggregate tags, and n is bit-length of the underlying MAC. Reduction loss means the ratio ϵ/ϵ', where ϵ and ϵ' are the success probabilities of adversaries' attacks against the corresponding construction and the underlying MAC, respectively.

Construction	#Func.-call		Parallel computation	Time complexity	Agg.-tag size	Reduction loss
	Primitive	#Call				
MT [9]	MAC	N		$N \cdot T_{\mathsf{MAC}} +$	n	n/a
	CRH	N		$(N-1)T_{\mathsf{CRH}}$		
HK [6]	MAC	N		$N \cdot T_{\mathsf{MAC}} +$	n	$O(Nq^2)$
	PRG	U		$U \cdot T_{\mathsf{PRG}}$		
EFG+ [5]	MAC	N		$N \cdot T_{\mathsf{MAC}} +$	n	$O(Nq^2L)$
	PRP	N		$N \cdot T_{\mathsf{PRP}}$		
SAMAC1	MAC	N	✓	$T_{\mathsf{MAC}} +$ $(N-1)T_{\mathsf{MUL}}$	n	$O(N(1 - 2^{-\frac{n}{4}})^{-N})$
SAMAC2	MAC	N	✓	$T_{\mathsf{MAC}} + T_{\mathsf{HF}}$	n	$O(N)$
	HF	1				

2   Preliminaries

In this paper, we use the following notations. For a positive integer n, let $[n] := \{1, 2, \ldots, n\}$. If we write a *negligible* function ε in λ, it means a function $\varepsilon : \mathbb{N} \to [0, 1]$ where $\varepsilon(\lambda) < 1/g(\lambda)$ for any polynomial g and a sufficiently large λ. We describe $\{x_i\}_{i \in [n]} := \{x_1, x_2, \ldots, x_n\}$ as a set of values x_i for all $i \in [n]$, and $(x_i)_{i \in [n]} := (x_1, x_2, \ldots, x_n)$ as a sequence of values x_i for all $i \in [n]$. We denote a polynomial in n by $\mathrm{poly}(n)$. Probabilistic polynomial time is abbreviated as PPT.

We define a deterministic message authentication code (MAC) as follows: A MAC scheme consists of three polynomial-time algorithms (KGen, Tag, Vrfy).

- $k \leftarrow \mathrm{KGen}(1^\lambda)$: KGen is a randomized algorithm which, on input a security parameter λ, outputs a secret key $k \in \mathcal{K}$.
- $t \leftarrow \mathrm{Tag}(k, m)$: Tag is a deterministic algorithm which, on input a secret key k and a message $m \in \mathcal{M}$, outputs a tag $t \in \mathcal{T}$.
- $1/0 \leftarrow \mathrm{Vrfy}(k, m, t)$: Vrfy is a deterministic algorithm which, on input a secret key k, a message m, and a tag t, outputs 1 (acceptance) or 0 (rejection).

Let $\mathcal{K}$ be a key-space, let $\mathcal{M}$ be a message-space, and let $\mathcal{T}$ be a tag-space. It is required that, for all $k \leftarrow \mathrm{KGen}(1^\lambda)$ and all $m \in \mathcal{M}$, we have $1 \leftarrow \mathrm{Vrfy}(k, m, \mathrm{Tag}(k, m))$.

We next define security notions of unforgeability against chosen message attacks (UF-CMA) and pseudorandomness for the MACs as follows: Let MAC = (KGen, Tag, Vrfy) be a MAC scheme.

UF-CMA. MAC meets UF-CMA, if for any PPT adversary $\mathcal{A}$ against MAC, the advantage of $Adv_{MAC,\mathcal{A}}^{uf\text{-}cma}(\lambda) := \Pr[\mathcal{A} \text{ wins}]$ is negligible, where $[\mathcal{A} \text{ wins}]$ is an event that $\mathcal{A}$ wins, in the following game:

   Setup: A challenger generates $k \leftarrow \mathrm{KGen}(1^\lambda)$ and sets $\mathcal{L}_{Tag} = \emptyset$.

   Tagging: The tagging oracle $\mathsf{Tag}_k(\cdot)$ takes a query $m \in \mathcal{M}$, returns $t \leftarrow \mathrm{Tag}(k,m)$, and sets $\mathcal{L}_{Tag} \leftarrow \mathcal{L}_{Tag} \cup \{m\}$. The number of queries submitted by $\mathcal{A}$ is at most $Q = \mathrm{poly}(\lambda)$.

   Output: When $\mathcal{A}$ outputs a forgery (m^*, t^*), $\mathcal{A}$ wins if the following holds: $1 \leftarrow \mathrm{Vrfy}(k, m^*, t^*)$, and $m^* \neq m$ for any $m \in \mathcal{L}_{Tag}$.

Pseudorandomness. MAC meets pseudorandomness, if the following holds: $Adv_{MAC,\mathcal{D}}^{pr}(\lambda) := \left| \Pr[\mathcal{D}^{\mathsf{Tag}_K(\cdot)}(1^\lambda) = 1] - \Pr[\mathcal{D}^{f(\cdot)}(1^\lambda) = 1] \right|$ is negligible. Here, $\mathcal{D}$ is a PPT algorithm which, on input an oracle either $\mathsf{Tag}_k(\cdot)$ or $f(\cdot)$, determines which oracle is given; $\mathsf{Tag}_k(\cdot)$ is the tagging oracle which, on input $m \in \mathcal{M}$, returns $t = \mathrm{Tag}(k,m)$; and $f(\cdot)$ is an oracle which, on input $m \in \mathcal{M}$, returns $f(m)$ for a random function $f : \mathcal{M} \to \mathcal{T}$.

3 Sequential Aggregate MACs: Our Model and Security

We introduce a new model of sequential aggregate MACs where an aggregation algorithm generates a sequential aggregate tag depending only on multiple and independent MAC tags without any secret-key, and we formally define security in this model.

Let MAC=(KGen, Tag, Vrfy) be a MAC scheme. Then, a sequential aggregate MAC scheme consists of a tuple of five polynomial-time algorithms (KGen, Tag, Vrfy, SeqAgg, SAVrfy) as follows, where N is the number of senders, $\mathcal{ID}$ is an ID-space, $\mathcal{K}$ is a key-space, $\mathcal{M}$ is a message-space, $\mathcal{T}$ is a tag-space, and $\mathcal{T}_{agg}$ is an aggregate tag-space. Let $\mathcal{S} := \{(id_{\ell_1}, id_{\ell_2}, \ldots, id_{\ell_{\widehat{N}}}) \mid \widehat{N} \leq N \wedge id_i \neq id_j \text{ if } i \neq j\}$, which means the set of all different sequences of IDs with length at most N:

- $k_{id} \leftarrow \mathrm{KGen}(1^\lambda, id)$: KGen is a randomized algorithm which, on input a security parameter λ and an ID $id \in \mathcal{ID}$, outputs a secret key $k_{id} \in \mathcal{K}$. Note that this is the same as KGen of the underlying MAC except for adding id.
- $t \leftarrow \mathrm{Tag}(k_{id}, m)$: Tag is a deterministic algorithm which, on input a secret key k_{id} and a message m, outputs a tag $t \in \mathcal{T}$. This is the same as Tag of the MAC.
- $1/0 \leftarrow \mathrm{Vrfy}(k_{id}, m, t)$: Vrfy is a deterministic algorithm which, on input a secret key k_{id}, a message $m \in \mathcal{M}$, and a tag t, outputs 1 (acceptance) or 0 (rejection). This is the same as Vrfy of the MAC.
- $\tau \leftarrow \mathrm{SeqAgg}(T)$: SeqAgg is a deterministic algorithm which, on input a sequence of tags $T = ((id_{\ell_i}, t_i))_{i \in [\widehat{N}]}$ such that $(id_{\ell_1}, \ldots, id_{\ell_{\widehat{N}}}) \in \mathcal{S}$, outputs an aggregate tag $\tau \in \mathcal{T}_{agg}$.

- $1/0 \leftarrow \text{SAVrfy}(K, M, \tau)$: SAVrfy is a deterministic algorithm which, on input a set of key/id pairs $K = \{(k_{id_i}, id_i)\}_{i \in [N]}$, a sequence of message/id pairs $((m_i, id_{\ell_i}))_{i \in [\widehat{N}]}$ for any $(id_{\ell_1}, \ldots, id_{\ell_{\widehat{N}}}) \in \mathcal{S}$, and an aggregate tag τ, outputs 1 (acceptance) or 0 (rejection).

We require that the following condition (i.e., correctness) holds:

- For all $id \in \mathcal{ID}$, all $k_{id} \leftarrow \text{KGen}(1^\lambda, id)$ and all $m \in \mathcal{M}$, we have $1 \leftarrow \text{Vrfy}(k_{id}, m, \text{Tag}(k_{id}, m))$.
- For all $id \in \mathcal{ID}$, all $k_{id} \leftarrow \text{KGen}(1^\lambda, id)$ and all $m \in \mathcal{M}$, for any $K = \{(k_{id_i}, id_i)\}_{i \in [N]}$ and any $M = ((m_i, id_{\ell_i}))_{i \in [\widehat{N}]}$ such that $(id_{\ell_1}, \ldots, id_{\ell_{\widehat{N}}}) \in \mathcal{S}$, we have $1 \leftarrow \text{SAVrfy}(K, M, \tau)$, where $T = ((id_{\ell_i}, \text{Tag}(k_{id_{\ell_i}}, m_i)))_{i \in [\widehat{N}]}$ and $\tau = \text{SeqAgg}(T)$.

We define the following relation for sequences of message/ID pairs in order to define security of sequential aggregate MACs in our model.

Definition 1. *For two sequences of message/ID pairs* $M^{(1)} = ((m_i^{(1)}, id_i^{(1)}))_{i \in [N^{(1)}]}$ *and* $M^{(2)} = ((m_i^{(2)}, id_i^{(2)}))_{i \in [N^{(2)}]}$, *we define* $(M^{(1)})_{i_1, i_2} \equiv (M^{(2)})_{i'_1, i'_2}$ *for* i_1, i_2, i'_1, i'_2 *such that* $i_1 < i_2 \le N^{(1)}$ *and* $i'_1 < i'_2 \le N^{(2)}$, *if the following holds:*

$$((m_{i_1}^{(1)}, id_{i_1}^{(1)}), \cdots, (m_{i_2}^{(1)}, id_{i_2}^{(1)})) = ((m_{i'_1}^{(2)}, id_{i'_1}^{(2)}), \cdots, (m_{i'_2}^{(2)}, id_{i'_2}^{(2)})).$$

If not, we denote $(M_1)_{i_1, i_2} \not\equiv (M_2)_{i'_1, i'_2}$.

We next define a security notion of *C-aggregate unforgeability against chosen message attacks (C-aggUF-CMA)* in our model.

Definition 2 (C-aggUF-CMA). *A sequential aggregate MAC scheme* SAMAC = (KGen, Tag, Vrfy, SeqAgg, SAVrfy) *meets C-aggUF-CMA, if for any PPT adversary $\mathcal{A}$ against* SAMAC, *the advantage* $\text{Adv}_{\text{SAMAC}, \mathcal{A}}^{\text{agg-uf}}(\lambda) := \Pr[\mathcal{A} \text{ wins}]$ *of $\mathcal{A}$ is negligible, where $[\mathcal{A}$ wins$]$ is an event that $\mathcal{A}$ wins, in the following game:*

Setup: *A challenger generates a set of secret-key/ID pairs $K = \{(k_{id_i}, id_i)\}_{i \in [N]}$ by using the KGen algorithm. Then, it sets lists $\mathcal{L}_{Cor} = \emptyset$ and $\mathcal{L}_{SA} = \emptyset$.*

Corrupt: *The corrupt oracle* Corrupt$(\cdot)$ *takes an ID $id \in \mathcal{ID}$ as input and returns the secret key k_{id} and sets $\mathcal{L}_{Cor} \leftarrow \mathcal{L}_{Cor} \cup \{id\}$, where $\mathcal{L}_{Cor}$ means a list of IDs whose corresponding secret keys are known by an adversary. The number of queries submitted by $\mathcal{A}$ is at most C.*

Tagging: *The sequential aggregate tagging oracle* SATag$_K(\cdot)$ *takes a sequence of message/ID pairs $M = ((m_i, id_{\ell_i}))_{i \in [\widehat{N}]}$ such that $(id_{\ell_1}, \ldots, id_{\ell_{\widehat{N}}}) \in \mathcal{S}$ and the number of not corrupted tags is at least $N - C$, where without loss of generality, we assume that $id_{\ell_1} \notin \mathcal{L}_{Cor}$ and $id_{\ell_{\widehat{N}}} \notin \mathcal{L}_{Cor}$. Then, it does the following:*

1. *Compute $t_i \leftarrow \mathrm{Tag}(k_{id_{\ell_i}}, m_i)$ for all $i \in [\widehat{N}]$,*
2. *Output $\tau \leftarrow \mathrm{SeqAgg}(((\widehat{id}_{\ell_i}, t_i))_{i \in [\widehat{N}]})$,*
3. *Set $\mathcal{L}_{SA} \leftarrow \mathcal{L}_{SA} \cup \{M\}$.*

The number of queries which $\mathcal{A}$ submits is at most $Q = \mathrm{poly}(\lambda)$. $\mathcal{A}$ is not allowed to access $\mathrm{Corrupt}(\cdot)$ after accessing $\mathrm{SATag}_K(\cdot)$. In addition, $\mathcal{A}$ is not allowed to query M such that for any $M' \in \mathcal{L}_{SA}$, it holds that $(M)_{1,1+\ell} \equiv (M')_{1,1+\ell}$ or $(M)_{\widehat{N}-\ell,\widehat{N}} \equiv (M')_{\widehat{N}'-\ell,\widehat{N}'}$, where $\ell := \min(\widehat{N}-1, \widehat{N}'-1)$ and $\widehat{N}'$ is the number of message/ID pairs in M'.

Output: *When $\mathcal{A}$ outputs $M^* = ((m_i^*, id_{\ell_i^*}))_{i \in [\widetilde{N}]}$ and τ^*, $\mathcal{A}$ wins if the following holds:*

- *$1 \leftarrow \mathrm{SAVrfy}(K, M^*, \tau^*)$,*
- *$(id_{\ell_1^*}, \ldots, id_{\ell_{\widetilde{N}}^*}) \in \mathcal{S}$ such that $id_{\ell_1^*} \notin \mathcal{L}_{Cor}$ and $id_{\ell_{\widetilde{N}}^*} \notin \mathcal{L}_{Cor}$, and the number of not corrupted IDs is at least $N - C$,*
- *$M^* \notin \mathcal{L}_{SA}$, and M^* is not any concatenation of queries in $\mathcal{L}_{SA}$ and a tag generated by a secret key of corrupted entities in $\mathcal{L}_{Cor}$.*

In principle, it is impossible in our model to guarantee the unforgeability against an adversary who can observe each MAC-tag before the aggregation. This reason is that, if the adversary obtains a sequence $\{(m_i, \mathrm{Tag}(k_{id_i}, m_i))\}_{i \in [\widehat{N}]}$ by accessing the tagging oracle, he can generate an aggregate tag for any sequential messages $(m_{\ell_i})_{i \in [N]}$ because SeqAgg algorithm is keyless. Thus, we consider the attacking model where an adversary makes a forgery by only accessing the sequential aggregate tagging oracle.

We next show a condition for a SeqAgg algorithm to achieve C-aggUF-CMA. For simplicity, we view a SeqAgg algorithm as a function $F : \mathcal{T}^N \to \mathcal{T}_{agg}$, where $\mathcal{T}$ is a MAC tag-space and $\mathcal{T}_{agg}$ is an aggregate tag-space. Then, the following proposition states that, for given $y \in \mathcal{T}_{agg}$, the equation $F(x) = y$ should not be correctly solved in polynomial time for achieving C-aggUF-CMA.

Proposition 1. *Let SAMAC = (KGen, Tag, Vrfy, SeqAgg, SAVrfy) be a sequential aggregate MAC scheme, and we identify SeqAgg with $F : \mathcal{T}^N \to \mathcal{T}_{agg}$. If we can compute a sequence of tags $(t_i)_{i \in [N]}$ from $F((t_i)_{i \in [N]})$ in polynomial time, then SAMAC does not meet C-aggUF-CMA.*

Proof. Let $\mathcal{A}$ be a PPT adversary against SAMAC. If $\mathcal{A}$ gets an aggregate tag τ on a sequence of messages $(m_i)_{i \in [N]}$ by accessing the sequential aggregate tagging oracle, $\mathcal{A}$ can compute each MAC-tag t_i on m_i for all $i \in [N]$. For a message sequence $(m_{\ell_i})_{i \in [N]}$ different from $(m_i)_{i \in [N]}$, $\mathcal{A}$ can make a forgery $\tau^* = F((t_{\ell_i})_{i \in [N]})$ on $(m_{\ell_i})_{i \in [N]}$. □

4 Construction of Sequential Aggregate MACs

4.1 Our Construction

We propose a generic construction of sequential aggregate MACs (SAMACs) in our model such that our SAMAC consists of any MAC scheme MAC =

(MAC.KGen, MAC.Tag, MAC.Vrfy) and a sequential aggregation algorithm-pair (SA.SeqAgg, SA.SAVrfy). This is well explained by the following construction of sequential aggregate MACs, GSAMAC = (KGen, Tag, Vrfy, SeqAgg, SAVrfy):

- $k_{id} \leftarrow$ KGen($1^\lambda, id$): Generate $k_{id} \leftarrow$ MAC.KGen(1^λ) and output k_{id}.
- $t \leftarrow$ Tag(k_{id}, m): Output a MAC-tag $t \leftarrow$ MAC.Tag(k_{id}, m).
- $1/0 \leftarrow$ Vrfy(k_{id}, m, t): Output $b \leftarrow$ MAC.Vrfy(k_{id}, m, t) $\in \{0, 1\}$.
- $\tau \leftarrow$ SeqAgg(T): Take a sequence of MAC tags $T = ((id_{\ell_i}, t_i))_{i \in [\widehat{N}]}$ as input and output $\tau \leftarrow$ SA.SeqAgg(T).
- $1/0 \leftarrow$ SAVrfy(K, M, τ): Take $K = \{(k_{id_i}, id_i)\}_{i \in [N]}$, $M = ((m_i, id_{\ell_i}))_{i \in [\widehat{N}]}$, and τ as input, and output a bit $b \leftarrow$ SA.SAVrfy(K, M, τ).

Therefore, it is enough to construct only a sequential aggregation algorithm-pair (SA.SeqAgg, SA.SAVrfy), and we propose two constructions called SA1 and SA2 for it. Consequently, we will obtain two constructions of SAMACs called SAMACi ($i = 1, 2$) starting from any MAC scheme and the aggregate algorithm-pair SAi.

We construct two aggregation algorithm-pairs SA1 and SA2. First, we describe the basic processes of SA1 informally as follows.

- SeqAgg algorithm:
    1. Each MAC-tag t_i is transformed into a matrix T_i,
    2. Output the product of these matrices $T_1 T_2 \cdots T_{\widehat{N}}$ as an aggregate tag τ.
- SAVrfy algorithm:
    1. Compute an aggregate tag τ' from $K = \{(k_{id_i}, id_i)\}_{i \in [N]}$ and $M = ((m_i, id_{\ell_i}))_{i \in [\widehat{N}]}$ following the SeqAgg algorithm,
    2. Output 1 (accept) if $\tau' = \tau$, or output 0 (reject) otherwise.

Our idea is based on non-commutativity of matrix multiplications. And, the order of messages is regarded as invalid, if the order of MAC-tags' matrices are changed. From this, we can construct sequential aggregate MAC schemes from any MAC schemes by transforming each MAC-tag into a matrix, and can give a security proof in the standard model. Also, we provide a simple construction SA2 by using hash functions, and give a security proof in the random oracle model. Furthermore, based on SA1, we can construct a history-free sequential aggregate MAC scheme from any MACs in Sect. 6. Although the existing construction [5] uses not only MACs but also pseudorandom permutations for constructing history-free sequential aggregate MACs, our construction requires only MACs.

Besides, it should be noted that we cannot achieve the security under consideration even if we slightly change inputs of the underlying MACs as follows: Suppose that, for each $i \in [N]$, the i-th sender computes $t_i \leftarrow$ Tag($k_{id_i}, i \parallel m_i$) and the resulting aggregate tag is $\tau = t_1 \oplus \cdots \oplus t_N$. However, it is easy to generate a valid forgery in the case where some IDs are corrupted. Actually, for an aggregate tag $\tau = t_1 \oplus \cdots \oplus t_N$ on $(m_i)_{i \in [N]}$, an adversary can compute $t_i' \leftarrow$ Tag($k_{id_i}, i \parallel m_i'$) with a corrupted ID's (i.e., id_i) secret key k_{id_i} and can generate a forgery $\tau' = \tau \oplus t_i \oplus t_i'$ without accessing the tagging oracle. Furthermore, even if an adversary does not corrupt any secret keys, he can break aggUF-CMA by submitting queries to the tagging oracle and receiving the following aggregate-tags:

$$\tau_1 = \mathrm{Tag}(k_{id_1}, 1 \parallel m_1) \oplus \mathrm{Tag}(k_{id_2}, 2 \parallel m_2) \oplus \mathrm{Tag}(k_{id_3}, 3 \parallel m_3) \oplus \cdots,$$
$$\tau_2 = \mathrm{Tag}(k_{id_1}, 1 \parallel m_1') \oplus \mathrm{Tag}(k_{id_2}, 2 \parallel m_2) \oplus \mathrm{Tag}(k_{id_3}, 3 \parallel m_3) \oplus \cdots,$$
$$\tau_3 = \mathrm{Tag}(k_{id_1}, 1 \parallel m_1) \oplus \mathrm{Tag}(k_{id_2}, 2 \parallel m_2') \oplus \mathrm{Tag}(k_{id_3}, 3 \parallel m_3) \oplus \cdots.$$

Then, he computes $\tau_1 \oplus \tau_2 \oplus \tau_3 = \mathrm{Tag}(k_{id_1}, 1 \parallel m_1') \oplus \mathrm{Tag}(k_{id_2}, 2 \parallel m_2') \oplus \mathrm{Tag}(k_{id_3}, 3 \parallel m_3) \oplus \cdots$, which is a valid forgery since the sequence $((m_1', id_1), (m_2', id_2), (m_3, id_3), \ldots)$ has never been queried. Therefore, this construction does not meet the security of sequential aggregate MACs in our model.

Construction 1. We propose a construction SA1 by transforming each MAC-tag t_i into a matrix as follows: Let n be bit-length of MAC-tag and we separate a MAC-tag $t_i \in \{0,1\}^n$ into $(t_{i,1} \parallel t_{i,2} \parallel t_{i,3} \parallel t_{i,4}) \in (\{0,1\}^{\frac{n}{4}})^4$. Then, we regard each $t_{i,j} \in \{0,1\}^{\frac{n}{4}}$ $(1 \le j \le 4)$ as an element of the finite field $GF(2^{\frac{n}{4}})$, and set $T_i := \begin{bmatrix} t_{i,1} & t_{i,2} \\ t_{i,3} & t_{i,4} \end{bmatrix}$. Here, we note that such a matrix T_i is invertible with an overwhelming probability if the MAC meets pseudorandomness. Based on this transformation, SA1 = (SA1.SeqAgg, SA1.SAVrfy) is constructed in the following way.

- $\tau \leftarrow$ SA1.SeqAgg$(((id_{\ell_i}, t_i))_{i \in [\widehat{N}]})$: Generate an aggregate tag as follows:

  1. For each $i \in [\widehat{N}]$, let $T_i := \begin{bmatrix} t_{i,1} & t_{i,2} \\ t_{i,3} & t_{i,4} \end{bmatrix}$ be a matrix transformed from t_i as mentioned above.
  2. Output $\tau := T_1 T_2 \cdots T_{\widehat{N}}$.
- $1/0 \leftarrow$ SA1.SAVrfy(K, M, τ): For $K = \{(k_{id_i}, id_i)\}_{i \in [N]}$ and $M = ((m_i, id_{\ell_i}))_{i \in [\widehat{N}]}$, verify (M, τ) as follows:

  1. For each $i \in [\widehat{N}]$, compute $t_i' \leftarrow \mathrm{MAC.Tag}(k_{id_{\ell_i}}, m_i)$ and $\tau' \leftarrow$ SA1.SeqAgg$(((id_{\ell_i}, t_i'))_{i \in [\widehat{N}]})$.
  2. Output 1 if $\tau' = \tau$, or output 0 otherwise.

Then, we show the following lemma.

Lemma 1. *Given two aggregate tags $\tau_1 \leftarrow$ SA1.SeqAgg$((id_{\ell_1}, t_1), \ldots, (id_{\ell_i}, t_i))$ and $\tau_2 \leftarrow$ SA1.SeqAgg$((id_{\ell_{i+1}}, t_{i+1}), \ldots, (id_{\ell_j}, t_j))$, if MAC meets pseudorandomness, the probability that $\tau_1 \tau_2 = \tau_2 \tau_1$ holds is negligible.*

Proof. We denote the matrices τ_1 and τ_2 by

$$\tau_1 = \begin{bmatrix} a_1 & b_1 \\ c_1 & d_1 \end{bmatrix}, \ \tau_2 = \begin{bmatrix} a_2 & b_2 \\ c_2 & d_2 \end{bmatrix},$$

where $a_i, b_i, c_i, d_i \in GF(2^{\frac{n}{4}})$ for $i \in \{1, 2\}$. We have

$$\tau_1 \tau_2 = \begin{bmatrix} a_1 a_2 + b_1 c_2 & a_1 b_2 + b_1 d_2 \\ a_2 c_1 + c_2 d_1 & b_2 c_1 + d_1 d_2 \end{bmatrix}, \ \tau_2 \tau_1 = \begin{bmatrix} a_1 a_2 + b_2 c_1 & a_2 b_1 + b_2 d_1 \\ a_1 c_2 + c_1 d_2 & b_1 c_2 + d_1 d_2 \end{bmatrix}.$$

Then, $\tau_1\tau_2 = \tau_2\tau_1$ is equivalent to the conditions:

$$b_1c_2 = b_2c_1, \tag{1}$$
$$a_1b_2 + b_1d_2 = a_2b_1 + b_2d_1, \tag{2}$$
$$a_2c_1 + c_2d_1 = a_1c_2 + c_1d_2. \tag{3}$$

Hence, the number of the equations that must hold is three, while the number of variables a_i, b_i, c_i, d_i ($i = 1, 2$) is eight. Therefore, if a_i, b_i, c_i, d_i ($i = 1, 2$) are chosen uniformly at random, the probability that the Eqs. (1)–(3) hold is $(2^{-\frac{n}{4}})^3 = 2^{-\frac{3}{4}n}$. Therefore, if the MAC meets pseudorandomness, the probability that the Eqs. (1)–(3) hold is negligible. $\square$

Construction 2. We construct SA2 = (SA2.SeqAgg, SA2.SAVrfy) by using hash functions in a simple way, and this construction is provably secure in the random oracle model. SA2 is given as follows: Let H be a random function $H : \{0,1\}^* \to \mathcal{T}$, where $\mathcal{T}$ is the tag space of a MAC scheme.

- $\tau \leftarrow$ SA2.SeqAgg$(((id_{\ell_i}, t_i))_{i \in [\widehat{N}]})$: Output $\tau := H(t_1, \ldots, t_{\widehat{N}})$.
- $1/0 \leftarrow$ SA2.SAVrfy(K, M, τ): Output 1 if $\tau = H(t'_1, \ldots, t'_{\widehat{N}})$, where $t'_i :=$ MAC.Tag$(k_{id_{\ell_i}}, m_i)$ for all $i \in [\widehat{N}]$, and output 0 otherwise.

By definition of random functions, we can see that the order of messages is guaranteed.

4.2 Security of Our Constructions

The following theorems show the security of our constructions.

Theorem 1. *If MAC meets pseudorandomness, SAMAC1 meets $(N - 2)$-aggUF-CMA.*

Theorem 2. *If MAC meets UF-CMA, SAMAC2 meets $(N - 2)$-aggUF-CMA.*

Proof of Theorem 1. We prove that SAMAC1 meets $(N - 2)$-aggUF-CMA. Let $\mathcal{A}$ be a PPT adversary against SAMAC1. We define the following events:

- Succ: An event that $\mathcal{A}$ outputs a forgery breaking aggUF-CMA.
- New: An event that for a new message which is never queried, $\mathcal{A}$ makes a forgery against a MAC scheme which is not corrupted.
- Pre: An event that $\mathcal{A}$ makes a forgery against SAMACi without generating any forgeries against MACs.
- Cor: An event that $\mathcal{A}$ does not break any MAC schemes, but uses new MAC-tags generated by using corrupted ID's keys.
- Replace: An event that $\mathcal{A}$ replaces the sequence of messages queried to the tagging oracle.

Because the events New and Pre are exclusive, we have

$$Adv^{agg-uf}_{SAMAC,A}(\lambda) := \Pr[\mathsf{Succ}] \leq \Pr[\mathsf{Succ} \wedge \mathsf{New}] + \Pr[\mathsf{Succ} \wedge \mathsf{Pre}]$$
$$\leq \Pr[\mathsf{Succ} \wedge \mathsf{New}] + \Pr[\mathsf{Succ} \wedge \mathsf{Pre} \wedge \mathsf{Replace}]$$
$$+ \Pr[\mathsf{Succ} \wedge \mathsf{Pre} \wedge \mathsf{Cor} \mid \overline{\mathsf{Replace}}] + \Pr[\mathsf{Succ} \wedge \mathsf{Pre} \wedge \overline{\mathsf{Cor}} \mid \overline{\mathsf{Replace}}].$$

Therefore, it is sufficient to prove the following:

- $\Pr[\mathsf{Succ} \wedge \mathsf{New}] \leq \frac{N}{P_{inv}} \cdot Adv^{uf-cma}_{MAC,\mathcal{F}}(\lambda)$ for a function P_{inv} of N.
- $\Pr[\mathsf{Succ} \wedge \mathsf{Pre} \wedge \mathsf{Replace}] \leq \varepsilon(\lambda)$ for a negligible function ε.
- $\Pr[\mathsf{Succ} \wedge \mathsf{Pre} \wedge \mathsf{Cor} \mid \overline{\mathsf{Replace}}] \leq \frac{(N-C)}{P_{inv}} \cdot Adv^{pr}_{MAC,\mathcal{D}}(\lambda) + \frac{1}{2^n}$.
- $\Pr[\mathsf{Succ} \wedge \mathsf{Pre} \wedge \overline{\mathsf{Cor}} \mid \overline{\mathsf{Replace}}] \leq \frac{(N-C)}{P_{inv}} \cdot Adv^{pr}_{MAC,\mathcal{D}}(\lambda) + \frac{1}{2^n}$.

Event [Succ∧New]: In this case, an adversary generates a forgery against a MAC scheme which the ID id fulfills $id \notin \mathcal{L}_{Cor}$. By using $\mathcal{A}$ breaking aggUF-CMA, we construct a PPT algorithm $\mathcal{F}$ breaking UF-CMA of MACs as follows.

Setup: Given the tagging oracle of a MAC, do the following.
1. Choose $id_i \in \mathcal{ID}$ for all $i \in [N]$,
2. Generate $k_{id_i} \leftarrow \mathsf{KGen}(1^\lambda, id_i)$ for all $i \in [N]$,
3. Set lists $\mathcal{L}_{Cor} = \emptyset$ and $\mathcal{L}_{SA} = \emptyset$.

Corrupt: When $\mathcal{A}$ submits an ID $id \in \mathcal{ID}$ to the oracle $\mathsf{Corrupt}(\cdot)$, return k_{id} and set $\mathcal{L}_{Cor} \leftarrow \mathcal{L}_{Cor} \cup \{id\}$. When $\mathcal{A}$ stops accessing Corrupt and moves to the Tagging phase, choose an ID $id^* \notin \mathcal{L}_{Cor}$ uniformly at random.

Tagging: For each query $M = ((m_i, id_{\ell_i}))_{i \in [\hat{N}]}$ to the oracle $\mathsf{SATag}_K(\cdot)$ where $K := \{(k_{id_i}, id_i)\}_{i \in [N]}$, do the following for all $i \in [\hat{N}]$.

- If $id_{\ell_i} \neq id^*$, compute $t_i = \mathsf{Tag}(k_{id_{\ell_i}}, m_i)$,
- If $id_{\ell_i} = id^*$, submit a message query m_i to the MAC oracle and receive the tag t_i.
  Return $\tau = \mathsf{SeqAgg}((id_{\ell_i}, t_i)_{i \in [\hat{N}]})$ to $\mathcal{A}$ and set $\mathcal{L}_{SA} \leftarrow \mathcal{L}_{SA} \cup \{M\}$.

Output: When $\mathcal{A}$ outputs $M^* = ((m_i^*, id_{\ell_i^*}))_{i \in [\tilde{N}]}$ and τ^*, do the following.
1. Move to the next step if the output of $\mathcal{A}$ meets the conditions of the security game except for $1 \leftarrow \mathsf{SAVrfy}(K, M^*, \tau^*)$, or abort this game otherwise.
2. For $i \in [\tilde{N}]$ and id_{ℓ_i} except for id^*, compute $\tau_i^* = \mathsf{MAC.Tag}(k_{id_{\ell_i^*}}, m_i^*)$.
3. Let i^* be the order of the ID id^* in M^* and compute T_{i^*} in the following way: $T_{i^*} = T^{*-1}_{i^*-1} \cdots T^{*-1}_1 \cdot \tau \cdot T^{*-1}_{\tilde{N}} \cdots T^{*-1}_{i^*+1} \in GF(2^n)$.
4. Recover a MAC-tag t_{i^*} from the matrix T_{i^*}.
5. Output (m_{i^*}, t_{i^*}) as a forgery of the MAC.

$\mathcal{F}$ simulates the environment of $\mathcal{A}$ completely. In Step 3 of Output phase, the probability that all matrices are invertible is at most $P_{inv} := (1 - \frac{1}{2^{n/4}})^{N-1}$. For all IDs $id_{\ell_i^*}$ ($i \in [\widetilde{N}]$) except for id^*, MAC tags t_i^* generated by using $k_{id_{\ell_i^*}}$ are valid. Therefore, t_{i^*} is also a valid MAC tag. Therefore, the success probability of $\mathcal{F}$ is at least $\frac{P_{inv}}{N} \cdot \Pr[\mathsf{Succ} \wedge \mathsf{New}]$.

Event [$\mathsf{Succ} \wedge \mathsf{Pre} \wedge \mathsf{Replace}$]: From Lemma 1, $\Pr[\mathsf{Succ} \wedge \mathsf{Pre} \wedge \mathsf{Replace}]$ is $2^{-\frac{3}{4}n}$ in SAMAC1.

Event [$\mathsf{Succ} \wedge \mathsf{Pre} \wedge \mathsf{Cor} \mid \overline{\mathsf{Replace}}$]: In this case, we consider the following adversaries: We assume that for a query M, there exists a corrupted pair (id, m, t) between not corrupted pairs $(id_{i_1}, m_{i_1}, t_{i_1})$ and $(id_{i_2}, m_{i_2}, t_{i_2})$ such that i_1 is the first order among not corrupted IDs and i_2 is the last order among not corrupted IDs, in M. An adversary tries to replace the message/tag pair (m, t) with (m^*, t^*) such that $m^* \neq m$ and $t^* = \mathsf{Tag}(k_{id}, m^*)$. He cannot replace the message/tag pair without knowing t_{i_1} and t_{i_2}. We show that the probability that the event happens is negligible if MACs meet pseudorandomness.

Let Game-0 be the standard security game and let C be the number of corrupted IDs. For $X \in [N - C]$, we define Game-X where for one of IDs $id \notin \mathcal{L}_{Cor}$, the MAC's tagging algorithm is replaced with a random function $f_{id} : \mathcal{M} \to \mathcal{T}$. Then, we show that in Game-$(X-1)$ and Game-X, the difference between the success probabilities of them is negligible from pseudorandomness of MACs. We construct a PPT algorithm $\mathcal{D}$ breaking pseudorandomness of a MAC scheme. $\mathcal{D}$ can be constructed in the same way as in the above $\mathcal{F}$ except for the process of Output phase. We describe the process of $\mathcal{D}$ at Output phase as follows: When $\mathcal{A}$ outputs $M^* = ((m_i^*, id_{\ell_i^*}))_{i \in [\widetilde{N}]}$ and τ^*, do the following.

1. Move to the next step if the output of $\mathcal{A}$ meets the conditions of the security game except for $1 \leftarrow \mathsf{SAVrfy}(K, M^*, \tau^*)$, or abort this game otherwise.
2. For each $id_{\ell_i^*}$ ($i \in [\widetilde{N}]$) except for id^*, compute t_i^* by using the key $k_{id_{\ell_i^*}}$.
3. Compute the MAC-tag t_{id^*} of id^* from τ^* and the other tags computed in Step 2.
4. Submit m^* to the tagging oracle and receive the tag t.
5. Output 1 if $t_{id^*} = t$ and (m^*, id^*) has never been queried, or output 0 otherwise.

In Game-$(N - C)$, all outputs of f_{id} and MAC tags are hidden statistically. Therefore, the probability is at most $\frac{(N-C)}{P_{inv}} \cdot Adv_{MAC, \mathcal{D}}^{pr}(\lambda) + \frac{1}{2^n}$.

Event [$\mathsf{Succ} \wedge \mathsf{Pre} \wedge \overline{\mathsf{Cor}} \mid \overline{\mathsf{Replace}}$]: In the same way as event [$\mathsf{Succ} \wedge \mathsf{Pre} \wedge \mathsf{Cor} \mid \overline{\mathsf{Replace}}$], we obtain $\Pr[\mathsf{Succ} \wedge \mathsf{Pre} \wedge \overline{\mathsf{Cor}} \mid \overline{\mathsf{Replace}}] \leq \frac{(N-C)}{P_{inv}} \cdot Adv_{MAC, \mathcal{D}}^{pr}(\lambda) + \frac{1}{2^n}$.

From the discussion above, we have

$$Adv_{SAMAC1, \mathcal{A}}^{agg\text{-}uf}(\lambda) \leq \frac{N}{P_{inv}} \cdot Adv_{MAC}^{uf\text{-}cma}(\lambda) + \frac{1}{2^{\frac{3}{4}n}} + 2\frac{(N - C)}{P_{inv}} \cdot Adv_{MAC}^{pr}(\lambda) + \frac{1}{2^{n-1}}$$

$$\leq 3\frac{N}{P_{inv}} \cdot Adv_{MAC}^{pr}(\lambda) + \left(\frac{N}{P_{inv}} + 2\right)\frac{1}{2^n} + \frac{1}{2^{\frac{3}{4}n}}.$$

We note that $Adv_{MAC}^{uf\text{-}cma}(\lambda) \leq Adv_{MAC}^{pr}(\lambda) + \frac{1}{2^n}$ holds (see [4]), and P_{inv} is $\left(1 - \frac{1}{2^{n/4}}\right)^{N-1}$. Therefore, the proof is completed. $\square$

Proof of Theorem 2. Let $\mathcal{A}$ be a PPT adversary against SAMAC2. Let $\mathcal{L}_H$ be the list of the query/answer pairs of $H(\cdot)$. Let Forge be an event that $\mathcal{A}$ breaks SAMAC2 by making a forgery of the underlying MAC, and let Coll be an event that $\mathcal{A}$ finds a collision of the random oracle H. Then, we have $Adv_{SAMAC2,\mathcal{A}}^{agg\text{-}uf}(\lambda) := \Pr[\mathsf{Forge}] \leq \Pr[\mathsf{Coll}] + \Pr[\mathsf{Forge} \wedge \overline{\mathsf{Coll}}]$.

In the event Coll, an adversary tries to find a collision of H. We note that this case includes an attack that he replaces MAC-tags queried to H. The success probability is at most $\frac{Q_h^2}{2^{n+1}}$.

Next, we consider the event $[\mathsf{Forge} \wedge \overline{\mathsf{Coll}}]$. We construct a PPT algorithm $\mathcal{F}$ breaking UF-CMA as in the proof of Theorem 1 except for the process of Output phase. In this phase, when $\mathcal{A}$ outputs $((m_i, id_{\ell_i^*}))_{i \in [\widetilde{N}]}$ and τ^*, $\mathcal{F}$ does the following process.

1. Move to the next step if the output of $\mathcal{A}$ meets the conditions of the security game except for $1 \leftarrow \mathsf{SAVrfy}(K, M^*, \tau^*)$, or abort this game otherwise.
2. Compute $t_i^* = \mathsf{MAC.Tag}(k_{id_{\ell_i^*}}, m_i)$ except for id^*,
3. Find a pair $((t_i^*)_{i \in [\widetilde{N}]}, \tau^*)$ except for a tag of id^* from $\mathcal{L}_H$. Abort this game if there exists no such pair in $\mathcal{L}_H$.
4. Output the id^*'s pair (m^*, t^*).

The pair $(t_1^*, \ldots, t_{\widetilde{N}}^*, \tau^*)$ is in $\mathcal{L}_H$ with overwhelming probability because the probability that it outputs τ^* such that $\tau^* = H(t_1^*, \ldots, t_{\widetilde{N}}^*)$ is negligible without accessing to the random oracle $H(\cdot)$. Thus, $\mathcal{F}$'s output is a valid forgery breaking a MAC scheme. Therefore, we have $\Pr[\mathsf{Forge} \wedge \overline{\mathsf{Coll}}] \leq N \cdot Adv_{MAC,\mathcal{F}}^{uf\text{-}cma}(\lambda)$.

From the above, we obtain $Adv_{SAMAC2,\mathcal{A}}^{agg\text{-}uf}(\lambda) \leq N \cdot Adv_{MAC,\mathcal{F}}^{uf\text{-}cma}(\lambda) + \frac{Q_h^2}{2^{n+1}}$, and the proof is completed. $\square$

5   Application: Sending Long Data by Data-Partitioning

Suppose that a device wants to send a long message in a wireless network, but the message is too long to directly transmit because of restrictions in the network. In this case, we usually utilize a data partitioning method to transmit the long data: We first divide a long message M into (at most) N pieces $m_1, m_2, \ldots, m_N$ (e.g., each piece may be called a packet); For each divided part m_j $(1 \leq j \leq N)$, the device generates a MAC tag $t_j \leftarrow \mathsf{Tag}(k, (m_j, j))$; The device sends $((m_j, j), t_j)$ for $j = 1, 2, \ldots, N$ by possibly different paths in the network; A receiver obtains $\{(m_j, t_j)\}_{j \in [N]}$, where we assume that divided parts $m_1, m_2, \ldots, m_N$ do not necessarily reach with the correct order (e.g., some of which may delayed in the network) and he will check the validity of both divided data and their ordering to correctly recover the message M. In this situation, we note that N tags are transmitted in the wireless network, which may cause a traffic problem if there are an enormous number of devices connected to the network and each device wants to send a long message. Our idea is to apply a sequential aggregate MAC under consideration in the previous sections in order to reduce the numbers of tags for divided data, so that we resolve the problem by reducing the amount of tags with the aggregation technique without changing the structure of the underlying MACs.

Formally, suppose that an existing authentication protocol utilizes a MAC scheme MAC=(KGen, Tag, Vrfy) as follows, where a secret key $k \leftarrow$KGen(1^λ) is already generated and installed in a device and such secret keys are generally different in devices:

- Transmission by Data-Partitioning:
    1. For a long message M, generate divided messages $(m_1, 1), (m_2, 2), \ldots, (m_N, N)$ from M by a data partitioning technique.
    2. For each (m_j, j), generate its tag $t_j \leftarrow$Tag($k, (m_j, j)$).
    3. It transmits $((m_j, j), t_j)$ for $j = 1, 2, \ldots, N$ by possibly different paths in the network.
- Verification: On receiving $\{((m_j, j), t_j)\}_{j \in [N]}$, it checks both the validity of both divided data and their ordering: If $1 \leftarrow$Vrfy($K, (m_j, j), t_j$) for every $j \in [N]$, M is recovered by the sequential data $(m_1, m_2, \ldots, m_N)$; otherwise, it rejects the data.

In order to resolve a traffic problem, we consider to embed a SeqAgg algorithm into a device and a SAVrfy algorithm into an verification protocol/system as an application of our sequential MACs. Then, we propose the following:

- Transmission by Data-Partitioning:
    1 and 2. The same in the above protocol.
    3. Compute $\tau \leftarrow$SeqAgg($((t_i, i))_{i \in [N]}$), and then transmit N pieces $((m_1, 1), T), (m_2, 2), \ldots, (m_N, N)$ by possibly different paths in the network, where we note that a tag is attached only to $(m_1, 1)$.
- Verification: On receiving $((m_1, 1), T)$ and $\{((m_j, j), t_j)\}_{2 \leq j \leq N}$, it checks both the validity of both divided data and their ordering: If $1 \leftarrow$SAVrfy($k, \tilde{M}, \tau$) where $\tilde{M} = ((m_1, 1), (m_2, 2), \ldots, (m_N, N))$, M is recovered by the sequential data $(m_1, m_2, \ldots, m_N)$; otherwise, it rejects the data.

Here, we note that in each device, the same key k is used for generating N tags $t_1, t_2, \ldots, t_N$. Therefore, if a device keeps the key secure, it is sufficient to apply C-aggUF-CMA secure sequential aggregate MACs with $C = 0$.

6   Our Construction of HF Sequential Aggregate MAC

We construct a partial invertible MAC scheme meeting computational almost universal from MAC schemes. By applying this construction to Construction 6.10 of [5], we can obtain a history-free (hf) sequential aggregate MAC scheme.

Let MAC = (KGen, Tag, Vrfy) be a MAC scheme. First, we define the following property of the MAC.

Partial Inversion. MAC meets partial inversion if there exists the following polynomial time algorithm: For any secret key k and any message m, and a tag τ given as input, the algorithm returns m' such that $\tau \leftarrow \text{Tag}(k, (m \parallel m'))$ for some $m' \in \{0,1\}^{\text{poly}(\lambda)}$.

Next, we construct a scheme meeting partial inversion and pseudorandomness from our SA1. Let MAC = (KGen, Tag, Vrfy) be the underlying MAC. Then, PIMAC = (PIMAC.KGen, PIMAC.Tag, PIMAC.Vrfy) is constructed as follows.

- $k \leftarrow \text{PIMAC.KGen}(1^\lambda)$: Output $k \leftarrow \text{KGen}(1^\lambda)$.
- $\tau \leftarrow \text{PIMAC.Tag}(k, m \parallel \tau')$: On input a secret key k and a message $(m \parallel \tau') \in \mathcal{M} \times \mathcal{T}_{agg}$ where any $\tau' \in \mathcal{T}_{agg}$ is a matrix of SA1, generate a tag τ in the following way.
  1. Compute $t \leftarrow \text{Tag}(k, m)$ and let T be a matrix for t based on SA1.
  2. Output $\tau := T \cdot \tau' \cdot T \in \mathcal{T}_{agg}$.
- $1/0 \leftarrow \text{PIMAC.Vrfy}(k, m \parallel \tau', \tau)$: On input a secret key k, a message $m \parallel \tau'$, and a MAC tag τ, verify the message/tag pair $(m \parallel \tau', \tau)$ as follows.
  1. Compute $\bar{\tau} \leftarrow \text{PIMAC.Tag}(k, m \parallel \tau')$.
  2. Output 1 if $\bar{\tau} = \tau$, or output 0 otherwise.

Then, we show the following lemma.

Lemma 2. *PIMAC meets partial inversion. Furthermore, if MAC meets pseudorandomness, PIMAC also meets pseudorandomness.*

Proof. First, we prove that PIMAC meets partial inversion by constructing the following partial inversion algorithm: It takes a secret key k, a message m, and τ as input, and does the following.

1. Compute $t \leftarrow \text{Tag}(k, m)$ and let T be a matrix transformed from t.
2. Output $\tau' := T^{-1} \cdot \tau \cdot T^{-1} \in \mathcal{T}_{agg}$.

Then, we can see that the output τ' is valid.

Second, we prove that PIMAC meets pseudorandomness. Let $\mathcal{A}$ be a PPT adversary breaking the pseudorandomness of PIMAC. We construct a PPT algorithm $\mathcal{B}$ breaking the pseudorandomness of the underlying MAC as follows: It is given the oracle of a MAC or a random function. When $\mathcal{A}$ submits a message query $m \| \tau'$, it submits m to the given oracle and receives the value t. Then, it computes τ following PIMAC.Tag algorithm and returns it. When $\mathcal{A}$ outputs the guessing bit $b' \in \{0, 1\}$, $\mathcal{B}$ also outputs b'.

If $\mathcal{A}$ breaks the pseudorandomness of PIMAC, $\mathcal{B}$ also breaks the pseudorandomness of MAC. This completes the proof.   □

Let HF-SAMAC be a sequential aggregate MAC obtained by applying PIMAC to Construction 6.10 of [5]. Then, by Theorem 6.11 of [5], we have:

Proposition 2. *If PIMAC meets pseudorandomness and partial inversion, HF-SAMAC meets the aggregate unforgeability of Definition 5.4 in [5].*

7   Conclusion

In this paper, we introduced a new model of sequential aggregate MACs where an aggregation algorithm generates a sequential aggregate tag depending only on multiple and independent MAC tags without any secret-key, and we formally defined security in this model. Our model and security are quite different from those of previous works [5,6,9]. In addition, we proposed two generic constructions, SAMAC1 and SAMAC2, starting from any MACs, with formal security proofs. And, we compared the existing ones and ours in terms of universal applicability, security, and efficiency. As a result, SAMAC2 is superior to others from all aspects of evaluation items, though the security proof is given in the random oracle model. It is interesting to consider SAMAC1 as well in the standard model, and it can be transformed into a history-free sequential aggregate MAC in the model of [5] without changing the input-formats of MACs or adding any other primitives except for MACs.

We note that, if a sequence of messages are rejected in our sequential aggregate MACs, we cannot identify which message has been invalid (e.g., some of them was forged, or their order was wrong). Hirose and Shikata [7] recently proposed (non-sequential) aggregate MACs in which we could identify which message was invalid, if a set of messages are rejected in their aggregate MACs. Our future work includes extension of [7] for sequential aggregate MACs.

Acknowledgements. The authors would like to thank the anonymous referees for their helpful comments. This research was conducted under a contract of Research and Development for Expansion of Radio Wave Resources funded by the Ministry of Internal Affairs and Communications, Japan.

References

1. NIST Special Publication 800–38G: Recommendation for block cipher modes of operation: the CMAC mode for authentication. National Institute of Standards and Technology (2005)
2. Bellare, M.: New proofs for NMAC and HMAC: security without collision resistance. J. Cryptol. **28**(4), 844–878 (2015)
3. Bellare, M., Canetti, R., Krawczyk, H.: Keying hash functions for message authentication. In: Koblitz, N. (ed.) CRYPTO 1996. LNCS, vol. 1109, pp. 1–15. Springer, Heidelberg (1996). https://doi.org/10.1007/3-540-68697-5_1
4. Bellare, M., Kilian, J., Rogaway, P.: The security of the cipher block chaining message authentication code. J. Comput. Syst. Sci. **61**(3), 362–399 (2000)
5. Eikemeier, O., et al.: History-free aggregate message authentication codes. In: Garay, J.A., De Prisco, R. (eds.) SCN 2010. LNCS, vol. 6280, pp. 309–328. Springer, Heidelberg (2010). https://doi.org/10.1007/978-3-642-15317-4_20
6. Hirose, S., Kuwakado, H.: Forward-secure sequential aggregate message authentication revisited. In: Chow, S.S.M., Liu, J.K., Hui, L.C.K., Yiu, S.M. (eds.) ProvSec 2014. LNCS, vol. 8782, pp. 87–102. Springer, Cham (2014). https://doi.org/10.1007/978-3-319-12475-9_7

7. Hirose, S., Shikata, J.: Non-adaptive group-testing aggregate MAC schemes. In: ISPEC. Lecture Notes in Computer Science, Springer (2018, to appear). Available at Cryptology ePrint Archive Report 2018/448
8. Katz, J., Lindell, A.Y.: Aggregate message authentication codes. In: Malkin, T. (ed.) CT-RSA 2008. LNCS, vol. 4964, pp. 155–169. Springer, Heidelberg (2008). https://doi.org/10.1007/978-3-540-79263-5_10
9. Ma, D., Tsudik, G.: Extended abstract: forward-secure sequential aggregate authentication. In: IEEE Symposium on Security and Privacy, pp. 86–91. IEEE Computer Society (2007)
10. Tomita, S., Watanabe, Y., Shikata, J.: Sequential aggregate authentication codes with information theoretic security. In: CISS, pp. 192–197. IEEE (2016)

Length-Preserving Encryption Based on Single-Key Tweakable Block Cipher

Xiangyang Zhang[1], Yaobin Shen[1], Hailun Yan[1], Ying Zou[1], Ming Wan[1],
Zheyi Wu[1], and Lei Wang[1,2(✉)]

[1] Department of Computer Science and Engineering, Shanghai Jiao Tong University,
Shanghai, China
{xiangyang.zhang,yb_shen,helenyan,zy_ask,wanming,wuzheyi,
wanglei_hb}@sjtu.edu.cn
[2] Westone Cryptologic Research Center, Beijing, China

Abstract. We present a Single-key Length Doubler built on an n-bit
Tweakable block cipher (SLDT), which is a length-preserving cipher on
the strings with bit length in integer interval $[n, n+1, \ldots, 2n-1]$. SLDT
is mainly motivated to reduce the key material size of a length doubler
proposed by Chen et $al.$ at FSE2018, since the key management is always
challenging in practice. We prove that SLDT is a strong pseudo-random
permutation (SPRP) if the underlying tweakable block cipher is SPRP.

Keywords: Length doubler · SLDT · Tweakable block cipher
Single key · Provable security · Birthday bound

1 Introduction

The encryption is always a fundamental functionality of cryptography, ever since
the secrecy has been desired. Nowadays the most popular approach of designing
an encryption scheme is to iterate a (tweakable) block cipher, which is usually called Mode of Operations. Examples include Cipher Block Chaining mode
(CBC), Electronic CodeBook mode (ECB), Cipher FeedBack mode (CFB), Output FeedBack mode (OFB) and CounTer mode (CTR). Nevertheless, a block
cipher is a fixed-input-length primitive. Throughout the paper, the block and
key sizes of (tweakable) block cipher are denoted as n and k respectively. A
block cipher is a deterministic algorithm $E : \mathcal{K} \times \mathcal{M} \to \mathcal{M}$, where $\mathcal{K} = \{0,1\}^k$,
$\mathcal{M} = \{0,1\}^n$ and for each key $K \in \mathcal{K}$, the mapping $E(K, \cdot)$ (sometimes written as $E_K(\cdot)$) is a permutation over $\mathcal{M}$ and easily invertible. A trivial iteration
of a block cipher can only proceed messages of multiple blocks long, that is
$i \times n$ bits long with some positive integer i. In order to handle arbitrarily long
messages, a solution widely adopted in practice is to use a padding algorithm
that pads a message M to be multiple blocks long, $e.g.$ $\mathrm{pad}(M) = M \| 10 \cdots 0$,
where $\|$ denotes concatenation. However, it brings a drawback that the cipher-
text is longer than the original plaintext. This is undesired, in particular for
low bandwidth network protocols, disk encryption, etc. Thus, an interesting and

© Springer Nature Switzerland AG 2018
J. Baek et al. (Eds.): ProvSec 2018, LNCS 11192, pp. 313–326, 2018.
https://doi.org/10.1007/978-3-030-01446-9_18

important research is the *length-preserving* encryption, which handles arbitrarily long messages, and yet produces ciphertexts of the same length with plaintexts.

There are roughly two approaches to build length-preserving encryption schemes. One is dedicated designs. Examples are EME [4], TET [5], HEH [13], HCTR [15], HCH [1] and XCB [8]. The other approach is *generic* transformations that can turn any mode of operations to be length-preserving. The first such transformation is XLS proposed by Ristenpart and Rogaway [11]. It utilizes block ciphers to build an encryption cipher for $(n + s)$-bit messages, where $s \in [1, \ldots, n-1]$, with length preserving. Hence such ciphers are referred to as *length doubler*. More formally, a length doubler is a deterministic function $\mathcal{E} : \mathcal{K} \times \mathcal{M} \to \mathcal{M}$, where $\mathcal{M} = \bigcup_{i=n}^{2n-1} \{0,1\}^i$. A length doubler can be attached to any encryption scheme for multiple-block messages to transform it to a length-preserving cipher. Unfortunately XLS was not secure, as Nandi found an attack [9]. Subsequently, two block-cipher-based length doublers DE and HEM are proposed by Nandi [14] and Zhang [16] respectively, which make four primitive calls.

Recently, Chen *et al.* [3] design a length doubler LDT, which for the first time uses tweakable block ciphers as underlying primitives. Interestingly it makes just two primitive calls. Tweakable block cipher has an additional public tweak compared with block cipher, $\widetilde{E} : \mathcal{K} \times \mathcal{T} \times \mathcal{M} \to \mathcal{M}$, where $\mathcal{K} = \{0,1\}^k$, $\mathcal{T} = \{0,1\}^t$, $\mathcal{M} = \{0,1\}^n$, and for any pair $(K,T) \in \mathcal{K} \times \mathcal{T}$, $\widetilde{E}(K,T,\cdot)$ (sometimes written as $\widetilde{E}_K(T,\cdot)$) is a permutation over $\mathcal{M}$ and easily invertible. LDT is proven secure up to $2^{n/2}$ adversarial queries, that is *birthday-bound* security.

Our Contributions

This research is motivated to further refine previous length doublers. An investigation on LDT finds that it requires two independent keys, one for each underlying tweakable block cipher, that is in total $2k$ key bits. It is well known that key management is very changing from the practical point of view. A long key size causes extra burden and potential risk on key exchange, storage and use. Thus, a conventional research line is to reduce the key size of cryptographic primitives while maintaining the same security level. Examples are [6,7]. Following this research line, we aim to reduce the key size of LDT [3], while maintaining the birthday-bound provable security.

We introduce a new length doubler SLDT, short for Single-key Length Doubler with Tweakable block cipher. SLDT uses a single key, and hence the key length is only k bits, that is half reduced from LDT. Our idea is largely inspired by Rogaway's XEX [12]. More specifically, we derive two tweakable block ciphers $(\widetilde{E}_1, \widetilde{E}_2)$ by masking a single tweakable block cipher $\widetilde{E}_K$ as below,

$$\widetilde{E}_1(\cdot, \cdot) = \widetilde{E}_K(\cdot, \cdot \oplus 2\Delta_1), \qquad \widetilde{E}_2(\cdot, \cdot) = \widetilde{E}_K(\cdot, \cdot \oplus 2\Delta_2)$$

where the masks are obtained by $\Delta_1 = \widetilde{E}_K(0,0)$ and $\Delta_2 = \widetilde{E}_K(0,1)$. Then we prove that $(\widetilde{E}_1, \widetilde{E}_2)$ are indistinguishable from two independent tweakable permutations up to the birthday bound security. Finally we replace the two underlying tweakable block ciphers of LDT by $(\widetilde{E}_1, \widetilde{E}_2)$, and obtain SLDT. By a standard hybrid proof procedure, we get that SLDT is a strong PRP up to the birthday bound $q^2/2^n$. A comparison of SLDT with previous length doublers are provided in Table 1.

Table 1. Comparison between SLDT and other length doublers.

Length doubler	Security $(\log_2)$	Key length	Cryptographic primitive calls	Mixing function	Reference
XLS	1	$2n$	3	ϵ-good	[9,11]
DE	$n/2$	$5n$	4	-	[14]
HEM	$n/2$	$3n$	4	ϵ-good	[16]
LDT	$n/2$	$2n$	2	Pure	[3]
SLDT	$n/2$	n	2	Pure	Section 4

2 Preliminaries

2.1 Notations

$\{0,1\}^n$ denotes the set of all n-bit strings. For any two strings $X, Y \in \{0,1\}^*$, $X \oplus Y$ denotes their bitwise exclusive or (XOR). $X\|Y$ denotes their concatenation. $|X|$ denotes the bit length of string X. We define $\{0,1\}^{[m,\ldots,n]} = \bigcup_{i=m}^{n}\{0,1\}^i$ for $m \leq n$ $(m, n \in \mathbb{N})$.

2.2 Tweakable Block Cipher and the Security Definition

A tweakable block cipher $\widetilde{E} : \mathcal{K} \times \mathcal{T} \times \mathcal{M} \to \mathcal{M}$ is a family of permutations on $\mathcal{M}$, which are indexed by two functionally distinct parameters: a key $K \in \mathcal{K}$ that is secret and used to provide the security, and a tweak $T \in \mathcal{T}$ that is public and used to provide variability. The tweak is assumed to be known or even controlled by the adversary. In this paper, we let $\mathcal{K} = \{0,1\}^k$ and $\mathcal{T} = \mathcal{M} = \{0,1\}^n$, where $k, n \in \mathbb{N}$. For a key $K \in \{0,1\}^k$. $\widetilde{E}_K^{-1}(T,\cdot)$ denotes the decryption.

A distinguisher $\mathcal{D}$ is an algorithm that has query access to one (or multiple) oracle of being either $\mathcal{O}$ or $\mathcal{Q}$, and outputs a single bit. The advantage of $\mathcal{D}$ in distinguishing these two primitives is defined as

$$\mathbf{Adv}(\mathcal{D}) = \left| \Pr\left[\mathcal{D}^{\mathcal{O}} \Rightarrow 1\right] - \Pr\left[\mathcal{D}^{\mathcal{Q}} \Rightarrow 1\right] \right|$$

Let $\widetilde{\mathsf{TWP}}$ be all functions $\widetilde{P} : \mathcal{T} \times \mathcal{M} \to \mathcal{M}$, where for each $T \in \mathcal{T}$, $\widetilde{P}(T,\cdot)$ is a permutation on $\mathcal{M}$. A function $\widetilde{P}$ is said to be an ideal tweakable block cipher if it is selected from $\widetilde{\mathsf{TWP}}$ uniformly at random, that is $\widetilde{P} \xleftarrow{\$} \widetilde{\mathsf{TWP}}$.

The security of tweakable block cipher is defined via upper bounding the advantage of all distinguishers $\mathcal{D}$ in the game defined as follows. $\mathcal{D}$ is given access to an oracle $\mathcal{O}$, which is either $\widetilde{E}_K$ with a secret key K randomly selected from $\mathcal{K}$ ($K \xleftarrow{\$} \mathcal{K}$) or an ideal tweakable block cipher $\widetilde{P}$. The advantage of $\mathcal{D}$ is defined as

$$\mathbf{Adv}_{\widetilde{E}}^{\mathrm{sprp}} = \left| \Pr\left[\mathcal{D}^{\widetilde{E}_K^{\pm}} \Rightarrow 1\right] - \Pr\left[\mathcal{D}^{\widetilde{P}^{\pm}} \Rightarrow 1\right] \right|$$

where the probability is taken over the choices of $K \xleftarrow{\$} \mathcal{K}$, $\widetilde{P} \xleftarrow{\$} \widetilde{\mathsf{TWP}}$ and $\mathcal{D}$'s coins if any.

Throughout this paper, we fix a model of computation and a choice of encoding. Then we define

$$\mathbf{Adv}_{\widetilde{E}}^{\mathrm{sprp}}(t, q) = \max_{\mathcal{D}} \mathbf{Adv}_{\widetilde{E}}^{\mathrm{sprp}}(\mathcal{D})$$

where the maximum is taken over all distinguishers whose time complexity is at most t and query complexity is at most q.

2.3   Length Doubler

A length doubler $\mathcal{E} : \{0,1\}^k \times \{0,1\}^{[n,\ldots,2n-1]} \rightarrow \{0,1\}^{[n,\ldots,2n-1]}$ is a set of permutations, indexed by two parameters: the secret key $K \in \{0,1\}^k$ and the block size $i \in [n,\ldots,2n-1]$. Let LB be the set of all the functions $\mathcal{E} : \{0,1\}^k \times \{0,1\}^{[n,\ldots,2n-1]} \rightarrow \{0,1\}^{[n,\ldots,2n-1]}$, where for each $K \in \{0,1\}^k$, $\mathcal{E}_K$ is a length-preserving permutation on $\{0,1\}^{[n,\ldots,2n-1]}$. A function π is said to be an ideal length doubler, if it is selected from LB uniformly at random, that is $\pi \xleftarrow{\$} \mathsf{LB}$. The security of a length doubler is defined via upper bounding the advantage of all distinguishers $\mathcal{D}$:

$$\mathbf{Adv}_{\mathcal{E}}^{\mathrm{vsprp}}(\mathcal{D}) = \left| \Pr\left[\mathcal{D}^{\mathcal{E}_K^{\pm}} \Rightarrow 1\right] - \Pr\left[\mathcal{D}^{\pi^{\pm}} \Rightarrow 1\right] \right|$$

where the probability is taken over the choices $K \xleftarrow{\$} \mathcal{K}$, $\pi \xleftarrow{\$} \mathsf{LB}$, and $\mathcal{D}$'s coins if any. Similarly with above, we define that

$$\mathbf{Adv}_{\mathcal{E}}^{\mathrm{vsprp}}(t, q) = \max_{\mathcal{D}} \mathbf{Adv}_{\mathcal{E}}^{\mathrm{sprp}}(\mathcal{D}),$$

where the maximum is taken over all distinguishers whose time complexity is at most t and query complexity is at most q.

2.4   Pure Mixing Function

We introduce the pure mixing function defined by Chen et al. [3]. A simple example is $\mathtt{mix}(A, B) = (B, A)$.

Definition 1 ([3, Sect. 2.4]).   *Let $m, n \in \mathbb{N}$ such that $m \leq n$. Let $\mathtt{mix} : \bigcup_{s=m}^{n}(\{0,1\}^s)^2 \rightarrow \bigcup_{s=m}^{n}(\{0,1\}^s)^2$ be a length-preserving permutation. Define by $\mathtt{mix}_L$ the left half of its evaluation and by $\mathtt{mix}_R$ its right half. The mixing function is called pure if for all $s \in [m \cdots n]$ we have:*

- $\mathtt{mix}_L(A, \cdot)$ *is a permutation for all $A \in \{0,1\}^s$,*

– $\mathtt{mix}_R(\cdot, B)$ *is a permutation for all* $B \in \{0, 1\}^s$.

A property of pure mixing function is found in [3].

Lemma 1 ([3, Sect. 2.4]). *Let* $\mathtt{mix}$ *be a pure mixing function as in Definition 1. Given* $B, D \in \{0, 1\}^s$, *there exists a unique value* $A \in \{0, 1\}^s$ *such that* $\mathtt{mix}_R(A, B) = D$ *and a unique value* $C \in \{0, 1\}^s$ *such that* $\mathtt{mix}_L^{-1}(C) = (A, B)$.

2.5 H-Coefficient Technique

The proof in this paper adopts the H-Coefficient technique [2,10]. Here we provide a brief description, which presents all necessary information to follow and verify our proof, and refer interested readers to [2,10] for completed definition. We focus on information-theoretic distinguisher $\mathcal{D}$ that is not computationally bounded. Hence, without loss of generality we assume $\mathcal{D}$ is deterministic. Suppose $\mathcal{D}$ interacts with one of two oracles, the "real world" oracle $\mathcal{O}$ or the "ideal world" oracle $\mathcal{Q}$. A view is the query-response tuples that $\mathcal{D}$ receives. Let X (resp. Y) be the probability distribution of the view when $\mathcal{D}$ interacts with $\mathcal{O}$ (resp. $\mathcal{Q}$). Let $\mathcal{V}$ be the set of all *attainable* views v when interacting with $\mathcal{Q}$, that is $\mathcal{V} = \{v \mid \Pr[Y = v] > 0\}$.

The H-Coefficient technique partitions $\mathcal{V}$ into disjoint subsets $\mathcal{V}_{\mathrm{good}}$ and $\mathcal{V}_{\mathrm{bad}}$ such that $\mathcal{V} = \mathcal{V}_{\mathrm{good}} \bigcup \mathcal{V}_{\mathrm{bad}}$. If there are two real values $0 \le \epsilon_1, \epsilon_2 \le 1$ such that

- for each $v \in \mathcal{V}_{\mathrm{good}}$, it has that

$$\frac{\Pr[X = v]}{\Pr[Y = v]} \ge 1 - \epsilon_1$$

- for a view v sampled from $\mathcal{V}$ uniformly at random, it has that

$$\Pr[v \in \mathcal{V}_{\mathrm{bad}}] \le \epsilon_2$$

then the advantage of $\mathcal{D}$ is upper bounded as

$$\mathbf{Adv}(\mathcal{D}) \le \epsilon_1 + \epsilon_2.$$

3 LDT [3] and an Attack on a Trivial Single-Key Variant

The specification of LDT [3] is depicted in Fig. 1. It uses two tweakable block cipher $\widetilde{E}_{K_1}$ and $\widetilde{E}_{K_2}$, and a pure mixing function $\mathtt{mix}$. We stress that K_1 and K_2 are independent. Here we give a brief description of the encryption of LDT, and its decryption can be easily derived.

Let M be an input message of bit length $n + s$, where $0 \le s \le n - 1$. Divide M into $M_1 \| M_2$, where M_1 is the first n bits of M and M_2 is the remaining s bits. LDT uses a Padding algorithm, and an example is $\mathtt{pad}(M_2) = M_2 \| 10^{n-1-s}$. The procedure is follows.

1. $Z \| M_3 \leftarrow \widetilde{E}_{K_1}(\mathtt{pad}(M_2), M_1)$;
2. $C_3 \| C_2 \leftarrow \mathtt{mix}(M_3, M_2)$;
3. $C_1 \leftarrow \widetilde{E}_{K_2}(\mathtt{pad}(C_2), Z \| C_3)$

Finally, $C_1 \| C_2$ is output as the ciphertext. We refer interested readers to the completed specification in [3].

3.1   An Attack for the Case $K_1 = K_2$

Let K denote the key, that is $K = K_1 = K_2$. We present a distinguishing attack that takes at most 3 queries, and succeeds with an overwhelming probability. The observation is that the attacker is able to obtain input-output tuples of $\widetilde{E}_K$ by exhausting the value of Z, when $|Z|$ is small, e.g. $|Z| = 1$. After that, by exploiting that the two layers use the same key, he can adaptively select a plaintext such that its input-output tuple of $\widetilde{E}_K$ at the first layer is equal to an input-output tuple of $\widetilde{E}_K$ at the second layer of some previous message, which enables him to examine some linear relation between the plaintext and the ciphertext, and hence to successfully distinguish from an ideal cipher. The attack procedure is detailed as follows.

1. Choose a plaintext $M = M_1 \| M_2$ with $|M_1| = n$ and $|M_2| = n - 1$, and get a corresponding ciphertext $C = C_1 \| C_2$ with $|C_1| = n$ and $|C_2| = n - 1$.
2. Compute intermediate states M_3 and C_3 from M_2 and C_2 due to Lemma 1. Note that $\widetilde{E}_K(\text{pad}(C_2), Z \| C_3) = C_1$.
3. Guess the value of Z randomly from $\{0, 1\}$.
4. Construct $M_1' \| M_2'$ as $M_1' = Z \| C_3$ and $M_2' = C_2$, and get a corresponding ciphertext $C_1' \| C_2'$:
5. Let $\text{LSB}_{n-1}(C_1)$ denote the $n - 1$ LSBs of C_1. Check if $\text{mix}_R(\text{LSB}_{n-1}(C_1), C_2)$ is equal to C_2'.
    - if yes, then output 1;
    - if no, change Z to the other value and repeat steps 4–5. If both values of Z have been examined, then output 0.

A straightforward analysis shows that $\Pr[\mathcal{D} \Rightarrow 1]$ is 1 when interacting with the LDT variant, and at most 2^{2-n} when interacting with an ideal cipher. Thus the advantage of $\mathcal{D}$ is at least $\mathbf{Adv}(\mathcal{D}) \geq 1 - 2^{2-n}$, which is overwhelming for typically $n = 128$.

4   Our Construction SLDT

In this section, we introduce our single-key length doubler SLDT, which is presented in Algorithm 1 and depicted in Fig. 1. It is a single-key variant of LDT, and hence is also based on Tweakable block cipher and pure mixing function.

Algorithm 1. $\mathcal{E}_K(M) = \text{SLDT}[\widetilde{E}, \text{mix}]$ encryption

---

Input: $K \in \{0, 1\}^k, M \in \{0, 1\}^{[n, \ldots, 2n-1]}$
Output: $C \in \{0, 1\}^{|M|}$

1: $s \leftarrow |M| - n$
2: $\Delta_1 \leftarrow \widetilde{E}_K(0, 0)$ and $\Delta_2 \leftarrow \widetilde{E}_K(0, 1)$
3: $M_1 \| M_2 \leftarrow M$, with $|M_1| = n$ and $|M_2| = s$
4: $Z \| M_3 \leftarrow 2\Delta_1 \oplus \widetilde{E}_K(\text{pad}(M_2), M_1 \oplus 2\Delta_1)$, with $|Z| = n$ and $|M_3| = s$
5: $(C_3, C_2) \leftarrow \text{mix}(M_3, M_2)$
6: $C_1 \leftarrow 2\Delta_2 \oplus \widetilde{E}_K(\text{pad}(C_2), (Z \| M_3) \oplus 2\Delta_2)$
7: **Return** $C_1 \| C_2$

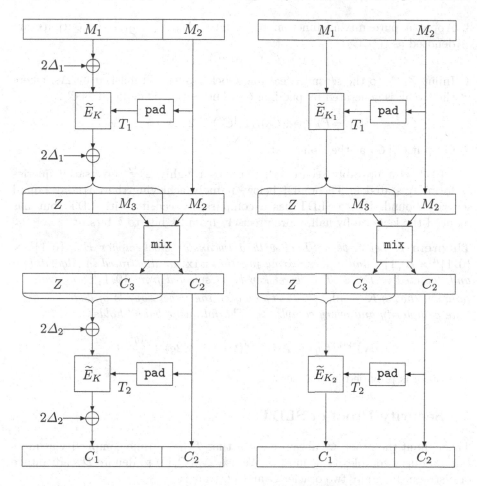

Fig. 1. Our SLDT (left) and LDT [3] (right)

SLDT uses two masks Δ_1 and Δ_2 such that $\Delta_1 = \widetilde{E}_K(0,0)$ and $\Delta_2 = \widetilde{E}_K(0,1)$. For a message $M \in \{0,1\}^{[n,\dots,2n-1]}$, the encryption procedure is as follows. The decryption procedure can be easily derived and hence omitted here.

1. Parse M to an n-bit string M_1 and a s-bit string M_2 ($s = |M| - n$) such that $M = M_1 \| M_2$.
2. Input M_1 into the first tweakable block cipher call masked by Δ_1, where the tweak is generated by padding M_2. The output is denoted as $Z \| M_3$, where Z is the first $n - s$ bits and M_3 is the remaining s bits.

$$Z \| M_3 = \widetilde{E}_K(\mathbf{pad}(M_2), M_1 \oplus 2 \cdot \Delta_1) \oplus 2 \cdot \Delta_1$$

where we note that the operation $\cdot$ is a finite field multiplication and often omitted in the description in this paper.

3. Apply a pure mixing function to update (M_3, M_2), and the outputs are denoted as (C_3, C_2).

$$(C_3, C_2) = \texttt{mix}(M_3, M_2).$$

4. Input $Z \| C_3$ to the second tweakable block cipher call masked by Δ_2, where the tweak is generated by padding C_2. The output is denoted as C_1.

$$C_1 = \widetilde{E}_K(\texttt{pad}(C_2), (Z \| C_3) \oplus 2 \cdot \Delta_2) \oplus 2 \cdot \Delta_2.$$

5. Output $C_1 \| C_2$ as the ciphertext.

SLDT is a provably secure SPRP up to roughly $2^{n/2}$ adversarial queries as formally stated in Theorem 1 below, namely achieving the birthday bound security bound. Hence SLDT has a comparable security with LDT, but has reduced the key size by half, more precisely from $2k$ bits to k bits.

Theorem 1. *Let $\mathcal{E}$ be a SLDT with a tweakable block cipher $\widetilde{E} : \{0,1\}^k \times \{0,1\}^n \times \{0,1\}^n$ and a pure mixing function* $\texttt{mix}$, *as illustrated in Algorithm 1 and depicted in Fig. 1. The secret key K is selected from $\{0,1\}^k$ uniformly at random, that is $K \xleftarrow{\$} \{0,1\}^k$. Let t and q be the upper bounds of distinguisher's time complexity and query complexity. The following bound holds*

$$\mathbf{Adv}_{\mathcal{E}}^{\mathrm{vsprp}}(t, q) \leq \mathbf{Adv}_{\widetilde{E}}^{\mathrm{sprp}}(t + O(q), 2q) + \frac{4q^2}{2^n} + \frac{5q}{2^n} \qquad (1)$$

The proof is provided in next section.

5   Security Proof of SLDT

Throughout the proof, we always assume that $\mathcal{D}$ has a time complexity at most t and a query complexity at most q. We use $\Delta_{\mathcal{D}}(\mathcal{O}, \mathcal{Q})$ to denote $\mathcal{D}$'s advantage of distinguishing any two oracles $\mathcal{O}$ and $\mathcal{Q}$, that is

$$\Delta_{\mathcal{D}}(\mathcal{O}, \mathcal{Q}) = \left| \Pr \left[\mathcal{D}^{\mathcal{O}} \Rightarrow 1 \right] - \Pr \left[\mathcal{D}^{\mathcal{Q}} \Rightarrow 1 \right] \right|.$$

Firstly, we replace the tweakable block cipher $\widetilde{E}_K$ with an ideal tweakable block cipher $\widetilde{P} \xleftarrow{\$} \widetilde{\mathsf{TWP}}$. Let $\mathcal{E}[\widetilde{E}_K]$ and $\mathcal{E}[\widetilde{P}]$ denote SLDT with underlying primitive $\widetilde{E}_K$ and $\widetilde{P}$, respectively. We have trivially that

$$\Delta_{\mathcal{D}}(\mathcal{E}[\widetilde{E}_K], \mathcal{E}[\widetilde{P}]) \leq \mathbf{Adv}_{\widetilde{E}_K}^{\mathrm{sprp}}(t + O(q), 2q). \qquad (2)$$

The remaining proof deals with ideal primitives. Hence we will only consider information-theoretic distinguisher $\mathcal{D}$ that has unlimited computation resource. Without loss of generality, we assume $\mathcal{D}$ is deterministic.

Secondly, let $\texttt{LDT}[\widetilde{P}_1, \widetilde{P}_2]$ be a LDT [3] with independent two ideal tweakable block ciphers $\widetilde{P}_1, \widetilde{P}_2 \xleftarrow{\$} \widetilde{\mathsf{TWP}}$. Let π be an ideal length doubler, that is $\pi \xleftarrow{\$} \mathsf{LB}$. It has been proven by Chen *et al.* in [3] that

$$\Delta_{\mathcal{D}}(\texttt{LDT}[\widetilde{P}_1, \widetilde{P}_2], \pi) \leq \frac{q(q-1)}{2^n}. \qquad (3)$$

We refer interested readers to [3, Theorem 1] for the proof of (3).

As $\mathbf{Adv}_{\mathcal{E}}^{\mathrm{vsprp}}(\mathcal{D}) = \Delta_{\mathcal{D}}(\mathcal{E}, \pi)$, we have the following upper bound via a straightforward hybrid argument.

$$\Delta_{\mathcal{D}}(\mathcal{E}, \pi) \leq \Delta_{\mathcal{D}}(\mathcal{E}[\widetilde{E}_K], \mathcal{E}[\widetilde{P}]) + \Delta_{\mathcal{D}}(\mathcal{E}[\widetilde{P}], \mathrm{LDT}[\widetilde{P}_1, \widetilde{P}_2]) + \Delta_{\mathcal{D}}(\mathrm{LDT}[\widetilde{P}_1, \widetilde{P}_2], \pi) \tag{4}$$

Combining the Eqs. (2), (3) and (4), we have that

$$\Delta_{\mathcal{D}}(\mathcal{E}, \pi) \leq \Delta_{\mathcal{D}}(\mathcal{E}[\widetilde{P}], \mathrm{LDT}[\widetilde{P}_1, \widetilde{P}_2]) + \mathbf{Adv}_{\widetilde{E}}^{\mathrm{sprp}}(t + O(q), 2q) + \frac{q(q-1)}{2^n}. \tag{5}$$

Therefore the remaining work is to upper bound $\Delta_{\mathcal{D}}(\mathcal{E}[\widetilde{P}], \mathrm{LDT}[\widetilde{P}_1, \widetilde{P}_2])$. Similarly with upper bounding $\Delta_{\mathcal{D}}(\mathcal{E}[\widetilde{E}_K], \mathcal{E}[\widetilde{P}])$, we can instead analyze the distinguishing distance between $(\widetilde{P}(\cdot, \cdot \oplus \Delta_1) \oplus \Delta_1, \widetilde{P}(\cdot, \cdot \oplus \Delta_2) \oplus \Delta_2)$ and $(\widetilde{P}_1, \widetilde{P}_2)$, which is the essential work in our proof. The pair of oracles are depicted in Fig. 2 and referred as oracles $\mathcal{X}$ and $\mathcal{Y}$ respectively. The proof adopts the H-coefficient technique introduced in Sect. 2.5. Here $\mathcal{X}$ and $\mathcal{Y}$ are referred to as so-called the real world and the ideal world respectively. Let X and Y be the probability distributions of the view when $\mathcal{D}$ interacts with $\mathcal{X}$ and $\mathcal{Y}$ respectively.

Views. At the end of $\mathcal{D}$ interacting with the oracle and before $\mathcal{D}$ outputting the bit, we reveal the values of the two masks (Δ_1, Δ_2) to $\mathcal{D}$. We stress that it only enlarges the advantage of $\mathcal{D}$, as he can simply ignore such information when making the final decision. In the ideal world, we randomly select two distinct values in $\{0,1\}^n$ as dummy Δ_1 and Δ_2, and release them to the distinguisher. Thus, the view of $\mathcal{D}$ is in the form

$$v = \left(\Delta_1, \Delta_2, (M_1^{(1)}, T_1^{(1)}, C_1^{(1)}), \ldots, (M_1^{(q)}, T_1^{(q)}, C_1^{(q)}), \right.$$
$$\left. (M_2^{(1)}, T_2^{(1)}, C_2^{(1)}), \ldots, (M_2^{(q)}, T_2^{(q)}, C_2^{(q)}) \right).$$

It is straight-forward that a view v to be attainable when interacting with $\mathcal{Y}$ should satisfy

- for any pair $(M_b^{(i)}, T_b^{(i)}, C_b^{(i)})$ and $(M_b^{(j)}, T_b^{(j)}, C_b^{(j)})$ with $T_b^{(i)} = T_b^{(j)}$, where $b \in \{1, 2\}$, $1 \leq i, j \leq q$ and $i \neq j$, it has that $M_b^{(i)} \neq M_b^{(j)}$ implies $C_b^{(i)} \neq C_b^{(j)}$ and $C_b^{(i)} \neq C_b^{(j)}$ implies $M_b^{(i)} \neq M_b^{(j)}$.

All such attainable views contribute to a set $\mathcal{V}$. Next, we partition $\mathcal{V}$ into two disjoint subsets $\mathcal{V}_{\mathrm{good}}$ and $\mathcal{V}_{\mathrm{bad}}$ such that $\mathcal{V} = \mathcal{V}_{\mathrm{good}} \bigcup \mathcal{V}_{\mathrm{bad}}$.

$\mathcal{V}_{\mathrm{bad}}$ *definition and* $\Pr[Y \in \mathcal{V}_{\mathrm{bad}}]$ *bound.* A view is said to be bad if (at least) one of the following cases happens.

- Case 1: there exists $1 \leq i, j \leq q$ such that $M_1^{(i)} \oplus M_2^{(j)} = 2 \cdot \Delta_1 \oplus 2 \cdot \Delta_2$ or $C_1^{(i)} \oplus C_2^{(j)} = 2 \cdot \Delta_1 \oplus 2 \cdot \Delta_2$;

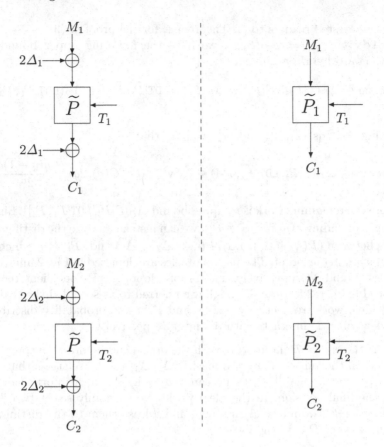

Fig. 2. Oracle $\mathcal{X}$ (left) and Oracle $\mathcal{Y}$ (right)

- Case 2: for $1 \leq i \leq q$, there exists $(M_1^{(i)}, T_1^{(i)} = 0)$ such that $M_1^{(i)} \oplus 2 \cdot \Delta_1 \in \{0, 1\}$, or there exists $(M_2^{(i)}, T_2^{(i)} = 0)$ such that $M_2^{(i)} \oplus 2 \cdot \Delta_2 \in \{0, 1\}$.
- Case 3: for $1 \leq i \leq q$, there exists $(C_1^{(i)}, T_1^{(i)} = 0)$ such that $C_1^{(i)} \oplus 2 \cdot \Delta_1 \in \{\Delta_1, \Delta_2\}$, or there exists $(C_2^{(i)}, T_2^{(i)} = 0)$ such that $C_2^{(i)} \oplus 2 \cdot \Delta_2 \in \{\Delta_1, \Delta_2\}$.

We can easily get the following upper bound, since the dummy Δ_1 and Δ_2 are randomly selected at the end of the interaction.

$$\Pr[Y \in \mathcal{T}_{bad}] \leq \Pr[\text{Case 1}] + \Pr[\text{Case 2}] + \Pr[\text{Case 3}]$$
$$\leq \frac{q(q-1)}{2^n} + \frac{4q}{2^n} + \frac{4q}{2^n}$$
$$= \frac{q(q-1)}{2^n} + \frac{8q}{2^n}, \tag{6}$$

$\Pr[X = v] / \Pr[Y = v]$ *for each* $v \in \mathcal{V}_{\text{good}}$. We write $\Omega_{\mathcal{X}}$ (resp. $\Omega_{\mathcal{Y}}$) for the set of all instance functions of the oracle $\mathcal{X}$ (resp. $\mathcal{Y}$), and its cardinality as $\|\Omega_{\mathcal{X}}\|$

(resp. $\|\Omega_{\mathcal{Y}}\|$). For a view v, we write $\mathrm{comp}_{\mathcal{X}}(v)$ (resp. $\mathrm{comp}_{\mathcal{Y}}(v)$) as the subset of $\Omega_{\mathcal{X}}$ (resp. $\Omega_{\mathcal{Y}}$) that are compatible with the view v. Namely if the oracle $\mathcal{X}$ (resp. $\mathcal{Y}$) is instantiated to a function in $\mathrm{comp}_{\mathcal{X}}(v)$ (resp. $\mathrm{comp}_{\mathcal{Y}}(v)$), $\mathcal{D}$ will receive v as its view during the interaction with $\mathcal{X}$ (resp. $\mathcal{Y}$). Thus, we have that

$$\Pr[X = v] = \frac{\|\mathrm{comp}_{\mathcal{X}}(v)\|}{\|\Omega_{\mathcal{X}}\|}, \qquad \Pr[Y = v] = \frac{\|\mathrm{comp}_{\mathcal{Y}}(v)\|}{\|\Omega_{\mathcal{Y}}\|}.$$

It is easily to get $\|\Omega_{\mathcal{X}}\| = (2^n!)^{2^n}$ and $\|\Omega_{\mathcal{Y}}\| = 2^n(2^n - 1)(2^n!)^{2^n}(2^n!)^{2^n}$.

Now we evaluate $\|\mathrm{comp}_{\mathcal{Y}}(v)\|$. We will group the query-response tuples according to the tweak value. Let w_1 and w_2 be the number of distinct tweak values in $\{(M_1^{(1)}, T_1^{(1)}, C_1^{(1)}), \ldots, (M_1^{(q)}, T_1^{(q)}, C_1^{(q)})\}$ and $\{(M_2^{(1)}, T_2^{(1)}, C_2^{(1)}), \ldots, (M_2^{(q)}, T_2^{(q)}, C_2^{(q)})\}$, respectively. We re-order the query-responses according to the tweak values and force the first tweak value be 0 if included. We denote by α_i (resp. β_i) the number of query-responses with the tweak $T_1^{(i)}$ for $1 \le i \le w_1$ (resp. $T_2^{(i)}$ for $1 \le i \le w_2$). As $v \in \mathcal{V}_{\mathrm{good}}$, we have $\sum_{i=1}^{w_1} \alpha_i = \sum_{i=1}^{w_2} \beta_i = q$. It is straightforward to get that

$$\|\mathrm{comp}_{\mathcal{Y}}(v)\| = (2^n!)^{2^n - w_1}(2^n!)^{2^n - w_2} \prod_{i=1}^{w_1}(2^n - \alpha_i)! \prod_{j=1}^{w_2}(2^n - \beta_j)!.$$

Next we evaluate $\|\mathrm{comp}_{\mathcal{X}}(v)\|$. Similarly we denote by w the number of distinct tweaks in $\{(M_1^{(1)}, T_1^{(1)}, C_1^{(1)}), \ldots, (M_1^{(q)}, T_1^{(q)}, C_1^{(q)}), (M_2^{(1)}, T_2^{(1)}, C_2^{(1)}), \ldots, (M_2^{(q)}\}$, where all query-response tuples are distinct due to $v \in \mathcal{V}_{\mathrm{good}}$. We re-order the query-responses according to the tweak value, and force the first tweak to be 0 if included. We denote by γ_i the number of query-responses with tweak $T^{(i)}$. It has that $\sum_{i=1}^{w} \gamma_i = 2q$. There are two cases as follows.

- the tweak 0 is included in the query-response tuples.

$$\|\mathrm{comp}_{\mathcal{X}}(v)\| = (2^n!)^{2^n - w}(2^n - 2 - \gamma_1)! \prod_{i=2}^{w}(2^n - \gamma_i)!$$

- the tweak 0 is not included in the query-response tuples.

$$\|\mathrm{comp}_{\mathcal{X}}(v)\| = (2^n!)^{2^n - w - 1}(2^n - 2)! \prod_{i=1}^{w}(2^n - \gamma_i)!$$

Overall, we have that

$$\|\mathrm{comp}_{\mathcal{X}}(v)\| \ge (2^n!)^{2^n - w}(2^n - 2 - \gamma_1)! \prod_{i=2}^{w}(2^n - \gamma_i)!$$

Up to now, we compute as follows

$$
\begin{aligned}
\frac{\Pr[X = v]}{\Pr[Y = v]} &= \frac{\|\mathrm{comp}_{\mathcal{X}}(v)\| / \|\Omega_{\mathcal{X}}\|}{\|\mathrm{comp}_{\mathcal{Y}}(v)\| / \|\Omega_{\mathcal{Y}}\|} \\
&\geq \frac{2^n (2^n - 1)(2^n - 2 - \gamma_1)! (2^n!)^{w_1 + w_2 - w} \prod_{i=2}^{w} (2^n - \gamma_i)!}{\prod_{i=1}^{w_1} (2^n - \alpha_i)! \prod_{j=1}^{w_2} (2^n - \beta_j)!} \\
&= \frac{\prod_{i=1}^{w_1} (2^n)_{\alpha_i} \prod_{j=1}^{w_2} (2^n)_{\beta_j}}{(2^n - 2)_{\gamma_1} \prod_{i=2}^{w} (2^n)_{\gamma_i}},
\end{aligned}
\tag{7}
$$

where $(i)_j = i! / (i - j)!$. We know that $(2^n - 2)_{\gamma_1} \leq (2^n)_{\gamma_1}$, so we can proceed (7) as follows.

$$
\begin{aligned}
(7) &\geq \frac{\prod_{i=1}^{w_1} (2^n)_{\alpha_i} \prod_{j=1}^{w_2} (2^n)_{\beta_j}}{(2^n)_{\gamma_1} \prod_{i=1}^{w} (2^n)_{\gamma_i}} \\
&= \frac{\prod_{i=1}^{w_1} (2^n)_{\alpha_i} \prod_{j=1}^{w_2} (2^n)_{\beta_j}}{\prod_{i=1}^{w} (2^n)_{\gamma_i}}.
\end{aligned}
\tag{8}
$$

In addition, $\sum_{i=1}^{w_1} \alpha_i = \sum_{j=1}^{w_2} \beta_j = q$, $\sum_{i=1}^{w} \gamma_i = 2q$ and $(x)_y (x)_z \geq (x)_{y+z}$. When $\gamma_i = 1$ for $1 \leq i \leq w$ and $w = 2q$, meaning that v has $2q$ distinct tweaks, the term $\prod_{i=1}^{w} (2^n)_{\gamma_i}$ can reach its maximum $(2^n)^{2q}$. we can proceed (8) as below:

$$
\begin{aligned}
(8) &\geq \frac{(2^n)_q (2^n)_q}{(2^n)^{2q}} \\
&\geq \frac{(2^n)_{2q}}{(2^n)^{2q}} \\
&= \sum_{i=1}^{2q-1} (1 - \frac{i}{2^n}) \\
&\geq 1 - \frac{q(2q - 1)}{2^n}.
\end{aligned}
\tag{9}
$$

From (7), (8) and (9), we get that for each $v \in \mathcal{V}_{\mathrm{good}}$,

$$
\frac{\Pr[X = v]}{\Pr[Y = v]} \geq 1 - \frac{q(2q - 1)}{2^n}.
\tag{10}
$$

Following the H-coefficient technique and the Eqs. (6) and (10), we have that

$$
\Delta_{\mathcal{D}}(\mathcal{E}[\widetilde{P}], \mathrm{LDT}[\widetilde{P}_1, \widetilde{P}_2]) \leq \frac{q(q - 1) + q(2q - 1)}{2^n} + \frac{8q}{2^n}
\tag{11}
$$

Finally, we can conclude from (5) and (11) that

$$
\begin{aligned}
\mathbf{Adv}_{\mathcal{E}}^{\mathrm{vsprp}}(t, q) &\leq \mathbf{Adv}_{\widetilde{E}}^{\mathrm{sprp}}(t + O(q), 2q) + \frac{q(q - 1) + q(2q - 1)}{2^n} + \frac{8q}{2^n} + \frac{q(q - 1)}{2^n} \\
&= \mathbf{Adv}_{\widetilde{E}}^{\mathrm{sprp}}(t + O(q), 2q) + \frac{4q^2}{2^n} + \frac{5q}{2^n},
\end{aligned}
$$

which completes the proof for Theorem 1.

Acknowledgment. The authors are supported by National Natural Science Foundation of China (61602302, 61472250, 61672347), Natural Science Foundation of Shanghai (16ZR1416400), Shanghai Excellent Academic Leader Funds (16XD1401300), 13th Five-year National Development Fund of Cryptography (MMJJ20170114).

References

1. Chakraborty, D., Sarkar, P.: HCH: a new tweakable enciphering scheme using the hash-encrypt-hash approach. In: Barua, R., Lange, T. (eds.) INDOCRYPT 2006. LNCS, vol. 4329, pp. 287–302. Springer, Heidelberg (2006). https://doi.org/10.1007/11941378_21

2. Chen, S., Steinberger, J.: Tight security bounds for key-alternating ciphers. In: Nguyen, P.Q., Oswald, E. (eds.) EUROCRYPT 2014. LNCS, vol. 8441, pp. 327–350. Springer, Heidelberg (2014). https://doi.org/10.1007/978-3-642-55220-5_19

3. Chen, Y.L., Luykx, A., Mennink, B., Preneel, B.: Efficient length doubling from tweakable block ciphers. IACR Trans. Symmetric Cryptol. **2017**(3), 253–270 (2017). https://doi.org/10.13154/tosc.v2017.i3.253-270

4. Halevi, S.: EME*: extending EME to handle arbitrary-length messages with associated data. In: Canteaut, A., Viswanathan, K. (eds.) INDOCRYPT 2004. LNCS, vol. 3348, pp. 315–327. Springer, Heidelberg (2004). https://doi.org/10.1007/978-3-540-30556-9_25

5. Halevi, S.: Invertible universal hashing and the TET encryption mode. In: Menezes, A. (ed.) CRYPTO 2007. LNCS, vol. 4622, pp. 412–429. Springer, Heidelberg (2007). https://doi.org/10.1007/978-3-540-74143-5_23

6. Iwata, T., Kurosawa, K.: OMAC: one-key CBC MAC. In: Johansson, T. (ed.) FSE 2003. LNCS, vol. 2887, pp. 129–153. Springer, Heidelberg (2003). https://doi.org/10.1007/978-3-540-39887-5_11

7. Kurosawa, K., Iwata, T.: TMAC: two-key CBC MAC. In: Joye, M. (ed.) CT-RSA 2003. LNCS, vol. 2612, pp. 33–49. Springer, Heidelberg (2003). https://doi.org/10.1007/3-540-36563-X_3

8. McGrew, D.A., Fluhrer, S.R.: The security of the extended codebook (XCB) mode of operation. In: Adams, C., Miri, A., Wiener, M. (eds.) SAC 2007. LNCS, vol. 4876, pp. 311–327. Springer, Heidelberg (2007). https://doi.org/10.1007/978-3-540-77360-3_20

9. Nandi, M.: XLS is not a strong pseudorandom permutation. In: Sarkar, P., Iwata, T. (eds.) ASIACRYPT 2014. LNCS, vol. 8873, pp. 478–490. Springer, Heidelberg (2014). https://doi.org/10.1007/978-3-662-45611-8_25

10. Patarin, J.: The "Coefficients H" technique. In: Avanzi, R.M., Keliher, L., Sica, F. (eds.) SAC 2008. LNCS, vol. 5381, pp. 328–345. Springer, Heidelberg (2009). https://doi.org/10.1007/978-3-642-04159-4_21

11. Ristenpart, T., Rogaway, P.: How to enrich the message space of a cipher. In: Biryukov, A. (ed.) FSE 2007. LNCS, vol. 4593, pp. 101–118. Springer, Heidelberg (2007). https://doi.org/10.1007/978-3-540-74619-5_7

12. Rogaway, P.: Efficient instantiations of tweakable blockciphers and refinements to modes OCB and PMAC. In: Lee, P.J. (ed.) ASIACRYPT 2004. LNCS, vol. 3329, pp. 16–31. Springer, Heidelberg (2004). https://doi.org/10.1007/978-3-540-30539-2_2

13. Sarkar, P.: Improving upon the TET mode of operation. In: Nam, K.-H., Rhee, G. (eds.) ICISC 2007. LNCS, vol. 4817, pp. 180–192. Springer, Heidelberg (2007). https://doi.org/10.1007/978-3-540-76788-6_15

14. Sarkar, P., Iwata, T. (eds.): ASIACRYPT 2014. LNCS, vol. 8873. Springer, Heidelberg (2014). https://doi.org/10.1007/978-3-662-45611-8
15. Wang, P., Feng, D., Wu, W.: HCTR: a variable-input-length enciphering mode. In: Feng, D., Lin, D., Yung, M. (eds.) CISC 2005. LNCS, vol. 3822, pp. 175–188. Springer, Heidelberg (2005). https://doi.org/10.1007/11599548_15
16. Zhang, H.: Length-doubling ciphers and tweakable ciphers. In: Bao, F., Samarati, P., Zhou, J. (eds.) ACNS 2012. LNCS, vol. 7341, pp. 100–116. Springer, Heidelberg (2012). https://doi.org/10.1007/978-3-642-31284-7_7

Applications

Modeling Privacy in WiFi Fingerprinting
Indoor Localization

Zheng Yang[1]([✉])[iD] and Kimmo Järvinen[2][iD]

[1] ITrust, Singapore University of Technology and Design, Singapore, Singapore
zheng_yang@sutd.edu.sg
[2] Department of Computer Science, University of Helsinki, Helsinki, Finland
kimmo.u.jarvinen@helsinki.fi

Abstract. In this paper, we study privacy models for privacy-preserving Wifi fingerprint based indoor localization (PPIL) schemes. We show that many existing models are insufficient and make unrealistic assumptions regarding adversaries' power. To cover the state-of-the-art practical attacks, we propose the first formal security model which formulates the security goals of both client-side and server-side privacy beyond the curious-but-honest setting. In particular, our model considers various malicious behaviors such as exposing secrets of principles, choosing malicious Wifi fingerprints in location queries, and specifying the location area of a target client. Furthermore, we formulate the client-side privacy in an indistinguishability manner where an adversary is required to distinguish a client's real location from a random one. The server-side privacy requires that adversaries cannot generate a fabricate database which provides a similar function to the real database of the server. In particular, we formally define the *similarity* between databases with a ball approach that has not been formalized before. We show the validity and applicability of our model by applying it to analyze the security of an existing PPIL protocol.

Keywords: Indoor localization · Wifi fingerprint
Security model · Privacy

1 Introduction

People spend significant amounts of their time in public indoor environments including shopping malls, libraries, airports, university campuses, etc. This has boosted the interest towards various indoor location-based applications [6,15] such as indoor-navigation or elderly assistance and emergency responding. However, in an indoor environment, the traditional Global Positioning System (GPS) may be not available due to weak signal strengths caused by blocking constructions. To obtain a location in a building, a client has to rely on certain *indoor location services* (ILS) provided by some server of the building. The most widely used approach for ILS is the one based on the Wifi fingerprinting technique [5,7–9,11,14,18,20,21]. This method is very effective and popular because it

© Springer Nature Switzerland AG 2018
J. Baek et al. (Eds.): ProvSec 2018, LNCS 11192, pp. 329–346, 2018.
https://doi.org/10.1007/978-3-030-01446-9_19

uses an existing Wifi infrastructure of a building. For a Wifi fingerprint based ILS, the server holds a geo-location database (e.g. [22, Table 1]) containing signal strengths of Wifi access points (AP) in various reference locations, as explained in Sect. 3. Roughly speaking, a client measures the signal strengths of Wifi APs in the client's current (unknown) location and send them to the server. The server calculates the client's location based on the geo-location database, e.g., by calculating the k-nearest Euclidean distances between the client's input and reference fingerprints in the database. Finally, the server sends the location to the client. However, this naive solution cannot prevent a malicious server from tracking its clients' locations, which of course violates the clients' privacy.

Recently, several solutions, e.g. [12,13,22,24], have been proposed to protect the clients' location privacy in ILSs. However, only a few pieces of research (e.g. [24]) have included a formal security model for privacy-preserving indoor localization (PPIL) schemes. This deficiency has resulted in the development of flawed protocols (e.g. [13,24]) which may take years to discover. Therefore, applying PPIL schemes without rigorous security proofs is inherently risky. For example, in INFOCOM 2014, Li et al. [13] presented a Wifi fingerprint localization system called PriWFL which was claimed to provide both clients' location privacy and server's database privacy (which will be referred to as client-privacy and server-privacy for short, respectively). PriWFL is based on the 'honest-but-curious' setting where the adversary does not change the protocol execution between an honest client and the server. Client-privacy roughly states that no passive adversary (including the server) can infer the honest client's location after intercepting all protocol messages. Server-privacy requires that a malicious client cannot use location queries for compromising the server's database. However, Yang and Järvinen [22] recently unveiled a practical attack (which will be called as chosen fingerprint attack) for breaking the server-privacy of PriWFL. In this chosen fingerprint attack, the malicious client chooses special fingerprints, such as all-zeros or single-one fingerprints, to compromise the whole server's database. Unfortunately, their attack idea can be applied to break also the protocol recently proposed by [24], as shown in [23]. One of the major problems here is that the server-privacy defined in [13,24] cannot cover the malicious client attack of [22]. Hence, PriWFL has not been provably demonstrated to provide security against such attack (due to lack of formal definitions). Namely, the curious-but-honest setting is not enough for proving the security for PPIL schemes.

To fix the problem of PriWFL, Yang and Järvinen proposed a new PPIL scheme (which will be referred to as YJ scheme) that relies on Paillier's public key encryption (PKE) [17] and garbled circuits based secure evaluation function (SFE). Intuitively, the YJ scheme satisfies both client- and server-privacy. However, we notice that its security is only informally justified in [22] without being analyzed under an appropriate security model. Hence, there are still open questions: (i) how many active attacks it can withstand and (ii) what the security assumptions of its build blocks and the corresponding security reductions should be. The primary motivation for this work is to develop a formal security model that allows formal analysis of the security of practical PPIL protocols.

We stress that the definitions on client- and server-privacy respectively are fundamental to the success of 'provably secure' PPIL schemes. It is therefore highly desirable to define a security model to cover the state-of-the-art attacks so that their securities can be formally proved to satisfy the security goals. Recently, Zhang et al. [24] made an effort to formulate the client- and server-privacy in a curious-but-honest setting. The definitions of client- and server-privacy in [24] can be seen as extensions from that in [13]. In the location privacy attack [24, Definition 1], a successful adversary should compromise either a client's Wifi fingerprint or location in a query. However, in practice, an adversary may violate client-privacy via learning (for instance) sensitive information about whether the client appeared at some place or its whereabouts, even without knowing its exact location or fingerprints. In particular, the definition of server-privacy is still vague in [24]. I.e., 'a certain level of accuracy' (in [24, Definition 2]) regarding ILS provided by an adversary is not clearly formalized. Specifically, there is no way to measure the accuracy of an adversary's ILS as there is no security experiment or any formulation about the adversary's advantage on breaking either client- or server-privacy. Furthermore, several important practical attacks are not modeled in [24]) such as: (i) chosen fingerprint attack introduced by Yang and Järvinen [22], (ii) known location attack (e.g. whether knowledge of an exposed (historical) location of a client affects the client's unexposed locations), and (iii) known sub-area attacks (e.g. a follower is curious about the direction of movement or location of a client within a specific area). It is still an open question on modeling these malicious attacks. Hence, we conclude that Zhang et al.'s model is rather weak and informal and it is not possible to give a thorough security analysis for a PPIL protocol using such model.

Our Results. In this paper, we present the first *unilateral-malicious* security model for Wifi fingerprint-based PPIL schemes to solve the open problems in existing models. Generally speaking, the unilateral-malicious setting is stronger than the traditional semi-honest setting but weaker than the fully malicious setting. In the unilateral-malicious setting, we particularly formulate the malicious behaviors relative to clients' sessions, e.g., manipulating Wifi fingerprints and exposing locations. We require the server to behave in semi-honest manner (for simplicity). Namely, the server may be curious about a client's location, but it should honestly run the protocol instance in order to provide a good service. We can weaken the security requirement of the server since a server's malicious behaviors (e.g., dishonest executions) would be easily caught in practice (and substantially punished) due to providing poor ILS. If the service is poor, then clients would likely just stop using the service and, consequently, make such an attack impossible. However, the server cannot easily identify a client's malicious behaviors. This is true especially when the client's messages are (non-deterministically) encrypted by its own public key. Hence, we define the first practical formal PPIL security model that focuses on modeling the most harmful malicious behaviors on the client side. We specifically apply our new security model to analyze the YJ scheme (as an example) to not only show the validity of our security model but also to exhibit another attractiveness of the YJ scheme in its provable security.

We consider the security model in a simulation environment (which covers the real world applications) with a single server and multiple clients, where each client may have multiple sessions for querying different locations. Unlike previous work [13,22,24], we formulate the attacks of an adversary via a series of oracle queries. Each query stands for a generic class of attacks. Under the unilateral-malicious setting, we assume that the adversary can only run protocol instances between the client and server by following the protocol specification. In spite of that, several important active attacks are defined via a series of oracle queries allowing an adversary to manipulate and learn sensitive information of sessions. Namely, an adversary can specify sessions' initial states such as Wifi fingerprint and target location area, record her own RSS measurements, or reveal a principal's long-term or ephemeral secret key and a client's location. The details of these queries can be found in Sect. 3.

The security goal of client-privacy is defined in an indistinguishable manner following the approach in [3]. Namely, a PPIL scheme is said to be client secure (informally) if no polynomial time adversaries can distinguish the location of an unexposed session from a random location. Whereas the security goal of server-privacy is achieved (informally) if all polynomial time adversaries are unable to generate a database D' which can provide a similar function of the server's real database D. A key problem required to be resolved is to formulate the notion of 'similar function'. Here we adopt a ball approach. Informally speaking, we say that the fabricated database D' generated by an adversary has a similar function to the real database D, if D' results in a fabricated location L' within a small ball that is centered at the corresponding real location L (which is calculated based on D for a certain location query) with a pre-defined *radius* ρ for most of the distinct location queries. Furthermore, each security goal is associated with a corresponding security experiment which defines the interactions between adversary and experiment simulator (challenger), rules of the adversary (on launching various attacks), and winning condition of the adversary. Eventually, we carefully define the client- and server- privacy in conjunction with the adversarial model, security experiment, and the corresponding adversaries' winning advantages. Here define a security model mainly for the Wifi fingerprint database. However, our security definitions and the adversarial model might be still generic enough to address the security for different kinds of PPIL schemes. It is not hard to see that the key elements (or formulation ideas) of our security model, such as adversary model, security experiment, and security definitions, can be simply applied to formulate other types of databases with small changes.

In the security analysis of the YJ scheme, we first show that the client-privacy can be linearly reduced to that of Paillier PKE and SFE. We also show that the YJ scheme does not leak any useful information about a server's database to the adversaries due to the large enough randomness space, and the security of SFE. Since adversaries cannot gain overwhelming advantages from the messages of YJ protocol, the security of the database is therefore determined by the secret entropy of the database itself.

Organization. The remainder of this paper is organized as follows. The security assumptions on the building blocks of the YJ scheme are reviewed in Sect. 2. In Sect. 3, we introduce a new security model for PPIL protocols. In Sect. 4, we review the YJ scheme and introduce the security analysis under our proposed model. Finally, we give conclusion remarks in Sect. 5.

2 Preliminaries

General Notations. We let $\kappa \in \mathbb{N}$ be the security parameter and 1^κ be a string of κ ones. Let $[n] = \{1, \ldots, n\} \subset \mathbb{N}$ denote the set of integers. Let $a \xleftarrow{\$} S$ denote the operation sampling a uniform random element from a set S. We use $\|$ to denote the concatenation operation of two strings. Let $|\cdot|$ denote an operation calculating the bit-length of a string, and $\#$ denote an operation calculating the number of elements in a set.

Paillier Public Encryption Scheme. Paillier public-key encryption (PKE) scheme [17] is a probabilistic encryption scheme. Let $\mathsf{PrimG}(\kappa)$ be a function which generates a set of primes of length κ. The Paillier PKE scheme mainly consists of the following three algorithms:

- **Key Generation** (KeyGen). Given the security parameter 1^κ, the algorithm chooses two large primes $p, q \xleftarrow{\$} \mathsf{PrimG}(\kappa/2)$, and computes $n = p \cdot q$. It also selects a group generator g for the multiplicative group $\mathbb{Z}_{n^2}^*$, such that the order of g is a non-zero multiple of n. The public key pk is a tuple (n, g) and the secret key sk is $\lambda = \mathrm{lcm}(p-1, q-1)$. This algorithm returns (pk, sk).
- **Encryption** (Enc). This algorithm takes a message $m < n$ and a public key (n, g) as inputs. It selects a random value $r \xleftarrow{\$} [n]$, and computes the ciphertext: $C = g^m \cdot r^n \bmod n^2$. The output of this algorithm is C. For simplicity, we may omit modulus n^2 in the rest of the paper.
- **Decryption** (Dec). This algorithm takes $C < n^2$ and the secret key λ as inputs, and outputs $m = \frac{L(C^\lambda) \bmod n^2}{L(g^\lambda) \bmod n^2} \bmod n$ where $L(u) = \frac{u-1}{n}$.

Paillier PKE scheme is additively homomorphic over the group $\mathbb{Z}_n$. Namely, for two ciphertexts $C_1 = \mathsf{Enc}(pk, m_1)$ and $C_1 = \mathsf{Enc}(pk, m_2)$, we have that $\mathsf{Dec}(sk, C_1 \cdot C_2 \bmod n^2) = m_1 + m_2 \pmod{n}$ and $\mathsf{Dec}(sk, C_1 \cdot C_2^{-1} \bmod n^2) = m_1 - m_2 \pmod{n}$, where the inverse can be computed via the exponentiation $C_2^{-1} = C_2^{n^2-1} \bmod n^2$. Using the above homomorphic additions, it is also possible to compute multiplications and divisions by a scalar $t \in [n]$: $\mathsf{Dec}(sk, C_1^t \bmod n^2) = t \cdot m_1 \pmod{n}$ and $\mathsf{Dec}(sk, C_1^{t^{-1} \bmod n} \bmod n^2) = m_1/t \pmod{n}$, where $t^{-1} \bmod n$ can be computed with the Extended Euclidean Algorithm.

We review the security of Paillier PKE scheme via the following definition.

Definition 1. *The security experiment for a Paillier PKE scheme* Pai= (KeyGen, Enc, Dec) *is defined in the following:*

$$\mathsf{EXP}^{ind-cpa}_{\mathsf{Pai},\mathcal{B}}(\kappa):$$
$$b \xleftarrow{\$} \{0,1\},\ p,q \xleftarrow{\$} \mathsf{PrimG}(\kappa/2),\ n = p \cdot q;\ g \leftarrow \mathbb{Z}^*_{n_2},$$
$$(m_0, m_1) \leftarrow \mathcal{B}(n, g),\ s.t.\ |m_0| = |m_1| and\ 0 \leq (m_0, m_1) < n;$$
$$r_0, r_1 \xleftarrow{\$} [n-1],\ C_0 := g^{m_0} \cdot r_0^n \mod n_2,\ C_1 := g^{m_1} \cdot r_1^n \mod n_2;$$
$$b' \leftarrow \mathcal{B}(pk, C_b);\ if b = b'\ return\ 1,\ otherwise\ return\ 0.$$

We define the advantage of $\mathcal{B}$ in the above experiment as: $\mathsf{Adv}^{ind-cpa}_{\mathsf{Pai},\mathcal{B}}(\kappa) := \left| \Pr[\mathsf{EXP}^{ind-cpa}_{\mathsf{Pai},\mathcal{B}}(\kappa) = 1] - \frac{1}{2} \right|$. *We say that the Paillier PKE scheme* Pai *is secure, if for all probabilistic polynomial time (PPT) adversary $\mathcal{B}$ the advantage* $\mathsf{Adv}^{ind-cpa}_{\mathsf{Pai},\mathcal{B}}(\kappa)$ *is a negligible function in κ.*

Two-party Secure Function Evaluation. We briefly review the formal notions regarding (circuit based) secure function evaluation (SFE) which is used by the YJ protocol. Given a public function $\hat{F}$, a classical SFE scheme allows two parties to run a protocol which results in party 1 learning only the outcome of $\hat{F}(x_1\|x_2)$, while party 2 learning nothing, where x_1 and x_2 are the private inputs of party 1 and party 2 respectively. We refer the reader to [2] for more details on the security notions and concrete example of SFE.

We let $\hat{f}$ denote a circuit for a certain function $\hat{F}$ with input size $n \in \mathbb{N}$ (that may be accessed as $\hat{f}.n$). And let $\mathsf{ev}(\hat{f}, x)$ be a canonical circuit evaluation function which takes as inputs $\hat{f}$ and a string x, and computes the output of the function $\hat{F}(x)$. Here we define a function $\Phi(\hat{f})$ to describe what we allow to be revealed regarding $\hat{f}$. With respect to a garbling scheme, Φ may reveal a circuit's size, topology, identity, or many others. More concrete side information functions can be found in [1,2].

In a two-party protocol, we suppose that party i ($i \in [2]$) has a private string x_i with length n_i, and party 2 has a circuit $\hat{f}$ where $n = n_1 + n_2$. We describe a two-party protocol (for executing a SFE scheme) via a pair of PPT algorithms $\Sigma = (\Sigma_1, \Sigma_2)$. Party $i \in \{1, 2\}$ will run Σ_i on its current state and the incoming message from its intended partner, to generate an outgoing message and a local output. The initial state of Σ_i includes the security parameter κ, a fresh random coin $\gamma_i \xleftarrow{\$} \mathcal{R}_i$ (chosen from a random space $\mathcal{R}_i$) and the (private) function input I_i of party i. The random coins γ_1 and γ_2 might be omitted (in the following descriptions) for simplicity, i.e., they are implicitly generated and used. In order to represent the protocol execution, we define a PPT algorithm View^i_Σ which takes as input security parameter 1^κ, and inputs (I_1, I_2) for the two parties respectively, and returns an execution view vw_i and output out_i of party i in a protocol instance. Nevertheless, we may denote an execution between two parties as $\mathsf{SF}.\Sigma(I_1, I_2)$ at a high-level view.

Then a SFE scheme is a tuple $\mathsf{SF} = (\Sigma, \mathsf{ev})$ where Σ is a two-party protocol with input (I_1, I_2) as above and ev is a circuit evaluation function. The correctness requirement states that, for all $\hat{f}$ and all $x \in \{0,1\}^{\hat{f}.n}$, we have $\Pr[\text{out}_1 = \text{ev}(\hat{f}, x)] = 1$, where $x = x_1 \| x_2$, $x_1 \in I_1$ and $(x_2, \hat{f}) \in I_2$. We here review the privacy of SFE in the honest-but-curious setting.

Definition 2. *For a SFE scheme* $\mathsf{SF} = (\Sigma, \text{ev})$, *a simulator* $\mathcal{S}$ *and an adversary* $\mathcal{E}$, *the security experiment relative to* Φ *is defined as follows:*

$$\mathsf{EXP}^{\text{pri.sim},\mathcal{S}}_{\mathsf{SF},\mathcal{E},\Phi}(\kappa, i):$$
$\quad b \xleftarrow{\$} \{0,1\};$
$\quad b' \leftarrow \mathcal{E}^{\mathsf{Excute}_{\mathsf{SF}}(b,i,\cdot,\cdot)}(\kappa, i);$
$\quad$ *if* $b = b'$ *return 1*,
$\quad$ *otherwise return 0.*

$\mathsf{Excute}_{\mathsf{SF}}(b, i, x_i, \hat{f}):$
$\quad$ *if* $x_i \not\subseteq \{0,1\}^{\hat{f}.n_i}$ *return* $\bot$;
$\quad x_{3-i} \xleftarrow{\$} \{0,1\}^{\hat{f}.n_{3-i}}$, $I_1 := x_1$, $I_2 := (x_2, \hat{f})$;
$\quad$ *if* $b = 1$ *return* $\mathsf{View}^i_\Sigma(1^\kappa, I_1, I_2)$;
$\quad$ *if* $i = 1$ *return* $\mathcal{S}(1^\kappa, \text{ev}(\hat{f}, x_1 \| x_2), \Phi(\hat{f}))$;
$\quad$ *if* $i = 2$, *return* $\mathcal{S}(1^\kappa, \hat{f}, |x_1|)$;

We define the advantage of $\mathcal{E}$, *which is allowed only a single* $\mathsf{Excute}_{\mathsf{SF}}$ *query, in the above experiment as:* $\mathsf{Adv}^{\text{pri.sim},\mathcal{S}}_{\mathsf{SF},\mathcal{E},\Phi}(\kappa, i) := \left| \Pr[\mathsf{EXP}^{\text{pri.sim},\mathcal{S}}_{\mathsf{SF},\mathcal{E},\Phi}(\kappa, i) = 1] - \frac{1}{2} \right|$. *We say that* SF *is secure relative to* Φ, *if for each* $i \in \{1,2\}$ *and all PPT adversaries* $\mathcal{E}$, *the advantage* $\mathsf{Adv}^{\text{pri.sim},\mathcal{S}}_{\mathsf{SF},\mathcal{E},\Phi}(\kappa, i)$ *is a negligible function in* κ.

3   A New Security Model for Privacy Preserving Indoor Location Schemes

In this section, we define a new unilateral-malicious security model for privacy preserving indoor location (PPIL) protocols which are based on Wifi fingerprints. The privacy for client and server is formulated respectively following the well-known game-based modeling approach [3,10].

Simulation Preliminary. We first describe the general simulation environment which will be exploited in the following security notions (in particular for security experiment). There are two types of entities considered: client C and server S. The server S is supposed to provide the indoor location service (ILS) of a building according to a client's request. The building area (which is covered by the location service) is assumed to be delicately divided into M reference locations $\mathsf{LT} = \{i, (x_i, y_i, z_i)\}^M_{i=1}$, e.g. the black dot in Fig. 1, where (x_i, y_i) denotes the horizontal coordinates and z_i denotes the vertical coordinate (e.g., the position of a floor). One could consider the unit of each coordinate is meter (m) for instance. Moreover, the building is deployed with N Wifi access points (AP) to provide network service, where each i-th ($i \in [N]$) access point may have a unique identity AP_i. Let $\mathsf{APT} = \{AP_j\}^N_{j=1}$ be list storing all identities of Wifi access points. In particular, each location has a so-called Wifi fingerprint which comprises of Received Signal Strength (RSS) values of certain Wifi AP, where each RSS value is from a range $\mathcal{R}_v = [v_{min}, v_{max}]$ and (v_{min}, v_{max}) are minimum and maximum values respectively. Consequently, the server is assumed to hold a pre-measured Wifi fingerprint database D which consists of a set of tuples

$< i, V_i = \{v_{i,j}\}_{j=1}^N >_{i=1}^M$ (See also in [22, Table 1]) , where i is an index of a reference location $L_i \in \mathsf{LT}$, each $v_{i,j}$ denotes the RSS value obtained at L_i from AP_j. Furthermore, we let Dist be a distance function which takes as input two locations L_i and L_j (with their corresponding coordinates (x_i, y_i, z_i) and (x_j, y_j, z_j)) and outputs the distance between them. One could consider Euclidean distance, i.e. Eq. 1, as a concrete example of Dist.

When C wants to know its location, it first measures the RSS values from all APs to get a real-time Wifi fingerprint $F = \{f_j\}_{j=1}^N$. Then it may 'privately' submit F to S as a location query, and calculate its location L from S's response. We refer the reader to [23, Sect. 2.1] for more details on the principle of Wifi fingerprint localization. Meanwhile, the private information of the client mainly includes its secret key sk, location query F and the corresponding location L. The secret of the server is the database D.

In order to emulate the behaviors of a set of entities (including λ clients and 1 server), we may realize a collection of oracles $\{\pi_\tau^s, \pi_{\lambda+1}^t : \tau \in [\lambda], s \in [d], t \in [\lambda \times d]\}$ for $(\lambda, d) \in \mathbb{N}$. Each oracle π_τ^s behaves as the s-th protocol instance (session) performed by the party τ for calculating one location. The special party $\lambda + 1$ is assumed to be server. Each party may have a pair of pubic/private key (pk_τ, sk_τ) for $\tau \in [\lambda + 1]$, where pk_τ can be accessed by all oracles. Moreover, each oracle π_τ^s for $\tau \in [\lambda]$ is supposed to keep the following internal state variables: (i) $ds_\tau^s \in \{\mathsf{accept}, \mathsf{reject}\}$ – final decision of a session; (ii) F_τ^s – fingerprint $F_\tau^s = \{v_j'\}_{j=1}^N$ for a location query; (iii) ins_τ^s – index selection set (INS) specifying the location indexes (in LT) which are close to the current location related to F_τ^s; (iv) er_τ^s – ephemeral randomness used to run the protocol instance; (v) T_τ^s – transcript recording all sent and received protocol messages; (vi) $L_\tau^s = (x_\tau^s, y_\tau^s, z_\tau^s)$ – location of party τ calculated in the s-th session. We assume the variable L_τ^s will be assigned if and only if $ds_\tau^s = \mathsf{accept}$ (meaning that a protocol instance is correctly executed in a session). The server's oracles only have ds_τ^s and T_τ^s.

In order to simulate a Wifi fingerprint used by a location query, we define a function $\mathsf{FPTSim}(i)$ which on input a reference location index i generates a Wifi fingerprint $F_i = \{f_j\}_{j=1}^N$ with the following steps: (i) $f_j \xleftarrow{\$} [v_{i,j} - \Delta, v_{i,j} + \Delta]$ where Δ is a pre-defined positive integer, where $v_{i,j} \in \mathsf{D}$; (ii) If $f_j \leq v_{min}$ or $v_{i,j} = v_{min}$ then $f_j := v_{min}$; (iii) Else if $f_j \geq v_{max}$ then $f_j := v_{max}$.

Adversarial Model. Here we define the power of an active adversaries. The active adversaries $\mathcal{A}$ in our model are considered as a probabilistic polynomial time (PPT) algorithms, which may interact with another PPT algorithm called simulator $\mathcal{C}$ via the following queries:

- **InitCorruptO**$(\tau, s, \tilde{F})$: The variables ds_τ^s, T_τ^s and L_τ^s (if any) of the client's oracle π_τ^s are initiated with an empty string $\emptyset$. This query initializes $\mathsf{ins}_\tau^s := [M]$. If $\tilde{F} \neq \emptyset$ and $\tau \neq \lambda + 1$, this query sets $F_\tau^s := \tilde{F}$. Each oracle can be initialized by this query only once.
- **InitHonestO**(τ, s, i, rds): This query first initializes ds_τ^s, er_τ^s, T_τ^s and L_τ^s with empty string $\emptyset$. Let $\widetilde{\mathsf{ins}} \subseteq [M]$ be a set of location indexes such that

$\forall j \in \widetilde{\text{ins}}$ the distance between $L_i = (x_i, y_i, z_i)$ and $L_j = (x_j, y_j, z_j)$ is smaller than rds, i.e., $\text{Dist}(L_i, L_j) \leq rds$. Note that $\widetilde{\text{ins}}$ may cover indexes within a ball centered at i with radius rds. If $\tau \neq \lambda + 1$ and $\#\widetilde{\text{ins}} \geq \lceil \chi \cdot M \rceil$ (for a threshold say $0.1 \leq \chi \leq 1$)[1], this query initializes F_τ^s as follows: (i) $j \xleftarrow{\$} \widetilde{\text{ins}}$; (ii) $F_\tau^s := \text{FPTSim}(j)$; (iii) $\text{ins}_\tau^s := \widetilde{\text{ins}}$. Again each client's oracle can be initialized by this query only once.

- **Execute$_{\text{PPIL}}(\tau, s, t)$**: This query executes the protocol instance between an unused and initialized client's oracle π_τ^s and a server's unused oracle $\pi_{\lambda+1}^t$, and returns the protocol transcript T_τ^s. We call π_τ^s and $\pi_{\lambda+1}^t$ proceeded in this query as *partner oracles*. The oracles run by this query are called *used*. All server's oracles here are assumed to be default initialized (without specific initiation query).
- **CorruptC(τ)**: This query responds with the τ-th client's secret key sk_τ.
- **CorruptS**: This query responds with the server's database D and secret key $sk_{\lambda+1}$ (if any).
- **RandReveal(τ, s)**: Oracle π_τ^s responds with the ephemeral secret key er_τ^s.
- **LocReveal(τ, s)**: Oracle π_τ^s responds with the location L_τ^s.
- **LocTest(τ, s)**: If the oracle has state $ds_\tau^s \neq$ accept or $\tau = \lambda + 1$, then this query returns a failure symbol $\perp$. Otherwise, it does the following steps: (i) flip a fair coin $b \xleftarrow{\$} \{0, 1\}$; (ii) choose a random index $j \in \text{ins}_\tau^s$, obtain $F_j := \text{FPTSim}(j)$, and calculate L_0 based on F_j and D (following the protocol specification) such that $L_0 \neq L_\tau^s$; (iii) set $L_1 := L_\tau^s$ (which is the real location). Eventually, the location L_b is returned. This query is allowed to be asked at most once during the following corresponding security experiment. We call the oracle π_τ^s selected in this query as *test oracle*.
- **DBLeak(i)**: If the index i has been queried via this query, then it returns a failure symbol $\perp$. Otherwise, this query responses with a similar Wifi fingerprint $F_i' \leftarrow \text{FPTSim}(i)$ according to the i-th row of database D.

InitCorruptO query is used to model the chosen fingerprint attacks against server's privacy (in the unilateral-malicious setting), i.e., the malicious client may choose special fingerprints (e.g. all zeros) to compromise the server's database. For example, the attack introduced in [22] is a kind of chosen fingerprint attack. An oracle initialized by this query is known as location exposed oracle.

InitHonestO query is used to initialize the honest (unexposed) oracle based on an area which is specified by an adversary in term of the reference location index i and a radius rds. We categorize the attacks modeled by this query as *known sub-area attacks*. Consider the attack scenario that an adversary loses his tracking target at a street corner (determined by i) and he wants to know the target's 'whereabouts' (within a range rds). In this case, the attacker may know an approximate area of the client within a range. Moreover, if rds is large enough then it may cover all location indexes in LT.

Execute$_{\text{PPIL}}$ query formulates the passive adversaries which only observe the communication between the client and server.

---

[1] If χ is too small, then there is no privacy at all.

CorruptC and **CorruptS** queries formulate the corruption of an honest principal's long-term credentials respectively. The corrupted party is known as dishonest or malicious one.

RandReveal query models the randomness exposure attacks which may be caused by malware or careless disposal.

DBLeak query 'approximately' formulates the attack that $\mathcal{A}$ measures and records the Wifi fingerprints $V_i{}'$ (which is similar to V_i of D) for certain location index i, say based on limited Wifi fingerprint samples.

LocReveal query models the known location attacks (ULA). The resilience of ULA requires that the exposed locations will not affect the others. For example, the PPIL scheme proposed in [12] is subject to known location attack. To get a location, the client in [12] would issue a set of camouflaged localization requests that follow a similar natural movement pattern. However, if one of the client's locations is exposed, e.g., by posting a picture, then the server can simply identify which location request is the real one.

LocTest query will be exploited to formulate the capability of an adversary on breaking the client's privacy. The job of the adversary is to distinguish the bit chosen by the **LocTest** query.

Note that we are the first one to generalize the practical attacks against PPIL schemes via the above generic queries which have not been formalized in previous work [13, 22, 24].

Client Privacy. We first define a security experiment as follows.

SECURITY EXPERIMENT $\mathsf{EXP}^{\mathsf{CP}}_{\Pi,\mathcal{A}}(\kappa, \mathsf{D})$: On input security parameter κ and a server's database D, the security experiment is carried out as a game between a simulator $\mathcal{C}$ and an adversary $\mathcal{A}$ based on a PPIL scheme Π, where the following steps are performed:

1. The simulator $\mathcal{C}$ first initiates the game by realizing a collection of oracles and generating all public/private key pairs for all $\lambda + 1$ honest parties and all other public information. $\mathcal{C}$ gives $\mathcal{A}$ all public information $\{pk_\tau\}_{\tau=1}^{\lambda+1}$, LT, APT and $\mathcal{PD}$.
2. $\mathcal{A}$ may adaptively issue a polynomial number of **InitCorruptO**, **InitHonestO**, **Execute**$_{\mathsf{PPIL}}$, **CorruptC**, **CorruptS**, **LocReveal**, and **RandReveal** queries. At some point, $\mathcal{A}$ may issue a single **LocTest**(τ^*, s^*) query.
3. At the end of the game, $\mathcal{A}$ may terminate and output a bit b' as its guess for b of **LocTest**(τ^*, s^*) query.
4. Meanwhile, the experiment would return a failure symbol $\perp$ if one of the following conditions is satisfied: (a) $\mathcal{A}$ has not issued a **LocTest**(τ^*, s^*) query; (b) The **LocTest**(τ^*, s) query returns a failure symbol $\perp$; (c) $\mathcal{A}$ asked an **InitCorruptO**(τ^*, s^*, F^*) query to the test oracle; (d) $\mathcal{A}$ asked a **CorruptC**(τ^*) query; (e) $\mathcal{A}$ asked either a **RandReveal**(τ^*, s^*) query or a **RandReveal**$(\lambda + 1, t^*)$ query, where $\pi_{\lambda+1}^{t^*}$ is the partner oracle of the test oracle; (f) $\mathcal{A}$ asked a **LocReveal**(τ^*, s^*) query to the test oracle $\pi_{\tau^*}^{s^*}$.
5. The experiment finally returns 1 if $b = b'$, and 0 otherwise.

We call an adversary as a 'legal' one if it runs an experiment without failure. A legal adversary should not violate the rules defined in the above step 4). Note that violating one of the rules (c) to (f) would 'trivially' break the client-privacy, i.e., asking the corresponding queries (specified in the rules) would enable the adversary to easily distinguish the bit b chosen in the **LocTest**(τ^*, s) query without breaking the underlying protocol. These situations should be therefore forbidden in the experiment. Otherwise, it would always return 1.

Definition 3 (Client-privacy). *The advantage of legal adversaries $\mathcal{A}$ in the above experiment is* $\mathsf{Adv}_{\Pi,\mathcal{A}}^{\mathsf{CP}}(\kappa, \mathsf{D}) := \left| \Pr[\mathsf{EXP}_{\Pi,\mathcal{A}}^{\mathsf{CP}}(\kappa, \mathsf{D}) = 1] - \frac{1}{2} \right|$. *We say that a PPIL scheme Π is client-secure, if for all PPT legal adversaries $\mathcal{A}$, the advantage* $\mathsf{Adv}_{\Pi,\mathcal{A}}^{\mathsf{CP}}(\kappa, \mathsf{D})$ *is a negligible function in κ.*

Server Privacy. Informally speaking, the server's privacy is achieved if all polynomial time adversaries are unable to generate a database D' which can provide a similar function as the server's real database D. We may call a location calculated based on D' as a *fabricated location*, and a location calculated based on D as *real location*. Given two databases D and D', we have the following similar event (as exemplified in Fig. 1):

- *Similar Event (SE)*: For a client's location query regarding Wifi fingerprint $F_i = \{f_j\}_{j=1}^{N}$, the corresponding location L_i and the fabricated location L_i' have distance at most ρ, i.e., $\mathsf{Dist}(L_i, L_i') \leq \rho$, where ρ is a pre-defined difference threshold (in meter).

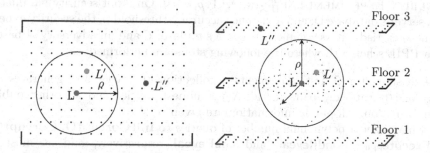

Fig. 1. Similar event occurrence examples in horizontal (left) and vertical (right) planes (right). The small black dots represent the reference locations in **LT**. The red dot represents the real location L. The green dot represents the fabricated location L' in which the similar event occurs. The blue dot represents the fabricated location L'' in which the similar event does not occur. (Color figure online)

The term on 'similar function' of two databases can be roughly illustrated as follows. Given a number of distinct client's location queries, the occurrence rate of SE is larger than a pre-defined success threshold α (e.g. $\alpha = 0.7$). Let TF be a test set that consists of $|TF| > M$ distinct fingerprints of random locations.

Table 1. Parameters of server-privacy.

Params	Description
D	Real database of server
ϕ	A security parameter specifying the number of **DBLeak** queries
ρ	Distance threshold between the real location and the fabricated location
α	Probability threshold of SE
TF	Test set of random fingerprints

For example, one could generate a fingerprint $F \in TF$ by randomly choosing an index $i \xleftarrow{\$} [M]$ and running $F := \mathsf{FPTSim}(i)$. Let $\mathsf{SimilarTest}$ be a function that is used to test the functional similarity between two databases. $\mathsf{SimilarTest}$ takes as input two databases D and D' with their related reference location lists LT and LT' (respectively), and a test set TF, and outputs the test result in $\{0, 1\}$. The execution steps of $\mathsf{SimilarTest}$ comprises of the following:

- Initiate a SE count variable $cnt := 0$. Suppose that for a fingerprint $F_i \in TF$ the real location which is calculated based on F_i, D and LT is $L_i = (x_i, y_i, z_i)$, and the fabricated location which is calculated based on F_i, D' and LT' is $L'_i = (x'_i, y'_i, z'_i)$. For $i \in [\|TF\|]$, if $\mathsf{Dist}(L_i, L'_i) \leq \rho$ then $cnt := cnt + 1$.
- Finally, it returns 1 if $\frac{cnt}{|TF|} > \alpha$; otherwise, 0 is returned.

The parameters, which are relevant to the formulation of the server-privacy, are summarized in Table 1.

SECURITY EXPERIMENT $\mathsf{EXP}^{\mathsf{SP}}_{\Pi, \mathcal{A}}(\kappa, \mathsf{D}, \mathsf{LT}, \rho, \alpha, \phi)$: On input security parameter κ, a server's database D, and a distance accuracy threshold ρ, the security experiment is carried out as a game between a simulator $\mathcal{C}$ and an adversary $\mathcal{A}$ based on a PPIL scheme Π, where the following steps are performed:

1. The simulator $\mathcal{C}$ first implements a collection of oracles and generates all public/private key pairs for all $\lambda + 1$ honest parties and all other public information. All public information are given to $\mathcal{A}$.
2. $\mathcal{A}$ may issue a polynomial number of queries to **InitCorruptO**, **CorruptC**, **Execute**$_{\mathsf{PPIL}}$, **RandReveal**, and **LocReveal** respectively, and at most ϕ **DBLeak** queries.
3. Eventually, $\mathcal{A}$ may return a database D' and a relevant reference location list LT' that has M' reference location. Meanwhile, the experiment would return a failure symbol $\bot$ if $\mathcal{A}$ asked either a **RandReveal**$(\lambda + 1, \cdot)$ query or more than ϕ queries to **DBLeak**.
4. Finally, the experiment returns $\mathsf{SimilarTest}(\mathsf{D}, D', \mathsf{LT}, LT', TF)$.

Definition 4 (Server-privacy). *The advantage of a legal adversary $\mathcal{A}$ in the above experiment is $\mathsf{Adv}^{\mathsf{SP}}_{\Pi, \mathcal{A}}(\kappa, \mathsf{D}, \mathsf{LT}, \rho, \alpha, \phi) := \Pr[\mathsf{EXP}^{\mathsf{SP}}_{\Pi, \mathcal{A}}(\kappa, \mathsf{D}, \mathsf{LT}, \rho, \alpha, \phi) = 1]$. We say that a PPIL scheme Π is server-secure, if for all PPT legal adversaries $\mathcal{A}$, the advantage $\mathsf{Adv}^{\mathsf{SP}}_{\Pi, \mathcal{A}}(\kappa, \mathsf{D}, \mathsf{LT}, \rho, \alpha, \phi)$ is a negligible function in κ.*

We define the above model based on Wifi fingerprint database as an example. Of course, one could simply modify our model for other types of PPIL schemes since each query aforementioned represents a generic class of attacks against PPIL schemes. One may only need to customize the simulation environment and slightly modify the queries if necessary.

Database Hardcore. The volume of a database D is determined by the number M of reference locations (that is related to the area of a building), the number N of APs, and bit size of each RSS value $|\mathcal{R}_v|$. However, there is a general problem on how hard it is for adversaries to generate a valid fabricated database D′ without any useful information from a PPIL scheme using D. I.e. is the D′ itself hard to build? This question is independent of any concrete PPIL schemes. If D′ is easy to generate without breaking the PPIL scheme, then we do not need a PPIL scheme at all. Since the server could just publish its database for all clients. Intuitively, the adversary should be very hard to generate a valid fabricated D′ that has a similar function as D since D′ also has a large number of bits to predict. In the following, we are going to give a formal definition regarding the security assumption of a database (that is non-relevant to PPIL schemes).

Definition 5. *The security experiment for testing the hardness of forging a similar database for a target database D is defined in the following:*

$$\mathsf{EXP}_{\mathcal{D}}^{\mathsf{DBH}}(\kappa, \mathsf{D}, \mathsf{LT}, \rho, \alpha, \phi):$$
$$(D', \mathsf{LT}') \leftarrow \mathcal{D}^{\mathsf{DBLeak}(\cdot)}(\mathsf{LT}, \rho, \alpha, \phi),\ Return\ \mathsf{SimilarTest}(\mathsf{D}, \mathsf{D}', \mathsf{LT}, \mathsf{LT}', \rho, \alpha, \phi).$$

*The advantage of $\mathcal{D}$ which can ask at most ϕ **DBLeak** queries in the above experiment is* $\mathsf{Adv}_{\mathcal{D}}^{\mathsf{DBH}}(\kappa, \mathsf{D}, \mathsf{LT}, \rho, \alpha, \phi) := \Pr[\mathsf{EXP}_{\mathcal{D}}^{\mathsf{DBH}}(\kappa, \mathsf{D}, \mathsf{LT}, \rho, \alpha, \phi) = 1]$. *We say that a database D is hard to forge, if for all PPT adversaries $\mathcal{D}$ the advantage $\mathsf{Adv}_{\mathcal{D}}^{\mathsf{DBH}}(\kappa, \mathsf{D}, \mathsf{LT}, \rho, \alpha, \phi)$ is a negligible function in κ.*

It is straightforward to see that D is hard to forge if only a small portion of D is leaked via **DBLeak** to the adversary and D has large M, N, and $|\mathcal{R}_v|$, e.g., $M = 505$, $N = 241$ and $|\mathcal{R}_v| = 8$ in the real database [16, BUILDING1_NEW] which has $M \times N \times |\mathcal{R}_v| = 973640$ bits at all. However, an open question is how hard it is to create a valid fabricated database. Such hardness might be closely related to the structure of specific building and database generation algorithm. In the future work, one is encouraged to formally analyze the database hardcore assumption in the setting with the leakage of side-channel information, such as adversaries' own RSS measurements modeled by **DBLeak** query. In this paper, we just focus on the formalism of server-privacy for PPIL schemes.

4   On the Security of the YJ Scheme

The YJ Scheme. We first review the PPIL scheme [22] recently proposed by Yang and Järvinen. The YJ scheme is built from Paillier PKE Pai = (KeyGen, Enc, Dec) and two-party SFE protocol SF = (Σ, ev). Paillier PKE scheme is used to protect a client C's fingerprint $F = (f_1, f_2, \ldots, f_N)$. In the YJ scheme, the server S should compute the distances between F and V_i (of its database D), where each distance d_i is assumed to be the following Euclidean distance:

$$d_i = ||V_i - F||^2 = \sum_{j=1}^{N} (v_{i,j} - f_j)^2 = \sum_{j=1}^{N} v_{i,j}^2 + \sum_{j=1}^{N} (-2v_{i,j}f_j) + \sum_{j=1}^{N} f_j^2. \quad (1)$$

SFE protocol is used to privately compute the location $L_C = (x, y, z)$ of C as the centroid of the k nearest reference locations indexed by $i_1, i_2, \ldots, i_k$, where $i_1, i_2, \ldots, i_k$ indicate distances such that $d_{i_1} \leq d_{i_2} \leq \ldots \leq d_{i_k} \leq d_j$ for all $j \neq i_1, i_2, \ldots, i_k$.

PROTOCOL DESCRIPTION. When C subscribes to the location service, it runs $(sk, pk) \xleftarrow{\$} \mathsf{KeyGen}(\kappa)$ to generate a key pair (sk, pk) for Paillier PKE scheme with a sufficiently large κ (e.g. $\kappa = 2048$) and sends $pk = (n, g)$ to S. The protocol execution is shown in Fig. 2.

Note that the randomness space $\mathcal{R}_R = \mathbb{Z}_n$ may result in the blinded distance being wraparound over $\mathbb{Z}_n$, i.e. a modular n operation is involved in the generation of the blinded distance.

C	S
$(sk, pk) \xleftarrow{\$} \mathsf{KeyGen}(1^\kappa)$	Database D
Location Retrieval with $F = (f_1, f_2, \ldots, f_N)$	
For $j \in [N]$:	For $i \in [M]$:
$\quad C_{j,0} := \mathsf{Enc}(pk, -2f_j)$	$\quad C_{\Delta_{i,1}} := \mathsf{Enc}(pk, \sum_{j=1}^{N} v_{i,j}^2)$
$\quad C_1 := \mathsf{Enc}(pk, \sum_{j=1}^{N} f_j^2)$	$\quad C_{\Delta_{i,2}} := \prod_{j=1}^{N} C_{j,0}^{v_{i,j}}$
	$\quad C_{d_i} := C_{\Delta_{i,1}} \cdot C_{\Delta_{i,2}} \cdot C_1$

$$\xrightarrow{\{\{C_{j,0}\}_{j=1}^{N}, C_1\}, pk}$$

$$(\theta, \{C_{\mathrm{Rcb},\iota}\}_{\iota=1}^{\theta}, \{R_\iota\}_{\iota=1}^{\theta})$$
$$\leftarrow Algorithm\ 1(\{C_{d_i}\}_{i=1}^{M}, M)$$

$$\xleftarrow{\{C_{\mathrm{Rcb},\iota}\}_{\iota=1}^{\theta}}$$

For $\iota \in [\theta]$:
$\quad \overline{d_\iota} := \mathsf{Dec}(sk, C_{\mathrm{Rcb},\iota})$ Produce $\hat{f}$
$\quad I_1 = x_1 := \{\overline{d_\iota}\}_{\iota=1}^{\theta}$ $x_2 := \{R_\iota\}_{\iota=1}^{\theta}$, $I_2 \leftarrow (\hat{f}, x_2)$

$$\xleftrightarrow{\mathsf{SF}.\Sigma(I_1, I_2)}$$

Obtain $\mathsf{SF.ev}(\hat{f}, x_1 || x_2)$

Fig. 2. The YJ Scheme

Security Analysis. The security results of our scheme are shown by the following theorems. Here we briefly analyze the theorems. The full proofs of them will be presented in the full version of this paper.

Algorithm 1. Pack Encrypted Distance Set

Input: $\{C_{d_i}\}_{i=1}^{M}$ and M
Output: θ, $\{C_{\mathrm{Rcb},\iota}\}_{\iota=1}^{\theta}$, and $\{R_\iota\}_{\iota=1}^{\theta}$
1   $\theta := 1$; $\mu := M$; $\mathcal{R}_R = \mathbb{Z}_n$
2   **while** $\mu > 0$ **do**
3     $t := \frac{\kappa - 1}{m}$
4   **if** $t > \mu$ **then**
5       $\lfloor \ t := \mu$
6     $C_{\mathrm{cb},\theta} := \prod_{i=1}^{t} C_{d_{\mu-i}}^{2^{(i-1)m}}$; $R_\theta \xleftarrow{\$} \mathcal{R}_R$; $C_{\mathrm{Rcb},\theta} := C_{\mathrm{cb},\theta} \cdot \mathsf{Enc}(pk, R_\theta)$
7     $\mu := \mu - t$
8   **if** $\mu \neq 0$ **then**
9       $\lfloor \ \theta := \theta + 1$

10 **return** $(\theta, \{C_{Rcb,\iota}\}_{\iota=1}^{\theta}, \{R_\iota\}_{\iota=1}^{\theta})$

Theorem 1. *Suppose that the Paillier PKE scheme* Pai *is secure and the SFE scheme* SF *is secure, then the YJ scheme with a database* D *is client-secure with* $\mathsf{Adv}_{\mathsf{YJ},\mathcal{A}}^{\mathsf{CP}}(\kappa, \mathsf{D}) \leq (d\lambda) \cdot ((N+1) \cdot \mathsf{Adv}_{\mathsf{Pai},\mathcal{B}}^{\mathsf{ind\text{-}cpa}}(\kappa) + \frac{M}{2} \cdot \mathsf{Adv}_{\mathsf{SF},\mathcal{E},\Phi}^{\mathsf{pri.ind}}(\kappa, 1)).$

We summarize the games of the proof in Table 2. We use a superscript '$*$' to denote an element of the test oracle.

Table 2. Sequence of games for client-privacy.

Game	Description and Modification
0	Real experiment. $\{\{C_{j,0}^*\}_{j=1}^{N}, C_1^*\}$ and $\{C_{\mathrm{Rcb},\iota}^*\}_{\iota=1}^{\theta}$ of the test oracle are computed with $F^* = \{f_\iota^*\}_{\iota=1}^{N} \xleftarrow{\$} \mathsf{FPTSim}(i^*)$
1	Abort if the challenger fails to guess the test oracle
2	$\{C_{\iota,0}^*\}_{\iota=1}^{N}$ are computed with $F^{*\prime} = \{f_\iota^{*\prime}\}_{\iota=1}^{N}$, but $\{C_{\mathrm{Rcb},\iota}^*, C_1^*\}_{\iota=1}^{\theta}$ are computed with $F^* = \{f_\iota^*\}_{\iota=1}^{N}$, where $f_1^{*\prime} \neq f_1^*$ but $\{f_\iota^{*\prime}\}_{\iota=2}^{N} = \{f_\iota^*\}_{\iota=2}^{N}$
3.j	Game 2 = Game 3.1
$j \in [N]$	In Game 3.j: $f_\iota^{*\prime} \neq f_\iota^*$ for $1 \leq \iota \leq j$, but $\{f_\iota^{*\prime}\}_{\iota=j+1}^{N} = \{f_\iota^*\}_{\iota=j+1}^{N}$
4	Generating C_1^* using a random squared RSS values. $\forall \{\{C_{j,0}^*\}_{j=1}^{N}, C_1^*\}$ and $\{C_{\mathrm{Rcb},\iota}^*\}_{\iota=1}^{\theta}$ are independent now
5	A random location is chosen to answer the **LocTest** query

Theorem 2. *Suppose that the SFE scheme* SF *is secure, the database* D *is hard to forge, then the YJ scheme is server secure with* $\mathsf{Adv}_{\mathsf{YJ},\mathcal{A}}^{\mathsf{SP}}(\kappa, \mathsf{D}, \mathsf{LT}, \rho, \alpha, \phi) \leq d \cdot \ell \cdot \mathsf{Adv}_{\mathsf{SF},\mathcal{E},\Phi}^{\mathsf{pri.ind}}(\kappa, 2) + \frac{\theta \cdot d \cdot \ell}{2^\kappa} + \mathsf{Adv}_{\mathcal{D}}^{\mathsf{DBH}}(\kappa, \mathsf{D}, \mathsf{LT}, \rho, \alpha, \phi).$

We summarize the proof of this theorem in Table 3.

Table 3. Sequence of games for server-privacy

Game	Description and modification
0	Real experiment
1	Abort if two random values are equal
2	The random values used to generate the ciphertexts $\{C^*_{\mathrm{Rcb},\iota}\}^{\theta}_{\iota=1}$ and corresponding SFE protocol instance are different
3	Apply database entropy assumption as Definition 5

5   Conclusion

We presented the first formal privacy model for Wifi fingerprint based PPIL schemes, where both client- and server- privacy are formulated in a unilateral-malicious setting to cover state-of-the-art active attacks. The client-privacy is defined based on the classic notion of indistinguishability, and the server privacy is defined in a computational manner. The proposed model is verified by applying it for proving a recent PPIL protocol. An interesting open question here is whether or nor our security analysis approach can be applied to prove other kinds of privacy-preserving schemes which have a similar construction (i.e., using Paillier PKE and SFE) to the YJ scheme, e.g., the protocols for face recognition [4,19]. For theoretical interesting, the reader is encouraged to define a stronger security model in the full malicious setting based on our model, and to proposed PPIL protocols which can be proven secure under such model. For example, one could allow the active adversaries to send her own messages to oracles (masquerading as either client or server). In the future work, it is also required to formally study the complexity of Definition 5. Nevertheless, it might be also interesting to consider whether or not it is possible to model the server-privacy based on indistinguishability.

Acknowledgments. This work was funded by the INSURE project (303578) of Academy of Finland, and the research project of the Humanities and Social Sciences of the Ministry of Education of China (Grant No. 16YJC870018), and supported by the project "Research on Cryptographic Techniques for Privacy Preserving Location Schemes" funded National Natural Science Foundation of China (Grant No. 61872051).

References

1. Bellare, M., Hoang, V.T., Keelveedhi, S.: Efficient garbling from a fixed-key block-cipher. In: IEEE Security and Privacy 2013, pp. 478–492 (May 2013)
2. Bellare, M., Hoang, V.T., Rogaway, P.: Foundations of garbled circuits. In: ACM CCS 2012, pp. 784–796. ACM, October 2012
3. Bellare, M., Rogaway, P.: Entity authentication and key distribution. In: Stinson, D.R. (ed.) CRYPTO 1993. LNCS, vol. 773, pp. 232–249. Springer, Heidelberg (1994). https://doi.org/10.1007/3-540-48329-2_21

4. Blanton, M., Gasti, P.: Secure and efficient protocols for iris and fingerprint identification. In: Atluri, V., Diaz, C. (eds.) ESORICS 2011. LNCS, vol. 6879, pp. 190–209. Springer, Heidelberg (2011). https://doi.org/10.1007/978-3-642-23822-2_11
5. Elnahrawy, E., Li, X., Martin, R.P.: The limits of localization using signal strength: a comparative study. In: SECON 2004, pp. 406–414. IEEE (2004)
6. Ferreira, A., Fernandes, D., Catarino, A., Monteiro, J.: Localization and positioning systems for emergency responders: a survey. IEEE Commun. Surv. Tutor. **19**(4), 2836–2870 (2017)
7. He, S., Chan, S.H.G.: WI-FI fingerprint-based indoor positioning: recent advances and comparisons. IEEE Commun. Surv. Tutor. **18**(1), 466–490 (2016)
8. Honkavirta, V., Perala, T., Ali-Loytty, S., Piché, R.: A comparative survey of WLAN location fingerprinting methods. In: WPNC 2009, pp. 243–251. IEEE (2009)
9. Hossain, A.M., Soh, W.S.: Cramer-Rao bound analysis of localization using signal strength difference as location fingerprint. In: INFOCOM 2010, pp. 1–9. IEEE (2010)
10. Jager, T., Kohlar, F., Schäge, S., Schwenk, J.: On the security of TLS-DHE in the standard model. In: Safavi-Naini, R., Canetti, R. (eds.) CRYPTO 2012. LNCS, vol. 7417, pp. 273–293. Springer, Heidelberg (2012). https://doi.org/10.1007/978-3-642-32009-5_17
11. Kaemarungsi, K., Krishnamurthy, P.: Modeling of indoor positioning systems based on location fingerprinting. In: INFOCOM 2004, pp. 1012–1022. IEEE, March 2004
12. Konstantinidis, A., Chatzimilioudis, G., Zeinalipour-Yazti, D., Mpeis, P., Pelekis, N., Theodoridis, Y.: Privacy-preserving indoor localization on smartphones. IEEE Trans. Knowl. Data Eng. **27**(11), 3042–3055 (2015)
13. Li, H., Sun, L., Zhu, H., Lu, X., Cheng, X.: Achieving privacy preservation in WIFI fingerprint-based localization. In: INFOCOM 2014, pp. 2337–2345 (2014)
14. Li, S., Li, H., Sun, L.: Privacy-preserving crowdsourced site survey in WIFI fingerprint-based localization. EURASIP J. Wireless Commun. Netw. **2016**(1), 123 (2016)
15. Liu, H., Darabi, H., Banerjee, P., Liu, J.: Survey of wireless indoor positioning techniques and systems. IEEE Trans. Syst. Man Cybern. Part C (Appl. Rev.) **37**(6), 1067–1080 (2007)
16. Lohan, E.S., et al.: Indoor WLAN measurement data. Data Set (2014). http://www.cs.tut.fi/tlt/pos/MEASUREMENTS_WLAN_FOR_WEB.zip. Accessed June 2017
17. Paillier, P.: Public-key cryptosystems based on composite degree residuosity classes. In: Stern, J. (ed.) EUROCRYPT 1999. LNCS, vol. 1592, pp. 223–238. Springer, Heidelberg (1999). https://doi.org/10.1007/3-540-48910-X_16
18. Roos, T., Myllymäki, P., Tirri, H., Misikangas, P., Sievänen, J.: A probabilistic approach to WLAN user location estimation. Int. J. Wirel. Inf. Netw. **9**(3), 155–164 (2002)
19. Sadeghi, A.-R., Schneider, T., Wehrenberg, I.: Efficient privacy-preserving face recognition. In: Lee, D., Hong, S. (eds.) ICISC 2009. LNCS, vol. 5984, pp. 229–244. Springer, Heidelberg (2010). https://doi.org/10.1007/978-3-642-14423-3_16
20. Swangmuang, N., Krishnamurthy, P.: Location fingerprint analyses toward efficient indoor positioning. In: PerCom 2008, pp. 100–109. IEEE (2008)
21. Talvitie, J., Renfors, M., Lohan, E.S.: Distance-based interpolation and extrapolation methods for RSS-based localization with indoor wireless signals. IEEE Trans. Veh. Technol. **64**(4), 1340–1353 (2015)

22. Yang, Z., Järvinen, K.: The death and rebirth of privacy-preserving WIFI finger-print localization with paillier encryption. In: INFOCOM 2018, April 2018
23. Yang, Z., Järvinen, K.: The death and rebirth of privacy-preserving WIFI fingerprint localization with paillier encryption. Cryptology ePrint Archive, Report 2018/259 (2018). http://eprint.iacr.org/2018/259
24. Zhang, T., Chow, S.S.M., Zhou, Z., Li, M.: Privacy-preserving WI-FI fingerprinting indoor localization. In: Ogawa, K., Yoshioka, K. (eds.) IWSEC 2016. LNCS, vol. 9836, pp. 215–233. Springer, Cham (2016). https://doi.org/10.1007/978-3-319-44524-3_13

Security Notions for Cloud Storage and Deduplication

Colin Boyd[1], Gareth T. Davies[1(✉)], Kristian Gjøsteen[1], Håvard Raddum[2], and Mohsen Toorani[3]

[1] NTNU, Norwegian University of Science and Technology, Trondheim, Norway
{colin.boyd,gareth.davies,kristian.gjosteen}@ntnu.no
[2] Simula@UiB, Bergen, Norway
haavardr@simula.no
[3] University of Bergen, Bergen, Norway
mohsen.toorani@uib.no

Abstract. Cloud storage is in widespread use by individuals and enterprises but introduces a wide array of attack vectors. A basic step for users is to encrypt their data, yet it is not obvious what security properties are required for such encryption. Furthermore, cloud storage providers often use techniques such as data deduplication for improving efficiency which restricts the application of semantically-secure encryption. Generic security goals and attack models have thus far proved elusive: primitives are considered in isolation and protocols are often proved secure under ad hoc models for restricted classes of adversaries.

We formally model natural security notions for cloud storage and deduplication using a generic syntax for storage systems. We define security notions for confidentiality and integrity in encrypted cloud storage and determine relations between these notions. We show how to build cloud storage systems that satisfy our defined security notions using standard cryptographic components.

1 Introduction

When handing over their data to third parties, it is natural that users regard security and privacy as critical concerns. Some users may be willing to trust a cloud storage provider (CSP) to secure their data, but as the Snowden revelations have shown, even well-meaning providers are not immune from compromise. Users increasingly want to manage confidentiality and integrity of their outsourced data without the need to trust the CSP.

It is perhaps surprising that up to now there seems to be no general model of security for remote storage. What are the essential components of a remote storage system, and how should users protect their data so that they can interact usefully with the system while maintaining security requirements? It may seem obvious that users should simply encrypt their data, but the remote storage scenario is different from that of communication or local storage. Multiple users interact and files are vulnerable to manipulation by the CSP. Moreover,

© Springer Nature Switzerland AG 2018
J. Baek et al. (Eds.): ProvSec 2018, LNCS 11192, pp. 347–365, 2018.
https://doi.org/10.1007/978-3-030-01446-9_20

efficiency factors may conflict with user goals. Specifically, CSPs extensively use *deduplication* for removing redundant copies of data and saving storage.

Security Goals for Cloud Storage. Users who trust their storage provider can send plaintext data for storage: this is today the most common situation. Several commercial storage providers, however, support client-side encryption so that the cloud provider cannot obtain the plaintext. It is not immediately obvious which security properties are most appropriate for client-side encryption. In this paper we create a fine-grained approach to adversarial capabilities in terms of compromise of both users and servers. We consider three different security goals and show how they can be achieved within our model.

IND This is the usual standard for strong confidentiality of encrypted data: *indistinguishability* of ciphertexts. We will show that this can be achieved in our cloud storage model by appropriate choice of encryption scheme.

PRV Deduplication cannot take place if strong encryption is deployed. Privacy under a *chosen distribution attack* (PRV-CDA) [4] is used to identify achievable security in the presence of message-derived keys. We will show how this primitive-level goal can be transferred to the protocol level using our model.

INT In many scenarios the user wishes to remove local copies of outsourced files so has no way checking if a retrieved file has been modified. We introduce a notion of integrity of ciphertexts for cloud storage schemes (INT-SC), with three flavors corresponding to differing levels of server compromise. Furthermore, we consider integrity in deduplicating schemes and link existing definitions of tag consistency to our framework.

Contributions. The literature on secure cloud storage has tended to focus on ad hoc solutions rather than generic models that capture classes of realistic adversaries. We fill this gap by providing a comprehensive definition of cloud storage in terms of the input/output behavior of the entities in the system. For various security properties we use our framework to define game-based notions.

We identify the limits of a number of key security properties in cloud storage and provide generic security models for encrypted storage and deduplication. Our framework covers many natural and practically-deployed cloud storage solutions and this approach enables practitioners to identify which components of a storage scheme need to satisfy certain criteria for a given security goal. Specifically, we:

- create a modular framework for security models in cloud storage;
- cast known and novel attack models and security notions in our framework;
- consider known attacks on schemes.

Previous Work. From the point of view of a single enterprise or an individual, secure outsourced storage seems straightforward: encrypt all files at the client side using strong symmetric encryption, use a message authentication code (MAC) or AE for integrity and keep the key(s) secret. In this mindset, cloud storage appears similar to disk encryption [11], and this is the approach recently taken by Messmer et al. [21]. Such an approach ignores more complex interactions between different clients and servers lacking mutual trust.

Moreover, the business model that allows CSPs to provide cheap storage relies on individuals not employing encryption so as not to interfere with data deduplication. Since the concept of convergent encryption [8] was formalized by Bellare et al. [4] there have been a number of proposals for secure deduplication [10,15,18,27], with each appearing to provide a new threat model. This has led to uncertainty over what security guarantees these schemes provide. For example, the protocol of Liu et al. (CCS '15) [18], as noted later in a revision to the ePrint version [19] and also in subsequent work by some of the same authors [20], only provides the security claims if one round of the protocol is considered: for more than one round, any user can infer whether or not any file is stored on the cloud – a side channel that can result in serious security issues [2,13].

Specific functionalities designed for the cloud storage scenario have been modelled and analysed extensively. These include, but are not limited to: protocols for proofs of retrievability (PoR) [14], proofs of data possession (PDP) [3], proofs of ownership (PoW) [12], secure auditing [29], and privacy of interactions (queries and results) between a data owner and a malicious server [26].

2   Preliminaries

We use the notation $a \leftarrow f(b)$ to denote assignment of a to the result of computing $f(b)$ if f is either a function or an algorithm. $a \xleftarrow{\$} D$ means that either a has been chosen from set D (uniformly) or according to some distribution D. If $\mathbf{a}$ is a vector then denote the ith component by $\mathbf{a}[i]$, with $|\mathbf{a}|$ denoting the number of components. We denote concatenation of two values, usually bit-strings, by $a||b$. If L is a list then the code $\mathsf{L} \xleftarrow{\cup} \{a\}$ indicates that a is appended to L.

Throughout this work we assume that all security parameters and public values are known to all parties (and algorithms). This means that if ever we need to initialize a primitive or protocol, generation of such values is implicit. In situations where algorithms are run with no inputs given, these public values are still provided. Our security experiments consider an adversary that possibly interacts with some oracles before terminating and providing an output. We use the concrete security framework throughout, thus we do not regard adversaries in terms of security parameters: in particular we avoid use of negligible advantage since in the cloud setting the (possibly adversarial) server can perform huge numbers of operations per second. In pseudocode for security games, $\textbf{return } b' \stackrel{?}{=} b$ is shorthand for $\textbf{if } b' = b \textbf{ then return } 1 \; // \; \textbf{else return } 0$, with output of 1 indicating successful adversarial behavior. We will use an init procedure to represent initialization of cloud storage systems – this encompasses a number of possible subroutines but for generality and brevity we use a single line. An oracle in a security game that corresponds to the environment simulating some functionality func is denoted by $\mathcal{O}.\mathsf{func}$ (the simulation may invoke some restrictions on func).

Cloud storage infrastructure includes some always-available *servers* (the CSP) and some *clients* (that act on behalf of *users*) that are sometimes available and interact with the servers. There may additionally be some parties that interact with the clients and servers to provide extra functionality, such as a key-server [15] or an auditing mechanism [29]. We regard *users* as the entities with distinct logins to a system, and *clients* as the devices that interact with the server on behalf of their owner, the user. This allows us to consider two clients that have the same key material, e.g. laptop and phone, of one user.

Symmetric-Key Encryption (SKE). Our results aim to build secure schemes from the most simple and well-understood building block in cryptography: symmetric encryption. In traditional SKE, two parties agree some key in advance and then communicate over some (presumed insecure) channel. In the context of outsourced storage the two parties are often the same user at different points in time. Additionally, the 'channel' is not only the communication lines between the user and the server but also the server's storage when the ciphertext is at rest. Our syntax and definitions of security follow standard practice and are given in the full version [6]; here we highlight some choices we have made to facilitate our results. Our games for IND-CPA, IND-CCA2 and AEAD represent multi-challenge left-or-right indistinguishability. We do not restrict what we regard as *files* for these notions due to the myriad of ways in which a file can be processed before, during and after the store procedure. Instead we insist that trivial wins are disallowed by *some restriction* on the relation between files sent in (F_0, F_1) calls to left-or-right oracles: normally this will mean that the segmentation procedure applied to both files must yield the same number of blocks. We also require PRV-CDA and tag consistency as given by Bellare et al. [4].

3   Modelling Cloud Storage

Our goal is to study security of cloud storage in terms of confidentiality and integrity of files. Such analysis is only possible if the model provides sufficient detail about adversarial capabilities. The challenge is to provide a sufficiently detailed model that allows analysis, yet is generic enough to facilitate study of natural schemes. It is desirable that the model can easily be extended to incorporate particular exotic design choices. We present here what is to our knowledge the first such model for (secure) outsourced storage that accommodates both widely-deployed (and conceptually straightforward) solutions as well as much of the literature (in particular schemes facilitating encrypted data deduplication). As for any storage scheme, a user of a cloud storage scheme should be able to store, retrieve and delete files. A user must be able to specify which previously stored files to retrieve or delete, and we shall achieve that by having the user choose a unique file handle (identifier) for each file when storing. Correctness can then be defined in the expected way, stated here for a notational introduction:

Definition 1 (Correctness). *If user* uid *previously stored* F *under handle* id *then when it later retrieves* id *the result will be* F, *unless client has sent* del(id).

init
01. $\mathsf{ST} \leftarrow \emptyset$

newu(uid)
02. $\mathsf{uk}_{\mathsf{uid}} \leftarrow \mathsf{kgen}$
03. $\mathsf{KT}_{\mathsf{uid}} \leftarrow \emptyset$
04. **return** $\mathsf{uk}_{\mathsf{uid}}$

del(uid, id)
05. $\mathsf{KT}_{\mathsf{uid}} \overset{\cup}{\leftarrow} \{(\bot, \mathsf{id})\}$
06. **if** $\exists\,\{\mathsf{uid}, \cdot, \mathsf{id}, 0\}$ in ST **then**
07. $\mathsf{ST} \overset{\cup}{\leftarrow} \{(\mathsf{uid}, -, \mathsf{id}, 1)\}$

upl(uid, c, id)
08. $\mathsf{ST} \overset{\cup}{\leftarrow} \{(\mathsf{uid}, c, \mathsf{id}, 0)\}$

store(uid, F, id)
09. $\mathsf{fk} \leftarrow \mathsf{fkeyGen}(\mathsf{F}, \mathsf{uk}_{\mathsf{uid}})$
10. $c \leftarrow \mathsf{E}_{\mathsf{fk}}(\mathsf{F}, \mathsf{id})$
11. $\mathsf{upl}(\mathsf{uid}, c, \mathsf{id})$
12. $\mathsf{KT}_{\mathsf{uid}} \overset{\cup}{\leftarrow} \{(\mathsf{fk}, \mathsf{id})\}$

retr(uid, id)
13. **if** $\exists\,(\mathsf{uid}, \cdot, \mathsf{id}, 1) \in \mathsf{ST}$ **or**
14. $\exists(\bot, \mathsf{id}) \in \mathsf{KT}_{\mathsf{uid}}$ **then**
15.   **return** $\bot$
16. **if** $\exists\,(\mathsf{uid}, c, \mathsf{id}, 0) \in \mathsf{ST}$ **and**
17. $\exists(\mathsf{fk}, \mathsf{id}) \in \mathsf{KT}_{\mathsf{uid}}$ **then**
18. $\mathsf{F} \leftarrow \mathsf{D}_{\mathsf{fk}}(c, \mathsf{id})$
19.   **return** F
20. **else**
21.   **return** $\bot$

Fig. 1. Definition of a cloud storage scheme CS.

We use storage handles, denoted by id, to indicate the value that the user wishes to use in the future to retrieve that file. We regard the generation of id as outside the scope of the model. It is perhaps easiest to think of id as a random value that is generated by the user's device for each file. In practice all a user sees is a list of filenames (which are certainly not suitable for our purposes due to non-uniqueness): this approach allows us to focus on issues directly related to confidentiality and integrity. This handle is distinct from the deduplication 'tags' used in prior literature on message-locked encryption [1,4,8]. In client-side-deduplicating systems the user first sends some short, message-derived tag (for example in convergent encryption [8] this is $\tau = \mathsf{H}(\mathsf{H}(C))$ for ciphertext C) and if the server already has this tag, informs the user not to send the full ciphertext and updates that ciphertext's metadata to indicate that the user can in future retrieve the ciphertext. Note that this process also occurs in deduplicating schemes that do not use any encryption. In this context, this tag is all that is required to claim ownership of a file. Our handles do not have this feature: they simply ensure that retrieve queries work 'correctly'. In Sect. 5 we will discuss integrity in the context of deduplicating and non-deduplicating cloud storage, and highlight the differences between our handles and these tags in more detail.

3.1   A Model for Cloud Storage

Our model for cloud storage is depicted in Fig. 1. A cloud storage scheme $\mathsf{CS}[\mathsf{SKE}, \mathsf{fkeyGen}] = (\mathsf{init}, \mathsf{newu}, \mathsf{store}, \mathsf{retr}, \mathsf{del})$ is parameterized by a symmetric-key encryption scheme $\mathsf{SKE} = (\mathsf{KG}, \mathsf{E}, \mathsf{D})$ and a file-key generation procedure $\mathsf{fkeyGen}$, and supports natural functionalities: init for initialization, newu for adding a new user, store for storing a file, retr for retrieval and del for deletion.

Each user is associated with a user identification uid, and each file is identified by a storage handle id. We define per-user keys uk and per-file keys fk. Each user has some (preferably small) local storage and the server maintains (what is from an abstract perspective at least) a vast data structure. Generation of per-user key material uk (line 02) may include keys for a number of different purposes. The user stores this material and their own KT ('Key Table') locally and the server(s) maintains a database ST ('Store Table') that it uses to track file ownership and retrieval handles. This means that there is only one ST but there could be many KTs. Our model retains generality: to our knowledge it incorporates almost all intuitive schemes and all protocols from the literature (more details in next subsection). We make no assumption about how files are handled in terms of segmentation, nor do we consider redundancy at the server's backend. The model that follows is, by design, modular and generic enough to cope with straightforward modifications to incorporate such processes.

We now discuss the design choices that require further attention. In line 02 we explicitly regard the per-user key generation procedure as occurring separately from the other procedures, this is to retain generality and to allow us to focus on file-key generation. ST tracks deletion status of each file for each user (lines 13–15), using a bit as the fourth value in each entry. In deployed systems this abstract procedure may not be done as directly as we describe. Line 07 indicates that the server may at this point delete the ciphertext for the deleted file, however we do not enforce this: the '1' flag indicates deletion has occurred[1] for user uid and handle id. Encryption algorithm E takes id as input (line 10): if SKE is an AEAD scheme then id could be the associated data – we model this construction later on. Lines 16–19 specify that the file can only be retrieved if it has not been removed either by the client or the server: in particular line 17 says that if there exists an fk such that $(fk, id) \in KT_{uid}$ then the retrieve is allowed to continue.

We differentiate between store – the entire process of storing a file on the server and updating the client's local storage – and upl– the specific action that occurs server-side. The definition generalizes to include the simplest and most widely-deployed solution, which is without any client-side encryption at all. Any scheme that distributes files among multiple servers is also included, incurring a rather complicated outsourced state ST, however the results in the remainder of this paper will mainly focus on the single server case. To satisfy correctness we require an implicit assumption that the CSP forwards all requests honestly: this approach reflects cryptographic models for key exchange. If fk used for store (encryption) is not the same as the one used for retr (decryption) then no scheme can be correct. The adversaries that we consider cannot modify KT so key symmetry is implicit in our model and for the rest of the paper.

---

[1] Many CSPs never actually delete files at the backend, and this is understandable: the cost of finding, accessing and removing a file and all its redundant copies is often considerable, and if the CSP uses client-side deduplication then if the user (or any other) uploads that file in the future this will incur a bandwidth cost.

	Scheme	fkeyGen(F, uk)
1	No encryption	fk ← ⊥
2	Per-user key	fk ← uk
3	Per-file key	fk ← KG
4	MLE [4]	fk ← H(F)
5	Liu et al. [18]	fk ← **PAKE.Out**(F)
6	DupLESS [15]	fk ← **OPRF.Out**(F)
7	Duan [10]	fk ← **DOKG**(F)
8	Stanek et al. [27]	fk ← **Thr.PKE.KG**(F)
9	CDStore [17]	fk ← **SS**(H(F))

Fig. 2. Specification for fkeyGen procedure for existing cloud storage schemes

3.2   Modelling Existing Schemes and Literature

In Fig. 2 we detail the file-key generation procedure for natural constructions and a number of schemes from the existing literature. The natural scenarios include a CSP that does not support client-side encryption (line 1), a CSP wherein each user holds a per-user key and encrypts all files with that key (line 2), and a CSP wherein a per-file key is randomly chosen at the point of the file being uploaded (line 3). The per-user key scenario (line 2) allows deduplication of a particular user's files (but not cross-user deduplication) which can still allow great savings, particularly in the backup setting. This case also reflects some enterprise scenarios in which an organization has a storage gateway (that may interact with trusted hardware, such as a hardware security module) that deduplicates files and encrypts (under one key) on behalf of all of its employees before sending to some public cloud (CSP). The per-file key scenario (line 3) intuitively provides increased confidentiality, but introduces challenging key management. A gateway can also be used in this case as described in the Omnicloud architecture [16]: this of course requires the gateway to additionally manage the vast number of keys that could be generated in the enterprise scenario.

Schemes in lines 4–9 all aim to provide 'secure cross-user deduplication' to some extent, providing more confidentiality than using no encryption (line 1) but at the risk of opening a side channel that may allow a user to learn if a file is already stored on the server [2]. In many schemes such as those of Keelveedhi et al. (DupLESS) [15] and Liu et al. [18], the fkeyGen procedure is not a single algorithm but a protocol run between the user and the key server or the other users in the protocol, respectively. Stanek et al. [27] use both convergent encryption and an outer layer threshold encryption scheme to produce ciphertexts, and the fkeyGen protocol interacts with two trusted third parties. Duan [10] attempts to avoid the single point of failure inherent in having a single (semi-trusted) key server (KS) in DupLESS-like schemes: fkeyGen generates encryption keys using a distributed oblivious key generation, instantiated using a (deterministic) threshold signature scheme. The CDStore protocol of Li et al. [17] distributes shares of a file to multiple cloud servers using so-called *convergent dispersal*.

The restriction to SKE in line 10 of Fig. 1 is for the purposes of results in Sects. 4 and 5. Note here that schemes 1–7 in Fig. 2 precisely fit our model while schemes 8 and 9 do not simply encrypt using SKE – for these schemes E represents some other encryption mechanism. In the schemes that do precisely fit our model, generation of file key fk could happen as part of the key generation procedure kgen: for example in the per-user key case (line 2 of Fig. 2) fkeyGen is the identity function. This is one of many potential modular extensions of our framework: we could of course consider a model in which (for example) the fkeyGen and E algorithms are general functions with arbitrary inputs.

Cloudedup [23] uses block-level convergent encryption to send ciphertexts to a third party that adds further (symmetric) encryption and manages metadata. Dang and Chang [7] similarly assume a trusted entity, in their case hardware. A trusted enclave uses an oblivious PRF (similarly to DupLESS) to get block-derived keys to allow the enclave to perform deduplication: the enclave acts as a deduplication gateway then applies randomized encryption before sending ciphertexts to the CSP. In these schemes encryption is done in two phases and the per-block keys are managed by the third party; this does not quite fit our model but it is straightforward to modify how KT (and SKE) works to analyze such schemes. Recently Shin et al. [25] attempted to distribute the role of the key server in DupLESS-like schemes by additionally using inter-KS deduplication. Again, allowing this type of scheme is a simple extension of our model.

To simplify much of our analysis later on we require that every time a new file is stored by a client, a new id is generated. This leads to the following assumption:

Assumption 1. *In all cloud storage schemes* CS *considered in this paper,* store *is never called on the same* id *twice.*

We emphasize that id is the retrieval handle chosen by the client, and is distinct from the deduplication 'tags' used in prior literature. This assumption (and the existence of the id) emphasizes that our handles are there to distinguish file uploads from one another: each $\{$uid, id$\}$ pair can only ever occur once.

4   Confidentiality

Now that we have defined a suitable syntax for cloud storage schemes, we can begin to consider the many ways in which security features can be obtained. In this section we turn our attention to confidentiality of files with respect to realistic adversaries. Defining confidentiality notions of security is a two-step process: We first define what we want to prevent the adversary from learning (the *goal*), and then we specify the adversary's capabilities.

There are several possible goals. The classical cryptographic goal is indistinguishability, where one of two adversary-chosen files was stored and the adversary is unable to decide which file was stored. This is similar to semantic security, where a file sampled from one of two adversary-chosen probability spaces was stored, and the adversary is unable to decide which distribution the file was sampled from. A weaker notion is to sample a file from one of two pre-chosen high-entropy probability spaces. The adversary has two distinct capabilities when attacking a cloud storage system. The first is the ability to influence the actions of the honest users. The second is the ability to influence the CSP.

When considering corruption of users, it is important to note that an adversary can usually create genuine logins to a system, and thus receive a valid uid and uk for an arbitrary number of users. We model this by distinguishing between two types of newu query: $\mathcal{O}$.newuC creates a valid (Corrupt) user and outputs its uk to the adversary, and $\mathcal{O}$.newuH that only creates a valid (Honest) user[2]. For its corrupted users the adversary may not necessarily use uk and fkeyGen correctly (which $\mathcal{O}$.store cannot handle): we model this capability by giving the adversary access to an $\mathcal{O}$.upl oracle that pushes some $\{(\text{uid}, c, \text{id}, 0)\}$ tuple to the server's storage table ST. We regard the minimum adversarial capability as being able to have full control over a number of corrupted users and to make honest users store files, we refer to this notion as a *chosen store attack* (CSA). The adversary may even be able to get honest users to retrieve files from the cloud storage system, a *chosen retrieve attack* (CRA). Analogously to encryption, CSA and CRA somewhat correspond to CPA and CCA, respectively.[3]

The adversary's control of the CSP can be usefully divided into three levels: the adversary may have no influence at all on the CSP then we have an honest CSP giving the adversary *zero access* (Z). The adversary may also be able to look at the CSP's storage and key material, but not tamper with anything, a *passively corrupt* (P) CSP. This models both honest-but-curious CSPs and snapshot hackers (of the cloud's storage servers or the communication channel). And finally, the adversary may have full control over the CSP, an *actively corrupt* (A) adversary. When the CSP is honest, it may seem that our model always guarantees confidentiality because the adversary would never have access to ciphertexts. However, this is not the case, since the file key generation procedure is regarded as a protocol and may leak information (as mentioned earlier with the protocol of Liu et al. [18]). Roughly speaking, we can say that when the CSP is honest, we consider only the security of the file key generation protocol. When the CSP is passively corrupt, we must additionally consider the confidentiality of the encryption used. When the CSP is actively corrupt, we must also consider integrity in the encryption mechanism. This separation of concerns is by design.

4.1 Defining Confidentiality for Cloud Storage

In combination we define a generic IND-atk-csp experiment with six distinct cases: atk $\in$ {CSA, CRA}, csp $\in$ {Z, P, A} and this IND-atk-csp experiment is detailed in Fig. 3. Just as in our general definition for storage protocols (Fig. 1) we keep track of the retrieval capability by using a table ST, initially set to empty.

---

[2] It is certainly possible to extend this model to adaptive corruptions, however this would add considerable extra complexity to any scheme.

[3] It is possible to define an equivalent of a passive adversary, however since our definitions are multi-challenge, the adversary can always call $\mathcal{O}$.LR$_b$ on $F_0 = F_1$ to mimic a store query (though it cannot query $\mathcal{O}$.retr on these ciphertexts).

$\underline{\mathrm{Exp}_{\mathsf{CS},\,\mathcal{A}}^{\mathsf{IND\text{-}atk\text{-}csp}}:}$
init
  $b \xleftarrow{\$} \{0, 1\}$
  $\mathsf{CL}, \mathsf{users_C}, \mathsf{users_H} \leftarrow \emptyset$
  $b' \leftarrow \mathcal{A}^{\mathrm{oracles}}$
  return $b' \overset{?}{=} b$

$\mathcal{O}.\mathsf{newuC}(\mathsf{uid}):$
  $\mathsf{users_C} \xleftarrow{\cup} \mathsf{uid}$
  $\mathsf{uk_{uid}} \leftarrow \mathsf{kgen}$
  $\mathsf{KT_{uid}} \leftarrow \emptyset$
  return $\mathsf{uk_{uid}}$

$\mathcal{O}.\mathsf{newuH}(\mathsf{uid}):$
  $\mathsf{users_H} \xleftarrow{\cup} \mathsf{uid}$
  $\mathsf{uk_{uid}} \leftarrow \mathsf{kgen}$
  $\mathsf{KT_{uid}} \leftarrow \emptyset$
  return $\perp$

$\mathcal{O}.\mathsf{store}(\mathsf{uid}, \mathsf{F}, \mathsf{id}):$
  do $\mathsf{store}(\mathsf{uid}, \mathsf{F}, \mathsf{id})$

$\mathcal{O}.\mathsf{upl}(\mathsf{uid}, c, \mathsf{id}):$
  if $\mathsf{uid} \in \mathsf{users_C}$ then
    do $\mathsf{upl}(\mathsf{uid}, c, \mathsf{id})$

$\mathcal{O}.\mathsf{del}(\mathsf{uid}, \mathsf{id}):$
  do $\mathsf{del}(\mathsf{uid}, \mathsf{id})$

$\mathcal{O}.\mathsf{LR}_b(\mathsf{uid}, \mathsf{F_0}, \mathsf{F_1}, \mathsf{id}):$
  if $\mathsf{uid} \notin \mathsf{users_H}$ then
    return $\perp$
  else
    $\mathcal{O}.\mathsf{store}(\mathsf{uid}, \mathsf{F}_b, \mathsf{id})$
    $\mathsf{CL} \xleftarrow{\cup} \{(\mathsf{uid}, \mathsf{id})\}$

$\mathcal{O}.\mathsf{retr}(\mathsf{uid}, \mathsf{id}):$ // CRA only
  if $\mathsf{uid} \notin \mathsf{users_H}$ or $(\mathsf{uid}, \mathsf{id}) \in \mathsf{CL}$ then
    return $\perp$
  else
    $\mathsf{F} \leftarrow \mathsf{retr}(\mathsf{uid}, \mathsf{id})$
    return F

$\mathcal{O}.\mathsf{peek}(\mathsf{uid}, \mathsf{id}):$ // P, A only
  return $\{(\mathsf{uid}, c, \mathsf{id}, 0/1) \in \mathsf{ST}\}$

$\mathcal{O}.\mathsf{erase}(\mathsf{uid}, \mathsf{id}):$ // A only
  $\mathsf{ST} \leftarrow \mathsf{ST} \setminus \{(\mathsf{uid}, \cdot, \mathsf{id}, \cdot) \in \mathsf{ST}\}$

$\mathcal{O}.\mathsf{insert}(\mathsf{uid}, c, \mathsf{id}, d):$ // A only
  $\mathsf{ST} \xleftarrow{\cup} \{(\mathsf{uid}, c, \mathsf{id}, d)\}$

Fig. 3. The experiment defining IND-atk-csp security for cloud storage, for atk $\in \{\mathsf{CSA}, \mathsf{CRA}\}$, csp $\in \{\mathsf{Z}, \mathsf{P}, \mathsf{A}\}$. All adversaries have access to $\mathcal{O}.\mathsf{newuC}$, $\mathcal{O}.\mathsf{newuH}$, $\mathcal{O}.\mathsf{store}$, $\mathcal{O}.\mathsf{upl}$, $\mathcal{O}.\mathsf{del}$ and $\mathcal{O}.\mathsf{LR}$. CRA additionally has access to $\mathcal{O}.\mathsf{retr}$, P additionally has the $\mathcal{O}.\mathsf{peek}$ oracle and finally A additionally has $\mathcal{O}.\mathsf{erase}$ and $\mathcal{O}.\mathsf{insert}$.

The security experiment keeps track of the $\mathcal{O}.\mathsf{LR}$ queries using a forbidden list CL to prevent trivial wins. In order to model the attacker's influence on the CSP, we introduce three new oracles: $\mathcal{O}.\mathsf{peek}$, $\mathcal{O}.\mathsf{erase}$ and $\mathcal{O}.\mathsf{insert}$. These are not functionalities of storage systems so they are not included in Fig. 1. $\mathcal{O}.\mathsf{peek}$ allows the adversary to see the ciphertext (and deletion status) for some user uid and some handle id, and this is available to a passively corrupt adversary (P). $\mathcal{O}.\mathsf{insert}$ and $\mathcal{O}.\mathsf{erase}$ model actively malicious (or completely compromised) CSPs, granting the ability to store or delete arbitrary items in the CSP's database: these two oracles are only available to an actively corrupt (A) attacker.

Definition 2 (IND-atk-csp *Security for Cloud Storage*). *Consider any cloud storage scheme* $\mathsf{CS} = (\mathsf{init}, \mathsf{newu}, \mathsf{store}, \mathsf{retr}, \mathsf{del})$. *The* IND-atk-csp *advantage for an adversary* $\mathcal{A}$ *and* atk $\in \{\mathsf{CSA}, \mathsf{CRA}\}$, csp $\in \{\mathsf{Z}, \mathsf{P}, \mathsf{A}\}$ *against* CS *is defined by*

$$\mathbf{Adv}_{\mathsf{CS},\,\mathcal{A}}^{\mathsf{IND\text{-}atk\text{-}csp}} = 2 \cdot \left[\mathbf{Pr} \left[\mathrm{Exp}_{\mathsf{CS},\,\mathcal{A}}^{\mathsf{IND\text{-}atk\text{-}csp}} = 1 \right] - \frac{1}{2} \right]$$

where experiment $\mathbf{Exp}_{CS, \mathcal{A}}^{IND\text{-}atk\text{-}csp}$ *is given in Fig. 3.*

On Our Model. Our weakest notion of server compromise, IND-atk-Z, refers to a very limited adversary, with no access to the server's database and only capable of making 'challenge' store queries (modelled by $\mathcal{O}.LR_b$) with users that it does not have key material for, resulting in ciphertexts that it cannot access. Thus even a scheme with no encryption can be secure under this notion. This is by design: the only schemes that do not meet this requirement are those that leak information about a file *to other users* during the store procedure.

It is possible to imagine adversaries that may wish to act without being noticed by the users they have infiltrated. This CRA adversary would thus retrieve but not store or delete – and yet seems to be more 'limited' than a CSA adversary that does perform store/delete operations and does not mind if the user notices its behavior. This is the nature of adversaries in cloud storage: the clear hierarchy that exists for encryption does not easily translate.

The concept of length equality for files in cloud storage is not as clear cut as it is for bitstrings in an IND-based game for encryption. If the encryption scheme is not length hiding and the adversary submits one $\mathcal{O}.LR$ query and one $\mathcal{O}.peek$ query: if the ciphertext lengths differ then the adversary trivially wins the game. As mentioned earlier, this means that an inherent restriction exists on $\mathcal{O}.LR$ queries: if the length of (the segmentation of) F_0 and F_1 differs then the experiment does not go ahead with the store procedure[4].

Relations Between Notions. While we have just defined six adversarial capabilities, in fact only three are distinct. Figure 4 summarizes how the notions relate to each other, and we detail these relations fully in the full version [6]. We give a brief intuition here. If notion A has strictly more oracles than notion B then any CS secure under A will also be secure under notion B. This means that IND-atk-A $\Rightarrow$ IND-atk-P $\Rightarrow$ IND-atk-Z for atk $\in \{CSA, CRA\}$, and also IND-CRA-csp $\Rightarrow$ IND-CSA-csp for csp $\in \{Z, P, A\}$. This leaves three equivalences and two separation results. IND-CSA-Z and IND-CRA-Z are equivalent since it is always possible to simulate the $\mathcal{O}.upl$ queries of an IND-CRA-Z adversary: this adversary can only use $\mathcal{O}.store$ to place items in ST that it can later retrieve (since $\mathcal{O}.LR$ and $\mathcal{O}.upl$ are forbidden), and by correctness this means a simulator can just keep track of these queries in a table. A similar approach can be used to show that IND-CSA-P and IND-CRA-P are equivalent. To show that IND-CSA-P and IND-CSA-A are equivalent, the simulator needs to successfully simulate $\mathcal{O}.insert$ and $\mathcal{O}.erase$ queries. This is indeed possible: the simulator keeps track of such queries in a table. As we have mentioned, the CS built using no encryption is IND-atk-Z. It is however not IND-CSA-P: the adversary simply performs one $\mathcal{O}.LR$ query with distinct files and then queries $\mathcal{O}.peek$ on that entry. We henceforth refer to these three distinct notions using IND-atk-Z, IND-CSA-P and IND-CRA-A.

---

[4] In deduplicating schemes segmentation can be a side channel in itself [24]. If the adversary can observe a distinguishable error symbol as part of its $\mathcal{O}.LR$ queries then this may cause issues. We strictly disallow this by not returning anything to the adversary and assuming a stringent restriction on allowed file pairs for $\mathcal{O}.LR$.

$$\text{IND-CSA-Z} \underset{\not\Rightarrow}{\Leftarrow} \begin{array}{c} \text{IND-CSA-P} \\ \text{IND-CRA-P} \\ \text{IND-CSA-A} \end{array} \underset{\not\Rightarrow}{\Leftarrow} \text{IND-CRA-A}$$

Fig. 4. Relations between IND notions for confidentiality of cloud storage systems.

4.2   Achieving Confidentiality in Cloud Storage

In the full version we show four straightforward reductions, showing that the intuitive protocols that we expect to meet all security goals – strong encryption with random file identifiers – do in fact provide confidentiality. Formal statements are omitted due to space constraints, but we summarize the results in Fig. 5. We show that if users encrypt using an IND-CPA-secure SKE scheme using their own fixed key then the overall system is IND-CSA-P secure (and thus also IND-CRA-P and IND-CSA-A secure). Specifically, key generation for CS outputs a random key to each user (or, kgen runs the SKE's KG algorithm) and fkeyGen(F, uk) outputs uk for all F. We go on to show that this same construction, when implemented with an AEAD scheme, yields an IND-CRA-A-secure cloud storage system, our strongest notion. The scenario in which a random symmetric key is created for each file, perhaps surprisingly meets the strongest IND-CRA-A notion of security even with IND-CPA-secure encryption. Finally we consider the secure deduplication setting with (a reduction to) PRV-CDA security of the underlying encryption: for this we need a modified security experiment (see full version). These theorems emphasize the simplicity and versatility of the model.

Theorem	Key Usage	Encryption	Conf of CS
1	Per-user	+ IND-CPA	$\Rightarrow$ IND-CSA-P
2	Per-user	+ AEAD	$\Rightarrow$ IND-CRA-A
3	Per-file	+ IND-CPA	$\Rightarrow$ IND-CRA-A
4	File-derived	+ PRV-CDA	$\Rightarrow$ PRV-CSA-P

Fig. 5. Summary of the composition results.

Deduplicating Systems Using File-Derived Keys. A natural way for using SKE in deduplicating systems is to derive encryption keys from the files themselves [4,8]. Cloud storage schemes with this property cannot achieve the usual indistinguishability notion because the adversary knows the possible files and therefore the possible encryption keys used. For such schemes, PRV-CDA [4] asks an adversary to distinguish ciphertexts when files are sampled from some pre-chosen high-entropy probability space and then encrypted. The probability space must be independent of the encryption scheme to avoid pathological situations, hence pre-chosen. This security notion can be achieved by both deterministic [4] and randomised schemes [1,4]. Based on such an encryption scheme, we define a natural cloud storage scheme by having fkeyGen simply run the encryption scheme's key derivation algorithm. We define a notion of security for such cloud storage similar to PRV-CDA, where we sample two vectors of files and store every file from one of those vectors. The adversary's task is to determine which vector was stored. In the full version we define this notion and prove the natural theorem, stated as the last line of Fig. 5.

4.3 Deduplicating Schemes with Non-trivial fkeyGen Procedures

The results so far in this section have only considered schemes for which fkeyGen is an operation that can be run locally, without the need for communicating with other users, the server or third parties (i.e. lines 1–4 of Fig. 2)[5]. While our model (Fig. 1) can handle deduplicating schemes with complex fkeyGen protocols such as that of Liu et al. [18], Duan [10] and Keelveedhi et al. [15], our security definitions do not fully capture them due to the 'unnatural' inputs to fkeyGen when 'called' by store. A simple extension to our framework allows analysis of such schemes: an $\mathcal{O}$.fkeyGen oracle that can be called on arbitrary inputs.

Our model is also easily extensible to the distributed storage context: the $\mathcal{O}$.peek oracle, instead of returning the tuple $\{(\mathsf{uid}, c, \mathsf{id}, 0/1)\}$, could take as input some indices that correspond to different servers and return the information stored on that subset of the servers, if any, under uid and id. This would enable a rigorous analysis of schemes such as CDStore [17].

It is straightforward to create a variant, D-IND, of our generic IND experiment for deterministic encryption: the adversary is not allowed to send the same file to $\mathcal{O}$.LR or $\mathcal{O}$.store. In particular, the experiment initializes an empty list, and on each F or (F_0, F_1) query to store, resp. $\mathcal{O}$.LR, that value is added to the list. If the adversary later attempts to perform $\mathcal{O}$.store or $\mathcal{O}$.LR with a file already on that list, return $\perp$. Certainly any scheme that is IND-atk-csp is also D-IND-atk-csp for some $\{\mathsf{atk}, \mathsf{csp}\}$, and furthermore D-IND-atk-csp $\Rightarrow$ PRV-atk-csp.

Since Duan [10] showed that the DupLESS system achieves D-IND$ (in the random oracle model), we would expect that DupLESS would meet strong security in our model. However given that the adversary has a fkeyGen oracle as described above, DupLESS does not even meet D-IND-CSA-P. The attack is straightforward: The adversary calls its fkeyGen oracle on F_0 to get fk_{F_0}; then again for some distinct F_1 to get fk_{F_1}; calls $\mathcal{O}$.LR$_b(F_0, F_1)$ for some (uid, id) and does $\mathcal{O}$.peek(uid, id) to receive the c that F_b is stored under. All that is left to do is to attempt to decrypt c using the two keys it got from fkeyGen earlier to get F_b, then output b. This indicates how weak a D-IND$ notion is: in a realistic attack setting, it is trivial for an adversary that has (even only snapshot) access to the cloud's storage to be able to distinguish ciphertexts.

---

[5] The threshold scheme of Stanek et al. [27] is a special case since fkeyGen is run locally but the encryption algorithm is not a symmetric encryption scheme.

5   Integrity

Once a user of a cloud storage system has decided to use encryption to ensure confidentiality of files, the user will also wish that integrity is retained for ciphertexts sent to the CSP. One approach to this requirement is proofs of retrievability (PoR) [14], where users embed some data in their files (ciphertexts) and periodically engage in a protocol with the CSP to check that the files have not been deleted or modified. We consider the simpler problem of ensuring that retrieved files are correct. Our approach is inspired by ciphertext integrity notions from the cryptography literature. As before, we focus on generic results rather than concrete instantiations. We formally define a notion of integrity of ciphertexts for cloud storage schemes, denoted INT-SC (INTegrity of Stored Ciphertexts). The experiment is given in Fig. 6. An adversary, in control of a number of users of the cloud storage scheme CS, wins the game by making a user retrieve a file that either the user had *previously deleted*, or that the user *did not store in the first place*. This rules out schemes for which possessing a file hash alone indicates ownership (Dropbox pre-2011 [9,22], content distribution networks, etc.): in Sect. 5.3 we discuss ciphertext integrity in such deduplicating systems.

5.1   Defining Integrity for Cloud Storage

What follows is a definition of integrity for cloud storage with three flavours corresponding to the different levels of server compromise detailed in Sect. 4.1. We call this notion INT-SC-csp for csp $\in \{Z, P, A\}$.

We use a second storage table TrueST to track all activities that the adversary makes the (notional) *users* do: store, retr and del. The other ST tracks all of these activities in addition to the oracles modelling active server compromise: $\mathcal{O}$.erase and $\mathcal{O}$.insert. In Sect. 5.2 we focus on actively corrupted servers manipulating the storage database: the adversary will always have access to $\mathcal{O}$.peek, $\mathcal{O}$.erase and $\mathcal{O}$.insert and this corresponds to INT-SC-A. We will later consider integrity in client-side deduplicating systems: there an adversarial client (INT-SC-Z) is (inherently) given more power by the mechanism that saves communication bandwidth. Note that in the description of $\mathcal{O}$.retr′, the code if $\{(\text{uid}, \cdot, \text{id}, \cdot) \in \text{ST}\} \neq \{(\text{uid}, \cdot, \text{id}, \cdot) \in \text{TrueST}\}$ means that for fixed uid and id, if there exists an entry in ST and an entry in TrueST such that the tuples are not exactly equal then this condition is met. Thus if the ciphertext component or the deletion bit (or both) being different means that this condition is achieved.

Definition 3 (INT-SC-csp for Cloud Storage). *Let* CS *be a cloud storage system based on symmetric encryption as in Fig. 1, and let* $\mathcal{A}$ *be an adversary. Then the* INT-SC-csp *advantage for an adversary* $\mathcal{A}$ *and* csp $\in \{Z, P, A\}$ *against* CS *is defined by*

$$\mathbf{Adv}_{\text{CS}, \mathcal{A}}^{\text{INT-SC-csp}} = \mathbf{Pr}\left[\mathbf{Exp}_{\text{CS}, \mathcal{A}}^{\text{INT-SC-csp}} = 1\right],$$

where experiments $\mathbf{Exp}_{\text{CS}, \mathcal{A}}^{\text{INT-SC-csp}}$ *are defined in Fig. 6.*

$$\frac{\mathsf{Exp}_{\mathsf{CS},\,\mathcal{A}}^{\mathsf{INT\text{-}SC\text{-}csp}} :}{b \leftarrow 0}$$
ST $\leftarrow \emptyset$
TrueST $\leftarrow \emptyset$
$\mathcal{A}^{\mathsf{oracles}}$
return b

$\mathcal{O}.\mathsf{del}'(\mathsf{uid}, \mathsf{id})$:
    do del(uid, id)
    if (uid, $\cdot$, id, 0) $\in$ TrueST then
       TrueST $\xleftarrow{\cup}$ (uid, $\cdot$, id, 1)

$\mathcal{O}.\mathsf{store}'(\mathsf{uid}, \mathsf{F}, \mathsf{id})$:
    do store(uid, F, id)
    TrueST $\xleftarrow{\cup}$ {(uid, c, id, 0)}, where
       (uid, c, id, 0) $\in$ ST

$\mathcal{O}.\mathsf{retr}'(\mathsf{uid}, \mathsf{id})$:
    do F $\leftarrow$ retr(uid, id)
    if {(uid, $\cdot$, id, $\cdot$) $\in$ ST} $\neq$ {(uid, $\cdot$, id, $\cdot$) $\in$ TrueST}
       and F $\neq \perp$
    then $b \leftarrow 1$
    return F

Fig. 6. The experiment defining INT-SC-csp for cloud storage. The adversary has access to $\mathcal{O}.\mathsf{newuC}$, $\mathcal{O}.\mathsf{newuH}$, $\mathcal{O}.\mathsf{store}'$, $\mathcal{O}.\mathsf{upl}$, $\mathcal{O}.\mathsf{del}'$ and $\mathcal{O}.\mathsf{retr}'$. If csp = P, the adversary additionally has access to $\mathcal{O}.\mathsf{peek}$; if csp = A, the adversary additionally has access to $\mathcal{O}.\mathsf{erase}$ and $\mathcal{O}.\mathsf{insert}$. Oracles that are not explicitly stated are as defined in Fig. 3.

Our definition of del in Fig. 1 firstly removes the KT entry and then updates ST if an applicable entry exists. This formulation makes it extremely difficult for an adversary to win the INT-SC-csp game by retrieving a file it previously deleted since it has no ability to edit KT. If del would only delete the KT entry after checking existence in ST then this would allow a trivial way to de-synchronize TrueST and ST. We believe this exposition gives the clearest possible definition of ciphertext integrity for cloud storage systems as we have defined them.

5.2 Achieving Integrity in Cloud Storage

In the full version [6] we show how to construct a cloud storage protocol that meets our strongest INT-SC-A notion. The construction is straightforward: each user holds their own symmetric key and uses an encryption scheme that is INT-CTXT secure during the store procedure (line 2 from Fig. 2). For this we require the syntax for an encryption scheme that can handle associated data – the associated data is the handle id.

Theorem 5. Per-user keys + SKE(AD = id) + INT-CTXT $\Rightarrow$ INT-SC-A.

Further, we prove an intuitive theorem inspired by Bellare and Namprempre's IND-CPA + INT-CTXT $\Rightarrow$ IND-CCA2 result for symmetric encryption [5].

Theorem 6. IND-CSA-P + INT-SC-A $\Rightarrow$ IND-CRA-A.

5.3 Integrity in Deduplicating Schemes

For deterministic schemes such as convergent encryption (fk $\leftarrow$ H(F)) an adversary with active server compromise can trivially create new ciphertexts that decrypt correctly. For this reason Bellare et al. (BKR) [4] discussed tag consistency (see full version for TC and STC exposition). BKR's tags served a different

<u>init</u>
01. $\mathsf{ST} \leftarrow \emptyset$

<u>newu(uid)</u>
02. $\mathsf{uk}_{\mathsf{uid}} \leftarrow \mathsf{kgen}$
03. $\mathsf{KT}_{\mathsf{uid}} \leftarrow \emptyset$
04. **return** $\mathsf{uk}_{\mathsf{uid}}$

<u>del(uid, id)</u>
05. $\mathsf{KT}_{\mathsf{uid}} \xleftarrow{\cup} \{(\bot, \mathsf{id}, \tau)\}$
06. **if** $\exists \{\mathsf{uid}, \cdot, \mathsf{id}, \tau, 0\}$ in ST **then**
07. $\mathsf{ST} \xleftarrow{\cup} \{(\mathsf{uid}, -, \mathsf{id}, \tau, 1)\}$

<u>store(uid, F, id)</u>
08. $\mathsf{fk} \leftarrow \mathsf{fkeyGen}(\mathsf{F}, \mathsf{uk}_{\mathsf{uid}})$
09. $c \leftarrow \mathsf{E}_{\mathsf{fk}}(\mathsf{F}, \mathsf{id})$
10. $\tau \leftarrow \mathsf{TGen}(c)$
11. $\mathsf{upl}(\mathsf{uid}, c, \mathsf{id}, \tau)$
12. $\mathsf{KT}_{\mathsf{uid}} \xleftarrow{\cup} \{(\mathsf{fk}, \mathsf{id}, \tau)\}$

<u>upl(uid, c, τ, id)</u>
13. $\mathsf{ST} \xleftarrow{\cup} \{(\mathsf{uid}, c, \mathsf{id}, \tau, 0)\}$

<u>retr(uid, id)</u>
14. **if** $\exists (\mathsf{uid}, \cdot, \mathsf{id}, \tau, 1) \in \mathsf{ST}$ **or**
15. $\exists (\bot, \mathsf{id}, \tau) \in \mathsf{KT}_{\mathsf{uid}}$ **then**
16.   **return** $\bot$
17. **if** $\exists (\mathsf{uid}, c, \mathsf{id}, \tau, 0) \in \mathsf{ST}$ **and**
18. $\exists (\mathsf{fk}, \mathsf{id}, \tau) \in \mathsf{KT}_{\mathsf{uid}}$ **then**
19. $\mathsf{F} \leftarrow \mathsf{D}_{\mathsf{fk}}(c, \mathsf{id})$
19a. $\tau' \leftarrow \mathsf{TGen}(c)$
19b.   **if** $\tau' \neq \tau$ **then**
19c.   **return** $\bot_{\mathsf{tag}}$
20.   **return** F
21. **else**
22.   **return** $\bot$

Fig. 7. Definition of a deduplicating cloud storage scheme DCS[SKE.Dedup].

purpose to our handles as their syntax assumes the server does not track the set of allowed users for each file (i.e. tag ownership is enough to retrieve). This assumption opens up systems to duplicate-faking attacks [28] in which a malicious client can find a tag collision for a target file, upload an ill-formed ciphertext under that tag, and stop genuine users from retrieving the target file. Assumption 1 rules out this type of attack, so we must consider a modified system model to include an additional tagging algorithm, formalized in Fig. 7.

A *deduplicating cloud storage scheme* is a tuple DCS = (init, newu, store, retr, del) as before, but in addition to SKE = (KG, E, D) and fkeyGen we also require a TGen algorithm. We follow BKR and define the TGen algorithm as acting on ciphertexts only: $\tau \leftarrow \mathsf{TGen}(c)$. This is without loss of generality: the HCE1, HCE2 and RCE schemes that they describe calculate $\tau \leftarrow \mathsf{H}(\mathsf{fk})$ to give a ciphertext formed as $\tau \| \mathsf{E}_{\mathsf{fk}}(\mathsf{F})$, then the TGen algorithm parses this value and outputs τ. Again following BKR we define a *deduplicating encryption mechanism* SKE.Dedup = (fkeyGen, E, D, TGen) that combines an SKE's encryption and decryption algorithms with the fkeyGen and TGen procedures. BKR called this primitive an MLE, and their definition was for generic KG: for our purposes it is sufficient to only consider the fkeyGen algorithm we have previously described since in the deduplicating scenario fkeyGen typically does not use any material that is unique to each user. This combined construction defines all the inputs to the wider cloud storage system: we write this as DCS[SKE.Dedup].

In a client-side deduplicating cloud storage system, the upl procedure will be a two stage process: first the user sends τ, gets a response indicating whether it should send the ciphertext or not, and finally sends the ciphertext if asked to.

In our syntax line 13 initially only requires $(\mathsf{uid}, \mathsf{id}, \tau)$ as inputs and checks its storage for a tag match: **if** $\exists \{\cdot, c, \cdot, \tau, \cdot\} \in \mathsf{ST}$ **then** $\mathsf{ST} \xleftarrow{\cup} \{(\mathsf{uid}, c, \mathsf{id}, \tau, 0)\}$. If a match is not found, the server sends a message, sometimes called a *deduplication signal* [2], to the user indicating that ciphertext transmission is necessary.

Lines 19a–c in Fig. 7 represent an optional tag check that has a (possibly distinguishable) error symbol: this operation is employed by the HCE2 and RCE schemes described by BKR. If the tag check procedure is enforced as part of retr, then using a SKE.Dedup that is STC does in fact yield a DCS that is INT-SC-A. The result is stated here informally; the proof is in the full version.

Theorem 7. *If* DCS[SKE.Dedup] *implements the tag check (lines 19a-19c in Fig. 7) and if* SKE.Dedup *is* STC *then* DCS *is* INT-SC-A.

Acknowledgements. We thank Frederik Armknecht and Yao Jiang for input to discussions. We also thank anonymous reviewers for useful feedback. This research was funded by the Research Council of Norway under Project No. 248166.

References

1. Abadi, M., Boneh, D., Mironov, I., Raghunathan, A., Segev, G.: Message-locked encryption for lock-dependent messages. In: Canetti, R., Garay, J.A. (eds.) CRYPTO 2013. LNCS, vol. 8042, pp. 374–391. Springer, Heidelberg (2013). https://doi.org/10.1007/978-3-642-40041-4_21

2. Armknecht, F., Boyd, C., Davies, G.T., Gjøsteen, K., Toorani, M.: Side channels in deduplication: trade-offs between leakage and efficiency. In: Karri, R., Sinanoglu, O., Sadeghi, A., Yi, X. (eds.) AsiaCCS 2017, pp. 266–274. ACM (2017). https://doi.org/10.1145/3052973.3053019

3. Ateniese, G., et al.: Provable data possession at untrusted stores. In: Ning, P., di Vimercati, S.D.C., Syverson, P.F., (eds.) CCS 2007, pp. 598–609. ACM (2007). https://doi.org/10.1145/1315245.1315318

4. Bellare, M., Keelveedhi, S., Ristenpart, T.: Message-locked encryption and secure deduplication. In: Johansson, T., Nguyen, P.Q. (eds.) Advances in Cryptology - EUROCRYPT 2013. Lecture Notes in Computer Science, vol. 7881, pp. 296–312. Springer, Heidelberg (2013). https://doi.org/10.1007/978-3-642-38348-9_18

5. Bellare, M., Namprempre, C.: Authenticated encryption: relations among notions and analysis of the generic composition paradigm. In: Okamoto, T. (ed.) ASIACRYPT 2000. LNCS, vol. 1976, pp. 531–545. Springer, Heidelberg (2000). https://doi.org/10.1007/3-540-44448-3_41

6. Boyd, C., Davies, G.T., Gjøsteen, K., Toorani, M., Raddum, H.: Security notions for cloud storage and deduplication. IACR Cryptology ePrint Archive 2017/1208 (2017). http://eprint.iacr.org/2017/1208

7. Dang, H., Chang, E.: Privacy-preserving data deduplication on trusted processors. In: Fox, G.C. (ed.) 10th International Conference on Cloud Computing, pp. 66–73. IEEE (2017). https://doi.org/10.1109/CLOUD.2017.18

8. Douceur, J.R., Adya, A., Bolosky, W.J., Simon, D., Theimer, M.: Reclaiming space from duplicate files in a serverless distributed file system. In: ICDCS 2002, pp. 617–624 (2002). https://doi.org/10.1109/ICDCS.2002.1022312

9. Drago, I., Mellia, M., Munafò, M.M., Sperotto, A., Sadre, R., Pras, A.: Inside drop-box: understanding personal cloud storage services. In: Byers, J.W., Kurose, J., Mahajan, R., Snoeren, A.C. (eds.) IMC 2012, pp. 481–494. ACM (2012). https://doi.org/10.1145/2398776.2398827

10. Duan, Y.: Distributed key generation for encrypted deduplication: achieving the strongest privacy. In: Ahn, G., Oprea, A., Safavi-Naini, R. (eds.) CCSW 2014, pp. 57–68. ACM (2014). https://doi.org/10.1145/2664168.2664169

11. Gjøsteen, K.: Security notions for disk encryption. In: di Vimercati, S.C., Syverson, P., Gollmann, D. (eds.) ESORICS 2005. LNCS, vol. 3679, pp. 455–474. Springer, Heidelberg (2005). https://doi.org/10.1007/11555827_26

12. Halevi, S., Harnik, D., Pinkas, B., Shulman-Peleg, A.: Proofs of ownership in remote storage systems. In: Chen, Y., Danezis, G., Shmatikov, V. (eds.) CCS 2011, pp. 491–500. ACM (2011). https://doi.org/10.1145/2046707.2046765

13. Harnik, D., Pinkas, B., Shulman-Peleg, A.: Side channels in cloud services: dedu-plication in cloud storage. IEEE Secur. Priv. 2010 8(6), 40–47 (2010). https://doi.org/10.1145/2046707.2046765

14. Juels, A., Kaliski, Jr., B.S.K.: PORs: proofs of retrievability for large files. In: Ning, P., di Vimercati, S.D.C., Syverson, P.F. (eds.) CCS 2007, pp. 584–597. ACM (2007). https://doi.org/10.1145/1315245.1315317

15. Keelveedhi, S., Bellare, M., Ristenpart, T.: DupLESS: server-aided encryption for deduplicated storage. In: King, S.T. (ed.) USENIX Security 2013, pp. 179–194. USENIX (2013). https://www.usenix.org/conference/usenixsecurity13/technical-sessions/presentation/bellare

16. Kunz, T., Wolf, R.: OmniCloud - the secure and flexible use of cloud storage ser-vices. Technical report Fraunhofer Institute SIT (2014). https://www.omnicloud.sit.fraunhofer.de/download/omnicloud-whitepaper-en.pdf

17. Li, M., Qin, C., Li, J., Lee, P.P.C.: CDStore: toward reliable, secure, and cost-efficient cloud storage via convergent dispersal. IEEE Internet Comput. 20(3), 45–53 (2016). https://doi.org/10.1109/MIC.2016.45

18. Liu, J., Asokan, N., Pinkas, B.: Secure deduplication of encrypted data without additional independent servers. In: CCS 2015, pp. 874–885 (2015). https://doi.org/10.1145/2810103.2813623

19. Liu, J., Asokan, N., Pinkas, B.: Secure deduplication of encrypted data without additional independent servers. In: IACR Cryptology ePrint Archive 2015/455 (2015). http://eprint.iacr.org/2015/455

20. Liu, J., Duan, L., Li, Y., Asokan, N.: Secure deduplication of encrypted data: refined model and new constructions. In: Smart, N.P. (ed.) CT-RSA 2018. LNCS, vol. 10808, pp. 374–393. Springer, Cham (2018). https://doi.org/10.1007/978-3-319-76953-0_20

21. Messmer, S., Rill, J., Achenbach, D., Müller-Quade, J.: A novel cryptographic framework for cloud file systems and CryFS, a provably-secure construction. In: Livraga, G., Zhu, S. (eds.) DBSec 2017. LNCS, vol. 10359, pp. 409–429. Springer, Cham (2017). https://doi.org/10.1007/978-3-319-61176-1_23

22. Mulazzani, M., Schrittwieser, S., Leithner, M., Huber, M., Weippl, E.R.: Dark clouds on the horizon: using cloud storage as attack vector and online slack space. In: USENIX Security 2011. USENIX (2011)

23. Puzio, P., Molva, R., Önen, M., Loureiro, S.: Cloudedup: secure deduplication with encrypted data for cloud storage. In: CloudCom 2013, pp. 363–370. IEEE (2013). https://doi.org/10.1109/CloudCom.2013.54

24. Ritzdorf, H., Karame, G., Soriente, C., Capkun, S.: On information leakage in deduplicated storage systems. In: Weippl, E.R., Katzenbeisser, S., Payer, M., Mangard, S., Androulaki, E., Reiter, M.K. (eds.) CCSW 2016, pp. 61–72. ACM (2016). https://doi.org/10.1145/2996429.2996432

25. Shin, Y., Koo, D., Yun, J., Hur, J.: Decentralized server-aided encryption for secure deduplication in cloud storage. In: IEEE Transactions on Services Computing (2017). https://doi.org/10.1109/TSC.2017.2748594

26. Song, D.X., Wagner, D.A., Perrig, A.: Practical techniques for searches on encrypted data. In: IEEE Security and Privacy 2000, pp. 44–55. IEEE (2000). https://doi.org/10.1109/SECPRI.2000.848445

27. Stanek, J., Sorniotti, A., Androulaki, E., Kencl, L.: A secure data deduplication scheme for cloud storage. In: Christin, N., Safavi-Naini, R. (eds.) FC 2014. LNCS, vol. 8437, pp. 99–118. Springer, Heidelberg (2014). https://doi.org/10.1007/978-3-662-45472-5_8

28. Storer, M.W., Greenan, K.M., Long, D.D.E., Miller, E.L.: Secure data deduplication. In: Kim, Y., Yurcik, W. (eds.) StorageSS 2008, pp. 1–10. ACM (2008). https://doi.org/10.1145/1456469.1456471

29. Yang, K., Jia, X.: An efficient and secure dynamic auditing protocol for data storage in cloud computing. IEEE Trans. Parallel Distrib. Syst. **24**(9), 1717–1726 (2013). https://doi.org/10.1109/TPDS.2012.278

Forward Secrecy of SPAKE2

José Becerra[✉], Dimiter Ostrev, and Marjan Škrobot

Interdisciplinary Centre for Security, Reliability and Trust,
University of Luxembourg, 6, Avenue de la Fonte,
4364 Esch-sur-Alzette, Luxembourg
{jose.becerra,dimiter.ostrev,marjan.skrobot}@uni.lu

Abstract. Currently, the Simple Password-Based Encrypted Key Exchange (SPAKE2) protocol of Abdalla and Pointcheval (CT-RSA 2005) is being considered by the IETF for standardization and integration in TLS 1.3. Although it has been proven secure in the Find-then-Guess model of Bellare, Pointcheval and Rogaway (EUROCRYPT 2000), whether it satisfies some notion of *forward secrecy* remains an open question.

In this work, we prove that the SPAKE2 protocol satisfies the so-called *weak forward secrecy* introduced by Krawczyk (CRYPTO 2005). Furthermore, we demonstrate that the incorporation of key-confirmation codes in SPAKE2 results in a protocol that provably satisfies the stronger notion of *perfect forward secrecy*. As forward secrecy is an explicit requirement for cipher suites supported in the TLS handshake, we believe this work could fill the gap in the literature and facilitate the adoption of SPAKE2 in the recently approved TLS 1.3.

Keywords: Provable security
Password Authenticated Key Exchange · Forward secrecy
Common Reference String

1 Introduction

1.1 SPAKE2 Protocol

Password Authenticated Key Exchange (PAKE) protocols allow two users, who only share a *password*, to agree on a high-entropy *session key* over a hostile network. The goal is to use the established session key to build a *secure channel* between the involved parties. The nature of passwords makes PAKEs vulnerable to *on-line* dictionary attacks, where an adversary tries to impersonate a user by guessing his password, engaging in a protocol execution and verifying if its guess was correct. An offline dictionary attack occurs when the protocol execution allows an adversary to launch an exhaustive offline search of the password. The intuition of security requires PAKEs to be vulnerable to online dictionary attacks only. The seminal work in this area is the Encrypted Key Exchange (EKE) protocol of Bellovin and Merritt [1]. Since then, various PAKE protocols

© Springer Nature Switzerland AG 2018
J. Baek et al. (Eds.): ProvSec 2018, LNCS 11192, pp. 366–384, 2018.
https://doi.org/10.1007/978-3-030-01446-9_21

have been proposed: PPK and PAK [2,3], J-PAKE [4,5], SRP [6], SPEKE [7] and SPAKE2 [8]. In parallel, prominent complexity-theoric security models for PAKEs have been proposed to get assurance on the claimed security properties by performing a rigorous analysis of the protocol in question [2,9–12].

The SPAKE2 protocol, proposed by Abdalla and Pointcheval [8], is a one-round PAKE protocol proven secure in the Find-then-Guess (FtG) model of Bellare et al. [9] without considering *forward secrecy*. It is a simple, yet efficient protocol that, in addition to the pre-shared password, requires the protocol participants to share two Common Reference Strings (CRS) prior to the execution of the protocol. The adoption of the CRS yields to an elegant construction that does not require full domain hash functions, which are hard to implement efficiently in practice. On the other side, the CRS requires extra security assumptions that might be easy to satisfy in some scenarios but may be very restrictive in others [13]. Also, as it is a one-round protocol, only *implicit authentication* can be satisfied. Fortunately, the incorporation of *key-confirmation codes* allows the protocol participants to explicitly authenticate each other [14] and [15, Chap. 40].

Recently, the Internet Engineering Task Force (IEFT) community has revisited the deployment of SPAKE2 protocol: (i) as stand alone specification [16], (ii) its usage as pre-authentication mechanism in Kerberos protocol [17] and (iii) its adoption in TLS 1.3 protocol, specifically in the *handshake* when *pre-shared* keys for authentication are available [18,19]. The discussion of forward secrecy in SPAKE2 has been a common factor in the aforementioned Internet Drafts.

1.2   PAKEs Adoption in TLS

Nowadays, the Transport Layer Security (TLS) is the *de-facto* standard to protect internet communications. It consists of two stages: the *Handshake* protocol where two parties agree on a session key, and the *Record* protocol where the communication is protected using the previously negotiated keys. Most of the TLS implementations provide only *unilateral* authentication, where client C authenticates server S during the handshake by means of public-key infrastructure (PKI), therefore identity disclosure of client to server is usually not supported.

While the unilateral server-authenticated approach might be sufficient for scenarios like internet surfing, it is certainly inadequate for real-world applications including email access, internet banking and social media, where client C needs to authenticate to server S to gain access to resources in S. In practice, the common approach for authenticating the client asks the client to send his user/password protected through a server-authenticated TLS channel. This approach protects the password against eavesdroppers but not against phishing attacks: An adversary can clone a legitimate website and fool the client to visit the fake website where he input his credentials. To make things worse, the adversary can manage to obtain a valid public-key certificate from a certification authority (CA) for his illegitimate web page. Indeed, the client may see on his web browser "secure connection" as a TLS connection may be established between the client and the cloned website controlled by the adversary.[1]

Fortunately, PAKEs stand as a strong candidate for scenarios where two parties require to *mutually* authenticate each other while intrinsically protecting their shared password. In fact, the Secure Remote Password (SRP) protocol [6] has been incorporated in previous versions of TLS and standardized in the form of RFC5054 [20]. Specifically, the SRP protocol was made available as cipher suite in the TLS handshake. Similarly, the IETF is currently considering the adoption of SPAKE2 in TLS 1.3 *handshake* [18], in particular in the TLS handshake, for scenarios where authentication is made using pre-shared password available between the Client and Server.

In the recently approved TLS 1.3, it has explicitly been a design goal to provide *forward secrecy* for the session keys used to construct the TLS channel. In particular, *static* RSA and Diffie-Hellman cipher suites were removed to favor public-key based key-exchange mechanism that guarantee forward secrecy. Therefore, formally proving that SPAKE2 satisfies some significant notion of forward secrecy would increase its possibilities of acceptance into TLS 1.3.

Remark: While PAKEs adoption in web authentication is a good approach to protect user's password during the authentication phase, there are still *usability* concerns that slow down the implementation of PAKEs in TLS to properly prevent phishing attacks. This implementation requires an easy to identify "safe area" available in the web browser where the passwords should be entered [21].

1.3   Forward Secrecy

Forward secrecy is a desirable property which has been explicitly a design goal in relevant AKE and PAKE protocols [3,4,22,23], and more recently in TLS 1.3 [19].[2] Roughly speaking, it ensures the protection of session keys even if the long-term secret of the participants gets later compromised [24]. For instance: (i) the password file at the server could be leaked or (ii) via phishing attacks a client could reveal his password to some malicious entity.

The notion of forward secrecy appeared first in [24] and was later formalized in [23,25–27] for AKE and in [9,28] for PAKE protocols. We distinguish *weak forward secrecy* (wFS) from perfect forward secrecy (PFS): The former protects session keys after compromise of long-term key material, but only those sessions created *without the active participation of the attacker* [23], while the latter protects all session keys which were negotiated before corruption, i.e. even those created with the active intervention of the adversary. It is generally accepted that PFS is difficult to satisfy in protocols which only guarantee *implicit authentication*. For instance, Krawczyk [23] states that PFS cannot be satisfied by two-flow protocols using *public-key* as authentication mechanism. Therefore Krawczyk proposed the notion of *weak Forward Secrecy* (wFS) as an attempt to satisfy

---

[1] A typical client should not be expected to verify the certificate details.

[2] However, in TLS 1.3, there still remains some configurations that do not satisfy forward secrecy.

some notion of security when long-term material is compromised but only for those sessions without the active participation of the adversary.

PFS and Key-Confirmation: The authors in [3,9,25] demonstrated that PFS can be satisfied when *explicit authentication* is added to protocols that initially satisfy only wFS. The idea is the following: Suppose P is a 2-flow PAKE protocol satisfying only implicit authentication. The adversary sends the first message to Bob masquerading as Alice, Bob computes the session key, sends back the second message and finishes his protocol execution. Then the adversary waits for the leakage of the long-term key and that could *possibly* help her to compute the same session key as Bob. For this scenario, the notion of PFS requires the adversary not to learn Bob's session key, which can be easily avoided by requiring key-confirmation, since then Bob will not accept the session key before he authenticates his communication partner.

1.4 Our Contribution

We propose a new version of SPAKE2 which we name PFS-SPAKE2. This is essentially SPAKE2 but with key-confirmation codes incorporated into the protocol. This well known approach allowed us to meet the PFS requirement in a provably secure way even in the case of active adversaries, making it a suitable candidate for standardization and adoption in the TLS 1.3 protocol. In addition, we prove that the original SPAKE2 satisfies weak forward secrecy.

2 Security Model with Forward Secrecy

Notation. We use calligraphic letters to denote adversaries, typically $\mathcal{A}$ and $\mathcal{B}$. We write $s \xleftarrow{\$} S$ for sampling uniformly at random from set S and $|S|$ to denote its cardinality. The output of a probabilistic algorithm A on input x is denoted by $y \leftarrow A(x)$, while $y := F(x)$ denotes a deterministic assignment of $F(x)$ to the variable y. Let $\{0,1\}^*$ denote the bit string of arbitrary length while $\{0,1\}^l$ stands for those of length l. Let λ be the security parameter, $negl(\lambda)$ denote a negligible function and PPT stand for probabilistic polynomial time.

Next we describe the well-known security model of Bellare, Pointcheval and Rogaway [9], which we use to prove the security of PFS-SPAKE2 and SPAKE2 protocol. Frequently referred as the Find-then-Guess (FtG) model, it is an extension of [29,30] to the password setting. We assume the reader is familiar with the model.

PAKE PROTOCOL. A PAKE protocol is defined by a pair of algorithms $(Gen, \mathcal{P})$. Gen is the password generation algorithm. It takes as input the dictionary D, a probability distribution Q and initializes the protocol participants with some password. The protocol description $\mathcal{P}$ defines how honest participants behave.

PROTOCOL PARTICIPANTS. Each participant is either a client $C \in \mathcal{C}$ or a server $S \in \mathcal{S}$. Let $\mathcal{U} = \mathcal{C} \cup \mathcal{S}$ denote the set of all (honest) users and $\mathcal{C} \cap \mathcal{S} = \varnothing$.

LONG-TERM SECRETS. Each client C holds a password π_C and server S holds a vector of passwords for all clients i.e. $\pi_S =< \pi_C >_{C \in \mathcal{C}}$ s.t. for each client C $\pi_S[C] = \pi_C$. We consider the client-server scenario where there is a single server S. The passwords are assumed to be independent and uniformly distributed.

PROTOCOL EXECUTION. $\mathcal{P}$ is a probabilistic algorithm that defines how users respond to signals from the environment. We assume the presence of a PPT adversary $\mathcal{A}$ with full control of the network and an unlimited number of *user instances*. Specifically, let Π_U^i denote the instance i-th of user $U \in \mathcal{U}$. In cases where distinction matters, let Π_C^i and Π_S^j denote the i-th and j-th instance of client $C \in \mathcal{C}$ and server S respectively.

Security is defined via a game played between the challenger $\mathcal{CH}$ and adversary $\mathcal{A}$ whose goal is to break the semantic security of the established session keys. $\mathcal{A}$ controls the oracle user instances with the following queries:

- **Send**(U, i, m): A message m is sent to instance Π_U^i and processed according to the protocol description $\mathcal{P}$. Its output is given to $\mathcal{A}$.
- **Execute**(C, i, S, j): This query causes an honest run of protocol $\mathcal{P}$ between Π_C^i and Π_S^j, the transcript of execution is given to $\mathcal{A}$.
- **Reveal**(U, i): The session key sk_U^i held at Π_U^i is given to $\mathcal{A}$. It requires the sk_U^i to be already computed, i.e. Π_U^i must be on *terminate* state.
- **Corrupt**(U). The adversary obtains the password of user U. If $U = C \in \mathcal{C}$, then $\mathcal{A}$ receives π_C, else if $U = S$, then $\mathcal{A}$ receives $\pi_S =< \pi_C >_{C \in \mathcal{C}}$.
- **Test**(U, i): $\mathcal{CH}$ flips a bit b and answers the query as follows: if $b = 1$ $\mathcal{A}$ gets the session key sk_U^i, otherwise she receives $r \xleftarrow{\$} \{0,1\}^\kappa$, where $\{0,1\}^\kappa$ denotes the length of the session key space.

2.1 Definitions

Partnering. Two instances, Π_C^i and Π_S^j, are partnered if both *accept*, holding $(sk_C^i, sid_C^i, pid_C^i)$ and $(sk_S^j, sid_S^j, pid_S^j)$ respectively and also:

1. $sk_C^i = sk_S^j$, $sid_C^i = sid_S^j$, $pid_C^i = S$, $pid_S^j = C$ and
2. no other instance accepts with the same session identifier *sid*, except with negligible probability.

The notion of freshness avoids scenarios where an adversary could trivially win the security experiment. Next we define two notions of freshness depending on the desired of forward secrecy guarantee: The first flavour models PFS, where the intuition is to consider as legitimate targets of a Test query those instances which session keys were negotiated *before* the corruption of any principal. The second variant models wFS, which does not guarantee the secrecy of those sessions keys which were negotiated with the *active* intervention of an adversary (determined via *partnering*) whenever some user has been corrupted.

PFS-Freshness. An instance Π_U^i is *PFS-fresh* unless:

- A Reveal query was made to Π_U^i or its partner or

– There was a Corrupt(U') and a Send(U, i, m) query, Π_U^i does not have a partner and the corruption of any user U' occurs **before** the Test query.

wFS-Freshness. An instance Π_U^i is *wFS-fresh* unless:

– A Reveal query was made to Π_U^i or its partner or
– There was a Corrupt(U') and a Send(U, i, m) query, Π_U^i does not have a partner and the corruption of any user U' occurs at any time.

Advantage of the Adversary. Let $\mathrm{Succ}_P^{\mathrm{PFS\text{-}FtG}}$ be the event where $\mathcal{A}$ asks a single Test query directed to a *PFS-fresh* instance that has terminated, $\mathcal{A}$ outputs his guess b' and wins i.e. $b' = b$. The advantage of $\mathcal{A}$ attacking protocol P is:

$$\mathrm{Adv}_P^{\mathrm{PFS\text{-}FtG}}(\mathcal{A}) = 2 \cdot \Pr\left[\mathrm{Succ}_P^{\mathrm{FtG}}(\mathcal{A})\right] - 1 \tag{1}$$

Definition 1 *(PFS-FtG security). Protocol P is FtG secure and satisfies perfect forward secrecy if for all PPT adversaries there exists a negligible function $\epsilon(\cdot)$ such that:*

$$\mathrm{Adv}_P^{\mathrm{PFS\text{-}FtG}}(\mathcal{A}) \leq n_{se}/|D| + \epsilon(\lambda),$$

where n_{se} is the number of Send queries and D is the password dictionary.

We similarly define FtG security with *weak* forward secrecy, the only change is in the advantage function, where the Test query must be made to a wFS-fresh instance. From inspection, it is easy to see that PFS-FtG $\rightarrow$ wFS-FtG security.

2.2 Cryptographic Hardness Assumptions

Let $\mathbb{G}$ be a multiplicative a group, with generator g and $|\mathbb{G}| = q$. For $X = g^x$ and $Y = g^y$, let $\mathrm{DH}(X, Y) = g^{xy}$, where $\{g^x, g^y, g^{xy}\} \in \mathbb{G}$.

Definition 2 *(Computational Diffie-Hellman (CDH) Problem). Given (g, g^x, g^y) compute g^{xy}, where $\{g^x, g^y, g^{xy}\} \in \mathbb{G}$ and $(x, y) \xleftarrow{\$} \mathbb{Z}_q^2$. Let the advantage of an algorithm $\mathcal{A}$ in solving the CDH problem be:*

$$\mathrm{Adv}_{\mathbb{G}}^{\mathrm{CDH}}(\mathcal{B}) = \Pr\left[(x, y) \xleftarrow{\$} \mathbb{Z}_q^2, X = g^x, Y = g^y : \mathcal{B}(X, Y) = DH(X, Y)\right].$$

Under the *CDH assumption* there exist sequences of cyclic groups $\mathbb{G}$ indexed by λ s.t. $\forall \mathcal{B}$ running in time t polynomial in λ, $\mathrm{Adv}_{\mathbb{G}}^{\mathrm{CDH}}(\mathcal{B})$ is a negligible function.

3 PFS-SPAKE2

Inspired by MacKenzie's work [3], we propose to incorporate key-confirmation codes into the SPAKE2 protocol [8] to achieve PFS in a provably secure manner.

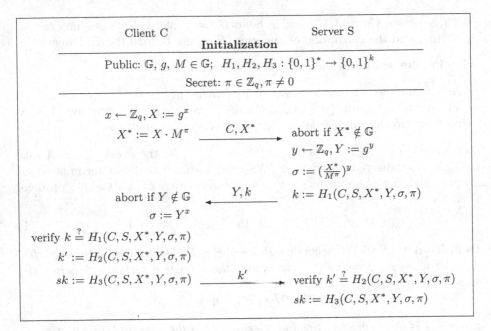

Fig. 1. PFS-SPAKE2 protocol.

3.1 Protocol Description

In Fig. 1 we provide the technical description of the proposed PFS-SPAKE2 protocol. Before the protocol is executed, public parameters must be chosen and published. These parameters include the description of group $\mathbb{G}$, hash functions H_1, H_2, H_3 and a CRS M – which we require to be choosen at random from $\mathbb{G}$ and its discrete logarithm to be kept secret. These constraints on the CRS can be achieved either by having a third trusted party or by assuming a public source of randomness to publicly derive M. Our protocol is instantiated over group $\mathbb{G}$, a q order subgroup of $\mathbb{Z}_p^*$ where CDH assumption holds and p, q are safe prime numbers. The protocol requires that passwords are encoded in $\mathbb{Z}_q$.

Comparison to Existing PAKEs. The efficiency of a PAKE protocol is defined by (i) the number of communication rounds until the protocol terminates, (ii) the total number messages exchanged and (iii) the computational cost of the protocol. Compared to the original SPAKE2, the proposed PFS-SPAKE2 protocol benefits from *explicit* authentication and strong security guarantees for PFS. It is also slightly less computationally expensive, as it requires the client to compute only three exponentiations instead of four, i.e. no need to compute $N^\pi \in \mathbb{G}$. These improvements usually come at the cost of increasing the number of rounds and message flows and unfortunately our protocol is not an exception [3,23].

Table 1. Comparison with existing PAKEs for Client-Server scenarios.

Protocol[a]	Commn.[b]	Computation[c]	Rounds/ Flows	Hardness Asm.[d]	Forward Secrecy	Key Confirm.
EKE [1,9]	$2 \times \mathbb{G}$	4 exp., 2 enc.	1/2	CDH	wFS	No
SPEKE [7,32]	$2 \times \mathbb{G} + 2\kappa$	4 exp.	2/4	DIDH	-	Yes
PPK [3]	$2 \times \mathbb{G}$	6 exp.	1/2	CDH	-	No
PAK [3]	$2 \times \mathbb{G} + 2\kappa$	5 exp.	3/3	CDH	PFS	Yes
J-PAKE[d] [4]	$12 \times \mathbb{G} + 6 \times \mathbb{Z}_q$	28 exp.	2/4	DSDH	PFS	No
J-PAKE* [4]	$12 \times \mathbb{G} + 6 \times \mathbb{Z}_q$	28 exp.	3/6	DSDH	PFS	Yes
SPAKE2 [8]	$2 \times \mathbb{G}$	6 exp.	1/2	CDH	wFS	No
PFS-SPAKE2	$2 \times \mathbb{G} + 2\kappa$	5 exp.	3/3	CDH	PFS	Yes

[a]J-PAKE* is simply J-PAKE but with an extra round for key-confirmation.
[b]Communication. $\mathbb{G}$ denotes a group element, $\mathbb{Z}_p$ a scalar and κ a κ-bit string.
[c]Exp. denotes an exponentiation in $\mathbb{G}$ and enc. an encryption and decryption operation.
[d]DSDH and DIDH stand for Decision Square and Decision Inverted-Additive Diffie-Hellman.

In Table 1 we summarize the comparison of PFS-SPAKE2 with other relevant PAKE protocols with full security proofs.[3] Notably J-PAKE satisfies PFS and requires only two communication rounds; however, it is computationally more expensive than PFS-SPAKE2 as the former requires 28 exponentiations while the latter only 5. Furthermore, J-PAKE with key-confirmation requires the same number of communication rounds as PFS-SPAKE2. Alternatively, PAK and PFS-SPAKE2 are similar in terms of efficiency, PFS and key confirmation guarantees, yet the usage of CRS in the latter allowed us to achieve *tighter* security reductions to the CDH assumption than the original results for PAK [3,31].

3.2 Security of PFS-SPAKE2

Theorem 1 *(Security in the PFS-FtG Model). Let P be the protocol specified in Fig. 1, instantiated in group $\mathbb{G}$ and with passwords uniformly distributed over dictionary D. Let $\mathcal{A}$ be an adversary that runs in time t polynomial in λ, makes at most n_{ex}, n_{se}, n_{ro} queries of type execute, send and random oracle. Then:*

$$\mathrm{Adv}_P^{\mathrm{PFS\text{-}FtG}}(\mathcal{A}) \leq \frac{n_{se}}{|D|} + \mathcal{O}\left(\frac{(n_{se}+n_{ex})(n_{se}+n_{ex}+n_{ro})}{q} + \right.$$

$$\left. n_{ro} \cdot \mathrm{Adv}_{\mathbb{G}}^{\mathrm{CDH}}(\mathcal{B}^{\mathcal{A}}) + n_{se}n_{ro} \cdot \mathrm{Adv}_{\mathbb{G}}^{\mathrm{CDH}}(\tilde{\mathcal{B}}^{\mathcal{A}}) + n_{ro}^2 \cdot \mathrm{Adv}_{\mathbb{G}}^{\mathrm{CDH}}(\hat{\mathcal{B}}^{\mathcal{A}}) \right),$$

where $\mathcal{B}^{\mathcal{A}}$, $\tilde{\mathcal{B}}^{\mathcal{A}}$ and $\hat{\mathcal{B}}^{\mathcal{A}}$ are CDH-solver algorithms running in time $t' = \mathcal{O}(t + (n_{se} + n_{ex} + n_{ro}) \cdot t_{exp})$, where t_{exp} is the time for an exponentiation in $\mathbb{G}$.

---

[3] The server usually stores some function $f(\cdot)$ of the password while the clients needs to compute $f(\pi)$ for every protocol run. This difference is relevant in (i) PPK, PAK and (ii) SPAKE2 and PFS-SPAKE2, as $f(\cdot)$ requires hashing into groups in (i) and group exponentiations in (ii).

To prove the security of PFS-SPAKE2, we introduce a sequence of protocols $P_0 \ldots P_7$, where P_0 is the original protocol and P_7 allows only online dictionary attacks. Let G_i be the security game associated to P_i. We borrow from [3] the structure and the nomenclature to prove the security of our PFS-SPAKE2 protocol and refer to Appendix A for the necessary terminology.

The security proof requires the random oracle model: each *new* random oracle query H_l for $l \in \{1, 2, 3\}$ is answered with a fresh random output, however, if the query has been previously made, it is answered consistenly with previous queries. In cases where it is clear enough, we write $H_l(\cdot)$ to refer to query of the form $H_l(C, S, X^*, Y, \sigma, \pi)$. For easiness of the proof we assume that for each $H_l(C, S, X^*, Y, \sigma, \pi)$ query made by $\mathcal{A}$, with $l \in \{1, 2, 3\}$, the corresponding $H_{l'}(\cdot)$ and $H_{l''}(\cdot)$ are also made, with $l', l'' \in \{1, 2, 3\} \setminus \{l\}$ and $l' \neq l''$. The simulator sets $M := g^m \in \mathbb{G}$, where $m \stackrel{\$}{\leftarrow} \mathbb{Z}_q$.

In the following games, we simply write $\mathrm{Succ}_{P_i}^{\mathrm{FtG}}$ instead of $\mathrm{Succ}_{P_i}^{\mathrm{PFS\text{-}FtG}}$ to denote the success probability of $\mathcal{A}$ winning in game G_i.

Game G_0: Execution of original protocol.
Game G_1: Uniqueness of honest sessions.

During the interaction with adversary $\mathcal{A}$, the challenger needs to simulate honest instances and generate the X^* and Y terms according to the protocol description. Let F_1 be the event where there is a collision between either an X^* or Y value, with previously seen X^* or Y values. If F_1 occurs, the challenger draws random values again until he arrives at a X^* or Y term that has not been previously seen. It is easy to show that the probability of F_1 occurring is bounded by the birthday paradox. Then for all $\mathcal{A}$:

$$\Pr\left[\mathrm{Succ}_{P_0}^{\mathrm{FtG}}(\mathcal{A})\right] \leq \Pr\left[\mathrm{Succ}_{P_1}^{\mathrm{FtG}}(\mathcal{A})\right] + \mathcal{O}\left(\frac{(n_{se} + n_{ex})(n_{se} + n_{ex} + n_{ro})}{q}\right).$$

Game G_2: Prevent Lucky Guesses on Hash Outputs.
This game forces $\mathcal{A}$ to query the random oracle whenever she needs to compute any hash $H(\cdot)_l$. As a result, this game rules out the possibility of $\mathcal{A}$ to output correct values k, k' or sk without calling the corresponding random oracle.

Let P_2 be a protocol identical to P_1, except that honest instances respond to Send and Execute queries without making any random oracle queries and subsequent random oracle queries made by $\mathcal{A}$ are backpatched to be consistent with previous queries. Next we detail the changes in P_2.

- In an Execute(C, i, S, j) query set $X^* = g^{\tau[C,i]}$ and $Y = g^{\tau[S,j]}$, where $\tau[\cdot] \stackrel{\$}{\leftarrow} \mathbb{Z}_q$, $k, k' \stackrel{\$}{\leftarrow} \{0,1\}^\kappa$ and $sk_S^j \leftarrow sk_C^i \stackrel{\$}{\leftarrow} \{0,1\}^\kappa$, where $\{0,1\}^\kappa$ denotes the session key space.
- In a CLIENT ACTION 0 query to Π_C^i, set $X^* = g^{\tau[C,i]}$, where $\tau[C, i] \stackrel{\$}{\leftarrow} \mathbb{Z}_q$.
- In a SERVER ACTION 1 query to Π_S^j, set $Y = g^{\tau[S,j]}$ and $k \stackrel{\$}{\leftarrow} \{0,1\}^\kappa$, where $\tau[S, j] \stackrel{\$}{\leftarrow} \mathbb{Z}_q$.

- In a CLIENT ACTION 1 query to Π_C^i proceed as follows:
  - If Π_C^i is paired with Π_S^j then set $k', sk_C^i \xleftarrow{\$} \{0,1\}^\kappa$.
  - Else if this query triggers a $\mathbf{testpw}(C, i, S, \pi_c, l)$ event, for some $l \in \{1, 2, 3\}$, then set k' and sk_C^i to the associated value of the event $\mathbf{testpw}$ $(C, i, S, \pi_c, 2)$ and $\mathbf{testpw}(C, i, S, \pi_c, 3)$ respectively.
  - Else Π_C^i aborts.

- In a SERVER ACTION 2 query to Π_S^j proceed as follows:
  - If Π_S^j is *paired with* Π_C^i *after* some CLIENT ACTION 1 query to Π_C^i, then set $sk_S^j \leftarrow sk_C^i$.
  - Else this query triggers a $\mathbf{testpw}(S, j, C, \pi_c, l)$, with $l \in \{1, 2, 3\}$, set sk_S^j to the associated value of the event $\mathbf{testpw}(S, j, C, \pi_c, 3)$.
  - Else instance Π_S^j aborts.
- In an $H_l(C, S, X^*, Y, \sigma, \pi)$ query made by $\mathcal{A}$, if it triggers a $\mathbf{testpw}$ (C, i, S, π_C, l), $\mathbf{testpw}(S, j, C, \pi_C, l)$ or $\mathbf{testexecpw}(C, i, S, j, \pi_C)$ event, then output the associated event of the corresponding event. Otherwise output $v \xleftarrow{\$} \{0,1\}^\kappa$.

Claim 1. *For all adversaries* $\mathcal{A}$, $\Pr\left[\mathrm{Succ}_{P_1}^{\mathrm{FtG}}(\mathcal{A})\right] \leq \Pr\left[\mathrm{Succ}_{P_2}^{\mathrm{FtG}}(\mathcal{A})\right] + \frac{n_{se}}{2^\kappa}$.

Proof. In SERVER ACTION 2 to Π_S^j, the input k' determines whether the instance Π_S^j should *terminate* or *abort*. Let F_1 be the event where in a SERVER ACTION 2 to Π_S^j, it terminates such that (i) Π_S^j is not paired with Π_C^i and (ii) $\mathbf{testpw}(S, j, C, \pi_C, l)$ event does not occur, for $l \in \{1, 2, 3\}$, i.e. $\mathcal{A}$ luckily guessed the correct k' value. Then $\Pr[F_1] \leq n_{se}/2^\kappa$. $\square$

Game G_3: Do not backpatch $H_l(\cdot)$ queries against Execute queries.
This game shows that there is no need to backpatch $H_l(\cdot)$ queries to maintain consistent views against Execute queries. More formally, let P_3 be identical to P_2 except that, in a $H_l(C, S, X^*, Y, \sigma, \pi_C)$ query made by $\mathcal{A}$, the simulator does not verify whether the $\mathbf{testexec}(C, i, S, j, \pi_C)$ event occurs or not. Let F_2 and F_3 denote the $\mathbf{testexec}(C, i, S, j, \pi_C)$ event occurring in P_2 and P_3 respectively.

Claim 2. *For all adversaries* $\mathcal{A}$, $|\Pr\left[\mathrm{Succ}_{P_2}^{\mathrm{FtG}}(\mathcal{A})\right] - \Pr\left[\mathrm{Succ}_{P_3}^{\mathrm{FtG}}(\mathcal{A})\right]| \leq \Pr[F_2]$.

Proof. P_2 and P_3 are identical protocols until the $\mathbf{testexec}(C, i, S, j, \pi_C)$ event occurs. The observation is that the events F_2 and F_3 are triggered as result of some interaction $\mathcal{CH}_2$ vs $\mathcal{A}$ and $\mathcal{CH}_3$ vs $\mathcal{A}$ respectively, however by definition they are identical. Then it follows that $\Pr[F_2] = \Pr[F_3]$ and to conclude the proof we simply apply Shoup's Difference Lemma [33]. $\square$

Claim 3. *Given* $\mathcal{A}$, *there exists a CDH-solver* $\mathcal{B}^{\mathcal{A}}$ *with running time* $t' = \mathcal{O}(t + (n_{se} + n_{ex} + n_{ro}) \cdot t_{exp})$ *such that:*

$$\Pr\left[\mathrm{Succ}_{P_2}^{\mathrm{FtG}}(\mathcal{A})\right] \leq \Pr\left[\mathrm{Succ}_{P_3}^{\mathrm{FtG}}(\mathcal{A})\right] + n_{ro} \cdot \mathrm{Adv}_{\mathbb{G}}^{\mathrm{CDH}}(\mathcal{B}^{\mathcal{A}}),$$

Proof. Let ϵ be the probability that **testexec**(C, i, S, j, π) event occurs in P_2. We build an adversary $\mathcal{B}^{\mathcal{A}}$ whose goal is to solve the CDH problem using adversary $\mathcal{A}$ as a subroutine and with success probability ϵ/n_{ro}. On input $(A = g^\alpha, B = g^\beta)$, $\mathcal{B}^{\mathcal{A}}$ *simulates* P_2 to $\mathcal{A}$ with the following changes:

1. For every Execute(C, i, S, j) query made by $\mathcal{A}$, the simulator $\mathcal{B}^{\mathcal{A}}$ sets $X^* = A \cdot g^{r_1}$, $Y = B \cdot g^{r_2}$, $k, k' \xleftarrow{\$} \{0,1\}^\kappa$ and $sk_S^j \leftarrow sk_C^i \xleftarrow{\$} \{0,1\}^\kappa$, where $r_1, r_2 \xleftarrow{\$} \mathbb{Z}_q$ are known to the simulator.
2. For every $H_l(C, S, X^*, Y, \sigma, \pi_C)$ query, where $l \in \{1, 2, 3\}$, X^* and Y are generated via an Execute(C, i, S, j) query, add γ to the set S-DH, where:

$$\gamma = \sigma \cdot B^{m \cdot \pi_C} \cdot M^{r_2 \cdot \pi_C} / B^{r_1} \cdot A^{r_2} \cdot g^{r_1 r_2}$$

3. When $\mathcal{A}$ finishes, the set S-DH contains at most n_{ro} elements, where each item a possible solution to DH(g^α, g^β). Then $\mathcal{B}^{\mathcal{A}}$ outputs $\gamma \xleftarrow{\$}$ L-DH.

The adversary $\mathcal{A}$ can only distinguish P_2 from P_3 once **testexec**(C, i, S, j, π) has occurred, but this happens with probability $\epsilon \le n_{ro} \cdot \text{Adv}_{G_q}^{\text{CDH}}(t')$. We make the observation that G_3 guarantees forward secrecy for session keys established via Execute queries.   □

Game G_4: Check for successful password guesses.
Let P_4 be identical to P_3, except that if **correctpw** event occurs, the protocol stops and the adversary automatically wins.

Claim 4. *For all PPT adversaries* $\mathcal{A}$, $\Pr\left[\text{Succ}_{P_3}^{\text{FtG}}(\mathcal{A})\right] \le \Pr\left[\text{Succ}_{P_4}^{\text{FtG}}(\mathcal{A})\right]$.

Proof. Obvious.   □

This game simply counts for an adversary who is successful in an online dictionary attack by impersonating either a Client or the Server. The implication is that from P_4, until either **correctpw** event or a Corrupt query occurs, no *unpaired* client or server instance will terminate.

Game G_5: Randomized session keys for paired instances.
Let P_5 be identical to P_4 except that if the **pairedpwguess** event occurs the protocol stops and the adversary fails.

In this game we will demonstrate that an adversary $\mathcal{A}$ who (i) may actively *corrupt* any Client or Server, i.e. $\mathcal{A}$ knows the corresponding *correct* password π_C and (ii) manages to compute k, k' or sk for *paired* instances Π_C^i and Π_S^j, is also a CDH-solver. Let F_4 and F_5 denote the **pairedpwguess** event occurring in P_4 and P_5 respectively.

Claim 5. *For all adversaries* $\mathcal{A}$, $\left|\Pr\left[\text{Succ}_{P_4}^{\text{FtG}}(\mathcal{A})\right] - \Pr\left[\text{Succ}_{P_5}^{\text{FtG}}(\mathcal{A})\right]\right| \le \Pr[F_4]$.

Proof. Identical to Claim 2.   □

Claim 6. *Given $\mathcal{A}$, there exists CDH-solver $\tilde{\mathcal{B}}^{\mathcal{A}}$ with running time $t' = \mathcal{O}(t + (n_{se} + n_{ex} + n_{ro}) \cdot t_{exp})$ such that:*

$$\Pr\left[\operatorname{Succ}_{P_4}^{\mathrm{FtG}}(\mathcal{A})\right] \leq \Pr\left[\operatorname{Succ}_{P_5}^{\mathrm{FtG}}(\mathcal{A})\right] + n_{se} \cdot n_{ro} \cdot \operatorname{Adv}_{\mathbb{G}}^{\mathrm{CDH}}(\tilde{\mathcal{B}}^{\mathcal{A}}),$$

Proof. Let ϵ be the probability of **pairedpwguess** event happening. We build $\mathcal{B}^{\mathcal{A}}$, a CDH-solver with success probability $\epsilon/(n_{se} \cdot n_{ro})$. On input $(A = g^{\alpha}, B = g^{\beta})$, $\tilde{\mathcal{B}}^{\mathcal{A}}$ sets $M = g^m \in \mathbb{G}$ for $m \xleftarrow{\$} \mathbb{Z}_q$, chooses $d \in \{1...n_{se}\}$ at random – a session target of the Test query – and *simulates* P_4 to $\mathcal{A}$ with the following changes:

1. In a CLIENT ACTION 0 query to Π_C^d with input S, set $X^* \leftarrow A$, where Π_C^d is the client instance that $\tilde{\mathcal{B}}^{\mathcal{A}}$ hopes it remains *PFS-fresh*.
2. In a SERVER ACTION 1 query to Π_S^j with input $\langle C, m \rangle$, where there was previous a CLIENT ACTION 0 query to Π_C^d with input S and output $\langle C, m \rangle$, set $Y = B \cdot g^{r_{S,j}}$, where $r_{S,j} \xleftarrow{\$} \mathbb{Z}_q$.
3. In a CLIENT ACTION 1 query to Π_C^d, if Π_C^d is *unpaired* then it aborts an also $\tilde{\mathcal{B}}^{\mathcal{A}}$ stops the simulation.
4. In a SERVER ACTION 2 query to Π_S^j, if it was *paired* with Π_C^d after its SERVER ACTION 1 but now is *not paired*, then Π_S^j aborts. However, the simulation continues as the instance Π_C^d may still be target of the Test query.
5. When $\mathcal{A}$ finishes, then for every $H_l(C, S, X^*, Y, \sigma, \pi_C)$, made by $\mathcal{A}$, with $l \in \{1, 2, 3\}$ and where (i) X^* and Y were generated by Π_C^d and Π_S^j respectively, (ii) Π_S^j was paired with Π_C^d after its SERVER ACTION 1 and (iii) Π_C^d was paired with Π_S^j, then add γ to the set S-DH, where:

$$\gamma = \sigma \cdot B^{m \cdot \pi_C} \cdot M^{r_{S,j} \cdot \pi_C} \cdot A^{-r_{S,j}}$$

6. The set S-DH contains at most n_{ro} elements, where each one is a possible solution to $\mathrm{DH}(g^{\alpha}, g^{\beta})$. Then $\tilde{\mathcal{B}}^{\mathcal{A}}$ picks $\gamma \xleftarrow{\$}$ L-DH as its output.

In this reduction the simulator $\tilde{\mathcal{B}}^{\mathcal{A}}$ has to guess the client instance target of the Test query, say Π_C^d. The freshness requirement guarantees that a Corrupt query is only possible after the Test query, directed to Π_C^d (or its partner), has been placed. Following the reductionist approach, we showed that the **pairedpwguess** event occurs at most with probability $\epsilon \leq n_{se} \cdot n_{ro} \cdot \operatorname{Adv}_{G_q}^{\mathrm{CDH}}(\tilde{\mathcal{B}}^{\mathcal{A}})$. $\qquad\square$

Game G_6: Prevent testing more two passwords per server instance.
In P_6 we restrict an adversary, who tries to masquerade as a client, from testing two passwords per session, say π_1 and π_2, in an online dictionary attack. Concretely, let P_6 be identical to P_5 except that if **doublepwserver** event occurs, the protocol stops and the adversary fails.

Let F_5 and F_6 denote the **doublepwserver** event occurring in P_5 and P_6 respectively. By definition it follows that $\operatorname{Succ}_{P_5}^{\mathrm{FtG}}(\mathcal{A}) \wedge \neg F_5 \Leftrightarrow \operatorname{Succ}_{P_6}^{\mathrm{FtG}}(\mathcal{A}) \wedge \neg F_6$.

Claim 7. *For all adversaries $\mathcal{A}$, $\left|\Pr\left[\operatorname{Succ}_{P_5}^{\mathrm{FtG}}(\mathcal{A})\right] - \Pr\left[\operatorname{Succ}_{P_5}^{\mathrm{FtG}}(\mathcal{A})\right]\right| \leq \Pr\left[F_6\right]$.*

Proof. Identical to Claim 2.   □

Claim 8. *Given $\mathcal{A}$, there exists a CDH-solver $\hat{\mathcal{B}}^{\mathcal{A}}$ with running time $t' = \mathcal{O}(t + (n_{se} + n_{ex} + n_{ro}) \cdot t_{exp})$ such that:*

$$\Pr\left[\operatorname{Succ}_{P_5}^{\text{FtG}}(\mathcal{A})\right] \leq \Pr\left[\operatorname{Succ}_{P_6}^{\text{FtG}}(\mathcal{A})\right] + n_{ro}^2 \cdot \operatorname{Adv}_{\mathbb{G}}^{\text{CDH}}(\hat{\mathcal{B}}^{\mathcal{A}}),$$

Proof. We construct an algorithm $\hat{\mathcal{B}}^{\mathcal{A}}$ that solves the CDH problem probability ϵ / n_{ro}^2, where ϵ is the probability of **pairedpwguess** event occurring. On input $(A = g^a, B = g^b)$, $\hat{\mathcal{B}}^{\mathcal{A}}$ simulates G_5 to $\mathcal{A}$ with the following changes:

1. Set $M := A$
2. In a SERVER ACTION 1 to Π_S^j with input $\langle C, X^* \rangle$ set $Y \leftarrow B \cdot g^y$, where $y \xleftarrow{\$} \mathbb{Z}_q$, and sends back $\langle Y, k \rangle$. From P_4 it holds that no unpaired instances can terminate. Specifically, unpaired client and server instances abort in CLIENT ACTION 1 and SERVER ACTION 2 respectively.
3. When $\mathcal{A}$ terminates, for every pair of queries $H_l(C, S, X^*, Y, \sigma_1, \pi_1)$ and $H_l(C, S, X^*, Y, \sigma_2, \pi_2)$, where $\pi_1 \neq \pi_2$, add γ to the S-DII, where:

$$\gamma = A^{-y} \cdot (\sigma_1 / \sigma_2)^{(\pi_2 - \pi_1)}$$

4. The set S-DH contains at most $(n_{ro})^2$ elements and each element in the set is a possible solution to $\mathrm{DH}(A, B)$. Then $\hat{\mathcal{B}}^{\mathcal{A}}$ outputs $\gamma \xleftarrow{\$} \text{S-DH}$.

P_6 and P_5 are identical unless the **doublepwserver** event occurs, however, this only occurs with probability $\epsilon \leq n_{ro}^2 \cdot \operatorname{Adv}_{G_q}^{\text{CDH}}(\hat{\mathcal{B}}^{\mathcal{A}})$. The quadratic degradation factor is due to $\hat{\mathcal{B}}^{\mathcal{A}}$ having to guess two queries $H_l(C, S, X^*, Y, \sigma_1, \pi_1)$ and $H_l(C, S, X^*, Y, \sigma_2, \pi_2)$ such that $\sigma_1 = \mathrm{DH}\ (X^*/M^{\pi_1}, Y)$ and $\sigma_2 = \mathrm{DH}\ (X^*/M^{\pi_2}, Y)$.   □

Game G_7: Internal password oracle.
In protocol P_7, we consider an internal password oracle $\mathcal{O}_\pi$ who handles every password request and is only available to the challenger. Specifically, the challenger queries the $\mathcal{O}_\pi$ to (i) assign passwords to users, (ii) answer Corrupt queries and (iii) determine if the **correctpw** event occurs.

Claim 9. *For all adversaries $\mathcal{A}$, $\Pr\left[\operatorname{Succ}_{P_6}^{\text{FtG}}(\mathcal{A})\right] = \Pr\left[\operatorname{Succ}_{P_7}^{\text{FtG}}(\mathcal{A})\right].$*

Proof. It follows from inspection.   □

Claim 10. *For all adversaries $\mathcal{A}$, $\Pr\left[\operatorname{Succ}_{P_7}^{\text{FtG}}(\mathcal{A})\right] \leq \frac{1}{2} + \frac{n_{se}}{2 \cdot |D|}.$*

Proof.

$$\Pr\left[\operatorname{Succ}_{P_7}^{\text{FtG}}(\mathcal{A})\right] = \Pr\left[\operatorname{Succ}_{P_7}^{\text{FtG}}(\mathcal{A}) \mid \text{correctpw}\right] \cdot \Pr\left[\text{correctpw}\right]$$
$$+ \Pr\left[\operatorname{Succ}_{P_7}^{\text{FtG}}(\mathcal{A}) \mid \neg\text{correctpw}\right] \cdot \Pr\left[\neg\text{correctpw}\right] \quad (2)$$

We know from P_6 that $\mathcal{A}$ can test at most one password per instance in an active attack, then $\Pr\left[\text{correctpw}\right] \leq n_{se}/|D|$. We examine the second term of

Eq. 2. The security experiment requires the adversary to make a Test query to some *PFS-fresh* instance Π_U^i of his choice. It is easy to show that the view of $\mathcal{A}$ is independent of the sk on which she is challenged: (i) P_1 prevents two or more instances accepting with the same *sid*, which would violate the partnering definition allowing $\mathcal{A}$ to trivially win, (ii) it follows from P_4 that, before any Corrupt query, only instances that are *paired* instances can reach terminate state – and therefore be target of a Test query – and (iii) from P_5 it holds that for such *paired* instances, the view of $\mathcal{A}$ is independent of sk for the session target of the Test query. Then $\Pr\left[\mathrm{Succ}_{P_7}^{\mathrm{FtG}}(\mathcal{A}) \mid \neg\mathrm{correctpw}\right] = 1/2$. ∎

4   The SPAKE2 Protocol

4.1   Security of SPAKE2

SPAKE2 protocol is already proven secure in the FtG model [8] without considering any notion of forward secrecy. Here, we show that SPAKE2 also satisfies *weak* forward secrecy in the FtG model assuming the CDH problem is hard in $\mathbb{G}$. The security proof of SPAKE2 is similar to that of PFS-SPAKE2 protocol; the biggest difference is game G_6, where $\mathcal{A}$ is prevented from testing two different passwords when she masquerades as C but also when masquerading as S. The later scenario does not occur in PFS-SPAKE2 since a client instance aborts the protocol whenever it receives an invalid key-confirmation code k.

Theorem 2. *Let P be the protocol specified in Fig. 2 instantiated in group $\mathbb{G}$ and with passwords uniformly distributed over dictionary D. Let $\mathcal{A}$ be an adversary that runs in time t polynomial in λ, makes at most n_{ex}, n_{se}, n_{ro} queries of type execute, send and random oracle. Then:*

<table>
<tr><td align="center">Client C</td><td align="center">Server S</td></tr>
<tr><td colspan="2" align="center">**Initialization**</td></tr>
<tr><td colspan="2" align="center">Public: $\mathbb{G}, g, M, N \in \mathbb{G}$; $H : \{0,1\}^* \to \{0,1\}^k$</td></tr>
<tr><td colspan="2" align="center">Secret: $\pi \in \mathbb{Z}_q, \pi \neq 0$</td></tr>
<tr>
<td align="center">$x \leftarrow \mathbb{Z}_q, X := g^x$
$X^* := X \cdot M^\pi$</td>
<td align="center">$y \leftarrow \mathbb{Z}_q, Y := g^y$
$Y^* = Y \cdot N^\pi$</td>
</tr>
<tr><td colspan="2" align="center">$\xrightarrow{ X^* }$
$\xleftarrow{ Y^* }$</td></tr>
<tr>
<td align="center">$\sigma := (\frac{Y^*}{N^\pi})^x$
$sk := H(C, S, X^*, Y^*, \sigma, \pi)$</td>
<td align="center">$\sigma := (\frac{X^*}{M^\pi})^y$
$sk := H(C, S, X^*, Y^*, \sigma, \pi)$</td>
</tr>
</table>

Fig. 2. SPAKE2 protocol.

$$\text{Adv}_P^{\text{wFS-FtG}}(\mathcal{A}) \leq \frac{n_{se}}{|D|} + \mathcal{O}\left(\frac{(n_{se} + n_{ex})(n_{se} + n_{ex} + n_{ro})}{q} + \right.$$

$$\left. n_{ro} \cdot \text{Adv}_{\mathbb{G}}^{\text{CDH}}(\mathcal{B}^{\mathcal{A}}) + n_{se}n_{ro} \cdot \text{Adv}_{\mathbb{G}}^{\text{CDH}}(\tilde{\mathcal{B}}^{\mathcal{A}}) + n_{ro}^2 \cdot \text{Adv}_{\mathbb{G}}^{\text{CDH}}(\hat{\mathcal{B}}^{\mathcal{A}})\right),$$

where $\mathcal{B}^{\mathcal{A}}$, $\tilde{\mathcal{B}}^{\mathcal{A}}$ and $\hat{\mathcal{B}}^{\mathcal{A}}$ are CDH-solver algorithms running in time $t' = \mathcal{O}(t + (n_{se} + n_{ex} + n_{ro}) \cdot t_{exp})$, where t_{exp} is the time for an exponentiation in $\mathbb{G}$.

Next we provide a sketch of the proof, where we simply write $\text{Succ}_{P_i}^{\text{FtG}}$ instead of $\text{Succ}_{P_i}^{\text{wFS-FtG}}$ to denote the success probability of $\mathcal{A}$ winning in game G_i:

Game G_0: Execution of original protocol.

Game G_1: Force uniqueness of honest instances.
If honest instances generate X^* or Y^* terms equals those seen in previous executions of the protocol, the the protocol stops and $\mathcal{A}$ fails.

$$\text{Succ}_{P_0}^{\text{FtG}} \leq \text{Succ}_{P_1}^{\text{FtG}} + \mathcal{O}\left(\frac{(n_{se} + n_{ex})(n_{se} + n_{ex} + n_{ro})}{q}\right).$$

Game G_2: Simulation without password.
The protocol is simulated without using password information, subsequent random oracle queries made by $\mathcal{A}$ are backpatch to generate consistent views. Also, $\mathcal{A}$ is forced to query the random oracle to compute $sk = H(\cdot)$.

$$\text{Succ}_{P_1}^{\text{FtG}}(\mathcal{A}) \leq \text{Succ}_{P_2}^{\text{FtG}}(\mathcal{A}) + \mathcal{O}(n_{se}/2^\kappa).$$

Game G_3: No need to backpatch $H_l(\cdot)$ queries against Execute queries.
We can show that the view of an $\mathcal{A}$ running in time t against P_2 is computationally indistinguishable from that of P_3 via a CDH reduction.

$$\text{Succ}_{P_2}^{\text{FtG}}(\mathcal{A}) = \text{Succ}_{P_3}^{\text{FtG}}(\mathcal{A}) + n_{ro} \cdot \text{Adv}_{\mathbb{G}}^{\text{CDH}}(\mathcal{B}^{\mathcal{A}}).$$

where $\mathcal{B}^{\mathcal{A}}$ is a CDH-solver algorithm running in time $t' = \mathcal{O}(t + (n_{se} + n_{ex} + n_{ro}) \cdot t_{exp})$ and t_{exp} the time for an exponentiation in $\mathbb{G}$.

Game G_4: Check for successful password guesses.
If before any Corrupt query, the adversary is successful on a password guess against a client or server instance, the protocol stops and the adversary wins.

$$\text{Succ}_{P_3}^{\text{FtG}}(\mathcal{A}) \leq \text{Succ}_{P_4}^{\text{FtG}}(\mathcal{A}).$$

Game G_5: Randomized session keys for paired instances. We build a CDH-solver algorithm from an adversary who manages to compute the sk established at paired instances Π_C^i and Π_S^j, even if $\mathcal{A}$ obtains π_C by adaptively corrupting any of the instances.

$$\Pr\left[\text{Succ}_{P_4}^{\text{FtG}}(\mathcal{A})\right] \leq \Pr\left[\text{Succ}_{P_5}^{\text{FtG}}(\mathcal{A})\right] + n_{se} \cdot n_{ro} \cdot \text{Adv}_{\mathbb{G}}^{\text{CDH}}(\tilde{\mathcal{B}}^{\mathcal{A}}).$$

Game G_6: Prevent testing more than one passwords per instance.
If before any Corrupt query, $\mathcal{A}$ manages to test more than one passwords per client or server instance, the protocol stops and the adversary fails. Via a CDH reduction, we show this may happend only with negligible probability.

$$\Pr\left[\,\text{Succ}_{P_4}^{\text{FtG}}(\mathcal{A})\,\right] \leq \Pr\left[\,\text{Succ}_{P_5}^{\text{FtG}}(\mathcal{A})\,\right] + 2n_{ro}^2 \cdot \text{Adv}_{\mathbb{G}}^{\text{CDH}}(\hat{\mathcal{B}}^{\mathcal{A}}).$$

Game G_7: Internal password oracle.
By inspection P_6 is statistically indistinguishable from P_7. Additionally, let Π_U^i be any instance that remains wFS-fresh and is the target of a Test query. In P_7, provided that $\mathcal{A}$ has not successfully guessed the password, the view of the adversary is independent of the sk_U^i. Then:

$$\Pr\left[\,\text{Succ}_{P_7}^{\text{FtG}}(\mathcal{A})\,\right] = \frac{1}{2} + \frac{n_{se}}{2 \cdot |D|}$$

5   Conclusion and Future Work

We proved that SPAKE2 protocol satisfies weak forward secrecy. Note that proving perfect forward secrecy for unmodified SPAKE2 seems to be a harder task. Consider the following scenario: $\mathcal{A}$ masquerades as a client and sends an arbitrary message X^* to a server instance Π_S^j, the latter computes Y^*, its session key, answers back with Y^* and *terminates*. Now $\mathcal{A}$ makes a Test(S, j) query, receives the challenge and then corrupts the tested server instance (as corruption occurred after the Test query the instance Π_S^j remains PFS-fresh). The difficulty is that, even though the proof shows that $\mathcal{A}$ cannot test two passwords per instance, in this particular scenario the simulator cannot determine the password to which $\mathcal{A}$ committed in X^* as she has not asked any random oracle query. Given the difficulty in proving perfect forward secrecy for SPAKE2, we modified the protocol by incorporating key-confirmation codes into it. We proved that the modified protocol satisfies perfect forward secrecy and therefore we called it PFS-SPAKE2.

In future work, we would like to study if the SPAKE2 and PFS-SPAKE2 protocols compose securely with symmetric-key encryption schemes. This question has practical relevance, as in TLS 1.3 the aforementioned primitives would be used not in stand alone operation but as a combined system.

Acknowledgements. The authors are especially grateful to the Luxembourg National Research Fund for supporting this work under CORE project AToMS.

A   Terminology from [3]

We introduce the terminology necessary to refer to adversary's actions.

We say "in a CLIENT ACTION k query to Π_C^i" to refer to "in a Send query directed to the client instance Π_C^i that results in CLIENT ACTION k procedure being executed" and "in a SERVER ACTION k" to refer to "in a Send query directed to the server instance Π_S^j that results in SERVER ACTION k procedure being executed".

A client instance Π_C^i is *paired with* server instance Π_S^j if there was a CLIENT ACTION 0 query to Π_C^i with output $\langle C, X^* \rangle$, a SERVER ACTION 1 to Π_S^j with input $\langle C, X^* \rangle$ and output $\langle S, Y, k \rangle$ and a CLIENT ACTION 1 to Π_C^i with input $\langle S, Y, k \rangle$. A server instance Π_S^j is *paired with* client instance Π_C^i if there was a CLIENT ACTION 0 query to Π_C^i with output $\langle C, X^* \rangle$ and a SERVER ACTION 1 to Π_S^j with input $\langle C, X^* \rangle$ and output $\langle Y, k \rangle$, additionally, if there is a SERVER ACTION 2 query with input k', then there was a previous CLIENT ACTION 1 to Π_C^i with input $\langle Y, k \rangle$ and ouput k'.

Next we define the events that will allow us to proof the security of the protocol by sequence of games.

testpw(C, i, S, π, l): Adversary $\mathcal{A}$ makes (i) an $H_l(C, S, X^*, Y, \sigma, \pi)$ query for some $l \in \{1, 2, 3\}$, (ii) a CLIENT ACTION 0 to Π_C^i with output $\langle S, X^* \rangle$ and (iii) a CLIENT ACTION 1 to Π_C^i with input $\langle C, Y, k \rangle$, where $X^* = X \cdot M^\pi$ and $\sigma = DH(X, Y)$. The associated value to this event is the output of the $H_l(\cdot)$ query, or the k, k', sk_C^i values, respectively for $l = 1, 2, 3$, whichever is set first.

testpw(S, j, C, π, l): $\mathcal{A}$ makes an $H_l(C, S, X^*, Y, \sigma, \pi)$ for some $l \in \{1, 2, 3\}$ and a SERVER ACTION 1 to Π_S^j with input $\langle S, X^* \rangle$ and output $\langle C, Y, k \rangle$, where $X^* = X \cdot M^\pi$ and $\sigma = DH(X, Y)$. The associated value to this event is the output of the $H_l(\cdot)$ query, or the k, k', sk_S^j values, respectively for $l = 1, 2, 3$, whichever is set first.

testpw!(C, i, S, π): In a CLIENT ACTION 1 query with input $\langle \mu, k \rangle$, causes a testpw$(C, i, S, \pi, 2)$ event to occurs, with associated value k.

testexecpw(C, i, S, j, π): $\mathcal{A}$ makes (i) an $H_l(C, S, X^*, Y, \sigma, \pi)$ for some $l \in \{1, 2, 3\}$, where $X^* = X \cdot M^\pi$ and $\sigma = DH(X, Y)$ and (ii) previously an Execute(C, i, S, j) which produces X^*, Y. The associated value to this event is the output of the $H_l(\cdot)$ query, or the k, k', sk_S^j values, respectively for $l = 1, 2, 3$, whichever is set first.

correctpw: Before any Corrupt query, either a testpw!(C, i, S, π_c) event occurs, for some C, i, S, or a testpw(S, j, C, π_c, l) event occurs for some S, j, C and $l \in \{1, 2, 3\}$, where π_c is the correct password.

pairedpwguess: For some client and server instance Π_C^i and Π_S^j respectively, both testpw(C, i, S, π_c, l) and testpw(S, j, C, π, l) event occurs for $l \in \{1, 2, 3\}$, where Π_C^i is paired with Π_S^j, and Π_S^j is paired with Π_C^i after its SERVER ACTION 1.

doublepwserver: Before any Corrupt query, both a testpw(S, j, C, π_1, l) and a testpw(S, j, C, π_2, l) event occurs, for some S, j, π_1 and π_2, with $\pi_1 \neq \pi_2$ and $l \in \{1, 2, 3\}$.

References

1. Bellovin, S.M., Merritt, M.: Encrypted key exchange: password-based protocols secure against dictionary attacks. In: 1992 IEEE Symposium on Research in Security and Privacy, SP 1992, pp. 72–84 (1992)

2. Boyko, V., MacKenzie, P., Patel, S.: Provably secure password-authenticated key exchange using Diffie-Hellman. In: Preneel, B. (ed.) EUROCRYPT 2000. LNCS, vol. 1807, pp. 156–171. Springer, Heidelberg (2000). https://doi.org/10.1007/3-540-45539-6_12
3. MacKenzie, P.: The PAK suite: protocols for password-authenticated key exchange. DIMACS Technical report 2002–46 (2002)
4. Hao, F., Ryan, P.: J-PAKE: authenticated key exchange without PKI. Trans. Comput. Sci. 11, 192–206 (2010)
5. Abdalla, M., Benhamouda, F., MacKenzie, P.: Security of the J-PAKE password authenticated key exchange protocol. In: IEEE Symposium on Security and Privacy, SP 2015, pp. 571–587. IEEE Computer Society (2015)
6. Wu, T.D.: The secure remote password protocol. In: Proceedings of the Network and Distributed System Security Symposium. The Internet Society (1998)
7. Jablon, D.P.: Strong password-only authenticated key exchange. ACM SIGCOMM Comput. Commun. Rev. 26(5), 5–26 (1996)
8. Abdalla, M., Pointcheval, D.: Simple password-based encrypted key exchange protocols. In: Menezes, A. (ed.) CT-RSA 2005. LNCS, vol. 3376, pp. 191–208. Springer, Heidelberg (2005). https://doi.org/10.1007/978-3-540-30574-3_14
9. Bellare, M., Pointcheval, D., Rogaway, P.: Authenticated key exchange secure against dictionary attacks. In: Preneel, B. (ed.) EUROCRYPT 2000. LNCS, vol. 1807, pp. 139–155. Springer, Heidelberg (2000). https://doi.org/10.1007/3-540-45539-6_11
10. Abdalla, M., Fouque, P.-A., Pointcheval, D.: Password-based authenticated key exchange in the three-party setting. In: Vaudenay, S. (ed.) PKC 2005. LNCS, vol. 3386, pp. 65–84. Springer, Heidelberg (2005). https://doi.org/10.1007/978-3-540-30580-4_6
11. Canetti, R., Halevi, S., Katz, J., Lindell, Y., MacKenzie, P.: Universally composable password-based key exchange. In: Cramer, R. (ed.) EUROCRYPT 2005. LNCS, vol. 3494, pp. 404–421. Springer, Heidelberg (2005). https://doi.org/10.1007/11426639_24
12. Chen, L., Lim, H.W., Yang, G.: Cross-domain password-based authenticated key exchange revisited. ACM Trans. Inf. Syst. Secur. 16(4), 15:1–15:32 (2014)
13. Goldreich, O., Lindell, Y.: Session-key generation using human passwords only. In: Kilian, J. (ed.) CRYPTO 2001. LNCS, vol. 2139, pp. 408–432. Springer, Heidelberg (2001). https://doi.org/10.1007/3-540-44647-8_24
14. Kunz-Jacques, S., Pointcheval, D.: About the security of MTI/C0 and MQV. In: De Prisco, R., Yung, M. (eds.) SCN 2006. LNCS, vol. 4116, pp. 156–172. Springer, Heidelberg (2006). https://doi.org/10.1007/11832072_11
15. Vacca, J.R.: Computer and Information Security Handbook, 2nd edn. Morgan Kaufmann Publishers Inc., San Francisco (2013)
16. Ladd, W., Kaduk, B.: SPAKE2, a PAKE. Internet-Draft draft-irtf-cfrg-spake2-05, IETF Secretariat, February 2018. http://www.ietf.org/internet-drafts/draft-irtf-cfrg-spake2-05.txt
17. McCallum, N., Sorce, S., Harwood, R., Hudson, G.: Spake pre-authentication. Internet-Draft draft-ietf-kitten-krb-spake-preauth-05, IETF Secretariat, February 2018. http://www.ietf.org/internet-drafts/draft-ietf-kitten-krb-spake-preauth-05.txt
18. Barnes, R., Friel, O.: Usage of spake with TLS 1.3. Internet-Draft draft-barnes-tls-pake-01, IETF Secretariat, April 2018. http://www.ietf.org/internet-drafts/draft-barnes-tls-pake-01.txt

19. Rescorla, E.: The transport layer security (TLS) protocol version 1.3. Internet-Draft draft-ietf-tls-tls13-28, IETF Secretariat, March 2018. http://www.ietf.org/internet-drafts/draft-ietf-tls-tls13-28.txt

20. Taylor, D., Wu, T., Mavrogiannopoulos, N., Perrin, T.: Using the secure remote password (SRP) protocol for TLS authentication. RFC 5054, RFC Editor, November 2007

21. Engler, J., Karlof, C., Shi, E., Song, D.: Is it too late for PAKE? In: Web 2.0 Security and Privacy Workshop 2009 (W2SP 2009), May 2009

22. Law, L., Menezes, A., Qu, M., Solinas, J., Vanstone, S.: An efficient protocol for authenticated key agreement. Des. Codes Cryptogr. **28**(2), 119–134 (2003)

23. Krawczyk, H.: HMQV: a high-performance secure Diffie-Hellman protocol. In: Shoup, V. (ed.) CRYPTO 2005. LNCS, vol. 3621, pp. 546–566. Springer, Heidelberg (2005). https://doi.org/10.1007/11535218_33

24. Diffie, W., Van Oorschot, P.C., Wiener, M.J.: Authentication and authenticated key exchanges. Des. Codes Cryptogr. **2**(2), 107–125 (1992). Jun

25. Shoup, V.: On formal models for secure key exchange. Cryptology ePrint Archive, Report 1999/012 (1999). http://eprint.iacr.org/1999/012

26. Canetti, R., Krawczyk, H.: Analysis of key-exchange protocols and their use for building secure channels. In: Pfitzmann, B. (ed.) EUROCRYPT 2001. LNCS, vol. 2045, pp. 453–474. Springer, Heidelberg (2001). https://doi.org/10.1007/3-540-44987-6_28

27. LaMacchia, B., Lauter, K., Mityagin, A.: Stronger security of authenticated key exchange. In: Susilo, W., Liu, J.K., Mu, Y. (eds.) ProvSec 2007. LNCS, vol. 4784, pp. 1–16. Springer, Heidelberg (2007). https://doi.org/10.1007/978-3-540-75670-5_1

28. Katz, J., Ostrovsky, R., Yung, M.: Forward secrecy in password-only key exchange protocols. In: Cimato, S., Persiano, G., Galdi, C. (eds.) SCN 2002. LNCS, vol. 2576, pp. 29–44. Springer, Heidelberg (2003). https://doi.org/10.1007/3-540-36413-7_3

29. Bellare, M., Rogaway, P.: Entity authentication and key distribution. In: Stinson, D.R. (ed.) CRYPTO 1993. LNCS, vol. 773, pp. 232–249. Springer, Heidelberg (1994). https://doi.org/10.1007/3-540-48329-2_21

30. Bellare, M., Rogaway, P.: Provably secure session key distribution: the three party case. In: Leighton, F.T., Borodin, A. (eds.) Proceedings of the Twenty-Seventh Annual ACM Symposium on Theory of Computing, STOC 1995, pp. 57–66. ACM (1995)

31. Becerra, J., Iovino, V., Ostrev, D., Šala, P., Škrobot, M.: Tightly-secure PAK(E). Cryptology ePrint Archive, Report 2017/1045 (2017). https://eprint.iacr.org/2017/1045

32. MacKenzie, P.: On the security of the SPEKE password-authenticated key exchange protocol. Cryptology ePrint Archive, Report 2001/057 (2001). http://eprint.iacr.org/2001/057

33. Shoup, V.: Sequences of games: a tool for taming complexity in security proofs. IACR Cryptology ePrint Archive 2004/332 (2004)

Short Papers

User-Mediated Authentication Protocols and Unforgeability in Key Collision

Britta Hale[✉]

Naval Postgraduate School (NPS), Monterey, CA, USA
britta.hale@nps.edu

Abstract. This research provides a computational analysis of the ISO 9798-6 standard's Mechanism 7a authentication protocol. In contrast to typical authentication protocols, ISO 9798-6 mechanism 7a requires user interaction and aims to authenticate data possession instead of identities. Consequently, we introduce a 3-party possession user mediated authentication (3-PUMA) model. Furthermore, we demonstrate the necessary security guarantees of the MAC primitive – which include non-standard assumptions – and introduce existential unforgeability under key collision attacks (EUF-KCA). The resulting analysis demonstrates a notable lack in the standard's requirements and has implications for other PUMA protocols.

Keywords: ISO 9798-6 · Authentication protocols · User interface MAC security · Key-collision attacks

1 Introduction

User interaction is largely unconsidered in protocol analysis, even in instances where the user takes an active role. This research addresses modeling of user-mediated authentication protocols and computationally analyzes the standardized ISO 9798-6 Mechanism 7a [8] (abbreviated ISO 9798-6.7a) authentication protocol. Unlike previously analyzed ISO 9798 protocols, those within the ISO 9798-6 standard employ an active user interface. These protocols present two intriguing modeling concerns: modeling of a 3-party authentication protocol and modeling of the user interface. While work has been done on modeling of 3-party – and more generally multi-party – key exchange protocols [4,12], 3-party authentication protocols are largely ignored. Analyses of many 3-party key exchange protocols handle the user as an out-of-band (OOB) information exchange [12]. Indeed, this follows from a standard device-to-device security perspective and modeling of the user is considered irrelevant or external to the cryptographic model. However, in a user-mediated protocol the user is an active participant relaying and confirming information and even generating nonces or keys. It is thus possible to consider a user-to-device "channel", e.g. a device keypad or display, as well as adversarial behavior such as via *a priori* access to a device.

This research was partially supported by and performed at SINTEF Digital, Trondheim, Norway.

J. Baek et al. (Eds.): ProvSec 2018, LNCS 11192, pp. 387–396, 2018.
https://doi.org/10.1007/978-3-030-01446-9_22

Notably, the goals of ISO 9798-6.7a differ also from those expected from typical mutual authentication protocols. In the absence of long-term keys and symmetric keys, etc., which could normally be used for entity authentication, the goal of ISO 9798-6.7a is to provide a mutually authenticated data string D, such that both parties are assured that the protocol partner has also agreed to the string. The only intended prevention mechanism against man-in-the-middle attacks is a user generated value, which again highlights the highly interactive nature of the protocol.

In addition to the protocols goals, the security goals of the underlying message authentication code (MAC) algorithm also differ from the accepted norm. ISO 9798-6.7a sends the MAC key in the clear, before verifying the MAC tag. Thus the MAC should be secure against an adversary that can produce a different but valid MAC key – essentially forging a key, given a message-tag pair. In order to address these demands, it is necessary to go beyond standard MAC assumptions (e.g. EUF-CMA and SUF-CMA) and formalize key collision attacks.

Related Work. Previous analyses of the ISO 9798 standard have addressed mechanisms in the standard which do not include a user interface [3,7,14]. These analyses include both formal modeling [3,14] and computational modeling [7]. None of these works cover any of the protocols of ISO 9798-6, but demonstrate the importance of analyzing such standardized protocols.

Classically, we assume that an adversary cannot access a secret key. Thus, both standard MAC security variants EUF-CMA and SUF-CMA required that the MAC key is fixed and unavailable to the adversary. Yet ISO 9798-6.7a contains a different scenario, one in which MAC tags are essentially "committed" to. Then, even if the key is revealed, the tag cannot be altered and an adversary must generate a message forgery that corresponds to the fixed tag, or produce an alternative key. Known Key, Chosen Key, and Related Key attacks bear some similarities to this security scenario, but differ from the present case. Known Key attacks (KKAs) were introduced in [11] and cover the case of block ciphers where an adversary knows a key and aims to exhibit non-random behavior in the cipher. KKAs [2] have been studied extensively. Chosen Key attacks (CKAs) consider a similar situation, but where an adversary may choose the key in question [6]. In a Related Key attack (RKA) [5] an adversary chooses a relation between a pair of keys for a blockcipher, but not the keys themselves, before launching a chosen plaintext attack. The goal of these attacks (e.g. non-random behavior in the cipher in the case of a KKA) differs from the goal of the MAC adversary exhibited in ISO 9798-6.7a (generating a new key for a given message-tag pair).

The concept of adversarial key guessing has surfaced previously under terms such as *key spoofing* and *key-collision*. The concept of *key spoofing* for symmetric encryption was briefly discussed in [1] as a situation where an adversary's goal is to find a new key which produces a given message-ciphertext pair. Later, the idea was revived in [13] (not peer-reviewed) under the term *key-collision* for digital signatures. Unlike in key spoofing, key collision demands only a fixed ciphertext – the adversary must find a new key and may additionally find a new message, which yields the given ciphertext. Still, these attacks do not consider

Table 1. Security experiment against a MAC algorithm with inpsuts into the verification oracle (key K, message m, or MAC tag t). If an adversary can generate a new input ($\checkmark$) when others are fixed (-), it wins the corresponding experiment. Other inputs which the adversary may manipulate are denoted (*). E.g. an adversary wins SUF-CMA if it can generate a new MAC tag, a new message or both. For visual completeness we include the trivial combinations where the adversary must generate a new key-tag pair for a message (given or of the adversary's choice).

MAC security experiments corresponding to verification inputs which are optionally generated by the adversary (*), required fresh for a win ($\checkmark$), and fixed (-)		
Security experiment	K	m	t
EUF-KCA	$\checkmark$	*	-
EUF-CMA	-	$\checkmark$	*
Forged tag	-	*	$\checkmark$
SUF-KCA	$\checkmark$	$\checkmark$	-
SUF-CMA = EUF-CMA + Forged tag	-	$\checkmark$	$\checkmark$
Trivial (win)	$\checkmark$	-	$\checkmark$
Trivial (win)	$\checkmark$	$\checkmark$	$\checkmark$
Trivial (impossibility)	-	-	-

a related-key case, where the adversary can exploit knowledge of the actual key. This leaves an open problem. How can we formulate MAC security for when the MAC key is intentionally provided to the adversary?

This research handles the situation where the adversary must guess a different valid key but is actually provided the correct key (which of course necessitates restriction of valid key use). We call this existential unforgeability under key collision attacks (EUF-KCA). Table 1 shows all possible forgeries an adversary can perform and the corresponding security game that captures such abilities. In all non-trivial cases, either the key or message tag is fixed. Note that classical SUF-CMA fixes the key while SUF-KCA fixes the tag. Discussion on SUF-KCA security is left for the full version.

Contributions. This work extends previous research on ISO 9798, providing a model for user-mediated authentication and analyzing a previously untouched protocol. Particularly:

- We introduce Existential Unforgeability under Key Collision Attacks (EUF-KCA) for a MAC. EUF-KCA security considers an adversary's ability to find a second key for a fixed MAC message-tag pair, given knowledge of the correct key.
- We initiate the study of 3-party Possession User-Mediated Authentication (3-PUMA) Protocols and provide a corresponding security model. This model handles 3-party authentication where one party is a user, with the explicit goal of authenticating possession of some data.

– We computationally analyze the ISO 9798-6.7a authentication protocol under the 3-PUMA model. Ultimately, we demonstrate that the MAC requirements stated in ISO 9798-6.7a are insufficient for the protocol's security.

2   Preliminaries

Here we introduce ISO 9798-6.7a and necessary MAC definitions.

2.1   ISO 9798-6 Mechanism 7a Authentication Protocol Specification

Both devices possess a "simple output interface", e.g. red and green lights. They also possess "standard input" interfaces which allow a user to input a bit-string into the devices. Figure 1 shows the ISO 9798-6.7a protocol with the following variables:

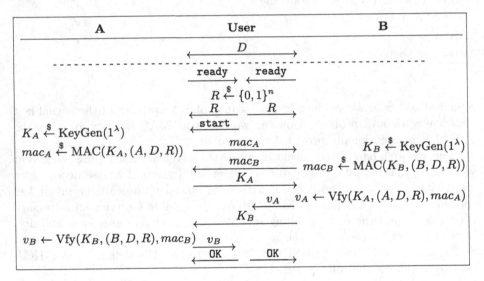

Fig. 1. ISO 9798-6 Protocol Mechanism 7a. Protocol flows are color-coded for the Device-to-Device channel and User-to-Device channel. Data string D and identities are pre-shared. (Color figure online)

– R: A 16–20 bit random bit-string generated by the user.
– D: A data string. D is the agreed upon data at the termination of the protocol run.
– K_I: A 128–160 bit short-term session key derived by identity I.
– mac_I: 128–160 bits output of a MAC algorithm, selected from ISO 9797 [9,10].
– ready: An indicating signal that the device is ready for the protocol to start.
– start: An initiation message.

- OK: An indicating signal that the protocol is completed successfully. If unsuccessful, `failed` is sent.

ISO 9798-6.7a does not define the distribution or freshness of the data string D, but the mechanism does not begin until after the data has been distributed. ISO 9798-6.7a does not specify how identities are obtained, but requires that identities are known prior to the start of the mechanism. Thus, we consider the identities to be transmitted out-of-band. ISO 9798-6.7a also does not specify how the random bit-string R is generated, but does require it to be kept secret (including during the user-to-device transfer of R). Following the specification, we assume that R is generated randomly. We do not consider "shoulder-surfing" attacks, where an adversary may observe R on input, in accordance with the strict specification on the secrecy of R to prevent MitM attacks.

A device outputs an indication of success/failure to the user based on the MAC verification step – we indicate this as $v = 1/0$. If both devices output an indication of success to the user ($v_B = v_A = 1$), then the user enters a confirmation of success (OK) into both devices. If either $v_B = 0$ or $v_A = 0$, the user enters an indication of failure `failed` into both devices; absence of a user response (OK/`failed`) within a specified time interval is interpreted as `failed` by the device. We say that a protocol instance of ISO 9798-6.7a *accepts* if: (1) it has received a value R from the user, and (2) it outputs a verification bit $v_{\text{partner identity}} = 1$, and (3) the last message received from the user is OK.

2.2 MAC Security

Due to space constraints the usual MAC definition and standard SUF-CMA security experiment $\text{Exp}_{\text{MAC},\mathcal{A}}^{\text{SUF-CMA}}$ is left for the full version. The one-time strong unforgeability (OT-SUF-CMA) experiment for MAC, $\text{Exp}_{\text{MAC},\mathcal{A}}^{\text{OT-SUF-CMA}}$, is as $\text{Exp}_{\text{MAC},\mathcal{A}}^{\text{SUF-CMA}}$ with the additional restriction that an adversary may only query MAC and MAC.Vfy once each.

Definition 1. *Let $\mathcal{A}$ be a PPT adversarial algorithm against the MAC. The existential unforgeability under key collision attacks (EUF-KCA) experiment for MAC, $\text{Exp}_{\text{MAC},\mathcal{A}}^{\text{EUF-KCA}}$ is given in Fig. 2. We define $\mathbf{Adv}_{\text{MAC},\mathcal{A}}^{\text{EUF-KCA}}(\lambda) := \Pr[\text{Exp}_{\text{MAC},\mathcal{A}}^{\text{EUF-KCA}}(\lambda) = 1]$.*

Definition 2 (Existential Unforgeability Under Key Collision Attacks). *We say that a MAC scheme is EUF-KCA secure if there exists a negligible function $\text{negl}(\lambda)$ such that for all PPT adversaries $\mathcal{A}$ interacting according to the experiment $\text{Exp}_{\text{MAC},\mathcal{A}}^{\text{EUF-KCA}}$ it holds that $\mathbf{Adv}_{\text{MAC},\mathcal{A}}^{\text{EUF-KCA}}(\lambda) \leq \text{negl}(\lambda)$.*

Since the MAC key is provided to the adversary following generation of a MAC tag, EUF-KCA security is naturally a one-time security game. Unlike in a brute-force search, the adversary in an KCA attack actually has a valid key at its disposal. It also possesses a complete message triple (K, m, t), with the goal of finding an alternative key.

$\mathrm{Exp}_{\mathrm{MAC},\mathcal{A}}^{\mathsf{EUF\text{-}KCA}}(\lambda):$

1: $K \xleftarrow{\$} \mathrm{Kgn}()$
2: $\mathsf{K} \leftarrow \bot, \mathsf{t} \leftarrow \bot$
3: $\mathcal{A}^{\mathrm{MAC}(\cdot),\mathrm{MAC.Vfy}(\cdot)}()$
4: **return** phase

$\mathrm{MAC}(m):$

1: **if** $(\mathsf{K}, \mathsf{t}) \neq (\bot, \bot)$
   then
2:    **return** $\bot$
3:   $\mathsf{t} \leftarrow \mathrm{MAC}(K, m)$
4:   $\mathsf{K} \leftarrow K, \mathsf{t} \leftarrow t$
5:   **return** (K, t)

$\mathrm{MAC.Vfy}(K, m):$

1: $v \leftarrow \mathrm{Vfy}(K, m, \mathsf{t})$
2: **if** $(v = 1) \wedge (K \neq \mathsf{K})$
   then
3:    phase $\leftarrow 1$
4:    **return** phase from
      experiment
5: **return** v

Fig. 2. EUF-KCA experiment for an algorithm $\mathrm{MAC} = (\mathrm{Kgn}, \mathrm{MAC}, \mathrm{Vfy})$ and adversary $\mathcal{A}$.

3   3-PUMA Model for Simple Output Devices

The 3-PUMA model considers the channel between devices (wired or wireless), as well as the third-party user interaction via channels between the user and devices.

Each device possesses a *simple output* interface, e.g. binary success/failure indication, as well as a *standard input* interface which allows a user to input a bit-string into the device. A participant in a 3-PUMA protocol is either a device $I \in \mathcal{ID}$ or a user U. As there is only one user interface, we do not model multiple users. The set of all participants is the union $\mathcal{ID} \cup \{U\}$. We refer to elements of $\mathcal{ID}$ alternatively as *devices* or *identities*. We model participants via *sessions*, such that π_i^P is the i-th session at P. that there may be multiple and simultaneous sessions at each participant.

Devices. Each device $I \in \mathcal{ID}$ is modeled via session oracles, where each session maintains a list of the following variables:

- $K \in \mathcal{K}$: a variable for storing an ephemeral key, where $\mathcal{K}$ is the protocol's key space.
- D: defined in Sect. 2.1.
- role $\in \{\mathsf{initiator}, \mathsf{responder}\}$: a variable indicating the role of I in the session.
- pid $\in \mathcal{ID}/\{I\}$: a variable for storing the partner identity for the session.
- $\delta \in \{\mathsf{accept}, \mathsf{reject}, *\}$: a variable indicating the session accepts, rejects, or has not yet reached a decision.
- sid: a variable for storing the session ID.

The internal state of each session oracle at identity I is initialized to $(K, D, \mathsf{role}, \mathsf{pid}, \mathsf{sid}) = (\emptyset, *, \emptyset, \emptyset, \emptyset)$, where $V = \emptyset$ indicates that the variable V is undefined and $*$ indicates that the variable value may or may not be defined. In the case of OOB exchange of D, D is initialized to the agreed value; otherwise, D is initialized to $\emptyset$. It is the explicit goal of the 3-PUMA protocol to authenticate possession of D at two sessions π_s^I and $\pi_s^{I'}$, versus mutually authenticating parties I and I', therefore we require that D be included in the sid. Rejection of the protocol run may occur at any time, but acceptance does not usually occur until the protocol is complete. We disallow $\mathsf{pid}_I = I$.

User. U is modeled via session oracles, where each session maintains the following:

- init $\in \mathcal{ID}$: a variable indicating the initiating identity.
- resp $\in \mathcal{ID}$: a variable indicating the responding identity.

The internal state of each session oracle at U is initialized to (init, resp) = $(\emptyset, \emptyset)$.

For devices we use a notion of partnering based on session IDs. Note that Device-to-Device (DtD) messages occur on a different channel than User-to-Device (UtD) messages. As there is a single user, we do not define partnering between the user and devices.

Definition 3. *Identities I and I' possess* matching session IDs *if* $\text{sid}_I = \text{sid}_{I'}$.

Remark 1. For analysis of ISO 9798-6.7a, we use $\text{sid} = (D, R, mac_A, mac_B, K_A, K_B)$. This is the full transcript between I and I', inclusive of OOB data D, but also includes elements *sent* to respective identities by the user, on the UtD channel.

Definition 4 (Partnering Device-to-Device). *We say that two sessions $\pi_s^I, \pi_{\bar{s}}^{I'}$, for $I, I' \in \mathcal{ID}$, are* partnered *if they both accept, and possess, respectively, $(\text{pid}_I, \text{sid}_I)$ and $(\text{pid}_{I'}, \text{sid}_{I'})$, where $\text{pid}_I = I'$, $\text{pid}_{I'} = I$, and $\text{sid}_I = \text{sid}_{I'}$.*

3.1 Adversarial Model

We consider a probabilistic polynomial-time (PPT) adversarial algorithm $\mathcal{A}$. We define the following abilities and queries of $\mathcal{A}$ in the 3-PUMA experiment $\text{Exp}_{\mathcal{A}}^{\text{3-PUMA}}$.

Device-to-Device (DtD). For messages between participants I and I', such that $I, I' \in \mathcal{ID}$, $\mathcal{A}$ is allowed to read, modify, replay, and delete messages.

User-to-Device (UtD). For messages sent between identities $I \in \mathcal{ID}$ and the user U, $\mathcal{A}$ may not modify a message's sender/recipient. We present three variants of adversarial behavior allowed on the UtD channel, where 3-PUMA$_i$ denotes i-th variant:

1. – Before the first DtD message, $\mathcal{A}$ is allowed to read, modify, replay, or delete UtD messages.
   – After the first DtD message is sent, $\mathcal{A}$ is allowed to read, replay, and delete messages, but may not modify UtD messages.
2. $\mathcal{A}$ is allowed to read, replay, and delete messages, but may not modify UtD messages.
3. – Before the first DtD message, $\mathcal{A}$ is allowed to replay or delete messages sent from a user to a device, but may not read or modify messages. $\mathcal{A}$ is allowed to replay, delete or read messages sent from a device to a user, but may not modify messages.

– After the first DtD message is sent, $\mathcal{A}$ is allowed to read, replay, and delete UtD messages, but may not modify messages.

We model the user as an honest, benign, and unauthenticated third party. However, we capture a CCA1 variant (3-PUMA$_1$).

Queries. $\mathcal{A}$ may use the following queries:

– SendDevice(π_s^I, m). Using this query, $\mathcal{A}$ sends a message m to a session oracle of its choice, where π_s^I is an oracle for session s at a participant $I \in \mathcal{ID}$. The message is processed according to the protocol and any response is returned to $\mathcal{A}$.

If a session oracle π_s^I, where $I \in \mathcal{ID}$, receives m as a first message, then the oracle checks if m consists of a special initiation message ($m = (\mathtt{init}, I')$), for $I' \in \mathcal{ID}$, to which it responds by setting $\mathtt{pid} = I'$ and outputting the first protocol message. Else it outputs $\perp$.

If at any point a session oracle π_s^I, where $I \in \mathcal{ID}$, receives a message m from U during a protocol run, such that m consists of a special role-setting message $m = \mathtt{start}$ and π_s^I has not received a message from another identity $I' \in \mathcal{ID}$, then π_s^I sets $\mathsf{role} = \mathsf{initiator}$ and responds according to the initiator role in the protocol. Else, if π_s^I receives a message from another identity $I' \in \mathcal{ID}$ according to the protocol without having received such a message $m = \mathtt{start}$ from U, it sets sets $\mathsf{role} = \mathsf{responder}$ and responds according to the responder role in the protocol.

– SendUser(π_s^U, m). Using this query, $\mathcal{A}$ sends a message m to a session oracle of his choice, where π_s^U is an oracle for session s at user U. The message is processed according to the protocol and any response is returned to the $\mathcal{A}$.

If a session oracle π_s^U, receives m as a first message, then the oracle checks of m consists of a special initiation message ($m = (\mathtt{init}, (I, I'))$), for $I, I' \in \mathcal{ID}$, to which it responds by setting $\mathtt{init} = I$ and $\mathtt{resp} = I'$. Else it outputs $\perp$.

– RevealEphKey(π_s^I). This query returns the ephemeral key K_{I_s} of the s-th session for the identity $I \in \mathcal{ID}$. If $K_{I_s} = \emptyset$, RevealEphKey returns $\perp$.

Definition 5 (Freshness). *A session oracle π_s^I for an identity $I \in \mathcal{ID}$ is fresh unless*

– *a* RevealEphKey *query on π_s^I occurs before the last DtD message is sent/received by π_s^I, or*
– *a* RevealEphKey *query on $\pi_{\bar{s}}^{I'}$ occurs before the last DtD message is sent/received by $\pi_{\bar{s}}^{I'}$, where $\pi_{\bar{s}}^{I'}$ is the partner of π_s^I.*

3.2   Security

Definition 6 (3-PUMA Experiment). *Let $\mathcal{A}$ be a PPT adversarial algorithm against 3-party possession user-mediated authentication, interacting with a challenger in the experiment $\mathsf{Exp}_{\mathcal{A}}^{\text{3-PUMA}}$ via the queries defined above. We say that the challenger outputs 1, denoted $\mathsf{Exp}_{\mathcal{A}}^{\text{3-PUMA}}(\lambda) = 1$, if either of the following conditions hold:*

1. Failure of (matching sid → acceptance). Oracles π_s^I and $\pi_{\bar{s}}^{I'}$ have matching sid and either π_s^I or $\pi_{\bar{s}}^{I'}$ does not accept.
2. Failure of (acceptance → matching sid). There exists a fresh oracle π_s^I which has accepted and there is no partner oracle $\pi_{\bar{s}}^{I'}$ which is fresh.

Otherwise the experiment outputs a random bit. We define the advantage of $\mathcal{A}$ in the experiment $\mathsf{Exp}_{\mathcal{A}}^{3\text{-PUMA}}(\lambda)$ as $\mathbf{Adv}_{\mathcal{A}}^{3\text{-PUMA}}(\lambda) := \Pr[\mathsf{Exp}_{\mathcal{A}}^{3\text{-PUMA}}(\lambda) = 1]$.

Definition 7 (Security of 3-PUMA). *We say that a 3-party possession user-mediated authentication protocol is* secure *if there exists a negligible function* $\mathsf{negl}(\lambda)$ *such that for all PPT adversaries $\mathcal{A}$ interacting according to the experiment* $\mathsf{Exp}_{\mathcal{A}}^{3\text{-PUMA}}(\lambda)$, *it holds that* $\mathbf{Adv}_{\mathcal{A}}^{3\text{-PUMA}}(\lambda) \leq \mathsf{negl}(\lambda)$.

As ISO 9798-6.7a requires strict privacy with regards to R, we use the 3-PUMA$_3$ model for analysis of ISO 9798-6.7a.

Theorem 1 (Security of ISO 9798-6.7a). *Let* ISO *be the ISO 9798-6.7a protocol and let $\mathcal{A}$ be a PPT adversarial algorithm against the 3-PUMA$_3$. Let q be a polynomial bound on the number of queries allowed to $\mathcal{A}$ and let $p = |\mathcal{ID}|$. Then we can construct adversaries $\mathcal{B}_0$ and $\mathcal{B}_1$ against the OT-SUF-CMA and EUF-KCA security of the MAC, respectively, such that*

$$\mathbf{Adv}_{\mathsf{ISO},\mathcal{A}}^{3\text{-PUMA}_3}(\lambda) \leq (2p^2+1) \cdot \mathbf{Adv}_{\mathsf{MAC},\mathcal{B}_0}^{\mathsf{OT\text{-}SUF\text{-}CMA}}(\lambda) + 2p^2 \cdot \mathbf{Adv}_{\mathsf{MAC},\mathcal{B}_1}^{\mathsf{EUF\text{-}KCA}}(\lambda) + q^2/2^n.$$

where n is the prescribed bit-length of R.

Due to space restrictions, the proof is left for the full version.

The reliance of ISO 9798-6.7a security on the EUF-KCA security of the MAC presents a significant issue. EUF-KCA security is not well understood and is non-standard. Consequently, it is unknown whether or not basic MAC primitives, such as are recommended for use in ISO 9798-6.7a, satisfy this security requirement.

References

1. Anderson, R., Needham, R.: Robustness principles for public key protocols. In: Coppersmith, D. (ed.) CRYPTO 1995. LNCS, vol. 963, pp. 236–247. Springer, Heidelberg (1995). https://doi.org/10.1007/3-540-44750-4_19
2. Andreeva, E., Bogdanov, A., Mennink, B.: Towards understanding the known-key security of block ciphers. In: Moriai, S. (ed.) FSE 2013. LNCS, vol. 8424, pp. 348–366. Springer, Heidelberg (2014). https://doi.org/10.1007/978-3-662-43933-3_18
3. Basin, D., Cremers, C., Meier, S.: Provably repairing the ISO/IEC 9798 standard for entity authentication. In: Degano, P., Guttman, J.D. (eds.) POST 2012. LNCS, vol. 7215, pp. 129–148. Springer, Heidelberg (2012). https://doi.org/10.1007/978-3-642-28641-4_8
4. Bellare, M., Rogaway, P.: Provably secure session key distribution: the three party case. In: 27th ACM STOC, pp. 57–66. ACM Press, May/June 1995
5. Biham, E.: New types of cryptanalytic attacks using related keys. J. Cryptol. **7**(4), 229–246 (1994)

6. Biryukov, A., Khovratovich, D., Nikolić, I.: Distinguisher and related-key attack on the full AES-256. In: Halevi, S. (ed.) CRYPTO 2009. LNCS, vol. 5677, pp. 231–249. Springer, Heidelberg (2009). https://doi.org/10.1007/978-3-642-03356-8_14
7. Hale, B., Boyd, C.: Computationally analyzing the ISO 9798-2.4 authentication protocol. In: Chen, L., Mitchell, C. (eds.) SSR 2014. LNCS, vol. 8893, pp. 236–255. Springer, Cham (2014). https://doi.org/10.1007/978-3-319-14054-4_14
8. ISO: Information technology - Security techniques - Entity Authentication - Part 6: Mechanisms using manual data transfer. ISO ISO/IEC 9798–6:2010, International Organization for Standardization, Geneva, Switzerland (2010)
9. ISO: Information technology - Security techniques - Message Authentication Codes (MACs) - Part 1: Mechanisms using a block cipher. ISO ISO/IEC 9797–1:2011, International Organization for Standardization, Geneva, Switzerland (2011)
10. ISO: Information technology - Security techniques - Message Authentication Codes (MACs) - Part 2: Mechanisms using a dedicated hash-function. ISO ISO/IEC 9797–2:2011, International Organization for Standardization, Geneva, Switzerland (2011)
11. Knudsen, L.R., Rijmen, V.: Known-key distinguishers for some block ciphers. In: Kurosawa, K. (ed.) ASIACRYPT 2007. LNCS, vol. 4833, pp. 315–324. Springer, Heidelberg (2007). https://doi.org/10.1007/978-3-540-76900-2_19
12. Nguyen, T., Leneutre, J.: Formal analysis of secure device pairing protocols. In: 2014 IEEE 13th International Symposium on Network Computing and Applications, pp. 291–295 (2014)
13. Rosa, T.: Key-collisions in (EC) DSA: attacking non-repudiation. Cryptology ePrint Archive, Report 2002/129 (2002). http://eprint.iacr.org/2002/129
14. Ziauddin, S., Martin, B.: Formal Analysis of ISO/IEC 9798–2 Authentication Standard Using AVISPA, July 2013

BAdASS: Preserving Privacy
in Behavioural Advertising
with Applied Secret Sharing

Leon J. Helsloot, Gamze Tillem$^{(\boxtimes)}$, and Zekeriya Erkin

Delft University of Technology, Delft, The Netherlands
leonhelsloot@gmail.com, {g.tillem,z.erkin}@tudelft.nl

Abstract. Online advertising forms the primary source of income for many publishers offering free web content by serving advertisements tailored to users' interests. The privacy of users, however, is threatened by the widespread collection of data that is required for behavioural advertising. In this paper, we present BAdASS, a novel privacy-preserving protocol for Online Behavioural Advertising that achieves significant performance improvements over the state-of-the-art without disclosing any information about user interests to any party. BAdASS ensures user privacy by combining efficient secret-sharing techniques with a machine learning method commonly encountered in existing systems. Our protocol serves advertisements within a fraction of a second, based on highly detailed user profiles and widely used machine learning methods.

Keywords: Behavioural advertising · Machine learning
Secret sharing · Privacy · Cryptography

1 Introduction

Online advertising forms a primary financial pillar supporting free web content by allowing publishers to offer content to users free of charge [4]. In recent years, however, an increasing number of people object to advertisements being shown on web pages they visit. A major concern for the users is their privacy which is threatened by the widespread data collection of advertising companies [14]. The collected data is used in behavioural targeting to determine which advertisements are shown to a user based on the user's browsing behaviour. Although such behavioural advertising is recognized as being beneficial to both users and publishers, a mistrust of advertising companies and a lack of control hinders acceptance of behavioural advertising [14].

The practice of showing advertisements based on previously exhibited behaviour is known as Online Behavioural Advertising (OBA). In OBA, user interests are inferred from data such as visited web pages, search queries, and online purchases. Based on these user interests, advertisements are typically personalized using campaign-specific supervised machine learning models that

© Springer Nature Switzerland AG 2018
J. Baek et al. (Eds.): ProvSec 2018, LNCS 11192, pp. 397–405, 2018.
https://doi.org/10.1007/978-3-030-01446-9_23

predict users' responses to advertisements. OBA utilises the Real-Time Bidding (RTB) model of buying and selling advertisements [15]. RTB facilitates real-time auctions of advertising space through marketplaces called ad exchanges (AdX), allowing buyers to determine bid values for individual ad impressions. Demand-Side Platforms (DSPs) provide advertisers, who may not possess the expertise required to accurately estimate impression values, with technologies to bid on individual impressions from multiple inventories. Likewise, Supply-Side Platforms (SSPs) support publishers in optimizing advertising yield.

In existing literature, a number of methods is proposed to address privacy concerns in OBA. These methods include blocking advertisements altogether [10], obfuscating browsing behaviour [3], and anonymization [11], as well as exposing only generalized user profiles to advertising companies [13]. Limiting the data that is available to advertising companies, however, is expected to decrease the targeting accuracy [5], and thus the value of advertisements to users, advertisers, and publishers. Other work proposes cryptographic approaches to aggregate click statistics [13] or select advertisements using secure hardware [1]. These approaches, however, are based on advertising models in which centralized networks perform simple keyword-based advertisement selection, and as such are unsuitable for use within the highly distributed RTB model. Recently, Helsloot et al. [8] proposed a protocol that uses threshold homomorphic encryption to preserve privacy in OBA within the RTB model. However, the use of expensive cryptographic operations throughout the protocol results in prohibitively large computational costs.

In this paper, we present BAdASS, a novel privacy-preserving protocol for OBA that is compatible with the RTB mechanism of buying ads and supports behavioural targeting based on highly detailed user profiles. BAdASS achieves significant performance improvements over the state of the art, using machine learning on secret-shared data to preserve privacy in OBA tasks. Our protocol uses the highly fragmented nature of the OBA landscape such that no single party can obtain sensitive information. We achieve performance multilinear in the size of user profiles and the number of DSPs, and perform the highly time-sensitive advertisement selection task in a fraction of a second.

2   Preliminaries

Logistic Regression: Logistic regression is one possible technique for user response estimation which has been commonly used by advertising companies [9]. Given a d-dimensional user profile vector $\boldsymbol{x}$ and model parameters $\boldsymbol{w}$, it estimates the probability of a binary outcome (click or no click) using the sigmoid function $\hat{y} = \sigma(\boldsymbol{w}^\mathsf{T}\boldsymbol{x}) = 1/1 + e^{-\boldsymbol{w}^\mathsf{T}\boldsymbol{x}}$. The model parameters are updated as $\boldsymbol{w} \leftarrow \boldsymbol{w} - \eta\boldsymbol{g}$ using the gradient of the logistic loss $\boldsymbol{g} = (\hat{y} - y)\boldsymbol{x}$ as in [9].

Feature Hashing: To avoid a high dimensional user vector in logistic regression, we use the hashing trick in [16] which enables to map the user profile into a lower-dimensional vector $\boldsymbol{x}$ by setting x_i to a count of the values whose hash is i. The resulting d-dimensional vector $\boldsymbol{x}$ (in [2], $d = 2^{24}$ is used) is the input feature vector to the logistic regression model.

Shamir Secret Sharing: Shamir's secret sharing scheme [12] is a t-out-of-n threshold scheme in which a secret $s \in \mathbb{Z}_p$ for a prime p is shared among n parties, from which any subset of size at least t can reconstruct the secret. We use the notation $\langle s \rangle$ to indicate a (t, n) secret sharing of a value s, for some predefined t and n, and $\langle \boldsymbol{v} \rangle$ denotes an element-wise sharing of the vector $\boldsymbol{v}$.

Universal Re-encryption: Universal re-encryption allows re-randomization of a ciphertext without access to the public key that was used during encryption. We use the notation $[\![x]\!]_u$ to denote the encryption of a value x under the public key of user u using the universal re-encryption scheme in [7].

3   Protocol Design

In BAdASS, we aim to 1. ensure profile privacy to prevent revealing information about user interests to any party other than the user, 2. ensure model privacy to prevent revealing model parameters of bidder to any party other than the bidder, and 3. make the design applicable to the RTB model and integrated into the OBA landscape. We assume a a semi-honest security model. Considering possible collusions between the AdX and DSPs, we introduce an additional entity called Privacy Service Provider (PSP). DSPs are the only parties that operate on user data. We define a DSP group Γ_i to be a set of DSPs. Computations on behalf of a DSP $\gamma_{i,j} \in \Gamma_i$ are performed entirely within Γ_i. The AdX only collect bids, and from these bids select the winner. SSPs are not considered in our protocol.

BAdASS is divided into four different phases: user profiling, bidding, auction, and model update. Prior to protocol execution, advertisers set up campaigns such that DSPs can bid on their behalf, and the PSP splits DSPs into groups of at least m parties. Moreover, each DSP shares campaign-specific parameters among the DSPs in their group. Finally, each user generates a key pair using any multiplicatively homomorphic cryptosystem and publishes their public key.

User Profiling Phase. In the user profiling phase, browsing behaviour is recorded locally within the user's web browser as in [6]. The resulting profile is captured in a d-dimensional feature vector $\boldsymbol{x}$ using feature hashing. To reduce the communication costs of sending the full d-dimensional feature vector for each request, feature vectors are cached at DSPs. To securely share a feature vector among DSPs, the user splits their profile into two additive shares, one of which is given to the AdX, the other to the PSP. Both the AdX and the PSP create Shamir shares from their additive shares, which are distributed among the DSP groups. Every DSP within the group receives two shares which are combined into a single share of the original value by calculating the sum of the two shares.

Bidding Phase. The bidding phase starts when a users contacts an AdX with an ad request. Receiving the ad request, AdX sends a bid request to DSP groups each of which cooperatively calculates the bidding prices for the campaigns they are responsible for. For each campaign, the user response $\hat{y}$ is estimated using a logistic regression model, and bidding values are derived from response estimations using linear bidding functions $B(\hat{y}) = c_1\hat{y} + c_2$ for campaign-specific constants c_1 and c_2. A challenge in logistic regression is to compute sigmoid function within the secret-shared domain. Following [8], we let the PSP compute the sigmoid function in the clear. In our setting, this is acceptable as the PSP knows neither the user, nor the campaign a value is associated with. To ensure profile privacy, each advertisement a_k is encrypted using the user's public key. The encrypted advertisement is submitted to the PSP, via the AdX such that the PSP cannot link the submission to a specific DSP, along with a random number r_k and the group descriptor Γ_i. Finally, the PSP stores a mapping $r_k \rightarrow (\llbracket a_k \rrbracket_u, \Gamma_i)$, which is used in the auction phase to retrieve the advertisement.

Auction Phase. The auction protocol uses a hierarchical auction in which each DSP group engages in a secure comparison protocol to select the highest of the bids within their group, along with associated information that is used in the model update phase. Shares of the information associated with the highest bid are stored for later use, after which each DSP group submits their highest bid to a global auction to select the final winner. Due to the use of secret sharing, the global auction cannot be performed by the AdX alone. In order to maintain the same level of trust as in the bidding protocol, at least m parties are required in the auction protocol. Therefore, the global auction is performed by a randomly selected DSP group Γ^*. Later, shares of a random identifier r associated with the highest bid are sent to the PSP, where the shares are combined to retrieve the encrypted advertisement and group descriptor associated with the highest bid. To ensure unlinkability between the encrypted advertisement retrieved from the PSP after the auction and the values submitted prior to the auction, the PSP performs re-randomization of the encrypted advertisement using universal re-encryption. Finally, the encrypted ad, the group descriptor, and the bid request identifier v are sent via AdX to the user, who decrypts and displays the advertisement.

Model Update Phase. In this phase, the response prediction model associated with the shown advertisement is updated using the update rule from Sect. 2. In order to ensure unlinkability between users and campaigns, the model update protocol is split into three stages: 1. The user identifier is revealed to the DSP group responsible for the shown advertisement in order to calculate shares of the update gradient $g = \eta(\hat{y} - y)x$. 2. Each DSP submits a set of multiple gradient shares to the PSP, which mixes the received shares via random rotation. The PSP then re-shares the set of gradient shares among the DSP group. 3. The campaign identifiers of the set of gradients are revealed to the DSP group, allowing the DSP group to apply the gradients calculated in the first stage to the correct parameter vector. Since the gradient shares have been mixed, the DSP group cannot link values revealed in the third phase to values revealed in the first phase.

4 Performance and Security Analyses

Computational Complexity. The computational complexity of BAdASS depends on a number of variables, in particular the user profile dimensionality d, the number of campaigns K, and the update aggregation threshold ζ. In the profile update protocol, the user creates d additive sharings, and the AdX and PSP both create d Shamir sharings. Moreover, each DSP performs d additions. If the profile update protocol is invoked for all DSP groups at once, the computational complexity becomes $O(dn)$, where n is the total number of DSPs. In the bidding protocol, each DSP performs a multiplication for every campaign within its DSP group to calculate the bid value, and an encryption of the advertisement for all its own campaigns. In the auction protocol, each DSP group Γ_i performs $K_i - 1$ comparisons, where K_i is the number of campaigns of Γ_i, followed by a single DSP group Γ^* performing $g - 1$ comparisons, where g is the number of groups. Since the group Γ^* is chosen at random out of g groups for every auction, the amortized complexity of the auction phase is $O(K)$. In the model update protocol, the total cost of the re-sharing is equal to that of dm multiplications. The group size m, however, can be considered a constant determined by the recombination threshold, resulting in an amortized complexity of $O(d)$.

Communication Complexity. Table 1 lists the amortized number of bits transmitted by each party for each subprotocol, and the number of rounds of communication required by each subprotocol. The round complexities of the profile update and bidding protocols, and the amortized round complexity of the model update protocol are constant. The round complexity of the auction phase is logarithmic in the number of campaigns since λ is logarithmic with respect to the number of campaigns, K. The communication complexities of the profile update and the model update phases are linear with respect to profile size d.

Table 1. Communication bandwidth in bits and number of communication rounds per invocation of each subprotocol. ϵ denotes the ciphertext size, and γ and τ the number of bits transferred in the comparison and truncation protocols. ρ is the round complexity of the comparison protocol, and T is the round complexity of the truncation protocol.

Protocol	Rounds	User	AdX	DSP	PSP
Profiling	2	$2d\sigma$	$dm\sigma$		$dm\sigma$
Bidding	2		$K\xi$	$(m+1)K_i\sigma + \kappa\xi$	$Km\sigma$
Auction	$\lambda(\rho+1)+3$		ξ	$(5K_i - 3)m\sigma + K_i\gamma + 2\frac{1}{g}\sigma$	ξ
Update	$T + 1\frac{3}{\zeta}$	$m\sigma$		$(d+1)m\sigma + \tau + (d+3)\sigma$	$(d+2)m^2\sigma$

Note that if the user profile is distributed among multiple DSP groups, the complexity of the user profiling phase becomes multilinear in the profile size and the number of DSPs. Likewise, the total communication complexity of the bidding and auction phase is linear in K.

Implementation. To measure the runtime of BAdASS, we made a proof-of-concept implementation in C++. Real values, such as model weights, are represented as 16-bit fixed-point numbers. Shamir shares are operated in a prime field of order $p = 2^{31} - 1$. The reconstruction threshold t is set to 3, resulting in a DSP group size m of 5. The key size for the ElGamal cryptosystem is set to 2048 bits. The tests were executed on a mobile workstation running Arch® Core™ i7-3610QM 2.3 GHz quad-core processor with 8 GB RAM.

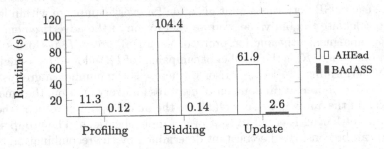

Fig. 1. Performance comparison between BAdASS and the state-of-the-art AHEad protocol. The measurements for AHEad are performed using a single DSP running a single campaign, whereas 5 DSPs with a total of 5 campaigns are used for BAdASS.

Figure 1 shows a comparison between the runtimes of BAdASS and the state-of-the-art AHEad protocol [8]. It is evident that, for a realistically large profile size $d = 2^{20}$, BAdASS provides significant performance improvements over AHEad. The computation time required by the model update far exceeds that of the profile update, bidding, and auction protocols, due to the large number of subshare recombinations performed by the DSPs, and the large number of sharings created by the PSP. When the computations performed by the DSPs are parallelized, the average time for the model update protocol for $d = 2^{20}$ can drop from 2.6 s to about 750 ms per invocation. The computation times of the bidding, auction, and the profile update phase are below 150 ms, and thus seem very well suited for use in a real-time setting as required by the RTB advertising model. The relatively large amount of computation performed in the model update phase is less time sensitive, and can thus be periodically performed as a background task without harming the user experience.

Security. The security of BAdASS is provided by the security of the underlying secret-sharing and encryption schemes in the semi-honest setting. In the non-interactive phases of the protocol, both the user profile and model parameters are shared among a DSP group using Shamir's secret sharing, which provides information-theoretic security as long as no more than $t - 1$ parties collude.

In the profile update protocol, the user profile is shared between the PSP and the AdX using a two-party additive secret sharing scheme, which, given the assumption that the PSP does not collude with any party, provides information-theoretic security. In the bidding protocol, the PSP obtains values $w_k^T x_u$ and $\hat{y}_k$ from DSP groups, but does not know the campaign k or user u to which the values belong, nor the specific DSP responsible for the campaign. Since the PSP knows neither w_k nor x_u, inferring the values of w_k or x_u from $w_k^T x_u$ is equivalent to the hardness of the subset-sum problem. If the PSP receives multiple values of $w_k^T x_u$ for the same w_k and x_u, the PSP can link these values to the same user, but cannot learn any information about the user's interests as the PSP cannot link response predictions to campaigns. The PSP also receives a mapping between a random number and an advertisement encrypted with the universal re-encryption, which is semantically secure under the DDH assumption [7].

In the model update protocol, the PSP obtains rotated shares of update gradients, bid values, and campaign identifiers. Given unbounded computational power, the PSP can perform an exhaustive search of rotation coefficients until recombination of shares results in likely values. Choosing sufficiently large values for the update period ζ and recombination threshold t makes exhaustive searches infeasible. After the PSP mixes the shares, DSPs receive shares of the same values submitted earlier in the model update phase. Since the shares are re-shared by the PSP, however, DSPs cannot link the shares received after mixing to shares submitted before mixing. Moreover, the random rotation performed by the PSP prevents DSPs from linking inputs to outputs.

5   Conclusion

In this paper we present a novel protocol using machine learning over secret-shared data to preserve privacy in OBA with minimal user-noticeable delays. Trust is distributed among DSPs using threshold secret sharing, allowing DSPs to collaboratively compute bid prices and determine the highest bid without gaining any knowledge of a user's interests. At no point are the contents of user profiles, shown advertisements, and actual user responses revealed to any party other than the user, nor are model parameters revealed to any party other than the DSP responsible for the campaign. Individual bid prices are not revealed to any party, but are aggregated for billing purposes. Finally, the protocols are integrated into the RTB setting by forming DSP groups from existing DSPs, with the addition of a single new party.

To the best of our knowledge, BAdASS is the first protocol to allow sub-second behavioural targeting of advertisements while preserving user privacy. The heavily fragmented shape of the online advertising landscape lends itself particularly well to the use of efficient secret-sharing techniques, giving advertising companies the opportunity to cooperatively move towards acceptable forms of behavioural advertising. Although the presented protocol should be adapted to the malicious setting, as DSPs may have an incentive to modify competitors' bid values, the results obtained with BAdASS show that it is possible to serve behaviourally targeted advertisements without disclosing those interests to any party, all within a fraction of a second. We believe that these results provide a first step towards adoption of privacy-preserving methods in the online advertising ecosystem.

References

1. Backes, M., Kate, A., Maffei, M., Pecina, K.: ObliviAd: provably secure and practical online behavioral advertising. In: IEEE Symposium on Security and Privacy, pp. 257–271. IEEE Computer Society, n.p. (2012)
2. Chapelle, O., Manavoglu, E., Rosales, R.: Simple and scalable response prediction for display advertising. ACM TIST **5**(4), 61:1–61:34 (2014)
3. Degeling, M., Herrmann, T.: Your interests according to Google -a profile-centered analysis for obfuscation of online tracking profiles. CoRR (2016). http://arxiv.org/abs/1601.06371
4. Deighton, J., Brierley, H.M.: Economic value of the advertising-supported internet ecosystem. Technical report, Interactive Advertising Bureau (2012)
5. Estrada-Jiménez, J., Parra-Arnau, J., Rodríguez-Hoyos, A., Forné, J.: Online advertising: analysis of privacy threats and protection approaches. Comput. Commun. **100**, 32–51 (2017)
6. Fredrikson, M., Livshits, B.: RePriv: re-imagining content personalization and in-browser privacy. In: 32nd IEEE Symposium on Security and Privacy, S&P 2011, pp. 131–146. IEEE Computer Society, n.p. (2011)
7. Golle, P., Jakobsson, M., Juels, A., Syverson, P.: Universal re-encryption for mixnets. In: Okamoto, T. (ed.) CT-RSA 2004. LNCS, vol. 2964, pp. 163–178. Springer, Heidelberg (2004). https://doi.org/10.1007/978-3-540-24660-2_14
8. Helsloot, L.J., Tillem, G., Erkin, Z.: AHEad: privacy-preserving online behavioural advertising using homomorphic encryption. IEEE International Workshop on Information Forensics and Security, WIFS 2017, pp. 1–6. IEEE, n.p. (2017)
9. McMahan, H.B., et al.: Ad click prediction: a view from the trenches. In: The 19th ACM SIGKDD International Conference on Knowledge Discovery and Data Mining, KDD 2013, pp. 1222–1230. ACM (2013)
10. Merzdovnik, G., et al.: Block me if you can: a large-scale study of tracker-blocking tools. In: 2017 IEEE European Symposium on Security and Privacy, EuroS&P 2017, pp. 319–333. IEEE, n.p. (2017)
11. Papaodyssefs, F., Iordanou, C., Blackburn, J., Laoutaris, N., Papagiannaki, K.: Web identity translator: behavioral advertising and identity privacy with WIT. In: Proceedings of the 14th ACM Workshop on Hot Topics in Networks. pp. 3:1–3:7. ACM, New York (2015)
12. Shamir, A.: How to share a secret. Commun. ACM **22**(11), 612–613 (1979)
13. Toubiana, V., Narayanan, A., Boneh, D., Nissenbaum, H., Barocas, S.: Adnostic: privacy preserving targeted advertising. In: Proceedings of the Network and Distributed System Security Symposium, NDSS 2010. The Internet Society, n.p. (2010)
14. Ur, B., Leon, P.G., Cranor, L.F., Shay, R., Wang, Y.: Smart, useful, scary, creepy: perceptions of online behavioral advertising. In: Symposium On Usable Privacy and Security, SOUPS 2012, pp. 4:1–4:15. ACM (2012)

15. Wang, J., Zhang, W., Yuan, S.: Display advertising with real-time bidding (RTB) and behavioural targeting. CoRR (2016). http://arxiv.org/abs/1610.03013
16. Weinberger, K.Q., Dasgupta, A., Langford, J., Smola, A.J., Attenberg, J.: Feature hashing for large scale multitask learning. In: Proceedings of the 26th Annual International Conference on Machine Learning, ICML 2009. ACM International Conference Proceeding Series, vol. 382, pp. 1113–1120. ACM (2009)

Signcryption with Quantum Random Oracles

Shingo Sato[✉] and Junji Shikata

Graduate School of Environment and Information Sciences,
Yokohama National University, Yokohama, Japan
sato-shingo-cz@ynu.jp, shikata@ynu.ac.jp

Abstract. Signcryption is a cryptographic scheme that achieves the functionalities of both public-key encryption and digital signatures. It is an important scheme for realizing a mechanism of sending and/or receiving messages in a secure way, since it is understood that signcryption is a public-key based protocol to realize a secure channel from an insecure channel. On the other hand, various post-quantum cryptographic schemes have been proposed so far. Recently, several cryptographic schemes have been proposed in the quantum random oracle model where an adversary can submit quantum queries to a random oracle. In this paper, we propose a generic construction of signcryption in the quantum random oracle model for the first time. Our construction achieves both of the strongest confidentiality and strongest integrity in the multi-user setting tightly.

Keywords: Signcryption · Post-quantum cryptography
Quantum random oracle

1 Introduction

To date, various constructions of cryptographic schemes resistant to attacks using quantum computers have been proposed. If quantum computers are realized, not only honest users but also adversaries can use the quantum computation. In addition, adversaries could attack cryptographic schemes by utilizing superpositions of states as queries to oracles (i.e., quantum queries). Therefore, it is interesting and important to consider cryptographic schemes which are secure against such adversaries. In particular, the *quantum random oracle model* is a model where a quantum adversary can utilize both classical and quantum queries to random oracles used in cryptographic schemes.

Regarding public key encryption (PKE) meeting indistinguishability against chosen ciphertext attacks (IND-CCA) in the quantum random oracle model (QROM), the constructions have been proposed so far [4,7,8,13,15]. In particular, the papers [8,13] proposed constructions meeting tight security of the existing ones. As for digital signatures (DSs), the papers [5,9] proposed generic constructions meeting strong unforgeability against chosen message attacks (sUF-CMA) by using some cryptographic primitives against classical adversaries.

© Springer Nature Switzerland AG 2018
J. Baek et al. (Eds.): ProvSec 2018, LNCS 11192, pp. 406–414, 2018.
https://doi.org/10.1007/978-3-030-01446-9_24

Signcryption is a cryptographic scheme that achieves both functionalities of PKE and DS, which was initially proposed in [17]. It is an important scheme for realizing a mechanism of sending and/or receiving messages in a secure way, since it is understood that signcryption is a public-key based protocol to realize a secure channel from an insecure channel. From the analysis of security of signcryption [2], it is desirable to consider security against insiders in the multi-user setting, called *multi-user indistinguishability against insider chosen ciphertext attack* (MU-IND-iCCA) and *multi-user strong unforgeability against insider chosen message attack* (MU-sUF-iCMA). There are several constructions satisfying both MU-IND-iCCA and MU-sUF-iCMA in the classical random oracle model [3,10,11] and in the standard model (i.e., without random oracles) [6,11,12,14].

Our main purpose is to propose a signcryption scheme in QROM, where queries to signcrypt and unsigncrypt oracles are classical. We propose a generic construction of signcryption which meets both MU-IND-iCCA and MU-sUF-iCMA in QROM for the first time. Our construction is provided from a PKE meeting one-wayness against chosen plaintext attacks (OW-CPA), a data encapsulation mechanism (DEM) meeting one-time security, and a lossy identification scheme (lossy ID scheme). Comparison of security bounds of our scheme and the existing constructions is given in Tables 1 and 2. Using these tables, we explain (dis)advantage of our construction as follows:

(i) Our construction for signcryption needs relatively weak primitives. In fact, in terms of confidentiality, our construction needs OW-CPA secure PKE and IND-OT secure DEM, which are weakest among the primitives required in Table 1. In addition, in terms of integrity, ours uses only a lossy ID scheme while the construction [9] uses not only a lossy ID scheme but also a pseudorandom function.
(ii) The security bounds of our construction for signcryption are better than those of existing constructions for PKE and DS. Namely, in terms of confidentiality, from Table 1, we can see that the security bound of ours is smaller than those of existing constructions of PKE. In addition, as for integrity, we compare ours with the construction of [9] because an ID schemes is not a stronger primitive than a trapdoor function or a digital signature. From Table 2, we can see that the security bound of ours is better than that of [9].

Table 1. IND-CCA (MU-IND-iCCA) Security bounds of PKE and our construction in QROM: Adv_{PKE} is the adversary's advantage breaking the underlying PKE and Adv_{DEM} is the adversary's advantage breaking the underlying DEM. δ is a probability that an correctness error of the underlying PKE happens, ϵ' is a negligible value, and q is the number of queries to quantum random oracles

Construction	Underlying primitive	Security bound
[7]	PKE(OW-CPA) and DEM(IND-CCA)	$q\sqrt{q^2\delta} + q\sqrt{Adv_{PKE}} + Adv_{DEM}$
[13]	PKE(IND-CPA) and DEM(IND-CCA)	$q\sqrt{Adv_{PKE}} + \epsilon' + Adv_{DEM}$
[8]	PKE(OW-CPA) and DEM(IND-CCA)	$q\sqrt{Adv_{PKE}} + q\sqrt{\delta} + \epsilon' + Adv_{DEM}$
Ours	PKE(OW-CPA) and DEM(IND-OT)	$q\sqrt{Adv_{PKE}} + q\sqrt{\delta} + Adv_{DEM}$

Table 2. sUF-CMA (MU-sUF-iCMA) Security bounds of DS and our construction in QROM: sUUF-RMA means strongly universal unforgeability against random message attacks. For each primitive $X \in \{\text{DS,PSF,TDP,ID,PRF}\}$, Adv_X is the adversary's advantage breaking X. ϵ' is a negligible value, and q is the number of queries to quantum random oracles

Construction	Underlying primitive	Security bound
[5]	DS(sUUF-RMA)	$Adv_{\text{DS}} + \epsilon'$
	Preimage sampleable function (PSF)	$Adv_{\text{PSF}} + \epsilon'$
	Trapdoor permutation (TDP)	$Adv_{\text{TDP}} + \epsilon'$
[9]	Lossy ID scheme	$(q^2 + q + 2)Adv_{\text{ID}} + \epsilon' + Adv_{\text{PRF}}$
	Pseudorandom function (PRF)	
Ours	Lossy ID scheme	$(q^2 + q + 2)Adv_{\text{ID}} + \epsilon'$

2 Preliminaries

In this paper, we use the following notation: A negligible function ϵ in n (or denoted by $\epsilon = \text{negl}(n)$) means a function $\epsilon : \mathbb{N} \to [0, 1]$ such that $\epsilon(n) < 1/g(n)$ for any polynomial g and sufficiently large n. For a randomized algorithm A and its input x, $A(x; r)$ is deterministic, where r is a random value used in A. Probabilistic polynomial-time is abbreviated as PPT.

We describe models and security definitions of several cryptographic primitives such as lossy ID schemes, public key encryption schemes, data encapsulation mechanisms, and signcryption schemes.

(Lossy) Identification Scheme. A lossy ID scheme ID consists of five polynomial-time algorithms (Setup, Gen, LossyGen, P, V). Let WSet be the set of commitments, let ChSet be the set of challenges, and let ZSet be the set of responses. Setup is a randomized (setup) algorithm that, given a security parameter k, outputs a public parameter prm. Gen is a randomized (key generation) algorithm that, given prm, outputs a public key pk and a secret key sk. LossyGen is a randomized (lossy key generation) algorithm which given prm, outputs a lossy key pk_{ls}. $P := \{P_1, P_2\}$ is a prover algorithm which given a secret key sk, consists of the following algorithms: P_1 is a randomized algorithm which, given sk, outputs a commitment $W \in$ WSet and a state st. P_2 is a randomized algorithm which, given sk, W, a challenge $c \in$ ChSet, and st, outputs a response $Z \in$ ZSet or $\perp$. V is a deterministic algorithm which, given pk, W, c, and Z, outputs 1 or 0.

To describe properties of ID, let $\text{Trans}(sk)$ be the transcript oracle of ID schemes which runs the protocol ID for $c \xleftarrow{U}$ ChSet and outputs (W, c, Z).

We require that a lossy ID scheme ID meets the following condition with correctness error δ: For all $prm \leftarrow \text{Setup}(1^k)$ and all $(pk, sk) \leftarrow \text{Gen}(prm)$, it holds that $V(pk, W, c, Z) = 1$ for all $(W, st) \leftarrow P_1(sk)$, all $c \in$ ChSet, and all $Z \leftarrow P_2(sk, W, c, st)$ with $Z \neq \perp$, and it also holds that $\Pr[Z = \perp \mid (W, c, Z) \leftarrow \text{Trans}(sk)] \leq \delta$.

We define the following properties of lossy ID schemes, *non-abort honest-verifier zero-knowledge* (naHVZK) and *computational unique response* (CUR), *lossyness*, and *lossy-soundness* (LS).

Definition 1 ([9]). *ID meets naHVZK, CUR, Lossyness, and LS if for all $prm \leftarrow \mathsf{Setup}(1^k)$, all $(pk, sk) \leftarrow \mathsf{Gen}(prm)$, and all $pk_{ls} \leftarrow \mathsf{LossyGen}(prm)$, it satisfies the following conditions:*

(i) naHVZK. *There exists a polynomial-time algorithm Sim meeting a condition that the statistical distance between the distributions of $(W, c, Z) \leftarrow \mathsf{Sim}(pk)$ and $(W', c', Z') \leftarrow \mathsf{Trans}(sk)$ is at most a negligible ε_{zk}.*

(ii) CUR. $Adv_{ID}^{CUR}(\mathcal{A}) := \Pr[Z \neq Z' \wedge V(pk, W, c, Z') = 1]$ *is negligible for any PPT algorithm $\mathcal{A}$ which takes pk and (W, c, Z) as input, and outputs (W', c', Z'), where $(W, c, Z) \leftarrow \mathsf{Trans}(sk)$.*

(iii) Lossyness. $Adv_{LID}^{LOSS}(\mathcal{A}) := \big| \Pr[\mathcal{A}(prm, pk_{ls}) \to 1] - \Pr[\mathcal{A}(prm, pk) \to 1] \big| \leq negl(k)$ *holds for any PPT algorithm $\mathcal{A}$.*

(iv) LS. $\Pr[V(pk_{ls}, W^*, c^*, Z^*) = 1]$ *is at most a negligible ε_{ls} for any PPT algorithm $\mathcal{A}$ which takes prm and pk_{ls} as input, and outputs (W^*, c^*, Z^*).*

Public Key Encryption (PKE). A PKE scheme consists of four polynomial-time algorithms (Setup, Gen, Enc, Dec). Let $\mathcal{M}$ be a message space. Setup is a randomized (setup) algorithm which, given a security parameter k, outputs a public parameter prm. Gen is a randomized (key generation) algorithm which, given prm, outputs an encryption key ek and a decryption key dk. Enc is a randomized (encryption) algorithm which, given ek and a message $\mu \in \mathcal{M}$, outputs a ciphertext e. Dec is a deterministic (decryption) algorithm which, given dk and e, outputs $\mu \in \mathcal{M}$ or $\perp$.

A PKE scheme PKE meets δ-correctness if the following holds: For all $prm \leftarrow \mathsf{Setup}(1^k)$, all $(ek, dk) \leftarrow \mathsf{Gen}(1^k)$, and all $\mu \in \mathcal{M}$, it holds that $\mathsf{Dec}(dk, e) = \mu$, where $e \leftarrow \mathsf{Enc}(ek, \mu)$, with at least probability $1 - \delta$.

Definition 2 (OW-CPA). *PKE meets OW-CPA, if the following advantage $Adv_{PKE}^{OW\text{-}CPA}(\mathcal{A}) \leq negl(k)$ holds for any PPT algorithm $\mathcal{A}$:*

$$Adv_{PKE}^{OW\text{-}CPA}(\mathcal{A}) := \Pr\left[\mu = \mu' \; \middle| \; \begin{array}{l} prm \leftarrow \mathsf{Setup}(1^k); \; (ek, dk) \leftarrow \mathsf{Gen}(prm) \\ \mu \xleftarrow{U} \mathcal{M}; \; e^* \leftarrow \mathsf{Enc}(ek, \mu); \; \mu' \leftarrow \mathcal{A}(prm, ek, e^*) \end{array}\right].$$

Data Encapsulation Mechanism (DEM). A DEM scheme DEM consists of two polynomial-time algorithm (Enc, Dec). Let $\mathcal{K}$ be a key space and let $\mathcal{M}$ be a message space. Enc is a deterministic (encryption) algorithm which, given a secret key $K \in \mathcal{K}$ and a message $\mu \in \mathcal{M}$, outputs a ciphertext e. Dec is a deterministic (decryption) algorithm which, given K and e, outputs μ or $\perp$. It is required that DEM meets the following condition: For any $K \in \mathcal{K}$ and all $\mu \in \mathcal{M}$, it holds that $\mathsf{Dec}(K, e) = \mu$, where $e \leftarrow \mathsf{Enc}(K, \mu)$.

Definition 3 (IND-OT). *DEM meets IND-OT, if the following advantage* $Adv_{DEM}^{IND\text{-}OT}(\mathcal{A}) \leq negl(k)$ *holds for any PPT algorithm* $\mathcal{A} := \{\mathcal{A}_1, \mathcal{A}_2\}$:

$$Adv_{DEM}^{IND\text{-}OT}(\mathcal{A}) := \left| \Pr\left[b = b' \mid \begin{array}{c} K \xleftarrow{U} \mathcal{K}; \ b \xleftarrow{U} \{0,1\}; \ (\mu_0, \mu_1, st) \leftarrow \mathcal{A}_1(\lambda); \\ e^* \leftarrow Enc(K, \mu_b); \ b' \leftarrow \mathcal{A}_2(\lambda, e^*, st) \end{array} \right] - \frac{1}{2} \right|.$$

Signcryption. A signcryption scheme SCS consists of five polynomial-time algorithms (Setup, KeyGen$_R$, KeyGen$_S$, SC, USC) as follows:

Setup is a randomized (setup) algorithm that, given a security parameter k, outputs a public parameter prm.

KeyGen$_R$ is a randomized (receiver's key generation) algorithm of receivers that, given prm, outputs a receiver's public/secret key-pair (pk_R, sk_R).

KeyGen$_S$ is a randomized (sender's key generation) algorithm of senders that, given prm, outputs a sender's public/secret key-pair (pk_S, sk_S).

SC is a randomized (signcrypt) algorithm that, given prm, pk_R, sk_S and a message $\mu \in \mathcal{M}$, outputs a ciphertext ct.

USC is a deterministic (unsigncrypt) algorithm that, given prm, pk_S, sk_R and ct, outputs $\mu \in \mathcal{M}$ or an invalid-symbol $\perp$.

It is required that for any $prm \leftarrow$ Setup(1^k), $(pk_R, sk_R) \leftarrow$ KeyGen$_R(prm)$, and any $(pk_S, sk_S) \leftarrow$ KeyGen$_S(prm)$, $\mu =$ USC$(prm, pk_S, sk_R,$ SC$(prm, pk_R, sk_S, \mu))$ holds with at least probability $1 - \delta$.

Definition 4 (MU-IND-iCCA and MU-sUF-iCMA). *SCS meets MU-IND-iCCA, if for any PPT adversary* $\mathcal{A} := \{\mathcal{A}_1, \mathcal{A}_2\}$ *in the following game, the advantage* $Adv_{SCS}^{MU\text{-}IND\text{-}iCCA}(\mathcal{A}) := \left| \Pr\left[b = b' \right] - \frac{1}{2} \right| \leq negl(k)$ *holds:*

Step 1: $prm \leftarrow$ Setup(1^k), $(pk_R, sk_R) \leftarrow$ KeyGen$_R(prm)$.

Step 2: $(pk_S^*, sk_S^*, \mu_0, \mu_1, st) \leftarrow \mathcal{A}_1^{USC(\cdot)}(prm, pk_R)$.

Step 3: $b \xleftarrow{U} \{0, 1\}$, $ct^* \leftarrow$ SC$(prm, pk_R, sk_S^*, \mu_b)$.

Step 4: $b' \leftarrow \mathcal{A}_2^{USC(\cdot)}(prm, pk_R, ct^*, st)$.

Unsigncrypt oracle USC(pk_S, ct) *returns* USC(prm, pk_S, sk_R, ct), $\mathcal{A}$ *is not allowed to query* ct^* *to the oracle* USC, *and* st *is state information.*

SCS meets MU-sUF-iCMA, if for any PPT adversary $\mathcal{A}$ *in the following game, the advantage* $Adv_{SCS}^{MU\text{-}sUF\text{-}iCMA}(\mathcal{A}) := \Pr[\mathcal{A} \text{ wins}] \leq negl(k)$ *holds:*

Step 1: $prm \leftarrow$ Setup(1^k), $(pk_S, sk_S) \leftarrow$ KeyGen$_S(prm)$.

Step 2: $(pk_R^*, sk_R^*, ct^*) \leftarrow \mathcal{A}^{SC(\cdot)}(prm, pk_S)$.

Signcrypt oracle SC(pk_R, μ) *returns* SC(prm, pk_R, sk_S, μ). *Let* q *be the number of queries to* SC. *Let* $[\mathcal{A} \text{ wins}]$ *be an event that* $\mu^* = $ SCS.USC$(prm, pk_S, sk_R^*, ct^*)$ *and* $(pk_R^*, \mu^*, ct^*) \neq (pk_{R,i}, \mu_i, ct_i)$ *for any* $i \in \{1, 2, \ldots, q\}$ *hold.*

In addition, we also define MU-IND-iCCA and MU-sUF-iCMA in QROM as follows: In the definition above, we add the condition that an adversary submits not only classical but also quantum queries to the random oracle.

3   Our Construction

We construct a signcryption scheme in QROM starting from an OW-CPA secure PKE, an IND-OT secure DEM, and a lossy ID scheme. Although our construction is based on the sign-then-encrypt methodology, it is shown in [2,11] that the construction, by combining IND-CCA secure PKE and sUF-CMA secure DS in a trivial way of this methodology, cannot achieve MU-sUF-iCMA while they can meet MU-IND-iCCA. The reason is as follows: Any inside adversary can obtain a valid pair of a message and a signature from a ciphertext ct by using his/her decryption key sk_R. Hence, the adversary can make a forgery in the MU-sUF-iCMA game by encrypting the pair again. To resolve this problem, we generate a signature on $\mu\|r$, where μ is a message and r is a random value used in the underlying PKE scheme. By doing this, even if an adversary decrypts μ and r, he/she has to generate a forgery of the underlying signature scheme.

The following primitives are used in our construction: PKE = (PKE.Setup, PKE.Gen, PKE.Enc, PKE.Dec) is a PKE scheme with a message space $\mathcal{M}_{pke}$, and the space $\mathcal{R}_{pke}$ of random values used in PKE.Enc algorithm. DEM = (DEM.Enc, DEM.Dec) is a DEM scheme with a key space $\mathcal{K}_{dem}$. ID = (ID.Setup, ID.Gen, ID.P, ID.V) is a lossy ID scheme with sets WSet, ChSet, and ZSet. Let H : $\{0,1\}^* \to$ ChSet, G : $\mathcal{M}_{pke} \to \mathcal{K}_{dem}$, and G' : $\mathcal{M}_{pke} \to \mathcal{R}_{pke}$ be random oracles.

We construct a signcryption scheme SCS-QRO = (Setup, KeyGen$_R$, KeyGen$_S$, SC, USC) as follows.

- $prm \leftarrow$ Setup(1^k): Generate $prm_{pke} \leftarrow$ PKE.Setup(1^k) and $prm_{id} \leftarrow$ ID.Setup(1^k). Output $prm := (prm_{pke}, prm_{id})$.
- $(pk_R, sk_R) \leftarrow$ KeyGen$_R(prm)$: Generate $(ek, dk) \leftarrow$ PKE.Gen(prm_{pke}). Output $pk_R := ek$ and $sk_R := dk$.
- $(pk_S, sk_S) \leftarrow$ KeyGen$_S(prm)$: Generate $(pk_{id}, sk_{id}) \leftarrow$ ID.Gen(prm_{id}). Output $pk_S := pk_{id}$ and $sk_S := sk_{id}$
- $ct \leftarrow$ SC(prm, pk_R, sk_S, μ): Compute a ciphertext on $\mu \in \mathcal{M}$ as follows:
  1. Let $\kappa := 0$ and do the following while $Z = \bot$ and $\kappa \leq \kappa_m$:
     - $\kappa \leftarrow \kappa + 1$, $r := r_1\|r_2 \overset{U}{\leftarrow} \mathcal{M}_{pke}$
     - $(W, st) = $ ID.P$_1(sk_{id}; r_1)$,
     - $Z = $ ID.P$_2(sk_{id}, W, c, st; r_2)$, where $c = $ H($W\|\mu\|r\|pk_R\|pk_S$).
  2. $e_1 = $ PKE.Enc($ek, r; \bar{r}$), where $\bar{r} = $ G'(r) $\in \mathcal{R}_{pke}$.
  3. $e_2 = $ DEM.Enc($K, \mu\|W\|Z$), where $K = $ G(r).
  4. Output $ct = (e_1, e_2)$.
- $\mu/\bot \leftarrow$ USC(prm, pk_S, sk_R, ct): Unsigncrypt $ct = (e_1, e_2)$ as follows:
  1. $M_1' = $ PKE.Dec(dk, e_1) and output $\bot$ if $M_1' = \bot$. Let $r' := M_1'$ otherwise.
  2. $M_2' = $ DEM.Dec(G(r'), e_2) and output $\bot$ if $M_2' = \bot$.
  3. Parse $M_2' = \mu'\|W'\|Z'$ and let $c' = $ H($W'\|\mu'\|r'\|pk_R\|pk_S$)
  4. Output μ' if ID.V(pk_{id}, W', c', Z') = 1, or output $\bot$ otherwise.

The security of SCS-QRO is shown by Theorem 1. We only describe its sketch proof due to the page limitation, and a complete proof will be given in a full version of this paper.

Theorem 1. *If PKE meets* OW-CPA *and DEM meets* IND-OT, *SCS-QRO meets* MU-IND-iCCA *in QROM. In addition, if ID meets* naHVZK, CUR, *lossyness, and* LS, *SCS-QRO meets* MU-sUF-iCMA *in QROM.*

Sketch Proof of MU-IND-iCCA. Let $\mathcal{A}$ be a PPT adversary against SCS-QRO. For each oracle $X \in \{USC, H, G, G'\}$, we define q_X as the number of queries which $\mathcal{A}$ submits to X. We consider the following games:

Game$_0$: The ordinary MU-IND-iCCA game.

Game$_1$: The same game as Game$_0$ except that the oracle $H(W\|\mu\|r\|pk_R\|pk_S)$ is replaced with $H_q(W\|\mu\|PKE.Enc(ek, r; G'(r))\|pk_S)$.

Game$_2$: The same game as Game$_1$ except that $G(r)$ is replaced with $G_q(PKE.Enc(ek, r; G'(r)))$.

Game$_3$: The same game as Game$_2$ except that $G(r)$ is replaced with $G_q(e_1)$.

Game$_4$: The same game as Game$_3$ except that in Challenge phase, $\bar{r}^* \in \mathcal{R}_{pke}$ and $K^* \in \mathcal{K}_{dem}$ are chosen uniformly at random.

Game$_5$: The same game as Game$_4$ except that when $\mathcal{A}$ submits i-th query to $G \times G'$, the challenger chooses $i \in \{1, \ldots, q_G + q_{G'}\}$ and measures the argument $\hat{r}$ of the i-th query.

Notice that $H_q(\cdot)$ and $G_q(\cdot)$ are random oracles to which $\mathcal{A}$ cannot access directly. For $i \in \{0, 1, \ldots, 5\}$, let S_i be the event that $\mathcal{A}$ wins in **Game$_i$**. We obtain the following: we have $|\Pr[S_0] - \Pr[S_1]| \leq 2q_H\sqrt{\delta}$ and $|\Pr[S_1] - \Pr[S_2]| \leq 2q_G\sqrt{\delta}$ by Lemma 37 of [1], $\Pr[S_2] = \Pr[S_3]$ holds conceptually, we get $|\Pr[S_3] - \Pr[S_4]| \leq 2(q_G + q_{G'})\sqrt{\Pr[S_5]}$ by Lemma 3 of [8], and $|\Pr[S_4] - \frac{1}{2}| \leq Adv_{DEM}^{IND-OT}(\mathcal{B}_2)$ holds in the same way as the security proof of KEM/DEM framework.

We next show $\Pr[S_5] = Adv_{PKE}^{OW-CPA}(\mathcal{B}_1)$ as follows: By Theorem 6.1 of [16], we can replace each oracle $X \in \{H_q, G_q, G'\}$ with a $2q_X$-wise independent hash function. We can construct $\mathcal{B}_1$ breaking OW-CPA as follows.

Setup. Take (prm_{pke}, ek) and the challenge ciphertext e_1^* as input, and generate $prm_{id} \leftarrow ID.Setup(1^k)$. Send $prm = (prm_{pke}, prm_{id})$ and $pk_R = ek$ to $\mathcal{A}$.

Queries. For queries to $X \in \{H, G, G'\}$, simulate these by using $2q_X$-wise independent hash functions. Simulate $USC(pk_S, ct)$ in the following way: Compute $\mu'\|W'\|Z' = DEM.Dec(K, e_2)$, where $K = G_q(e_1)$. Return μ' if $V(pk_S, W', c', Z') = 1$, or return $\perp$ otherwise.

Challenge. When $\mathcal{A}$ submits $(pk_S^*, sk_S^*, \mu_0, \mu_1)$, do the following:

    Step 1. $b \xleftarrow{U} \{0, 1\}$, $K^* \xleftarrow{U} \mathcal{K}_{dem}$.
    Step 2. Generate (W^*, c^*, Z^*) on $\mu_b\|e_1^*\|pk_S^*$ following SC algorithm,
    Step 3. $e_2^* \leftarrow DEM.Enc(K^*, \mu_b\|W^*\|Z^*)$.
    Step 4. Return $ct^* := (e_1^*, e_2^*)$.

Output. In the i-th query to G and G', measure the arugument $\bar{r}$ of the query, and then output $\bar{r}$.

From the above, we obtain the following inequlity, which complets the proof:

$$Adv_{\text{SCS-QRO}}^{\text{MU-IND-iCCA}}(\mathcal{A}) \leq 2(q_G + q_{G'})\sqrt{Adv_{\text{PKE}}^{\text{IND-CPA}}(\mathcal{B}_1)} + 4q_G\sqrt{\delta} + Adv_{\text{DEM}}^{\text{IND-OT}}(\mathcal{B}_2).$$

Sketch Proof of MU-sUF-iCMA. We consider the following games:

Game$_0$: The ordinary MU-sUF-iCMA game.

Game$_1$: The same game as Game$_0$ except for using the simulator Sim of ID in the process of the oracle SC($\cdot$).

Game$_2$: The same game as Game$_1$ except that the challenger outputs $\perp$ if $c^* \neq \tilde{H}(W^*\|\mu^*\|r^*\|pk_R^*\|pk_S^*)$.

Game$_3$: The same game as Game$_2$ except that pk_S is a lossy key pk_{ls}.

For $i \in \{0, 1, 2, 3\}$, let S$_i$ be an event that $\mathcal{A}$ wins in **Game**$_i$. In the same way as the proof of Theorems 3.2 and 3.3 of [9], we obtain $|\Pr[\text{S}_0] - \Pr[\text{S}_1]| \leq \kappa_m q_{sc} \cdot \varepsilon_{zk}$, $|\Pr[\text{S}_1] - \Pr[\text{S}_2]| \leq 2^{-\alpha+1} + Adv_{\text{ID}}^{\text{CUR}}(\mathcal{B}_1)$ where α is the min-entropy of W, $|\Pr[\text{S}_2] - \Pr[\text{S}_3]| \leq Adv_{\text{ID}}^{\text{LOSS}}(\mathcal{B}_2)$, and $\Pr[\text{S}_3] \leq 8(q_H + 1)^2 \varepsilon_{ls}$, where q_H is the number of queries to H.

Therefore, we have $Adv_{\text{SCS-QRO}}^{\text{MU-sUF-iCMA}}(\mathcal{A}) \leq \kappa q_{sc} \cdot \varepsilon_{zk} + 2^{-\alpha+1} + Adv_{\text{ID}}^{\text{CUR}}(\mathcal{B}_1) + Adv_{\text{ID}}^{\text{LOSS}}(\mathcal{B}_2) + 8(q_H + 1)^2 \varepsilon_{ls}$, which completes the proof. $\square$

References

1. Ambainis, A., Rosmanis, A., Unruh, D.: Quantum attacks on classical proof systems: the hardness of quantum rewinding. In: FOCS, pp. 474–483. IEEE Computer Society (2014)
2. An, J.H., Dodis, Y., Rabin, T.: On the security of joint signature and encryption. In: Knudsen, L.R. (ed.) EUROCRYPT 2002. LNCS, vol. 2332, pp. 83–107. Springer, Heidelberg (2002). https://doi.org/10.1007/3-540-46035-7_6
3. Baek, J., Steinfeld, R., Zheng, Y.: Formal proofs for the security of signcryption. J. Cryptol. **20**(2), 203–235 (2007)
4. Boneh, D., Dagdelen, Ö., Fischlin, M., Lehmann, A., Schaffner, C., Zhandry, M.: Random oracles in a quantum world. In: Lee, D.H., Wang, X. (eds.) ASIACRYPT 2011. LNCS, vol. 7073, pp. 41–69. Springer, Heidelberg (2011). https://doi.org/10.1007/978-3-642-25385-0_3
5. Boneh, D., Zhandry, M.: Secure signatures and chosen ciphertext security in a quantum computing world. In: Canetti, R., Garay, J.A. (eds.) CRYPTO 2013. LNCS, vol. 8043, pp. 361–379. Springer, Heidelberg (2013). https://doi.org/10.1007/978-3-642-40084-1_21
6. Chiba, D., Matsuda, T., Schuldt, J.C.N., Matsuura, K.: Efficient generic constructions of signcryption with insider security in the multi-user setting. In: Lopez, J., Tsudik, G. (eds.) ACNS 2011. LNCS, vol. 6715, pp. 220–237. Springer, Heidelberg (2011). https://doi.org/10.1007/978-3-642-21554-4_13
7. Hofheinz, D., Hövelmanns, K., Kiltz, E.: A modular analysis of the Fujisaki-Okamoto transformation. In: Kalai, Y., Reyzin, L. (eds.) TCC 2017. LNCS, vol. 10677, pp. 341–371. Springer, Cham (2017). https://doi.org/10.1007/978-3-319-70500-2_12

8. Jiang, H., Zhang, Z., Chen, L., Wang, H., Ma, Z.: IND-CCA-secure key encapsulation mechanism in the quantum random oracle model, revisited. In: Shacham, H., Boldyreva, A. (eds.) CRYPTO 2018. LNCS, vol. 10993, pp. 96–125. Springer, Cham (2018). https://doi.org/10.1007/978-3-319-96878-0_4

9. Kiltz, E., Lyubashevsky, V., Schaffner, C.: A concrete treatment of Fiat-Shamir signatures in the quantum random-oracle model. In: Nielsen, J.B., Rijmen, V. (eds.) EUROCRYPT 2018. LNCS, vol. 10822, pp. 552–586. Springer, Cham (2018). https://doi.org/10.1007/978-3-319-78372-7_18

10. Libert, B., Quisquater, J.-J.: Efficient signcryption with key privacy from gap Diffie-Hellman groups. In: Bao, F., Deng, R., Zhou, J. (eds.) PKC 2004. LNCS, vol. 2947, pp. 187–200. Springer, Heidelberg (2004). https://doi.org/10.1007/978-3-540-24632-9_14

11. Matsuda, T., Matsuura, K., Schuldt, J.C.N.: Efficient constructions of signcryption schemes and signcryption composability. In: Roy, B., Sendrier, N. (eds.) INDOCRYPT 2009. LNCS, vol. 5922, pp. 321–342. Springer, Heidelberg (2009). https://doi.org/10.1007/978-3-642-10628-6_22

12. Nakano, R., Shikata, J.: Constructions of signcryption in the multi-user setting from identity-based encryption. In: Stam, M. (ed.) IMACC 2013. LNCS, vol. 8308, pp. 324–343. Springer, Heidelberg (2013). https://doi.org/10.1007/978-3-642-45239-0_19

13. Saito, T., Xagawa, K., Yamakawa, T.: Tightly-secure key-encapsulation mechanism in the quantum random oracle model. In: Nielsen, J.B., Rijmen, V. (eds.) EUROCRYPT 2018. LNCS, vol. 10822, pp. 520–551. Springer, Cham (2018). https://doi.org/10.1007/978-3-319-78372-7_17

14. Tan, C.H.: Signcryption scheme in multi-user setting without random oracles. In: Matsuura, K., Fujisaki, E. (eds.) IWSEC 2008. LNCS, vol. 5312, pp. 64–82. Springer, Heidelberg (2008). https://doi.org/10.1007/978-3-540-89598-5_5

15. Targhi, E.E., Unruh, D.: Post-quantum security of the Fujisaki-Okamoto and OAEP transforms. In: Hirt, M., Smith, A. (eds.) TCC 2016. LNCS, vol. 9986, pp. 192–216. Springer, Heidelberg (2016). https://doi.org/10.1007/978-3-662-53644-5_8

16. Zhandry, M.: Secure identity-based encryption in the quantum random oracle model. In: Safavi-Naini, R., Canetti, R. (eds.) CRYPTO 2012. LNCS, vol. 7417, pp. 758–775. Springer, Heidelberg (2012). https://doi.org/10.1007/978-3-642-32009-5_44

17. Zheng, Y.: Digital signcryption or how to achieve cost(signature & encryption) << cost(signature) + cost(encryption). In: Kaliski, B.S. (ed.) CRYPTO 1997. LNCS, vol. 1294. Springer, Berlin (1997). https://doi.org/10.1007/BFb0052234

Formal Treatment of Verifiable Privacy-Preserving Data-Aggregation Protocols

Satoshi Yasuda[1(✉)], Yoshihiro Koseki[1], Yusuke Sakai[3], Fuyuki Kitagawa[2,3], Yutaka Kawai[1], and Goichiro Hanaoka[3]

[1] Mitsubishi Electric, Kanagawa, Japan
Yasuda.Satoshi@ea.MitsubishiElectric.co.jp,
Koseki.Yoshihiro@ak.MitsubishiElectric.co.jp,
Kawai.Yutaka@da.MitsubishiElectric.co.jp
[2] Tokyo Institute of Technology, Tokyo, Japan
kitagaw1@is.titech.ac.jp
[3] National Institute of Advanced Industrial Science and Technology (AIST), Tokyo, Japan
{yusuke.sakai,hanaoka-goichiro}@aist.go.jp

Abstract. Homomorphic encryption allows computation over encrypted data and can be used for delegating computation: data providers encrypt their data and send them to an aggregator, and then the aggregator performs computation for a receiver with the data kept secret. However, since the aggregator is merely the third party, it may be malicious, and particularly may submit a result of incorrect aggregation to the receiver. Ohara et al. (APKC2014) studied secure aggregation of time-series data while enabling the correctness of aggregation to be verified. However, they only provided a concrete construction in the smart metering system and only gave an intuitive argument of security. In this paper, we give general syntax of their scheme as *verifiable homomorphic encryption* (VHE) and introduce formal security definitions. Further, we formally prove that Ohara et al.'s VHE scheme satisfies our proposed security definitions.

1 Introduction

A homomorphic encryption scheme is a useful building block for various cryptographic protocols. This cryptographic primitive allows computation over encrypted data with the data kept secret from the entity that performs the computation. This useful property has been utilized for decades.

One of the attractive applications of homomorphic encryption is secure data aggregation. In this application, a set of data providers provides a large dataset, for example, time-series data from sensor devices. A third party called the aggregator performs the resource-demanding computation over the dataset. Finally the aggregator provides the result of the computation to another party called the receiver, and the receiver utilizes the result of computation for statistical

© Springer Nature Switzerland AG 2018
J. Baek et al. (Eds.): ProvSec 2018, LNCS 11192, pp. 415–422, 2018.
https://doi.org/10.1007/978-3-030-01446-9_25

analysis. In this scenario, it is highly desirable that the aggregator is unable to access the dataset as plaintext, but only helps the receiver to obtain the result of the computation.

In this scenario, a set of security issues arises. Firstly, the data aggregator must be unable to know the data subject to the aggregation. Secondly, the receiver must be able to know only the aggregated dataset, but unable to know the original dataset, say, for the privacy reason. Lastly, even when the aggregator is malicious, it is unable to submit an incorrect result of aggregation.

Toward addressing these three issues, Ohara et al. [7] initialized a cryptographic problem of verifying correctness of homomorphic data aggregation. While they focused only on a smart-metering setting, their solution is an important first step toward a general-purpose protocol of verifiable data aggregation.

1.1 Our Contribution

Motivated by Ohara et al.'s work [7], we formalize the aforementioned scenario as a cryptographic primitive named *verifiable homomorphic encryption* (VHE). This formalization is based on Ohara et al.'s work [7], where, in our terminology, they studied secure aggregation of time-series data while enabling the correctness of aggregation to be verified. We formalize their scheme as verifiable homomorphic encryption. Further, since they only provided an intuitive argument of security, we define security notions for a VHE scheme and prove that the scheme satisfies the security definitions.

In this paper, we define unforgeability and privacy for a VHE scheme. The unforgeability assures that a valid ciphertext should not be generated without a data provider's secret key. Further, the unforgeability assures that the aggregator cannot submit a valid ciphertext of a result of incorrect computation to the receiver. We prove that Ohara et al.'s scheme satisfies the unforgeability.

Further, we introduce two kinds of privacy and call them an aggregator privacy and a receiver privacy. The aggregator privacy requires that an aggregator cannot obtain any information about the encrypted message from ciphertexts without the receiver's secret key. The receiver privacy represents that even the receiver that has the secret key should be unable to know the dataset before computation, but only able to know the result of the computation. This property is important for keeping the data providers' original data secret. We prove that Ohara et al.'s scheme satisfies these privacy notions.

1.2 Related Work

As far as we know, some VHE schemes have already been proposed [2,4,5,8]. However, the existing schemes focus on outsourcing computation to the aggregator with the receiver's own data in our terminology, and thus they are defined in symmetric key setting, that is, it requires the same key to encrypt a message and decrypt a ciphertext. Therefore, they cannot be used in our scenario where there exists many data providers and they encrypt their own data. In contrast, our formalization for VHE is done in public key setting in order to apply VHE schemes in scenarios with many participants.

Verifiable aggregator oblivious encryption [3,6] can compute an aggregated sum of data with keeping the privacy of data providers. Further, it can publicly verify the correctness of computation done by the aggregator. However, it requires an honest dealer that generates secret keys for the data providers and the aggregator. In contrast, our formalization for VHE does not need a trusted third party like the honest dealer.

2   Preliminaries

For a positive integer n, $[n]$ represents a set $\{1, \ldots, n\}$. Let S be a set, then $a \leftarrow S$ represents that $a \in S$ is chosen uniformly at random from S. For a function f, we write $f(\lambda) = \mathsf{negl}(\lambda)$ if f is negligible in λ. PPT stands for probabilistic polynomial time.

We will work in bilinear groups of the form $\Lambda = (q, \mathbb{G}_1, \mathbb{G}_2, \mathbb{G}_T, e, g, h)$ where

- q is a λ-bit prime, where λ is a security parameter.
- $\mathbb{G}_1, \mathbb{G}_2$ and $\mathbb{G}_T$ are order q groups with efficiently computable group operations, membership tests and map $e : \mathbb{G}_1 \times \mathbb{G}_2 \to \mathbb{G}_T$.
- g generates $\mathbb{G}_1$, h generates $\mathbb{G}_2$, and $e(g, h)$ generates $\mathbb{G}_T$.
- The map e is bilinear, that is, $^\forall a \in \mathbb{G}_1, {}^\forall b \in \mathbb{G}_2, {}^\forall x, y \in \mathbb{Z}_q : e(a^x, b^y) = e(a, b)^{xy}$.

Let $\mathcal{G}$ be a PPT algorithm that takes a security parameter λ as input and generates a set of parameters of bilinear groups $\Lambda = (q, \mathbb{G}_1, \mathbb{G}_2, \mathbb{G}_T, e, g, h)$.

3   Verifiable Homomorphic Encryption

In this section, we introduce a notion of verifiable homomorphic encryption (VHE) and security definitions for a VHE scheme.

3.1   Syntax

First, we formalize VHE and this formalization is based on Ohara et al.'s work [7]. They proposed the framework that allows to delegate computation to an untrusted aggregator with the data kept secret and verify the correctness of the computation performed by the aggregator. Their framework is specialized in a smart grid system, and thus we formalize their framework as VHE for general purposes.

There are three kinds of participants in a typical application of VHE, that is, data providers, an aggregator and a receiver. In the following formal definition, data providers and a receiver corresponds to signers and a verifier, respectively.

Definition 1 (Verifiable Homomorphic Encryption). *A VHE scheme for the class $\mathcal{F}$ of functions is a tuple of PPT algorithms* VHE = (Setup, SKGen, VKGen, Enc, Eval, Dec) *defined as follows:*

- pp ← Setup(1^λ): *given a security parameter λ, outputs a public parameter* pp.
- (spk, ssk) ← SKGen(pp): *given a public parameter* pp, *outputs a signer public key* spk *and a signer secret key* ssk.
- (vpk, vsk) ← VKGen(pp): *given a public parameter* pp, *outputs a verifier public key* vpk *and a verifier secret key* vsk.
- c ← Enc(pp, ssk, vpk, τ, m): *given a public parameter* pp, *a signer secret key* ssk, *a verifier public key* vpk, *a tag τ and a message m, outputs a ciphertext c.*
- $\tilde{c}$ ← Eval(pp, vpk, (spk$_1$, c_1), ..., (spk$_n$, c_n), f): *given a public parameter* pp, *a verifier public key* vpk, *pairs of a ciphertext and an associated signer public key* (spk$_1$, c_1), ..., (spk$_n$, c_n) *and a function $f \in \mathcal{F}$, outputs a ciphertext $\tilde{c}$.*
- $\tilde{m}$ or $\bot$ ← Dec(pp, vsk, (τ_1, spk$_1$), ..., (τ_n, spk$_n$), c, f): *given a public parameter* pp, *a verifier secret key* vsk, *pairs of a tag and a signer public key* (τ_1, spk$_1$), ..., (τ_n, spk$_n$), *a ciphertext c and a function $f \in \mathcal{F}$, outputs a message $\tilde{m}$ or a special symbol $\bot$.*

Correctness. *For any positive integers λ and n, for all functions $f \in \mathcal{F}$, for all tags $\tau_1, ..., \tau_n$ and for all messages $m_1, ..., m_n$, the following experiment succeeds with probability one: generate a public parameter* pp ← Setup(1^λ), *signer key pairs* (spk$_i$, ssk$_i$) ← SKGen(pp) *for each $i \in [n]$, a verifier key pair* (vpk, vsk) ← VKGen(pp), *and ciphertexts* c_i ← Enc(pp, ssk$_i$, vpk, τ_i, m_i) *for each $i \in [n]$, let c* ← Eval(pp, vpk, (spk$_1$, c_1), ..., (spk$_n$, c_n), f) *and finally test whether* Dec(pp, vsk, (τ_1, spk$_1$), ..., (τ_n, spk$_n$), c, f) = $f(m_1, ..., m_n)$.

3.2 Security Definitions

Below, we introduce security definitions for a VHE scheme. In Ohara et al.'s work [7], they only provided an intuitive argument of security for their framework, and thus we formally argue the security notions.

Unforgeability. First, we formally define an unforgeability for a VHE scheme. The unforgeability assures that a valid ciphertext should not be generated without a signer secret key. Further, it assures that the aggregator cannot submit a valid ciphertext of a result of incorrect computation to the receiver. If the aggregator submits a ciphertext of incorrect computation to the receiver, the receiver can find that the ciphertext is invalid.

In the following definition, when an adversary outputs a forgery that satisfies the condition (1), the forgery represents a valid ciphertext generated without a signer secret key. On the other hand, when the forgery satisfies the condition (2), it represents a ciphertext of incorrect computation.

Definition 2 (Unforgeability). *Let* VHE = (Setup, SKGen, VKGen, Enc, Eval, Dec) *be a VHE scheme for the class $\mathcal{F}$ of functions. For any integer n, we define the following game between an adversary $\mathcal{A}$ and a challenger:*

- *Setup Phase: The challenger generates a public parameter* $\mathsf{pp} \leftarrow \mathsf{Setup}(1^\lambda)$, *signer key pairs* $(\mathsf{spk}_i, \mathsf{ssk}_i) \leftarrow \mathsf{SKGen}(\mathsf{pp})$ *for* $i \in [n]$ *and a verifier key pair* $(\mathsf{vpk}, \mathsf{vsk}) \leftarrow \mathsf{VKGen}(\mathsf{pp})$ *and sends* pp, $\{\mathsf{spk}_i\}_{i \in [n]}$, *and* vpk *to* $\mathcal{A}$. *Let* L_{tag} *be an empty set.*
- *Encryption Query Phase: On input a tag* τ_j, *an index of the signer public key* i_j, *where* $i_j \in [n]$, *and a message* m_j *by* $\mathcal{A}$, *if* $\tau_j \in L_{tag}$, *then the challenger returns* $\perp$ *to* $\mathcal{A}$. *Otherwise, the challenger adds* τ_j *to* L_{tag}, *generates a ciphertext* $c_j \leftarrow \mathsf{Enc}(\mathsf{pp}, \mathsf{ssk}_{i_j}, \mathsf{vpk}, \tau_j, m_j)$ *and returns* c_j. $\mathcal{A}$ *can make an encryption query polynomial times.*
- *Forgery Phase: $\mathcal{A}$ outputs pairs of a tag and an index of the signer public keys* $(\tau_1^*, i_1^*), \ldots, (\tau_N^*, i_N^*)$ *where* $i_1^*, \ldots, i_N^* \in [n]$, *a ciphertext* c^* *and a function* $f^* \in \mathcal{F}$.

In this game , the adversary wins if either condition is satisfied:

- *(1) When* $\tau_\ell^* \notin L_{tag}$ *for some* $\ell \in [N]$, *it holds* $\mathsf{Dec}(\mathsf{pp}, \mathsf{vsk}, (\tau_1^*, \mathsf{spk}_{i_1^*}),$ $\ldots, (\tau_N^*, \mathsf{spk}_{i_N^*}), c^*, f^*) \neq \perp$.
- *(2) When* $\tau_\ell^* \in L_{tag}$ *for all* $\ell \in [N]$, *it holds* $\mathsf{Dec}(\mathsf{pp}, \mathsf{vsk}, (\tau_1^*, \mathsf{spk}_{i_1^*}),$ $\ldots, (\tau_N^*, \mathsf{spk}_{i_N^*}), c^*, f^*) \notin \{\perp, f^*(m_1, \ldots, m_N)\}$, *where* m_ℓ *for* $\ell \in [N]$ *is the message queried with* τ_ℓ^* *as the encryption query.*

We say that VHE *satisfies the unforgeability if for any PPT adversary* $\mathcal{A}$ *and for any* $n = n(\lambda)$, *it holds* $\mathsf{Adv}_{\mathcal{A}}^{UF}(\lambda) = \Pr[\mathcal{A} \text{ wins}] = \mathsf{negl}(\lambda)$.

Privacy. We formalize two kinds of privacy and call them the aggregator privacy and the receiver privacy. The aggregator privacy is almost the same as the IND-CPA security for a public key encryption scheme. That is, no one can obtain any information about the encrypted message from ciphertexts without the verifier secret key.

Definition 3 (Aggregator Privacy). *Let* $\mathsf{VHE} = (\mathsf{Setup}, \mathsf{SKGen}, \mathsf{VKGen}, \mathsf{Enc}, \mathsf{Eval}, \mathsf{Dec})$ *be a VHE scheme for the class* $\mathcal{F}$ *of functions. We define the following game between an adversary* $\mathcal{A}$ *and a challenger:*

- *Setup Phase: The challenger generates a public parameter* $\mathsf{pp} \leftarrow \mathsf{Setup}(1^\lambda)$, *a signer key pair* $(\mathsf{spk}, \mathsf{ssk}) \leftarrow \mathsf{SKGen}(\mathsf{pp})$ *and a verifier key pair* $(\mathsf{vpk}, \mathsf{vsk}) \leftarrow \mathsf{VKGen}(\mathsf{pp})$ *and sends* $\mathsf{pp}, \mathsf{spk}$, *and* vpk.
- *Challenge Phase: On input a tag* τ *and messages* (m_0, m_1) *by* $\mathcal{A}$, *the challenger chooses a random bit* $b \in \{0, 1\}$, *generates a ciphertext* $c^* \leftarrow \mathsf{Enc}(\mathsf{pp}, \mathsf{ssk}, \mathsf{vpk}, \tau, m_b)$ *and returns* c^* *to* $\mathcal{A}$.
- *Guess Phase: $\mathcal{A}$ outputs a bit* $b' \in \{0, 1\}$.

In this game, the adversary $\mathcal{A}$ *wins if* $b' = b$. *We say that* VHE *satisfies the aggregator privacy if for any PPT adversary* $\mathcal{A}$, *it holds* $\mathsf{Adv}_{\mathcal{A}}^{A\text{-}Privacy}(\lambda) = |\Pr[\mathcal{A} \text{ wins}] - 1/2| = \mathsf{negl}(\lambda)$.

The receiver privacy represents that even the receiver that has the verifier secret key should be unable to know the dataset before computation, but only able to know the result of the computation.

Definition 4 (Receiver Privacy). *Let* $\mathsf{VHE} = (\mathsf{Setup}, \mathsf{SKGen}, \mathsf{VKGen}, \mathsf{Enc},$ $\mathsf{Eval}, \mathsf{Dec})$ *be a VHE scheme for the class* $\mathcal{F}$ *of functions. For any integer* n, *we define the following game between an adversary* $\mathcal{A}$ *and a challenger:*

- *Setup Phase: The challenger generates a public parameter* $\mathsf{pp} \leftarrow \mathsf{Setup}(1^\lambda)$, *signer key pairs* $(\mathsf{spk}_i, \mathsf{ssk}_i) \leftarrow \mathsf{SKGen}(\mathsf{pp})$ *for* $i \in [n]$ *and sends* $\mathsf{pp}, \{\mathsf{spk}_i\}_{i \in [n]}$ *to* $\mathcal{A}$.
- *Challenge Phase: On input a verifier public key* vpk, *indices of the signer public keys* $(i_1, \ldots, i_N)$, *where* $i_1, \ldots, i_N \in [n]$, *tags* $(\tau_1, \ldots, \tau_N)$, *messages* $(m_{01}, \ldots, m_{0N}), (m_{11}, \ldots, m_{1N})$ *and* $f \in \mathcal{F}$, *where* $f(m_{01}, \ldots, m_{0N}) =$ $f(m_{11}, \ldots, m_{1N})$ *by* $\mathcal{A}$, *the challenger chooses a random bit* $b \in \{0, 1\}$, *generates ciphertexts* $c_j \leftarrow \mathsf{Enc}(\mathsf{pp}, \mathsf{ssk}_{i_j}, \mathsf{vpk}, \tau_j, m_{bj})$ *for all* $j \in [N]$ *and* $c^* \leftarrow \mathsf{Eval}(\mathsf{pp}, \mathsf{vpk}, (\mathsf{spk}_{i_1}, c_1), \ldots, (\mathsf{spk}_{i_N}, c_N), f)$ *and returns* c^*.
- *Guess Phase:* $\mathcal{A}$ *outputs a bit* $b' \in \{0, 1\}$.

In this game, the adversary $\mathcal{A}$ *wins if* $b' = b$. *We say that VHE satisfies the receiver privacy if for any PPT adversary* $\mathcal{A}$ *and for any* $n = n(\lambda)$, *it holds* $\mathsf{Adv}_{\mathcal{A}}^{R\text{-}Privacy}(\lambda) = |\Pr[\mathcal{A} \ wins] - 1/2| = \mathsf{negl}(\lambda)$.

4 Construction

We describe a construction of a VHE scheme $\mathsf{VHE} = (\mathsf{Setup}, \mathsf{SKGen}, \mathsf{VKGen},$ $\mathsf{Enc}, \mathsf{Eval}, \mathsf{Dec})$ in Fig. 1. We employ the scheme proposed by Ohara et al. [7] as concrete VHE scheme. Their scheme uses the ElGamal encryption, the lifted ElGamal encryption, the AFG+ commitment [1] and a digital signature scheme $\Sigma = (\mathsf{Gen}, \mathsf{Sig}, \mathsf{Ver})$ as building blocks.

We assume that the size of the massage space of VHE is polynomial since messages are encrypted by the lifted ElGamal encryption, and thus the discrete logarithm of h^m needs to be computed in polynomial time. We stress that the class $\mathcal{F}_{\mathsf{ws}}$ of the functions is restricted to the one of the weighted sums described like $f(x_1, \ldots, x_n) = w_1 x_1 + \cdots + w_n x_n$ because the lifted ElGamal encryption only has additive homomorphic property. Further, it is necessary to choose the suitable weights w_i so that the resulting ciphertext from homomorphic evaluation can be decrypted efficiently.

Correctness. To see the correctness, we consider ciphertexts $c_i = (\psi_i, \psi_i', C_i, \sigma_i)$ for $i \in [n]$, where $\psi_i = (\psi_{i.1}, \psi_{i.2}) = (h^{r_i}, h^{m_i} \cdot y^{r_i})$, $\psi_i' = (\psi_{i.1}', \psi_{i.2}') = (h^{r_i}, R_i \cdot y^{r_i})$, $C_i = e(G_R, R_i) e(G_1, h^{m_i})$ and a function $f(x_1, \ldots, x_n) = w_1 x_1 + \cdots + w_n x_n$. Here, let $R_i' = \log_h R_i$. Then, the output ciphertext of Eval is $\tilde{c} = (\tilde{\psi}, \tilde{\psi}', (C_1, \ldots, C_n), (\sigma_1, \ldots, \sigma_n))$, where

$$\tilde{\psi} = (\tilde{\psi}_1, \tilde{\psi}_2) = (\textstyle\prod_{i=1}^n \psi_{i.1}^{w_i}, \textstyle\prod_{i=1}^n \psi_{i.2}^{w_i}) = (h^{\sum_{i=1}^n w_i r_i}, h^{\sum_{i=1}^n w_i m_i} \cdot y^{\sum_{i=1}^n w_i r_i}),$$

$$\tilde{\psi}' = (\tilde{\psi}_1', \tilde{\psi}_2') = (\textstyle\prod_{i=1}^n \psi_{i.1}'^{w_i}, \textstyle\prod_{i=1}^n \psi_{i.2}'^{w_i}) = (h^{\sum_{i=1}^n w_i r_i}, h^{\sum_{i=1}^n w_i R_i'} \cdot y^{\sum_{i=1}^n w_i r_i}).$$

In Dec, it first computes $\tilde{m} = \log_h(\tilde{\psi}_2 \cdot \tilde{\psi}_1^{-s}) = \sum_{i=1}^n w_i m_i$ and $\tilde{R} = (\tilde{\psi}_2' \cdot \tilde{\psi}_1'^{-s}) = h^{\sum_{i=1}^n w_i R_i'}$. This can be computed efficiently if $f(m_1, \ldots, m_n)$

$pp \leftarrow \mathsf{Setup}(1^\lambda):$ $\quad \Lambda = (q, \mathbb{G}_1, \mathbb{G}_2, \mathbb{G}_T, e, g, h) \leftarrow \mathcal{G}(1^\lambda);$ $\quad G_R \leftarrow \mathbb{G}_1; \; r_1 \leftarrow \mathbb{Z}_q; \; y = h^s; \; ck = (G_R, G_1);$ $\quad$ Output $pp = (\Lambda, ck).$	$\tilde{c} \leftarrow \mathsf{Eval}(pp, vpk, (spk_1, c_1), \dots, (spk_n, c_n), f):$ $\quad c_i = (\psi_i, \psi'_i, C_i, \sigma_i);$ $\quad \psi_i = (\psi_{i.1}, \psi_{i.2}); \; \psi'_i = (\psi'_{i.1}, \psi'_{i.2});$ $\quad \tilde{\psi} = (\prod_{i=1}^n \psi_{i.1}^{w_i}, \prod_{i=1}^n \psi_{i.2}^{w_i});$ $\quad \tilde{\psi}' = (\prod_{i=1}^n \psi_{i.1}'^{w_i}, \prod_{i=1}^n \psi_{i.2}'^{w_i});$ $\quad$ Output $\tilde{c} = (\tilde{\psi}, \tilde{\psi}', (C_1, \dots, C_n), (\sigma_1, \dots, \sigma_n)).$
$(spk, ssk) \leftarrow \mathsf{SKGen}(pp):$ $\quad (vk, sk) \leftarrow \mathsf{Gen}(1^\lambda);$ $\quad$ Output $(spk, ssk) = (vk, sk).$	
$(vpk, vsk) \leftarrow \mathsf{VKGen}(pp):$ $\quad s \leftarrow \mathbb{Z}_q; \; y = h^s;$ $\quad$ Output $(vpk, vsk) = (y, s).$	$\tilde{m} \leftarrow \mathsf{Dec}(pp, vsk, (\tau_1, spk_1), \dots, (\tau_n, spk_n), c, f):$ $\quad c = (\psi, \psi', (C_1, \dots, C_n), (\sigma_1, \dots, \sigma_n)); \; vsk = s;$ $\quad$ 1. $b = \mathsf{Ver}(spk_i, C_i \| \tau_i, \sigma_i);$ $\qquad$ If $b = 1$ for all i, go to the next step. $\qquad$ Otherwise, output $\bot$ and terminate.
$c \leftarrow \mathsf{Enc}(pp, ssk, vpk, \tau, m):$ $\quad ssk = sk; \; vpk = y; \quad r, r' \leftarrow \mathbb{Z}_q; \; R \leftarrow \mathbb{G}_2;$ $\quad$ 1. $\psi = (h^r, h^m \cdot y^r);$ $\quad$ 2. $C = e(G_R, R)e(G_1, h^m);$ $\quad$ 3. $\psi' = (h^{r'}, R \cdot y^{r'});$ $\quad$ 4. $\sigma \leftarrow \mathsf{Sig}(sk, C \| \tau);$ $\quad$ Output $c = (\psi, \psi', C, \sigma).$	$\quad$ 2. $\psi = (\psi_1, \psi_2); \; \tilde{m} = \log_h(\psi_2 \cdot \psi_1^{-s});$ $\quad$ 3. $\psi' = (\psi'_1, \psi'_2); \; \tilde{R} = \psi'_2 \cdot \psi_1'^{-s};$ $\quad$ 4. If $\prod_{i=1}^n C_i^{w_i} = e(G_R, \tilde{R})e(G_1, \tilde{m})$ holds, $\qquad$ output $\tilde{m}.$ $\qquad$ Otherwise, output $\bot.$

Fig. 1. The concrete VHE scheme

is in the polynomial size message space and we see that it holds $\tilde{m} = f(m_1, \dots, m_n)$. Finally, we see if the commitment can be opened correctly in step 4 of Dec. For the commitments $C_1, \dots, C_n$, it holds $\prod_{i=1}^n C_i^{w_i} = \prod_{i=1}^n (e(G_R, R_i)e(G_1, h^{m_i}))^{w_i} = e(G_R, h^{\sum_{i=1}^n w_i R_i'})e(G_1, h^{\sum_{i=1}^n w_i m_i})$. Thus, it is clear that Dec outputs the correct message $\tilde{m}$.

Security. For the security of VHE, the following theorems hold.

Theorem 1. VHE *satisfies the aggregator privacy for the class* $\mathcal{F}_{ws}$ *of functions if the decisional Diffie-Hellman assumption in* $\mathbb{G}_2$ *holds.*

Theorem 2. VHE *satisfies the unforgeability for the class* $\mathcal{F}_{ws}$ *of functions if the symmetric external Diffie-Hellman assumption holds and the signature scheme* $\Sigma = (\mathsf{Gen}, \mathsf{Sig}, \mathsf{Ver})$ *satisfies the EUF-CMA security.*

Due to the page limitation, we omit the security proofs of Theorems 1 and 2 here. See our full paper for the detailed proofs.

Theorem 3. VHE *satisfies the receiver privacy for the class* $\mathcal{F}_{ws}$ *of the functions.*

Proof. Let $\mathcal{A}$ be an adversary in the receiver privacy game against VHE. We consider the following Game_0 and Game_1.

- Game_0: This is the original receiver privacy game. In this game, since the adversary $\mathcal{A}$ can generate the verifier key pair (vpk, vsk) by himself, $\mathcal{A}$ can decrypt the challenge ciphertext, and thus $\mathcal{A}$'s view is $\{f(m_{b1}, \dots, m_{bN}),$ $f(\tilde{R}_1, \dots, \tilde{R}_N), C_i = e(G_R, R_i)e(G_1, h^{m_i})$ for $i \in [N]\}$ where $R_i \leftarrow \mathbb{G}_2$ and $R_i = h^{\tilde{R}_i}$. Here, let $R = \log_g G_R$ and $r_1 = \log_{G_R} G_1$.

- Game_1: Same as Game_0 except following. In the challenge phase, the challenger randomly chooses R'_i, and computes $\tilde{R}_i = R'_i - r_1 m_{bi}$.

In Game_1, since R'_i is chosen uniformly at random, $\tilde{R}_i = R'_i - r_1 m_{bi}$ is also uniformly random. Thus, Game_0 and Game_1 are information theoretically indistinguishable.

To complete the proof, we show that the view of $\mathcal{A}$ in Game_1 does not contain the bit b. While $\mathcal{A}$ can potentially know the value of $\alpha_i = \log_{e(g,h)} C_i = R(R'_i - r_1 m_{bi}) + r_1 R m_{bi} = R R'_i$, $\mathcal{A}$ cannot obtain any information about the bit b from α_i for $i \in [N]$. Further, for $f(\tilde{R}_1, \ldots, \tilde{R}_N)$, since f is a linear function, the following equation holds: $f(\tilde{R}_1, \ldots, \tilde{R}_N) = f(R'_1 - r_1 m_{b1}, \ldots, R'_N - r_1 m_{bN}) = f(R'_1, \ldots, R'_N) - r_1 f(m_{b1}, \ldots, m_{bN})$. Thus, from the restriction that $\mathcal{A}$ should make a challenge query satisfying $f(m_{01}, \ldots, m_{0N}) = f(m_{11}, \ldots, m_{1N})$, $\mathcal{A}$ does not obtain the bit b from $f(\tilde{R}_1, \ldots, \tilde{R}_N)$. From the above discussion, $\mathcal{A}$ cannot obtain the information of the bit b in Game_1, and thus VHE satisfies the receiver privacy. □

References

1. Abe, M., Fuchsbauer, G., Groth, J., Haralambiev, K., Ohkubo, M.: Structure-preserving signatures and commitments to group elements. In: Rabin, T. (ed.) CRYPTO 2010. LNCS, vol. 6223, pp. 209–236. Springer, Heidelberg (2010). https://doi.org/10.1007/978-3-642-14623-7_12
2. El-Yahyaoui, A., El Kettani, M.D.E.C.: A verifiable fully homomorphic encryption scheme to secure big data in cloud computing. In: WINCOM, pp 1–5. IEEE (2017)
3. Emura, K.: Privacy-preserving aggregation of time-series data with public verifiability from simple assumptions. In: Pieprzyk, J., Suriadi, S. (eds.) ACISP 2017. LNCS, vol. 10343, pp. 193–213. Springer, Cham (2017). https://doi.org/10.1007/978-3-319-59870-3_11
4. Fiore, D., Gennaro, R., Pastro, V.: Efficiently verifiable computation on encrypted data. In: ACM Conference on Computer and Communications Security, pp. 844–855. ACM (2014)
5. Lai, J., Deng, R.H., Pang, H., Weng, J.: Verifiable computation on outsourced encrypted data. In: Kutyłowski, M., Vaidya, J. (eds.) ESORICS 2014. LNCS, vol. 8712, pp. 273–291. Springer, Cham (2014). https://doi.org/10.1007/978-3-319-11203-9_16
6. Leontiadis, I., Elkhiyaoui, K., Önen, M., Molva, R.: PUDA – privacy and unforgeability for data aggregation. In: Reiter, M., Naccache, D. (eds.) CANS 2015. LNCS, vol. 9476, pp. 3–18. Springer, Cham (2015). https://doi.org/10.1007/978-3-319-26823-1_1
7. Ohara, K., Sakai, Y., Yoshida, F., Iwamoto, M., Ohta, K.: Privacy-preserving smart metering with verifiability for both billing and energy management. In: AsiaPKC@AsiaCCS, pp. 23–32. ACM (2014)
8. Tran, N.H., Pang, H., Deng, R.H.: Efficient verifiable computation of linear and quadratic functions over encrypted data. In: AsiaCCS, pp. 605–616. ACM (2016)

Author Index

Printed in the United States
By Bookmasters